D0213575

RACE

RACE AND AMERICAN CULTURE

Arnold Rampersad and Shelley Fisher Fishkin
General Editors

Love and Theft
Blackface Minstrelsy and the American Working Class
Eric Lott

The Dialect of Modernism
Race, Language, and Twentieth-Century Literature
Michael North

Bordering on the Body
The Racial Matrix of Modern Fiction and Culture
Laura Doyle

"Who Set You Flowin'?"
The African American Migration Narrative
Farah Jasmine Griffin

"Doers of the Word"
African-American Women Speakers and Writers in the North (1830–1880)
Carla L. Peterson

Race, Rape and Lynching
The Red Record of American Literature, 1890–1912
Sandra Gunning

Scenes of Subjection
Terror, Slavery, and Self-Making in Nineteenth-Century America
Saidiya V. Hartman

Racechanges
White Skin, Black Face in American Culture
Susan Gubar

Race
The History of an Idea in America, New Edition
Thomas F. Gossett

RACE

The History of an Idea in America

New Edition

THOMAS F. GOSSETT

New York   Oxford
Oxford University Press
1997

East Baton Rouge Parish Library
Baton Rouge, Louisiana

Oxford University Press

Oxford   New York

Athens   Auckland   Bangkok   Bogota   Bombay   Buenos Aires
Calcutta   Cape Town   Dar es Salaam   Delhi   Florence   Hong Kong
Istanbul   Karachi   Kuala Lumpur   Madras   Madrid   Melbourne
Mexico City   Nairobi   Paris   Singapore   Taipei   Tokyo   Toronto   Warsaw

and associated companies in
Berlin   Ibadan

Copyright © 1963, 1997 by Thomas F. Gossett

Published by Oxford University Press, Inc.,
198 Madison Avenue, New York, New York 10016

Oxford is a registered trademark of Oxford University Press

All rights reserved. No part of this publication may be reproduced,
stored in a retrieval system, or transmitted, in any form or by any means,
electronic, mechanical, photocopying, recording, or otherwise,
without the prior permission of Oxford University Press.

Library of Congress Cataloging-in-Publication Data
Gossett, Thomas F., 1916–
Race : the history of an idea in America / by Thomas F. Gossett.
—New edition
p.   cm.—(Race and American culture)
Includes bibliographical references and index.
ISBN 0-19-509777-7; ISBN 0-19-509778-5 (pbk.)
1. Racism—United States.   2. Race awareness—United States.
3. United States—Race relations.   4. Minorities—United States.
I. Title.   II. Series.
E184.A1G6   1996
305.8'00973—dc20   96–38769

1 3 5 7 9 8 6 4 2

Printed in the United States of America
on acid-free paper

For Louise

Foreword to the
New Edition

THOMAS GOSSETT'S *Race: The History of an Idea in America* is a work of considerable personal and professional significance to us, the editors of this series of books from Oxford University Press in which Gossett's volume is now republished after being out of print for some years.

We moved to reprint *Race: The History of an Idea in America* in small part as an acknowledgment of our personal debt to Thomas Gossett for having written a book that helped to shape our careers. Far more important, however, in reprinting this volume we are trying to ensure that serious readers today and in the foreseeable future will have access to one of the most important books published in the United States in the last fifty years on the vital subject of race as an idea in the development of American culture.

When we set out around 1992 to launch our series of books for Oxford University Press, interest in race as a subject in the American academy was both of long standing and also so new as to be almost faddish. Racial science, or pseudo-science, once occupied a secure place in the American academy and American intellectual culture in general. The key undergirding of twentieth-century American racial thought may be located, as Professor Gossett himself has done, in the appearance in this country of two landmark foreign texts. In 1911 came a translation of Houston Stewart Chamberlain's highly influential *Foundations of the Nineteenth Century* (first published in Germany in 1899). The following year, 1912, saw the appearance here of an abbreviated translation of Arthur de Gobineau's classic *Essay on the Inequality of Human Races* (originally published in

France between 1853 and 1855). However, if there was ever a "golden age" of American intellectual interest in race as a subject (we use the term "golden" ironically here), it was probably in the decade or so after the end of World War I. In those years, a flood of books, some of them of wide appeal, sought to apply putatively scientific theories of race to an assessment of American national life; many of these books were interventions in the ongoing debate about immigration to the United States and the resultant threat posed by "lesser" races to Aryan or Nordic supremacy (these terms were ever slippery) here and around the world. Such works include the Princeton University psychologist Carl C. Brigham's *A Study of American Intelligence* (1923); the Harvard psychologist William MacDougall's *Is America Safe for Democracy?* (1921), and the Harvard-trained historian Theodore Lothrop Stoddard's best-selling *The Rising Tide of Color against White World-Supremacy* (1920) and *The Revolt against Civilization: The Menace of the Under Man* (1923).

Behind most of these books was a near-absolute faith in the scientific basis of race as a concept as well as an unshakeable belief in white supremacy. Such faith left its mark on subsidiary debates, such as that over race and intelligence (IQ tests were already widely accepted and applied) and race and moral disposition. However, faith in the scientific basis of race as an idea was shattered for many people in the 1930s, when Nazi ideas about Aryan racial supremacy, backed by the German war machine, wreaked destruction in Europe and threatened the extinction of Jews as a people. In the process, this tragic record not only utterly discredited the notion of Aryan racial superiority but also made any sustained discussion of race largely taboo in most American universities and other intellectual circles. In its very subtitle, Jacques Barzun's invaluable *Race: A Study in Modern Superstition* (1937) echoed the virtual collapse of the prestige of race as a subject in American intellectual life.

Accordingly, the prestige of racial science sank to its lowest level in this century during the decades following the start of World War II. By the early 1990s, however, when we began our series of books, race once again had become widely recognized as one of the principal topics of investigation among scholars and critics of American literature and culture. Starting in the late 1970s or thereabouts, the troika of race, class, and gender had steadily emerged as perhaps the most compelling collective focus of cultural criticism in America, at least in the universities. Race was probably the last of the three great subjects to assert itself in a comprehensive way. However, by the early 1990s it had become clear that no systematic analysis of American reality, including American literature, music, and art, could ignore the subject of race as an idea. Proof of this new recognition has come in the steady flow of books on the subject emerging from university and trade presses in the past few years, with little sign of abatement. As in the 1920s, some of these volumes, such as Charles Murray and Richard Herrnstein's *The Bell Curve* and Cornel West's *Race Matters,* became bestsellers.

Why did race once again become recognized as a legitimate, even urgent topic within university and other intellectual circles? A generation ago, when we the editors of this series were either completing or beginning our years of graduate study, race was a concept generally ignored by our professors even as the civil rights movement and its aftermath, including Black Power, underscored the significance of racial antagonism as a problem in American life and culture. In the course of our training as literary scholars in the late 1960s and 1970s, perhaps the main source of enlightenment came with our deeper reading in African-American literature, where the idea of race has a natural investment. Not surprisingly, given the anti-black bias of most earlier race-thinkers, as well as the harsh conditions under which African-Americans were forced to live historically, the will to question race as an idea and to examine closely its implications within literary and other cultural activity was a notable feature of the work of earlier African-American intellectuals. W.E.B. DuBois, in *The Souls of Black Folk* (1903) and even more trenchantly in his autobiography *Dusk of Dawn* (1940), probed the changing meanings of race as an intellectual construction and attempted to measure some of the more important implications of those changes. Other scholars, such as Alain Locke and Sterling Brown of Howard University, also brought a probing intelligence to bear, mainly in essays, on the subject of race and literature. However, writers like DuBois, Locke, and Brown were hardly staples of American university life in general. They, and "Black Studies" in general, were decidedly on the margin.

For some Americans, of course, race could never be simply on the margin. During our student years we were well aware of the active championing of race as an idea by many contemporary African-American cultural nationalists, a championing that seemed understandable and indeed justifiable because of the history of social injustice in America. Nevertheless, such faith in race and racial difference came up sharply against the discourse of liberalism prodominant in the humanities, where notions of racial superiority, inferiority, and difference were on the whole decried even as the reality of our lives suggested that such ideas were real and potent. In addition, we had to deal with the particular disdain, especially within university departments of literature, of race or any other quasi-political concept as an appropriate tool of critical analysis. The New Criticism, with its putative contempt for politics, died slowly; indeed, it is not dead. For many professors in the humanities, to talk of race was, and still is, to talk dirty.

On the whole, white literary critics, including the most eminent and influential, steered clear of race as a subject. (In the field of history, the prominence of the subject of American slavery made for a different situation. If most historians did not probe the question of race with any degree of diligence, the topic of American slavery by definition compelled them to observe the social differences between blacks and whites and thus kept them relatively close to the subject of race at almost all times.) With the exception of a few scholars, such as Robert Kerlin in the 1920s, Vernon Loggins in the 1930s, and Robert Bone and Seymour Gross in the 1960s, white professors of literature more or less ignored black writing altogether as a subject worthy of inquiry. And even a writer as concerned with race as Herman Melville, who inspired a vast body of literary criticism, drew little attention on the question of race; scholars such as Michael Rogin and Carolyn Karcher, with their incisive studies of race and slavery in Melville, were decidedly in the future. The case of Leslie Fiedler, whose *Love and Death in the American Novel* (1966) sought to bring the topics of race and sexuality into the criticism of American literature in a major way, was instructive. Fiedler's work, though widely praised, was not warmly received by all of the more prestigious elements in the academy. The often chilly response to his probing of the interplay between race and sexuality could serve only as a caution to younger American scholars.

Today, the situation concerning race as a subject in the academy is generally transformed. Although many scholars continue to avoid the subject even when it appears appropriate and others approach it reluctantly and with evident discomfort, the potential importance of race in evaluations of American cultural phenomena is widely acknowledged. In 1995, when Shelley Fisher Fishkin made a systematic survey of recent writing on the subject, she found more than a hundred articles and books to review for her article "Interrogating 'Whiteness,' Complicating 'Blackness': Remapping American Culture" [see *American Quarterly* 47:3 (September 1995): 428–466].

Appearing in 1963, *Race: The History of an Idea in America* had much to do with laying the foundation for this change. Professor Gossett's book emerged quietly but soon became a resource to which many younger scholars turned as they sought a more honest and open understanding of American culture. The volume was both searching in its scope and highly readable. Its readability perhaps had something to do with the fact that Thomas Gossett was by training a professor of English—he was one of us—and thus was concerned with matters of clarity and style. In addition, his grounding in literature also made him sensitive to the impact of race as an idea beyond the scientific and pseudoscientific books and papers and especially on the work of novelists and other artists. Clearly, skeptical about race as a science and alert to the force of racism, Professor Gossett never gave in to simple-minded invective. Instead, he maintained a balanced tone as his timely book negotiated what were at that time the largely uncharted waters of American racial history.

In the thirty-three years since *Race: The History of an Idea in America* first appeared, a wealth of new bibliographic material has surfaced, and there is increased awareness of the significance of some material that had been known in Gossett's day and that now perhaps deserves to be emphasized. As in the case of gender, the standards applied today in the academy to the vocabulary appropriate to a discussion of race are more stringent than they were in 1965, when this book first appeared. Whether some of our standards in this respect are too severe, as some critics have claimed, is another matter. At our invitation, Professor Maghan Keita of Villanova University, who has made the history of race his special subject, has provided us with a detailed commentary on bibliographic and other matters pertaining to the text. Professor Keita's commentary should make this volume even more useful to the scholar of race today. Also at our invitation, Professor Gossett has provided a personal essay on the occasion of this reprinting of *Race: The History of an Idea in America,* in which he recounts some of the circumstances that led to his decision to take on this project.

However, the text as published in 1963 is reproduced here without change. In some passing way, no doubt, the text may shed a little light unwittingly on attitudes to the subject of race current in the 1960s, when the book was written. In a far more significant way, this work splendidly fulfills the promise of its title and subtitle: it offers an invaluable and as yet unsurpassed guide to the history of our understanding of this crucial aspect of American reality that is race.

Shelley Fisher Fishkin
Arnold Rampersad

Preface to the
New Edition

I HAD TWO DIFFERENT but complementary purposes in writing this book. Primarily, I meant to produce a history of race theory as it developed in this country. Such theory nearly always was developed by whites and almost as often was indistinguishable from racism. Sometimes race theory developed by Anglo-whites was used against other white groups such as German, Irish, Jewish, and other European immigrant groups. More commonly it was directed against such non-white groups as Indians, blacks, Hispanics, and Asiatics.

Because race theory in European thought had a great effect upon American race theory, it was necessary to trace in some detail the nature of that influence. In the nineteenth century, Charles Darwin, though scarcely a racist at all himself, had developed an evolutionary theory which could be and often was used to "explain" the backwardness of non-white races. This so-called backwardness was often an excuse for discrimination against these peoples.

My other purpose in the book was to examine the history of race relationships in this country. This meant, for the most part, a history of the relations of the other ethnic groups with the dominant Anglo-whites. How did Indians, for example, fare in their contacts with whites? And how did blacks, Hispanics, various European immigrant groups, and Asiatics fare? With this many subjects I knew that my treatment of any one of them would have to be brief if I did not mean to write a long book. I could only hope that the examples which I chose would be similar enough to the experiences of other ethnic groups which I had discussed more briefly or sometimes had omitted altogether. The purpose of the book, then, was to combine a history of race theory in this country with a history of ethnic groups here. These two purposes, I hoped, would merge into one. The book would be both a general history of race theories and a history of the way these theories had worked out in practice.

Most researchers have probably begun their studies of race in one or more of the social sciences. Mine, on the other hand, started from my study and teaching of American literature. I had a master of arts in English (largely British literature) and a doctorate in American Studies which I received in 1953 from the University of Minnesota. In this program I had had courses in American history, philosophy, politics, sociology, and art history as well as courses in literature. On the other hand, I had had no courses in biology, anthropology, or psychology. I wrote the book in the late 1950s and the early 1960s while I was teaching American literature at small universities in the South. None of the biologists I knew was a specialist in the history of the discipline and none of the institutions where I taught had a department of anthropology. The result was that nearly all of what I learned from these disciplines came from my own reading.

I did read a great deal, but I was never sure that the books and articles I chose were the right ones. I feared making some elementary mistake in biology, anthropology, psychology, or some other discipline which almost any graduate student in these disciplines would recognize immediately. The reviewers rarely mentioned my mistakes or inadequacies, but the reason may have been that only a few of them were specialists in particular academic disciplines. I now hope to take a shorter period of American history than the one I took in *Race,* perhaps from about 1880 to about 1950, and to write a book more narrowly focused. The reading I have done in recent years will enable me, I think, to write a more coherent and perceptive account of the ways in which race theories have developed in American thought and also the ways in which race theories justifying inequality of treatment of ethnic minorities have been challenged.

I made Franz Boas, the anthropologist, the intellectual and moral hero of *Race.* I thought then, and I still do, that he did more to combat theories of racial superiority and inferiority than any other person in history. It was only after *Race* was published, however, that further reading convinced me that I had partially misrepresented his opinions about race. He did not argue, as I thought when I was writing that book, that races are necessarily equal. He conceded that there might be differences in intelligence, for example, between whites and blacks. On the other hand, he did not think that culture-free examinations of racial intelligence had been or presumably ever would be developed. His position was that if race differences in intelligence existed at all, they were minor. Though Boas saw culture as the determinant of the traits of members of particular ethnic groups, he did not deny that there might be genetic differences in intelligence among them.

In the original edition of *Race* I said almost nothing about myself. The little I said was in the preface and it was omitted in the paperback edition—the edition which most people probably read. Three years ago I met Professor C. Vann Woodward at a scholarly meeting commemorating the work of W. J. Cash. Professor Woodward told me that he had read my book, but he added, in a friendly way, I thought, that he had assumed it had been written by a foreigner. Someone broke into the conversation and I did not find out why he thought that. It may have been because I had paid a good deal more attention to social scientists than to historians. I had already discovered, however, that if you say nothing about yourself in a book, people will inevitably make erroneous assumptions about you. Some people have thought that I was black myself. Others have thought that I must be either a social scientist, probably a sociologist, or a historian. Letters addressed to me at Wake Forest University, where I taught for twenty years before I retired in 1987, usually were sent to the sociology or history department, not the English department. Once I received a questionnaire from a sociological society. It listed several dozen of types of sociologist and asked me to check the categories which most nearly fitted me.

Long before I went to college or thought about writing books, I had had experiences which influenced my attitudes toward race and yet they were often so indirect that they are difficult to judge in terms of their influence on my thinking. I was born in 1916 in Dallas. The neighborhood where I lived did not, of course, seem odd to me in my youth, but it does now. It was four miles from downtown—Dallas was not then a large city—and across the Trinity River in the suburb of Oak Cliff. My own neighborhood was middle class and overwhelmingly white and Protestant. The schools were segregated and therefore, of course, I met no blacks in them. I do not remember whether any blacks lived in our neighborhood. More surprisingly, I do not remember either in elementary or high school ever meeting a Hispanic, a Jew, a descendant of an immigrant from southern or eastern Europe, an Indian, or an Asiatic. There were many Jews in Dallas, but most of them lived at that time across the river from us in the suburb of south Dallas. I do not remember meeting even a single Catholic in grade school, and I knew of only one in high school. He was a friend of mine but was disinclined to discuss religion.

For all my isolation, I did know that segregation and discrimination existed. Dallas was not, of course, deep South, but it was deeper than one might suppose. Early in the 1920s when I was about five or six years old, the Ku Klux Klan had a mammoth night parade there. My father, mother, sister, brother, and I saw it from my father's office on the fifth floor of a building on Main Street in the center of town. Both my parents were strongly anti-Klan and it is a puzzle to me why we were there at all. We must have been there by design, probably the design of my father, since it would have been unlikely for us to go to the office at any time and especially not at night. I probably would not remember the parade at all if my father had not held me out of the window of his office so that I could see it clearly. It frightened me to look down from such a height. I saw hundreds of sheeted figures and the fiery torches which many of them carried. I am sure that I had not the remotest notion of the meaning of the parade. Later when I became more aware of the realities of racial discrimination, I would recall the scene of the march.

On most issues my parents were kind and moral people, but they had little to say about other races, especially not about blacks. I would have been in trouble with them, and particularly with my mother, if I had ever used the word "nigger," as my school fellows sometimes did. The way in which I most obviously encountered

segregation and discrimination was on the streetcars (we had no buses then). There were moveable wooden signs with the word "white" on one side and "colored" on the other. The whites sat in front and the blacks in back, and the signs were moved according to the point at which the racial division took place. Though I did not challenge segregation, I was aware of one of its injustices. When white passengers got off a car, they left an unoccupied seat on it unless they had been standing before. To allow standing blacks in the rear of the car to sit down, seated white passengers in the front would usually move forward and occupy new seats. Sometimes whites would not budge from their seats and blacks would be left standing in the back. I thought their doing so was most unjust. I complained about this lack of consideration of the white passengers to my parents. I do not think it occurred to me, however, that the situation was an inevitable result of segregation. Like the air, segregation too was so obviously there that I did not challenge it. I suppose I thought of it as a necessary part of the rules of society.

The most dramatic incident of racial discrimination that I experienced occurred in the summer of 1931 when I was fifteen years old. My parents owned a farm with a forty-acre peach orchard in east Texas. Other parts of the farm were worked by tenants, but when the peaches were ripe our whole family would go to the country to pick them. By this time the depression of the 1930s had seriously affected my father's income, and perhaps that is the reason that he hired only black laborers to help pick the peaches. He hired them because he would have to pay them less. White people in the area discovered that all the peach pickers on the farm were black, and they sent a delegation to my father to protest. I did not attend this meeting nor was I told what the members of the delegation had said. I did see what happened the next morning. My father called the black workers together, gave each one of them a quarter, and fired them.

I knew my father was reluctant to do this. He may have feared violence from the white people in the neighborhood if he did not discharge the black workers. Still, his decision was a great shock to me. I had worked alongside the black workers and I knew how desperately they needed work. Though I did not immediately be-

come a civil rights activist or even a particularly vocal critic of segregation and discrimination, something had occurred inside me. I knew that racial discrimination was wrong.

Probably the most important event which determined my later attitudes toward race was my entering Southern Methodist University in 1934. A year later I became the student assistant of Henry Nash Smith. He would become a famous scholar in American literature and history. Even then when he was still in his twenties his colleagues and students expected great things of him. I immensely admired and respected him. As nearly as anyone could, he woke me up to what it meant to be a serious student. Though I knew that he was racially tolerant, I do not now remember any particular statements he made on the subject of race. I do remember that he was a committed and articulate anti-Nazi. He understood long before most people in this country did that Hitler was something more than a temporary dictator, that he was, in fact, an international menace.

Race was written at a time when the South was convulsed by problems of segregation and racial discrimination. I considered writing a book about the details of the battles for civil rights which were then taking place. I concluded, rightly I think, that better books on that subject could and would be written by people closer to the battles than I was. My subject was race theory and its relation to the mistreatment of ethnic minorities. It was a subject, I thought, which gave me all the scope I needed.

The conclusion of *Race* turned out to be naive. In 1963 racist theory seemed to me to be in full retreat. In addition, the federal government had become more and more resolved to end all legal forms of racial discrimination. In the last sentence of the book I said there was hope that race might be reduced from a major to a minor issue in American society.

Of course, it has not happened that way. The problems of race are different now, but they are as pressing as they were in 1963. It is true that the open expression of white racism is less common than it was, much less common I think, but many of the old attitudes remain. Many blacks are better off than they were then, but many are not. In addition, the problems of other ethnic minorities leave much

to be desired. It may be that in time our society may become more equitable and just, but the process will probably be a slow one. In the meantime, we should do what we can to keep the racial fires damped down.

I was fortunate in having excellent editors at the Southern Methodist University Press in 1963 when I first began to think about publication of *Race*. Margaret Hartley and Allen Maxwell greatly helped in transforming a bulky and diffuse manuscript into a book that was shorter, better organized, and more readable. My debt to them is certainly incalculable.

Preface

MY EFFORT HAS BEEN to understand and explore how ideas of race have affected currents of thought in America. I have been more interested in what people thought about race than in what they did about it. On the other hand, since ideas of race have nearly always gone hand in hand with definite programs of action, I have also attempted to describe what was happening in race relations at the time the theorists were propagating their doctrines. This book is, then, both a history of race theory and a history of bigotry.

Like many other students, I am deeply indebted to Henry Nash Smith, who first led me to a serious interest in the history of ideas. In particular, it was he who suggested to me the subject of race as a rewarding area of study.

I am also indebted to J. W. W. Daniel of Macon, Georgia—a man now nearing ninety—who helped me to see in some perspective the tragic background of the history of race relations in the South. Other men who have influenced my thinking have been Mulford Q. Sibley, Edgar T. Thompson, Willis B. Glover, Carl Bennett, William J. Hinson, and James F. Govan. It should be stated, however, that no one of these men has read more than a small portion of this book in manuscript, and that any errors in it are wholly mine.

A grant given me by the American Council of Learned Societies while I was a graduate student in American Studies at the University of Minnesota enabled me to devote a year wholly to this study, and subsequently I have received grants from the Duke University Visiting Scholar Fund, from the Southern Fellowships Fund, and from Trinity University. The encouragement given me by members of the faculty and administration of Trinity has been especially stimulating and heartwarming.

I am particularly grateful to Mr. and Mrs. Joseph B. Young, my father-in-law and mother-in-law, of Rainelle, West Virginia, who provided me a quiet place to work in the country at the family farm near Lewisburg, West Virginia.

Finally my hope is that this book may help readers understand the cruelty and the absurdity of racism.

THOMAS F. GOSSETT

San Antonio, Texas
November 26, 1963

Contents

I. Early Race Theories 3

II. England's American Colonies and Race Theories 17

III. Eighteenth-Century Anthropology 32

IV. Nineteenth-Century Anthropology 54

V. The Teutonic Origins Theory 84

VI. The Study of Language and Literature 123

VII. Race and Social Darwinism 144

VIII. The Social Gospel and Race 176

IX. Literary Naturalism and Race 198

X. The Indian in the Nineteenth Century 228

XI. The Status of the Negro: 1865–1915 253

XII. Anti-Immigration Agitation: 1865–1915 287

XIII. Imperialism and the Anglo-Saxon 310

XIV. World War I and Racism 339

XV. Racism in the 1920s 370

XVI. The Scientific Revolt Against Racism 409

XVII. The Battle Against Prejudice 431

Notes 461

Bibliographic Essay 503

Index 511

RACE

I

Early Race Theories

WHEN THE ENGLISH COLONISTS first landed in this country, they immediately encountered one race "problem" in the Indians. In a few years they imported another when, in 1619, the first boatload of Negro slaves arrived. What had been the history of ideas about race up until that time? Is the problem of race an age-old one in human relations, or is it mainly the result of revolutions of thought in biology and anthropology which took place in the eighteenth and nineteenth centuries?

Now that the idea of race consciousness has spread all over the world, it is frequently assumed that any conflict in history which cannot be readily explained in some other way must have been due to race antagonism. On the other hand, before the eighteenth century physical differences among peoples were so rarely referred to as a matter of great importance that something of a case can be made for the proposition that race consciousness is largely a modern phenomenon. What is certain is that the tendency to seize upon physical differences as the badge of innate mental and temperamental differences is not limited to modern times. The racism of ancient history, even though it had no science of biology or anthropology behind it, was real, however difficult it may be for us to judge the extent of its power.

In India, race prejudice manifested itself perhaps as long as five thousand years ago. In the Rig-Veda there is a description of an invasion by the Aryas, or Aryans, of the valley of the Indus where there lived a dark-hued people. The god of the Aryas, Indra, is described as "blowing away with supernatural

might from earth and from the heavens the black skin which
Indra hates." The dark people are called "Anasahs"—noseless
people—and the account proceeds to tell how Indra "slew the
flat-nosed barbarians." Having conquered the land for the
Aryas, Indra decreed that the foe was to be "flayed of his black
skin."[1]

In early Chinese thought we occasionally discover ideas
which are explicitly racist. The historians of the Han Dynasty in
the third century B.C. speak of a yellow-haired and green-eyed
barbarian people in a distant province "who greatly resemble
monkeys from whom they are descended." Other Chinese historians relate a legend which explains the differences between
themselves and certain barbarian mountain tribes. A Chinese
emperor, so the story goes, swore a mighty oath he would give
his daughter in marriage to whoever would kill a hated insub-
ordinate chieftain. The palace dog astonished the king by showing up one day with the head of the enemy. Loath to go back on
his word, the king awarded his daughter to the dog, who took
her into remote and inaccessible mountains. The children of this
union, according to the legend, were "fond of living in high
altitudes and averse to plains" and they developed characteristics
of both dogs and men.[2]

In Egypt, there is an indication of the early recognition of
race differences in the portraits on the walls of tombs from as
early as 1350 B.C. Four colors were used for the complexions of
the peoples represented: red for the Egyptians themselves, yellow
for their enemies to the east, white for people from the north,
and black for Negroes. Color prejudice, says one writer, depended on which ethnic group held sway. When the lighter-skinned
Egyptians were dominant they referred to the darker group as
"the evil race of Ish." On the other hand, when the darker-
skinned Egyptians were in power, they retorted by calling the
lighter-skinned peoples "the pale, degraded race of Arvad."[3]

Among the Jews, the prophet Ezra preached the abomination
of mixing the seed of Israel with that of the Ammonite and the
Moabite. All alien wives and children were deported and all fu-

ture mixed marriages were brought under a strong ban. This, said Ruth Benedict, shows that "fanatic racism . . . occurred in Israel long before the days of modern racism." Another modern writer believes that the "first recorded slur" against the Negro in the Bible is that of the prophet Jeremiah who asked, "Can the Ethiopian change his skin or the leopard his spots?"[4]

The most famous example of racism among the Jews is found in the legends which grew up concerning Ham, the son of Noah. The account in Genesis tells of Ham's expressing contempt for his father because Noah had become drunk and was lying naked in a stupor. Noah's other sons had covered their father's nakedness, averting their eyes so as not to witness his shame, but Ham had not averted his eyes. Noah blessed the descendants of Shem and Japheth, his other sons, but cursed the descendants of Ham. There is some confusion in the account in Genesis because it is not clear whether the curse was to be visited upon Ham or upon Canaan, the son of Ham. Modern critics usually regard the story as having been told originally of Canaan, Ham being a later insertion. Nothing is said in Genesis about the descendants of either Ham or Canaan being Negroes. This idea is not found until the oral traditions of the Jews were collected in the Babylonian Talmud from the second century to the sixth century A.D. In this source, the descendants of Ham are said to be cursed by being black. In the Talmud there are several contradictory legends concerning Ham—one that God forbade anyone to have sexual relations while on the Ark and Ham disobeyed this command. Another story is that Ham was cursed with blackness because he resented the fact that his father desired to have a fourth son. To prevent the birth of a rival heir, Ham is said to have castrated his father. Elsewhere in the Talmud, Ham's descendants are depicted as being led into captivity with their buttocks uncovered as a sign of their degradation.[5]

Sometimes ancient writers speculated upon the causes of race differences. In Greece, the legend of Phaethon, the son of the god Helios, contains one of the explanations of the origin of race. Phaethon persuaded his father to let him drive the sun chariot for a day. Unable to control the fiery steeds, Phaethon drove the chariot too close to the earth in some regions, burning the people there black, and drove it too far from the earth in other regions, whose inhabitants turned pale from the cold. Hippocrates may have been familiar with this legend when in the fifth century B.C. he attempted to account for race differences on the basis of climate and geography. The Greeks were superior to Asiatics, he said, because the bareness and infertility of the soil made them hardy and self-reliant. The climate in Greece was "more likely to steel the temper and impart to it a fierce passion than in a monotonous sameness." Luscious vegetation and plenteous crops, on the other hand, led to softness and a lack of war spirit. Thus the Asiatics were "feeble," "less warlike," and "more gentle." Hippocrates attributed the differences of skull formation among peoples to customs. A tribe he identified as the "long heads" had, he says, originally induced this peculiarity by remodeling the heads of their children at birth when they were soft and pliable and by applying restricting bandages. Eventually the shaping of the heads was no longer necessary because the peculiarity had become hereditary.[6]

Aristotle thought that both physical and temperamental race differences were caused by climate, particularly heat and cold:

This is a subject which can be easily understood by anyone who casts his eye on the more celebrated states of Hellas, and generally on the distribution of races in the habitable world. Those who live in a cold climate and in Europe are full of spirit, but wanting in intelligence and skill; and there they retain comparative freedom, but have no political organization, and are incapable of ruling over others. Whereas, the natives of Asia are intelligent and inventive, but they are wanting in spirit, and therefore they are always in a state of subjection and slavery. But the Hellenic race, which is situated between them, is likewise intermediate in character, being high-spirited and also intelligent. Hence it continues free, and is the best-governed of any nation, and if it could be formed into one state, would be able to rule the world.[7]

In the first century Vitruvius, historian of architecture in Rome, paused to reflect on the superiority of Romans to other peoples. He attributed the keen intelligence of his countrymen to the rarity of the atmosphere and to the heat. The less fortunate northern peoples, "being enveloped in a dense atmosphere, and chilled by moisture from the obstructing air," he observed, "have but a sluggish intelligence." A somewhat similar idea is found in a North American Indian legend, which has it that both the black man and the white man were created before God had mastered his technique. In baking the first man, God cooked him too long and he emerged black. The white man, also a culinary failure, had not been baked long enough. It was only with his third attempt that God was able to produce the properly golden brown Indian.[8]

Among ancient peoples, discrimination against minorities had a racist basis less often than might be supposed. In India, for example, anthropometric records have shown that on the whole high-caste individuals had lighter skins and narrower noses than others; but there is nothing infallible about this test, even in restricted areas. There is no inconsistency between high caste and a dark skin or a flat nose. If race ever was the original basis of caste in India, it did not remain so. In Greek civilization, we find that there was apparently no relationship between slavery and race. Negroes, as captured peoples, might be slaves; but there is no indication that they were either more or less suitable than others for this state. In neither Greece nor Rome does there appear to have been much prejudice against Negroes because of their race. In Greek thought, we find environmental and cultural explanations even for such qualities as courage and military prowess. Hippocrates, for example, after commenting on the cowardice of the Asiatics, suggests this explanation:

Now where men are not their own masters and independent, but are ruled by despots, they are not keen on military efficiency but on not appearing warlike. For the risks they run are not similar. Subjects are likely to be forced to undergo military service, and to be parted from their wives, their children, and their friends. All their worthy, brave deeds merely serve to aggrandize and raise up their lords, while the harvest they themselves reap is danger and death.[9]

Late in the history of Rome, a theory of race developed which might, under other circumstances, have become immensely powerful. It was that of Julian the Apostate, who succeeded Constantine as emperor in the fourth century A.D.

Julian questioned the idea that all mankind is descended from a single pair. He pointed out "how very different in their bodies are the Germans and Scythians from the Libyans and Ethiopians." Even more do these people differ in their dispositions and intelligence. "Come," declares Julian, "tell me why it is that the Celts and the Germans are fierce, while the Hellenes and the Romans are, generally speaking, inclined to political life and humane, though at the same time unyielding and warlike?" Egyptians are "more intelligent and more given to crafts," Syrians "unwarlike and effeminate" but at the same time "intelligent, hot-tempered, vain, and quick to learn." He argued that mankind could not possibly be all descended from one pair because the world had not existed long enough to be peopled under such an arrangement, "even if the women used to bear many children at a time to their husbands, like swine." But his principal point is that "if we were descended from one man and one woman, it is not likely that our laws would show such a great divergence."[10]

Julian preferred to accept another account of creation, that found in Plato's *Timaeus*. There mankind is said to have originated from drops of sacred blood which fell from Zeus. Whereas Zeus was the creator of all men, different peoples have inherited their peculiar characteristics from lesser deities. Ares passed on his character to warlike peoples; Athene gave other peoples both wisdom and military ability; Hermes was the father of those who were intelligent but not bellicose; and so on. And then Julian draws explicitly racist conclusions. "Can we suppose," he asks, "that there is not some mark or symbol indelibly stamped upon the souls of men, which will accurately indicate their descent and vindicate it as legitimate? . . . When a man has virtuous progenitors and is himself like them, he may with confidence be described as nobly born."[11]

Julian died in his early thirties, too soon to see the fate of his ideas. From its inception, Christianity had emphasized the unity of mankind. Jesus made it clear that he had not come to save only the Jews. Paul gave the idea of unity explicit statement. God "hath made of one blood all nations in the earth to dwell. . . ." A few years after the death of Julian, we find St. Augustine proclaiming a doctrine opposite to that of Julian's racism. We may hear of "monstrous races," says Augustine, "people who have one eye in the middle of their foreheads, people with no mouths, people with doglike heads, people who are but one cubit high." He doubts whether such people exist, but if they do exist there is no more reason to suspect that they are of different descent from ourselves than there is to suspect that deformed people, like hermaphrodites or people with six fingers, are of a different order of creation:

But whoever is anywhere born a man, that is, a rational mortal animal, no matter what unusual appearance he presents in colour, movement, sound, nor how peculiar he is in some power, part or quality of his nature, no Christian can doubt that he springs from that one protoplast. We can distinguish the common human nature from that which is peculiar, and therefore wonderful.[12]

When the Catholic church began extensive missionary operations, the idea of the unity of mankind was emphasized. In the thirteenth century, we find an indication of how far the Middle Ages were from the idea of race prejudice. In France, Pierre Dubois proposed that more sensible than Crusades against the Moslem would be intermarriage. Well-educated French gentlemen and ladies should marry the Moslem nobility in order to convert them to Christianity and monogamy, and incidentally to pave the way for French domination of the Middle East and Orient.[13]

It is true that the essentially religious prejudice against Jews sometimes became indistinguishable from race prejudice. Instead of being the Chosen People, the Jews became, in the Christian mind, the accursed people, the *deicidae,* God's murderers. Ani-

mosity of Christians toward Jews came very early in the history
of the church. Some modern biblical scholars have suggested
that in the Gospels themselves there is an attempt to place the
blame for the crucifixion of Jesus upon the Jews rather than
upon the Romans. Pilate's reluctance to condemn Jesus is sometimes interpreted as an attempt by the scribe to make it easier
for the Romans to accept Christianity by minimizing their part
in the opposition to Jesus. In the Gospel of Matthew, the Jews reply to Pilate's plea for leniency for Jesus: "His blood be upon
us, and on our children," a passage which could be interpreted
as making all Jews everywhere and at all times guilty for the
death of Christ.[14]

In the early history of the Catholic church, the Jews had not
fared too badly. Gregory the Great, Pope from 590 to 604, had
forbidden persecution of Jews and for five hundred years his
example was generally followed. Christians of this time still
hoped for their conversion, but it was generally felt that the
means to convert them should be peaceable. Though there were
restrictions against Jews and the niceties of tolerance were not
always observed, the Jews were usually allowed liberty to worship. Toward the end of the eleventh century, however, the attitude of Christians toward Jews changed radically for the worse.
Some historians have attributed this change to the Crusades. In
1095 Pope Urban II preached a sermon before the Council of
Clermont which summoned all Christendom to recover the Holy
Land from the clutches of the infidel. The passions thus aroused
against Moslems were apparently transferred to the Jews, the
"infidels" in the very midst of Christendom. Within six months
after Urban's appeal, the Jews at Worms were massacred by
Crusaders. A few saved themselves by baptism and others found
refuge in the palace of the Bishop of Worms, who did his best
to save as many as possible.[15]

From then on, the Jews became the most frequent scapegoat
of Christian societies. The most fantastic legends arose concerning them, accusing them of water poisoning, sorcery, ritual
murder of children, image and host desecration. An explanation

of sorts can be found for the last charge. The Jews were believed to have an uncontrollable desire to pierce the host until it bled. The bacterium, *Micrococcus prodigius*, leaves a small red stain on certain foods when exposed to air, the wafer among them, and the discovery of this red stain on wafers led to pogroms. Prejudice spread to all levels of society. Even the mild and gentle Prioress of Chaucer's *Canterbury Tales* could say of the Jews: "Our firste fo, the Serpent Sathanas, that hath in Jewes herte his waspes nest."[16]

Unquestionably, this persecution of the Jews did show similarities with modern racism. Jews were frequently regarded by Christians as loathsome creatures who had bad physical, mental, and moral characteristics which they apparently inherited and passed on to their descendants. Even horned Jews are sometimes described. (One explanation for this idea comes from a translation of Exodus 34:29, "And behold the skin of his face sent forth beams." The Aquila and the Vulgate, the standard texts used by the Roman church, misinterpreted the passage to mean that Moses had horns.) Jews were thought to have a peculiar and unpleasant odor. The beard of the Jewish man was said to resemble that of the goat, notorious as a lecherous beast. Jews were believed to suffer from diseases, particularly of the blood, that were unknown to Christians. Jewish men were believed to menstruate. Jews were thought to have malodorous sores which produced a constant flux. Jewish children, it was said, were born with their right hands attached to their heads so that a minor operation was necessary to release them, and thus from birth they were bloodstained. These diseases of blood and irregularities of birth were significant because it was also believed that Jews could cure themselves of their disorders only through the use of Christian blood—the basis for the charge of ritual murder. "Really I doubt whether a Jew can be human," observed Peter the Venerable of Cluny, "for he will neither yield to human reasoning, nor find satisfaction in authoritative utterances, alike divine and Jewish." At the time of the Spanish Inquisition, the Curate of Los Palacios expressed the charitable wish that "the whole accursed race of Jews, male and female, of twenty years and upwards, might be purified with fire and fagot!" In 1575, a book of illustrated wonders announced that a Jewish woman near Augsburg had given birth to two little pigs. There were instances in which Christian men were tried for sodomy because they had married or cohabited with Jewish women."[17]

During the age of exploration, an even more explicit racism developed from the contacts of Europeans with native peoples all over the world. In Spain a debate continued throughout the sixteenth century on the question of whether the Indians in the New World were really men, or whether they were beasts or perhaps beings intermediate between beasts and men. As in the case of the Jews, we find arguments that the Indians were an accursed people. In 1540, the novel argument was put forth that they were the modern descendants of the Ten Lost Tribes of Israel, condemned to wander forever. Gonzalo Fernandez de Oviedo, the official historian of the Spanish conquest, described the Indians as

naturally lazy and vicious, melancholic, cowardly, and in general a lying, shiftless people. Their marriages are not a sacrament but a sacrilege. They are idolatrous, libidinous and commit sodomy. Their chief desire is to eat, drink, worship heathen idols, and commit bestial obscenities. What could one expect from a people whose skulls are so thick and hard the Spanish had to take care in fighting not to strike on the head lest their swords be blunted.[18]

The great Spanish opponent of Indian slavery and of the theory that Indians were beasts rather than men was Bartolomé de Las Casas, the Bishop of Chiapas, known to posterity as the "Apostle of the Indians." Las Casas came to Hispaniola as a conquistador in 1502. Eight years later, however, he entered the priesthood, being the first to take holy orders in the New World. At first he did not question the institution of slavery; in fact, he owned slaves himself. In 1514, however, he experienced a change of heart. He writes that he was preparing a sermon when his eye fell upon a verse in Ecclesiastes: "He that sacrificeth of a thing wrongfully gotten, his offering is ridiculous, and the gifts of unjust men are not accepted." After pondering on this text for several days, Las Casas decided "that everything done to the Indians thus far has been unjust and tyrannical." He immediately freed his slaves and began to preach against the institution of slavery.[19]

Las Casas was a resolute man; he was also learned in argument and in languages. He was not easily silenced by opponents in Spain who justified slavery by appeals to Aristotle, to theology, and to astrology. Throughout his long life—he lived to be ninety-two—he worked tirelessly for the cause of the Indians, defending them particularly against the charge that they were not true men. In addition, he wrote accounts which became famous of their unjust treatment by the Spaniards. He probably exaggerated the number of Indians who were killed outright or worked to death by the Spaniards—a figure he estimated in the millions. In most respects, however, Las Casas' treatment of facts has been taken seriously by modern historians.[20]

After years of effort, Las Casas was able to secure the support of both the King of Spain and the Pope in his battle against the enslavement of the Indians. In 1530, he obtained a royal cedula prohibiting slavery in Peru, and he himself delivered the edict to the governor of the colony. In 1537, Pope Paul III, largely because of the efforts of Las Casas, issued a proclamation that the Indians are "truly men" and should not be treated as "dumb brutes" or deprived of their freedom or property. With both the Spanish Crown and the Pope opposed to the enslavement of Indians, one might imagine that the main battle was over. There remained, however, enormous obstacles to the application of the edicts to the colonies. Most of the remainder of Las Casas' life was spent in the New World defending the cause of the Indians against the colonists. He made a number of visits to Spain in which he engaged in debates on the subject of Spanish policy with regard to the Indians, debates which frequently involved discussions of the innate characteristics of the Indians.[21]

What actually happened with regard to the Spanish prohibition of slavery is a complicated story. In some colonies slavery was abolished outright. In many of them, however, every device which the local authority could utilize to prolong the institution, in fact if not in name, was adopted. Nevertheless, Las Casas' accomplishment was formidable. Indians had been admitted to equality with Spaniards under the law. By the pronouncement of the Pope, the Indians had the status of rational beings, and henceforth it was heretical to maintain the contrary. These were no small victories, and it was Las Casas who more than any other single man was responsible for them.[22]

Some of the arguments which opponents of Las Casas employed against the Indians were also utilized to explain the character of Europeans. In seventeenth-century France, Jean Bodin worked out a complicated system, an amalgam of geography, climate, and astrology, to explain all human differences everywhere. People who lived in the hills tended to be violent and rebellious; look at the tumultuous history of the Romans. People who lived in the lowlands were prone to despotic governments. Those who lived near the sea favored governments which were a mixture of aristocracy and democracy. The planet Mars made the northern Europeans more warlike than others and also gave them a practical inventiveness valuable in designing engines of war as well as other useful tools. The southern peoples, ruled by Saturn, were marked by a zeal for contemplation and a love of learning. It was they who had developed mathematics, religion, and astrology. Unfortunately, Saturn also made the southern peoples cruel and cowardly. The planet Jupiter ruled over the middle regions—by which Bodin meant essentially France. These peoples were the best for managing affairs. "If anyone reads all the writings of the historians," says Bodin, "he will judge that from men of this type institutions, laws, and customs first came, and the best method of directing the state; then, also commerce, government, rhetoric, dialectic, and finally the training of a general."[23]

Occasionally we find thinkers who argued that primitive peoples come of a stock altogether separate from that of Europeans. Paracelsus declared in 1520 that the children of Adam occupy only a small part of the earth and that Negroes and other peoples have a wholly separate origin. "God could not endure to have the rest of the world empty and so by his admirable wisdom filled the earth with other men." In 1591, Bruno asserted that no thinking person would imagine that the Ethiopians had the same ancestry as the Jews. Exploration and commerce, he said, were destroying the natural barriers between peoples and bringing about a harmful mixture among those whom nature had intended to live apart. Lucilio Vanini argued in 1619 that the Ethiopians must have had apes for ancestors because they were the same color as apes. Undoubtedly, he added, the Ethiopians had once walked on all fours.[24]

In 1655, Isaac de la Peyrère, a French Protestant, published a book in which he argued that there had been two separate creations of human beings. In the first chapter of Genesis, a man and a woman are given dominion over every living thing, but it is not until the second chapter that anything is said of the creation of Adam and Eve. Therefore, argued Peyrère, a race of men must have existed before Adam. It was from this race that Cain had chosen his wife when he was cast off by his own people for the murder of Abel. It was the pre-Adamite races from whom the natives of Africa, Asia, and the New World were descended.[25]

Both astrology and theories of the separate origin of races, however, were in time repudiated by the Roman Catholic church. In 1559, Pope Paul IV placed astrology and other methods of divination such as the cult of physiognomy on the Index. The church acted even more strongly against the theory of separate origin of primitive peoples. Vanini and Bruno were burned at the stake for their various heresies. Peyrère was imprisoned for six months and released only on condition that he retract his heretical beliefs, among them his belief in pre-Adamite races. There is understandably some doubt that his retraction was genuine.[26]

It would be a mistake to imagine, however, that it was merely the power of the church to condemn and punish heresy which prevented theories of separate origin of races from developing. It is probable that only a few men reflected on this idea. Leonardo da Vinci, who was certainly no slavish believer in the authority of the church and was perfectly capable of contradicting its dogma when he disagreed with it, was convinced that mankind really is unified and that physical differences among races could be explained by environment. He thought that men born in hot countries are black because they find the cool dark nights refreshing and do much of their work at that time and thus become dark, while the peoples of northern climates are blond because they work during the day.[27]

Race theory, then, had up until fairly modern times no firm hold on European thought. On the other hand, race theory and race prejudice were by no means unknown at the time when the English colonists came to North America. Undoubtedly, the age of exploration led many to speculate on race differences at a period when neither Europeans nor Englishmen were prepared to make allowances for vast cultural diversities. Even though race theories had not then secured wide acceptance or even sophisticated formulation, the first contacts of the Spanish with the Indians in the Americas can now be recognized as the beginning of a struggle between conceptions of the nature of primitive peoples which has not yet been wholly settled.

II

England's American Colonies
And Race Theories

ALTHOUGH in the seventeenth century race theories had not as yet developed any strong scientific or theological rationale, the contact of the English with Indians, and soon afterward with Negroes, in the New World led to the formation of institutions and relationships which were later justified by appeals to race theories. In the area of race relations the experience of the English as colonists was both similar to and different from that of the Spanish. Like the Spaniards, the Englishmen frequently professed that conversion of the Indians and Negroes was one of their chief aims. On the other hand, they did not succeed so well as did the Spanish in converting the Indians or in assimilating Indians and Negroes into their own society.

When England began to plant colonies in the New World, the works of Las Casas were translated and the accounts of the cruelty of the Spanish toward the Indians aroused considerable indignation. Richard Hakluyt in his *Discourse on Western Planting* (1584) included some of the goriest passages on Spanish cruelties related by Las Casas, apparently to warn Queen Elizabeth of the perfidy of Spain.[1] Sir Walter Raleigh recognized in Las Casas' descriptions of the horrors of Spanish atrocities a valuable propaganda weapon for the English. He suggested that Las Casas' *Very Brief Account of the Destruction of the Indies* be translated into the native language of the Indians of Peru with gruesome pictorial illustrations to warn the Indians of their probable fate under the Spanish.[2]

This anti-Spanish propaganda often implied that the English

would handle things differently in their colonies. Accordingly, we find the conversion of the Indians given a good deal of prominence by the colonists in their bids for financial support both from the government and from private sources. In one of their earliest official publications, the Virginia colonists emphasized that the

Principal and Maine Ends [of the new colony] . . . were first to preach and baptize into Christian Religion and by propagation of the Gospell, to recover out of the arms of Divell, a number of poore and miserable soules, wrapt up unto death, in almost invincible ignorance; . . . and to add our myte to the Treasury of Heaven.[3]

The charter of the Massachusetts Bay Colony stated that it was the principal aim of the plantation to "Winn and incite the natives of the country to the knowledge and obedience of the onlie true God and Savior of Mankinde, and the Christian Faythe." The seal of the colony bore a figure of an Indian with the words inscribed, "Come over and help us."

These expressions of intention were not necessarily hypocritical, nor were the contacts between white men and Indians invariably hostile. For example, when King James I objected to the marriage of John Rolfe and Pocahontas, it was not for a reason which would give much comfort to anyone seeking for early racism. His objection apparently came from his feeling that Rolfe, a commoner, was giving himself airs by marrying an Indian princess. It has been suggested that King James was less concerned about the niceties of protocol than he was about the possibility that Rolfe or his descendants might lay claim to the colony of Virginia because of Pocahontas' royal blood. Rolfe's attitude toward Pocahontas was not one to bear out the romantic legend. Although liaisons between English men and Indian women were not uncommon, marriages were rare.[4]

Both in Virginia and in New England, attempts were made to convert the Indians. In 1619 Sir Edwin Sandys, treasurer of the Virginia Company, urged that a college be founded which would accept both Indian and whites, and plans were also made for a preparatory school. The Indian massacre of 1622, however, checked any further attempts at Indian education in Virginia until the opening of William and Mary College in 1688.[5] In New England, Roger Williams began to study the language of an Indian tribe and to engage in missionary work. In 1636, the Plymouth Colony enacted laws to provide for the preaching of the gospel among the Indians. In 1646, the General Court of Massachusetts directed the ministers to select each year two of their number to serve as Indian missionaries.[6]

The best known of the missionaries is John Eliot. He began this work in 1646, and after some initial failures, the missions began to grow. Eliot studied the language of the tribe intensively. In 1661 he published an Indian translation of the New Testament, and in 1663 a translation of the Old Testament. Towns of "Praying Indians" were formed. By 1675 there were fourteen such towns in Massachusetts, and in all of New England there were perhaps as many as 2,500 converted Indians. Apparently, Eliot did not plan that Indians should become assimilated in white communities. He tells us that the Indians themselves desired to be segregated from the whites, and he seems to have believed separation to be wise. In November, 1648, he wrote to Governor Winslow in London:

The Indians are not willing to come to live near to the English, because they have neither tools, nor skill, nor heart to fence their grounds, and if it be not well fenced their Corne is spoyled by the English cattle, which is a great discouragement to them and to me. A place must be found somewhere remote from the English, where they must have the word constantly taught, and government constantly exercised.[7]

But one must regretfully dismiss these efforts to convert the Indians as exceptions rather than the rule. Actual contact with the Indians seems to have engendered fear and hatred rather than the desire to convert. After the massacre of 1622, the Virginia colonists sent a report to London which seemed to imply that the "principal end" of the colony was no longer to convert the Indians. The report expressed some satisfaction that the rebellious incident had occurred, because "our hands, which before were tied with gentleness and fair usage, are now set at liberty by the treacherous violence of the savages," and it added that "the way of conquering them is much more easy than of civilizing them."[8]

In New England, the Indian outbreak known as King Philip's War, which lasted from 1675 to 1676, effectively squelched most missionary activities on behalf of the Indians. This war, which is estimated to have taken a toll of one-sixteenth of the white male inhabitants of New England, was fought with great cruelty on both sides, and for a long time afterward the idea of Indians as potential Christians was received among the colonists with considerable skepticism. Even the Praying Indians were suspect. Early in the war, one of their settlements was moved, not because of any charges against them, but because they were believed to be potentially a source of trouble. One chief among the Praying Indians was noted for his piety and "had so good a memory that he could rehearse the whole catechism, both questions and answers." However, "Old Jacob"— as he was known among the white settlers—was among those who participated in an Indian raid and helped to murder the wife and three or four of the children of a white colonist.[9]

The conviction that the Indians were and presumably always would be bloodthirsty savages deepened after King Philip's War. The accounts of the scalping expeditions naturally stressed the tortures and cruelties of the Indians. Mary Rowlandson, who was herself a captive of the Indians for eleven weeks, wrote one of the most stirring of the popular accounts of the inhuman ferocity of the Indians in their attacks on white settlements—a book which has gone through as many as thirty editions. Mrs. Rowlandson described the Indians as "murtherous wretches," "merciless Heathen," "hell-hounds," and "Barbarous Creatures."[10] Increase Mather, in his account of the discovery of a settler who had been burned at the stake by the Indians, tells us that the colonists found him soon after his death, while the fire was still burning. "He was left for Us, to put out the Fire with our

Tears!" And Mather exclaims, "Reader, Who should be the Father of these Myrmidons?" Mather also says that John Eliot had some years before made an effort to convert King Philip himself, but that "monster" merely grabbed a button on the coat of the missionary and declared that he "cared for his gospel just as much as he cared for that button." Mather drew the conclusion that the "world has heard what a terrible ruine soon came upon that monarch, and upon all his people."[11]

What hope was there, the white colonists reflected, for the conversion of such a cruel and inhuman people? As early as 1648, John Cotton had tended to discourage the hope that the Indians would be converted, except for a scattered few:

There may be doubt that for a time will be no great hope of any national conversion, till Anti-christ be ruined, and the Jews converted: because the Church of God is said to be filled with smoke, till the seven plagues (which are to be poured upon the Anti-christian state) be fulfilled: And till then, no man (that is, no considerable number of men out of the Church, as Pagans be) shall be able to enter into the Church, Rev. 15, 8. Yet nevertheless, that hindreth not, but that some sprinklings, and gleanings of them may be brought home to Christ.[12]

With King Philip's War, the settlements of the Praying Indians disintegrated and John Eliot saw his work undone. "There is a cloud," he said in his old age, "a dark cloud upon the work of the Gospel among the poor Indians. The Lord revive and prosper that work, and grant that it may live when I am dead."[13]

That some of the Puritans were uneasy in their consciences concerning the failure of the Indian missions is indicated by Increase Mather in his history of King Philip's War, published in 1676. Mather apparently thought his remarks might be offensive to some of his fellow colonists, since he begins by saying, "I have desired to approve myself as in the sight of God, speaking what I believe God would have me speak, without respect to any person in this world." He then says there are "some that make a wrong use" of John Cotton's opinion that the conversion of the Indians must not be expected before certain prophecies

mentioned in the Book of Revelation are fulfilled. "It is far
from my purpose to contradict that Great Author," Mather says
of Cotton, who was his father-in-law, but he feels that the
colonists have misinterpreted Cotton's idea. Cotton had never
"intended that that Assertion should be improved so as to discourage the prosecution of that which was the professed, pious,
and a main design of the *Fathers* of this *Colony:* viz. *To propa-*
gate the Gospel and Kingdom of Christ among these Indians,
who in former Ages had not heard of his fame and Glory."
While not denying that Cotton's interpretation of the prophecies was correct, Mather argues that even "the Salvation of a few
immortal Souls is worth the labour of many all their lives."[14]
And he proceeds to praise the work of John Eliot.

One reason why Mather felt uncomfortable about the failure
to convert the Indians was that Catholics had apparently done
better elsewhere. "It troubleth me, when I read how the *Papists*
glory in that they have converted so many of the *East* and *West*
Indians to the *Christian Faith,* and reproach Protestants, because
they have been no more industrious in a work of that nature."
Of course, he says—apparently forgetting for the moment that
there were slaves in New England—the Catholics convert the
Indians only so they can enslave them. He comforts himself with
the reflection that the Catholics are merely converting the Indians to "Heresies" and thus they are *"twofold more the child-*
ren of Hell, than they were before." Besides, the conversions
were in name only. He quotes a story he has heard of a Fran-
ciscan in the New World who wrote to a friend in Europe that
in a period of twenty-six years of living among the Indians he
had converted many thousands of them to the Faith, "and he
desired his Friend to send him a Book called the *Bible,* for he
heard there was such a Book in *Europe,* which might be of some
use to him."[15]

A stronger impulse than this was needed if the Puritans were
to keep alive their missionary spirit. When John Eliot died in
1690, the attempt to Christianize the Indians had all but ceased.
In the middle of the eighteenth century, William Douglass

wrote a history of the American colonies in which he praised Eliot's goodness but questioned his judgment. He pointed out that the tribe of Natick Indians for whom Eliot had translated the Bible had been reduced to fewer than twenty families, "and scarce any of these can read." And Douglass reflected: *"Cui bono!"*[16] With the ending of missionary enterprise, the conviction was free to grow that the only good Indian was a dead Indian.

One explanation of the differences between Spanish and English opinions of Indians is to be found in the different characters of the Indians whom the two nations encountered. The Indians of Mexico, the Caribbean islands, and South America had—with some exceptions—tended to be agriculturalists rather than hunters, settled into stable villages and towns, and were generally less proficient in warfare. They were easier to subdue and did not represent the danger on the frontier that the northern Indians frequently did. Thus, among the Spanish we find Indians frequently characterized as gentle people. Las Casas says of them:

God made this numerous people very simple, without trickery or malice, most obedient and faithful to their natural lords, and to the Spaniards, whom they serve; most humble, most patient, very peaceful and manageable, without quarrels, strife, bitterness or hate, none desiring vengeance. They are a very delicate and tender folk, of slender build, and cannot stand much work, and often die of whatever sicknesses they have; so that even our own princes and lords, cared for with all conveniences, luxuries and delights, are not more delicate than these people . . . who possess little, and who do not desire many worldly goods; nor are they proud, ambitious, or covetous. . . . They have a very clear and lively understanding, being docile and able to receive all good doctrine, quite fitted to understand our holy Catholic faith, and to be instructed in good and virtuous habits, having less hindrances in the way of doing this than any other people in the world. . . . Certainly these people would be the happiest in the world if only they knew God.[17]

While it is unlikely that the Indians were quite this admirable, Las Casas is undoubtedly describing people different from those encountered by the English in North America. Among the Spanish we find plenty of contempt for the Indians, but we do not find great fear of them because of cruelty or barbarity.

Another obstacle which Englishmen encountered in converting the Indians was that their Protestant ideas of conversion were frequently more rigorous than those of the Catholic missionaries. Religion was for them a matter of much study. They limited full church membership to only a minority among themselves, and thus they were hesitant to accept the conversion of alien peoples like the Indians. The Catholics, on the other hand, tended to accept conversions which they must have realized were purely nominal, in the hope that such conversions would some day become genuine.

One indication that the relationships of the Spanish and French with Indians were more amicable than those of the English is that the Noble Savage tradition flowered mainly in the Latin countries. Benjamin Bissell has argued that the cult of the Noble Savage flourished when the Indian was encountered in a tropical climate. The proper environment for Elysium could not be found in the North American climate where the English colonists were.[18] This explanation would seem to fit the cult of the Noble Savage in Spain, but it does little to explain it in France. The French explorers in Canada had found no tropical Eden, and the Indians there were often as savage and uncivilized as those south of the St. Lawrence. The French experience with the Indians was, it is true, less unpleasant than that of the English. They came as traders rather than as settlers like the English, who enclosed land for farming and thus made it unavailable for hunting, and so the French were more welcome.

The idea of the Noble Savage throve best among those who had little or no experience with Indians. It was more characteristic of the eighteenth century than of the sixteenth or seventeenth, although it probably had its beginnings in modern times in the accounts of the early explorers eager to advertise the attractions of the New World. English explorers such as Drake and Raleigh sometimes portrayed the Indians as noble and almost godlike creatures, handsome in form and civil in manner, but this view tended to be radically altered once the Englishmen became more familiar with Indians.[19] Favorable comments among the English colonists in the latter part of the seventeenth century tended to be limited to the Indians' proud stoicism, their prowess, and their endurance. Otherwise, the picture of the Indians was that of cruel and treacherous foes.

From the standpoint of future race theory, the most important characteristic of the English colonists was probably the fact that—unlike the French and the Spanish—they did not intermarry in significant numbers with the Indians, although they frequently did interbreed with them. Nineteenth-century American historians often regarded this reluctance of their forefathers to marry Indians as the proud self-consciousness of a superior Anglo-Saxon race.[20] Other explanations, however, seem more probable.

Arnold Toynbee believes that the emphasis upon the Old Testament among the English colonists encouraged the idea of a Chosen People divinely commissioned to exterminate the infidel.[21] Among the Puritans the idea was particularly strong. The synod of 1679 declared that

the ways of God toward this His people are in many respects like unto his dealings of old. It was a great and high undertaking of our fathers when they ventured themselves and their little ones upon the rude waves of the vast ocean, that so they might follow the Lord into this land.

Just as the Israelites conquered the inhabitants of Canaan, so the Israelites of the Massachusetts Bay Colony had conquered the Indians. "The Lord hath planted a vine, having cast out the heathen, prepared room for it and caused it to take deep root. . . . We must ascribe all these things, as unto the grace and abundant goodness of the Lord our God, so to His owning a religious design and interest."[22]

Yet the English have tended to be racially exclusive when they were not obsessed with the Puritan conviction of being a chosen people. Frederick Hertz has pointed out that the Protestant Dutch have been much more tolerant than the English in their contact with other races, a fact which is strange if racial exclusiveness is related to Protestantism. Although it is true that the Spanish were racially tolerant in the New World, Hertz continues, they strongly disapproved of intermarriage with the Jews and the Moors in their own country. Clearly, something besides the differences between Catholicism and Protestantism is involved in the idea of racial exclusiveness.[23]

Hans Kohn has attributed the seemingly more powerful appeal of racial exclusiveness to Protestant nations to their early separation of religion and politics. Luther left the settlement of all specifically nonreligious questions to the state, argues Kohn, and this decision led in turn to the creation of powerful nationalist and racist doctrines on the part of the state.[24] Yet, as Hertz says, Calvin did not share Luther's approval of the separation of religion and politics, and on this point the New England Puritans tended to follow Calvin rather than Luther. Calvin not only subjected the state to the church but shared the Catholic view that one should subordinate all areas of life to the precepts of religion. On the other hand, it is an interesting fact that Calvin was not concerned with the conversion of heathen peoples. Allowance must be made, says one of his biographers, for his interest in the multifarious problems in Europe and for the practical difficulties in the way of his undertaking missionary enterprises; but there is little indication in his writings that he felt the pressure of a foreign missionary problem. "Love ought to extend itself to all mankind," he wrote, "but those ought to be preferred whom God hath joined to us more closely and with a more holy tie."[25]

There is some truth in the idea of differences between Catholics and Protestants in the matter of racial exclusiveness. We have seen how the Catholic church and the Spanish Crown took a strong stand against the idea that the Indians of the New World might be less than human. In the Catholic church, the priest had an authority which was far more independent of local community opinion than was the authority of Protestant clerics. We have seen how much trouble Las Casas had in convincing the Spanish colonists that the Indians were "true men." If he had been a Protestant, his task would have been even more difficult. John Eliot could only gently exhort the Puritans to treat the Indians better, but Las Casas could employ the full authority of the Catholic church in dealing with Spanish colonists.

Probably more important than any of these explanations is the fact that the English were colonists and often brought their families with them, while the Spanish and French came more often as traders and left their families at home. Those Englishmen who left the settlements in order to become traders in Indian territory showed little tendency to maintain the idea of racial exclusiveness. In his *History of Carolina*, published in 1709, John Lawson spoke from the experience of his own travels among the Indians when he said:

The English trader is seldom without an Indian female for his bedfellow, alleging these reasons as sufficient to allow for such familiarity. First, they being remote from any white people, that it preserves their friendship with the heathens, they esteeming a white man's child much above one of their own getting. . . . And lastly, this correspondence makes them learn the Indian tongue much the sooner.[26]

William Byrd, the redoubtable old Virginia aristocrat and planter, criticized Englishmen in America for not having intermarried with the Indians. Merely educating a few Indians was not enough, he declared. Indians had attended William and Mary College, where they had been taught "the principles of the Christian religion until they came to be men." Yet when they returned to their own tribes, "instead of civilizing and converting the rest, they have immediately relapsed into barbarism themselves." But this failure did not lead Byrd to reflect on the innate and unchanging inferiority of the Indians. He had decided after much reflection, he tells us, that there was "but one way of converting these poor infidels and reclaiming them from barbarity, and that is charitably to intermarry with them, ac-

cording to the modern policy of the most christian king in Canada and Louisiana." If the English had been foresighted enough
to do this when they first settled in America, "the infidelity of
the Indians had been worn out at this day, with their dark complexions, and the country had swarmed with people more than
it does with insects."

It was certainly unreasonable, Byrd goes on to say, for the
colonists to think themselves too good for such alliances. "All
the nations of men have the same natural dignity, and we know
that very bright talents may be lodged under a very dark skin."
Besides, under a civilized regime it would not be long before the
Indians changed their appearance. Byrd declared:

Even their copper colored complexion would admit of blanching, if
not in the first, at the farthest in the second generation. I may safely
venture to say that the Indian women would have made altogether as
honest wives for the first planters as the damsels they used to purchase
from aboard the ships.

And with that mixture of practicality and idealism which was
characteristic of the period, Byrd adds—though probably his wit
intrudes here—that it seems strange to him that any good Christian should have "refused a wholesome straight bedfellow when
he might have had so fair a portion of her as the merit of saving
her soul."[27]

It would be interesting to know what Byrd's fellow colonists
would have thought of his suggestion. He himself seems to have
felt that the time when the plan for intermarriage might have
succeeded had already passed. Religion and customs as well as
race discouraged any widespread intermarriage. Probably the
fact that among English traders relationships with Indian wom-
en tended to be casual alliances made it all the more difficult for
intermarriage between the races to be accepted.

It was the white man's relationship with the Negro rather
than his relationship with the Indian which was eventually
rationalized into the most powerful racist doctrine this country
has known. It is true that Indians, too, were sometimes enslaved,

but only sporadically. The Indian was not adapted for the kind of work the white man required and slavery was alien to him, whereas the Negro slave frequently found himself in a position in the colonies which was not wholly different from his position in Africa under a tribal chieftain. Slavery first began when "twenty Negars" were landed at Jamestown in 1619, but it did not become an important source of labor until more than sixty years later. The institution spread after 1680 because not enough English bond-servants could be secured, because English and Dutch slave traders redoubled their activities, and because competition among tobacco farmers intensified the search for cheap labor.[28]

The importance of Negro slavery in generating race theories in this country can hardly be overestimated, but it must be remembered that there was a minimum of theory at the time the institution was established. The theory of any political or social institution is likely to develop only when it comes under attack, and the time for opposition to slavery was still far in the future. Oscar Handlin has written an excellent account of how the institution of slavery developed in Virginia. The Negroes were pushed into a society where most of the people were bond-servants and therefore to some degree unfree. Since the word *slave* had no meaning in English law, the Negro was thought of as a servant and not as a slave. The fact that no time for the ending of the Negro's servitude was set is no proof that the Negroes really were considered as slaves, argues Handlin. The reason was that in England, where there was a plentiful labor supply, the employer was accustomed to a system in which the expiration of a term of service had little meaning because the servant was nearly always obliged by his circumstances simply to sign up for another term of service.[29]

The labor system in the colonies tended to work to the advantage of the white bond-servant. In order to combat the publicity given to harsh treatment of servants in the colonies, the term of indentured service was shortened, first for Englishmen and later on for Irishmen and other aliens. The Negro, on the other hand, did not have to be placated in this way because there was no need to encourage more Negroes to come to the colonies or to combat adverse opinion in Africa. As the term of service for white bond-servants was decreasing, the demand for labor was increasing. In these circumstances, the number of Negroes imported greatly increased. In the 1660's, the status of Negroes was finally recognized as different from that of other servants. The Maryland House enacted a bill which stated, "All Negroes and other slaves shall serve Durante Vita." Virginia law was at first more indirect. In an act of 1661 imposing penalties on runaways it recognized that some Negroes were to be slaves for life. It was not until 1670 that Virginia law specified that "all servants not being christians" who were brought into the colony by sea were to be slaves for life.[30]

The fact that the legal condition of the first Negroes who arrived in America was not different from that of white bond-servants has led to interesting speculations concerning the extent to which the white colonists were concerned with the matter of race differences. Slavery, it has sometimes been argued, was first considered in the colonies as an interim institution designed to convert both Negroes and Indians to Christianity. It is sometimes further argued that the early white colonists were little troubled about their physical differences from the Negroes.[31]

There is evidence, however, that there was a caste barrier between whites and Negroes before the institution of slavery legally came into being. Guy B. Johnson observes that it is extremely doubtful whether the white people of the colonies felt the same toward Negroes as they did toward their white bond-servants. He points out that an early court record of Virginia in 1630 reads as follows: "Hugh Davis to be soundly whipt before an assembly of Negroes and others for abusing himself to the dishonor of God and shame of Christianity by defiling his body in lying with a Negro, which fault he is to acknowledge next Sabbath day." It could be argued that Davis was punished for fornication and not because his partner was a Negro. However, the fact that mulattoes were already spoken of as "spurious issue" or "abominable mixture" indicates that the early colonists wished to keep the races separate. In New England, a white woman married a Negro in 1681, lived with him for years, and bore him children, but she was completely ostracized by her family and by the community.[32]

It is interesting, however, that among the colonists of the seventeenth and early eighteenth centuries it is the heathenism of the Negroes and Indians, rather than their race, which is emphasized as a basis for their enslavement. In 1710, Cotton Mather founded a school for slaves. While admitting that the slave trade is "a spectacle that shocks humanity," he wondered whether the Negroes' coming to this country might not represent the obscure workings of Providence.

God, whom you must remember to be "your Master in heaven," has brought them, and put them into your hands. Who can tell what good he has brought them for? How if they should be the elect of God, fetched from Africa, or the Indies, and brought into your families, on purposes, that by the means of their being there, they may be brought home unto the Shepherd of souls!

In the South, when the institution of slavery came under heavy attack in the nineteenth century, a principal justification offered for it was that it was a means of converting the heathen. In the eighteenth century, however, when slavery was virtually unchallenged in the South, we find little reliance upon this particular argument. At least, Bishop Berkeley testified in 1731 that American slaveholders had "an irrational contempt of the blacks, as creatures of another species, who had no right to be instructed or admitted to the sacraments."[33]

III

Eighteenth-Century
Anthropology

IN 1684, François Bernier, a French physician who had traveled widely, published an article in a Paris journal on the subject of human differences. "The geographers up until this point," says Bernier, "have divided the world only according to the different countries or regions." His own travel had suggested to him a different method of classification—that based upon the facial lineaments and bodily conformations of the people. For Bernier, there are four general classifications of what would now be called races—the Europeans, the Far Easterners, the "blacks," and the Lapps. The Indians of America are not a separate people, he maintains, although he does not specify to which of the four categories they belong.[1]

Bernier admits that Europeans differ a good deal from country to country, but even so he considers all Europeans—with the exception of the Lapps—as members of the same race. He does not describe the Europeans, perhaps because he thought that such a description would be unnecessary for his readers, but he does describe the other races. The "blacks" of Africa have thick lips and flat noses. Their skin has a polished look and their hair is like a species of wool or like the hair of some spaniels. Their teeth are as white as the finest ivory. The Far Easterners have a peculiar "turn" to their faces and oddly shaped eyes. The Lapps are short with large feet and large shoulders. They are the only "race" he describes with evident distaste. These people have faces similar to those of bears, he tells us, and are "quite frightful." He admits that he has seen only two Lapps himself, but he adds

32

that other people have confirmed him in his impression that the Lapps are "villains animaux."[2]

The significance of Bernier's observations lies in the fact that his is probably the first attempt in history to classify all the races of mankind. Biologically, classification even of the lower animals was then primitive and rudimentary. The attempt to explain the universe in terms of natural laws had made possible the development of the sciences of physics and chemistry, but not that of biology. The best scientific minds of the seventeenth century were engrossed with such problems as the laws of motion and the effect of gravity. To illustrate the difference between the problems of the physicist and those of the biologist, A. R. Hall compares the theories of Galileo with those of Darwin. He remarks that less mental effort is required to grasp the plausibility of the laws of inertia than to understand the evidence for the concept of evolution. A presentation of the theory of evolution demanded an elaborate discussion of varied and obscure evidence. Galileo's *Discourse on Two Sciences,* on the other hand, relied upon evidence which could be verified fairly quickly by an intelligent observer. Darwin's theory was the result of more than twenty years of the patient filling of notebooks with materials relating to his problem. Even this accumulation would probably not have been possible, Hall goes on to say, had not Darwin been able to rely upon a tradition of descriptive natural history which had been painstakingly built up—largely after the seventeenth century.[3]

This lag was important in the development of race theory. The scientists of the seventeenth and eighteenth centuries did not infer general laws concerning organic phenomena in any sense comparable to the laws of motion in physics. The result was that biology remained a subject generally outside the mechanistic propositions which were applied in physics and chemistry. Just as the astronomers before Galileo had assumed that angels governed the movements of the planets, so scientific thought in the seventeenth and eighteenth centuries usually assumed that the Creator must personally have attended to the fabrication of every animal and plant on earth. An organism was what it was because God had decided it should be so. Its similarities with other organisms were evidence of God's glory but in themselves were incidental and unimportant. All this meant that the study of race differences, like the study of biology itself, was in its infancy.[4]

Even if the situation in the biological sciences had been different, the temper of the eighteenth century would have found it difficult to assimilate theories of race superiority and inferiority. The emphasis upon universal reason was then enough to keep the philosophers of the Enlightenment uncomfortable in the presence of theories which implied conceptions of innate character and intelligence. It was the hope and belief of the Enlightenment that at birth the mind of a child is a *tabula rasa,* an empty receptacle. Education and environment could make this child into a completely reasonable and intelligent being. The idea that character is innate belonged, in this view, to discredited Calvinist ideas of predestination. If the mind of man should prove not to be a *tabula rasa* at the time of birth, then hopes for universal progress would receive a crushing blow. Thus race theories were considered a challenge to the optimism of the Enlightenment.[5]

For example, we find Leibnitz objecting, in 1737, even to the relatively mild and harmless system of race classification developed by Bernier. "I recollect reading somewhere, though I cannot find the passage," says Leibnitz, "that a certain traveller had divided man into certain tribes, races or classes. He made one special race of the Lapps or Samoyedes, another of the Chinese and their neighbors, another of the Caffres and Hottentots." Leibnitz is willing to admit that both the physical appearance and the dispositions of men are different in different parts of the world. Among the Indians in the Americas, for example, the "Galibs" and the "Caribs" are brave and spirited, but the Indians of Paraguay "seem to be infants, or in pupilage all their lives." But these differences are not enough to make Leibnitz accept the idea of separate races. "That . . . is no reason," he says, "why all men who inhabit the earth should not be of the same race, which has been altered by different climates, as we see that beasts and plants change their nature, and improve or degenerate."[6]

In eighteenth-century anthropology a distinction was made between *species,* on the one hand, and *varieties* on the other. Species were regarded as immutable prototypes, "separate thoughts in the mind of God," perfectly designed for their role in the divine economy of nature. Varieties, by contrast, were merely those members of a single species who—because of such conditioning factors as climate and geography—had changed their appearance in one way or another.[7]

The idea of the fixity of species is the basis of the classification system for all living organisms devised by Linnaeus. "There are as many species," he stated as a law, "as there are forms produced in the beginning by the Infinite Being." Linnaeus was little interested in varieties, except to distinguish them from true species. Since he considered the races of man varieties and not different species, he has comparatively little to say of them. His contribution to science lies almost wholly in his system of nomenclature. He considered his work done when he had classified a biological organism, assigned it to a place, and tagged it with a name so that in the future it could be identified. He divided mankind into four varieties: *Homo Europaeus, Homo Asiaticus, Homo Afer,* and *Homo Americanus.*[8]

One of the most influential authorities in natural history in the eighteenth century was George Louis Leclerc Buffon. Over a period of fifty-five years—from 1749 to 1804—his work appeared in forty-four volumes, the unfinished portions being edited after his death by an assistant. He was neither a profound investigator nor sufficiently skeptical of his sources—later on his great work was dubbed the "unnatural" *Natural History*— but he did collect a great deal of information and stimulate interest in his subject. Most of his attention was given to the lower biological orders, but he does have something to say concerning the variety of human races.[9]

For Buffon, the white race is the norm. It is to that we must look for the "real and natural color of man." All other races are exotic variations, but it would be wrong to think of them as different species. "Classes and genera are only the arbitrary operations of our own fancy," he declared. Excessive heat has made the Negroes black. As they darkened under a tropical sun, their descendants eventually acquired blackness as a hereditary characteristic. If the Negroes should be imported to Europe, over a period of generations their descendants would gradually lighten in color, eventually to a shade "perhaps as white as the natives of that climate." The fact that excessive cold tends to darken the skin explains the relatively dark complexions of the Laplanders and Greenlanders. Differences which cannot be explained by temperature he attributes to the altitude of the land, the nearness to the sea, the diet and social customs of the people. Race, therefore, is not a constant. It "persists as long as the milieu remains and disappears when the milieu is changed."[10]

Buffon does mention the fact that travelers in Africa have found Negro tribes so primitive that they cannot count beyond the number three, and he is willing to concede that the Negroes have "little genius." But then he adds that "the unfortunate Negroes are endowed with excellent hearts, and possess the seeds of every human virtue." One wonders whether he thought that stupidity among Negroes would disappear—just as their dark skin would—in a colder climate. In his *Natural History,* he pauses from his scientific labors at one point to denounce the advocates of slavery: "How can men, in whose breasts a single spark of humanity remains unextinguished, adopt such detestable maxims? How dare they, by such barbarous and diabolical arguments, attempt to palliate those oppressions which originate solely from their thirst for gold?"[11]

An Englishman who was influenced by Buffon was Dr. John Hunter, a famous surgeon who in 1775 published a widely discussed theory of the causes of race differences. Like Buffon, Hunter regarded climate as the main determinant of race. He recognized, however, that Europeans who live in the tropics do not acquire a naturally darker skin even after residence there over a period of generations, nor do Negroes who come to Europe lighten in color if they interbreed only among themselves. More than climate was necessary to change the color of one's skin. To achieve this result, one must "try those modes and ways of life" which are typical of a given country. Climate was only one of the causes of change. That it was important he had no doubt, and as proof he mentions the fact that Negroes are born white and remain so for several hours, the sun and air being agents in turning the skin to a black color. In addition, he thought the fact that a blister or burn on a Negro is likely to be white is an indication that this was the original color of his remote ancestors. Hunter encouraged the study of natural history in England, developing an extensive museum of zoölogical specimens.[12]

Johann Friedrich Blumenbach, a professor of medicine at the University of Göttingen, had a lifelong interest in the study of race differences. His doctoral thesis, "On the Natural Variety of Mankind" (1775), was the first of his long series of ethnological studies of the meaning of race. He collected specimens of human skeletons, particularly crania, from all over the world. He became famous as a cofounder with Buffon of the science of anthropology and in his own right as the "father of craniology." Like Buffon, he was convinced that no precise data could be developed to differentiate and classify the races. "Innumerable varieties of mankind," he declared, "run into one another by insensible degrees." Although he thought any system of classification was arbitrary and subject to many exceptions, Blumenbach did believe it possible to divide mankind into five varieties—Caucasian, Mongolian, Ethiopian, American, and Malay. This is roughly the same classification still often found in geography textbooks and sometimes codified in law, although the terms are usually different. Most often, the races are named by colors: white, yellow, black, red, and brown. It was Blumenbach who coined the word *Caucasian* to describe the white race. It is curious that this word—which is still widely used—is based

upon a single skull in Blumenbach's collection which came from
the Caucasian mountain region of Russia. Blumenbach found
strong resemblances between this skull and the crania of the
Germans. Therefore, he conjectured that possibly the Caucasus
regions may have been the original home of the Europeans.[13]

Blumenbach was a careful investigator of the theories of
race differences current at the time. He finds none of the explanations wholly satisfactory. He quotes the opinion that Belgians have oblong skulls because the Belgian women have the
habit of letting their children sleep on their sides in swaddling
clothes. If this is true, he asks, why is it that animal breeders
cannot artificially induce a new variety by mutilations carried
out over several generations? He would be willing to go along
with those who believe that acquired characters can be inherited,
he says, if they "could explain why the peculiarities of the same
sort of conformation, which are first made intentionally or accidentally, cannot be in any way handed down to descendants."[14]

He thought that differences in color among races might have
been created, not by climate precisely, but by a combination of
climate and other factors. He thought that blackness in Negroes,
for example, might have been caused by a tendency in the tropics
for carbon to become imbedded in human skin. Carbon in contact with oxygen would darken. Perhaps such a theory might
explain why Negro babies turn black after having been born
white. Or perhaps there might be other explanations for the
blackness of Negroes. It was significant, he thought, that the
liver is frequently more active in a European when he goes to the
tropics. The endemic and bilious complaints which white people
developed in such climates might be related to bodily changes
which take place over generations and eventually create different races. Or perhaps there might be some connection between
the blackness which white women sometimes develop during
pregnancy and the blackness which Negroes have developed as
their permanent attribute. For Blumenbach, all these ideas were
entirely speculative, and he had no solution to the question of
the cause of race differences.[15]

He frequently directed his satire, however, against those who thought races were superior or inferior. Those who chose to rank the races in order of their beauty especially irritated him. "If a toad could speak," he observed, "and were asked which was the loveliest creature upon God's earth, it would say simpering, that modesty forbade it to give a real opinion on that point." He protests against those who compare the races by putting an ugly Negro opposite a Greek god. He considers Negroes, Indians, and Mongolians as potentially valuable members of society and is convinced that they bear no hereditary taint. He notes with interest that Benjamin Rush in America was acquainted with a Negro who was a mathematical genius. Blumenbach himself collected a library of books written by Negroes, to demonstrate that they are not inherently stupid.[16]

In the United States, Reverend Mr. Samuel Stanhope Smith wrote, in 1787, an ethnological treatise on race animated by the same optimism concerning human differences which actuated Buffon, Hunter, and Blumenbach. Smith was a Presbyterian minister and a professor of moral philosophy at the College of New Jersey, later to become Princeton. He was, however, interested in science. When he became president of the college in 1795, he raised funds for scientific apparatus and brought to the faculty John Maclean, the first teacher of chemistry and natural science in this country. Convinced that race differences were caused by climate and that Negroes were innately the same as whites, Smith wrote a treatise, *Essay on the Causes of the Variety of Complexion and Figure . . .* , to expound his ideas on racial equality.[17]

Attributing color mainly to climate, Smith said that dark skins might well "be considered as a universal freckle." As one moved toward the tropics he would find successively darker shades of skin. He himself had noticed, he tells us, that the white inhabitants of the southern part of New Jersey were darker in color than the people of Pennsylvania. The white people of Maryland and Virginia were darker still, and Carolinians "degenerate to a complexion that is but a few shades lighter than

that of the Iroquois," especially in those classes exposed constantly to the sun. In time, he believed, the dark color of these
people would become hereditary. Like Buffon, Smith explained
the fact that the shades of complexion of some people did not
match the degree of darkness which their latitude on earth
should indicate by arguing that one must also take into account
the "elevation of the land, its vicinity to the sea, the nature of
the soil, the state of cultivation, the course of winds, and many
other circumstances." Since the causes of race differences were
so numerous and complex, he concluded that there could be no
accurate system of classification of races. "It is impossible to
draw the line precisely between the various races of men," he
says, "or even to enumerate them with certainty," and it would
be "a useless labor to attempt it."[18]

Smith was convinced that all that stood in the way of the
advancement of Negroes and other nonwhite races was their bad
environment. Social factors even influenced bodily conformation and facial lineaments, he declared. As a young man he had
had a pastorate in Virginia. There, he tells us, he detected great
differences between field slaves and house slaves. The field slaves
had "ill shaped" features, the "African lips, and nose, and hair,"
and appeared to be "sleepy and stupid." The house slaves, on the
other hand, had "agreeable and regular features" and "the ex-
pressive countenance of civilized society." He thought that if
the Negroes "were perfectly free, enjoyed property, and were
admitted to a liberal participation of the society, rank and privileges of their masters, they would change their African peculiarities much faster."[19]

What seemed to be a dramatic confirmation of Smith's theory about the influence of climate upon human skin color was the
case of Henry Moss. Born a slave in Virginia, Moss had joined
the Continental Army and had fought in the Revolution. After
years of living in the North, he began to develop white spots on
his body and in three years he had become almost entirely white.
In 1796 he was exhibited in Philadelphia as a curiosity of science.
Smith declared that Moss was living proof that the human spe-

cies is a unity, that Negroes would in time change their complexion to white if they lived in a northern climate. Smith noted that "wherever there were rents in the thin clothes which covered him there were generally seen the largest spots of black," proof that the sun was the determinant of a dark color.[20]

Did other Americans of the time share Smith's optimism concerning the potentialities of the Negroes and Indians? Informed opinion was undoubtedly on his side on the issue of the unity of human races. On this point, both science and theology were in agreement except for a few dissenters. In 1795, a debating society at Dickinson College in Pennsylvania discussed the question of the unity of the races and the side which won maintained that "the races of man are descended from a common original." On the idea that a favorable environment could work wonders for Negroes and Indians, Smith also had considerable support, at least among the intellectuals, though here the support was much more qualified. The Declaration of Independence did, it is true, say that "all men are created equal," and to some this meant not merely a presumed equality before the law, but equality in native endowment. Benjamin Rush, the friend of Jefferson and one of the eminent scientists and philanthropists of his time, subscribed to the idea of the innate equality of the races. "The history of the creation of man and of the relation of our species to each other by birth, which is recorded in the Old Testament," Rush maintained, "is the . . . strongest argument that can be used in favor of the original and natural equality of all mankind." And Rush was as impressed by the case of Henry Moss as Smith was, although his explanation of the phenomenon was slightly different. Blackness in Negroes, in his view, was a mild and apparently uncontagious form of a disease. He explained to a meeting of the American Philosophical Society that "the Black Color (as it is called) of the Negroes is derived from the LEPROSY," but Moss was, for some reason, undergoing a cure induced by nature itself and was thus reverting to his natural white color.[21]

Americans were already sensitive to the charge that for all

their talk of freedom they were slaveholders. "How is it that we hear the loudest *yelps* for liberty," crusty old Samuel Johnson is reported as saying, "among the drivers of negroes?" Thomas Jefferson strongly disapproved of slavery himself, but—in spite of his writing in the Declaration that "all men are created equal" —did not really believe that Negroes are inherently the equals of white men. In his *Notes on Virginia* (1786), he set down his reasons for believing that the Negro is condemned by nature to an inferior status.[22]

Jefferson argues, first of all, that the Negro is ugly. He asks whether the blushes, those "fine mixtures of red and white," which lend to the "expressions of every passion" in the white race are not superior to the "eternal monotony,—that immovable veil of black which covers the emotions of the other race?" In addition, the Negroes have "a very strong and disagreeable odor." The "flowing hair" and "more elegant symmetry of form," says Jefferson, convinces the Negroes themselves that the whites are more beautiful. "The circumstance of superior beauty is thought worthy attention in the propagation of our horses, dogs, and other domestic animals," Jefferson reflects. "Why not in that of men?"[23]

It is the mental and moral characteristics of Negroes, how-ever, which Jefferson cites as the most obvious proof of their inferiority. He admits that they are "at least as brave, and more adventuresome than the whites." But he quickly adds that this bravery "may proceed from a want of forethought." They may have some musical ability since they are "capable of imagining a small catch," but he doubts whether they would be able to learn a complicated melody. "They are more ardent after their female; but love seems with them to be more an eager desire, than a tender delicate mixture of sentiment and sensation." Their "griefs are transient." Their existence "appears to participate more of sensations than reflections." "In memory they are equal to the whites; in reason much inferior," and "in imagination they are dull, tasteless, and anomalous."[24]

Jefferson argues that the absence of Negro achievement cannot be wholly due to lack of opportunity. The Indians have had no more advantages than the Negroes, but they "often carve figures on their pipes not destitute of design or merit." The Indians have

a germ in their minds which only wants cultivation. They astonish you with strokes of the most sublime oratory; such as prove their reason and sentiment strong. But never yet could I find a black had uttered a thought above the level of plain narration; never saw even an elementary trait of painting or sculpture.

If the lack of imagination in Negroes were due to their situation, Jefferson continues, we should at least expect to find some poetry among them, since "misery is often the parent of the most affecting touches in poetry." But Negroes are incapable of such productions. "Among the blacks is misery enough, God knows, but no poetry." Love is "the peculiar oestrum of the poet." But for the Negro it only "kindles the senses." "Religion has produced a Phyllis Wheatley [the Negro poetess], but it could not produce a poet. The compositions published under her name are below the dignity of criticism." Imagination in Negroes is "wild and extravagant, escapes incessantly from every restraint of reason and taste, and, in the course of its vagaries, leaves a train of thought as incoherent and eccentric, as is the course of a meteor through the sky."[25]

It is not an argument, Jefferson declares, to say that the Negroes are slaves and have had no opportunities to cultivate the arts. Under the Romans the condition of slaves was "much more deplorable" than that of American slaves. But because Roman slaves were superior to Negroes they were able to become "rare artists" and learned men, "tutors to their masters' children," examples being Epictetus, Terence, and Phaedrus. Jefferson will concede only that Negroes are generally kindly and humane. "Whether further observation will or will not verify the conjecture, that nature has been less bountiful to them in the endowments of the head," he says, "I believe that in those of the heart she will be found to have done them justice." Jefferson had read Buffon and was perhaps uneasily aware that his own opinion of Negroes was not shared by most of the men of his time who were specialists in natural history. We cannot "degrade a whole race of men from the work in the scale of beings which their creator may perhaps have given them," he says. "I advance it, therefore, as a suspicion only, that the blacks, whether originally a distinct race, or made distinct by time and circumstance, are inferior to the whites in the endowment both of body and of mind."[26]

At this point, Jefferson was very near a much more explosive issue than the question of Negro equality. The idea that the Negroes might be a "distinct race" was then associated with atheism and blasphemy. One of its advocates in France was Voltaire. Though he never gave the subject of race detailed attention, Voltaire did pour ridicule on those foolish enough to imagine that human races—as different as they are—should all have descended from Adam and Eve. In characteristic fashion, he begins one of his essays, "The People of America," by relating how all the wise men of Europe had declared when America was first discovered that it could not exist. Then, after its existence was incontestable, they began ransacking ancient books to find which one of "Noah's great-grandsons" had taken the trouble to people this great wilderness. And then, continues Voltaire, the scholars began to find all kinds of analogies between the Indians of the Americas and other peoples. Father Laffiteau, the Jesuit, for example, noted that "the Mexicans, in the violence of their grief, tear their garments; some Asiatics do the same; therefore they are the ancestors of the Mexicans." Is there any real proof that the American Indians are related to the peoples of the Old World? And Voltaire triumphantly answers his own question: "None."[27]

To Voltaire, the Indians and Negroes are separate species from the Europeans and therefore it is futile to look for significant physical or cultural relationships. "As the negro of Africa has not his original from us whites," he argues, "why should the red, olive, or ash-colored peoples of America come from our countries?" His chief reason for believing in separate origin is simply that the races are quite different in physical appearance. "The negro race is a species of men as different from ours," he declares, "as the breed of spaniels is from that of greyhounds. The mucous membrane, or network, which nature has spread between the muscles and the skin, is white in us and black or copper-colored in them." But it is not only their appearance—it is their state of civilization and intelligence which leads Voltaire to reject them as relations of white men. "If their understanding is not of a different nature from ours," he says, "it is at least greatly inferior. They are not capable of any great application or association of ideas, and seem formed neither for the advantages nor the abuses of philosophy."[28]

Among Voltaire's contemporaries, one of the best-known advocates of the separate origin of races idea was Lord Kames, the Scottish jurist who wrote books on a great variety of subjects —law, mathematics, metaphysics, aesthetics, the history of social institutions. In his *Sketches of the History of Man* (1774), Kames criticizes Buffon's definition of a species as composed of those organisms which are able to produce fertile offspring among themselves. If Buffon would look more closely at the animal world, said Kames, he would find that animals which are undoubtedly different species are still sometimes able to inter-breed and produce fertile offspring—examples being sheep and goats, camels and dromedaries, hares and rabbits. It was no more logical to argue that Negroes and white men are of the same species, says Kames, than to assume that these examples from the animal world are of the same species. He doubted that all dogs are of the same species, and from this example he proceeds to a human analogy: "There are different species of men as well as of dogs: a mastiff differs not more from a spaniel, than a white man from a negro, or a Laplander from a Dane."[29]

Kames ridicules the idea that climate has caused the differ-ences among the races. How can climate explain the low stature of the Eskimos, the smallness of their feet, or their large heads? How can the cold climate have caused the low stature and ugliness of the Laplanders when the Finns and Norwegians in a climate just as cold are "tall, comely, and well-proportioned"? How can Buffon contend that climate determines color when in Malabar there is a colony of industrious Jews of the same complexion which Jews have in Europe, although the Malabar community claims to have been there since their ancestors fled from the captivity of Babylon? Buffon is "totally silent upon a fact that alone overturns his whole system of colour," says Kames, "viz. that all Americans [Indians] without exception are of a copper colour, tho' in that vast continent there is every variety of climate."[30]

Even more important than outward appearance, Kames argues, are the inward traits of character and temperament. Great variations in courage and cowardice are found among the different races. Such qualities "must depend upon a permanent and invariable cause." The reason cannot be climate, because examples of courageous and cowardly peoples can be found in all climates. The northern nations of Europe and Asia have always been remarkable for their courage, he observes, but then so have the inhabitants of the South Seas who attack European ships of war armed with nothing but poniards. It is nonsense, he continues, to think as Lucan did that the courage of the Scandinavians comes from their belief that it is a small matter to die since they will be happy in another world. All nations have believed the soul is immortal, but sometimes the bravest peoples —the ancient Caledonians, for one example—have taken the gloomiest view of the future existence of the soul. The only conclusion one can logically draw from all these differences, says Kames, is that each race is a separate species.[31]

Orthodox enough to believe that his ideas on race ought to find support in the Bible, Kames makes a not very convincing attempt to reconcile his theory with Genesis. If there were no "counter-balancing evidence," he says, we should be obliged to believe "that God created many pairs of the human race, differing from each other both externally and internally." But this opinion, however plausible, is in direct conflict with the biblical account of creation. "Tho' we cannot doubt of the authority of Moses," says Kames, "yet his account of the creation of man is not a little puzzling." It does not explain, for example, how men were conditioned to live in different climates or how some of the progeny of Adam—in spite of the fact that "he certainly must have been an excellent preceptor to his children"—degenerated into a savage state.[32]

If the races were not separated at the time of creation, he reasons, they must have been re-created later as separate races. Kames decides that the separation took place at the time of the building of the Tower of Babel:

Here light breaks forth in the midst of darkness. By confounding the language of men, and scattering them abroad upon the face of the earth, they were rendered savages. And to harden them for their new habitations, it was necessary that they should be divided into different kinds, fitted for different climates. With an immediate change of bodily constitutions, the builders of Babel could not possibly have subsisted in the burning region of Guinea, or in the frozen region of Lapland; especially without houses, or any other convenience to protect them against a destructive climate.[33]

It was Dr. Charles White, an eminent English physician and surgeon, who most clearly developed scientific arguments in favor of the idea of the multiple origin of races. White is known for a single brief work on race entitled *An Account of the Regular Gradation in Man* (1799). In this work, he has a series of drawings which trace cranial development from the lower to the higher animals. At first glance, the drawings would seem to be a demonstration of the theory of evolution, but White is not an evolutionist. He does not suggest that species evolve into one another but merely that they are arranged in a kind of hierarchy, a "great chain of being": "From man down to the smallest reptile, whose existence can be discovered only by the microscope, Nature exhibits to our view an immense chain of beings, endued with various degrees of intelligence and active powers, suited to their stations in the general system."[34]

Negroes, White argues, occupy a different "station" on the chain from the whites. In his opinion, the Negro is an intermediate species between the white man and the ape. The differences between Negroes and whites which he emphasizes are chiefly anatomical. The feet of the Negroes are flatter, their fingers and toes are longer, and their thumbs are shorter. Their hair is coarser. Their cheekbones project more, their lower arms are considerably longer, and their chins, instead of projecting outward, recede as do those of apes. Their skulls are smaller in internal capacity. Their nerves are larger and their brains are smaller. Their bodies exude an unpleasant odor, a characteristic which is accentuated in apes.[35]

There are important sexual differences, White says.

That the *Penis* of an African is larger than that of an European, has, I believe, been shown in every anatomical school in London. Preparations of them are preserved in most anatomical museums; and I have one in mine. I have examined several living negroes, and found it invariably to be the case. . . . In *simiae* the penis is still longer, in proportion to the size of their bodies.

The sexual organs of Negro women are also larger than those of European women, and "in the females of the ape and the dog, the *clitoris* is still longer." It is a fact, he continues, that "women of colour have easier parturitions, in general," than white Europeans. "Apes and baboons menstruate less than negresses, monkeys still less." White refers to the accounts of travelers who report that the breasts of Hottentot women are so long that they can suckle their children upon their backs "by throwing the breast over the shoulders." These and other characteristics are cited to prove that Negroes are intermediate between the whites and the apes.[36]

Mental and emotional differences between Negroes and Europeans are just as striking. White quotes a traveler who finds that "the inhabitants of the warmer climates have a dull torpid brain, and are less keen and sharp than the Europeans. They have a power of thinking, but not profoundly, and consequently conversation among them is rather trifling." He also quotes another traveler who asserts that Negroes are not subject to nervous diseases, an indication that their minds are less complex and therefore less likely to become deranged. Negroes can also bear pain better than whites. "I have amputated the legs of many negroes," White quotes a surgeon as saying, "who have held the upper part of the limb themselves." The logical conclusion is, of course, not that such Negroes are brave but that they are insensitive to pain. Negroes have not the delicate sense of touch of whites, "since both the cuticle and *rete mocosum* are thicker in them." White has heard it said that Negroes are superior to Europeans in memory, but his explanation is that "those domestic animals with which we are best acquainted, as the horse and the dog, excel the human species in this faculty."[37]

Negroes, says White, are closer to apes than they are to white Europeans. "In whatever respect the African differs from the European," he declares, "the particularity brings him nearer to the ape." To the argument that Negroes have abilities which apes have not, White remarks that the apes themselves have frequently been underrated by Europeans. "They have been taught to play upon musical instruments, as the pipe and the harp. They have been known to carry off negro boys, girls, and even women," he adds, "with a view of making them subservient to their wants as slaves, or as objects of brutal passion; and it has been asserted by some, that women have had offspring from such connections." He admits, however, to some skepticism on this last point.[38]

To the argument that Negroes and Europeans are able to interbreed successfully and to product fertile offspring, White replies that mulattoes—like mules—tend to be barren. One of White's friends who lived in Jamaica had told him, he says, that he had never known a case in which two mulattoes were able to have offspring. Those instances in which mulattoes are known to have had children, White explains, must have occurred when one or the other of the parents was either all Negro or all white. Even if mulattoes could be proved sometimes to have children

among themselves, says White, the fact that they are less prolific than pure whites or pure Negroes would indicate that the
two races are separate species.[39]

Like Lord Kames, White attempts to square his theory of
race with the story in Genesis. Nowhere do we read of Adam
and Eve having any daughters, he declares, so there must have
been in existence other peoples of which the Bible makes no
mention. Other peoples are hinted at when the biblical account
relates that Cain was expelled from his own people and married
a woman who conceived a son. "Who then was Cain's wife,"
asks White, "and whence did she come?" And if there were
other people created then, why could not other races have been
created just as easily?[40]

White insists that he has no ulterior motives in formulating
his theory of separate origin. It was the proponents of the theory
of the unity of the human race, he maintained, who were doing
more to degrade humanity than the proponents of the theory of
diversity. If it is true that Negroes are the same species as white
men, "it would be easy to maintain the probability that several
species of *simiae* are but varieties of the species *Man*." And one
never knew where such kinship would stop. If the argument was
extended, "almost all the animal kingdom might be deduced
from one pair, and be considered as one family." He says he has
"no desire to elevate the brute creation to the rank of humanity,
nor to reduce human species to a level with brutes." His only
purpose is "to investigate a proposition in natural history." He
hopes that nothing he has said will be construed "to give the
smallest countenance to the pernicious practice of enslaving
mankind, which he wishes to see abolished throughout the
world." Nor does he wish to see Negroes suffer any penalties
such as social stigma because they are a separate species. They are
at least "equal to thousands of Europeans, in capacity and responsibility; and ought, therefore, to be equally entitled to freedom and protection. Laws ought not to allow greater freedom
to a *Shakespear* or a *Milton*, a *Locke* or a *Newton*, than to men
of inferior capacities."[41]

The idea that Negroes are a separate species was still a curiosity in the eighteenth century, though the arguments of Voltaire, those of Kames, and especially those of White were to be repeated *ad nauseam* in nineteenth-century defenses of slavery. The great handicap which the theory of separate origin encountered was the fact that it cast doubt upon the biblical narrative, or at least required a rather special interpretation of it. In spite of his attempts to make the theory of separate origin of races square with scripture, Kames was severely castigated for the expression of infidel opinions. Even Samuel Stanhope Smith, who usually wrote in a broad-minded and open manner, was scandalized by Kames's argument. One of Smith's reasons for writing his book on race was that he wished to refute the pernicious idea of Kames. "When ignorance or profligacy pretends to sneer at revelation and at opinions held sacred by mankind, it is too humble to provoke resentment," said Smith, "but when a philosopher affects the dishonest task, he renders himself equally the object of indignation and contempt."[42]

Though less severe toward Jefferson's opinions with regard to Negroes, Smith was equally critical of them. In a second edition of his book on race, published in 1810, Smith attacks particularly Jefferson's idea that Negroes ought to have developed conceptions of art and poetry through their association with their white masters. The cultivation of genius, Smith says, requires "freedom" and "the reward at least of praise." The condition of the Negro in America, "condemned to the drudgery of perpetual labor, cut off from every means of improvement, conscious of his degraded state in the midst of free men who regard him with contempt, and in every word and look make him feel his inferiority," is such that it is grossly unfair, Smith maintains, for Jefferson to expect the Negro to develop his mind and tastes to anything approaching a cultivated level. It is especially unfair, Smith continues, to argue that Negroes ought to produce works of art because they have seen excellent examples of it brought from abroad to the homes of their masters. "What is intended in this remark," exclaims Smith,

I can hardly conceive. Does the writer mean statues, pictures, or household furniture? I believe few of them have seen the most exquisite productions in any of these departments; and those who have, I presume, have contemplated them with the same eyes with which other coachmen, hostlers, and footmen view them. . . . And why are these exquisite works of genius said to be *from abroad*? If the ingenious whites have never yet produced them *at home*, why are the poor negroes degraded from their rank in the scale of rationality, because their enslaved genius has not towered above that of their masters?[43]

Smith also rejects the argument that Negroes ought to have produced poetry because of the close relation of misery and literature. In order to invest misery with imagination, says Smith, one must have a refined sensibility and a carefully cultivated taste. "When have we seen the miseries of Newgate or the gallies produce a poet? . . . With what fine tints can imagination invest the rags, the dirt, or the nakedness so often seen in a quarter of negro labourers?" And it is unfair to compare the achievement of Negroes in the United States with that of the slaves of the Romans. In ancient times, men frequently became slaves when they were "an ingenious and enlightened people, and practiced in all the liberal arts." In addition, their learning was respected by their masters. "They were philosophers, and poets, and artists before they became slaves." On the other hand, the condition of the Negro under American slavery is wholly different. It is out of the question, Smith maintains, to expect the Negro in such circumstances to develop his artistic talents.[44]

Jefferson himself modified his ideas concerning Negro ability. In 1809—more than twenty years after he had written his opinions on Negroes in *Notes on Virginia*—he answered a letter of a Frenchman who objected to his unfairness. "My doubts were the result of personal observation on the limited sphere of my own state," Jefferson concedes, "when the opportunities for the development of their genius were not favorable, and those of exercising it still less so. I expressed them, therefore, with great hesitation; but whatever be their degree of talents, it is no measure of their rights." And Jefferson goes on to say that the intellectual superiority of Isaac Newton should not therefore make him "lord of the person or property of others." The Negroes, says Jefferson, "are gaining daily in the opinions of nations, and hopeful advances are making towards their reestablishment on an equal footing with the other colors of the human family."[45]

On this last point, Jefferson's optimism proved to be in error. Though in the eighteenth century scientific and informed opinion generally favored the idea of the potential intelligence and virtue of Negroes and other nonwhite races, in the nineteenth century this view rapidly waned in influence until it almost disappeared. Jefferson assumed that the situation of the Negroes would become better and not worse. What he could not foresee was that racial theory explaining inherent inferiority and superiority would make great inroads not merely in popular thought but also in that of the scientists and scholars. The Negro would have to wait a long time before impressive voices were raised in behalf of his innate intellectual and temperamental equality with the whites.

IV

Nineteenth-Century Anthropology

THE OPTIMISM of the Enlightenment on the subject of race faded quickly in the nineteenth century. We can see the change clearly in the continuing debates over whether the human races were one or many species. Though the debate was acrimonious, the contestants do not now seem nearly as far apart as they seemed to themselves. The leading exponents of both schools of thought came more and more to believe that the Negro is innately inferior and that neither education nor environment can do much to improve him. Other nonwhite races fared scarcely better. The nonwhites stood to gain more from the advocates of the proposition that all races are a single species, but sometimes the only benefit they won from the monogenist school was the concession that they had the right to the consolations of religion. The advocates of the polygenist theory, on the other hand, frequently denied that the nonwhite races were people at all and maintained that missionary efforts among them were wholly wasted.

In the first half of the nineteenth century, the anthropologist who took the most favorable view of the potentiality of the Negro was James Cowles Prichard, an English physician who entered the medical profession mainly for the opportunities it gave him to pursue his researches on race theory. Prichard was the son of learned Quakers, and his works show a strong ethical bent. His doctoral thesis, *De Humani Generes Varietate*, completed at the University of Edinburgh in 1808, was followed over the next forty years by a series of multivolume studies of race. He maintained that the human race had originally been black and that whiteness was a later development. In support of his position, he developed a series of analogies with the lower animals. He was convinced that domesticated breeds become lighter in color, and he thought that civilized life had had a similar effect upon the whites. Where people are still to be found in the savage state, they are almost invariably dark in color. In addition, primitive peoples seem to be physiologically better adapted to the conditions of savage life—their senses of smell, sight, and hearing are superior to those of civilized peoples. Their women have less difficulty in childbirth. Negroes sometimes have white children—albinos—but white people never have Negro children without miscegenation, an indication that the black skin is the basic type and the white skin a variation.[1]

Prichard argues that new races are created by biological "sports." Though climate and other external influences condition the change, they do not cause it. "Whatever varieties are produced in the race have their beginning in the original structure or some particular ovum or germ," he contended, "and not in any qualities superinduced by external causes in the progress of its development." Because he was unable to give any clear examples of biological "sports" which had become new races, his theory remained substantially without proof. He was strongly convinced, however, that mankind is a single species.[2]

Prichard also attacked the problem of the origin of the races from the standpoint of comparative philology. An accomplished linguist, he published in 1831 a study of the relationship of the Celtic languages to Sanskrit, attempting to trace the kinship of Celtic peoples to the Indo-Europeans. In addition, Prichard made a comparative study of the social institutions, philosophies, and religions of the major races. One of his works was a treatise on Egyptian mythology in which he attempted to prove a direct relationship between the Hindus and the Egyptians, basing his argument upon the similarity of their social castes and other institutions. This project he regarded as part of his larger task of demonstrating the essential unity of all human races.[3]

Because he was a learned man and a tireless researcher, Prichard had a considerable reputation among scientists and historians. He has been called, with justice, the founder of English anthropology. His influence was circumscribed by the fact that he was much more interested in the scientific features of anthropology than in their political and social implications. His books have such a prolix style and they are so cautious in their generalizations that the reader finds it difficult to discover what the author really thought. Moreover, since careful studies of primitive peoples were almost nonexistent when he was writing, he was obliged to rely on the frequently inaccurate accounts of travelers. Prichard did serve as an opponent of the polygenist theory of race and presented a careful refutation of the arguments of those who found characteristics in Negroes which would justify their being assigned to a separate species.[4]

Prichard's optimism concerning the nonwhite races was not, however, typical of his time. The changing attitude toward race is evident in a series of lectures which were delivered from 1816 to 1818 by Sir William Lawrence, a physician at the Royal College of Surgeons in London. Lawrence thought that the human race was one species, but his point of view toward "lower" races is similar to that of Dr. Charles White, the advocate of the polygenic origin theory. Like White, Lawrence insists that the superiority of the white race does not justify it in enslaving or mistreating inferior races. On the other hand, he thinks it is foolish to argue that superiority and inferiority of races is not a fact of nature which must be taken into account:

The different progress of various nations in general civilization, and in the culture of the arts and sciences, the different characteristics and degrees of excellence in their literary productions, their varied forms of government, and many other considerations, convince us beyond the possibility of doubt, that the races of mankind are no less characterised by diversity of mental endowments, than by . . . differences of . . . body structure. . . .

He admits that there are individual members of lower races who are intellectually the equal of any white man, but the law of averages is against them. The Negroes belong at the bottom of the scale. "That the Negro is more like a monkey than the European," says Lawrence, "cannot be denied as a general observation."[5]

Lawrence is one of the first of the anthropological theorists to carry the idea of superior and inferior races into Europe itself. "I think . . . it will appear," he observes, "that most of the virtues and talents which adorn and ennoble men, have existed from early times in a higher degree among the Celtic German than among the Slavonic and oriental people; while the latter have usually displayed a more sensual character than the former." He also noted differences in the crania of different nations. What these meant must "await the result of more numerous and accurate comparisons." Lawrence could not have known what a fateful question this last was to become in the heated nationalism of the nineteenth and twentieth centuries.[6]

In Europe, the question of the unity or diversity of human races was indirectly involved in a famous debate which took place in 1830 between Baron Cuvier and Geoffroy Saint-Hilaire, two of the most celebrated French naturalists. Cuvier, a man with an immense scientific reputation—he was called the "dictator of biology"—maintained that all living organisms are descendants of ancestors identical in structure with themselves. Saint-Hilaire was a precursor of Darwin. He argued that all living organisms are related to one another and that higher forms are descended from lower. At the time of the debate, he undertook to prove specifically that there is a fundamental similarity of structure between the inkfish and the vertebrates. Cuvier, on the other hand, said of the inkfish: "They have not resulted from the development of other animals, nor has their own development produced any animal higher than themselves." Saint-Hilaire was a brilliant speculator, but not so thoroughly grounded in the study of comparative anatomy as was Cuvier. Thus, Cuvier was able in the debate to point out absurd errors Saint-Hilaire had made in comparing the structures of organisms.

By his superior knowledge of anatomy, Cuvier was able to give the argument for the immutability of species an impressiveness which it did not deserve. In most circles, the argument for unity of types was regarded as settled in favor of Cuvier. This victory was a temporary defeat for the idea of evolution, with the implication that the account of creation in the Bible was correct. An incidental effect of the victory was that the idea of polygenic origin of the races received a check, being considered as part of the discredited doctrine of Saint-Hilaire. The unity-diversity debate in Europe thus lost most of its intensity.[7]

In the United States, on the other hand, the idea that the Negroes might be a separate species made a more determined last stand and, in fact, for a time came near dominating the thinking of scientific men on the subject. The leader of the polygenist school of thought in this country was not, as we might suppose, an apologist for slavery. He was Dr. Samuel George Morton (1799-1851), a lifelong resident of Philadelphia, famous both as a physician and as a researcher in natural history. At first, his natural history studies were in the field of paleontology; he described the fossils collected by the Lewis and Clark Expedition and thus was the founder of invertebrate paleontology in this country. For a time, he was corresponding secretary and later president of the Academy of Natural Sciences in Philadelphia. Benjamin Silliman of Yale, the editor of the *American Journal of Science,* regarded Morton as the outstanding American authority in geology.[8]

As early as 1820, Morton was interested in the collection of skulls of both animals and men. Later his wide acquaintance among scientists enabled him to secure human crania—to which his interest was now largely directed—from all over the world. His collection eventually came to hold hundreds of crania. The largest collection in the world at the time, it came to be known as the "American Golgotha." Oliver Wendell Holmes, in a letter to Morton, indicates the eminence of Morton as a scientist:

The more I read on these subjects [Morton's studies on race], the more

I am delighted with the severe and cautious character of your own most extended researches, which, from their very nature, are permanent data for all future students of Ethnology, whose leader on this side of the Atlantic, to say the least, you have so happily constituted yourself by well-directed and long-continued efforts.[9]

The key to the separate origin of races, argued Morton, was to be found in hybrids or mulattoes. Since Linnaeus, the test of species in natural history had been the ability of two organisms to produce fertile offspring. The eighteenth-century advocates of the polygenic origin theory had challenged this definition of species, and Morton echoed their argument that there were many examples on record in which animals of different species had been able to propagate fertile offspring. Among human races, he admitted that mulattoes were fertile, but his own research into crosses between whites and Negroes indicated that mulatto women bear children only with great difficulty. If these women mated only with other mulattoes, Morton argued, the descendants of this union would be even less fertile and the progeny would eventually die out. From his conviction that half-breeds cannot propagate themselves indefinitely, Morton was led to the conclusion that whites and Negroes are not varieties of a single race but entirely different species. Prichard's doctrine of "sports" or "accidental varieties" was rejected. Nobody had ever seen or heard of a Negro who was born as an accidental variety from parents who were pure Caucasians. And then Morton went on to reflect on the innate mental and temperamental differences between races. Indians were "averse to cultivation, and slow in acquiring knowledge; restless, revengeful, and fond of war, and wholly destitute of maritime adventure." Negroes were "joyous, flexible, and indolent," representing the "lowest grade" of the races.[10]

The polygenists received strong support from Louis Agassiz, the famous Swiss naturalist, who settled in the United States in 1846. Agassiz maintained that there had been not one creation of organic life in one part of the earth but a series of creations in different parts of the world. It was an error to ascribe "to all

living beings upon earth one common centre of origin" with
subsequent migrations explaining their changed appearance in
distant lands. There were several geographic regions of the world
where the flora and fauna were peculiar to the region and different from those of other regions. This "arrangement" was the
result of "a premeditated plan" on the part of the Creator.
Furthermore, the geographic areas of separate species of plants
and animals tended to correspond roughly with distribution of
human races before the modern age of exploration.[11]

Agassiz steadfastly maintained that he had no political or
social motivation for his conclusions. Whatever their origin, he
declared, all races of men were "endowed with one common nature, intellectual and physical, derived from the Creator of all
men,—were under the same moral government of the universe,
and sustained similar relations to the Deity." Privately, however,
Agassiz confessed that his first association with Negroes in
America had amazed and repelled him. He wrote to his mother
about the Negro waiters at the hotel in which he stayed in Philadelphia. He was so struck by their anatomical differences—their
color, the peculiar shape of their limbs, their thick lips, and their
woolly hair—that he could hardly restrain himself from re-
treating from the room in fear and disgust. This experience convinced him that the Negro was not the same species as the white
man and he predicted that the great numbers of them living in
the South would cause the downfall of the Republic. Even in the
North, he added, they were excluded everywhere from white
society by a feeling of instinctive repugnance.[12]

The principal scientific proponent of the monogenic theory
of the origin of the races was, surprisingly enough, a southerner,
an owner of slaves, and a clergyman. John Bachman, minister
of St. John's Lutheran Church in Charleston, South Carolina,
brought some impressive arguments to bear against Morton's
theory. Although Morton was sometimes inclined in the heat of
argument to write off his opponent as a mere "clerical adversary," Bachman was a good deal more than this. He was born in
New York State, but had moved to South Carolina as a young

man to recover from consumption and remained there for the rest of his long life. Known as the "Hunting Parson," he had from his youth developed a serious interest in natural history and had corresponded with the naturalists of the United States and Europe. He was a friend and close associate of John James Audubon. He collaborated with Audubon in several scientific enterprises. Together they wrote *The Quadrupeds of North America*. Bachman was able to refer to something besides the Bible in his battles with Morton. Frequently he was a skilful opponent.[13]

Perhaps Bachman's strongest argument was his skepticism concerning the numerous out-of-the-way examples of fertile animal hybrids which Morton had cited. "You hie to Africa," said Bachman, to find an account of a hybrid "produced between the ass and the cow"; then off Morton goes to Paraguay to learn that "our common cat, on the plains, performs a double miracle by producing fertile hybrids, with not only one, but two species of the wild cats of South America." And then to the Bay du Croc "to listen to a recital" about "a wild caribou breaking into a sheepfold, at night, in pursuit of a cow," and "consequent conjectures that she might have been impregnated. My good friend," said Bachman, "I confess it is a severe infliction to be obliged to follow you so far out of the track of civilization." And Bachman reminded Morton that there was "scarcely a vulgar error in existence that could not be supported by an overwhelming mass of testimony . . . witchcraft, for instance."[14]

Bachman contended that no species of animals in the natural world was known to have developed from the union of two separate species. All known hybrids, he maintained, are absolutely sterile and not relatively sterile. Thus, even if Morton had been able to establish as a fact that mulattoes were relatively sterile, said Bachman, there would still be no proof that Negroes and whites belonged to separate species. In addition, Bachman maintained, mulattoes were just as fertile as "pure" races, whether they mated among themselves or with whites or Negroes. He had been able to find instances in which mulattoes had intermarried among themselves for as long as five generations with no apparent loss in fertility. In addition, he attacked Morton's theory that there is a "natural repugnance" between races which makes them reluctant to intermingle with one another and especially to propagate with one another. Morton had admitted that this repugnance had been partially overcome by "centuries of proximity" among separate races. On this point, Bachman had a different opinion. He said that many immigrants from Europe who came to Charleston had no inherent aversion to cohabiting with Negro women. If they have any repugnance at all, says Bachman, it fades away "not after the lapse of centuries but in a very few days."[15]

Bachman also attacked Agassiz's contention that there are clear geographical divisions in the world for all types of flora and fauna as well as for human races. Bachman maintains that it would not be possible to draw the lines of division for any considerable number of animals and plants with any degree of clarity and that it would be even less feasible to draw such a line for the races of mankind. The Arctic, for example, was one of the geographical divisions designated by Agassiz, who therefore considered Eskimos to be a separate species from other races. If this were true, said Bachman, one wondered how man originally had subsisted there. The Deity, if he created man specifically for the Arctic, would certainly have had to equip the Eskimos with hooks, lines, sinkers, and baits and the knowledge to use them. Also, if Eskimos were a separate species especially created for the Arctic, it was strange that the Creator had not given them carnivorous teeth—since there was only meat there for them to eat.[16]

In spite of his knowledge of natural history and his ability in argument, Bachman was seriously compromised both by his religious ideas and by his commitment to slavery. The fact that the Negro is a member of the same race as the white man, Bachman is quick to concede, does not mean that he is the white man's equal. At this point Bachman drops arguments based upon scientific evidence and appeals to Holy Scripture. He tells how Noah had blessed the descendants of Shem who became the "parent of the Caucasian race—the progenitor of the Israelites and our Saviour." Japheth was the ancestor of the Mongolians, and—just as the Bible had prophesied—many of the sons of Japheth were "to this day dwelling in tents" in the Far East. The third son of Noah was Ham. Though we cannot regard his descendants as "accursed," says Bachman, Negroes certainly are "still everywhere the 'servants of servants.' "[17]

Thus, Negro slavery was wholly justifiable. "We have been irresistibly brought to the conviction," Bachman declares, "that in intellectual power the African is an inferior variety of our species. His whole history affords evidence that he is incapable of self-government." This inferiority was not proof that the Negro should be degraded from the ranks of mankind. "Our child that we lead by the hand, and who looks to us for protection and support," he concluded, "is still of our own blood notwithstanding his weakness and ignorance." If the theory of separate origin of races were accepted, "infidelity must unquestionably spring up in the very bosom of the Christian church, since the scriptures would be said to contradict themselves." Morton replied that the theory of polygenic origin was not inconsistent with the Bible, but he could not resist the taunt that "what is miscalled *Theology* is a Protean compound, that has made as little progress in ten centuries, as any branch of human knowledge."

In 1851, in the midst of a series of heated exchanges between Morton and Bachman, Morton suddenly died. At the time, the argument seemed to be going in his favor. He had convinced most of the scientific community, at least, that the theory of separate species among human races was the most logical explanation for the differences between races. Aside from his controversial articles against Bachman, Morton was at the time of his death preparing a chapter for one of Henry Rowe Schoolcraft's volumes on Indians and also working on an article on human races for the *Iconographic Encyclopaedia of Science, Literature, and Art*. Bachman's arguments, on the other hand, were increasingly being rejected as unscientific.[18]

With the death of Morton, advance of the polygenic origin theory was left to two of his disciples—Josiah Clark Nott and George Robin Gliddon. Nott was a physician and surgeon who practiced medicine in Mobile. A native South Carolinian, he had received his medical degree from the University of Pennsylvania and afterward had gone to Europe, where he remained for three years studying medicine and natural history. In Mobile he had a large practice and wrote a good many articles on medicine which were published in the best journals of the time on this subject. He had real ability, though his delight in furious controversy and his habit of thinking up amusing epithets for his opponents may have compromised his reputation as a serious student. Gliddon was born in England, the son of a successful mercantile businessman. He first represented his father's business in Malta and then in Alexandria. Though an Englishman, he was for a time the vice-consul for the United States in Cairo. He became a student of Egyptology, and his connection with Americans in Cairo led him to a correspondence with Morton. Eventually he became Morton's agent in collecting Egyptian and other Middle Eastern crania. Later, Gliddon came to the United States with relics from ancient Egypt and set up as a traveling lecturer in this country. Gliddon was one-half serious student and one-half P. T. Barnum. Even more than Nott, he delighted in nothing so much as a good verbal brawl.[19]

Both Nott and Gliddon were proslavery, but this subject was less important to them than their warfare on conservative theology. They enthusiastically seized upon portions of the polygenist argument which cast doubt upon Holy Scripture, whereas Morton had been more circumspect. It was because Bachman supported the biblical account of creation as much as because he argued for the unity of the human races that they singled him out for special attack. Both Nott and Gliddon delighted in what Nott described as "parson skinning." Constantly appealing to the necessity of adhering to scientific truth, they castigated their opponents as advocates of murky theology and benighted superstition.[20]

Nott and Gliddon collaborated on a voluminous study of eight hundred pages entitled *Types of Mankind*. Published in 1854, this book added little that was new to the argument over separate origin. The title is misleading because by "types" Nott and Gliddon meant not variations within a species, but separate species. From the standpoint of science, it was important chiefly because it collected a good deal of Morton's work; but it also spread the polygenist idea of the origin of races to a wider and more popular reading public. Even at the price of $7.50, the first printing sold out immediately, and before the end of the century the book had gone through at least nine editions.[21]

The idea which appears over and over again in this book is that the nonwhite races are incapable of taking the first step toward civilization when they are of unmixed blood. It was an invariable rule, asserted Nott, that no Negro or Indian or other nonwhite man could show evidence of high intelligence unless he had at least one white ancestor. Sequoyah, the famous "Cherokee Cadmus" who had devised an alphabet for his people, was "a half-breed, owning his inventive genius to his Scotch father." One contributor in the book described Indians as "colored vermin." To anyone who has had experience with Indians, says Nott, "it is in vain to talk of civilizing them. You might as well attempt to change the nature of a buffalo." The Negro was closer to the chimpanzee and the orangutan than he was to the Caucasian. Even among the white races, there were some who were doomed by nature to barbarism. The instability of the French government, says Nott, was due to the turbulent dark men in the nation. The government of France would be wise "simply to chop off the head of every demagogue who was not a blond *white*-man. . . . *Dark*-skinned races, history attests, are only fit for military governments. It is the unique rule genial to their physical nature: they are unhappy without it, even now, at Paris."[22]

The theory of the polygenic origin of races would have supplied the South with an excellent rationale for the defense of slavery. With the exception of Bachman, the monogenic origin theory had no real champion among men of science. If the South had been willing to contend that Negroes should be slaves because they are a separate species from the whites, it would have found itself a powerful partner in the science of the time. The state of anthropology was such that it was virtually useless to the abolitionists, and they generally kept clear of the subject. Frederick Douglass, the Negro slave who gained his freedom and became famous as an abolitionist orator, questioned the political motivation of Nott and Gliddon. To their claim that Negroes had never produced a civilization of any consequence, Douglass retorted that the ancient Egyptians had had a generous admixture of Negro blood. On this point, however, Douglass could find few students of Egyptology who agreed with him.[23]

The South would have nothing to do with the arguments of the polygenists. In 1854, the fire-eating *Richmond Enquirer* declared that some might accept the "infidel" doctrine of diversity because it seemed to be an excellent defense of slavery, but they would be wrong. Southerners could afford no such defenders as Nott and Gliddon if the Bible was to be "the price it must pay for them." Were not the abolitionists attempting to undermine the Bible in rejecting its clear recognition and justification of the institution of slavery? George Fitzhugh, one of the most rabid defenders of slavery and of the innate inferiority of the Negro, nonetheless considered the Negro to be the same species as the white man. William Stanton, the modern authority on the race theory of this period, has pointed out that "when the issue was clearly drawn, the South turned its back on the only intellectually respectable defense of slavery it could have taken up."[24]

What ended the monogenist-polygenist controversy was, of course, Charles Darwin's theory of evolution. Even without Darwin, the polygenist theory would soon have encountered serious opposition. In 1859, Dr. Theodore Waitz in Germany carefully examined the theory of polygenic origin and—on non-evolutionary grounds—rejected it. The races of man are alike in too many ways, he argued, to countenance a theory of separate origin. Gliddon died in 1857, but Nott lived until 1873—long enough to see polygenic origin discredited scientifically. As early as 1859, Nott wrote to a friend that he had been able "to skim Darwin's book—the man is clearly crazy, but it is a capital dig into the parsons. . . ." Asa Gray, in his attempts to soften religious opposition to Darwin's theory, pointed out that it provided a means of refuting the theory that Negroes and other nonwhite races are a separate species and are not human. "One good effect is already manifest," he said of Darwin's *The Origin of Species*. Darwin had refuted "the hypothesis of a multiplicity of human species." It was now scientifically respectable to maintain that the human species is one for "the very first step backwards" into the evolutionary past "makes the Negro and the Hottentot our blood-relations." Nott himself eventually came around to an acceptance of the evolutionary thesis, though hardly for Gray's humanitarian reasons.[25]

Darwin left no doubt that all human races belong to a single species. He wrote:

Although the existing races of man differ in many respects as in color, hair, shape of skull, proportions of the body, etc., yet if their whole structure be taken into consideration they are found to resemble each other closely in a multitude of points. Many of these are so unimportant or of so singular a nature that it is extremely improbable that they should have been independently acquired by aboriginally distinct species or races.

Most of the defenders of the monogenic origin theory in this country believed in the literal inspiration of the Bible, and thus they would hardly have chosen Darwin as their champion. Though they were willing to accept all human races as kin to the white race, they were hardly prepared to accept the whole animal world as well.[26]

Darwin changed the basis of race theory, but he did not change the argument that some races are superior to others. Even before *The Origin of Species* was published, the direction which the new racism would take had been indicated. In 1843, Robert Chambers, an Edinburgh publisher and an amateur scientist, had anonymously published *Vestiges of Creation,* a book which advanced an evolutionary hypothesis. Chambers was not a trained student in natural history, and he made some glaring errors, thus discrediting the theory of evolution itself. His idea of evolution as applied to race was exactly what millions of people would come to believe when evolution became respectable. Chambers argues that man began as a Negro, passed through Malay, Indian, and Mongolian phases, and finally emerged as a Caucasian. "The leading characters . . . of the various races of mankind are simply representations of the development of the highest, or Caucasian type."[27]

Darwin is much more cautious than Chambers in describing how the evolution of human races came about. He does not attempt to place each race in its proper position on the evolutionary scale, nor does he assume that the direction of evolution is clearly toward the superior Caucasian. He believed that changes came about through sexual selection. Men or women who were more vigorous or attractive would have an advantage in mating and in propagating themselves. Slight changes of body conformation might be advantageous in attracting a mate. In this way, he believed new races had eventually been created. Traits might be superior for a particular time and in particular circumstances, but Darwin does not attempt to point out traits which are universally superior.[28]

Darwin did believe that human races differ a good deal from one another both outwardly and inwardly and that many of these differences could be measured. "There is . . . no doubt that the various races, when carefully compared and measured," he declared, "differ much from each other,—as in the texture of the hair, the relative proportions of all parts of the body, the capacity of the lungs, the form and capacity of the skull, and even in the convolutions of the brain." Concerned with problems of biology among the lower orders, Darwin never got around to a thorough study of the ways in which human races differ.[29]

The theory of evolution stimulated a movement which was

already the chief interest of many nineteenth-century anthropologists—the measurement of race differences. If the races represented different stages of evolution, then it was important to measure their differences. These measurements might well indicate the direction in which evolution had proceeded. Only when the norms of the different races had been established could students of race speak of their field with something like the confidence with which biologists described species and varieties among the lower members of the natural world. Ambitious schemes for the measurement of race differences multiplied. The nineteenth century was a period of exhaustive and—as it turned out—futile search for criteria to define and describe race differences.[30]

The most obvious way in which races might be said to differ and the way in which popular opinion still tends to differentiate them is by their color. The eighteenth-century idea that there was a correlation between climate and color was challenged in Europe by Peter Simon Pallas in 1780, but students of anthropology continued to hope that some correlation between race and color might be established as a base of measurement. In 1870, Thomas Henry Huxley in England divided the races of Europe into the *xanthrochroid* (the fair) and the *melanochroid* (the dark)—but both groups were found to differ from, and resemble, each other in so many other ways that his system of classification was not generally adopted. Paul Broca, who founded the Anthropological Society in Paris in 1859, used thirty-four shades of skin color in an attempt to differentiate the races, but no scheme of classification emerged. Color as a race determinant has in the final analysis been one of the least satisfactory of the methods tried.[31]

Probably the most ambitious attempts to classify the races came from the study of crania. Even in the eighteenth century students of race were busy measuring and comparing skulls. In Germany, Peter Camper advanced the theory that races could be classified in a hierarchy according to the "facial angle"—that is, by the angle that an imaginary line from the bottom of the

chin to the top of the forehead forms with a horizontal line at
the bottom of the chin. *Orthognathous* and *prognathous* were
the terms which this theory brought into currency. Camper
measured the profiles of Greek statues and concluded that the
ancient Greeks had a facial angle so orthognathous that it often
measured as much as 100 degrees. Negroes, according to Camper,
were the most prognathous of races, with a facial angle of from
60 to 70 degrees. Blumenbach criticizes Camper's theory as a
basis for differentiating the races. In his own collection he had
two skulls, one belonging to a Lithuanian and the other to an
Ethiopian, which had identical facial angles. In all other characteristics, the two skulls were as unlike as possible. "The more
my daily experience, and, as it were, my familiarity with my
collection of skulls of different nations increases," Blumenbach
concluded, "so much the more impossible do I find it to reduce
these racial varieties . . . to the measurement of any single
scale."[32]

Blumenbach's attack on the theory of the facial angle as an
index of race did not prevent it from enjoying a long and excit-
ing life. In this country, the opponents of the idea of unity of
human origin frequently appealed to it. Samuel S. Kneeland, a
Boston naturalist and one of the followers of Dr. Morton, declared that "those animals with the longest snouts are always
considered the most stupid and gluttonous," and that the "animal aspect" of the prognathous Negroes could not "fail to strike
an unprejudiced observer." After the Civil War, the name of
the "distinguished Professor Camper" was heard among the
speeches made in Congress in opposition to the adoption of the
Fifteenth Amendment.[33]

Kneeland's comparisons of the jaws of Negroes to the
"snouts" of animals is in the tradition of the pseudoscience of
physiognomy, which frequently used animal analogies in attempting to read the character of people on the basis of their
physical characteristics. Physiognomy was known to the ancients
—Aristotle wrote a treatise on it—and it was widespread in
Europe from the time of the Middle Ages, experts in the art

frequently being astrologers as well. It was outlawed in England in 1743, but it was later popularized on the Continent by Johann Kaspar Lavater. In 1775-78 he published a handsomely illustrated text with engravings which would enable his readers to interpret character by examining physical—usually facial and cranial—features. In 1831, Charles Darwin narrowly missed being turned down as one of the members of the expedition of the *Beagle* because of his physiognomy. The captain of the ship was an ardent student of Lavater and he doubted, Darwin tells us, "whether any one with my nose could possess sufficient energy and determination for the voyage."[34]

Phrenology was an outgrowth of physiognomy. It is important to remember that this study developed originally under most reputable auspices. Franz Joseph Gall, a German physician of eminence, had from his student days been convinced that there is a relationship between physiognomy, particularly the shape of the head, and human character. One of his ideas was that those of his fellow students who had large eyes also had exceptionally good memories, and from this assumption he argued that the organ of memory must be directly behind the eyeballs. About the year 1800, Gall developed his theory of the mind which assumed that there were thirty-seven faculties and that an experienced "reader" could determine character by examining the size and shape of various areas of the human skull. These "faculties" were described by such terms as "acquisitiveness," "secretiveness," "combativeness," "conjugality," "ideality," "sublimity," "firmness," and "self-esteem." By the time of his death in 1828, Gall had a tremendous reputation. He was a student of anatomy of real ability, but it was his scheme of reading character that made him famous. Metternich, for example, declared that Gall was the greatest mind he had ever encountered.[35]

Johan Gaspar Spurzheim was one of Gall's associates and pupils, but his ideas were significantly different from those of his teacher. Gall had accepted evil as one of the characteristics of man which his new science could be utilized to detect. Spurzheim, on the other hand, thought all the human "faculties" were potentially good. It was only their abuse which could lead to evil. Under Spurzheim, phrenology—a word he coined—was not a determinist science under which the defects and limitations of man could be measured. Rather, it was a device by which the human race might perfect itself by developing its strong points. Evil was recognized by the Spurzheim school of phrenology in a backhanded way, but the whole emphasis of his approach was optimistic. It was hardly more determinist than are the various kinds of "personality inventories" which are a popular fad of our time.[36]

Although the new science of phrenology had attracted some attention in the United States before, it was the visit of Spurzheim to this country in 1832 which raised interest in the subject to a considerable degree of excitement. "With only one exception, Lafayette, no stranger ever visited the United States who . . . possessed the power at once so fully to absorb and gratify the public mind," declared Professor Benjamin Silliman of Yale. In New Haven, Spurzheim performed before the medical profession a brilliant brain dissection to which the physicians reacted with "great satisfaction." He proceeded to Boston, where he gave a series of lectures at the Athenaeum which had to be transferred to the Masonic Temple because of the crowds who came to hear them.[37]

Samuel Gridley Howe, Horace Mann, President Quincy of Harvard, Emerson, Poe, and Whitman were all disposed to endorse phrenology to one degree or another. None of them went so far as Horace Greeley, who suggested that the new science be used to select railway trainmen who would not be what the psychologists would now call "accident prone." It was almost inevitable that this high level of performance would not be maintained and that quacks would begin to set up in business. If we want to know how phrenology ended, we should think back to Huck Finn's companion, the Duke of Bridgewater, who advertised himself along the Mississippi as the "celebrated Dr. Armand de Montalban of Paris who would lecture on the Science of Phrenology at ten cents admission, and furnish charts of character at twenty-five cents apiece."[38]

Phrenology had no great direct influence on race theories in this country, perhaps partially because it throve principally in the optimistic atmosphere of New England. Its attitude toward evil, conceiving it as merely "the absence of good," was not greatly different from that of Emerson. Fanny Kemble, the English actress who married a slaveholder and lived for a time in Georgia, shrewdly observed that George Combe, one of the most famous of the phrenologists, would have had a great career in America if he had scientifically rationalized the institution of slavery. When asked what light his science had on this issue, Combe answered cautiously that the Negro's skull was inferior to that of the white man but that he was by no means without abilities. He was not unfit for free labor. What was needed was a vigorous program of education. Had not the free Negroes in the North shown what education might do? For some reason, the phrenologists were more severe with regard to the Indian. Both Spurzheim and Combe pronounced the Indian not only inferior in intelligence but, because of the peculiar organization of the faculties of his brain, almost hopelessly savage and intractable.[39]

It was Morton, in the United States, who made the most widespread and careful comparisons of human skulls. With his collection of eight hundred crania from areas over many parts of the world, he was able to compare and contrast human races better than any of his contemporaries either in this country or abroad. Confronted by the complexity of problems of comparison, Morton decided to measure cranial capacity alone. The system which he adopted was that of filling his skulls with some material which would pack closely, such as shot pellets or white pepper seed. In this way he attempted to determine the comparative sizes of the crania in his collection and to compare the sizes of skulls of different races and nationalities. He arrived at the conclusion that the larger the size of the cranium, the greater the average of intelligence.

Measuring the skulls did not prove to be a simple matter. It was difficult to develop a uniform method for closing the openings of the skull and for deciding when to stop pouring shot pellets or pepper seed. Morton discovered that second and third measurements frequently did not correspond with the first measurement. He first thought that the trouble might stem from the carelessness of assistants, but after dismissing some of them he was obliged to look to other causes for the discrepancies. In one of his studies he admitted that it "is not merely possible but probable" that there are errors of measurement in his tables. Nonetheless, he continued in his efforts to measure cranial capacity and to find the relationship between race and skull capacity. In 1849, one of his studies included the following results: the English skulls in his collection proved to be the largest, with an average cranial capacity of 96 cubic inches. The Americans and Germans were rather poor seconds, both with cranial capacities of 90 cubic inches. At the bottom of the list were the Negroes with 83 cubic inches, the Chinese with 82, and the Indians with 79.[40]

The numbers of skulls he possessed in the different racial categories of his collection varied a great deal. In the category of the English "race" there were five skulls, in the American seven, and in the German eighteen. On the other hand, there were 338 Indian and 85 Negro skulls. No attempt was made to distinguish between male and female skulls, because neither then nor now has any method ever been perfected for determining from a skull the sex of its former owner. The skulls in the three highest categories had nearly all belonged to white men who had been hanged as felons. It would have been just as logical to conclude that a large head indicated criminal tendencies. Instead, Morton argued that if he had been able to obtain the skulls of white men who had not been criminals, their cranial capacity would have been even larger.[41]

After Morton's death, Josiah Clark Nott continued the work of skull measurement. He wrote to famous men requesting them to measure the circumference of their skulls. From the Boston physician who had performed an autopsy upon Daniel Webster, he learned that the great statesman's head was unusually large, measuring 23¾ inches. "There are several heads in Boston," the doctor wrote with a pardonable pride, "larger than Mr. Webster's." Nott also obtained from a clothing manufacturer in New Jersey an analysis of hat sizes required in different sections of the United States. In the western states where there was a large proportion of Germans, Nott discovered, the hats were, on an average, one-fourth of an inch larger than in the rest of the nation.[42]

What about individual Negroes and Indians and Chinese who had large heads? Was it to be admitted that they were superior to those white men who had small heads? Bachman was quick to point out this difficulty. Nott, in turn, argued that no reliable indication of an individual person's intelligence could be obtained from his skull measurement. It was only where groups of skulls were compared that comparisons could justifiably be made. In addition, it was not merely the overall size of the skull which determined intelligence, but the comparative size of the parts. Since Morton's experiments had not attempted to show the comparative size of the parts of the skull, Nott's conclusion was no more than a prejudiced guess.[43]

In 1856, Gratiolet in France advanced the theory that in Negroes the coronal suture of the skull closes at an early age, gripping the brain in a prison and arresting its growth. For this reason, although young Negro children are as intelligent as white children, at the age of thirteen or fourteen they begin to fall behind because their skulls prevent their intellectual development. This argument was sometimes used in opposition to Negro education in the North. The assumption was that any intensive mental work by a Negro would lead to his physical and mental breakdown.[44]

Another method of studying crania was developed by Anders Retzius in Sweden. In 1842 he published his researches which attempted to explain the physical differences between the Finns, whom he believed to be an indigenous race, and the Swedes, whom he believed to have come from central Asia. In the course of his studies, he hit upon a new way to measure skulls. By dividing the length of the skull into the breadth and multiplying the quotient by 100 to eliminate decimals, Retzius obtained the cephalic index. Long, narrow skulls, those with an index of 80 or less, were termed *dolichocephalic*. All the skulls with an index above 80 were *brachycephalic*. On this basis, the brachycephalic Finns were found to differ from the dolichocephalic Swedes.[45]

The most ingenious disciple of Retzius was Paul Broca. With an enormous enthusiasm for research, he published treatises filled with statistics and complicated diagrams. He arranged his collection of two thousand skulls in Paris into sixty series. His studies are so complex that it is next to impossible for a nonspecialist to follow the details. From some of his remarks, however, we can discover why he failed in his attempts to establish a system of race classification. He found that two anthropologists rarely got the same figure in measuring the diameter of the same skull. Even worse, one anthropologist frequently got a different figure in a second measurement of the same skull. The human head is too irregular, he concluded, to allow accurate comparison on a statistical basis. The confusion was compounded when the dolichocephalics and the brachycephalics were further split into several subdivisions. When this happened, a minute difference in measurement resulted in the placing of the same skull in different categories, according to whose figures were used. These difficulties dampened the enthusiasm of some of the "anthropometrists," but not all. In 1900, one of them achieved the dubious triumph of measuring a single skull in five thousand different ways. The measurement of crania became impossible in its complexity. A whole new vocabulary appeared to describe types of skulls with terms like "Pentagonoides acutus" and "Ellipsoides embolicus," which, as the twentieth-century anthropologist Ernest A. Hooton has pointed out, "are hard to pronounce and almost impossible to apply, except as opprobrious epithets."[46]

By the 1880's, it was clear that measurement of crania did

not provide a method for distinguishing races from one another. Professor A. H. Keane, an English anthropologist, pointed out that craniology could not be depended upon to supply "sufficient, or even altogether trustworthy, materials for distinguishing the main divisions of mankind." Dolichocephaly and brachycephaly were not, he declared, constant in any group, and in many cases where some degree of uniformity might reasonably be expected the most astonishing diversity prevailed. Eskimos were commonly grouped with the brachycephalic Mongol division, but were themselves inclined to extreme dolichocephaly. No norms could be established for any of the races. The Caucasian race especially contained every variety of head shape. Johannes Ranke of Munich, a careful student of craniometry and craniology, declared in 1894 that there was no basis for the belief that the cranial index is a race characteristic. Rudolph Virchow, also an eminent German anthropologist, said it was impossible to decide from the examination of a skull to which race its owner had belonged. Even Broca came to the conclusion that "individual variations are always greater within a given race, than the distance which separates it not only from neighboring races but sometimes from all other races." As a method of classifying races, craniometry was a complete failure.[47]

Another method which seemed to promise light on race differences was the examination of human brains. In 1838, F. Tiedeman, an anatomist at the University of Heidelberg, conducted an experiment to determine whether or not it was true that the brains of Negroes were different from those of white men. After examining the brains of fifty cadavers of both races, he found no appreciable difference. The Negro brains were as large as white brains and were similar in structure. "We must conclude," said Tiedeman, "that no innate difference in the faculties can be admitted to exist between the negro and European races." This experiment caused consternation among the advocates of the polygenic origin theory in the United States. Josiah Clark Nott challenged the validity of the conclusion. Part of the error, said Nott, could be attributed to the fact that Tiedeman had included Egyptians and Hindus as white men, whereas these peoples had heavy infusions of Negro blood.[48]

Charles Darwin himself believed that brain size was related to intelligence and that some races had larger and better brains than others. He explained:

> With civilized nations, the reduced size of the jaws from lessened use, the habitual play of different muscles serving to express different emotions, and the increased size of the brain from greater intellectual activity, have together produced a considerable effect on their general appearance in comparison with savages.

But the differences still remained to be proved. Joseph Deniker, a Frenchman, collected data on eleven thousand European and Negro brains and announced in 1900 that the average weight for the brains of both groups was almost identical. In 1906, Dr. Robert Bennett Bean, an assistant professor of anatomy at Johns Hopkins University and later president of the New Orleans Academy of Science, compared 150 white and 150 Negro brains and found significant racial variations. The frontal lobes of the Negro brains, he reported, were smaller in relation to the posterior lobes than was the case with the white men's brains. From this variation, Bean concluded that Negroes have some faculties—smell, sight, the ability to sing and to build things with their hands—better developed than do white men. On the other hand, they were inherently deficient in self-control, will power, ethical and aesthetic insight, and reason. One of Bean's colleagues at Johns Hopkins, Dr. Franklin P. Mall, undertook to weigh and measure the same brains used in Bean's experiment. Mall's conclusion was that he could find no observable qualitative race differences in the white and Negro brains.[49]

It may be that investigators on both sides of this particular controversy were unconsciously prejudiced, and that this prejudice affected their conclusions. A number of more modern investigators have come to the conclusion that there is a small, but measurable, difference in the size of the brains of different races. In 1929 Professor Raymond Pearl made a study of Negroes and whites and found that "the temporal lobe of the brain is smaller and differently shaped in Negroes." Professor M. F. Ashley Montagu concludes that the Negro has an average cranial capacity of 1,400 cubic centimeters, 50 cubic centimeters less than the white man, but he denies that the difference has any significance as an indicator of comparative inherent intelligence. He points out that the Kaffirs and Amaxosa of Africa have larger brains than whites and so do the Japanese, the Eskimos, and the Polynesians. The fact that Neanderthal man had a brain 200 cubic centimeters larger than that of modern white men, Montagu says, did not make him superior in intelligence. Ruth Benedict admitted that the size of the brains of the Pygmy tribes of Africa is probably significantly smaller than that of other ethnic groups, but she contended that it might be smaller merely because their bodies are smaller. Some modern authorities still maintain that there is a small but demonstrable correlation between a large brain and high intelligence. They admit, however, that there are many exceptions. When an autopsy was performed upon Anatole France, for example, he was discovered to have a brain which weighed about 300 grams less than that of the average adult. The idea of a relationship between brain size and intelligence is still unproved.[50]

The convolutions of the brain have also figured in theories of race differences. John Fiske, the eminent historian of science, was convinced that it was not mainly the weight of the brain which mattered but the number and complexity of the brain's fissures and convolutions. The cerebral surface of an infant's brain, Fiske explained, was smooth "like that of an ape." In an adult savage or in a European peasant, the furrowing was "somewhat marked and complicated." But the brain of "a great scholar" has "furrows" which are "very deep and crooked, and hundreds of creases appear which are not found at all in the brains of ordinary men." Darwin, as we have seen, thought that races differed in the convolutions of their brains. Subsequent research has failed to discover, however, any significant racial differences. Even the relationship of convolutions to intelligence has not been demonstrated. The *Iconographic Encyclopaedia* (1886) admitted that the subject was a confused one:

> The complexity of the convolutions of the brain has been asserted by some to stand in direct relation to intellectual power; and it has been triumphantly pointed out in support of this theory that the brains of the higher apes are much more simple in their convolutions, and therefore have less gray matter, than that of men. This is true, but comparative anatomy has also discovered the opposing fact that the brain of the dog has much simpler convolutions than that of the sheep, which is notoriously a stupid animal in comparison.

As late as 1935, Dr. Robert B. Bean—then a professor of anatomy at the University of Virginia—published a study in which he found Negro brains deficient in the number and complexity of their convolutions. In this conclusion, however, Dr. Bean stood almost alone.[51]

The structure of human hair has been considered as a possible index to race. Blumenbach attempted to classify races by their hair, but discovered that peoples who resembled one another in other respects differed so much in their hair structure that no racial system of classification was possible. In the 1840's, Peter A. Browne, a Philadelphia lawyer with scientific interests, invented a variation of the microscope which he called the "trichometer" for measuring the various properties of hair and wool. At first, he was interested in the subject for its commercial possibilities and studied the hair and wool of lower animals. When he came to study human hair, he discovered that there are three kinds—some oval, some cylindrical, and some "eccentrically elliptical." These three kinds corresponded, he said, to the white race, the Indian race, and the Negro race. "Pile" was the word he coined to describe both hair and wool, and he found that Negro hair was more like wool than like the hair of a white man. Thus, he noted that "the hair of the white man *will not felt*, but the wool of the Negro *will felt*." There was no difference between Negro hair and that of sheep except in "degree of felting power." This discovery was enough for Browne to proclaim that he had "no hesitancy in pronouncing" that Negroes and whites "belong to *two distinct species*." There is an account in a book of the period of a Negro pastor who quieted the fears of his congregation when they had heard this "proof" that they were a different species from the white man. He assured them that they were under the special protection of God, since they were the lambs of the world with wool instead of hair.[52]

Prichard devoted a chapter of one of his studies of race to proving that the Negro possesses true hair and not wool. At the time, most of the proponents of the idea that the Negro is a separate species thought they had more convincing arguments than those which Browne based upon hair, and thus they regarded his studies as interesting rather than deeply significant. Later in the century, however, when the promise of craniometry upon which the anthropologists had placed so much hope had receded, a number of students of race turned again to hair as a possible basis of race classification. Broca, Muller, Huxley, Haeckel, and Keane all studied human hair for this purpose. All their intensive research uncovered was that hair was a more constant basis of differentiation than were skull measurements. This was not saying much, however, and hair too was finally abandoned as a determinant of race differences.[53]

Even body lice were at one time seriously considered as a possible index of race differences. In 1861, Andrew Murray, an English entomologist, collected lice from the inhabitants of a number of countries and reported that they differed not only in color but also in structure. His experiments showed that the body lice of some races could not live on the bodies of individuals of other races. Murray's researches led Darwin to think that a racial scale might be worked out by exposing doubtful cases to different varieties of lice, but no such method of differentiation was ever devised. In 1886, the *Iconographic Encyclopaedia* ridiculed the theory. Schoolteachers in the United States, the author of the article on ethnology declared, could have told Darwin something about the ease with which lice move from unkempt children of one race to those of another.[54]

Although he was not so ambitious as to think he could work out a complete method of race classification, Lewis H. Morgan, the American ethnologist, hoped to correlate race with social customs. In 1871, Morgan published a volume analyzing "systems of consanguinity and affinity" of peoples all over the world. Where family and social relationships seemed to be similar, Morgan assumed that the groups in question were probably descended from a common stock. All the difficulties which this method presented did not shake Morgan's faith. He found that the system of family relationships of the Seneca-Iroquois tribes of Indians of western New York was almost identical with that of the Tamil people of southern India. In spite of the distance separating the two peoples and their diversity in many other respects, Morgan declared that the most satisfactory explanation of their similarities was to suppose them to be descended from "a once common household." But Morgan's method was apparently impossible to apply except in isolated instances.[55]

The confusion over methods of determining race differences shows up most sharply in the widespread disagreement over the number of human races. Linnaeus had found four human races; Blumenbach had five; Cuvier had three; John Hunter had seven; Burke had sixty-three; Pickering had eleven; Virey had two "species," each containing three races; Haeckel had thirty-six; Huxley had four; Topinard had nineteen under three headings; Desmoulins had sixteen "species"; Deniker had seventeen races and thirty types. Jean Finot, one of the critics of race theorizing, concluded in 1906 that the methods of classification were so different that "the facility with which human races may be created at will can easily be imagined." We should be gratified, says Finot, that the anthropologists differ so little. "Far from being astonished at the number of races already extant, we must bless Heaven for having preserved us from a thousand million races and consequent classifications!"[56]

There was a fundamental fallacy behind this whole vast nineteenth-century search for methods to measure race differences. Many a racist awaited breathlessly some scheme of race classification which would withstand the testing methods of science and was prepared—once such a method was found—to pile mountains of *ad hoc* theory concerning the character and temperament of the races onto any discoveries concerning their measurable physical differences. How little the search really mattered may be seen in the tendency of racists, when a physical basis of measurable race differences eluded them, to assume immense innate psychological differences in any case. They did not really need proof for what they *knew* was there.

When the evidence began to be overwhelming that none of their systems worked, why did the anthropologists not consider the possibility that there are no "hierarchies" of race? Some of them were bold enough to come to exactly this conclusion, but for others the idea of race was so real that no amount of failure could convince them that it might be an illusion. It is interesting to read the admissions of defeat in the search for racial character. "Race," said the French anthropologist Topinard in 1879, "in the present state of things, is an abstract conception, a notion of continuity in discontinuity, of unity in diversity. It is the rehabilitation of a real but directly unattainable thing." Dr. John Wesley Powell, Director of the Bureau of Ethnology of the Smithsonian Institution in the 1880's, flatly declared that "there is no science of ethnology," by which he meant the determination of race differences. But many anthropologists hoped that a method of determining and classifying races might still be found, and racists in general were hardly daunted at all by the failures of the anthropologists.[57]

V

The Teutonic Origins Theory

IN THE EIGHTEENTH CENTURY, America showed little interest in race theories which made invidious distinctions among white men. The country needed manpower and, in general, was not much concerned with which particular branch of the white race a man came from. In Europe, however, there were already a few theorists who, to defend the claims to eminence of a particular class or nation, were relying on race theory. In France, for example, the Count de Boulainvilliers (1658-1722) developed a racist theory to explain the special privileges of the nobles. The Franks, he said, had been the ancient tribe in France. They were the *Germani*, a blond, courageous, chaste, and self-governing people. In their conquest of Gaul they had acquired rights over the Gallo-Romans. The nobility of France were descendants of the *Germani;* the commoners were descendants of the plebeian Gallo-Romans.[1]

The most important early source of Teutonic racism was Tacitus (*ca.* 55-120 A.D.). His name was invoked in France, in Germany, in England, and eventually in the United States to explain differences in capacity and virtue among "races" of white men. The irony of this development is that there is doubt whether Tacitus was actually a racist at all. He admired the barbarian people to the north, but the reason probably was that he hoped to convince the Romans, in a time of decay and corruption, of the necessity for recapturing the ancient virtues.

Among the English historians of the eighteenth century, the name of Tacitus conveyed no particular magic. The Anglo-

Saxon tribes were recognized as a branch of the Germanic people, but they were generally regarded merely as uncivilized bar-barians. As we have seen, the philosophers of the Enlightenment generally resisted the idea that the character of peoples is deter-mined by race. The emphasis of the period upon environmental explanations for human conduct made many of the historians regard racism with skepticism. Both of the leading historians of the time, Edward Gibbon and David Hume, attempted to write from a judicious perspective and above personal partialities, and they looked with contempt upon writers who tended to glorify the history of their own people. Gibbon, for example, thought that the Irish and Scottish historians wished to idealize their an-cestors, and he observed that "a people dissatisfied with their present condition grasp at any visions of their past or future glory." Hume, too, complained of the "rather fabulous annals, which are obtruded on us by the Scottish historians."[2]

Gibbon and Hume did not regard the overthrow of Rome by the northern tribes as the triumph of a superior race. They tend-ed to think of the period from the destruction of Rome until the Renaissance as one of unrelieved darkness and superstition. Thus we find Hume contemptuous of the early Germanic tribes and of the Anglo-Saxons in particular. They were

in general a rude, uncultivated people, ignorant of letters, unskilled in the mechanical arts, untamed to submission under law and government, addicted to intemperance, riot, and disorder. Their best quality was their military courage, which yet was not supported by discipline or conduct. Their want of fidelity to the prince, or to any trust reposed in them, appears strongly in the history of their later period; and their want of humanity in all their history.

Thus, he was convinced that "the skirmishes of kites or crows as much merited a particular narrative, as the confused transac-tions and battles of the Saxon Heptarchy." Gibbon regarded the debilitating effects of Christianity rather than the superior vir-tues of the Teutonic tribes as responsible for the fall of Rome.

Some English historians were attracted to the ideal of liberty among the Anglo-Saxons. As early as 1745, Samuel Squire had written *An Enquiry into the Foundation of the English Consti-tution,* in which he discussed the ideas of Tacitus, including the "invincible love of liberty" shown by the ancient Germans.[3]

Toward the end of the century, a few historians were draw-ing race distinctions more tightly. In 1787 John Pinkerton published his *Dissertation on the Origin of the Scythians or Goths,* one of the first histories in England to rely heavily upon race theory.[4] Less extreme in this respect than Pinkerton was Sharon Turner, whose *History of the Anglo-Saxons* was publish-ed in several volumes between 1799 and 1805. Turner admitted that the Saxons, with their "attachment to piratical expeditions," their unrestrained drinking and brawling, their blood feuds, and their fondness for raw meat, were not wholly admirable fore-fathers. His main point, however, was that they had deeply in-fluenced modern England. And he was the first to underline the significance of the story of Beowulf for historical study.[5]

Nor were the English themselves the only ones to feel that modern English ideas of government had come from Anglo-Saxon and Teutonic ancestors. Early in the century Montesquieu formulated this concept, drawing upon Tacitus for his descrip-tion of the system of government of the Germanic tribes. Eng-land, he said, had developed the most perfect expression of par-liamentary government, the roots of "that beautiful system having been devised in the woods."[6]

Hume was aware of these attempts to find representative in-stitutions among the Teutonic tribes, but he disparaged them. Some people have argued, he said, that the council, the *witenage-mot,* was an ancestor of the British Parliament. "The matter would probably be of difficult discussion, even were it examined impartially," he observed, and the proponents of both sides had been "captious and deceitful." The modern monarchical "fac-tion" were maintaining that "these *wites,* or *sapientes,* were the judges, or men learned in the law; the popular faction assert them to be representative of the boroughs, or what we now call the commons." Hume thought the advocates of the power of the monarch had the better case.[7]

In the United States, Thomas Jefferson was sufficiently interested in the question of the extent to which representative government and English law had descended from the Anglo-Saxons to take up the study of the ancient language. He devised an Anglo-Saxon grammar himself, but his numerous other activities prevented him from pursuing his Anglo-Saxon studies as far as he would have liked to carry them, and he was never able to trace to the ancient sources English and presumably American institutions.[8]

In the first half of the nineteenth century, the racism of British historians was still comparatively mild. In 1832 Sir Francis Palgrave published his *Rise and Progress of the English Commonwealth*. Palgrave was not a racist. Himself the son of Meyer Cohen, a Jew, he had no particular reason to glorify the Anglo-Saxons. His book is an attempt to reassure the conservatives who feared any change and to caution the advocates of change to proceed deliberately and wisely. He argued that the English had derived their ideas of government from both the Romans and the Teutons—from Rome the idea of monarchy, which enabled them to avoid becoming a collection of little satrapies, and from the Teutons the idea of limiting the power of the monarch. The love of liberty with definite safeguards against arbitrary power had, he said, always been characteristic of the Teutonic forebears. It was the tradition, not the race, of the Anglo-Saxons which interested Palgrave; he was appealing to their institutions to bring some sort of peace between two warring domestic factions in England.[9]

But when the next important historian of the Anglo-Saxons appeared in England, the climate of opinion concerning social change was different. The revolutions of 1848 had dampened enthusiasm for reform and strengthened the hand of the conservatives. In 1849, John Mitchell Kemble attempted to show in his *The Saxons in England* why his native land had escaped the upheavals so common on the Continent. "On every side of us," Kemble declares, "thrones totter, and the deep foundations of society are convulsed." By contrast, Queen Victoria was safe up-

on her throne, "secure in the affections of a people whose institutions have given to them all the blessings of an equal law."
And Kemble comes close to a racist explanation for this good
fortune. "The Englishman has inherited the noblest portion of
his being from the Anglo-Saxons," he tells us. "In spite of
every influence, we bear a marvellous resemblance to our forefathers."[10]

In the United States, nineteenth-century histories which appeared before the Civil War sometimes reflect the kind of generalized reliance upon race theory found in English histories of
the period. In this country, the Teutonic origins theory of representative institutions appealed even more than in England to
historians who had great faith in democracy. The theory was
useful in defending representative institutions against the attacks of conservatives—both at home and abroad—who maintained that democracy as a theory of government had not been
able to withstand the test of time. Representative government
could be shown to have a long, honorable, and successful history. Although freedom was the major theme, there was sometimes another, more chilling note—the idea that freedom was
the race heritage of the Germanic peoples but perhaps not that
of other peoples.

George Bancroft, for example, represented a mild version of
the theory that freedom is somehow the special characteristic of
Teutonic races. "Of all the nations of the European world," he
declares in his *History of the United States* (1834), "the chief
emigration was from that Germanic race most famed for the
love of personal independence." Bancroft had studied in Germany, and there is some evidence, at least, that he favored the
Germanic element over others in American history. Ordinarily,
however, he had little interest in racist explanations of history.
His main purpose was to show that the will of God had determined the triumph of democracy. History yields eternal evidence, he declared, "that tyranny and wrong lead inevitably to
decay," but "freedom and right, however hard may be the
struggle, always prove resistless."[11]

Like Bancroft, John Lothrop Motley was inspired by the ideals of democracy and freedom. "If ten people in the world hate despotism a little more and love religious liberty a little better in consequence of what I have written," he said of his *The Rise of the Dutch Republic* (1856), "I shall be satisfied." Motley was struck by the similarities between the struggle for independence of the Dutch against Spain and that of the American colonists against England. Americans, he thought, should have a special interest in the Dutch struggle because Dutchmen and Americans were racially akin. The United States, "in whose Anglo-Saxon veins flows much of that ancient and kindred blood received from the nation . . . tracking its own political existence to the same parent spring of temperate human liberty—must look with affectionate interest upon the trials of the elder commonwealth." The history of the Dutch "is a portion of the records of the Anglo-Saxon race—essentially the same, whether in Friesland, England, or Massachusetts."[12]

Motley divides the Dutch nation into two races—the *Belgae* (or Celts) and the Germans. The *Belgae* were "the bravest of all the Celts." They were "inflammable, petulant, audacious." The Celtic fighting man, of vast stature and with "yellow hair floating over his shoulders," was superior to the Roman soldiers. In fact, the "gigantic Gaul derided the Roman soldiers as a band of pigmies." But the *Belgae* were just as plainly inferior to the Germanic tribes in Holland. For one thing, they were "a priest-ridden race," even before they were converted to Catholicism. The German, on the other hand, "in his simplicity, had raised himself to a purer belief than that of the sensuous Roman or the superstitious Gaul. He believed in a single, supreme, almighty God, *All-Vater* or All-father. This Divinity was too sublime to be incarnated or imaged, too infinite to be enclosed in temples built with hands." It was not fair to accuse the early Germans of practicing human sacrifice. "It must be confessed that . . . a criminal or a prisoner . . . was occasionally immolated," but such lapses were due to the fact that the "purity of their religion was . . . stained by their Celtic neighborhood."[13]

Though the Celts were great warriors, the Germans were greater still. "The Gaul was irascible, furious in his wrath, but less formidable in a sustained conflict with a powerful foe." The difference between the two races had been apparent in their struggle against the Romans and it was just as significant, much later, in their joint struggle against the Spanish. The Celts "were the first to assault and to defy the imperial power in both revolts," while the Germans were "slower to be aroused, but of more enduring wrath, were less ardent at the commencement, but, alone, steadfast at the close of the contest." Perhaps most importantly, the two races differed in their political systems. "The Gallic tribes were aristocracies, in which the influence of clanship was a predominant feature; while the German system, although nominally regal, was in reality democratic,"[14] according to Motley.

All this appears to be the most throughgoing kind of racism, but actually it is comparatively mild. Motley has every opportunity to compare the Germanic race in Holland with the Latin race of Spain, but he has nothing to say on this subject. He blames Catholicism, rather than the racial characteristics of the Spanish people, for the evils of the Spanish occupation as well as for the character of Spanish rulers, particularly that of Philip II. Philip himself, says Motley, was a Goth and not a Latin. Even his tendency to persecute heretics came from "the ancient ardor, which in heroic centuries had animated the Gothic champions of Spain," although in Philip this ardor "had degenerated into bigotry." Thus, the conflict between Spain and Holland is hardly racial at all; it is religious and political. Though Motley appeals to race theories, his major interests are clearly democracy and freedom.[15]

Other writers who dealt with the history of institutions were sometimes more racist than Bancroft or Motley. William Hickling Prescott, Francis Lieber, and Francis Parkman were less ecstatic in their attachment to democracy and representative institutions. They were a little more at ease in praising the courage of the Anglo-Saxon than in lauding his instinct for democracy.

When they treated the latter theme at all, they paid tribute to the supposed inherent caution and good sense of the Anglo-Saxons or of the Teutonic peoples, which kept them from making representative institutions too representative or from leaving them unchecked by other powers. To trust everything—or even very much—to the native good sense of the Anglo-Saxon was a doctrine too risky for these writers.

William Hickling Prescott sometimes referred with satisfaction to the stern virtues of the Anglo-Saxons, particularly to their self-reliance, their willingness to see changes come gradually, their distrust of utopian schemes of reform. In his *Conquest of Peru* (1847), Prescott also praises the character of the Spanish warriors, but he indicates serious reservations concerning them. In the Spanish character "meaner influences were strangely mingled with the loftier, the temporal with the spiritual." The courage of the Spanish soldier was "sullied with cruelty, the cruelty that flowed equally—strange as it may seem—from his avarice and his religion." The defects of the Spaniards are contrasted with the virtues of the Englishmen who settled in North America:

What a contrast did these children of Southern Europe present to the Anglo-Saxon races who scattered themselves along the great northern division of the western hemisphere! For the principle of action with these latter was not avarice, nor the more specious pretext of proselytism; but independence—independence religious and political. To secure this, they were content to earn a bare subsistence by a life of frugality and toil. They asked nothing from the soil, but the reasonable returns of their own labor. No golden visions threw a deceitful halo around their path, and beckoned them onwards through seas of blood to the subversion of an unoffending dynasty. They were content with the slow but steady progress of their social polity. They patiently endured the privations of the wilderness, watering the tree of liberty with their tears and with the sweat of their brow, till it took deep root in the land and sent up its branches high towards the heavens; while the communities of the neighboring continent, shooting up into the sudden splendors of a tropical vegetation, exhibited, even in their prime, the sure symptoms of decay.[16]

In a letter to a friend in Spain, written during the period of the revolution of 1848, Prescott wondered whether the continental European countries were suited for free institutions. Spain was in "a charming state of disorganization." The consolidation of the German empire was "a noble idea," but he doubted whether it was "practicable." The "liberation of Italy from the barbarians" was a "beautiful old dream" which could probably not be realized. "The republicanism of France is a chimera, I fear. The volatile spirits of that people must be hooped with iron. An iron rule, I suspect, is the rule for them." All these difficulties were presumably due to the racial character of these countries. "Liberty and equality seem to be too great stimulations for some constitutions. They suit the Anglo-Saxon better than any." In addition to his good sense with regard to political institutions, the Anglo-Saxon deserved the gratitude of mankind for his ability to apply science to the useful arts.[17]

In his histories, however, Prescott portrayed the Spaniard in a more complimentary way than these quotations would suggest. In the struggle with the Indians, the Spaniard is allowed to represent the forces of enlightenment struggling against those of barbarism, and his virtues are emphasized. He is a "high-mettled cavalier," "a paladin of romance," with his "nice point of honor" and his "proud . . . vaunt." In Prescott's histories, the Spaniard does not appear in conflict with the Anglo-Saxon. His warfare is directed against the Aztec and the Inca—or in the European histories, with the Moors in Spain. In all these conflicts, Prescott enthusiastically champions the cause of the Spaniard. To a friend he wrote that he had spent so much time in considering the history of Spain that he felt almost as if he were a Spaniard himself.[18] He had little sympathy to waste upon the Indians for the cruelties which they had suffered in Mexico and South America. He thought that Las Casas had vastly overstated the case for the Indians. "However good the motives of its author," Prescott says of Las Casas' *Short Account of the Destruction of the Indies,* "we may regret that the book was ever written." Las Casas "lent a willing ear to every tale of violence and rapine, and thus diminished his own influence and consequent usefulness." And Prescott's attitude toward the injustice which the Indians suffered is suggested in his saying of the Aztecs, "Who shall lament their fall?"[19]

When Prescott turned to contemporary politics in the United States, he had comparatively little to say about race. We find him uneasy in the presence of the idea that the Anglo-Saxons have representative institutions in their very blood, and very lukewarm to the apostles of Jacksonian democracy. On one occasion he observed that the phrase "the good sense of the people" had more of humbug in it "than he once thought." Prescott had only a limited admiration for race as the explanation for American democracy.[20]

Francis Lieber was a political scientist—the first notable one in an American college—and not a historian. Like the historians, however, he attempts to relate the institutions of representative and constitutional government to race. As a youth in Germany, he had been an ardent opponent of tyranny, but he lost a good deal of his enthusiasm when he went to Greece in 1822 to help the patriots fight Turkish tyranny. The Greeks were less noble than he had thought they would be; in fact, he found them incompetent and cowardly. Disillusioned, he wished to leave, but it was only after considerable difficulty that he was allowed to do so. Suspected as a radical when he returned to his native country, he went first to England and then to the United States. Beginning in 1835, he taught for more than twenty years at the College—now the University—of South Carolina. In 1857, he was appointed to a chair at Columbia University. He continued to teach as a member of the Columbia faculty until his death in 1872.[21]

Lieber was an advocate of effective checks by the judiciary on both executive and legislative authority. In his works we find much praise of the "Anglican" race, by which he seems to have meant, practically, the English and American nations. These countries alone had developed a system of restraints upon liberty which were necessary if liberty itself was to survive. "We belong to the Anglican race," he says somewhat inconsistently, since he himself had come from Germany,

which carried Anglican principles and liberty over the globe, because, wherever it moves, liberal institutions and common law full of manly rights and instinct with the principle of an expansive life accompany it. We belong to that race whose obvious task it is, among other proud and sacred tasks, to rear and spread civil liberty over vast regions in every part of the earth, on continent and isle. We belong to that tribe alone which has the word Self-Government.

Other races also have characteristic tendencies. The ancient Greeks had an "instinct" for aesthetics and the Romans one for "law." The modern "Gallican race," on the other hand, was easily swayed by mass appeals.[22]

Yet Lieber was too shrewd to find race theories a satisfactory explanation for everything. As early as 1833, he sent a questionnaire to the officials at Sing Sing Prison, where the inmates were not segregated by race. The replies convinced him that there were no significant innate differences in intelligence between whites and Negroes. He was convinced that the Negroes would never develop their abilities unless they were accorded social equality, but he opposed such a solution because he thought it would lead to intermarriage, an idea he strongly disapproved. In his later years he found racism, particularly nationalistic racism, less and less satisfactory as an explanation of history. All Europeans and their American descendants, he said, belong to the same race, the "Cis-Caucasian." He insisted that no race had a monopoly on the right to civil liberty. Near the end of his life he came near rejecting the word *race* itself. In 1871 he declared, "the word race has probably been abused in modern times more than any other," so that "even to use it was virtually a confession of ignorance or evil intent."[23]

In the histories of Francis Parkman we find a heavy reliance upon racism. In his studies of the French in Canada, Parkman devotes considerable attention to the political institutions which he believed to be responsible for the fall of French Canada, but behind these institutions he sees all-important race characteristics. It would be easy to imagine, says Parkman, that the difference between the French and English colonies was "a difference of political and religious institutions," but this explanation "does not cover the ground." The important factor was race. "The Germanic race, and especially the Anglo-Saxon branch of it, is peculiarly masculine," Parkman says, "and, therefore, peculiarly fitted for self-government. It submits its action habitually to the guidance of reason, and has the judicial faculty of seeing both sides of a question." On the other hand,

the French Celt is cast in a different mould. He sees the end distinctly, and reasons about it with an admirable clearness; but his own impulses and passions continually turn him away from it. Opposition excites him; he is impatient of delay, is impelled always to extremes, and does not readily sacrifice a present inclination to an ultimate good. He delights in abstractions and generalizations, cuts loose from unpleasing facts, and roams through an ocean of desires and theories.

It would not have helped if the French had tried to imitate the government of the English colonists. "The institutions of New England were utterly inapplicable to the population of New France," says Parkman, "and the attempt to apply them would have wrought nothing but mischief. . . . Freedom is for those who are fit for it. The rest will lose it, or turn it to corruption."[24]

By this time, the currents of racism were running strongly on both sides of the Atlantic. In Scotland, to cite one example, Dr. Robert Knox, a professor of anatomy at the Edinburgh College of Surgeons, wrote a book which shows the more violent new tone of such studies. "Race is everything," says Knox. "Literature, science, art, in a word, civilization, depend on it."[25] He rejects all theories which imply that primitive races can be civilized. His main thesis is that the Saxon must win the inevitable war which impends against the Celt. He can detect in the Know Nothing riots in the United States the cosmic workings of history and portents of the future. He had thought, he said, that the inevitable conflict of the Saxon and Celt would be put off for a number of years, but he had been wrong. The struggle has already appeared in one of the northern states, the Saxons assembling tumultuously, and burning a Roman-catholic church, with other acts of violence toward the frequenters of that church, who of course are Celtic. We shall see: time unfolds all events; the war of race will some day shake the Union to its foundation. They never will mix—never commingle and unite.[26]

It is, of course, the Celt who causes the trouble. The elements of Celtic character are "furious fanaticism: a love of war and disorder; a hatred for order and patient industry; no accumulative habits; restless, treacherous, uncertain; look at Ireland." For Knox, the Irish and the French are essentially the same race because both are Celts. Their common Celtic qualities are shown, for example, in their religion. He finds everywhere their "monkeries and mummeries, their nunneries, and seigniories, feudality and primogeniture." Even when the Celts are not Catholic they still show the characteristics of that religion. In Wales and Scotland, for example, "the reformed Celts have never joined the churches 'as by law established.' It is the Saxon who accepts of his religion from the lawyers; the Celt will not. Accordingly, the Welsh and Caledonian Celt are strictly evangelical." And their religion is accompanied by "a laxity of morals which would astonish the world, if fairly described."[27]

In America, Knox found both Saxons and Celts displaying their true racial characters. The Saxons are "democrats by their nature, the only democrats on the earth, the only race which truly comprehends the meaning of the word liberty." They rely upon themselves and have only contempt for the mob. The Celt, on the other hand, relies upon closely-knit societies and upon mass opinion. "See him cling to the banks of rivers, fearing to plunge into the forest; without self-reliance; without self-confidence." In England, Knox does not hesitate to suggest a drastic solution for the racial problem which the Celts present. "The source of all evil lies in the *race*, the Celtic race of Ireland. . . . The race must be forced from the soil; by fair means, if possible; still they must leave. England's safety requires it. I speak not of the justice of the case; nations must ever act as Machiavelli advised: look to yourself."[28]

In spite of Knox's opinion, Celtic "depravity" played a less important part than we might suppose in the Know Nothing agitation in the United States. We find, of course, some appeals to racism. One sharp-tongued member of the upper class in Boston could say, "Our Celtic fellow citizens are almost as remote from us in temperament and constitution as the Chinese." There was a joke about the wheelbarrow being the greatest invention of all time because it had been the means of teaching the Irishman to walk on his hind legs. Even the Know Nothings, however, depended far more on the evils of Popery than they did on racism in pressing their cause. One Know Nothing editor declared that the Irish were "our natural enemies, not because they are Irishmen, but because they are the truest guards of the Papacy." The best known of the histories of the Know Nothing movement scarcely mentions race as a specific factor in the conflict.[29]

Ralph Waldo Emerson read Knox's book on race. He was repelled by its wild exaggerations but felt that it nonetheless was "charged with pungent and unforgettable truths." In Emerson's writings we find a much more restrained theory of race, and yet a significant one. One of the chapters of his book, *English Traits,* is entitled "Race." Here Emerson develops the idea that just as a son inherits the physical character and the innate character as well of his parents, so do races inherit their outer appearance and inward nature. "We look to find in the son every mental and moral property that existed in the ancestor. In race, it is not the broad shoulders, or litheness, or stature that gives advantage, but a symmetry that reaches as far as to the wit. Then the miracle and renown begin." Therefore, race is an indispensable factor in the understanding of human history:

It is race, is it not? that puts the hundred millions of India under the dominion of a remote island in the north of Europe. Race avails much, if that be true, which is alleged, that all Celts are Catholics, and all Saxons are Protestants; that Celts love unity of power, and Saxons the representative principle. Race is a controlling influence in the Jew, who for two millenniums, under every climate, has preserved the same character and employments. Race in the negro is of appalling importance. The French in Canada, cut off from all intercourse with the parent people, have held their national traits. I chanced to read Tacitus "On the Manners of the Germans," not long since, in Missouri, and the heart of Illinois, and I found abundant points of resemblance between the Germans of the Hercynian forest, and our *Hoosiers, Suckers,* and *Badgers* of the American woods.[30]

The harsh, imperious note characteristic of Knox's racism was to be found increasingly among the historians of England in the latter half of the nineteenth century. Bishop William Stubbs and Edward A. Freeman, both professors of history at Oxford and leaders of what was known as the Oxford School, agreed in their conviction that it was largely race which explained human history. They traced nearly everything good in English civilization back to the Teutonic forebears. Stubbs stated the thesis in this way:

It is to Ancient Germany that we must look for the earliest trace of our forefathers, for the best part of almost all of us is originally German; though we call ourselves Britons, the name has only a geographical significance. The blood that is in our veins comes from German ancestors. Our language, diversified as it is, is at bottom a German language; our institutions have grown into what they are from the common basis of the ancient institutions of Germany. The Jutes, Angles, and Saxons were but different tribes of the great Teutonic household; the Danes and Norwegians, who subdued them in the north and east, were of the same origin; so were the Normans: the feudal system itself was of Frank, *i.e.* also German origin. Even if there is still in our blood a little mixture of Celtic ingredient derived from the captive wives of the first conquerors, there is no leaven of Celticism in our institutions.

Stubbs and Freeman assigned themselves the duty of tracing modern British political and legal institutions back to their primitive "germs" among the Teutonic forebears, relying heavily upon Tacitus' *Germania* and the early Anglo-Saxon chronicles. But they were not content to restrict the virtues of the Teutonic races to their genius for devising political institutions.

Up until this time, the Anglo-Saxon had been prevented from becoming a really powerful race symbol by the belief that he possessed certain innate defects. The theory had been that he was brave and liberty-loving but sluggish and stupid. "The polite luxury of the Norman," Macaulay had observed, "presented a striking contrast to the coarse voracity of his Saxon neighbors." Even Knox, extravagantly as he admired the Saxons for their courage and ability to govern themselves, thought little of their taste or their powers of abstract thought.

Now Stubbs and Freeman set about the task of refurbishing the moral, intellectual, and aesthetic characteristics of the Anglo-Saxons. They regarded the Anglo-Saxons and the Normans as racially the same people, and the Normans had shown themselves able to absorb what was best in French civilization. It was unjust, moreover, to stigmatize the Anglo-Saxons as being no better than savages. "You must remember," said Freeman, "that we were then both a heathen and a barbarous people, and that it is not fair to judge our fathers by the same rules as if they had been either Christians or civilized men." In any case, the barbarism of the Anglo-Saxons was open and aboveboard, not like the lying craftiness of the Celts and Latins.

Whatever its drawbacks, the early barbarism of the Anglo-Saxons had insured the racial purity of England. "It has turned out much better in the end," philosophized Freeman, "that our forefathers did thus kill or drive out nearly all the people whom they found in the land. The English were thus able to grow up as a nation in Britain, and their laws, manners, and language grew up with them, and were not copied from those of other nations." When the stern duties of exterminating the enemy were over, the Anglo-Saxon had proved himself capable of the highest culture. "Have we not our Homer after Homer in the heroic lay of Beowulf? Have we not our Milton before Milton in the sacred song of Caedmon?"[31]

The Anglo-Saxons, Freeman argues, changed the Normans more than the Normans did the Anglo-Saxons. Through the Anglo-Saxons, the Normans recovered ideas of ancient freedom which they had temporarily forgotten in their association with the "Romanic" races in France.[32]

Neither Stubbs nor Freeman had much that was favorable to say concerning non-Teutonic races. In 1859 Stubbs supported Austria in her war against "those wretched Italians," and on another occasion he denounced "those horrid Poles." In a letter to a German scholar, he rejoiced that the Jews there were considering returning to Israel. "If the Jews are on their way back to Palestine," he asked, "could not the Irish be prevailed on *antiquam exquirer matrem,* and emigrate in search of Scota, Pharaoh's daughter?"[33]

Freeman's comments on races he did not like were much stronger. His hatred of the Celts found expression in his deep satisfaction over the defeat of France in 1871. "I should like to cut up the whole Gal-welshry into bits," he wrote to a friend, "as its unity is clearly a standing menace to . . . the world generally." He had a special hatred for Jews. In 1882 he wrote to a friend of his disgust that there should be an uproar because "the Russians have punched some Hebrew heads irregularly" and because Chinese immigrants in California had been mistreated. "There is no religious persecution in either case," he declared, "only the natural instinct of any decent nation to get rid of filthy strangers."

Stubbs and Freeman exerted at least some influence upon the most popular English historian of the period. John Richard Green dedicated his *Short History of the English People* (1874) to his "Two dear Friends, my Masters in the Study of English History." Green was not so completely racist as Stubbs and Freeman in his interpretation of history. He could deprecate Freeman's "overpowering Teutonism," and could exhibit some sympathy for racial minorities like the Irish. But the influence of race theory is still strong in him. Whereas Stubbs and Freeman had admitted a slight Celtic admixture in the modern Englishman, Green apparently makes him solidly Teutonic. "Not a Briton remained as subject or slave on English ground" after the invasion of the Anglo-Saxons, he says. "Sullenly, inch by inch, the beaten men drew back from the land which their conquerors had won; and eastward of the border-line which the English sword had drawn, all was now purely English." We are not surprised to learn, therefore, that "with the landing of Hengest, English history begins." Like Stubbs and Freeman, Green traces the British Parliament back to "the little body of farmer-commonwealths" in Germany, and like them he finds Teutonic characteristics in English literature. "Caedmon is a type of the new grandeur, depth, and fervour of tone which the German race was to give to the religion of the East." Even the German devil was a superior devil. "The human energy of the German race, its sense of the might of individual manhood, transformed in Caedmon's verse the Hebrew Tempter into a rebel Satan, disdainful of vassalage to God." Also in Caedmon, "we catch the new pathetic note which the Northern melancholy was to give our poetry."[34]

For about a quarter of a century the Teutonic origins theory was the dominant school of thought among American historians. In 1870, Professor William F. Allen, a classical scholar at the University of Wisconsin, advanced the idea that American conditions might offer peculiarly rewarding means of testing Tacitus' ideas concerning the German tribes, because the primitive conditions of the ancient race found their counterpart in this country in relatively recent times. He wrote a letter to the *Nation* suggesting to Sir Henry Maine, an English legal historian, that the early settlements of the English colonists in New England had been strikingly similar to those described by Tacitus. Maine had argued that private property was not an early and primitive human institution but came only when a people became civilized. Allen thought that this idea could be borne out in early New England. There, the colonists "had a free field before them, like the Saxon conquerors of Britain." They had experimented, it is true, with joint ownership of property, but they discovered the theory was unworkable and eventually rejected it.[35]

Allen had studied Greek and Latin at Göttingen and Berlin.

His *Short History of the Roman People* (1890) shows strongly the influence of the Teutonic school. He explains that it was not the Germans who despoiled the Roman Empire. It was the Huns who were guilty, and the Huns were a "Tartar race" from central Asia, "small, dark-hued, and hideous of feature." The Germans had, long before, sent emissaries to Rome, and citizens of German blood there had occupied "the highest places of government and administration." The Germans had not been numerous enough, however, to rescue Rome from the barbaric invasions from the east. It took centuries for the Germans to restore civilization in Europe to a semblance of its former grandeur. Allen was an enthusiastic admirer of Tacitus and published an edition of the *Germania* in this country.[36]

In other writings, Allen seems to have had some second thoughts about the innate character of the Germans. He was disturbed because German immigrants in this country did not always behave as history said they were supposed to; they showed a tendency to espouse socialism. The Germans must have been corrupted when they were closely associated with Rome. There labor had been "left to slaves" and "a freeman was disgraced by labor." Therefore, "in those countries of the Continent which have derived their institutions and civilization by an unbroken succession from the Roman Empire, industry has continued to be held in the same contempt." Thus Allen explained the labor "agitations" which "threaten to subvert our social organization." Germans, like other Europeans, had been infected with the same contagion. It must be admitted that Germany was "the home of Socialism. . . . It is . . . a Teutonic country . . . but it was brought at a very early date . . . into close connection with the Romance nations; was thoroughly feudalized, and, while never losing entirely its primitive local liberties, was reduced under the rule of absolutism as completely as its southern neighbors."[37]

Thus, for Allen, England and not Germany is the true inheritor of the early German councils described by Tacitus. "The English," says Allen, "having come less directly under the influence of Roman traditions than any other of the leading nations of Europe, and having therefore preserved more completely their primitive free institutions and the democratic spirit of which these were the outgrowth, are the foremost representatives and pioneers of this movement." They are the champions of representative government. In addition, "the English race stands for the dignity of labor." This does not mean that they will permit "anti-social" theories. "Labor contests there may no doubt be; but schemes to destroy society itself could never have originated in an Anglo-Saxon community."[38]

In 1871, one of the most discerning minds in America became interested in the Teutonic origins theory. At Harvard, where he was then a professor of history, Henry Adams set himself the task of learning the Anglo-Saxon language in order to determine whether something explicit could be garnered from the confusion which surrounded the study of sources of modern political and legal institutions. In Adams' historical studies there is not the passionate focus upon race characteristics which we find in Freeman. One of his biographers has suggested that Adams was drawn to the Teutonic theory for use as a weapon in defense of representative institutions, which were then under serious attack by intellectuals both in Europe and in America. "In an age highly critical of the pretensions of democracy," says Ernest Samuels, "the theory supplied an ancestry for American institutions that made them venerable and not merely virtuous." Adams had not yet developed the pessimism concerning democracy which was soon to be a major element in his philosophy.[39]

During the academic year 1873-74, Adams conducted a special seminar of "candidates for honors" in the study of Teutonic and Anglo-Saxon institutions. The work was so satisfactory to Adams that he established at Harvard at his own expense a class of doctoral candidates to carry on for another year the research already begun. "It matters very little what line you take," Adams wrote to one of his eminent pupils, Henry Cabot Lodge, "provided you can catch the tail of an idea to develop with solid reasoning and thorough knowledge." It was in something of this nondoctrinaire spirit that Adams wrote the leading essay in the collection, *Essays in Anglo-Saxon Law* (1876), which also contained essays by members of his class.[40]

The tone of Adams' contribution to the volume is favorable to democracy, and there are no appeals to racism. The divine right of kings was, in his opinion, "a mere historical blunder." It is soon apparent that he is in favor of the theory of checks and balances in government. His effort is to discover the workings of a similar system in the conflicts between nobles and kings in England and still farther back in the tribal customs of the Anglo-Saxons and their ancestors in Germany. Adams believed that the antiquity of representative government "gives to the history of Germanic, and especially of English, institutions a roundness and philosophic continuity, which add greatly to their interest, and even to their practical value."

Adams raised so many objections to the links of continuity which previous historians had formulated, however, that his contemporaries must sometimes have doubted whether he subscribed to the Teutonic theory at all.[41] "Great as is Mr. Freeman's parade of knowledge," Adams wrote to Lodge, "he has never written anything really solid." More sharply still, Adams could observe that apparently it did not trouble Freeman that the English race of the eleventh century, which was supposed to be indomitable, was "conquered twice in half a century and held permanently in subjection by races inferior to itself in wealth and power." Adams could even maliciously declare that Freeman's serious historical works were less successful than his *Early English History for Children*. Against Stubbs, Adams alleged that he had not proved what he set out to prove. Stubbs had been misled by "a sentiment of patriotism" to assume that Parliament was the direct descendant of the Anglo-Saxon *Witan* or royal council. The *Witan*, Adams contended, had "perished with the class it represented," and furthermore "two whole centuries elapsed between the last genuine meeting of the *Witan* and the first meeting of Parliament." Adams was, in fact, criticizing the Teutonic origins theory on the grounds which eventually caused historians generally to reject it.

But Adams himself, even though he believed he had destroyed Stubbs's and Freeman's arguments in favor of Teutonic origins, thought he had hit upon a way to save the theory itself.[42] It was not the idea of a parliament, said Adams, which the Teutons and the Anglo-Saxons had passed on to their descendants. It was the principle of law. Adams undertook to prove that the Germans had bequeathed a fundamental body of laws to the Anglo-Saxons. This system of laws underwent severe stresses and strains, Adams admitted, in the later confusion of Anglo-Saxon kingdoms and still more under the Norman invaders, but it had never been wholly destroyed. The essentials of these legal principles were private property, jury trials, the settlement of disputes by compromise, and the relegation of private matters to family control. Not parliament but the rule of law over that of the personal caprice of a ruler, Adams argued, had an unbroken history back to the Germanic tribes. The student who attempts to trace "the slender thread of political and legal thought," he declared, "no longer loses it from sight in the confusion of feudalism, or the wild lawlessness of the Heptarchy." Instead, he "follows it safely and firmly until it leads him out upon the wild plains of northern Germany." There, the blessings of law "embraced every free man, rich or poor, and in theory at least allowed equal rights to all." It was not necessary, said Adams, to try to trace the idea even farther back. "The State and the Law may well have originated here."[43]

It was a magnificent theory, but was it true? Years later Adams dismissed the whole thesis of inheritance from the Anglo-Saxons. In 1901 he wrote to Henry Osborne Taylor, the famous medievalist, that his own studies of "dreary Anglo-Saxon law" had been "a *tour-de-force* possible only to youth." He had not then understood the combination of solid practical sense and poetry which characterized the Normans. "Never," said Adams, "did any man go blind on a career more virtuously than I did, when I threw myself so obediently into the arms of the Anglo-Saxons." What had changed his mind, Adams tells Taylor, was the ability of his friend John La Farge to teach him how to look at Norman castles and churches. "Between Bishop Stubbs and John La Farge," Adams said, "the chasm has required lively gymnastics. The text of a charter of Edward the Confessor was uncommonly remote from a twelfth-century window. To clamber across the gap has needed many years of La Farge's closest instruction to me, on the use of eyes, not to say feet."[44]

Rather conveniently, Adams shifted the great qualities which he had previously admired in the Anglo-Saxons over to the Normans. In them, he thought he could discern the stern qualities of the great age of New England. "A great age it was," he wrote in 1895 to Brooks Adams concerning the Norman period, "and a great people our Norman ancestors." They were "rather hard and grasping, and with no outward show of grace." They were "given to use of the sword and plough rather than the chisel, and with apparently little or none of the brush and with no sense of color comparable to that of other races." Still, our "Norman grandpapas did great things in art, or at least in the narrow field of art that reflected their lives." Their one great artistic talent was in architecture, and Americans should recognize the merits of their ancestors. "I have rarely felt New England at its highest ideal power," he exclaimed, "as it appeared to me, beatified and glorified, in the Cathedral of Coutances." But by this time Adams was a disillusioned old man and he thought New England itself was in its final decline. Like the Normans, he said, New Englanders "have lost their religion, their art, and their military tastes. . . . They have kept only the qualities which were most useful, with a dull instinct recalling dead associations. So we get Boston."[45]

In the 1880's, Herbert Baxter Adams was the most prominent advocate of the Teutonic origins theory in America. Like many of his scholarly predecessors, he had studied in Germany under the great Von Treitschke. As one of the organizers of the graduate school at Johns Hopkins University when it opened in 1876, he introduced the German seminar method there. In 1883, he began publication of the *Johns Hopkins Studies in History and Political Science*; and for years he served as its editor. In

1884, he founded the American Historical Association. Woodrow Wilson described Herbert Baxter Adams as "a captain in the field of systematic and organized scholarship."[46]

When we turn to the works of Herbert Baxter Adams, however, it is difficult to find the power in them that many of the historians of his generation saw. Adams was a placid soul who abhorred controversy and had little interest in applying the lessons of history to modern events. He had something of the same kind of gentle pride in tracing back the institutions of his country to ancient sources that genealogists derive from contemplating the achievements of their remote ancestors. It was the tracing itself which was important to Adams in his historical writings, not the relevance of the past to the present.[47]

The method of research employed by Herbert Baxter Adams was different from that of Stubbs, Freeman, and Henry Adams. He did not study Anglo-Saxon documents. Instead, he made direct comparisons between the institutions and customs described in Tacitus' *Germania* and those found in the communities of Colonial New England. The early American system of individual allotment of land, the system of communal pasturage, the duties of certain town officials, the methods of building blockhouses and spiked barricades—all these could find their counterparts, said H. B. Adams, in Tacitus' account. Above all, the New England town meeting was a resurrection of the Teutonic tribal council, a direct embodiment of ancient freedom which had been "lost" a thousand years.

The effect of H. B. Adams' historical method was, to a large extent, to bypass the Anglo-Saxons of England or at best to treat them as a comparatively unimportant link between the Americans and the Germans. In themselves, the Anglo-Saxons of England were "merely one branch of the great Teutonic race, a single offshoot from the tree of liberty which takes deep hold upon all the past." It was not that Adams was anti-British, but he apparently wished both the Americans and the British to recognize their close connection with the Germans.[48]

Occasionally H. B. Adams does attempt to explain American

traits on the basis of the innate character of the Teutons. On one occasion, he describes the cruelty of the Puritans to criminals and Indians and invokes a racist explanation. All these practices, he says, resulted from the stern Saxon nature of the Puritan. We can see modern survivals of such practices in the institutions of "convict labor, southern chain-gangs, and Delaware whipping-posts." We must not criticize too severely either the cruelty of the Puritans or that of their modern descendants. "It is folly to heap reproaches upon the Pilgrim Fathers," said Adams. "We Americans whether in the North or at the South, are of the same English blood; we have inherited kindred institutions, with much the same virtues and about the same vices."[49]

Yet this kind of theorizing is not typical of H. B. Adams. His position usually is only that Teutonic blood is very good blood indeed and that we should be grateful if we have it. On the question of what should be the relationship between Teutonic and non-Teutonic races, he is silent. If his Germanic theories ever suggested to him that immigration should be restricted, that racial minorities should be kept in check, that the United States should pursue a foreign policy related to the needs of its racial kinsmen overseas, or any such consequence, he does not say so. In reading Adams, one gets the impression that he thought of history as interesting wholly for its own sake. It had, it would seem, no particular relevance to contemporary ideas.[50]

On one occasion, however, H. B. Adams received an assist from one of the real dynamos among the historians. In 1881, Edward A. Freeman made a lecture tour in the United States and everywhere he sang the praises of Herbert Baxter Adams and the Johns Hopkins graduate school. His major theme, however, was that the Teutonic race in its "three homes"—England, Germany, and the United States—was the source of world civilization. Former disputes among the three should be forgotten, he proclaimed. England should realize that George Washington was a spiritual as well as a racial descendant of the Teutonic folk heroes. The American Revolutionaries had rediscovered the an-

cient Anglo-Saxon freedom which had temporarily been neglected in England. Their example in lighting the fires of freedom
had inspired their English brothers overseas to effect a non-
violent but equally thoroughgoing political revolution. In "the
wider view of the English folk, in the wider view of England,"
said Freeman, "it was in truth in and for England that they [the
American Revolutionaries] lighted it." In typical fashion, Freeman went on to extol the need for racial solidarity:

How can we be strangers and foreigners to one another, how can we
be other than kinsfolk and brethren of the same hearth, when we think
that your forefathers and mine may have sailed together from the oldest England of all in the keels of Hengest or of Cerdic—that they
may have lurked together with AElfred in the marshes of Athelney—
that they may have stood side by side in the thick shield-wall on the
hill of Senlac—that they may have marched together as brethren to
live and die for English freedom alike on the field of overthrow at
Evesham and on the field of victory at Naseby?[51]

If only Freeman could have stopped on this note, all might
have been well. But Freeman was not a man of half-measures.
He did not realize that already in the United States the power
of minorities was great enough to be embarrassing for his hosts
and troublesome for himself. On his lecture tour, Freeman came
near getting into serious trouble because he said that "the best
remedy for whatever is amiss in America would be if every
Irishman should kill a negro and be hanged for it." Freeman
may have surmised himself that this statement should be amend-
ed, or perhaps he was told. In one of his lectures at an unnamed
city which must have contained a sizable Irish population, he
said, "I tremble as I speak of Aryan settlers who are not of the
Teutonic race; I have heard of other lecturers in this city who
have suffered some persecution for not speaking with due respect
of some who come under that head." He had always thought the
Irish were a witty people, he added, and would know that he
was only joking in his comments about them and about the
Negroes. To avoid "dangerous ground," he would only add that

"while all Teutons are very near to us, no European Aryan is very far from us."[52]

To a friend in England, however, he wrote in a very different vein. "The really queer thing is the niggers who swarm here," he said. "I find it hard to feel that they are men acting seriously: 'tis . . . easier to believe they are big monkeys dressed up for a game." He was particularly disturbed that there was no law forbidding Negroes to hold public office. "I feel a creep when I think that one of these great black apes may (in theory) be President. Surely treat your horse kindly; but don't make him consul. I told a man here my notions of citizenship, which were these—1. Dutchmen, High and Low, at once, 2. Other Aryans in third generation, 3. Non-Aryans not at all." Back in England, he resumed his truculent anti-Irish diatribes. In a published account of his tour, he said,

Very many approved when I suggested that the best remedy for whatever was amiss would be if every Irishman should kill a negro and be hanged for it. Those who dissented dissented most commonly on that ground that, if there were no Irish and no negroes, they would not be able to get any domestic servants. The most serious objection came from Rhode Island, where they have no capital punishment, and where they had no wish to keep the Irish at the public expense.[53]

The Teutonic origins theory of government dominated the thinking of American historians at this period. The Germanic source of American institutions, said Albert Bushnell Hart in 1887, is a fundamental principle which should be "sharply defined in the minds of students at Harvard." Andrew D. White and Moses Coit Tyler stressed the theory at Cornell. At Washington University in St. Louis, both John Fiske and James E. Hosmer poured forth a steady stream of books which emphasized it. Henry Cabot Lodge in his histories of New England spoke of the ancient institutions which the Puritans had inherited from their forefathers. In the field of political science, John W. Burgess of Columbia was an ardent advocate of the Teutonic theory.[54]

The Teutonists developed into local variations, some with mutually contradictory ideas. There were, in general, three schools of thought. Some scholars emphasized the close relationship between German and American institutions. A few men emphasized the Norman contribution. A far larger group than either of these placed the emphasis on the Anglo-Saxon contribution. Herbert Baxter Adams was a member of the first school, the German wing, but he was a moderate. The real fire-eater among those who felt they could detect a close relationship between the institutions of the United States and those of Germany was John W. Burgess.

A student at the universities of Göttingen, Leipzig, and Berlin, Burgess had absorbed far more of the racism and nationalism then characteristic of much German thought than most American students there. He arrived in Germany just after the end of the Franco-Prussian War and witnessed the return of the victorious army to Berlin. He regarded the German triumph over France as the triumph of Teutonic justice over Latin "gilded barbarism." In Germany, he studied under the great historians who were then proclaiming an ecstatic nationalism—Mommsen, Droysen, Von Treitschke, and Von Gneist. Burgess identified himself wholly with German philosophy, science, literature, music, and militarism, and all these things he identified with civilization itself.

Burgess had grown up in a slaveholding family in Tennessee, but the family was strongly Unionist and he himself had served in the Union Army. At this time he conceived a dislike for the British because of the sympathy that existed in England for the Confederacy, and this dislike was intensified in his student days in Germany. He always chafed under the connection which the Teutonic origins theory had implied between Americans and Englishmen, and he set himself the task of getting rid of it. The English, he said, were not really Teutons. During the Norman Conquest they had suffered a fatal infusion of French blood, which had completely changed their character. When the English came to America, however, the pioneer hardships of the wilderness had in some way stripped the "Norman-French" veneer from the colonists and brought "the German element in the English character again to the front." In addition, a heavy immigration from Germany to America had helped to work out some of the remnants of the Norman taint. "The German Nation," concluded Burgess, "stands closer, ethnically, than any other European Nation, to the American people."[55]

It followed that Germany and the United States had characteristics in common which England did not share. In both England and France, said Burgess, the government could theoretically operate unhampered, and therefore in those nations Caesarism was a constant threat. In Germany and in the United States, on the other hand, there were constitutional restraints upon the will of the majority. Burgess feared the day, it is true, when American safeguards might not prove strong enough, when the "masses" might capture control of the government and proceed to distribute the wealth of the "classes." One of his chief aims was to awaken his students to the danger, and he was willing to advocate severe remedies. "There is not the slightest doubt in my own mind," he wrote in 1895, "that our prodigality with the suffrage has been the chief source of the corruption of our elections. We must begin with the cause if we would remove the effect." What should be done he mentioned only in large and vague terms. "The Teutonic element, when dominant," he said, "should never surrender the balance of power . . . to other elements. Under certain circumstances, it should not even permit limited participation of the other elements in political power."

In his *Political Science and Comparative Constitutional Law* (1893), Burgess argued that there is "a diversity of gifts among nations as among individuals, and political genius seems no more to have been bestowed equally than other kinds of genius." The Greek, for all his artistic genius, had no talent for political organization; neither had the Slav. "The psychology of the Celt is," he added, "if anything, still more unpolitical than that of the Greek and the Slav." Only the Teutonic races had been imbued with the ability to build stable governments. They may have learned something from the Romans, but "education can only develop what already exists in seed and germ," so we can safely conclude that "no amount of Roman discipline, which was distinctly anti-national in its universality, could have evolved the national idea unless this had been an original principle of Teutonic political genius." The Teutons in Spain, Portugal, France, Belgium, England, the Scandinavian countries, Germany, Holland, Switzerland, and Austria had been "the dominant elements in the creation of these modern national states," and they were at that very time proceeding to organize political states in Greece, in Rumania, in the principalities along the Danube, and even in Russia.[56]

This talent of the Teutonic races, this ability to form stable governments even in countries where they were a minority, involves them in a tremendous responsibility. They must recognize that the talent for organization belongs to them alone. While it is unjust to withhold participation in the government in nations composed of Teutonic elements, it is not wrong elsewhere. Other races must necessarily "remain in a state of barbarism or semi-barbarism, unless the political nations undertake the work of state organization for them." The civilized state thus "may righteously go still further than the exercise of force in imposing organization. If the barbaric populations resist the same, *a l'outrance*, the civilized state may clear the territory of their presence and make it the abode of civilized man." Above all, the dominant Teuton power "should not be troubled in its conscience about the morality of this policy when it becomes manifestly necessary." There is far too much "weak sentimentality abroad in the world" on this subject and it springs mainly from a "lack of discrimination in regard to the capacities of races."[57]

Burgess' position on race questions inevitably involved him in controversies with minority groups. On the question of immigration, he said in 1907 that immigrants from Teutonic countries "are people with a conscience, with a basis of self-control, and, therefore, prepared for the enjoyment of civil liberty."

Immigrants from southern and eastern Europe, on the other
hand, "are inclined to anarchy and crime. . . . They are, in
everything which goes to make up folk character, the exact opposite of genuine Americans."

In his thirty-six years as a teacher at Columbia, Burgess exerted an enormous influence upon higher education in the United
States. Herbert Baxter Adams tells us that Burgess sent "shoals"
of his students to Germany where they became known as "the
Burgess school." They went to hear his old favorites lecture and
came home "with trunks full of Droysen's *Preussische Politik*
and the writings of Leopold von Ranke." By 1905, Burgess himself could speak of "the virtual control of American universities by men educated at German universities." Burgess' great
hope in founding the school of political science at Columbia had
been that it would become the training school for the future
rulers of the country.[58]

The wish seems to have been dramatically fulfilled in Theodore Roosevelt, who enrolled as a student under Burgess in 1880.
While Roosevelt was a student, Burgess regarded him with affection and approval. Roosevelt, on his side, had an immense admiration and respect for Burgess. They first disagreed over the
Spanish-American War. Burgess was opposed to the war because
he believed the conquered territories would eventually become
a part of the nation and thus members of "mongrel races" from
overseas would become American citizens. Moreover, he thought
that British diplomacy had tricked the United States into declaring war. In 1908, however, Burgess had forgiven Roosevelt
sufficiently to refer to him and Kaiser Wilhelm as "the two
greatest men and statesmen among the rulers of the world."
Some critics of Roosevelt have thought that he was considerably influenced by Burgess, especially in willingness to extend
American control over other countries without granting political rights to the inhabitants. Roosevelt never came anywhere
near Burgess' admiration for the Germans, however; he was too
much of an American nationalist for that.[59]

During World War I, Burgess' version of Teutonism led him

to an all-out defense of Germany's cause. Germany, he declared, was a country of equal opportunity and economic democracy. He was convinced that the Kaiser had done everything possible to prevent the war. Once begun, the war defined itself as a battle for "Teutonic civilization" against the "oriental Slavic quasi-civilization" of Russia and "the decaying Latin civilization" of France. The British were motivated chiefly by jealousy of Germany's overseas trade. The attitude of the German government toward the Wilson administration, Burgess contended, was in every respect moderate and just. Only British perfidy and wily propaganda kept America from recognizing its real friends. In 1914-15, Burgess served as a visiting professor in Austrian universities. After the war, he castigated the Allies because they did not restore Germany to the rank of a first-rate power in order to counter the menace of "Asiatic bolshevism." By this time, of course, Burgess' position was generally thought to be an extremist one and he no longer had strong political support.[60]

The second school of Teutonic origins, that which emphasized the contributions of the Normans to civilization, was small. Its best-known advocate, Henry Cabot Lodge, did not use the theory as a political weapon. Lodge, it will be recalled, had been one of Henry Adams' students who helped trace institutions back to primitive charters. Lodge wrote the second essay in the collection, *Essays in Anglo-Saxon Law*, following that of Henry Adams himself. Although he accepted the thesis that our system of law came down to us from the Anglo-Saxons, Lodge in his essay showed himself to be not wholly satisfied with this interpretation. Where the Anglo-Saxons should have had a well-developed legal system, he complained, he could find only a chaos of contradictions. "The extreme clumsiness of the Anglo-Saxon mind," Lodge declares, "is apparent to anyone who has closely studied their legal history." This "mental awkwardness led them to cling to their primitive ideas."[61]

In his speeches and writings, Lodge sometimes referred, probably for political purposes, to the virtues of Anglo-Saxons. He declared that New England farmers were descended from sturdy Anglo-Saxon stock. He noted that Daniel Webster had revised his speeches by carefully throwing out effete words of Latin and French derivation and had depended upon strong and forceful Anglo-Saxon words. In opposing the movement for initiative, referendum, and recall, he argued that such practices were alien to the vital experience of the Anglo-Saxon race. Yet his writings sometimes show less enthusiasm for the Anglo-Saxons. In England they had loved "fighting for fighting's sake." They were "narrow, slow of perception, brutal at times, and neither adaptable nor adroit." A certain praiseworthy conservatism and a crude intuition of the value of law were the characteristics which saved them from utter barbarism. Lodge did not like the Anglo-Saxons nearly so well as he did the Normans.[62]

In shifting his allegiance, Lodge probably was performing an act of filiopiety. The family ancestor whom he most admired was George Cabot. Of "pure Norman extraction," Lodge tells us, Cabot was descended from one of the men who had accompanied William the Conqueror from Normandy to England. His ancestors were "of that Norman race which did so much for the making of England." From this point on, the racism proceeds in an accustomed groove. Lodge accepted Edward A. Freeman's contention that the Normans had been Frenchmen only in name:

They were Saxons who spoke French . . . the most remarkable of all people who poured out of the Germanic forests. . . . To them we owe the marvels of Gothic architecture, for it was they who were the great builders and architects of medieval Europe. They were great military engineers as well and revived the art of fortified defense. . . . They were great statesmen and great generals, and they had been in Normandy about a hundred years when they crossed the English Channel, conquered the country, and gave to England for many generations to come her kings and nobles.[63]

Lodge's admiration for the Normans did not lead him into the advocacy of any particular relationship between the United States and any of the European countries. He was too much a nationalist to care about alliances or close associations with foreign countries. He thought little of Germans and Frenchmen and only a little, if any, more of Englishmen. The American Revolution in which his ancestors had rebelled against England still loomed large with him. His own desire was that the United States should pursue a course independent of that of all other countries, and in the controversy over the League of Nations after World War I he was able to insure the triumph of an isolationist policy. On the other hand, Lodge's version of the theory of Teutonic origins did lead him to hate and fear certain classes of immigrants to the United States. He recalled with nostalgia the Boston of his boyhood before the city had been changed beyond all recognition by the influx of foreigners. In his histories, he sometimes depicts the Irish as a quarrelsome and disorderly lot, although he was obliged—for political purposes—to express quite different views in his later public addresses. For many years, he was perhaps this country's most active proponent of immigration restriction.[64]

The English school of Teutonic origins appealed to the largest number of historians, but no single one of them was as enthusiastic as were members of the German and Norman schools. We have already seen that William F. Allen had propounded a version of the theory which emphasized the English virtues. John Fiske objected to the term *Anglo-Saxon* because he thought it should properly apply merely to the small group of tribes which conquered England, not to everyone of English descent. Having substituted the word *English,* however, Fiske wrote much as the Anglo-Saxon enthusiasts did. Anglo-Saxons had first developed the theory of democracy, said Fiske, and the Normans had not radically changed it. James K. Hosmer, a prolific writer among the historians, also accepted the idea of the superiority of the Anglo-Saxon as the central fact of American history and explained nearly everything good in the nation on the basis of its racial character.[65]

It would be a mistake to imagine, however, that the different schools held their positions inflexibly. By a little judicious tampering, the historians and political scientists could adapt racial theory to the needs of the moment. If they wished to demonstrate our racial kinship with England, they could say that both nations were basically Anglo-Saxon. If they wished to maintain that Americans were not all plebeian, they could refer to the Norman blood which ran in American veins. If they admired Germany or if they wished to cast aspersions on southern and eastern European immigrants, they could say that we were Teutons—a term which could, on occasion, include the people of England, Germany, Holland, and the Scandinavian countries. If they wished to include virtually all of Europe—for example, if they wished to demonstrate the solidarity of the white man against colored races or Christians against Jews—then they could refer to Americans as Caucasians or Aryans. The fact that race has no precise meaning has made it a powerful tool for the most diverse purposes.[66]

When opposition to the theory of Teutonic origins arose, the point at issue was whether our modern institutions were really descended from primitive "germs" among our racial ancestors and whether they were really radically different from the institutions of all other nations and peoples. Edward Channing was among the skeptical historians. The Teutonists had been misled, said Channing, into mistaking "analogies" for "identities." Similarity of institutions did not necessarily mean direct relationship. It was not Teutons alone who had built blockhouses and defensive works like those described by Tacitus. The French settlers had built similar ones in Canada. If the Teutonists insisted on these analogies, then they might end up by inadvertently "proving" relationships which they had never intended. "The argument that because a New England town and a German village were each surrounded by a defensive wall, the one is descended from the other," said Channing, "proves too much. A similar line of argument would prove the origin of New England towns to be the Massai enclosure of Central Africa."[67]

Channing was, however, unwilling to follow up his argument with an attack upon the Teutonists' racial assumptions. His own theory of the origin of New England towns is not wholly free from racism. In his view, American institutions were derived from the seventeenth-century English parish, but they were also influenced by the character of the "English race," one of whose traits is "a conservatism in adhering to that which is old for no other reason than because it is that which exists." Elsewhere, Channing shows a certain narrowness of outlook. In the *Guide to the Study of American History* (1896), which he wrote in collaboration with Albert Bushnell Hart and Frederick Jackson Turner, Channing said, "There is little significance to present-day readers in American history earlier than the discovery by Columbus." Among the Indians there were no developed political institutions, "and hence little history in the modern sense." In addition, Latin American countries had "pursued a separate road and developed a civilization and history of their own." Therefore, "it is common and allowable . . . for the people of the United States to use the term 'American History' to cover the lands now a part of the continental United States and subject to the dominance of Anglo-Saxon ideas and institutions." None of this is particularly virulent, but it does help to explain why Channing, though he did criticize details of the Teutonic origins theory, did not attack the racial hypothesis inherent in it.[68]

Charles Francis Adams was skeptical of the theory that New England institutions such as the town meeting had descended from early Teutonic or Anglo-Saxon prototypes, partly because he was skeptical of democracy itself and particularly of the town meeting as the ideal agent for deciding questions of governmental policy. Having served as the moderator of the town meetings in Quincy, Massachusetts, Adams said that the "ideal town-meeting" was very different from "the actual town-meeting." The Teutonists might change some of their ideas if they knew more about modern town meetings. "To the theorist in history who should attend one," said Adams, "it would, not improbably, be the rude dispelling of a fanciful delusion. He would come away from it rather amazed that civilized government was possible through such a system than understanding how New England had been built up on it." Town meetings in New England, Adams believed, had generally been unable to solve problems of advancing industrialism and growth of slums. Yet he did not attack the racist thesis of the Teutonist historians. He was himself, in fact, an advocate of the doctrine of Anglo-Saxon superiority, although he drew his arguments from Social Darwinism and not from the Teutonic origins theory.[69]

One of the critics of the racist assumptions of the historians was Herbert Levi Osgood. Unfortunately, he never developed his objections into any sustained indictment, although he did specifically deny the possibility of establishing a relationship between racial qualities and tendencies of history. He had been a pupil of Burgess at Columbia and had gone to Germany where he studied under Von Treitschke. Perhaps he felt it would not be good manners to attack the work of men whom he admired. He did, however, go to the heart of the matter when, on a number of occasions, he rejected attempts to explain politics on the basis of race. "It is useless to claim that . . . [anarchism] is wholly a foreign product," he wrote at one point,

and for that reason to clamor for restriction upon immigration. Newspaper utterances on this phase of the subject have consisted too largely of appeals to ignorance and prejudice. There probably are good reasons why immigration should be restricted, but this should weigh very lightly among them. . . . Anarchism, so far as it has a scientific basis, is, like socialism, a natural product of our economic and political conditions. . . . It is as much at home on American soil as on European.

Though in his books Osgood laboriously traces American institutions from their English beginnings, these are virtually all institutions which were found in seventeenth-century England. There are no grandiloquent appeals to a dim past in the Teutonic forest or to the magic qualities of race in developing the principles of representative government.[70]

Frederick Jackson Turner did not directly attack the Teutonic thesis, but his own work tended to emphasize environment rather than race. In 1883 Turner, along with Woodrow Wilson, had been a student of Herbert Baxter Adams at Johns Hopkins. Some of Turner's friends who wrote theses about the western parts of the United States under the direction of Adams saw in the vast territories of that section of the country another "homeland" of the Teutonic race. Turner's thesis, though written under Adams' direction, contains no trace of the Teutonic origins theory. When Turner returned to Wisconsin, he compromised with the Teutonist historians there, being willing to ascribe weight both to the racial character of the Americans and to the frontier environment as determinants of institutions. The latter influence won out, however, in 1893 when at the Chicago exposition he read his famous essay, "The Significance of the Frontier in American History." In the second paragraph of this work, he gives the Teutonic origins theory an amiable brush-off: "All peoples show development; the germ theory of politics has been sufficiently emphasized." Although Turner occasionally fell back on mildly racial interpretations of history, his theory of the frontier did much to focus the attention of historians upon environment and away from race as an explanation for human institutions.[71]

In 1898, Charles A. Beard, then twenty-four years old, examined in detail and rejected the thesis of William Stubbs that representative institutions were directly descended from the councils of the Anglo-Saxons. For some reason, Beard's essay was not printed until thirty-four years later. In 1902, William A. Dunning could dismiss the Teutonic origins theory rather wearily. "It is hardly too much to say that our knowledge of primitive political thought is as vague as it is vast," he wrote.

Recent research has enormously extended our acquaintance with primitive institutions, but the interpretation of those institutions tends to be rather advanced than primitive. What idea the early Teuton associated with his customs he has nowhere recorded; the political theory that passes for his is likely to be in reality that of Tacitus, lamenting the Roman Republic, or of Freeman, preaching the unity of history.[72]

Like so many ideas, the Teutonic origins theory was not suddenly and dramatically rejected. It died so gradually that its death was scarcely noticeable outside the craft of historians. In the twentieth century, it still turned up fairly often among the speeches of men in public life who had absorbed it in one way or another. In 1908, Nicholas Murray Butler, the president of Columbia University, apparently still accepted the theory as respectable among the historians. It was the "extraordinary persistence of the Anglo-Saxon impulse," said Butler, which was the "chief cause" that "brought the United States of America into existence. For the origin of that impulse one must go back to the Teutonic qualities and characteristics of the people so admirably described by Tacitus." From these ancient sources had come modern American conceptions of government and industry which were designed to insure that "every opportunity was accorded to individual initiative," but liberty was distinguished from license and justice was preferred to force.[73]

In England, as in Germany, the Teutonic origins theory had had mainly nationalist implications. It is true that in England the theory had class implications as well. It was sometimes directed against the Irish, but the Teutonist historians generally insisted that the English people themselves were Teutonic and racially homogeneous. Class differences were smoothed over; *race* and *nation*, they argued, were somewhat similar terms. In the United States, the theory began as a justification for representative government. As in England, it was a rationale for the superiority of our institutions and incidentally of our nation. As it developed, however, it came more and more to mean that the "old Americans"—those of English and northern European antecedents—were the "real Americans." As time passed, it lost its strong and simple pride in democratic institutions and drew its racial lines more exclusively.

VI

The Study of Language
And Literature

A MOVEMENT similar to the Teutonic origins theory was the attempt to equate race and language. Since languages were known to have a long history, so the theory ran, perhaps it would be possible by philological comparison to determine basic racial affinities among peoples. Those peoples whose languages were similar might generally be assumed to be of the same race or at least of closely related races. Toward the end of the eighteenth century, Sir William Jones, the British orientalist, was contending that the relationships of most of the languages of modern Europe could be explained only under the assumption that they all had a common ancestral tongue. The original language, Jones believed, had long since disappeared, but Sanskrit was its closest surviving relative. Jones's theory was later greatly expanded by the German linguist Franz Bopp, who argued that all modern European languages except Finnish, Turkish, Magyar, and Basque were related to one another and that they had a common ancestral tongue similar to Sanskrit. Neither Jones nor Bopp, however, was moved to draw racial implications from the suggestion that the languages were related.[1]

In Sanskrit literature there were legends about a tall, blond, and muscular people who had vanquished the dark-skinned peoples of India and Persia. The name of these people, the Aryans, was translated by some philologists to mean *noble*, by others to mean *pure*. These blond people, so the theory went on, had spread to Europe, where—although in many countries they were a small minority—they introduced civilization and became the

123

political and intellectual leaders. Since the northern Europeans tended to be blonds, the corollary of the theory was that here were the purest descendants of the original Aryans. Thus the cult of Aryanism was born.[2]

Perhaps the most enthusiastic proponent of the Aryan theory was Adolphe Pictet, a Swiss scholar. Originally an advocate of the theory of Celtic supremacy, Pictet shifted in the middle of his career to the new cult of Aryanism. In a two-volume work, *Indo-European Origins, or the Primitive Aryas* (1859), Pictet attempted to demonstrate the importance of philology for ethnology. The original Aryans, he said, had migrated in all directions from their original home in Persia; and world civilization itself might be said to have begun with this event. The Aryan race was "destined by Providence some day to dominate the entire globe." It was "privileged by the beauty of its blood and the gifts of its intelligence," and the proof of its superiority was to be found in the "richness, vigor, harmony, and perfection of form of its language."[3]

In England, Aryanism enjoyed a popular vogue in the 1860's. The chief proponent of the theory there was Friedrich Max Müller, a German who was professor of oriental languages at Oxford. Müller had a popular following as well as a commanding academic reputation. From 1861 to 1864, his lectures in London were taken up by the fashionable set and extensively reported by British newspapers. His theme was that of a mighty people who had spread out in waves from their Aryan center somewhere in the East, emigrating mostly to Europe where they were the harbingers of civilization and culture. It was the Teutonic peoples, including the English, who were the purest modern representatives of the ancient Aryans.[4]

In the United States, for obvious reasons, the Aryan theory had much less compelling power at this time than it had in Europe. The race problem here was concerned with differences between whites and Negroes or between whites and Indians, and the country was not yet ready for a race theory which in important ways set one group of whites against another group of whites. In addition, there were few men here with the requisite training in languages to follow the complexities of the theory. During the Civil War, Charles Loring Brace undertook to utilize the theory of Aryanism in dealing with contemporary problems. He was drawn to the subject by his dismay at the rising propaganda against Negroes and Indians in the North. The lynching of Negroes during the draft riots of 1863 convinced him that racism might split the North and prevent its victory in the war. He accepted the idea of a powerful and intellectual Aryan people, but rejected the notion that other races are incapable of civilization. Within the contemporary frame of reference, the tendency of his study was to minimize the importance of race.[5]

In Europe, the Aryan thesis came in for serious criticism. For one thing, the measurements of anthropometrists increasingly disclosed that language was not an accurate measure of race differences. Peoples who were anthropometrically similar spoke different languages; peoples who were anthropometrically different spoke the same language or related languages. The people of a given nation might come from the opposite ends of the earth, critics of Aryanism declared, and still speak a common tongue. As philology itself progressed, there were discovered throughout the world nearly a thousand languages almost entirely unrelated to one another. The question naturally arose whether or not all these languages belonged to separate races. What methods could be devised to determine when language indicated a racial relationship? No philologist was able to suggest a satisfactory method of surmounting objections to the theory.[6]

Aryanism received a serious blow in the 1880's when Max Müller himself abandoned the idea that race and language are necessarily related. He stripped the word *Aryan* of all its connotations of blood brotherhood. In the remaining years of his life he sought to correct the misimpression which he had helped to spread. He became impatient when he discovered that Aryanism, having once been set in motion, was not easy to stop:

I have declared again and again that if I say Aryans, I mean neither blood nor bones nor hair nor skull; I mean simply those who speak an

Aryan language. . . . To me an ethnologist who speaks of Aryan race, Aryan blood, Aryan eyes and hair, is as great a sinner as a linguist who speaks of a dolichocephalic dictionary or a brachycephalic grammar. It is worse than a Babylonian confusion of tongues—it is downright theft. We have made our own terminology for the classification of languages; let ethnologists make their own for the classification of skulls, and hair, and blood.

Nonetheless, for a long time people continued unabashedly to speak of an Aryan race. In 1899, William Z. Ripley—an American ethnologist—complained that the "latest and best" geographical book in the nation was still teaching the "unity of the European or 'Aryan' race." Aryanism did gradually decline but only to be revised in megalomaniac form by the Nazis in Germany in the 1920's and 1930's. It is a sobering thought that the cult of Aryanism—which led to the death of millions in concentration camps—had so fragile an intellectual basis for its sweeping conclusions.[7]

In the United States, the way in which race and language were first and most obviously combined was in the teaching of the Anglo-Saxon language. The first man in America who is known to have been interested in this language in any systematic way was, as we have seen, Thomas Jefferson. As a young man, Jefferson had taken up its study and, confused by the inadequate textbooks then available, had set himself the task of deriving the grammar on his own. There is some ambiguity in Jefferson's statements about his reasons for interest in Anglo-Saxon. He tells us that he first became interested in it when he attempted to discover the historical meaning of "a multitude of law terms." He was familiar with the thesis then developing in England that representative institutions had come from the Teutonic forests. Jefferson mentions favorably the institutions of the ancient Germans and says that we are "beholden to the Northern nations" for the theory of constitutional government. He thought that the system of law and government of the Anglo-Saxons in England had been corrupted and almost destroyed by the Normans and that it had taken centuries for the English people even to recover partially the rights they had lost. In a letter of 1824 to Major John Cartwright in which he praises a book of Cartwright's on the English constitution, Jefferson indicates his own belief that freedom had descended from the Anglo-Saxons. He tells Cartwright that he has read his book with "pleasure and much approbation" and believes that "it has deduced the Constitution of the English from its rightful root, the Anglo-Saxon. . . ." Jefferson goes on to say that "although this Constitution was violated and set at naught by Norman force, yet force cannot change right. A perpetual claim was kept up by the nation, by their perpetual demand of a restoration of their Saxon laws; which show they were never relinquished by the will of the nation."[8]

What Jefferson hoped to do with his own study of Anglo-Saxon is not really clear. He may have wished to prove that the American system of government was, in fact, older than the tyrannical government of England against which the colonists had rebelled. Jefferson goes on in his letter to Cartwright to say: "It has ever appeared to me, that the difference between the Whig and the Tory of England is that the Whig deduces his rights from the Anglo-Saxon source, and the Tory from the Norman." It may be that Jefferson meant to use his Anglo-Saxon studies to gather arguments against archaic survivals in law—such as the law of entail in Virginia. And yet Jefferson also realized that any system of government which derived its ultimate sanction from the past would play into the hands of conservatives who would resist all change. Thus in 1800 we find him writing to Joseph Priestley in strong opposition to the "Gothic idea that we are to look backwards instead of forwards . . . and to recur to the annals of our ancestors for what is most perfect in government, in religion & in learning, is worthy of those bigots in religion & Government, by whom it has been recommended, & whose purposes it would answer."[9]

Jefferson tells that he was unable to continue his study of Anglo-Saxon because of the pressure of other activities, and he expresses his regret that he was obliged to stop. One wonders, however, if one reason he gave it up was that he surmised that the history of ancient Anglo-Saxon institutions would eventually strengthen the hand of the opponents of change rather than that of the innovators. When, late in life, he persuaded the trustees of the University of Virginia to offer a course in Anglo-Saxon—the first such course taught in America—he says nothing about deriving the institutions of ancient freedom. He does mention that the study of the language would have importance for the historians of law, but his emphasis is on such reasons as that it would enable Americans "to read Shakespeare and Milton with a superior degree of intelligence and delight." Also, it would serve to promote "the kind affections of kindred blood" between this country and Great Britain.[10]

The study of Anglo-Saxon spread slowly in the United States and was carried on for many years by a few isolated scholars. Randolph-Macon College began offering a course of instruction in that language in 1839, Amherst in 1841, and Harvard in 1851. Professor W. C. Fowler lectured on Anglo-Saxon at Amherst in the early 1840's. "He had imported Anglo-Saxon books, then curiosities," recalled one of his students in later years. "He held them up and exhibited them to us, as he lectured, exactly as the natural history men did precious shells, or minerals. He said there were only two or three men living who knew anything about the language." After the Civil War, however, there was an upsurge in Anglo-Saxon studies. By 1875, the language was offered in twenty-three colleges over the country, but even then the study of Anglo-Saxon proceeded without any strong connection with race theory.[11]

In the last decade of the nineteenth century, the study of Anglo-Saxon became the glory of English departments in American universities. This came about largely because the English language, more than the literature, would yield to "scientific" study according to the German methods of scholarship which became popular after the Civil War. In order to justify the dominant position which Anglo-Saxon came to occupy in the curriculum, English professors put forth arguments which had very little to do with the strict merits of the case for studying the language. Of course, not all the reasons advanced for the study of Anglo-Saxon were racist in nature. It was argued, for example, that it is impossible to speak and write modern English effectively without a knowledge of its early history. In studying Anglo-Saxon, asked Horace H. Furness, "are we not acquiring at the same time, a knowledge that will help us throughout life to express our thoughts in honest, homespun, vigorous phrases?" Passages expressing the conviction that the study of Anglo-Saxon would improve the use of modern English are plentifully sprinkled through English and educational journals of the period.[12]

Though this argument may have been specious, it was relatively harmless; but strong racial reasons were also given why the students in this country should learn Anglo-Saxon. In answer to the objection—sometimes heard from professors of Greek and Latin—that Anglo-Saxon contained no body of great literature comparable to that of the classical languages, the professors of English began to find all sorts of beauties and felicities in Anglo-Saxon literature. Moreover, they were beauties and felicities which illustrated the character of the Anglo-Saxon race. Some of the professors even found it possible to discover the characteristics of the race throughout the entire history of English literature.

"If we study Homer to learn the early poetic working of the Hellenic mind, the beginnings of ancient culture," declared Professor James M. Garnett of the University of Virginia in 1890, "we should study Old English poetry to learn the early manifestation of the Teutonic mind, the beginnings of modern culture. . . ." Why he believed that "modern culture" began with the Anglo-Saxons, Professor Garnett does not tell us; but he does maintain that a study of the Anglo-Saxon language would make abundantly clear to students what is really essential in our great racial heritage. "Just as in the language itself the basis is pure English, the bone and sinew of the Anglo-Saxon stock," he declared, "so in the literature there exist the qualities of the

Anglo-Saxon mind, the plain-straightforward commonsense, the earnest vigor, the patient endurance, characteristic of the people. . . . " As the student read the literary classics of Anglo-Saxon and reflected "that all this is the indication of the life of a mighty people," Professor True W. White said, "he cannot fail to be thrilled with an increased pride that he, too, is a part of this great life."[13] As late as 1925, Dr. Morgan Callaway, Jr. of the University of Texas was still carrying on the same ecstatic note:

Some of the deepest notes in English literature were struck first in Old English poetry. In the Caedmonian poems we find the high seriousness that is characteristic of Sidney Lanier and of Robert Browning. Note the similarity—almost the identity—of sentiment concerning woman attributed to the Early Germanic peoples by Tacitus, who tells us that the Teutons saw something divine in woman, and that expressed by Lanier in "The Symphony" or by Coventry Patmore in *The Angel in the House*. No deep student of Beowulf can fail to see that in our first epic are exhibited many of the fundamental characteristics of modern Englishmen of the highest type. . . .[14]

By 1893, Professor Francis A. March of Lafayette College could speak with satisfaction of the victory—of the "great advances" which the study of Anglo-Saxon had made in the college curriculum. "The press has teemed with critical studies, as well as textbooks," said March. "This Anglo-Saxon study, delightful and important in itself to specialists, seems also to be necessary for a solid and learned support to the study of Modern English in college."

Most of the American intellectual movements of the time which involved the theory of Anglo-Saxon superiority had their close counterparts in England. The theory of the Teutonic origins of government had strong adherents, for example, both in England and in the United States. Enthusiasm for the study of Anglo-Saxon languages and literature, however, seems to have been more of an American than an English phenomenon during this period. A contemporary professor of Anglo-Saxon at Cambridge has observed that the study of Anglo-Saxon literature declined in England after 1850. It is true, Professor H. Munro Chadwick concedes, that the work of English historians such as Stubbs and Freeman led to an extensive use of Anglo-Saxon historical and legal works, but even these were nearly always read in translation. Interest in Anglo-Saxon literature in England, says Chadwick, was much more limited, a result which he attributes to the zeal for comparative philology which English scholars absorbed from German universities.[15]

American scholars of the late nineteenth century were aware of the decline of Anglo-Saxon language studies in England and felt it opened up to them a unique opportunity. "Anglo-Saxon is *utterly* neglected in England," observed Professor Francis J. Child of Harvard in 1875. "At present there is but one man in England that is known to know anything of it. . . . Two or three American scholars, devoted to Anglo-Saxon, would have a great field to distinguish themselves in, undisputed by Englishmen."

As the movement for the teaching of Anglo-Saxon grew in the United States, there were men who could find vaguely racist reasons for the preponderance of its study here. It was no accident that there had been a previous resurgence of the study of Anglo-Saxon in England in the seventeenth century, declared Professor Albert S. Cook of Yale, because in Cromwell's rebellion Anglo-Saxon Puritans were arrayed against Norman cavaliers, against a feudal aristocracy. It was natural that in such stirring times there should be a resurgence of interest in Anglo-Saxon literature. Likewise, there was nothing strange in the fact that Americans were more interested than Englishmen in exploring the literature of their Anglo-Saxon forebears. The British lack of interest in Anglo-Saxon, declared Cook, was "in some measure due to the aristocratic traditions which cling to the ancient seats of learning in that country." British men of learning ignored, depreciated, or even opposed the progress of the study of Anglo-Saxon. "The reason is plain: these classes of persons have been the representatives of prescription and authority, and have therefore felt in the advance of English the approaching triumph of a natural foe." Americans were more

receptive to Anglo-Saxon language and literature because here
flourished "democracy and individualism, the spirit of nationality, the methods of physical science, and the sensational and
utilitarian philosophy, to which may be added the growing influence of women, and, in part as the cause of this influence, the
pervasive and vitalizing effect of essential Christianity."[16]

Strangely enough, later on in the same book Professor Cook
argues that it is democracy which is responsible for the opposition to the study of Anglo-Saxon and English literature in general. "A democracy does not readily tolerate superiority of any
kind," he complained. "A materialistic age does not contemplate
with rapturous satisfaction the things of the spirit. . . . Those
who . . . consider no evil so dire as poverty . . . have their own
realms of gold to travel in, and think those of Keats mean in
comparison."[17] This apparent change of sides was due to the fact
that Cook was now defending English departments against the
advocates of utilitarian education. When he was praising democracy, he was defending English departments against the advocates of heavy emphasis on Greek and Latin.

Not satisfied with triumphs in colleges and universities, some
English teachers dreamed of the day when Anglo-Saxon would
be required in elementary and high schools. "Why should it not
be equally possible," asked Professor Mark H. Liddell of the
University of Texas,

to put . . . [Anglo-Saxon] in the place that dogmatic grammar used
to occupy? . . . It would not be difficult to teach any boy to read Old
English at the time when he begins to read Latin, to continue the work
by teaching him to read Middle English, and then to put upon this
elementary work . . . a more or less thorough training in English historical grammar.[18]

Sidney Lanier endorsed the regimen prescribed by the professors. Nearly every boy in high school could give some account
of the death of Hector, he observed, but few boys—or few men
for that matter—would do more than stare if asked to relate the
death of Byrhtnoth.

Yet Byrhtnoth was a hero of our own England in the tenth century, whose manful fall is recorded in English words that ring on the soul like arrows on armor. Why do we not draw in this poem—and its like—with our mother's milk? Why does not the serious education of every English-speaking boy commence, as a matter of course, with the Anglo-Saxon grammar?

The proponents of the teaching of Anglo-Saxon language and literature in grade school and high school could easily dismiss the argument that such a method was suitable only for the more intelligent pupils. One enthusiastic handbook for teachers of English argued that Old English and Middle English would be most useful to those students who never intended to put pen to paper except for the most rudimentary purposes and who had no intention of going on to college. Pointing out that the complexities of Anglo-Saxon grammar would provide an excellent discipline for the young mind, this manual added that Anglo-Saxon tales of heroism would increase the student's knowledge of literature. Last of all, the study would "widen his whole mental horizon by bringing him into close relation, at first hand, with the great monuments in the history of his race."[19]

This last reason runs through many of the arguments for the teaching of Anglo-Saxon. However much they depended upon a conviction that a knowledge of the language would be helpful in understanding modern English and in developing a vigorous prose style, few professors of English were willing to leave matters there. It was F. A. Barbour, a professor in a teachers' college in Michigan, who stated the racist thesis most bluntly:

Yes, I am persuaded that a final fruit of this glance at the old speech might lead to a more manly and vigorous expression of thought. Along with its simplicity of style let the boy and girl learn something of the rugged strength of his fathers. Let him hear Beowulf's sword-fellow, unchristianized, without hope in the hereafter, cry out from his noble soul:—"Death is better than life of shame." Yes, let every English and American youth thank God that he is descended from that plucky race that under Danish invasion, and Norman conquest and contempt, clung with unyielding tenacity to the native speech, and bequeathed it to him, his richest inheritance in the nineteenth century.[20]

The emphasis of English departments upon Anglo-Saxon language and literature was matched by a corresponding neglect of modern literature, particularly American literature. Those men who did take it upon themselves to write histories and criticism of American literature frequently did so in an attitude of apology. "We must . . . think of our literature, not only as a provincial continuation of the English," said Henry S. Pancoast in his *Introduction to American Literature* (1898), "but as a beginning at a comparatively late period in the life of that race of which we are a branch." Pancoast called upon his readers to be proud of the fact that they were descended from the same illustrious forebears as their English cousins. "We inherit the same civilization, the same traditions, the same classics, the same national traits; we are sprung from the same race, and the speech of Shakespeare—England's poet and ours—is on our lips." Pancoast had no corresponding pride, however, in American literary figures and concerning their achievements he seldom went beyond a very modest enthusiasm. His great hope was that as the nation grew it would produce more literary geniuses than it had in the past.[21]

More explicitly racist than Pancoast was Barrett Wendell, who argued that the greatness of New England letters in the period from 1830 to 1860 was to be attributed to the fact that the region was then almost racially homogeneous. For Wendell, the literature of New England was the only American literature which counted. So provincial was his *Literary History of America* (1900) that Professor Fred Lewis Pattee advanced a proposal to retitle it *A Literary History of Harvard University, with Incidental Glimpses of the Minor Writers of America.* An extreme conservative as well as an extreme racist, Wendell felt that democracy was the evil doctrine which had corrupted American ideals. While deploring the atheism of Nietzsche, he evinced considerable sympathy for Nietzsche's attacks on popular government. "I find his views of democracy very like mine," he wrote to a friend, "and his views of elastic aristocracy as well." Democracy had corrupted England as well as America, Wendell believed, especially since the adoption of the Reform Bill of 1832. "The old system, where a great gentleman often carried half a dozen boroughs in his pocket," Wendell declared,

made it easy to find a seat in the House for any young man of promise; to go no further, it was to this system that we owe the parliamentary career of Burke. There can be little doubt that with the progress of democratic temper in England, the House of Commons has tended personally to deteriorate.[22]

One of the great virtues of the Anglo-Saxon race, Wendell believed, was its "marked power for assimilating whatever came within its influence." It was this trait which "centuries before had made the conquered English slowly but surely assimilate their Norman conquerors. . . ." The ideas of democracy and equality were, on the other hand, fundamentally alien to the genius of the race. The trouble had begun in this country, Wendell believed, when the great men of the American Revolution began to develop an "unscientific enthusiasm for freedom." Americans had learned the false doctrine of democracy "rather from the philosophical vagaries of Eighteenth-Century France than from the practical experience we inherit from law-abiding England." While our conduct had been "generally based on the sound old English traditions," our doctrine had been "more than we have generally realized, borrowed from the cloud-spun theories of clever Frenchmen. We have never yet dreamed that our conduct and our speech do not agree."[23]

Sometimes Wendell felt that the strength of the Anglo-Saxon race would be sufficient to overcome all obstacles. World history, he declared, "is bound to be the history of the domination of that race which in the struggle of the ages proves most worthy to survive. And that race, I hope and believe, is the race of which we form a part and in a certain sense the advance guard. . . ." In addition, the power to assimilate other races was a trait which "the Yankees of our own day have not quite lost. . . . In Modern America no fact is more noteworthy than that, for all the floods of immigration which have seemed to threaten almost every political and social landmark, our native type still absorbs the foreign."[24]

Likewise, in spite of the evil which had been caused by democracy, Wendell sometimes believed that the innate conservative good sense of the Anglo-Saxon race in the United States might prevent the worst effects of the vicious doctrine. He was encouraged by the checks on popular government exercised in some of the recent decisions of the Supreme Court. "In no way . . . has America evinced its English origin more clearly," he declared, "than by the serenity with which it has forbidden logic to meddle with the substantial maintenance of legal institutions." All the virtues of the Anglo-Saxons, Wendell believed, were distilled in the best of English and American literature. "Whatever else, this literature is the most spontaneous, the least formal and conscious, the most instinctively creative, the most free from the rankness and the debility of extreme culture, and so seemingly the most normal."[25]

Yet Wendell was more often a pessimist than an optimist concerning the future of Anglo-Saxons, and in his later years his pronouncements became progressively more gloomy. He lost his faith that American Anglo-Saxons would preserve their distinctive characteristics in the face of the tide of degenerate immigrants pouring in. "The racial agony in which we are being strangled by invading aliens, who shall inherit the spirit of us, grows heavier with me," he wrote to a friend, "as the end of me—and of ours—comes nearer." He came to regard the triumph of democracy as inevitable and as an unrelieved disaster. Worst of all, he wavered in his faith that Anglo-Saxons possessed all the racial virtues which he had liked to ascribe to them. Some of his eastern friends, he tells us, were inclined to trace the western agrarian agitation of the 1890's either to foreign immigration or to the incursion of southern "poor whites." But Wendell did not agree with his friends:

It seems more likely that these Western regions whose political and moral condition now leaves most to be desired are those where native Northern blood preponderates. If this be true, the shiftless immigrants of Mrs. Kirkland's day, evidently what we should now call social degenerates, have proved a more important factor in our history than tradition has remembered.[26]

The literary histories of America written by Charles F. Richardson would seem to be, on first glance, as racist as those of Wendell. Like Wendell, Richardson believed that the "Saxon characteristics" of "honesty, rugged independence, reverence for women and love of home and children" were ingrained in the early Americans. His *American Literature, 1607-1885* (1886) begins with an account of the Indian mound-builders, but it soon shifts to the remarks of Tacitus upon the Germans. The character of the early Germans, he declared, had been inherited by modern Americans. "The critic of American literature," he wrote, "should be thoroughly acquainted with both English and American political, social, and literary history; should perceive clearly that in England and America is a dominant and assimilating Saxon folk, working out a similar problem on similar lines." The way to understand our literature was to understand the character of our race. "The United States, like every Teutonic nation, works through the individual on moral lines. . . ."[27]

Richardson was a better critic than these quotations would indicate. "Behind literature is race," he argued, but he also thought that "behind race" were "climate and environment." He thought that the superior moral character of New Englanders was probably the result of their rigorous cold winters. In most of his works he relied more upon the environment which is "behind" race than he did upon race itself. Unlike Wendell, he had great hopes for democracy. He dreamed of the day when American letters would become "the literature of a cultured and genuine Democracy, a sort of Saxon-Greek Renaissance in the New World." "If such a literature cannot exist and be true and grow great," he added, "then all the predictions of wise men from Plato to Milton, from Cicero to Victor Hugo, have been at fault."[28]

There are a good many evidences in Richardson of an ungenerous attitude toward the immigrants in America who were not Anglo-Saxons. "Rascals and ignoramuses vote in the United States, while intelligent women and bright and ingenuous youths are denied the right," he declared. "Unqualified immigrants and freedmen have full powers of self-government, so far as the law can give them those powers." He could speak of New York as "the receptacle of the residuum of a part of debased foreign society." Yet for all this, Richardson had great hopes for the powers of assimilation in America. "The characteristics of the first English settlers remain strongly marked upon the composite people," he contended, "and the American Irishman, or German, or Frenchman . . . soon loses somewhat of his former nature, under the potent influence of new conditions and of the dominant Saxon temper." This is still a racist analysis, and it is significantly silent about whether other immigrants—those from southern and eastern Europe, for example—can be assimilated by the "dominant Saxon temper." Yet it clearly seems to be moving toward a more tolerant attitude regarding the race of immigrants.[29]

Among the historians, the Teutonic origins theory was a fairly specific thing. It proposed to trace modern institutions back to primitive progenitors; it also assumed that the ability to create these institutions was imbedded in the biological character of the Teutonic or Anglo-Saxon race. Thus, its opponents had a definite theory to attack. When it became apparent that the ancient forebears had, for example, cared less for representative government and the rule of law than their descendants had hoped, the whole Teutonic origins theory began to crumble. In the American colleges of the last decade of the nineteenth century, racism pervaded English departments as much as it did history departments; but in English departments the theory of Anglo-Saxon superiority was not tied to anything so definite as an evolving parliament or court of law. Among the literary scholars, racism was vaguer and therefore harder to disprove. In English departments a kind of "germ" theory did prevail, which held that the characteristics of English and American literature were essentially race characteristics that could best be understood by being studied in their pure form in the "classics" of Anglo-Saxon. Thus it is that we are more likely to find remnants of racism in the literary histories of the twentieth century than in histories generally.

In one recent textbook anthology of English literature, for example, we are told that if we wish to understand "so practical a people" as the English who at the same time have "made so great a poetry," we must, among other things, "consider the number of racial strains . . . to be found among them." The "Anglo-Saxon element is fundamental" in the ancestry of the English. We are left to infer what precisely this element has contributed, but we get an idea of it by the comparison of English with continental European writers. "In matters of structure, form, and the 'feeling for the whole,' " the editors tell us, "English writers have usually lagged behind the European. . . . It is in sheer fecundity and in over-mastering masculine force that they have won their supremacy." In addition to the Anglo-Saxons, the English owe their character to other "races." The Normans, for example, were "a people of swift and keen intelligence, with a gift for government and an insatiable lust for power." The Danes and Norsemen also "contributed largely to the blood of those 'true-born Englishmen' whose contempt for foreigners has been, at various times, among their more amusing traits." The Celts are also praised, but the nature of their achievement is left undescribed. The editors content themselves with saying that the Celtic contribution "has been precious and pervasive beyond computation."[30]

Another recent literature textbook invokes race to explain the character of the hero Beowulf. There is something "solid and sure" about him. His bravery is not "of the fiery impetuous type like Roland's or The Cid's. It is stubborn, unyielding, somber—in short, Teutonic rather than Latin." Elsewhere, the same textbook explains the shift from Neoclassicism to Romanticism in the latter part of the eighteenth century at least partly by an appeal to the character of races. The standards of the Neoclassical movement were "imposed upon the Englishman," presumably

by foreigners, and lasted only "a century and a half." Because
of "the introspective quality of the Anglo-Saxon, his energy and
adventurousness, plus the quick audacity of the Norman and the
wit and fancy of the Celt—it is inconceivable that the literary
formalities of the neo-classical age could have prevailed for
long."[31] One wonders why if the Celts in England were restive
under the restrictions of Neoclassicism they were apparently less
so in France where they were supposed to be far more numerous.
Apparently, it was the racial character of the Anglo-Saxons and
the Normans which turned out to be decisive in turning the
English away from Neoclassicism. Racial explanations of cultural differences quickly bog down in contradictions. Those surviving in contemporary English literature textbooks are usually
merely remnants of the nineteenth century's confident racism.

One unfortunate corollary of the theory that the "pure"
character of the Anglo-Saxon race is found in Anglo-Saxon literature is the assumption that literature is less interesting the
farther it is removed from its ancient source. Anglo-Saxon scholars have sometimes seemed to feel that even an interest in someone as late as Shakespeare was not quite academically respectable,
and any deep interest in modern or American literature was
deemed almost quixotic. In 1928, a survey of American college
catalogues disclosed that, on the average, American literature
was considered to be about one-fifth as important as Latin literature, one-fifth as important as Greek literature, one-tenth as important as English literature, and about equal in importance to
Scandinavian literature. The situation was better when Howard
Mumford Jones made a similar survey in 1944, but he could find
only two or three colleges or universities where American literature was given anything like full attention. Since that time, however, the number of courses in American literature has grown
so rapidly that even some specialists have publicly worried over
whether the tendency may not have gone too far and thus have
obscured the importance for students of literature of the English
literature background.[32]

Obviously, other factors besides the teaching of Anglo-Saxon contributed to the low esteem in which American literature was held in many colleges and universities of this country until quite recently. And obviously, the teaching of Anglo-Saxon can be justified on other than racist grounds. Increasingly, as scholars have become more aware of the fallacies of race theories, the argument for learning Anglo-Saxon has been cultural rather than racist. But this change in emphasis has raised the question whether modern English and American literature does not owe far more to the ideas of Greek and Roman literature and to continental European literature than to the relatively crude and simple ideas of the Anglo-Saxons.

Among historians of American literature, the racist thesis developed by Pancoast, Wendell, and Richardson went substantially unchallenged until 1913, when John Macy published his *Spirit of American Literature.* "In literature," Macy declared firmly, "nationality is determined by language rather than by blood or geography"; and he pointed out that Maeterlinck belonged to French literature in spite of the fact that he was born in Belgium, and Joseph Conrad belonged to English literature in spite of his having been born in Poland. "Of the ancestors of English literature," he brusquely added, " 'Beowulf' is scarcely more significant, and rather less graceful, than our tree-inhabiting forebears with prehensile toes; the true progenitors of English literature are Greek, Latin, Hebrew, Italian, and French." This point of view was then so unusual that Howard Mumford Jones has maintained that Macy's book "inaugurated the modern interpretation" of American literature.[33]

Ironically, one of the first really effective attacks on the Anglo-Saxon element in literature came not from a critic of racism but from one of its enthusiastic advocates. H. L. Mencken has been rightly credited with having broken the way for American writers whose ancestors had not been British and whose foreign-sounding names handicapped them in their literary careers. Mencken hailed the work of authors of more recent immigrant stock—such men as Theodore Dreiser and Ring Lardner.[34]

But Mencken merely fought fire with fire and combated Anglo-Saxon racism by inverting all the old racist shibboleths. "Whenever the Anglo-Saxon, whether of the English or of the American variety, comes into sharp conflict with men of other stocks, he tends to be worsted," Menken trumpeted. "That this inferiority is real must be obvious to any impartial observer."

One of Mencken's pet hatreds was the South, and next to the South he detested New England. For him, the defects of the inhabitants of both regions had been inherited from their ancestors. The South is backward, he maintained, because, aside from a small class of superior gentry, it was originally settled by some of the most debased stock in England, that which was to be found among indentured servants and ne'er-do-wells who had emigrated to America. What good blood the region had originally possessed was destroyed, he maintained, in the Civil War. An ethnological survey of the "racial strains" and "cranial indices" conducted by competent authorities would prove, he was convinced, that white southerners as well as Negroes (Mencken had very little faith in Negro potentiality) were handicapped by their hopeless heredity.[35]

The Colonial fathers in New England were also drawn from "the botched and unfit," and it was thus not surprising that "New England has never shown the slightest sign of a genuine enthusiasm for ideas." Even the supposed age of greatness of New England literature, the period from 1831 to 1861, was the "work of women and admittedly second-rate men." By a little ingenious footwork, Mencken deprives New England of two of its chief nineteenth-century luminaries. Emerson and Hawthorne, he says, "stood outside the so-called tradition of their time." Some of the nineteenth-century figures he admires in American literature were good writers, he maintains, because they were not pure Anglo-Saxons. Poe, Whitman, and Twain were rejuvenating forces in American literature because they were not descended from the "exhausted strains" of Anglo-Saxons but were the "products . . . of crosses."[36] A saner view of race questions is not to be found in Mencken.

Eventually, literary historians wearied of these arguments concerning racial virtues and vices. Frederick Jackson Turner had directed the attention of American historians away from race and toward the influence of environment in developing civilization. What Turner did in clearing away antique rubbish for the historians, Vernon L. Parrington eventually did nearly thirty-five years later for American literary chroniclers. Every page of Parrington's *Main Currents in American Thought,* the three volumes of which appeared from 1927 to 1930, is an implicit rebuke to racist theories of literature. Until Parrington had shown what could be done in literary history by explaining movements and ideas on the basis of their social and economic background, there was no really effective answer to those who would explain literature largely on the basis of racial composition.[37]

VII

Race and Social Darwinism

ONE DOES NOT have to read very far in the writings of nine-teenth-century social scientists to discover the immense influence of race theories among them. In studying human societies, they generally assumed that they were also studying innate racial character. Races were thought to represent different stages of the evolutionary scale with the white race—or sometimes a subdivision of the white race—at the top. Accordingly, any given society represented the power and influence of its various racial stocks and the amount and quality of the intermixture among them. Heredity was considered immensely more important than environment in conditioning the development of society, and to many of the social theorists heredity meant mainly race.

Acceptance of the Darwinian theory of evolution led to the acceptance of the idea of evolving institutions and civilizations, but it was thought that societies change only very gradually, as slowly perhaps as biological organisms change their physical characteristics. Any attempt, therefore, to change the nature of a society or a people was regarded with suspicion by most of the nineteenth-century theorists who were influenced by Darwin. No society apparently could be much improved beyond the level to which the natural forces of evolution had brought it. Any attempt to change society would, in fact, have catastrophic results. Society could be changed by design only for the worse.

Eric Voegelin has pointed out that in the first half of the nineteenth century, when economics was the fashion, "symbols had to be based on economic materials, as in the system of Marx."

In the second half of the century, Voegelin adds, the symbols
tended to shift to those of evolution and genetics.[1] Racism was
able to subsist under both sets of symbols. Marx himself, for
example, relied heavily on race theories when they suited his purpose.[2] There is no doubt, however, that racism thrived as the ideas
of biological evolution began to make themselves felt. We have
already seen some of the ways in which Darwin affected race
theory. He shattered the prevailing traditional, mystical, and theological views concerning man's origin and nature. He made the
arguments of both the polygenists and the monogenists seem absurd to the point of quaintness. Despite the fact that he destroyed the basis for much of the old racism, Darwin provided
a new rationale within which nearly all the old convictions about
race superiority and inferiority could find a place. Darwin's influence upon race theory arose not so much from anything
specific which he himself said on the subject—he was as far as
possible from the vulgarity of a Gobineau or a Houston Stewart
Chamberlain—as from certain analogies which his followers
drew between relationships among the lower species in the animal world, on the one hand, and among men in human societies
on the other. The idea of natural selection was translated to a
struggle between individual members of a society, between members of classes of a society, between different nations, and between different races. This conflict, far from being an evil thing,
was nature's indispensable method for producing superior men,
superior nations, and superior races.

Such were the chief ideas of Social Darwinism, and the man
who did the most to give them form and substance was Herbert
Spencer (1820-1903). It requires a real effort of the imagination to see the universe as Spencer saw it. His philosophy is based
upon a complex system of analogies. He argued that the forces
of nature—both mechanical and biological—proceed from inevitable laws from which a common pattern may be derived. Accepting Von Baer's law in biology that the individual proceeds
from the homogeneous to the heterogeneous, Spencer declared
that astronomy confirmed the same thesis in its laws of motion.

The nebular hypothesis represented a similar development of the homogeneous to the heterogeneous, and both astronomy and biology proclaimed the existence of a law, "the persistence of force." The working of the same grand laws could be seen in every aspect of the natural universe, and therefore astronomy, geology, biology, psychology, and sociology handle "a connected aggregate of phenomena . . . admitting only of conventional separations . . . exhibiting in common the law of transformation and the causes of transformation. And clearly therefore, they should be arranged into a coherent body of doctrine."[3]

The monumental lifetime task which Herbert Spencer set himself was to show the essential relationships of all these fields of study and thus develop a universal philosophy. The remarkable thing is that he really did carry out his project.

Even before the publication of Darwin's *The Origin of Species* in 1859, Spencer had worked out the essentials of his version of the theory of evolution. The main thing he gained from Darwin was an explanation of how variation takes place— that is, by natural selection. It was Spencer, in fact, who coined two of the terms commonly associated with the idea of evolution, "the struggle for existence" and "the survival of the fittest."[4]

Spencer drew an analogy, which became famous as a basic idea of his sociology, between individual biological organisms on the one hand and society on the other. In this view, society has many points in common with a living organism and the tenets of biological evolution are generally applicable to it. A society improves very slowly through the process of evolution, but it cannot be changed for the better by other means. In Spencer's ideal society, government seems to have represented an exception to the general law of development from homogeneity to heterogeneity. In his primitive condition, argued Spencer, man necessarily resorted to violence and warfare. Warfare had a eugenic effect by "killing off the inferior races," thus producing "a balance of advantage during the earlier stages." As mankind developed industrial societies, however, the conflicts among men would become economic rather than military, and warfare as an instrument of policy would eventually disappear. A strong government was necessary in the early primitive or "military" phases of society's evolution, but would be less necessary when society had achieved its "industrial phase." Then "the purifying process," that is, the survival of the fittest through natural selection, would be "carried on by industrial war." As man became more civilized, government would become less and less necessary and finally would disappear altogether.[5]

Spencer saw the proper role of government in his time as that of keeping the conflicts in society from exploding into open violence while restraining itself as much as possible from interference with economic processes. The chief task of the sociologist, as Spencer saw it, was to convince mankind that society would improve in proportion as the powers of government and the sentimental idealism of charity were restrained from interfering with "free" economic forces. As Spencer explained in one of his letters, it is not what government must do but what it must not do that is important:

No adequate change of character can be produced in a year, or in a generation, or in a century. All which teaching can do—all which may, perhaps, be done by a wider diffusion of principles of sociology, is the checking of retrograde action. The analogy supplied by an individual life yields the true conception. You cannot in any considerable degree change the course of individual growth and organization—in any considerable degree antedate the stages of development. But you can, in considerable degree, by knowledge put a check upon those courses of conduct which lead to pathological states and accompanying degradations.[6]

Thus, Spencer was opposed to public education, to free libraries, to a government post office, and to the mint. All these "socialistic" institutions would end not by improving society but by paving the way to its degeneration. People should pay for the education of their children if they wanted to have them educated. Free libraries merely led to the stocking of "trashy novels." He was opposed to sanitation laws, to efforts to license doctors and nurses, and to compulsory vaccination. People who were stupid enough not to avail themselves of proper medical care ought to be allowed to reap the consequences of their folly. In the ideal society there would be no social legislation, no regulation of industry, no poor relief, nothing which would interfere with the laws of natural selection.[7]

All this—at least in Spencer's early and middle life—is coupled with a serenely optimistic belief that if man could only restrain himself from meddling with society, if he could attain the discipline of laissez faire, the resulting progress would be amazing. Progress resulted "from a law underlying the whole organic creation," and by its beneficent operation, "so surely must man become perfect."[8] In his later life Spencer became progressively more disillusioned, not with the doctrine of laissez faire, but with the possibility of convincing the governments and peoples of the evils of regulation, and thus his optimism was seriously compromised. The letters of his later years are filled with anguished outcries as the government invaded area after area where he was convinced it had no rightful concern.[9]

Spencer's social theory had, of course, race implications. Rousseau's idea of "the primitive equality of men" was "absurd" and "quite inconsistent with the evolutionary doctrine." Little or nothing could be done for primitive peoples because their civilization merely reflected the stage of their biological evolution. On the other hand, primitive peoples presented the sociologist with a fascinating subject of study, because he could help to discover the process by which evolution had taken place. Spencer was convinced, for example, that the idea of monogamy had been developed by the higher races until it had become "innate" in their germ plasm. Thus, the evolutionary stage of a race would be indicated by its attitude toward marriage.[10]

At one time, Spencer envisioned for himself the task of tracing the psychological development of man in a manner similar to that employed by Darwin in tracing biological evolution. In an essay published in 1875, Spencer outlined his proposed plan of study. "How races differ in respect of the more or less involved structures of their minds," he observed, "will best be understood on recalling that unlikeness between the juvenile mind and the adult mind among ourselves, which so well typifies the unlikeness between the minds of savage and civilized." Here Spencer is apparently thinking of one of the spectacular confirmations of the theory of evolution in the discovery of recapitulation in embryos. At a certain stage in their development, the embryos of the higher vertebrates, including man, were found to have vestigial gill slits, with arterial systems capable of supplying blood to them, which later disappeared—thus recapitulating the fish and amphibian stages of evolution. Spencer reasoned, by analogy, that the mind of a child recapitulates the history of human races in a development from savagery to civilization. To understand the mind of primitive races, said Spencer, the civilized races should examine the character of the minds of their own children. Among such children we find "an absorption in special facts" but an inability to generalize. They have little interest in political or social matters. They have a "vanity about clothes and small achievements, but little sense of justice: witness the forcible appropriation of one another's toys." The minds of primitive races had all the limitations of the minds of children, except that their childhood of intellect was permanent.[11]

Spencer was willing to admit that the children of savage or semicivilized races show "great precocity," but he concluded that such intelligence is merely "in conformity with the biological law that the higher the organisms the longer they take to evolve," and thus "members of the inferior human races may be expected to complete their mental evolution sooner" than the members of superior races. And Spencer goes on to cite the general agreement among travelers that the precocity of primitive children is followed by mental stagnation during their adolescence. Spencer thinks that this difference should be much more closely studied. We do not need proof that a "general contrast" exists among the races, but "there remains to be asked the question, whether it is consistently maintained throughout all orders of races, from the lowest to the highest—whether, say, the Australian differs in this respect from the Hindu, as much as the Hindu does from the European."[12]

Just how all these comparisons are to be made Spencer does not say. This was well before the era of intelligence tests, but even a modern tester might blanch before the kind of comparison Spencer had in mind. Besides "mental complexity," by which Spencer meant intelligence, there was the matter of "mental mass." We have all noticed, he says, that the intelligence of some people,

high though it may be, produces little impression on those around; while there are some who, when uttering commonplaces, do it so as to affect listeners in a disproportionate degree. . . . Behind the intellectual quickness of the one there is not felt any power of character; while the other betrays a momentum capable of bearing down opposition—a potentiality of emotion that has something formidable about it. Obviously the varieties of mankind differ much in respect of this trait.

In fact, Spencer is convinced that the "dominant races overrun the inferior races mainly in virtue of the greater quantity of energy in which this greater mental mass shows itself." One wonders whether the "commonplaces" of the conquering races might not make a deeper impression because they are backed up by gunboats, but Spencer ignores this kind of explanation. Instead, he suggests the possibility of attempting to relate "mental mass" to such factors as the size of the bodies of the different races, the size of their brains, the richness of their blood, their social state, whether nomadic or settled, predatory or industrial, etc.[13]

It is interesting to see Spencer's application of his race theories to specific peoples. We find him attributing failure and success among the nations to the qualities of their race and the degree of their intermixture. When France was defeated in 1871, Spencer wrote to a friend that the nation had been in decline for many years past "from some cause difficult to trace (race, or the particular mixtures of race, being perhaps at the root)," and he had little hope of any future regeneration.[14] On the other hand, the race mixture among the Americans was predominantly a good thing. "From biological truths it is inferred," Spencer declared in a speech when he visited the United States, "that the eventual mixture of the allied varieties of the Aryan race . . . will produce a more powerful type of man than has hitherto existed. . . . I think . . . the Americans may reasonably look forward to a time when they will have produced a civilization grander than any the world has known."[15]

But intermixture of unlike peoples was always a bad thing. In 1892, Spencer, replying to the letter of a Japanese political leader who asked his opinion concerning the intermarriage of Japanese with foreigners which was then "much agitated among our scholars and politicians," wrote that there should be "no difficulty at all" about the proper answer to such a question. Intermarriage should be "positively forbidden. It is not at root a question of social philosophy. It is at root a question of biology." Animal breeders had long known that the random intermixture of stocks could only lead to degeneration. And one had only to look at the Eurasians in India and the half-breeds in America to see that the same was true of human races.

The physiological basis of this experience appears to be that any one variety of creature in course of many generations acquires a certain constitutional adaptation to its particular form of life, and every other variety similarly acquires its own special adaptation. The consequence is that, if you mix the constitutions of two widely divergent varieties which have severally become adapted to widely divergent modes of life, you get a constitution which is adapted to the mode of life of neither—a constitution which will not work properly, because it is not fitted for any set of conditions whatever. By all means, therefore, peremptorily interdict marriages of Japanese with foreigners.[16]

Some of Spencer's ideas on race, however, proved annoying to racists more thoroughgoing than himself. Spencer accepted the main outlines of Darwin's theory of evolution, but he did not follow Darwin on one important point. Darwin argued that organisms change through accidental variations which turn out to have survival value and thus perpetuate themselves, but Spencer adopted the Lamarckian idea that acquired characteristics are inherited—that is, that the giraffe inherits his long neck because generations of his ancestors stretched their necks to reach food. Spencer thought he himself had inherited small hands because his ancestors had been schoolmasters and thus had not engaged in manual labor which would have enlarged their hands. He thought the Germans tended to be nearsighted because for generations they had been "notoriously studious." At one time he was investigating the possibility that Quakers are more given to color blindness and tone deafness than other peoples because of their ancestors' aversion to colors and to music. Thus, Spencer's conception of innate racial character tended to be more malleable than that of many of his contemporaries. As an example of race modification he observed after a trip to the United States that "the descendants of the immigrant Irish lose their Celtic aspect, and become Americanised. . . ."[17] Spencer also annoyed racists who favored imperialist domination of the primitive races. Laissez faire meant to him, among other things, letting the native peoples *alone*. "First men are sent to teach the heathens Christianity, and then Christians are sent to mow them down with machine guns. . . . The policy is simple and uniform—bibles first and bomb-shells after."[18]

But the misgivings which racists came to feel concerning Spencer resulted from something less tangible than his Lamarckianism or his anti-imperialism. In common with his age, Spencer freely attributed race characteristics to almost any human phenomenon which did not have some other ready explanation. On the other hand, his reflective and far-reaching mind led him to a careful study of the institutions and social life of primitive peoples. Over a period of fourteen years, he supervised the compilation of a comprehensive series of volumes by various writers on *Descriptive Sociology,* of which eight parts on different racial areas had been published by 1881. Because the venture was a financial failure, Spencer suspended the project, but in his will he left a sum of money to insure its continuance. As racist explanations of civilization began to lose their strength, the sociologists could find much in Spencer which would suggest nonracist explanations for the character and civilization of peoples. When Madison Grant, one of the more thoroughgoing twentieth-century American racists, published his *The Passing of the Great Race* in 1916, Henry Fairfield Osborn declared in the introduction that Grant was reacting against the environmentalism of Taine and Herbert Spencer.[19]

In the United States, the influence of Spencer on the developing discipline of sociology was tremendous. Charles H. Cooley thought that most of the people who took up the study of sociology in this country between 1870 and 1890 were drawn to the subject chiefly through Spencer's writings.[20] Spencer's popularity was not merely academic. As an advocate of laissez faire, he was lionized by the business classes when he visited this country. His prestige among conservatives undoubtedly led many boards of trustees of American universities to look with favor upon the idea of founding departments of sociology.[21]

Spencer's chief American disciple was William Graham Sumner, a professor of political science at Yale and one of the founders of American sociology. Sumner was only a little less rigorous than Spencer in drawing the line between legitimate and illegitimate state activity. He did support public education, but he was opposed to all poor laws, to all eleemosynary institutions, to any regulation of hours and working conditions in factories, and to laws preventing abuses of convict labor by private contractors. Like Spencer, Sumner frequently compared society to a living organism, and he used the analogy to combat the ideas of labor organizers, Greenbackers, Populists, socialists, and single taxers. What reformers failed to realize, Sumner declared, was that talking about altering "the system" was like "talking of making a man of sixty into something else than what his life has made him."[22]

The battles against economic reformers took most of Sumner's energy, and race theory plays a comparatively small direct part in his sociology. He certainly was not a race egalitarian. He opposed Negro suffrage. He said that if you had asked Thomas Jefferson whether the statement "All men are created equal" was meant to include Negroes, Jefferson would have replied that "he was not talking about negroes." If you asked modern reformers whether it included Russian Jews, Hungarians, or Italians, all of them would "draw the line somewhere."

If you should meet with a man who should say . . . that all men ought to have an equal chance to do the best they can for themselves on earth, then you might ask him whether he thought the Bushmen, Hottentots, or Australians were equal to the best educated and most cultivated white men. He would have to admit that he was not thinking of them at all.

On another occasion, Sumner wrote, "A man may curse his fate because he is born of an inferior race," but he will get no answer from heaven for his "imprecations."[23]

More closely related to Spencer's ideas on race are the writings of G. Stanley Hall. In 1878, Hall received the Ph.D. in psychology from Harvard, the first doctorate in this field in America. He founded the psychological laboratory at Johns Hopkins in 1883 and the *American Journal of Psychology* in 1887. A specialist in child psychology, Hall expanded Spencer's idea that the mind of a child recapitulates the history of the human race in its development from savagery to civilization. Thus Hall advocated a type of education designed to fit a child's biogenetic stages. At the proper times he should be taught to trap small game, to fish, and—within limits, at least—to fight with his companions. If the child was not allowed to work out these vestigial savage compulsions at the proper phylogenetic stage, they would reappear later in a suppressed and perverted form.[24]

Like Spencer, Hall employed the idea of recapitulation to explain the characteristics of races as well as those of children. Primitive races, he declared, were in an early evolutionary stage, something like that of an arrested childhood. They should thus be given tender and sympathetic treatment by their phylogenetic "elders," and we should be ashamed to make war upon them.[25] This idea was sometimes taken over by imperialists in their softer moods. The "little brown brother" Filipino as described by William Howard Taft and the native who was "half devil, half child" in Rudyard Kipling's fiction probably both owed something to the theory of biogenetic recapitulation. Kindly treatment did not, of course, imply potential equality of status. Hall, for example, was opposed to the movement for educating American Indians because he believed they were incapable of profiting from the white man's civilization and would be happier if permitted to live in their traditional ways. He was also pessimistic about the possibilities for educating and assimilating the great numbers of immigrants who were then coming to the United States from southern and eastern Europe.[26]

Race consciousness was also sharpened among social scientists in this country about this time by the beginnings of the eugenics movement. The eugenicists were primarily interested in attempting to prove that geniuses tend to come from superior human stock, and that feeblemindedness, criminality, and pauperism are also strongly influenced by hereditary factors. The movement began in England where its leader was Francis Galton, a cousin of Charles Darwin. It was Galton who coined the word "eugenics" as well as the popular catch-phrase "nature and nurture," which precipitated so much controversy over the relative importance of heredity and environment. Galton was also the originator of mental tests and of the statistical method for dealing with the measurement of individual differences.[27]

In *Hereditary Genius* (1869) Galton attempted to show by tables compiled from biographical research that men of high intellectual distinction in Great Britain tended to come from a relatively small number of families and to be related to one another. Galton minimized the effect of social and economic conditions in producing genius, assuming that men with real ability would inevitably make their mark in the world. He was convinced that "the men who achieve eminence, and those who are naturally capable, are, to a large extent, identical." If a man had intellectual capacity, for example, there was no method by which the exhibition of this intelligence could be "repressed." No "social hindrances" could keep a genius from attaining eminence, and, on the other hand, "social advantages are incompetent to give that status to a man of moderate ability." All this led, of course, to a cult of the elite. "I am sure that no one who has had the privilege of mixing in the society of the abler men of any great capital, or who is acquainted with the biographies of the heroes of history," declared Galton, "can doubt the existence of grand human animals, of natures pre-eminently noble, of individuals born to be kings of men."[28]

Naturally, the theory had its race implications: Galton was convinced that there are not merely grades of men within each race, but also grades of races. "The average intellectual standard of the negro race," he declared, "is some two grades below our own." Negroes might sometimes attain an eminence as high as that of Anglo-Saxons of the second or third order of ability, said Galton, a phenomenon which accounted for occasional Negroes of ability, men such as Toussaint l'Ouverture. The average of Negro ability, however, was very low and Galton was convinced it would remain low. Anyone could ascertain for himself that great numbers of Negroes are "half-witted," said Galton, by consulting any book from America which discussed the subject of Negro house servants. As additional proof of Negro inferiority, Galton cited the extensive travel literature concerning Africa. "It is seldom that we hear of a white traveller meeting with a black chief," Galton observes, "whom he feels to be the better man." He had often discussed the subject with "competent persons," Galton tells us, and could recall only "a few cases of the inferiority of the white man." Other primitive races were also congenitally defective. "Any amount of evidence might be adduced," declared Galton, "to show how deeply Bohemian habits of one kind or another, were ingrained in the nature of men who inhabited most parts of the earth now overspread by the Anglo-Saxon and other civilized races."[29]

Nor was it merely the nonwhite races which were inferior. Galton looked across the English Channel and explained the low state of European civilization on the basis of defective human stock. The qualities of the white races there had been sapped by the policies of a repressive church and repressive governments. The celibacy required of Catholic orders meant, for example, that many of the most gifted men and women of Europe did not reproduce their kind. In addition, the persecution of heretics by the church decimated a large number of those who were "the most fearless, truthseeking, and intelligent." The Church of Rome "practiced the arts which breeders would use, who aimed at creating ferocious, currish, and stupid natures." In France, this catastrophe had been succeeded by the Revolution. Then "the guillotine made sad havoc among the progeny of her abler races." Persecution and revolution explained the decline of Italy as well as "the formation of the superstitious, unintelligent Spanish race of the present day." It was no wonder that Europe had declined. "The wonder is," said Galton, "that enough good remained in the veins of Europeans to enable their race to rise to its present, very moderate level of natural ability."[30]

In the United States, as in England, the eugenics movement flourished. In 1877 Richard Dugdale published his study of the Jukes, a family in which mental deficiency predominated through several generations. Dugdale gave more credit to environmental factors than did many of the later eugenicists, but he did lend credence to the view that mental and emotional qualities are largely a matter of heredity.[31] In the 1880's and 1890's, the books of G. Stanley Hall and James Mark Baldwin spread the idea of the importance of heredity to psychologists and educators. Baldwin popularized a version of heredity which he called "organic selection." His theory was an adaptation of Lamarckian evolution to the mind. In Baldwin's view, peoples adapt themselves to the conditions of their environment and transmit this adaptation to their offspring. Mental and emotional traits eventually become a part of the germ plasm, and therefore the children of educated people receive biological as well as environmental advantages from the mental activity of their ancestors. By 1900, the idea was widely accepted that both intelligence and traits of character tend to be inherited, and one of the proofs or this contention was believed to be found in race differences.[32]

In one respect, the eugenicists were different from the Social Darwinist individualists. The eugenicists did not believe in laissez faire. Galton was convinced that "the vigorous classes" failed to produce enough children, whereas "the incompetent, the ailing, and the desponding" succeeded all too well in reproducing large numbers of like children. The upper classes should be encouraged to have more children and the lower classes should be induced—or perhaps compelled—to have fewer.[33] It was around this program of increasing the "fit" elements of the population and decreasing the "unfit" elements that the eugenics movement developed. It was a racist movement in so far as social classes reflected race divisions, but its racism was more frequently implicit than explicit.

It is probably no accident that the rise of the eugenics movement was accompanied by a greatly increased interest in genealogy. "If there is one thing more than another about which the American of the present day is concerned," wrote Professor L. Sears of the University of Vermont in 1886, "it is his ancestry. He would rather know who was his grandfather in the year 1600, than to know who will be the next president. To find out who this ancestor was he will cross the Atlantic to England, search town records, look for the flagstone under which he was laid in the parish church, and find . . . memorial brasses on the walls."[34] Goldwin Smith, an English historian who first came to live in the United States and then settled in Canada, observed with wonder in 1902 that there was an American "Burke" containing "upwards of seven hundred coats of arms of American families, with their lions rampant, helmets, men in armour, and feudal mottoes."[35] John Graham Brooks noted in 1903 that

heraldry now is a charmed word for multitudes of very humble people. Librarians are suddenly plagued by the importunity for genealogical evidence of distinguished ancestry. Daughters of this and daughters of that; clubs, coteries, everywhere springing into life, bound to discover proof that they are not quite like other people.[36]

Genealogy was taken seriously, however, not merely by those people who were uncertain about their social status but also by some Americans of old stock who felt that the study might be a method of separating real from spurious achievement in a society which was becoming increasingly conglomerate. It was for these that Henry Cabot Lodge spoke when he argued that genealogy was more than an idle occupation. "The waves of democracy have submerged the old and narrow lines within which the few sat apart," explained Lodge, "and definition of a man's birth and ancestry has become more necessary. Moreover, Darwin and Galton have lived and written, Mendel has been discovered and revived, and the modern biologists have supervened, so that a man's origin has become a recognized part of his biographer's task."[37]

The Social Darwinist individualists and the eugenicists were agreed that it was solely the heredity of the poor classes which kept them poor. "Poverty, dirt, and crime," declared David Starr Jordan, president of Stanford University, are due to poor human material. "It is not the strength of the strong but the weakness of the weak," he added, "which engenders exploitation and tyranny."[38] Employers were not unjust to badly paid wage earners, insisted the sociologist Franklin H. Giddings. The poor were "unfree task-workers, not because society chooses to oppress them," he explained, "but because society has not yet devised or stumbled upon any other disposition to make of them."[39] G. Stanley Hall ridiculed reform the aim of which was not to improve the basic human stock of the country. "The scores of alluring programs of reformers are at best only palliatives," he declared, "and their helpfulness is usually at best only transitory." And he launched into the familiar Social Darwinist dogma that pity for the failures of society was dangerous, because by aiding defectives we might well be interfering with the processes of wholesome natural selection. Sterilization and segregation of the unfit were the only reform measures about which he could feel any degree of enthusiasm.[40]

It is an ironic fact that the men who challenged the conclusions of Social Darwinist individualism, who championed the cause of the lower classes and argued that their low state was not generally to be explained by their poor heredity, were, if anything, more given to racist theorizing than were their opponents. They substituted for Social Darwinist individualism a kind of Darwinian collectivism which involved them in certain conclusions about the inherent character of races. Men whom we generally think of as liberals and who did the most to loosen the grip of the social and economic "laws" propounded by Spencer and Sumner accomplished part of their task by appeals to race theory.

The man who most clearly represents the paradoxical position into which the rebels against Social Darwinist individualism maneuvered themselves was Lester F. Ward. Born in 1841 in Illinois of obscure parents, taken as a boy to Iowa in a covered wagon, Ward struggled against the odds of his crude surroundings to achieve intellectual eminence. As a boy he conceived a genuine passion for learning, taught himself Greek, and kept a diary in French. When he was wounded as a soldier in the Civil War, he was rewarded with a clerkship in Washington. For the next forty years, he was a minor official in various government bureaus, but in his spare time he developed his studies until he became one of the most learned men in America. Toward the end of his life, he gained recognition not only as a paleobotanist but as a sociologist. In 1906, when he was sixty-five, an age when many professors nowadays retire, Ward was finally made a professor of sociology at Brown University. Ralph W. Gabriel has justly described Ward as "the St. Augustine of the American cult of science" and has credited him with doing more than anyone else to formulate the basic pattern of the American concept of the planned society.[41]

Ward set out to break the stranglehold of the conservatives on the disciplines of sociology and economics. Accepting Spencer's dictum that social phenomena are, like physical phenomena, uniform and governed by law, Ward opposed Spencer's position that social phenomena are not amenable to human control. "It is only through the artificial control of natural phenomena that science is made to minister to human needs," argued Ward, "and if social laws are really analogous to physical laws, there is no reason why social science may not receive practical applications such as have been given to physical science." It followed that Ward opposed Spencer's analogy of society with a biological organism, believing that a more accurate way to describe society was to compare it to a mechanism which men might learn how to control. Human society, Ward believed, unlike animal groups which were essentially "instinctive," was basically rational.[42]

Ward never tired of demonstrating the inconsistencies of the laissez faire position. In a review of William Graham Sumner's *What Social Classes Owe to Each Other* (1883), he said he was puzzled at Sumner's moral crusade against reformers. Sumner apparently forgot, Ward observed, that "these very troublesome persons are merely products of society and *natural.*" The reformers belonged to society just as much as the hated paupers and worthless invalids whom Sumner would abandon to the laws of nature. Why couldn't Sumner leave the reformers in peace? "Why meddle with the natural course of things? In fact what is the *raison d'être* of this earnest book that wants to have so much done? On his own theory, the author should let his deluded victims alone, should *laisser faire.* . . ."[43]

Ward dealt even more sharply with conservative businessmen who used laissez faire as a cloak for control of the government for the benefit of one economic class. "Nothing is more obvious today than the signal inability of capital and private enterprise to take care of themselves unaided by the state," Ward declared,

and while they are incessantly denouncing "paternalism,"—by which they mean the claim of the defenseless laborer and artisan to a share of this lavish state protection,—they are all the while besieging legislatures for relief from their own incompetency, and "pleading the baby act" through a trained body of lawyers and lobbyists.

Ward urged the active intervention of human intelligence and foresight in order to control the processes of evolution. "Even the economists are beginning to see," he declared in 1903, "that 'free competition' in business is a myth unless it be protected from the universal tendency of all competition in nature speedily and surely to end in monopoly."[44]

Ward was equally hostile to the kind of determinism propagandized by the eugenicists. Convinced that education could discover and develop latent ability among the lower classes, Ward criticized the conclusions of Galton. In *Hereditary Genius,* Galton had observed that it was always a great pleasure to him to see a collection of England's great leaders gathered together. Being physically as well as mentally superior to the great mass of men, such men were usually "massive, vigorous, capable-looking animals."[45] Ward agreed that successful men might be physically superior to the unsuccessful, but he thought that Galton had misinterpreted the reason for this superiority. Instead of being successful because they are superior, Ward contended, "it would be more nearly true to say that they are superior because they are where they are." Their physical and intellectual superiority was chiefly the result of their environment, he maintained. In society, there is operating a law of social primogeniture. "Only the first born, *i.e.,* the specially favored, receive the legacy; the rest are disinherited, although they may embrace the flower of the family."[46]

At a meeting of the American Sociological Society in 1906, Ward vigorously opposed the position that the most effective method for improving society is to improve the heredity of its individual members. One of the speakers at the conference advocated that the unfit and dependent should be eliminated from society, chiefly by eugenical methods. In reply, Ward branded such a program as an example of the "oligocentric world-view" which was gaining influence among the upper classes. Society would not be improved, Ward insisted, by cultivating the abilities of only a few and ignoring all the rest. The poor, he contended, were not inherently inferior:

So far as the native capacity, the potential quality, the "promise and potency," of a higher life are concerned, these swarming, spawning millions, the bottom layer of society, the proletariat, the working class, the "hewers of wood and drawers of water," are by nature the peers of the boasted "aristocracy of brains" that now dominates society and looks down upon them, and the equals in all but privilege of the most enlightened teachers of eugenics.[47]

With such views as these, we might expect Ward also to attack the racism which was a part of Social Darwinist philosophy. The lower classes of society, which Ward declared contained as much potentiality of intellect as the highest classes, certainly were not all Anglo-Saxons. At this point, however, Ward faltered. We can see him grappling with the problem and attempting to minimize the importance of race differences. "It is . . . clear," he observed, "that there is no race and no class of human beings who are incapable of assimilating the social achievement of mankind and of profitably employing the social heritage." Again, Ward indicated the essential liberality of his point of view when he said that "evidence is rapidly accumulating to show that not only between individuals of the same race but also between the races of men the substratum differs far less than was supposed. . . ."[48]

Ward had other views, however, which were difficult to reconcile with race egalitarianism. Like Spencer, he believed in the Lamarckian theory of the transmission of acquired characteristics. He himself employed the theory to promote an optimistic sociology. To opponents of Lamarckianism, he granted that acquired knowledge could not be directly transmitted by heredity, but he argued that the capacity to acquire knowledge could be so transmitted. As education became more widespread, he believed, men would improve their germ plasm and their offspring would find the process of education less difficult. If the opponents of Lamarck were correct and "use inheritance" was impossible, Ward feared, then education would have "no value for the future of mankind" and its benefits would be "confined exclusively to the generation receiving it." If Lamarckianism was a delusion, Ward found it so persuasive an argument for the diffusion of education among all classes that, unless overwhelming proof could be marshaled against it, we should "hug the delusion."[49]

Ward apparently failed to recognize that his acceptance of the Lamarckian theory could easily be turned against him. If the capacity to learn was increased over the generations by the transmission of acquired characteristics, then those families which had a long record of learning and achievement could transmit to their offspring qualities which would make them innately superior to those children whose ancestors had not been learned men. Further, Lamarckianism could easily be adapted to race theories. One can easily visualize an imperialist agreeing with Ward that primitive peoples might at some future time develop a civilization as high as that of the white races but that it would take hundreds if not thousands of years for the germ plasm of the inferior races to improve to this extent.

Ward may have realized that his position in favor of Lamarckian inheritance involved him in possible contradictions with his other ideas. Significantly, we find him arguing that there are no important differences in the "use inheritance" which has come down to the various races of Europe. Whether "Aryan or Semitic," he contended, the aggregate of European races "has held close enough together for all to profit by the achievement of any, so that it forms a continuous and unbroken line of social heredity and has maintained the continuity of the social germ-plasm. Of this entire race at least . . . intellectual equality . . . can with safety be predicted." But what about the others? Unfortunately, the case was different with them. Ward drew a distinction between the "historic" or "favored" races which had originated in Europe and the other great groupings of black, red, and yellow races. While arguing that these races had more ability than they had been given credit for, Ward acknowledged their innate inferiority. On one occasion, he cited approvingly Auguste Comte's statement that the black races are as much superior to the whites in feeling or sentiment as they are below them in intelligence and that the yellow races are superior to both the whites and the blacks in "activity" though they are inferior in "intelligence and feeling."[50]

Equally important in his attitudes toward race was Ward's acceptance of the theories of the conflict school of sociologists, represented most prominently by two European writers, Ludwig Gumplowicz and Gustav Ratzenhofer. Their theory was that society evolves and improves through race conflict. Two races engage in a war with one another. Sometimes these wars end in extermination for the losing side, but more often the winners find it expedient to come to some sort of compromise with the losers. What follows is a society based upon rigid caste lines. The upper caste discovers in time, however, that it needs the cooperation of the lower caste in order to carry out measures of public policy or to assist in protection against outside enemies. Thus originates the idea of the state in which classes have both rights and duties. Eventually, there is so much intermarriage and interbreeding between the racial castes that the society becomes more or less one homogeneous people united by a common patriotism. This society, in time, engages in war with some outside society and the process of racial assimilation is repeated.[51]

The conflict theory of society might have been maintained, perhaps, without any reliance upon the idea of the inequality of races. Ward himself denied that military success could be considered as an indication of innate superiority. The trouble was that Ward relied so heavily on biological analogies to support the theory of racial conflict that a more insistent racism was the almost inevitable result. For example, Ward compared the process of the amalgamation of the races to fertilization in biology. The conquering race was the spermatozoa and the conquered race was the ovum, "the former active and aggressive, the latter passive and submitting, resulting in a crossing of strains."[52] The process of conflict between races was "natural" and therefore a positive good. "Without race conflict there can be no state and no political development," Gumplowicz had argued, "and without blending there can be no culture and no civilization."[53] Ward

echoed this view. "Races, states, peoples, nations are always forming, always aggressing, always clashing and clinching, and struggling for the mastery, and the long, painful, wasteful, but always fruitful gestation must be renewed and repeated again and
again." Perhaps some day new and peaceful forms of assimilation might supersede the violent conflicts of the past and present. There was no immediate prospect of peace, however, and it
was inevitable that the primitive races of the world must be conquered by the civilized races. A cessation of race conflict, Ward
feared, would only lead to general social stagnation. He spoke
frankly of "superior," "inferior," and "decadent" races.⁵⁴

One curious aspect of Ward's version of the role of conflict
in the evolution of society was his attitude toward the question
of the rape of white women in the South by Negroes. The lower
races, Ward maintained, experience an unusual amount of sexual desire for members of the higher races because they dimly
and instinctively realize that the improvement of their own race
is involved. A Negro who rapes a white woman, Ward declared,
is impelled by something more than mere lust. "This is the same
unheard but imperious voice of nature commanding him at the
risk of 'lynch law,' " said Ward, "to raise his race to a little higher level." On the other hand, the fury of the white community
in which such an act takes place is equally natural.

Although the enraged citizens who pursue, capture, and "lynch" the
offender do not know any more than their victim that they are impelled to do so by the biological law of race preservation, still it is this
unconscious imperative, far more than the supposed sense of outraged
decency, that impells them to the performance of a much greater and
more savage "crime" than the poor wretch has committed.

Luckily, Ward did not conclude that a cycle of raping and
lynching is also necessary for the improvement of society. Instead he discovered still another natural "law," which said that
"the men of any race, in default of women of a higher race, will
be content with women of a lower race." In addition, he believed that the understanding by both races of the biological rea-

sons for these urges would tend to prevent their violent expression.[55] There is little evidence that the southerners—either white or Negro—ever saw the problem in quite that light.

We might imagine that Ward's acceptance of the race conflict theory would seriously modify his social optimism, specifically his belief in a planned society and in democracy. It would seem useless to plan in a society which, in order to progress, must engage in constant race wars. Yet Ward managed to retain an optimistic and democratic view of human society, to reconcile in his philosophy all dissident elements. He was even successful in converting Gumplowicz to his cheerful point of view.[56] Modern interpreters of Ward have seen clearly, however, that his theories of race conflict cannot be reconciled with his theories of a democratic society. It is his attacks upon Social Darwinist individualism and eugenic determinism and not his race theories which have won him a secure place in the history of social thought in this country. One observer has said that Ward's preoccupation with race conflict theories was "unfortunate," and another has argued that they "found but a small place" in his work.[57] Still, we can easily see why he was not able to extend his attack upon Social Darwinist individualism to an effective attack upon Social Darwinist racism.

Unfortunately, the other liberal sociologists and social scientists who attacked the theories of Spencer and Sumner were even more comfortable in the midst of race theorizing than was Ward. One of these was Charles H. Cooley. In his writings we discover, in somewhat more subdued form, the same contradictions between a passion for democracy and an addiction to race theories that are found in Ward. Cooley was one of the most effective of the opponents of Social Darwinist individualism. In his volume, *Human Nature and the Social Order* (1902), he ridiculed the notion that self-reliant individualism was the fine fruit of evolution by pointing to the gorilla as the one perfect individualist. He concluded from his observations of children that human nature is more the product of social living than it is of individual competition. Likewise, he subjected the eugenic theories of Francis Galton to a searching analysis and wrote an essay which Ward described as "the most consistent and satisfactory answer" to Galton ever published.[58]

Cooley's liberalism, however, did not extend to race questions. He attributed the success of the Anglo-Saxons, it is true, to "the intrinsic cantankerousness of the race." By "cantankerousness," however, he seems to have meant no more than "restlessness" and "dissatisfaction with things as they are." Because the Anglo-Saxon wanted a place of his own he had become a "world-winning pioneer." He had more need for heroes than had less strenuous peoples. Somewhat inconsistently, Cooley goes on to say that the peoples of northern Europe were less given to hero worship than those of southern Europe, because they were "less given to blind enthusiasm for popular idols." Hero worship among the northern peoples was "more constructive . . . in building up ideals," because the races were "more sober and independent in their judgment. . . ." Above all, the Anglo-Saxons had courage, and it was no accident that Beowulf long ago had declaimed, "Death is better for every clansman than coward life."[59]

The most spectacular of the rebels against Social Darwinist individualism was undoubtedly Professor E. A. Ross of the University of Wisconsin. A commanding figure six feet six inches tall, an advocate of the strenuous life, a friend of Theodore Roosevelt, the author of twenty-four books which sold more than 300,000 copies, Ross was a vigorous opponent of social and economic conservatism. In 1894, when he was a professor at Stanford University, Ross wrote to Ward, his "master," that he was about to lock horns with the laissez faire interpretation of the theory of evolution in a lecture entitled "Dollars and Darwinism." He could not see eye to eye with President David Starr Jordan of Stanford, whose lectures seemed to link up the "repulsive dog-eat-dog practices of current business and politics with that 'struggle for existence' which evoked the higher forms of life."[60] From the beginning of his career, Ross was the champion of the laboring man and the foe of the "interests." "Those

who have the sunny rooms in the social edifice have . . . a powerful ally in the suggestion of Things-as-they-are," he wrote.
"With the aid of a little narcotizing teaching and preaching, the
denizens of the cellar may be brought to find their lot proper
and right." Ross denounced laissez faire individualism as "a caricature of Darwinism, invented to justify the ruthless practices
of business men." A friend of the Populists and later of the
muckrakers, Ross did much to make sociology a popular subject.[61]

Ross was much less diffident about his racism than was Ward.
He seemed to accept racism as just one more weapon in the battle for social justice. He was opposed to immigration because it
made the formation of unions more difficult and the control of
unorganized workers by businessmen more certain. Aliens would
be content with paltry wages, he argued, and would see no harm
in "scabbing" or strikebreaking. Political questions, such as the
relation of the church to the state, the church to the school, and
the state to the child, which had been settled in America, would
have to be reopened if large numbers of European immigrants
were allowed to come here. "We are forced to thresh over this
old straw," says Ross, "when we ought to be thinking of such
questions as the protection of labor, the control of monopoly,
and the conservation of natural resources."[62] Ross could have developed his arguments concerning immigration without recourse
to race theories, but he could not resist falling back on the old
easy explanations of the backwardness of the immigrants from
southern and eastern Europe.

Like many a racist, Ross was unable—for most of his life, at
least—to recognize his own prejudices. In 1901, he wrote in an
article that the error "which exaggerates the race factor and re-
gards the actual differences of people as hereditary and fixed"'
was "vulgar" and was growing in power. Americans, he cautioned, "ought to beware of it." In the identical article Ross
coolly argues that "the energy and character" of America was
"lowered by the presence in the South of several millions of an
inferior race." Some races, he added, were "over-emotional and

poised unstably between smiles and tears." Bedouins loved violence for its own sake. Abyssinians were "fickle and uncertain," and the courage of the Mongol was merely "a sudden blaze of pugnacity" rather than true intrepidity. He recalled Carlyle's comparison of Gallic fire which is "as the crackling of dry thorns under a pot" with the Teutonic fire which "rises slowly but will smelt iron." The Anglo-Saxon had less patience and financial acumen than the Jew, but he was able to meet "finesse with force," so that "despite his less developed value sense, more and more the choice lands and the riches of the earth come into his possession and support his brilliant yet solid civilization." Ross concluded that "the superiority of a race cannot be preserved without *pride of blood* and an uncompromising attitude toward the lower races."[63]

Unlike Ward and Cooley, Ross was a friend of the eugenics movement. In his declarations in favor of eliminating the unfit, in fact, Ross seems uncomfortably close to the essential beliefs of his old enemies, the Social Darwinist individualists. "The Christian cult of charity as a means of grace has formed a shelter under which idiots and *cretins* have crept and bred," he declared. "The state gathers the deaf mutes into its sheltering arm, and a race of deaf mutes is in process of formation." There was no reason why

society should convert itself into a moral sanitarium and free dispensary, administering precepts to moral paupers, and poisoning the hale with hospital air in order to preserve the sick. The shortest way to make this world a heaven is to let those so inclined hurry hell-ward at their own pace.

And Ross makes a not very convincing effort to turn the eugenist argument against the upper classes and in favor of the lower classes. "Among the privileged the fools and weaklings are not winnowed out, as they are among plain people, but propagate their kind unhindered."[64] Ross urged Anglo-Saxons to have larger families. Already the Irish and the French Canadians had swamped New England, he observed, and the victory of the alien races had been facilitated by the low native birth rate there. Anglo-Saxons, he declared, were committing "race suicide."[65]

In his autobiography, written in 1936 at the age of seventy, Ross tells us that after much study and a tour of the Far East in 1908 he abandoned his race theories. "I lost faith," he says, "in Race as a key of social interpretation." An examination of his writings after 1908 discloses that the abandonment cannot always be depended upon. "That the Mediterranean peoples are morally below the races of northern Europe is as certain as any social fact," he wrote in 1913. "Even when they were dirty, ferocious barbarians, these blonds were truth-tellers." Americans bear the palm for coolness, orderly saving of life, and consideration for the weak in shipwreck, he declared, but if they do not check immigration they "will lose these traits in proportion as they absorb excitable mercurial blood from southern Europe." Ross did make increasing attempts to abandon race theories and to explain the differences among peoples on the basis of culture and environment. Yet at the end of his career, he confessed in sorrow that he had not been able to bring himself to feel more than a very limited sympathy for Negroes and Indians. "Their faces," he said, "are a script I have not yet learned to read."[66]

Even his nonracist explanations of human conduct, written after he had ostensibly abandoned racism, show the effects of the old theories. He was convinced, for example, that the vertical rays of the sun in tropical regions stimulate the people who live there to a constant and voracious sexual appetite. He discovered in South America, he tells us, that both the descendants of the Spaniards and the Indians indulged in orgies of sexuality unknown in northern climates. "I came to the conclusion that at bottom this [sensuality] is the direct effect of the torrid sun, not of *heat* for it is just as marked on the bleak uplands as on the steaming lowlands." From fellow Americans who were working in South America, Ross drew out confidences that within three or four weeks after arriving in the tropics they experienced a great sharpening of sex appetite, which stayed with them as long as they remained, but left them on the voyage home or soon after. The result of this theory was to suggest, of course, that restraint and discipline could never be a characteristic of tropical peoples. In a similar fashion, Ross attempted to explain the traits of northern peoples after he had discarded his race theories. Did early Western man, he asked in 1932, get "that capacity for reflection so necessary to conscience" from "the long cold of his winters, which by depriving him of the out-door, sensuous life of the South threw him back upon his thoughts?" By this time, Ross was cautious enough to answer, "We do not know." He did go on to suggest, however, that it is by "a sifting of some sort or another" that the characteristics of a people are developed.[67]

Still another social thinker of the period whose racism seems strangely at variance with his democratic idealism was the liberal economist, John R. Commons. More of a man of action than a theorist, Commons was less interested in destroying the theory of Social Darwinist individualism than he was in demonstrating that democracy and co-operation could be employed to improve society. Beginning as a Christian Socialist, Commons lectured at Chautauqua and served on the editorial board of George Herron's radical religious magazine, *The Kingdom*, and in 1894 published a series of essays on *Social Reform and the Church*. Later, Commons was brought to the University of Wisconsin by Richard T. Ely to teach economics. Closely associated with the reforms of the elder LaFollette, Commons drafted a new civil service law for the state, engineered the formation of an Industrial Commission whose principles have since been copied by liberal legislation in many states, and helped to reorganize the municipal government of Milwaukee under a reform administration. "In his pragmatism, his opportunism, his talent for compromise and for common sense, his shrewdness and curiosity, his humor and simplicity, his suspicion of theory and of theorists, his versatility and industry, and his idealism," declares Henry Steele Commager, "Commons was one of the representative men of his generation."[68] All these virtues Commons probably had, but like many liberals of his time he was also a racist.

As with Ross, Commons' racism was allied to his opposition to immigration and his hopes for the strengthening of labor unions. Only northern Europeans, he believed, were capable of democracy, because they alone had the basic and innate qualities of intelligence, manliness, and co-operation. "If they [these qualities] are lacking, democracy is futile." The question for America was whether democracy could survive very much more alien infusion from immigration. "Race differences are established in the very blood and physical constitution," he maintained. "They are most difficult to eradicate and they yield only to the slow processes of the centuries." All tropical races were "indolent and fickle." The Negro was "generally acknowledged to be lacking in 'the mechanical idea.' " Only "ambitious races" could be industrialized. The peasants of Europe, especially those of southern and eastern Europe, had been "reduced to the qualities similar to those of an inferior race that favor despotism and oligarchy rather than democracy."[69]

The calm complacency represented by Spencer and Sumner, their conviction that economic and social conditions are as they must be because of immutable biological law, makes it easy for us to understand their racism. It is, in fact, similar to that which still so largely survives in the popular mind. Its central idea is that the nonwhite races are oppressed, poverty-stricken, and of an inferior social status for no other reason than their innate lack of capacity.

But we have more difficulty in comprehending the racism of the young rebels against Social Darwinist individualism. The racism of Ward, Cooley, Ross, and Commons—and others like them—seems at first sight quite inconsistent with their general social optimism, with their suspicion of closed systems, and with their opposition to other forms of tyranny. Since they successfully attacked Spencer's and Sumner's use of biological analogies to justify ruthless competition in business, it would seem logical that they would have followed up their success with an intensive examination of race theories which were also largely dependent upon analogies with biological evolution. The contrast between the opposition to social determinism and the racism of these men is such that modern liberal historians have sometimes chosen to ignore their racism or pass over it lightly, perhaps the better to present them as heroes fighting against black reaction.[70]

If there is one conviction which unites modern liberals, it is a resistance to the idea of explaining innate character and capacity on the basis of race. We need to understand that liberalism only recently acquired this conviction. The liberals of the latter part of the nineteenth century and the first part of the twentieth were frequently not, it is painfully clear, liberal on the subject of race. Part of the reason why racism flourished so mightily in this period is that it had no really effective opposition where one might have expected it, since it also flourished among the liberals. Some of their racism is explicable on the basis of the practical problem they faced in the almost unrestricted immigration of the time. With a good deal of logic on their side, some of them—especially Ross and Commons—believed that as long as hundreds of thousands of immigrants came to America from southern and eastern Europe every year it would be impossible to protect the native workers from exploitation. Their racism is thus closely allied to their convictions about immigration.

Their racism was also, however, the result of the methods they chose in their war with Social Darwinist individualism. When they began to think of means by which the immense power of laissez faire based upon evolution might be broken, they turned back to the pure gospel of Darwin himself and attempted to prove that his theories had been misinterpreted. They argued that co-operation and state intervention were just as logical conclusions from the theory of evolution as was the doctrine of laissez faire. They attempted to reconcile biological law with the preconceptions of democracy.

In order to escape the implications of the theory that man is engaged in a struggle for existence with all other men, these liberals quite rightly attempted to show that man survives by co-operation with his fellows more often than he does by competition with them. They attempted to prove that societies are aggregates of groups at least as much as they are aggregates of individuals. Not all the groupings which the liberals pointed to were dangerous for the cause of democracy which they sought to defend. As long as it was the family, the tribe, or the social class which concerned them, they were on firm ground. They understood that all these groups were subordinate to the needs of society itself. But when they turned to race as the greatest of the natural divisions of society, they tended to fall into an error which, on other occasions, they had rightly charged to their opponents. They relied too heavily on biological analogies. In their theories, the different races of men have a relationship to one another something like that of different species among the lower animals. Struggle among the species in the lower animal world became, when applied to men, a struggle among races. Thus, while they attacked theories of society based upon conflict among individuals, they actually encouraged theories of society based upon conflict among races. As long as this line of thought persisted, the result almost inevitably was more and more racism.

VIII

The Social Gospel and Race

IT IS HARD to think of any period in which religious thought underwent a more painful readjustment than in that following the publication of Darwin's *Origin of Species* in 1859. It was not merely that conceptions of man's origin and the inerrancy of scripture had to be revised, although these are the aspects of the battle that are best known. Nor was it merely that the theory of evolution led to the Social Darwinist thought in which it was considered wrong to help the poor and helpless, an idea difficult to square with Christianity. The clergymen of the time who made an effort to keep abreast of contemporary thought could hardly afford to ignore evolution or fail to realize that the theory had important implications for their faith. Still another effect of the theory of evolution—and the one which most directly concerns us here—was that it provided new arguments for the superiority and inferiority of races, arguments which the clergymen had to face.

Looking back at the religious controversies over science and social justice in the latter part of the nineteenth century, we can admire both the courage and the intelligence of the leaders of the Social Gospel movement. Such men as Theodore Munger, Washington Gladden, Josiah Strong, Lyman Abbott, Walter Rauschenbusch, and George T. Herron, widely as they differed from one another in their economic and political attitudes, were at one in their concern that the theory of evolution should not, on the one hand, be ignorantly dismissed by religious leaders or, on the other hand, be used to justify the exploitation of the weak. It was not an easy thing for these men to come to grips with social and economic ideas which had traditionally not been regarded as the proper province of clergymen, and the fact that they were willing to face all the enormous obstacles to such a confrontation is greatly to their credit.

When we have said all this, however, we cannot help noticing that the Social Gospel clergymen spoke out much more strongly in the area of specific economic injustices—the abuse of the laboring class in unhealthful working conditions, long hours, and poor wages, for example—than they did on matters of racial injustice. Part of the reason was that the Social Gospel clergymen were genuinely uncertain in the area of race theory. The doctrine of evolution seemed to have as one of its necessary concomitants the idea that human races represented different stages of evolution and therefore were innately unequal. Henry Adams, in commenting on the enormous influence of evolution among scientists and social scientists, said that to question any of its implications was "to range oneself with curates and bishops."[1] The prestige of the theory was not lost on the clergymen themselves. Those who studied the ideas of the evolutionists with any care could hardly escape the conclusion that racial inequality was taken for granted among them. Just as the clergymen had been obliged to accept the lower primates as the ancestors of man, so it seemed they would have to accept the nonwhite races as varieties of the species in a relatively primitive stage of evolution.

The force of the idea of hereditary inequality, whether among classes or races, can be gauged from the apologetic air which the opponents of Social Darwinist individualism assumed when confronted with it. Washington Gladden, a leading exponent of the Social Gospel and a champion of the fight against economic abuses, still acknowledged the power of heredity to create beggars and felons. "Heredity, too," he declared, "is a great factor in the production of pauperism and crime. The paupers and the criminals bring forth with great fecundity after their kind, and a careless pseudo-charity has encouraged them to persevere."[2]

Bishop Spalding, the liberal Catholic educator, was almost as much on the defensive. "When we have said a thousand things in praise of education," he observed, "we must, at last, come back to the fundamental fact that nearly everything depends on the kind of people of whom we are descended. . . ." Having granted this concession, Spalding made a valiant but not very convincing effort to recover some of the ground he had conceded. "Nearly everything, but not quite everything," he continued, "and it is this little which . . . makes us children of God and masters of ourselves."[3] The optimism of some of the most enlightened men of the period was heavily qualified by eugenic determinism. William James observed regretfully, for example, that most of the American nation, and probably of the European nations as well, was "white trash."[4]

One of the most influential of the Social Gospel clergymen, Josiah Strong, decided that fundamental race inequality was not a painful fact which one would somehow have to become accustomed to. Rather, it was a triumphant demonstration of the workings of the Almighty. Far from lamenting the gradual disappearance of the American Indian, for example, we should see in his extinction merely the reflection of the will of God in preparing the land for a better race, the Anglo-Saxons. Similarly, the troubles of the native peoples over the world—as vexing as they might be—were merely local manifestations of a cosmic process, the replacing of inferior with superior stock. Just as Strong was able to reconcile the theory of evolution, the struggle for existence, and the survival of the fittest with an optimistic Protestant theology, so he was able to view the ascendancy and decline of races as part of the providence of God.

The idea that the nonwhite races might best fulfil the will of God simply by disappearing was not, of course, invented by Strong, nor was it wholly the consequence of a theology conditioned by Social Darwinism. "God cast out the heathen to make room for his people," one Puritan divine explained, referring to the spurious claims of the dispossessed Indians. Another Puritan discovered "the special interposition of Providence in reducing by disease the Indians in Massachusetts from thirty thousand to three hundred."⁵ Probably with his tongue in his cheek, Benjamin Franklin later expressed a rather similar idea, declaring in his *Autobiography* that rum was "the appointed means" of fulfilling "the design of Providence to extirpate these savages in order to make room for the cultivators of the earth."⁶

Likewise, the early English colonists had thought of themselves as a chosen people long before the laws of biology were invoked to justify their superiority. The Puritans frequently compared their relationship to God to that of the Israelites of old. In the American Revolution, the phrase was revived to induce patriotism among the colonists. After the war, the theme of an "American Israel" formed the keynote of a sermon delivered in 1783 by Ezra Stiles, president of Yale.⁷ Two years later Jefferson proposed that the seal of the United States should represent the children of Israel led by a pillar of light.⁸ In 1787 Timothy Dwight referred frankly to Americans as "this chosen race."⁹

The idea of an elect people was sometimes employed to further the cause of American idealism. In 1801, for example, Jefferson spoke of the United States as "the world's best hope" and in 1805 he declared in his second inaugural address that "God led our forefathers, as Israel of old," implying that American institutions had the seal of divine approval.¹⁰ These convictions merged easily with the accumulating racism of the nineteenth century. By the 1840's the idea of the chosen people had become associated with convictions regarding the superior merits of the Anglo-Saxon "race." In 1846 Senator Thomas Hart Benton, for example, declared that the Anglo-Saxons—with the help of the Celts—would advance to the shores of the Pacific and then begin the even grander project of colonizing Asia. These two branches of the Caucasian race, Benton declared, "had alone received the divine command, to subdue and replenish the earth," and they would become "the reviver and the regenerator of the inferior and torpid yellow peoples."¹¹ Just how the Asiatics would be revived and regenerated is not entirely clear, but there is less doubt about what was in store for the Indians in this country. The Indians, Benton declared, had no claim to the land, but the white races did have such a claim because "they used it according to the intentions of the CREATOR."[12] During the Mexican War, one of the persistent arguments advanced by the war's proponents was the divine mission of the Anglo-Saxon to populate the continent.[13]

Ideas like these were not limited to rambunctious westerners intent upon extending the territory of the United States. They also appealed to two of the best known among the religious reformers, Horace Bushnell and Theodore Parker. Bushnell was a rebel against theological orthodoxy, one of the most persuasive of the anti-Calvinists. His theology was intuitive rather than intellectual; he emphasized free will, mysticism, and "Christian nurture" rather than election as the means of salvation. He was not an abolitionist, because he shrank from a sudden and violent solution to the problem of slavery, but he did hope that slavery would eventually disappear and he was on friendly, if critical, terms with William Lloyd Garrison. It was Bushnell who served as a model for Washington Gladden, one of the leading exponents of the Social Gospel. A prominent twentieth-century Protestant clergyman has declared that Bushnell was one of the three Americans most influential in American church history—the other two being Jonathan Edwards and Walter Rauschenbusch.[14]

Bushnell argued that there were two methods by which the kingdom of God was being extended. One was the process of conversion of the heathen. The other was the expansion of Christian peoples into the four corners of the earth. A look at history would reveal, said Bushnell, that the Anglo-Saxon race by "a grand law of increase" was "rolling out and spreading over the world." It might be that the divine intention was not merely that the Anglo-Saxon should regenerate the "feebler and more abject races." "What if it should be God's plan," Bushnell wondered, "to people the world with better and finer material?" Of course, we still had an obligation to convert the heathen. "It is for God to say what races are to be finally submerged," he cautioned, "and not for us." Yet, he could not help noticing that the Anglo-Saxons were everywhere increasing their power and the native races of foreign lands were disappearing. "Whatever expectations we may indulge," he declared, "there is a tremendous overbearing surge of power in the Christian nations, which, if the others are not speedily raised to some vastly higher capacity, will inevitably submerge and bury them forever."[15]

Even the intelligent and sensitive Theodore Parker had similar blind spots with regard to the future of the nonwhite races. Unlike Bushnell, Parker was an active opponent of slavery, though he died the year before the outbreak of the Civil War. The contrast between Parker's idealism and his racism is particularly glaring. On the one hand, he insisted upon fair treatment for racial minorities. "If the nation play the tyrant over her weakest child, if she plunder and rob the feeble Indian, the feebler Mexican, the Negro, feebler yet," he admonished his Boston congregation, "why the blame is yours."[16] And yet the Anglo-Saxon had a very different future from that of the other races. "Of all races," says Parker, "the Caucasian has hitherto shown the most . . . instinct of progress." Of the various "families" of the Caucasian race, it was the Teutonic which was the most progressive. Of the Teutons, it was the Anglo-Saxons, "especially that portion of them in the Northern states of America," who were "advancing most rapidly in their general progress." The Anglo-Saxon had a particularly brilliant future if he would only cleanse himself of the "plague-spot" of slavery:

Then by peaceful purchase, the Anglo-Saxon may acquire the rest of this North American continent. The Spaniards will make nothing of it. Nay, we may honorably go further south, and possess the Atlantic and Pacific slopes of the Northern continent, extending the area of freedom at every step. We may carry thither the Anglo-Saxon vigor and enterprise, the old love of liberty, the love also of law; the best institutions of the present age,—ecclesiastical, political, social, domestic. Then what a nation we shall one day become! America, the mother of a thousand Anglo-Saxon States, tropical and temperate, on both sides of the equator, may behold the Mississippi and the Amazon uniting their waters, the drainage of two vast continents, in the Mediterranean of the Western world; may count her children at last by the hundreds of millions—and among them all behold no tyrant and no slave!¹⁷

Parker showed his ambivalent attitude toward race questions particularly when, in 1843, he wrote an unfavorable review of William Hickling Prescott's *Conquest of Mexico*. One charge against Prescott was that his social conscience was callous, that he showed insufficient concern over the Spanish mistreatment of the Aztecs. Prescott was unfair to the Indians, says Parker, just as he was unfair to the Moors in Spain where he "glozes over the injustice shown towards them." It does not trouble him that in Mexico "the Spaniards did not attempt to pretend to buy a title to the land. Their claim was the claim of the pirate." They thought they had sufficient title to America, Parker satirically observes, from the Pope as "head of the human race, trustee for all mankind, and vice-regent of the Almighty." Of course, the title had been given on condition that the heathen be converted, but "we shall see how this was attended to."¹⁸

How differently affairs had been handled in New England! "The Spaniard could not plead necessity, like the pilgrims,— poor, persecuted, and just escaped from the ocean who took a few fish and some corn in their extremity, when they landed on Cape Cod, and carefully paid for both when, months afterwards, they found the owners!" The Puritan as well as the Pilgrim understood that

he had no right, whatever necessity compelled him, to take from the savages, against their will, all that they had or anything that they had, without returning them a complete equivalent thereof. So these settlers of New England did not rely on the grant of the English king for their title to the Indian land; they bought it of the Indians, took a deed, recorded the transfer, and honestly paid for it—a small consideration, but enough to extinguish the title, and more than it was worth to the Indians themselves.

On the other hand, the Saxons, unlike the Spaniards, did not intermarry with the Indians. Though regrettably "like other conquerors forgetting his dignity in loose amours," the Saxon would not "mix his proud blood in stable wedlock with another race," showing an "antipathy" which was "almost peculiar to this remarkable tribe." Of course, he was concerned over the spiritual welfare of the Indians. "In New England," says Parker,

more pains were taken than elsewhere in America, to civilize, and to convert the sons of the wilderness; but yet here the distinction of race was always sharply observed. . . . The Puritan hoped to meet the Pequods in heaven, but wished to keep apart from them on earth, nay, to exterminate them from the land.[19]

How the Saxon could hope to civilize and convert the Indians while he was also exterminating them from the land, Parker does not make clear.

But Parker's chief criticism of Prescott is that he does not understand the grand truths which underlie human history. Instead, he fills his pages with accounts of particular events. "It is not very important to know," Parker says, "whether General Breakpate commanded on the right or the left, whether he charged uphill or downhill, whether he rode a bright chestnut or a dapple gray, nor whether he got dismounted by the breaking of his saddle-girth or the stumbling of his beast." Prescott has too many details like these. "The book lacks philosophy to a degree exceeding belief. The author seems to know nothing of the philosophy of history. . . ." Parker thinks Prescott should have made more of an effort to understand currents of thought, the way in which civilization developed. He ought to have told more about the ordinary concerns of the people. "A few facts from the every day life of the merchant, the slave, the peasant, the mechanic," observes Parker, "are often worth more, as signs of the times, than a chapter which relates the intrigues of a courtier, though these are not to be overlooked."[20]

More important than any of this, Prescott had generally ignored the racial implications of history. At one point, it is true, Prescott had mentioned, although incidentally, what should have been his major theme. The Aztecs had thought that the Span-

iards were "white gods." "This 'random shot of prophecy,' as
Mr. Prescott calls it," said Parker, "seems to have hit the mark,
and prepared the nation for conquest. . . . Then the Spaniards were Caucasians and had the organic superiority of that
race. . . ." But Prescott erred in not showing that the decline of
the Indian civilization would be followed by the decline of the
Spaniard, and for the same reason—racial inferiority. Of Spanish
civilization, Parker says:

> Surely it cannot stand before the slow, strong, steady wave of the
> Anglo-Saxon tide, which seems destined ere long to sweep it off, or
> hide it in its own ample bosom. The consequence is always in the cause,
> there but hidden. The historian of the conquest of Mexico, writing so
> long after the events he chronicles, while those consequences are patent
> to all the world, might describe to us the cause; nay, the history is not
> adequately written until this is done. Without this, a work is history
> without its meaning, without philosophy. We must complain of Mr.
> Prescott's work, in general, that he has omitted this its most important
> part. True, he was only writing of the conquest of the country and
> the immediate colonization; but this is not adequately described until
> the other work is done.[21]

One other racist idea which antedates the theory of evolution was the conviction that northern Europeans generally and
Anglo-Saxons in particular had an innate racial character which
made Protestantism especially congenial to them. In 1850, Robert Knox, the Scottish physician and ethnologist, had ridiculed
the attempts of the Frenchman Daubigny to assign historical
causes for the acceptance of the Reformation by some nations
and its rejection by others. "Let him look to the map," declared
Knox, "and he will find that, with a slight exception, . . . the
Celtic race universally rejected the Reformation of Luther; the
Saxon race as certainly adopted it. There need be no mystery in
stating so simple a fact."[22] In 1851, the Reverend Robert Baird
in this country was convinced that not only were the Anglo-
Saxons divinely ordained to be Protestant but so was the United
States. "Had De Soto, when he sailed from Cuba . . . turned his
prow to the east of the peninsula of Florida, instead of the west,"

declared Baird, "he would have discovered the Atlantic coast of what is now the United States, and that great country might have had a Spanish instead of an Anglo-Saxon,—a Roman Catholic, instead of a Protestant,—population. It is said that a very trifling circumstance decided him!" Clearly, the United States had had a very narrow escape. "But all was ordered by that Being who knows how to make the most insignificant as well as the greatest occurrence subserve His glorious purposes."[23]

We can see from the racist ideas of the foregoing men— nearly all of them clergymen—that adapting religious ideas to the theory of evolution would not prove to be as difficult as we might have thought. In Bushnell and Parker we find most of the characteristics of the later racism. There is a disposition to see civilization as a matter of good forces winning out over bad, a conviction that the Anglo-Saxon is in the forefront of progress, and an ambiguous attitude toward the "lower" races—we should be kind to them but our kindness should not blind us to the fact that their days are numbered. To adapt these theories to the theory of evolution, all that was necessary was to relate racial ascendancy and decline to such biological terms as "struggle for existence" and "survival of the fittest." In addition, we should recognize that the biblical record is erroneous in some of its details—such as the creation—however much it may be right in its general conceptions of God and man.

The clergyman who did the most to correlate his optimistic conviction that the Anglo-Saxon was a superior race designed by God to conquer and populate the world with theories of evolution and Social Darwinism was Josiah Strong, a Congregational minister. A graduate of Western Reserve University and for years pastor of a church in Topeka, Kansas, Strong in the 1880's became an official of the Congregational Home Missionary Society. An advocate of a liberal theology, Strong defended the theory of evolution from the attacks of theological conservatives. He wrote a great deal and his writings were distributed widely. The secret of his popularity seems to have been in his ability to adapt popular science, especially evolutionary theories, to the convictions and prejudices of rural and small-town Protestant America.[24]

Strong is usually mentioned as a leader of the fight against economic abuses and an advocate of the Social Gospel. Some of his utterances would seem to justify this classification. In an angry moment he could lash out at business monopoly:

This is modern and republican feudalism. These American barons and lords of labor have probably more power and less responsibility than many an olden feudal lord. They close the factory or the mine, and thousands of workmen are forced into unwilling idleness. . . . We have developed a despotism vastly more oppressive and more exasperating than that against which the thirteen colonies rebelled.[25]

Yet Strong's attitude toward capitalism was not as critical as this quotation would suggest. On one occasion he said that wealth in America was inequitably distributed and that excessive concentration of power was dangerous, but he was not a socialist. He added that "the enrichment of one is for the benefit of all, and the greater part of a rich man's wealth serves the public far more than it serves him." Investments were the means of building railways, steamships, factories, and all the other instruments necessary for the progress of mankind. Rich men could not build any of these things, said Strong, "without giving employment to labor, which receives more of the earnings than capital."[26]

Strong was constantly cautioning his fellow "reformers" not to go too far. We should remember, he declared, that "evolution is the method of social progress." More important than any outward reform, he declared, was our discovery of the invisible workings of Providence in our society. He found it reassuring "to know that there is a Power in the world which makes for progress. Under its unseen guidance life blindly worked its way upward through many gradations to conscious man." Since that time Providence had been "able to overrule human ignorance and folly and greed so as to make them tributary to the progress of the race."[27]

Strong's essential conservatism is apparent in an appeal he made on one occasion for financial support of home missionaries in the West. "You can hardly find a group of ranch-men or miners from Colorado to the Pacific," he quoted one of the ministers in that region as saying, "who will not have on their tongues' end the labor slang of Dennis Kearney, the infidel ribaldry of Robert Ingersoll, the socialistic theories of Karl Marx."[28] One of the obvious advantages of missionaries there would be not merely to save the souls of the ranchers and miners but to cure their economic heresies.

The real limits of the liberalism of Strong are most apparent, however, in his discussion of the intentions of God with regard to the races. Throughout the world of nature, he declared, we can perceive that "the lower was intended as a means to the higher. . . ." Mold gives way to grass, grass gives way to the herd, and the herd gives way to man. Likewise, the inferior races give way to the superior. "Thus the Finns were supplanted by the Aryan races in Europe and Asia, the Tartars by the Russians," he reasoned, "and thus the aborigines of North America, Australia and New Zealand are now disappearing before the all-conquering Anglo-Saxons. It would seem as if these inferior tribes were only precursors of a superior race, voices in the wilderness crying 'Prepare ye the way of the Lord!' "[29]

The religious life of the Anglo-Saxon race, declared Strong, was "more vigorous, more spiritual, more Christian than that of any other." Anglo-Saxons were not, of course, morally perfect. "They will have to answer for many sins against weaker races and against the weaker of their own race," Strong admitted. "They produce as worldly, as gross, as selfish and beastly men and women as do any other people." Yet he went on to say, "But for all that, they exemplify a purer Christianity and are to-day a mightier power for righteousness on earth than any other race." And he asked, "Is there room for doubt that this race, unless devitalized by alcohol and tobacco, is destined to dispossess many weaker races, assimilate others, and mold the remainder, until, in a very true and important sense, it has

Anglo-Saxonized mankind?" In expressing ideas like these, Strong was, of course, reflecting a very strong current of the social thought of his time. John Fiske maintained, for example, that the vigor and independence of the Anglo-Saxon had enabled him to develop societies based upon the ideals of individualism, industrialism, and Protestantism.[30]

Strong was consumed with the optimistic American passion for statistics. One of his favorite mental exercises was to compute the probable increase in the numbers of Anglo-Saxons in future generations. In his calculations, the Anglo-Saxons of England would serve a comparatively minor role. It was the United States which was to be the center of Anglo-Saxon power:

By 1980 the world Anglo-Saxon race should number at least 713,000,-000. Since North America is much bigger than the little English isle, it will be the seat of Anglo-Saxondom.

If human progress follows a law of development, if "Time's noblest offspring is the last," our civilization should be the noblest; for we are "The heirs of all the ages in the foremost files of time," and not only do we occupy the latitude of power, but *our land is the last to be occupied in that latitude.* If the consummation of human progress is not to be looked for here, if there is yet to flower a higher civilization, where is the soil that is to produce it?[31]

Nearly a decade before Frederick Jackson Turner in his famous essay declared that public lands in the United States were nearly all taken up and thus an era had ended, Strong made the same statement. Unlike Turner, Strong did not feel that this event was any reason for pessimism. The result of this depletion, said Strong, would be merely that the Anglo-Saxons would expand overseas:

Then will the world enter upon a new stage of its history—*the final competition of races for which the Anglo-Saxon is being schooled.* If I do not read amiss, this powerful race will move down upon Mexico, down upon Central and South America, out upon the islands of the sea, over upon Africa and beyond. And can anyone doubt that the result of this competition will be the "survival of the fittest"?[32]

One of Strong's grimly amusing inconsistencies is his custom of hailing the conversion of the heathen and then consigning them forthwith to extinction. "If I were a Christian African or Arab, I should look into the immediate future of the United States with intense and thrilling interest," he declared, "for, as Professor Hoppin of Yale has said: 'America Christianized means the *world* Christianized.' " But America—Christianized or not— also seems to have meant annihilation for Africans, Arabs, and members of non-Anglo-Saxon races generally. "Whether the extinction of inferior races before the advancing Anglo-Saxon seems to the reader sad or otherwise," Strong declared, "it certainly appears probable."[33] Perhaps Strong had in mind some distinction between those members of other races who accepted Christianity and those who did not, but he does not say so.

Like many a racist, Strong was ostensibly opposed to race prejudice. "Let us not imagine that we can do much either to Americanize or to Christianize the mixed multitude of the downtown city," he admonished, "so long as we can speak of any human being as 'sheeny,' or 'dago,' or 'coon.' Such characterizations are an insult to our common human nature, and degrade those who are guilty of using them." Since the United States was a Christian nation, it was "peculiarly favorable to the eradication of race prejudice and the cultivation of a broad sympathy which must precede the coming brotherhood of man." But Strong did not always maintain this high moral tone. In describing a tour through the slums of New York, he mentioned seeing "a snoring, disgusting negro wench; an opium-eating, licentious Italian, *et al!*"[34]

Our Country (1885), Strong's most blatantly racist book, sold more than 175,000 copies in American editions and was translated into European and oriental languages. His biographer tells us that the book "made Strong a national figure, brought him repeated requests for lectures and speeches, and was the occasion of his appointment as Secretary of the American Evangelical Alliance. . . ." He traveled a great deal and met with a particularly hearty reception in England, where the way had been paved by an immense circulation of his writings. The book appealed to reformers as well as to conservatives. Richard T. Ely, the Johns Hopkins economist, declared it to be a "valuable" book containing "precisely the information people need."[35]

While Strong was basing his claim of the superiority and inevitable triumph of the Anglo-Saxons upon the idea of evolution with incidental glances in the direction of Holy Scripture, a curious fundamentalist sect of the time was developing the same racist conclusions but with the reasons for them reversed. The Anglo-Israelites also believed that the Anglo-Saxons were God's chosen race; but according to them it was in the Bible, not in the writings of biologists, that one could find proof of their superiority. The movement had begun in England as early as 1837. The Reverend Mr. John Wilson, a nonconformist clergyman, encountered a verse of Scripture in which Jacob pronounced a glorious destiny for his son Joseph. Wilson hit upon the idea that the praise of Joseph's bow and arrow in this verse was somehow a prophecy of the English yeoman with his longbow. Clearly, the English were the descendants of Joseph. The ten tribes of Israel had been carried away by the Assyrians in the eighth century B.C. They had disappeared into the mists of history, but now at last they had been found. They were the Anglo-Saxons of England.[36]

It might be objected that the Englishmen had changed a good deal in their physical appearance, but some of Wilson's followers had an ingenious explanation. Originally the Jews had been a blond people very similar to modern Anglo-Saxons. Did not the Bible say that David had a "ruddy" and "beautiful" countenance? Did not Solomon declare in the canticles, "Behold, thou art fair, my love"? After the crucifixion of Christ, according to one exegete, the physiognomy of the Jews had greatly altered for the worse. "Then, indeed, the Jews became marked, so that all men should know them as heretofore Cain." But the Jews who were members of the ten tribes retained their blondness and their beauty. The Anglo-Saxons were the true Jews, God's chosen people.[37]

In the 1870's the Anglo-Israelite movement spread to America, and in 1884 the parent group in England sent one of their missionaries, the Reverend Mr. Edward Hine, to this country. Where Wilson had been willing to admit all Teutonic peoples as descendants of the Ten Tribes, Hine set the movement on a firmly nationalist basis. In England, he had founded the Anglo-Israel Association, the name of which was later changed to British-Israel Association to meet the objections of its Scotch adherents. One of the most curious figures in the history of religious dissent, Hine was moved by a boundless optimism concerning the coming conversion of America. From Garden City, Long Island, he reported his activities in a letter to one of his friends in England:

I have now held eight drawing-room meetings and delivered five lectures. At one I converted Bishop Littlejohn and Dr. Drone, at another I converted Gen. Hancock who put up for president, and only lost by a few votes; he is much thought of. At another I converted Mr. Grace, Mayor of New York; . . . everywhere I have the ear and the respect of the people. The Rev. Mr. Ingersoll writes me saying the Col. Bob Ingersoll [the militant agnostic] is looking into the Identity [one of Hine's pamphlets], and is much struck by it, and he augurs a new life for this man.

Colonel Ingersoll remained an agnostic and Hine's early successes were not borne out by later events. His lectures did not meet his expenses and he was obliged to write his English adherents for money. A few months later we find him writing, "Humanly speaking, I think I came out too early. Divinely speaking, I think not." When he returned to England three years later, he was almost destitute.[38]

Hine's principal convert in this country was Lieutenant Charles A. L. Totten, a professor of military tactics at Yale. Hine, who was a guest in Totten's home for several weeks, apparently imbued his disciple with the conviction that the Anglo-Saxons are God's chosen race and with a passion for biblical research. Totten founded a periodical entitled *Our Race, Its Origin and Its Destiny,* which lasted from 1890 until 1915 and which

Totten himself edited until his death in 1909. It is filled
with prophecy of events to come, with passionate disputes over
whether the Americans or the British are the true chosen people,
and with paeans of tribute to the racial superiority of the Anglo-
Saxons. The Anglo-Israelite movement continues to this day
both in England and in this country as a religious curiosity.[39]

The theme of the superiority of the Anglo-Saxons and especially the idea that they were destined to replace other races
was not one which appealed to a great many clergymen of the
time. Among them, we find a great deal of praise of Josiah
Strong for his efforts in the home missionary field and his effectiveness as a speaker, but little mention of his favorite theme of
racial superiority. Missionaries abroad were nearly always expansionists and they were supported by powerful religious leaders in this country, but they were not willing to echo Strong's
message that it was the destiny of the nonwhite races to melt
away. Probably more typical than Strong on this point was the
Reverend Mr. John H. Barrows, who declared:

God has placed us like Israel of old, in the center of nations, . . . while
to the west of us is that Asiatic world of immeasurable greatness which
when awakened out of sleep, will combine with America to make the
Pacific ocean the chief highway of the world's commerce . . . and
wherever on pagan shores the voice of the American missionary and
teacher is heard, there is fulfilled the manifest destiny of the Christian
republic. . . .[40]

Perhaps the most authentic disciple of Strong among the
clergy was the Reverend Mr. John Brandt, a Disciples of Christ
minister. In 1915, thirty years after the appearance of Strong's
Our Country, Brandt published his *Anglo-Saxon Supremacy*, a
book which resembles it in some ways. Brandt's blindness to
social and economic forces may be inferred from what he has
to say concerning domestic servants and slums. It was an interesting fact, he observed, that one did not often find Anglo-
Saxon women as house servants or Anglo-Saxons in slums.
Anglo-Saxon women did not think domestic service "beneath

their station," but they sought "a more congenial position in life." These "inferior stations" were filled by German, Austrian, Italian, and Irish women. "That the Anglo-Saxon women know how to do such work is evident from the fact that tens of thousands of them attend to their own household duties, as a matter of economy and independence." In the cities, Brandt tells us, one sees that "those we term foreigners are huddled together in slum districts, along dirty alleys, in illy ventilated tenement houses, whereas the Anglo-Saxons seek for quarters where there is more space, purer atmosphere, better drainage and more congenial surroundings." Like Strong, Brandt approved of American expansionism, but he was a little more sensitive to the problem of the welfare of the natives overseas. Our mission there was "to promote the happiness and comfort of the people." There is no indication that this task included helping the natives to learn how to govern themselves.[41]

If Josiah Strong was not followed by clergymen in his zeal for the coming victories of the Anglo-Saxons, neither was he criticized for his racist theories. No clergymen of the period, it would appear, ever attacked him for his unfeeling attitude toward the rights of nonwhite races. From those men from whom we might have expected criticism—such Social Gospel figures as Theodore Munger, Washington Gladden, Walter Rauschenbusch, Lyman Abbott, and George T. Herron—it was not forthcoming. Strong was apparently approved by these men because he joined with them in their attacks upon economic injustice. They may have thought that since so many men within the churches were poles apart from them in their theological and economic liberalism, it was impolite to examine too closely the ideas of a man who was generally inclined to throw in his lot with them. On a number of occasions, they praised Strong as one of the great pioneers of the Social Gospel movement.[42]

Though it is certainly unlikely that other leaders of the movement shared Strong's ideas on race, one soon notices in their writings a timidity and a general discomfort in the area of racial theory or the rights of racial minorities. Washington Gladden, it is true, did attack the idea that Negroes in the South should be given only vocational education for the lower trades. "If, as seems to be determined, there is to be social separation between the races," he declared in 1909, "that is itself a decisive reason why the black man must have access to the highest culture." These are brave words, but Gladden has other ideas which would seem to cancel them out. He never directly asserts his belief in the innate inferiority of Negroes, but he quotes with apparent approval men who do say or imply that Negroes are innately inferior. For example, Gladden sympathizes with a white southern educator who speaks of the "unexampled difficulties" of educating the "morally undeveloped" Negroes who are "a race, a thousand years behind. . . ." Again, Gladden quotes another southerner who argues that it is wrong "for a superior race to hold down an inferior one that the superior may have the services of the inferior. . . ." And at a time when virtually all the southern states were reducing the proportion of their educational funds devoted to Negro schools, Gladden wrote: "The southern states, it may be said, are making provision for the education of negroes, and it is better to leave the business in their hands."[43]

Occasionally, some of the Social Gospel leaders attempted to explain the successes of the Anglo-Saxons on nonracist grounds. The Anglo-Saxons had produced a superior civilization, said the Reverend Mr. George T. Herron, not because they were innately superior but because they had benefited from the accidents of history. "The commercial and political supremacy of the Anglo-Saxon peoples is largely due," he said, "to the faith of Calvin and Cromwell in the divine government of the world." Such a faith had led to the doctrine of progress and to an unswerving belief in their own destiny, and thus had enabled the Anglo-Saxons to persevere against all odds.[44] Walter Rauschenbusch argued that the ancient free institutions of the Aryans had helped them to create a superior civilization. In addition, Christianity had helped the early Anglo-Saxons to create a society which favored the idea of freedom. "In the Anglo-Saxon communities especially . . . ," Rauschenbusch said, "the spirit of Christianity has been set free sufficiently to do its work in the field of political life, and has found one great outlet for its power in creating a passionate love for freedom and equality." On the other hand, Rauschenbusch argued, the difficulties of other peoples in forming democratic governments might not be the result of racial inferiority. "The chronic difficulty encountered by the Latin nations of Southern Europe and Southern America in making free institutions work," he observed, "is probably not due to any inefficiency of blood or race, but partly to the anti-democratic spirit constantly flowing out from the Roman Church into the national life of peoples, under her control."[45]

On other occasions, Rauschenbusch abandons these attempts to explain civilizations on the basis of institutions and tacitly assumes that racial inequality may after all be the final judgment of science. He argues that large-scale immigration from Catholic countries is bad because their racial stock has been damaged by the celibacy of the clergy. By "sterilizing the best individuals," the Catholics had unwittingly done a disservice to the stock of whole nations. Immigration from these nations to this country had lowered wages and depressed the morale of native Americans, but its worst result had been that it "checked the propagation of the Teutonic stock" and "radically altered the racial future of our nation." This kind of argument is not wholly typical of Rauschenbusch. Mainly, he expressed good will toward all races; but his statements on the subject are marred by feebleness and uncertainty of expression. In 1914, he declared that the problem of Negroes in the South had seemed to him so tragic and insoluble that he had never ventured to discuss it in public, but he knew it must sometime be faced:

We of the North . . . realize . . . we cannot solve it for the South, but no solution by Southern men can be permanent which does not satisfy the Christian consciousness of the whole nation, and no solution will satisfy the Christian spirit of our united Nation which does not provide for the progressive awakening of hope and self respect in the individual Negro and the awakening of race pride and race ambition in all Negro communities.[46]

Lyman Abbott, a prominent member of the Social Gospel movement, did not champion the cause of Anglo-Saxon superiority, but he apparently did believe that the nonwhite races were inferior and he was not a champion of the rights of ethnic minorities. In an article written in 1898 which took the position that Indian reservations should be abolished, Abbott said: "Treat them [the Indians] as we have treated the negro. As a race the African is less competent than the Indian, but we do not shut the negroes up in reservations. . . ." Abbott had heard Henry W. Grady speak in 1886 and had apparently been convinced that the North should allow the white South to settle the "racial problem" in its own way. In 1890, he opposed the bill championed in the Senate by Henry Cabot Lodge which would have guaranteed Negroes the right to vote in federal elections. "The negro problem," said Abbott, "must be worked out by the negroes and the white men of the South with the aid of the North, not by the North or the Federal government over the heads of the white men." Later, when nearly all the Negroes in the South had been disfranchised, he disapproved of the federal government's taking any action; attempts to force political or social equality would inflict "incalculable" injury on the Negro and on the nation.⁴⁷

Thus we see that some of the most advanced thinkers among the clergymen of the time betrayed a curious attitude toward race. At the worst, we find a tremendous blind spot in the sympathies of figures like Horace Bushnell, Theodore Parker, and Josiah Strong who are justly renowned for their willingness to champion unpopular causes and to speak out for the weak and helpless. It apparently never seriously occurred to them that where they saw the mysterious law of God in the disappearance of the nonwhite races before the advancing Anglo-Saxon, a disappearance which apparently occurred without anyone's willing it or doing anything to bring it about, the actual process was a brutal one of oppression, dispossession, and even extermination. In Parker's unstinted praise of the Puritan fathers for their treatment of the Indians, we find optimism so invincible that it no longer has contact with reality. None of these three men shows any sign of having recognized the fact that though they might assign the disappearance of the nonwhite races to the mystic laws of Providence, there were plenty of frontiersmen and other white men who would be only too happy to hasten the process along by killing any natives who got in their way.

None of the Social Gospel clergymen who were contemporaries of Josiah Strong was a racist in the sense that he was. In the context of their times, all the others were spokesmen for moderation and conciliation in racial as well as in other matters. But the fact that the Social Gospel did not produce even one opponent of Strong's racist ethic is significant. Whereas the Social Gospel ministers spoke out openly and fearlessly against other injustices of society, they said nothing with real meaning about racial injustice. It is probable that their hesitation was partly due to their conviction that if they opposed ideas of racial superiority and inferiority, they would seem to be attacking one facet of evolution—the idea of a hierarchy of human races. They were sensitive to the charge that they were sentimental idealists unwilling to take account of the discoveries of science.

If the clergymen of the period most concerned about problems of social and industrial justice were unwilling to champion the cause of the nonwhite races or even that of the immigrants who were not of English or Teutonic stock, we can readily guess just how willing other people were to do so. At the end of the nineteenth century and well into the twentieth, racism greatly restricted the idealism concerning minority ethnic groups in this country which a man could entertain without seeming to fly in the face of the findings of science. The trouble which afflicted the clergymen of the Social Gospel movement was similar to that of the economists, sociologists, and historians of the period who genuinely wished to see a society which was not divided into unbridgeable classes. Before any substantial reforms could come to improve the lot of the minorities, there would have to be a change in the thinking of those people who would be their most logical champions, a change to a view which no longer saw a man as doomed to mediocrity or positive evil because of his race.

IX

Literary Naturalism and Race

RACE PLAYED an important part in American literature long before the era of literary naturalism when Social Darwinist ideas
turned the attention of writers increasingly to biological and
evolutionary explanations of human character. In the novels of
James Fenimore Cooper, early in the nineteenth century, we find
fairly complete the popular stereotypes of racial character—
Negroes of jovial disposition but with very limited intelligence
(one of them has a skull so thick that he is almost immune to
Indian tomahawk attacks), Indians who are naturally wild and
ferocious except for the few "good" Indians made necessary by
the demands of plot, sly and wily half-breeds, and so forth. By
the end of the century, however, racism had greatly expanded
its influence. In earlier novels, such as those of Cooper, the
heroes and heroines are usually presumed to be Anglo-Saxon or
perhaps Norman, with the implicit conviction that these "races"
are superior; but race is most often used to identify quickly and
easily the characteristics of minor figures in the plot. By 1900,
however, racism had become much more definite as an underlying philosophy in fiction. There was an increasing tendency
to describe the characteristics of the heroes and heroines as well
as those of the villains and minor characters in terms of race. In
fact, race for some novelists came to be the principal means of
explaining and understanding all the characters in a novel.

No American writers have done more to publicize race theories and to glorify the Anglo-Saxons than have Frank Norris,
Jack London, and Owen Wister. None of these authors is a ma-

jor figure in American literature, but all of them—and especially London and Wister—wrote books which sold a great many copies.[1] These books are undoubtedly a major source of the spread of popular Social Darwinism, a theory of human experience adapted for literary purposes to explain the importance both of conflict and of heredity, especially of race, in explaining human conduct.

By this time, racism was so much a part of contemporary thought that authors were able to derive explanations for the minds and characters of their literary creations from a great variety of racist sources. The man who did the most to translate race theory into an explicit force in literature was Hippolyte Taine (1828-1893). Although it is uncertain how much he directly influenced the novelists we have mentioned, we can certainly discover ideas similar to his in their writings. Taine represents the union of the forces of Social Darwinism, and its resultant scientific determinism, with those of racism. His theory of civilization is wholly determinist. "History is a mechanical problem," he observes. "The only difference is that it cannot be measured by the same means." This idea leads him to the logical corollary that "virtue and vice are products like vitriol and sugar." The task of the novelist, like that of the literary critic, is to determine the elements which have led to the development of either an individual person, a group of people, or even a nation. These elements, says Taine, can be divided into three kinds: the race, the milieu, and the particular moment in history. Thus, the task of the novelist and the literary critic is to analyze the importance of each of these three influences. His own particular task as a literary critic, for example, was to explain writers in terms of their race, their environment, and the particular time in history in which they wrote.[2]

Taine's ideas on heredity and race are a mixture of Lamarckian ideas of evolution and the pre-Mendelian dependence upon "blood" as the explanation of inherited characteristics. For example, the Saxons in England were "cool-blooded" and "of a cold temperament," so much so that they were essentially nonliterary. His explanation for the decline of English literature in the period following the Norman invasion was that Norman blood had mingled with Saxon blood. The modifications that come about with time are also to be attributed, however, to inheritance of acquired characteristics. "Under this steady pressure the character forms," Taine explained. "That which was habit becomes instinct; the form acquired by the parent is found hereditary in the child." Thus, the character of races can presumably be changed if a sufficiently long period elapses for the ideas of civilization to become a part of their innate character.[3]

Taine also argues that the writing of literature can and ought to be wholly dispassionate and objective. Luckily, he does not seem to have followed this dictum in his own writings. A real attempt to be objective would certainly have been singularly arid, as Edmund Wilson has pointed out. In addition, what he regarded as a reliance upon race theory can easily be translated by the modern reader into a reliance upon literary tradition. For example, he attempts to explain Chaucer in terms of his "racial heritage." All this turns out to mean, however, is that in Chaucer is found a mixture of the imaginative courtly romance of the French literature of his time and "English positive common sense."[4] To handle really doubtful cases, Taine tends to deemphasize the importance of race theory. He can say that it is an oversimplification to treat heredity as if it were "a matter of the transmission of gross aggregates of characters," and he can even say that the "blood" theory of race has definitely been refuted. Or he can say that race is a force which is still insufficiently understood.[5]

Taine's method was to find the dominant trait (*pensée maîtresse*) in the person or nation or race he was considering and build his conceptions around this one trait. Livy he explains, for example, on the basis of his "oratorical instinct." This method, as we might guess, works better with minor figures than it does with major ones, and it really gets into difficulties when it is used to explain whole nations or races. For Taine, the French and the Italians were "races." Their differences can be observed in the fact that "the French, more northern, more prosaic, and more social," have had as their special province "the systematizing of pure ideas, that is to say, the method of reasoning and the art of conversation." On the other hand, the Italian race, "more southern, more artistic, and more given to imagery, has had for its province the ordination of sensible forms, that is to say, music and the arts of design." The German "race," as we might expect, does not come out so well. Taine said he regarded "the human animal" of the Germanic race "as inferior on comparing him with the Italian or southern Frenchman."[6]

Taine's method of explaining individuals, nations, and races on the basis of a single trait has been criticized by Edmund Wilson. "Taine feeds history into a machine which automatically sorts out the phenomena," says Wilson, "so that all the examples of one kind of thing turn up in one section or chapter and all the examples of another kind in another, and the things which do not easily lend themselves to Taine's large and simple generalizations do not turn up at all."[7] In reading Taine, most of us must feel sympathy with Amiel's impression of him: "This writer has a trying effect on me like a creaking of pulleys, a clicking of machines, a smell of the laboratory."[8]

Norris could easily have been influenced by Taine through one of his teachers, Professor Lewis E. Gates. In the composition classes of Professor Gates at Harvard, Norris wrote large portions of his novels *Vandover and the Brute* and *McTeague,* and he declared that he had learned more about writing from Gates than from anyone else.[9] Gates, in turn, described Taine's *History of English Literature,* a work which develops Taine's race theories in some detail, as "a magnificent achievement and a work of the greatest possible significance." On another occasion, he declared that Taine "stands as the one great representative of the scientific method in the study of literature."[10] Even if Norris did not learn of Taine's ideas from Gates, he may well have absorbed them from Emile Zola, who had views on heredity and environment very similar to those of Taine. Zola exerted a tremendous influence upon Norris. Not only his ideas but the details of plot structure and characterization of his novels are closely reflected in Norris' work.[11] All three writers—Norris, London, and Wister—were concerned with hereditary and race tendencies in such a way as to suggest the influence of either Taine or Zola, or perhaps of both.

The similarity between the ideas of Taine and Norris seems unusually close. On one occasion, Norris mentioned the study of race tendencies as one of the most important of the novelist's duties. There are three kinds of novels, he declared. "The ordinary novel merely tells something, elaborates a complication, devotes itself primarily to *things*." The second class of novel is more complicated, dealing with "the workings of temperament," devoting itself to "the minds of human beings." The last variety is the "best class." This kind of novel, said Norris, "proves something, draws conclusions from a whole congeries of forces, social tendencies, race impulses, devotes itself not to a study of men but of man."[12]

The evidence that the three American writers were influenced by Taine is indirect, but the influence of another writer who undoubtedly affected their use of race theories was frankly admitted by all three of them. Frank Norris discovered Rudyard Kipling while in his freshman year in college, and from then on the Englishman was his "adored and venerated author."[13] He was just as much a hero for Jack London. Just as Benjamin Franklin had copied essays in *The Spectator* to improve his style, London served his early writing apprenticeship, his biographer tells us, by "laboriously, in longhand, and for days on end" copying story after story by Kipling.[14] In 1891, Owen Wister came back to his home in the East after several summers in Wyoming, where he had gone to recover his health. In reply to the suggestion of a friend who wanted to know why some Kipling wasn't "saving the sagebrush for American literature," Wister decided to undertake the task himself. A strong admirer of Kipling, Wister in 1895 actually met the great man, and even conferred with him on the subject of a title for a collection of short stories.[15]

What was it in Kipling that these three men admired? Partly it was his vigorous style, his ability to convey the thoughts and language of virile and audacious men. But probably more important than his style was the fact that Kipling offered an escape from the humdrum life of industrialized countries and presented in its place tales of pure adventure. Like the comic books of the present day, some of Kipling's stories written for children were more often read by adults. In *The Jungle Book* (1894), Kipling carries his exaltation of strength and savagery into lands far from the laws of civilization. The boy Mowgli is reared by the wolf pack and learns from his animal companions the law of the struggle for existence and the survival of the fittest. In other stories, Kipling wrote of heroes in distant lands fighting for the cause of Empire or sometimes for the sake of the ideal of courage alone. Proclaiming the indomitable fighting spirit of the Anglo-Saxon and disdaining "the lesser breeds without the law," Kipling represented the active life which appealed to the founders of American literary naturalism.

Kipling's cult of force and energetic enterprise found its reflection in Frank Norris' work. Norris remarked to a friend that his concern was with the "raw man," adding that he was not interested in writing about the orderly and conventional gentleman. He wanted to write of "man with his shirt off, stripped to the buff and fighting for his life."[16] Jack London exhibited a similar liking for unbridled and ruthless heroes who are ready at any time for a crude contest of strength. The hero of his novel *Adventure* cannot explain why he has come to the South Sea islands, but the heroine is able to tell him. "Blind destiny of race," she explains. "We whites have been land-robbers and sea-robbers from remotest time. It is in our blood, I guess, and we can't get away from it." The hero replies thoughtfully, "I never thought about it so abstractly."[17] Owen Wister's cowboy heroes are men who usually settle their difficulties with guns or sometimes with their fists. They are a little casual in their attitude toward law, on occasion seeming to prefer lynch law to any other kind.[18]

Other sources of the race theory of these writers are more difficult to trace. Norris entitled one of his short stories "A Case for Lombroso," but he gives no more specific evidence of interest in the famous criminologist's theories of physiognomy.[19] One way in which he may have developed his race theories was by reading ancient sagas concerning the exploits of folk heroes. His academic record at the University of California indicates that he did well in only one of his literature courses, a study of medieval English poetry. One of his biographers conjectures that Norris' interest in German and Scandinavian sagas may well have come from the reading he did in this course.[20]

Jack London was probably drawn to theories of race by the prejudices of his mother. In the autobiographical *John Barleycorn*, a book written in the cause of temperance, London discusses his early introduction to race theory:

> My mother had theories. First, she steadfastly maintained that brunettes and all the tribe of dark-eyed humans were deceitful. Next, she was convinced that the dark-eyed Latin races were profoundly sensitive, profoundly treacherous, and profoundly murderous. Again and again, drinking in the strangeness and the fearsomeness of the world from her lips, I had heard her state that if one offended an Italian, no matter how slightly and unintentionally, he was certain to retaliate by stabbing one in the back. That was her particular phrase—"stab you in the back."[21]

As a boy of seven, London came near suffering disaster because of his mother's theory about Italians. He had wandered into a saloon and a drunken Italian there offered him a half-glass of strong wine. Although he hated the taste, London remembered what his mother had said about what would happen if he made an Italian angry, and he gulped down the wine exactly as if it had been medicine. Surprised to see the wine disappear so readily, the Italian offered the child another glass and then another. The men in the saloon gathered around to see the miraculous child who could drink an indefinite amount of wine. He drank so much and became so ill that years later he wondered how his heart and brain stood the terrible aftereffects.[22]

London could ridicule the race superstitions of his mother, but they are hardly more extreme than those which he himself maintained throughout his life.

From his writings, it is impossible to tell much about the source of his ideas. His daughter, Joan London, has said that although he read Darwin, Spencer, Nietzsche, and Marx, he was far more concerned with the dramatic value of their ideas for his fiction than he was with their strict truth. The influence of Nietzsche especially, she says, was based on little else than her father's penchant for such phrases as "the blond beasts," "the glad perishers," "the superman," and "live dangerously!"[23] One sociologist who seems to have influenced him was Benjamin Kidd, an Englishman whose book, *Social Evolution,* was immensely successful on both sides of the Atlantic in 1894. It was Kidd's thesis that the Anglo-Saxon race, though it was the most profoundly altruistic of all the races, had a degenerating effect on the inferior races with which it came into contact. When confronted with the Anglo-Saxons, the inferior races tended naturally to die off. Nothing could stay this mighty law, this "destiny which works itself out irresistibly." Whatever the Anglo-Saxons might intend, "the weaker races disappear before the stronger through the effects of mere contact."[24] This theory was useful to London because it absolved his heroes from responsibility for the fate of the "inferior" races, since they would disappear anyway. Thus, he could present the heroes as both altruistic and predatory.

One of the curious contradictions in London's thought is that between his socialism and his racism. He believed in a cooperative society, he said on one occasion, but only for white men. In an interview in 1900 he is quoted as saying that he believed democracy could be achieved by all peoples whose institutions, ideals, and traditions were Anglo-Saxon; but he was silent on the chances for democracy among other peoples. Several months later, he ruled out the possibility that any system could alleviate tensions among the races. In another interview, he declared:

Socialism is not an ideal system, devised by man for the happiness of all life; nor for the happiness of all men; but it is devised for the happiness of certain kindred races. It is devised so as to give more strength to these certain kindred favored races so that they may survive and inherit the earth to the extinction of the lesser, weaker races. The very men who advocate socialism may tell you of the brotherhood of all men, and I know they are sincere; but that does not alter the laws— they are simply instruments, working blindly for the betterment of these certain kindred races, and working detriment to the inferior races they would call brothers. It is the law; they do not know, perhaps; but that does not change the logic of events.[25]

At a meeting of the Socialist party in San Francisco some of the members once tried to argue with London that an emphasis upon the "Yellow Peril" and race doctrines in general were harmful to the party and inconsistent with its program. London is said to have met their arguments by pounding on the table and exclaiming, "What the devil! I am first of all a white man and only then a Socialist!"[26]

Owen Wister rarely refers to any kind of source or authority in setting forth his race doctrines. He wrote one novel with a South Carolina setting in which there is a good deal of discussion concerning race problems in the South. In this novel, *Lady Baltimore*, there is an unnamed German whose hobby is ethnology and who has a collection of skulls in Charleston. The ethnologist attempts to explain to the hero, who has come from the North and is critical of the South's handling of its race problems, why all attempts to raise the Negro to the level of the white man must fail. He places the skull of a Negro between that of an ape and that of a white man. "There was a similarity of shape, a kinship there between the three, which stared you in the face," the hero reflected, "but in the contours of the vaulted skull, the projecting jaws, and the great molar teeth—what was to be seen? Why, in every respect that the African departed from the Caucasian, he departed in the direction of the ape. Here was zoölogy mutely but eloquently telling us why there had blossomed no Confucius, no Moses, no Napoleon, upon that black stem; why no Iliad, no Parthenon, no Sistine Madonna,

had ever risen from that tropic mud."²⁷ The hero comes to see
that his former attitude was sentimental humanitarianism and
hopelessly unscientific. Apparently, Wister means to convert his
readers to the belief that craniology is a science which clearly
differentiates superior from inferior races.

Sometimes Wister appears to have been influenced by racist
theories of Teutonic origins. He attempts to compare, at one
point, the essential differences in outlook between two justices of
the Supreme Court, Oliver Wendell Holmes and Louis Brandeis.
Because these two men have sometimes taken the same view in a
given case, Wister observes, the uninformed have tended to class
them together. Such a conclusion Wister believed to be a profound mistake, and he exclaims, "I doubt if any gulf exists more
impassable than the one which divides the fundamental processes of a Holmes from those of a Brandeis. . . ." The difference
is that Holmes has behind him "the English Common Law,
evolved by the genius of a people who have built themselves the
greatest nation in a thousand years." Brandeis, on the other
hand, is descended "from a noble and ancient race which has
radiated sublimity in several forms across the centuries, but has
failed in all centuries to make a stable nation of itself."²⁸

Wister attempts to isolate the implications of this difference
between the two justices by referring to a particular legal case.
The owners of a tract of land had sold it with the agreement
that the buyers would not have recourse for damages through
the sinking of the surface caused by mining operations. Forty-
three years later a state law was passed which forbade mining
companies to disturb the surface of land near a dwelling house.
After the law was passed, the owner of the dwelling house sued
a coal company because of damage caused by the sinking of his
land. The coal company maintained that on this particular property the law was not applicable because of the prior contract.
The Supreme Court sustained the contention of the coal company. Justice Holmes agreed with the decision that the coal company could not be forced to pay damages, but Justice Brandeis
wrote a dissenting opinion, arguing that enforcement by the

state of its law was a legitimate exercise of police power. Holmes realized, said Wister, that the duty of a justice was to declare what the law is and "never to assert or to further any humanitarian or political bent." As long as Holmes's concept was maintained, Wister concluded, the Commonwealth would stand secure. If Brandeis' concept became generally accepted, our nation would crumble just as the Jewish nation "crumbled in ancient days despite the sublime genius of its Oriental race." And Wister added, "That there are no short cuts to anything except perdition, is a legal concept beyond an Oriental mind, when humanitarian considerations, such as a hardship done to a poor man by a rich company, tempt it to alleviate an individual at the expense of a principle."[29]

We can discover a good deal about the racism of these three authors by examining the appearance and character of their heroes and heroines. Nearly all of these are tall and athletic blonds with blue or gray eyes. Billy Roberts, the hero of Jack London's *The Valley of the Moon*, is typical. A teamster and an ex-prizefighter, Billy has golden hair, blue-gray eyes, and big muscles. He has a "short, square-set nose," "rosy cheeks," a "firm, short upper lip" and a "well-modeled, large clean mouth where red lips smiled clear of white, enviable teeth." He reminds the heroine of the novel, Saxon Brown, of a picture she had cherished since childhood of the Anglo-Saxon invasion of England:

Between bold headlands of rock and under a gray cloud-blown sky, a dozen boats, long and lean and dark, beaked like monstrous birds, were landing on a foam-whitened beach of sand. The men in the boats, half naked, huge-muscled and fair-haired, wore winged helmets. In their hands were swords and spears, and they were leaping waist-deep, into the sea-wash and wading ashore. Opposed to them, contesting the landing, were skinclad savages, unlike Indians, however, who clustered on the beach or waded in the water to their knees. The first blows were being struck, and here and there the bodies of the dead and wounded rolled in the surf. One fair-haired invader lay across the gunwale of a boat, the manner of his death told by the arrow that transfixed his breast. In the air, leaping past him into the water, sword in hand, was Billy. There was no mistaking it. The striking blondness, the face, the eyes, the mouth were the same.[30]

The heroes of Frank Norris' novels usually bear a close resemblance to those of London's. He too admired the "big-boned, blond, long-haired type—the true Anglo-Saxon. . . ." In a historical tale of early Anglo-Saxon freebooters, Norris has a character whom apparently he means to be archetypical, an ancient hero described in battle as having "great bare shoulders gleaming with his blood, the long braids of yellow soaked with it. Awful, gigantic, suddenly a demi-god, he stood colossal, a man made more than human." Sometimes Norris makes his heroes less handsome than those of London, probably to emphasize their crude power. Ward Bennett, the hero explorer of Norris' novel, *A Man's Woman,* is described as an "ugly man. . . . His lower jaw was huge almost to deformity, like that of the bulldog, the chin salient, the mouth close-gripped, with great lips, indomitable, brutal. The forehead was contracted and small, the forehead of the men of single ideas, and the eyes, too, were small and twinkling."[31]

Wister's heroes usually are less spectacular and more conventionally handsome. One of them is described as a man "powerful, blue-eyed, his mustache golden, his cheek cleancut, and beaten to shining health by the weather." Another has "blue and merry eyes" and "sunny yellow" hair. Wister's most famous hero, the Virginian, is an exception to the general rule of blondness. Although he is a "slim young giant," the Virginian not only has black hair, but is even described as "swarthy." However, the Virginian is "of old stock in Virginia English" with one Scotch-Irish grandmother, so there is no question about his race.[32] The heroes of London, Norris, and Wister are often described as "bronzed by the sun," partly that their outdoor character may be emphasized, perhaps, but there may have been some feeling that a man with too blond a complexion would run the risk of being thought effeminate.

The heroines, too, of these three writers are usually tall, athletic, with blue or gray eyes. With one exception, they are not so muscular and intrepid as the heroes, but they are still likely to be a little startling to anyone accustomed to conventional heroines. It is Norris who carries the idea of the physically powerful heroine to the farthest extreme. Moran, the daughter of a Norwegian sea captain in his novel *Moran of the Lady Letty,* is not identified as an Anglo-Saxon, though Norris seems to have felt that the qualities of Norwegians and Anglo-Saxons were identical. Moran is "not pretty." Her body is "too massive," her hands are red and hard, and "even beneath the coarse sleeve of the oilskin coat one could infer that the biceps and deltoids were large and powerful." Still, her "fine animal strength of bone and muscle," her "splendid ropes" of yellow hair, and her "heavy contralto voice" give her "a certain amount of attraction." When Moran joins the hero in combat against a group of Chinese seamen, she apparently achieves a kind of atavistic communion with her old Norse forebears. "With a voice hoarse from shouting," Norris tells us, "she sang, or rather chanted, in her long-forgotten Norse tongue, fragments of old sagas, words, and sentences, meaningless even to herself." Norris' other heroines are somewhat more feminine, although they still belong to the athletic convention. Lloyd Seabright in *A Man's Woman* is "regal" and "very straight as well as very tall." She can "look down upon most women and upon not a few men." Travis Bessemer, the heroine of *Blix,* is tall and "solidly, almost heavily built," with "broad" shoulders, a "deep chest," and a "round and firm" neck. She has "stamina, good physical force, and fine animal vigour." Her hair is "not golden nor flaxen, but plain, honest yellow."[33]

A curiosity of Norris' fiction is that many of his heroines have masculine names. Although his own daughter was christened with the name of Jeannette, he is said never to have called her by any name but Billy. Norris admired the forthright Gibson Girl of the 1890's. "The Gibson girl is more serious perhaps [than other girls]," he wrote on one occasion, "and you must keep keyed pretty high to enjoy her society. But somehow you feel she's a 'man's woman' and could stand by a fellow and back him up if things should happen." None of his other heroines, however, are as powerful as Moran. At one point Norris is enthusiastic enough to describe her as stronger in muscle than even the hero, Ross Wilbur, but this extravagance of language is not borne out by events. Later in the novel Moran challenges Ross to personal combat; he accepts, and she undergoes the ignominy of defeat.[34]

Neither London nor Wister cared as much as Norris did for lady wrestler types. The heroines of London usually have a good deal of the femininity of the conventional heroine, although they are fit helpmeets for the muscular heroes. The unnamed heroine in his short story, "Amateur Night," has "a robustness in a finer than the wonted sense, a vigorous daintiness, which gave an impression of virility with none of the womanly left out." Joan Lackland, the heroine of his novel, *Adventure,* is described as "the most masculine and at the same time the most feminine woman" whom the hero had ever met. This device of giving his heroines both feminine and masculine traits was apparently not always satisfactory to London. In one of his later novels, he solved the problem by giving the heroine a slightly different racial inheritance from that of the hero. Billy Roberts, the hero of *The Valley of the Moon,* is a pure example of the Anglo-Saxon, but the heroine, Saxon Brown, has a slight but significant intermixture of blood. "She was a flower of Anglo-Saxon stock," but she did not have the traditional heaviness, size, and strength of the Anglo-Saxon. She was "a rarity in the exceptional smallness and fineness of hand and foot and bone and grace of flesh and carriage—some throw-back across the face of time to the foraying Norman French that has intermingled with the sturdy Saxon breed."[35]

Wister, perhaps because he spent his early years in a more genteel society than did either Norris or London, is content with a more old-fashioned kind of heroine. The women of his fiction are high-spirited, but they do not challenge anyone to physical combat and they have no traits which are identifiably masculine. The gentility of Wister's heroines is illustrated by Molly Wood, a girl who has come West from Vermont and who nurses the Virginian back to health after he has been shot by Indians. The

Virginian has to undergo the embarrassment of revealing part of his past. Has he, Molly asks him, ever been shot before?

Only once, he told her. "I have been lucky in having few fusses," said he. "I hate them. If a man has to be killed—"
"You never—" broke in Molly. She had started back a little. "Well," she added hastily, "don't tell me if—"
"I shouldn't wonder if I got one of those Indians," he said quietly.

Further in the book, Wister tells us more concerning the Virginian's attitude toward women:

It was his code never to speak ill of any man to any woman. Men's quarrels were not for women's ears. In his scheme, good women were to know only a fragment of men's lives. He had lived many outlaw years, and his wide knowledge of evil made innocence doubly precious to him.[36]

A code like this would never have appealed to the heroes of Norris and London.

Wister was aware that athletic and forcefully direct women were emerging both in American life and in American fiction, but he seems not to have liked them. Hortense Rieppe, the evil woman in his novel, *Lady Baltimore,* is apparently created as a protest against the vigorous and emancipated women then attracting attention in this country. The narrator of the novel speaks of Hortense's arrogant beauty and reflects that "she contained nothing of the past, and a great deal of tomorrow." But it is clear that he prefers the past:

I basked myself in the memory of her achieved beauty, her achieved dress, her achieved insolence, her luxurious complexity. She was even later than those quite late athletic girls, the Amazons of the links, whose big, hard, football faces stare at one from public windows and from public prints, whose giant, manly strides take them over leagues of country and square miles of dance-floor, and whose bursting, blatant, immodest health glares upon sea-beaches and round supper-tables.[37]

The eyes of the heroes and heroines in the fiction of the three writers were, as we have seen, likely to be either blue or gray, but one characteristic they frequently share is that the color of their eyes is somewhat uncertain and it changes under the excitement of emotion. Joan Lackland in London's novel, *Adventure*, is described as having "flashing gray eyes," but they change color when their owner is angry or excited. Owen Wister's heroine, Molly Wood, could not decide what color the Virginian's eyes were. "That strange color of the sea-water, which she could never name," Wister tells us at a tender moment in the story, "was lustrous in his eyes." Wolf Larsen, the superman ship captain in London's *The Sea-Wolf*, has eyes of a "baffling protean gray which is never twice the same" and they change according to the mood of their owner:

They were eyes that masked the soul with a thousand guises, and that sometimes opened, at rare moments, and allowed it to rush up as though it were about to fare forth nakedly into the world on some wonderful adventure,—eyes that could brood with the hopeless sombreness of leaden skies; that could snap and crackle points of fire like those which sparkle from a whirling sword; that could grow chill as an arctic landscape, and yet again, that could warm and soften and be all a-dance with love-light, intense and masculine, luring and compelling, which at the same time fascinate and dominate women till they surrender in a gladness of joy and of relief and sacrifice.

London apparently thought that a distinguishing mark of Anglo-Saxons was the fact that their eyes change color. Saxon Brown is aware that the eyes of her rugged sweetheart, Billy Roberts, are not the eyes of a Scandinavian. "So blond was he," says London, "that she was reminded of stage-types she had seen, such as Ole Olson and Yon Yonson; but there the resemblance ceased. It was not a matter of color only, for the eyes were dark-lashed and -browed, and were cloudy with temperament rather than staring a child-gaze of wonder. . . ." Another apparent distinguishing mark of Anglo-Saxon eyes is that they are wide apart. London says of Wolf Larsen that his eyes are "wide apart as the true artist's are wide."[38]

Blond hair, although not an indispensable mark of the Anglo-Saxon, was one of the usual recognizable characteristics.

London, at one point, attempted to divide the characters in a novel into two groups of blond and brunet and to assign general characteristics to both groups. In *The Mutiny of the Elsinore* the unnamed narrator notes that the men in command of the ship on which he is a passenger are nearly all blonds, whereas most of the crew are brunets. "Every one of us who sits aft in the high place is a blond Aryan," he observes.

For'ard, leavened with a ten per cent of degenerate blonds, the remaining ninety per cent of the slaves that toil for us are brunettes. . . . The best of the food and all spacious and beautiful accommodation is ours. . . . For'ard is a pigsty and a slave pen. As a king, Captain West sits above all. . . . Miss West [his daughter] is a princess of the royal house.[39]

Speculation upon the heredity, including the racial heredity, of their characters is a prominent feature of all three novelists. In his short story, "Thoroughbred," for example, Norris constructs a brief parable intended to illustrate the power of good blood. "Once there were two men in love with the same girl," he forthrightly begins, "and this is the story of how the one was taken and the other left." One of the suitors is Jack Brunt, "a tower of leathery muscles and hard, tough sinew and fibre, and used to crack walnuts in the hollow of his arm." He is a handsome man, "with fine, high colouring, brown eyes, and a drooping brown moustache." Nor is he merely handsome. He is a "self-made man, true son of the people, a man whom other men, children, and *some* women like," although his manners are rather coarse. He has made his money by hard work, and when businessmen speak of him they say he is "a good *earnest* fellow with no nonsense about him."[40]

The other candidate for the girl's hand is Wesley Shotover, who appears on the surface at least to be much inferior to Jack Brunt. His hair is blond, his eyes are blue, and he has "almost the face of a girl, smooth, guiltless of beard, and invariably calm." It is "just saved from effeminacy by certain masculine dints about the nostrils and between the cheek bones and the angle of the jaw." He is a thoroughly frivolous young man, spending his time smoking cigarettes, eating chocolate nougats, and drinking French vermouth. In addition, he does "many things which cannot be noted here." Because he has inherited a million and a half dollars, he can afford to waste his time. Women are fond of Shotover, Norris observes, but men are not. They say he will "never amount to much, which in America is the very worst thing one man can say of another."⁴¹

But Brunt's advantages over Shotover are illusory. His trouble is bad heredity. One grandfather had been "a stone cutter from Colusa." Nor are his American ancestors of the best. In the eighteenth century they were being leased out to labor contractors "to grub and grapple under the whip with the reluctant colonial soil." Shotover's ancestors, however, were "framing laws, commanding privateers, and making history generally in the days of the *Constitution* and the *Bonhomme Richard*." Still, Norris adds, both the ancestors of Brunt and those of Shotover were mainly Americans "and a certain document that a Shotover had helped to draw up told them both that all men are created equal." An incident occurs which shows that the two men are essentially and innately different. Both suitors come to call on the heroine at the same time and while they are sitting on the veranda of her home in San Francisco, a gang of opium-crazed Chinese attack them with the intent of looting the place. Shotover springs to the heroine's defense and masters the whole mob with only a whip, but Brunt makes a cowardly retreat into the house. When the trouble is over, he comes out with the flimsy excuse that he had gone searching for a revolver. "They never saw very much of Brunt after that day," Norris concludes, and of course Shotover wins the heroine.⁴²

In Wister's novels, both pride of family and pride of race are strong. Cowboys are sometimes natural heroes and thus the conventions of a good genealogy do not always matter very much, but it is significant that the Virginian is equipped with a long line of fighting ancestors, including some who fought under Old Hickory. In one of Wister's essays, "The Evolution of the

Cow-Puncher," there is a revealing comparison between the aristocracy of the cowboy and that of the English nobleman. Wister mentions having shared a railway coach in England with a nobleman and a cowboy from Texas. "The peer leisurely took brandy, and was not aware of our presence," Wister tells us. The Englishman had all the trappings of comfort—traveling rugs, cut glass containers for his liquor, a sandwich box displaying his monogram. "He had understood life's upholstery and trappings for several hundred years, getting the best to be had in each generation of his noble descent." Wister obviously admires the Englishman, but the cowboy in the compartment did not, presumably because the Englishman didn't offer to share his liquor. "I'll trouble you for a light," the cowboy said to the aristocrat, and Wister detects in his voice "his poor opinion of feudalism." But the Englishman is entirely equal to the occasion. "His lordship returned the drawl—not audibly, but with his eye, which he ran slowly up and down the stranger. His was the Piccadilly drawl; the other made use of the trans-Missouri variety; and both these are at bottom one and the same—the Anglo-Saxon's note of eternal contempt for whatever lies outside the bent of his personal experience."[43]

This casual incident has a rather unusual sequel. Later, Wister heard, the nobleman fell into some kind of disgrace with his family in England and was obliged to emigrate. He went to Texas. "Directly the English nobleman smelt Texas," Wister tells us, "the slumbering untamed Saxon awoke in him, and mindful of the tournament, mindful of the hunting-field, galloped howling after wild cattle, a born horseman, a perfect athlete, and spite of the peerage and gules and argent, fundamentally kin with the drifting vagabonds who swore and galloped by his side. The man's outcome typifies the way of his race from the beginning."[44] Real Anglo-Saxon aristocracy, then, can generally be counted upon to meet the demands of vigorous frontier life, to master the feats of strength and agility required of the American cowboy.

For London, pride of race was apparently a substitute for

pride of family. Perhaps because he himself had been an illegitimate child, London has only sneering things to say of those who are proud of their family genealogy. Such pride he usually equates with pride of wealth, and as a vehement socialist he is intent upon proving that wealth is a mere accident, not necessarily the reward of innate virtue. To his rich and cultivated passenger, Humphrey Van Weyden, Wolf Larsen in *The Sea-Wolf* makes a querulous speech about his disadvantages as a youth. He might have been a ruler and conqueror of the whole world, he maintains, had he been given the advantages of study and development available to young men with wealthy parents. Sometimes London liked to have women of high birth in his novels. Vesta Saxon in *The Scarlet Plague*, for example, is the daughter of a multimillionaire industrial magnate and is "the perfect flower of generations of the highest culture this planet has ever produced." For his heroes, however, London seems to prefer poor and humble beginnings.[45]

On the other hand, the racial ancestry of London's heroes is most important. With the captain's daughter, Margaret West, London's unnamed narrator in the novel *The Mutiny of the Elsinore* climbs aloft in the rigging of the ship. He tells her that he has a dim racial memory of seafaring life:

It is nothing new. I have been here before. In the lives of all my fathers have I been here. The frost is on my cheek, the salt bites my nostrils, the whining wind chants in my ears, and it is an old happening. I know, now, that my forebears were Vikings. . . . With them I have raided English coasts, dared the Pillars of Hercules, forayed the Mediterranean, and sat in the high place of government over the sun-warm peoples. I am Hengist and Horsa; I am of the ancient heroes even legendary to them. I have bearded and bitted the frozen seas, and, aforetime of that ever the ice ages came to be, I have dripped my shoulders in reindeer gore, slain the mastodon and the saber-tooth, scratched the record of my prowess on the walls of deep-buried caves—aye, and suckled she-wolves side by side with my brother cubs, the scars of whose fangs are now upon me.

Miss West apparently can think of no proper reply to all this, but she approves of it and "laughs deliciously."[46]

The important point for the heroes of all three novelists is not so much whether they have or do not have wealth but that they do not depend upon it. Curtis Jadwin, the hero of Norris' *The Pit,* is a powerful, virile capitalist, but he is obliged to begin life over at the end of the novel when the market goes against him, and apparently he suffers no fall in the author's scale of status. London's heroes sometimes strike it rich as prospectors or adventurers of one kind or another, but much more important than money to them is the ability to wield power over men, to dominate them by sheer physical strength. A Wister cowboy hero usually owns no more than his horse and saddle. The Virginian does settle down after he falls in love, it is true, but he merely becomes the trusted foreman of another man's ranch, not a capitalist in his own right. A contempt for money, a willingness to risk everything on a hand of poker, Wister seems to feel, is an admirable cowboy trait. When he is writing about easterners, however, he employs rather different standards. Then his heroes are generally wealthy, or at least affluent enough so that the making of money is not one of their major interests. Wister seldom emphasizes the race of his eastern heroes, but he nearly always does that of his cowboy heroes. Apparently his eastern heroes are Anglo-Saxons too, but in a more civilized society the fact of race is presumably less important.

Sometimes other races are admirable and brave in the novels of the three authors, but this is rare and when it happens it is usually explained away. Wister, for example, recognizes that Mexicans had demonstrated their ability as *vaqueros* before the Anglo-Saxon cowboy came along, but he is not much impressed by them:

I do not think that he [the cowboy] rode with bolder skill than the Mexicans, but he brought other and grittier qualities to bear upon that wild life, and also the Saxon contempt for the foreigner. Soon he had taken what was good from this small, deceitful alien, including his name, *Vaquero,* which he translated into Cow-boy. He took his saddle, his bridle, his spurs, his rope, his methods of branding and herding—indeed, most of his customs and accoutrements—and with them he went rioting over the hills. His playground was two thousand miles long and a thousand miles wide.[47]

Other non-Anglo-Saxon races had even fewer of the qualities necessary for success as cowboys. No country had suffered as much as the United States, declared Wister, from the influx of "debased and mongrel" immigrants from southern and eastern Europe, "encroaching alien vermin, that turn our cities to Babels and our citizenship to a hybrid farce, who degrade our common-wealth from a nation into something half pawn-shop, half broker's office." Fortunately, it required "courage," "the spirit of adventure," and "self-sufficiency" to survive in "the clean cattle country," and thus inferior races generally did not venture there. "You will not find," declared Wister, "many Poles or Huns or Russian Jews in that district."[48]

The contempt of Norris and London for some of the non-Anglo-Saxon races fully matches that of Wister. One of London's favorite themes is that some races are naturally born to servitude, since it is part of their very nature. One of his Alaskan heroes is obliged to draw a gun to assert his rights in a poker game. He says of one of his cardshark opponents, "Look at the fat Jew there. This little weapon's sure put the fear of God in his heart. He's yellow as a sick persimmon."[49] Jews in Norris' stories are usually cowardly, venal, and deceitful. Even worse is the half-breed:

Imagine the Mongolian and African types merged into one. He should have the flat nose, and yet the almond eye; the thick lip, and yet the high cheek bone; but how as to his hair? Should it be short and crinkly, or long and straight, or merely wavy? But the ideas of the man, his bias, his prejudices, his conception of things, his thoughts—what a jumble, what an amorphous, formless mist![50]

What would be considered murderous brutality in other races sometimes shows up as splendid raw courage in the Anglo-Saxon heroes of these three writers. Wister's cowboys are cruel enough when their code demands cruelty, but they usually have a horror of the man who refuses to live by the rules, the outlaw. Norris and London, on the other hand, admired courage and strength so much that they sometimes seem to be saying that these are the only virtues which matter. Ward Bennett in Norris' *A Man's Woman* springs to the aid of Lloyd Seabright, his sweetheart, when her horse goes out of control. Bennett seizes a hammer and without a moment's hesitation crushes the horse's skull. "There was a primitiveness, a certain hideous simplicity in the way Bennett had met the situation," Norris tells us, "that filled her [Lloyd] with wonder and with even a little terror and mistrust of him." And yet, on reflection, the girl admires Ward for his directness and strength. She admires "a force and a power of mind that stopped at nothing to attain its ends, that chose the shortest cut, the most direct means, disdainful of hesitation, holding delicacy and finessing in measureless contempt." Later in the book, Lloyd has apparently expanded this idea almost into a philosophy. "The world wants men," she says, "great, strong, harsh, brutal men—men with purposes, who let nothing, nothing, nothing stand in their way." Ross Wilbur, the hero of *Moran of the Lady Letty,* has an even more ferocious outlook. "Did you ever kill a man, Jerry?" Wilbur asks an inexperienced friend. "No? Well, . . . Kill one some day. . . ."[51]

London, too, admires intensely the superman who sweeps all opposition before him. "I believe that life is a mess," declares Captain Wolf Larsen in *The Sea-Wolf.*

It is like yeast, a ferment, a thing that moves and may move for a minute, an hour, a year or a hundred years, but that in the end will cease to move. The big eat the little that they may continue to move, the strong eat the weak that they may retain their strength. The lucky eat the most and move the longest, that is all.

Fulfilling this philosophy, Larsen brutally dominates the crew of his ship. To punish the ship's cook, for example, he has him dangled over a school of sharks and one of them bites off his foot. London attempts to excuse the evil of Captain Larsen by presenting it, not as calculated wrong, but as a necessary consequence of his tremendous and primordial virtues. Larsen is "a perfect type of primitive man, born a thousand years or generations too late and an anachronism. . . ." Viewed in this light, he is "not immoral, but merely unmoral." The men under his command exhibit a different kind of evil. They are "suffering brutes that grovelled before him and revolted only in drunkenness and in secrecy." Their faces exhibit "hard lines and the marks of the free play of the passions." Larsen, on the other hand, is a "mighty spirit" whose desire to achieve makes it necessary for him brutally to break other men's wills. His features display "no such evil stamp." There is nothing "vicious" in them, London tells us. "True, there were lines, but they were the lines of decision and firmness. It seemed, rather, a frank and open countenance. . . ."[52]

Neither Norris nor London is wholly comfortable with eulogies of brute force. Sometimes they both show signs of recognizing that moderation and restraint might be virtues worth cultivating. Characteristically, when these qualities appear in their novels, they belong exclusively to Anglo-Saxons; and previous praise of the magnificent contempt which Anglo-Saxons feel for moral quibbling is ignored. At a picnic, Presley, the poet in Norris' *The Octopus*, reflects that the California ranchers and farmers are kindly Anglo-Saxons:

It was Homeric, this feasting, this vast consuming of meat and bread and wine, followed now by games of strength. An epic simplicity and directness, an honest Anglo-Saxon mirth and innocence, commended it. Crude it was; coarse it was, but no taint of viciousness was here. These people were good people, kindly, benignant even, always readier to give than to receive, always more willing to help than to be helped. They were good stock. Of such was the backbone of the nation—sturdy Americans every one of them.

On a community rabbit hunt, the kindliness of Anglo-Saxons is contrasted with the cruelty of other races. When the rabbits are trapped in an enclosure, the half-breed helpers of the ranchmen and farmers move in for the kill. "Blindly, furiously, they struck and struck," Norris tells us. "The Anglo-Saxon spectators round about drew back in disgust, but the hot, degenerated blood of

Portuguese, Mexican, and mixed Spaniard boiled up in excitement at this wholesale slaughter."[53]

Although he obviously admires his character Wolf Larsen intensely, London is unwilling wholly to endorse his Social Darwinist philosophy. The effete and wealthy Humphrey Van Weyden, the narrator passenger who fell from the rail of his own ship and was later picked up by Wolf Larsen, is allowed to triumph to some degree over his tormentor. Deserted by his crew and unable to save his ship from destruction, doomed by cerebral cancer which causes him to go blind, Larsen is finally defeated. Van Weyden wins the girl whom Larsen had tried to win. Though Larsen dies, he dies a magnificent pagan and one who still maintains the philosophy to which London himself often seems to be more than half converted.

London sometimes equips his Anglo-Saxons with an innate regard for law, a quality which would seem to be inconsistent with the creed that power is all that matters. In one short story, Edith Whittlesey, an English servant girl, emigrates to America and marries Hans Nelson, a Swedish immigrant. Hans is "a large-muscled, stolid sort of man, in whom little imagination was coupled with immense initiative, and who possessed, withal, a loyalty and affection as sturdy as his strength." Edith and Hans go to Alaska to prospect for gold, pooling their resources with three men. One of their partners is Dennin, an Irishman, who turns out to be a murderous villain. When the group discovers gold, Dennin wants it all for himself. He kills the two other partners and attempts to kill Hans and Edith, but Hans is able to overpower him before he can load his gun for another shot."[54]

At this point in the story, a respect for law turns out to be an Anglo-Saxon but not a Teutonic race characteristic. Hans is Teutonic and he wants to kill Dennin immediately, but Edith insists that—even though there are only the three of them in the wilderness—Dennin must be given a trial. "Nor was it a sense of piety, nor obedience to the 'Thou shalt not' of religion," London tells us. "Rather was it some sense of law, an ethic of her race and early environment, that compelled her to interpose her body between her husband and the helpless murderer." Although London does give some recognition here to forces of environment, more important for him is that Edith "could not escape . . . from the blood that was in her." Hans, on the other hand, has no innate feeling concerning law and gives in to his wife's judgment on this matter only because he recognizes that she has qualities superior to his own.[55] Hans and Edith are so far from civilization that they are obliged to serve as judge, jury, and executioner for Dennin, but we can't expect instinct to take care of everything.

Only faint echoes of the old argument that the Anglo-Saxon has no artistic or literary genius occur in the fiction of these three writers. London is apparently willing to admit that the Anglo-Saxon is not musical. Billy Roberts, one of his heroes whose racial virtues are most strongly emphasized, sings a song, "Bury Me Not on the Lone Prairie," for Saxon Brown. She reflects that she has "discovered the first flaw in him. He was tone-deaf. Not once had he been on the key."[56]

London does not openly admit that the Anglo-Saxon is deficient in ideas or in imagination, but sometimes he seems to be working from this assumption. He creates characters in which the lack of such qualities does not matter. Captain West in *The Mutiny of the Elsinore* is obviously not a reader or thinker. "He has all the poise and air of a remote and superior being," reflects the narrator, "and yet I wonder if it be not poise and air and nothing else. . . . I now find myself almost forced to conclude that his touch of race, and beak of power, and all the tall, aristocratic slenderness of him have nothing behind them." When the narrator offers West a copy of William James's *Varieties of Religious Experience*, West returns it with the comment that it does not interest him. All other attempts to engage the captain in discussion of books or ideas likewise fail. So determined is London to make Captain West into an impressive man that he converts the indifference into a positive virtue. Captain West is like George Washington, the narrator decides, a man of action and not a man of ideas. He has a "lonely eminence" and a freedom from "the strivings of the elements." In short, he is above the uncertainties of ordinary men. He is "a samurai." Sheldon, the hero of *Adventure,* is another of London's great silent men. "Life pulsed steadily and deep in him," we are told, "and it was not his nature needlessly to agitate the surface so that the world could see the splash he was making." The effect of talk was "to make him retreat more deeply within himself and wrap himself more thickly than ever in the nerveless, stoical calm of his race."[57]

Norris, too, seems to feel defensive on the subject of the intelligence and imagination of the Anglo-Saxon. "The United States . . . ," he says truculently, "does not want and does not need Scholars, but Men—Men made in the mould of the Leonard Woods and the Theodore Roosevelts. . . ." Though he depended often enough himself on race dogma, Norris was reluctant to see the tables turned against the Anglo-Saxon by European critics who assumed the race had no artistic genius. It was not fair, Norris argued in his essay, "The Responsibilities of the Novelist," to say that the American was inherently incapable of creating works of the imagination. "When you have choked the powers of imagination and observation, and killed off the creative ability, and deadened the interest in life," he admonished philistines in the United States, "don't call it lack of genius." It was unfair to conclude, "when some man of a different race than ours, living in a more congenial civilization, whose training from his youth up has been adapted to a future artistic profession, succeeds in painting the great picture, composing the great prelude, writing the great novel," that he had the innate ability to do these things. "Don't say he was born a 'genius,' " Norris insists, "but rather admit that he was made 'to order' by a system whose promoters knew how to wait."[58] Even the most insistent of racists will fall back upon environmental explanations if it suits their purpose.

For all their admiration of the courage and strength of the Anglo-Saxon, London and Wister seem worried about his chances for survival. London especially presents the Anglo-

Saxon as doomed. Perhaps an instinctive knowledge of their approaching end explains their frequent moody reverie. Wolf Larsen, London's sea captain, is oppressed by nameless longings. "He is oppressed," Humphrey Van Weyden reflects, "by the primal melancholy of the race." This conclusion causes Van Weyden to reflect with a new understanding on the truth of old Scandinavian legends concerning the sadness of the heroes. "The frivolity of the laughter-loving Latins is no part of him," Van Weyden decides. "When he laughs it is from a humor that is nothing else than ferocious. But he laughs rarely; he is too often sad. And it is a sadness as deep-reaching as the roots of the race." It is the Anglo-Saxon heritage, in fact, which has made the race "sober-minded, clean lived, and fanatically moral," and it explains such English contributions to civilization as the Reformed Church and Mrs. Grundy. Larsen's "brutal materialism" will not permit him the consolations of religion. When his blue moods come on him, "nothing remains for him but to be devilish."[59]

London had read a curious ethnological study by Major Charles E. Woodruff, an American army surgeon. Woodruff's book, entitled *The Effects of Tropical Light on White Men* (1905), advanced the thesis that the fair-haired and blue-eyed races of northern Europe had subjected themselves to inevitable doom by moving out of the small climatic zone which was suitable for their development. In a corner of northwest Europe the heavy clouds protected them from the rays of the sun, to which they were peculiarly susceptible. Outside this zone—even England was regarded by Woodruff as unsuitable for the Anglo-Saxon, and America much more so—the race would gradually deteriorate and eventually die. Thus, although the Anglo-Saxons were superior to other races in intelligence, in physique, and in will power, argued Woodruff, they were inferior to other races in their ability to survive in a climate where the rays of the sun beat down directly upon them. In the tropics, they would soon die off. In the United States they would gradually disappear and be replaced by immigrants from southern and eastern Europe whose dark skins would not be injured by the rays of the sun.

"It is a very tenable hypothesis," says the narrator of London's novel, *The Mutiny of the Elsinore*.[60]

For London, the theory seemed to be consistent with all that he had said concerning Anglo-Saxon melancholy. The narrator of *The Mutiny of the Elsinore* observes that the upper caste members aboard ship are all Anglo-Saxons and they belong to a superior but decaying race. The officers of the crew are "all fair-skinned, blue-eyed, and perishing, yet mastering and commanding, like our fathers before us. . . ." "Ah well," he concludes, "ours is a lordly history, and though we may be doomed to pass, in our time we shall have trod on the faces of all peoples, disciplined them to obedience, taught them government, and dwelt in the palaces we have compelled them by the weight of our own right arms to build for us."[61]

Owen Wister does not say that the Anglo-Saxon race is doomed in America, and yet he develops a curiously similar thesis for his cowboy heroes. The cowboys are a disappearing "race," he laments, because they have not propagated their breed. "The woman they saw," Wister reflects, "was not the woman a man can take into his heart," and often was not of his race. Therefore, few cowboys "begot sons to continue their hardihood." "That their fighting Saxon ancestors awoke in them for a moment and made them figures of poetry and romance," Wister proclaimed, "is due to the strange accidents of a young country. . . ." For thirty years, the "cow-puncher, the American descendant of Saxon ancestors," had flourished in the West, but "because he was not compatible with Progress," he had now "departed, never to return." In place of him, the West was now composed of "the querulous Populist and Free-Silverite." The tragedy of the cowboy, said Wister, was that he "had no poet to connect him with the eternal, no distance to lend him enchantment." Not even his courage and skill had merited him a tribute. "Though he has fought single-handed with savages, and through skill and daring prevailed, though he has made his nightly bed in a thousand miles of snow and loneliness, he has not, and never will have, the 'consecration of memory.'"[62]

For London and for Wister, then, the destiny of the Anglo-Saxons was a tragic one. London relied on an ethnological theory to explain the coming extinction of the Anglo-Saxon. Wister—for other reasons, it is true—traced the decline of the cowboy, who for him was the highest type of Anglo-Saxon. It is debatable whether the hundreds of thousands of readers of these two writers agreed with them that the Anglo-Saxon of the highest type was disappearing, but those readers who did agree could hardly be expected to look with a kindly eye on the races who were replacing this heroic figure. More likely, it was Anglo-Saxon courage and strength which most of the readers remembered from the novels of London and Wister—and also from those of Norris. It is certainly true that a popularized version of Social Darwinist racism was spread far and wide by these three writers.

X

The Indian
In the Nineteenth Century

THE PATTERN of the treatment of the Indian by the English colonists had been set in the seventeenth century. It was not the kindly attitude of Roger Williams, John Eliot, and the Quakers which generally prevailed. When the Indians gave trouble, the colonists made war against them, often adopting customs as savage as those of the Indians themselves. As early as 1653, the English had begun the system of reservations—assigning each warrior fifty acres of land and the privilege of hunting in unoccupied territory. As the white men moved west, they developed a pattern with regard to the land of the Indians which was repeated over and over again. The Indians would be assigned to a reservation. In time, the white men would covet their land and by one means or another seek to acquire it. They would send to the Indians agents who would offer gifts—often trinkets or whiskey—in exchange for vast tracts of land. Sometimes they would choose some chief or chiefs willing to sign away the land for a price and then assume arbitrarily that this man or these men spoke for all the members of a tribe or of many tribes. Old treaties which had promised eternal boundaries for Indian lands were ignored. If cajolery, trickery, or threats failed, the white men would use force to move the Indians westward.[1]

When the United States became a nation, the policy toward the Indians had already been set in motion. From the beginning, however, there was often a glaring discrepancy between high-sounding statements of policy and actual practice. The Northwest Territory Ordinance of 1787 would seem to be a model document so far as the treatment of the Indians was concerned:

The utmost good faith shall always be observed toward the Indians, their lands and property shall never be taken from them without their consent; and in their property, rights, and liberty, they shall never be disturbed, unless in just and lawful wars authorized by Congress; but laws founded in justice and humanity shall from time to time be made, for preventing wrongs being done to them, and for preserving peace and friendship with them.[2]

It is difficult to equate the language of this document with the fact that territorial governments sometimes offered white citizens bounties for the Indian scalps they brought in. The Dutch had done this as early as 1641 and later on the Puritans engaged in the practice. In the early nineteenth century, it was sometimes argued that if frontiersmen and farmers could be encouraged to kill Indians on a commission basis, the governments could save money because this method would be less expensive than paying soldiers to do it. The last American scalp bounty was offered by the Territory of Indiana in 1814 as an "encouragement to the enterprise and bravery of our fellow citizens."[3]

Because of the savagery of many Indians, it is not surprising that frontiersmen—who were most often the men in conflict with the Indians—should have developed the firm conviction that the only good Indian was a dead Indian. The frontiersmen were frequently violent toward the men in their own group who violated their rules or got in their way, and they were still more violent against the Indians—who neither lived by nor understood the rules of the white man. The idea expressed by Cotton Mather in the seventeenth century that the Indians were the devil's minions, damned from birth by God and incapable of redemption, shifted in the nineteenth century to the conviction that the Indians were damned by biology—that they were inherently incapable of taking the first step toward civilization. At best the Indians were an inferior breed of men and at worst no more than savage beasts. Hugh Brackenridge, the jurist and novelist, indicated the direction of the shift when he wrote in 1782 that "extermination" would be most fitting for "the animals vulgarly called Indians. . . ."[4]

The Constitution mentioned the Indians only briefly. One can infer from the section dealing with them that—following Colonial precedent—the Founding Fathers thought of the Indians not as citizens, real or potential, but as members of autonomous foreign nations. The Constitution declares, for example, that "Congress shall have the power to regulate commerce with foreign nations, and among the several states, and with the Indian tribes." A treaty would imply that the government had no specific obligation to extend the blessings of citizenship to the Indians. This point of view was not limited to the conservatives, who were inclined to interpret individual rights of people rather narrowly. Thomas Paine, one of the most ardent apostles of liberty in the American Revolution, had little inclination to extend the blessings of American citizenship to alien peoples— to the French and the Spanish in the Southwest, for example— much less to the Indians. After the Louisiana Purchase in 1803, a Louisiana delegation was sent to Washington asking for the privileges of citizenship for French and Spanish settlers. Paine declared that the fact that Americans had fought for their own rights did not make it "incumbent upon us to fight the battles of the world for the world's profit." Paine was equally indifferent to the idea of the rights of citizenship for Indians.[5]

John Quincy Adams was reflecting a widespread conviction when he said in 1800 that the Indian tribes had a "questionable foundation" to land:

But what is the right of a huntsman of the forest of a thousand miles, over which he has accidentally ranged in quest of prey? . . . Shall the exuberant bosom of the common mother, amply adequate to the nourishment of millions, be claimed exclusively by a few hundreds of her offspring?

Adams suggested that the title of Indians to land was valid only when they had settled upon it and cultivated it. This meant, in effect, that in order to acquire title to land the Indians had to stop being hunters and become farmers, a transformation which would have been very difficult for them to bring about even if they had been able to comprehend and had agreed to the reasons for it.[6]

The process of encumbering Indian lands went steadily on, but an important change occurred in 1825. Up until that time, the aim of Indian policy had been to confine the Indians in the eastern part of the nation to reservations in which they could take up farming. However, as these lands were more and more coveted by white settlers, this solution no longer was satisfactory. The federal government decided that all Indians should be moved to new reservations west of the Mississippi. At that time, there was a general conviction that the treeless plains of the West were unsuitable for habitation by white men, and thus the removals were apparently planned as a permanent solution to the Indian "problem."[7]

In Illinois, the forcible removal of the Sauk and Fox tribes led to the Black Hawk War in 1832. Black Hawk was a chieftain who refused to cede tribal lands. In 1831, when civilian frontiersmen had gathered to drive the Sauk tribe out, Black Hawk and his followers had retreated west across the Mississippi. The tribe spent a miserable winter in the Iowa country, since they had arrived too late to plant crops. Black Hawk's apparent intention was to return peacefully to Illinois to ask the white man for permission to settle on what had been the Sauks' own land. The fact that the whole tribe—including women and children—accompanied him was proof that his party was not warlike. Nevertheless, a wave of panic swept the white settlers. The Indians were attacked, and at the end of the ensuing "war" of nearly three months' duration, only 150 of the 1,000 Indians who had begun the march from the Iowa country were still alive. The other Indian tribes of the Middle West got the point that it was better to give up their lands and move west than to be exterminated. From 1832 to 1837, the Indians ceded nearly two million acres in the Northwest, and by 1846 the last of the Indian tribes had been transported—whether they wanted to go or not—to their new "home" in the West.[8]

In Georgia, the Cherokees—a tribe of about seventeen thousand—met the requirement that they live upon and farm their land. They maintained schools and had a written constitution based upon the American model with an executive, a legislative, and a judicial branch. Sequoyah, one of their chiefs, had invented an alphabet for the Cherokee language with eighty-five characters and had published parts of the Bible and edited a newspaper, the *Cherokee Phoenix*. None of this prevented them from losing their land. Both the federal government and the state of Georgia were determined that they should be removed.[9]

In 1828, Congress appropriated $50,000 for the removal of the Cherokees. The War Department agents were authorized to offer the Indians land in the West, transportation, a blanket, a rifle, a kettle, five pounds of tobacco, a year's supplies, and fifty dollars in cash. The Indians refused the offer and stayed where they were. Then the state legislature of Georgia declared all Cherokee laws to be void, denied the Indians the right to be a party in a legal suit or to testify in court against any white man, and denied them also the right to prospect for gold on their own lands, though white men could do so. In 1830, Congress passed a Removal Bill which authorized the President to resettle any eastern tribe—by force, if necessary, and without regard to any treaties which the government had previously signed. The land of the Cherokees was ruthlessly taken over by white settlers, debts owing to them were declared canceled, and government agents attempted to induce factions of them to rebel against their leaders. Three white missionaries protested against the policy of the state and national governments and, as "citizens" of the Cherokee nation, refused to swear an oath of allegiance to the state of Georgia. They were arrested, chained, and forced to walk twenty-one miles behind a wagon. Later they were sentenced to four years of hard labor in the state penitentiary. When the Cherokee case came before the Supreme Court, Chief Justice John Marshall, in the famous *Worcester vs. Georgia* decision, declared that the Cherokees were a "domestic dependent nation" under the protection of the federal government and that the state of Georgia had no right to molest them. In reply, President Andrew Jackson, an old Indian fighter himself, declared: "John Marshall has rendered his decision; now let him enforce it."[10]

In 1834, federal agents were finally successful with the old trick of bribing a minor faction to deed the tribe's land. General Winfield Scott, with seven thousand troops and followed by "civilian volunteers," invaded the Cherokee domain, seized all the Indians they could find, and, in the middle of winter, sent them on the long trek to Arkansas and Oklahoma. The "civilian volunteers" appropriated the Indians' livestock, household goods, and farm implements and burned their homes. Some fourteen thousand Indians were forced to travel the "trail of tears," as it came to be called, and about four thousand of them died on the way. An eyewitness to the exodus reported: "Even aged females, apparently ready to drop into the grave, were travelling with heavy burdens attached to their backs, sometimes on frozen grounds and sometimes on muddy streets, with no covering for their feet."[11]

Alabama and Mississippi, following Georgia's lead, acted to rid themselves of the Indians in their midst. They forbade tribes to meet or Indian chiefs to exercise their offices—a device to make it easier for Indian agents to bribe minority factions. The Choctaws and the remnants of the Creeks were forced to join the Cherokees in their pitiful exodus. It is little wonder that General Sam Houston could say after the Mexican War that he saw no reason why the United States government should not appropriate the lands of the Mexicans. Americans, said Houston, had always cheated Indians and since the Mexicans were no better than the Indians, "I can see no reason why we should not go on the same course now, and take their land."[12]

Up until 1849, the Bureau of Indian Affairs of the federal government was under the control of the War Department, but it was then transferred to the Interior Department. On its face, this would seem to be an improvement, in that it transferred the Indians to civilian control; but it was not. The Interior Department was then the agency through which Congress could dispose of public lands, and it proved too strong a temptation in the distribution of these lands to include the Indian property as well. The War Department had initiated a policy of dissolving tribal societies, since it was organization which gave the Indians their cohesiveness and enabled them to resist encroachment. Under the Interior Department, the Indian Bureau set about more systematically than had the War Department to dissolve tribal societies and to "liquidate" the Indian title to land, selling it to white settlers and to speculators.[13]

The Indian titles to the lands in the West were immediately in danger as soon as the white man got around to wanting them. In 1851, the Indian Bureau negotiated treaties with 119 of the tribes of California. The Indians surrendered more than half the state and in exchange were offered perpetual ownership of 7,500,000 acres. By a ruse, the Indian Bureau deprived the Indians of this land. Because of pressure from white politicians in California, the Senate in Washington did not confirm these treaties but merely kept them in its files. The Indians were not told that the treaties were invalid and at the time had no means of discovering the intricacies of American law. The treaties remained in the files of the Senate until 1905, still unratified; the 7,500,000 acres were sold to white settlers and speculators. How strongly the Indian Bureau felt about engaging in honest dealings with the Indians or keeping its word is indicated by the frank comment of General Francis C. Walker, Commissioner of Indian Affairs, in 1871. "When dealing with savage men, as with savage beasts, no question of national honor can arise. Whether to fight, to run away, or to employ a ruse, is solely a question of expediency." Walker was referring to outright warfare with the Indians, but his comment is also relevant to the political and legal aspects of the policy of the American government.[14]

The Indian tribes steadily declined in numbers. In California, for example, the number of Indians was estimated in 1850 to be from 110,000 to 130,000, but by 1880 their number had declined to fewer than 20,000. What happened to the Indians? Some of them, it is true, died from the diseases of the white man to which they had acquired no immunity. Nobody knows how many were murdered, but in most parts of the West killing an Indian was rarely considered a crime. Some of the Indians died because, forced off their own land, they were obliged to move to areas so barren that they could not maintain an existence there. Undoubtedly, the shock of losing their land, the security of their tribal life, and their accustomed ways of farming and hunting led to a decline in their numbers. Sometimes the white people wondered, with a cynicism or a naïveté which is well-nigh incredible, what it was that made the Indian disappear from the land. "There seems to be something in our laws and institutions, peculiarly adapted to the Anglo-Saxon-American race, under which they will thrive and prosper," said Congressman Alexander Duncan in 1845, "but under which all others wilt and die. . . . There is something mysterious about it." This "Lo, the Poor Indian" tradition in American thought is surprisingly widespread.[15]

If the land reserved for Indians was desirable to the white men, especially if any discovery was made which enhanced the value of the land—for example, the existence of gold or silver—the great probability was that the Indian title would soon be extinguished. In 1881, Helen Hunt Jackson wrote *A Century of Dishonor*, a record of the white man's injustice in dealing with Indians in this country. She found that this injustice followed a remarkably consistent pattern:

It makes little difference . . . where one opens the record of the history of the Indians; every page and every year has its dark stain. The story of one tribe is the story of all, varied only by differences of time and place; but neither time nor place makes any difference in the main facts. Colorado is as greedy and unjust in 1880 as was Georgia in 1830, and Ohio in 1795; and the United States Government breaks promises now as deftly as then, and with an added ingenuity from long practice.[16]

As recently as 1880, Congress had debated a bill which was designed to force the Colorado Ute Indians to sell their lands because gold and silver had been discovered on them. American miners must be given the privilege of taking up claims on this land, declared Representative James B. Belford of Colorado, and Congress must "apprise the Indian that he can no longer stand as a breakwater against the constantly swelling tide of civilization." Thus would be settled the doctrine that

an idle and thriftless race of savages cannot be permitted to guard the treasure vaults of the nation which hold our gold and silver, but that they shall always be open, to the end that the prospector and miner may enter in and by enriching himself enrich the nation and bless the world by the results of his toil.[17]

The final episode of white violence against an Indian tribe took place in 1890. The battle was comparatively minor, but as clearly as any single example it illustrates the cruelty and stupidity of the government's policy toward Indians. Wovoka was a Paiute Indian of Nevada who, on a day when there was an eclipse of the sun, went into a trance and proclaimed a vision of a heavenly messiah who would return to earth, cause the white man to disappear, and restore the Indian to his former status. Wovoka did not advocate violence against the white man. Instead, he maintained that the Indians should simply wait patiently for the great spirit to appear. The news of Wovoka's vision spread to Indian tribes all over the western half of the United States. The Sioux Indians of South Dakota began engaging in "Ghost Dances" to bring about the appearance of the messiah. The U.S. Army chose to see these dances as a preparation for warfare and at the Battle of Wounded Knee massacred ninety-eight disarmed warriors and two hundred Indian women and children.[18]

Hatred and contempt for the Indians were strong among those who stood most to gain from appropriation of Indian lands. A frontiersman writing to the Illinois State Register in 1846 said of the California Indians that those "reptiles" must "either crawl or be crushed." Some of the leading scientific students of race were scarcely less harsh. Dr. Samuel George Morton, the authority on craniology, asserted in 1839 that Indians were inherently savage and intractable. Morton believed that all native tribes in North and South America were members of one race "peculiar and distinct from all others" and that the differences in the cultures of the Indians were superficial. Josiah Clark Nott, Morton's disciple in anthropology and coauthor of the popular *Types of Mankind* (1856), had an extremely low opinion of the inherent character of the Indians. In spite of all the "glowing accounts" from missionaries, said Nott, there was no such thing as a "civilized *full-blooded* Indian." Nott had seen Indians in Alabama who were farmers and who had partially absorbed the white man's civilization, but he thought they were little different from the savages of the West. They were "scarcely a degree advanced above brutes of the field, quietly abiding their time." Education and religion were alike helpless, said Nott, to change their nature. The study of crania disclosed, he maintained, that whereas Caucasians had those parts of the skull developed which indicated intellect, the Indian skulls indicated strong "animal propensity." Another contributor to *Types of Mankind*, Dr. Henry S. Patterson, wrote of a young friend who had been killed by Utah Indians while on a surveying expedition for a proposed railroad to the Pacific. "We have had too much of sentimentalism about the Red-man," declared Patterson. If only this young man could be restored to life, his resurrection would be "cheaply purchased back if it cost the extermination of every miserable Pah-Utah under heaven!"[19]

If anti-Indian racism had declined in volume and virulence by the end of the nineteenth century, a major reason was that the Indians were no longer a threat to the safety of the whites and that they no longer had huge tracts of valuable land. We still find the opinion widely held that it was the Indians' race which was their single but insuperable handicap. Theodore Roosevelt castigated Helen Hunt Jackon's *A Century of Dishonor* as "beneath criticism" as history and important only because the high character of the author and her excellent literary work in other directions have given it a fictitious value and made it much quoted by a large class of amiable but maudlin fanatics concerning whom it may be said that the excellence of their intentions but indifferently atones for the invariable folly and ill effect of their actions.

The real fault of the policy of the white Americans toward the Indians had been, Roosevelt maintained, that it had been irresolute and was unwilling to "resort to the ultimate arbitrator— the sword." Of his own opinion of the Indian, Roosevelt said:

I suppose I should be ashamed to say that I take the Western view of the Indian. I don't go so far as to think that the only good Indians are the dead Indians, but I believe nine out of every ten are, and I shouldn't inquire too closely into the case of the tenth. The most vicious cowboy has more moral principle than the average Indian.[20]

Of course, not all nineteenth-century opinion concerning the Indians was unfavorable. Sometimes they were highly praised for their courage and skill as warriors, their ability to endure pain, and their loyalty to their friends. One can find in nineteenth-century America much more praise of the Indian than of the Negro, though the Negro was allowed to survive as a slave whereas the Indian was either slaughtered or banished to lands where it was impossible for him to thrive. De Tocqueville observed that the Negro and the Indian were fundamentally different in character. "The servility of the one dooms him to slavery," he said, and "the pride of the other to death."[21]

One of the genuine friends of the Indian early in the nineteenth century was the Reverend Mr. Jedidiah Morse, well known not only as a clergyman but as a geographer. In 1820, he visited many of the major Indian tribes to prepare a report for the secretary of war. Morse had genuine insight into the character of the Indians. "There is as visible a difference of character among the different tribes," he observed, "as there is in our own population," and therefore, "few general observations . . . will apply to them as a body." He does, however, come to some general conclusions concerning Indians. He thinks they are inferior to whites in physical strength. He likes their custom of not talking when they have nothing to say. He finds them "not vociferous, noisy, or quarrelsome, in their common intercourse, but mild and obliging." He thinks they often have "a high sense of honor, justice, and fair dealing, and great sensibility, when advantage is taken of their weakness and ignorance, to deprive them of their property, and in other ways, to trespass on their rights." To the charge of the white men that the Indians are cruel, Morse replied, "Physician, heal thyself."[22]

Morse recognized clearly that the policy of the white men toward the Indians was wrong and that it might ultimately lead to their extinction. He quotes an Indian chief as saying, "Where the white man puts down his foot, he never takes it up again." Morse criticizes the policy of taking Indian lands by fraud or by force. He says that the result of such a policy is that the Indians are "constrained to leave their homes . . . either to go into new and less valuable wildernesses, and to mingle with other tribes, dependent on this hospitality, for a meagre support; or without the common aids of education, to change at once all their habits and modes of life. . . ." If they choose the latter, "they become insulated among those who despise them as an inferior race, fit companions to those only, who have the capacity and the disposition to corrupt them." Morse's remedy is that the Indians should become wards of the government. He reacted with horror to a proposal which had been submitted to Congress calling for their extermination under the theory that they were irrevocably savage and unchangeable in their character. Morse said the Indians were a race which "on every correct principle ought to be saved from extinction, if it be possible to save them."[23]

James Fenimore Cooper was, in general, favorably disposed toward the Indians. In some of his novels, at least, the Indian appears as a truly admirable character—the intrepid adventurer, the master of forest lore, the trusted friend. Chingachgook, the friend of the white hero Natty Bumppo, is only one of a series of noble Indian characters who appear in Cooper's fiction.

Cooper's knowledge of the Indians was not extensive and one may reasonably suspect that the Indians in his novels were sometimes quite unlike real Indians. Because his novels were widely read, however, it is probably true that many Americans drew their conclusions regarding the character of Indians from Cooper.

In *The Redskins* (1846), one of Cooper's novels, the Indian chief Susquesus is compared with Jaaf, a Negro slave. Susquesus is "vastly the superior of the black." The intelligence of the Negro "had suffered under the blight which seems to have so generally caused the African mind to wither," but Susquesus possesses "the loftiness of a grand nature," one which has developed under "the impetus of an unrestrained, though savage, liberty." Susquesus is "a gentleman, in the best meaning of the word; though he may . . . want a great deal in the way of conventional usages." In *Satanstoe* (1845), another Indian chief and Negro slave are contrasted with one another. When an amusing incident occurs, the Negro "laughed in fits, . . . rolled over on the rocks, . . . shook himself like a dog that quits the water, laughed again, and finally shouted." On the other hand, the Indian

took no more notice of these natural but undignified signs of pleasure . . . than if the latter had been a dog, or any other unintellectual animal. Perhaps no weakness would be so likely to excite his contempt, as to be a witness of so complete an absence of self-command, as the untutored negro manifested on this occasion.[24]

Cooper solves the problem of Indian character a little too neatly by dividing Indians into the good Indians and the bad Indians. The good Indians, we may justifiably suspect, are good partly from the demands of derring-do plots—there needs to be a good Indian or two to warn the whites what the bad Indians are up to. Or there needs to be a tribe of "good Indians" like the Delawares to aid the whites in their warfare against the "bad Indians"—for example, the Mingoes. At one point in *The Pathfinder* (1840), a young white companion of Leatherstocking asks how a good and merciful God could have created beings so thoroughly evil as the Mingoes, and Leatherstocking replies:

I have passed days thinking of them matters, out in the silent woods, and I have come to the opinion, boy, that, as Providence rules all things, no gift is bestowed without some wise and reasonable end. If Injins are no use, Injins would not have been created; and I do suppose, could one dive to the bottom of things, it would be found that even the Mingo tribes were produced for some rational and proper purpose, though I confess it surpasses my means to say what it is.

One gets the impression, from his subsequent adventures in the novel, that Leatherstocking, even while calmly picking off a hated Mingo with his unerring aim, is willing to affirm that the Indian represents part of the grand design of Providence. In another novel, *The Pioneers* (1823), Leatherstocking reflects on the unequal merits of the differing races and concludes that in heaven these inequalities will be resolved. "There is One greater than all, who'll bring the just together at his own time, and who'll whiten the skin of a blackamoor, and place him on a footing with princes." In this life, however, the "inferior" races must submit to the will of the "superior."[25]

Cooper's belief that the Indian was the superior of the Negro did not mean, of course, that he was superior to the white. An interesting revelation of the defects of the Indian chief Susquesus occurs when Mordaunt Littlepage, the narrator of *The Chainbearer* (1845), learns that Susquesus is being pursued by white men:

I trembled for Susquesus; though I knew he must anticipate a pursuit, and was so well skilled in throwing off a chase as to have obtained the name of Trackless. Still, the odds were against him; and experience has shown that the white man usually surpasses the Indian even in his own peculiar practices, when there have been opportunities to be taught.

Elsewhere in the novel, Littlepage explains to the Indian chief what it is that has enabled the white man to triumph over the

Indian. "The white man is stronger than the redman," says Littlepage, "and has taken away his country, because he knows most." Another reason for the superiority of the white man, Littlepage continues, is his respect for the laws of property. Susquesus is not eloquent enough or perhaps he is too polite to give his opinion of the white man's respect for Indian property. He does not reply to Littlepage's rationalization of the claims of the white man.[26]

Other men than Cooper compared the Indian and the Negro, nearly always to the advantage of the Indian. "The indomitable, courageous, proud Indian," exclaimed Louis Agassiz, "in how very different a light he stands by the side of the submissive, obsequious, imitative negro, or by the side of the tricky, cunning, and cowardly Mongolian!" We can find considerable difference in the attitude toward Indians and Negroes even in the popular prints of Currier and Ives, which were widely distributed throughout the last half of the nineteenth century. These prints nearly always show Negroes in such a way as to excite amusement or contempt. They are either performing some activity in a ludicrously inept manner—such as manning a fire brigade, riding in a train, playing baseball or tennis, or pulling a mule up a hill—or they are putting on absurd airs far above those suitable for their "natural" station in life. In "The Darktown Hunt—the Meet," Negroes are shown on a fox hunt riding broken-down nags and dressed in extravagant costumes which are a caricature of the costume worn by an English or Virginia gentleman. In "The Aesthetic Craze," a Negro is shown, sunflower in hand, in the supposedly languid style of Oscar Wilde. Indians, on the other hand, are consistently displayed with respect. They are depicted in ritual dances, in family groups, hunting buffalo, dressing meat, or looking on in a benign and friendly manner as wagon trains of whites cross the prairie. Nothing in the Currier and Ives prints of the Indians suggests that they might excite hatred or contempt.[27]

An opinion of the Indians commonly expressed in the nineteenth century was that they have some virtues but that, either because of a decision by the Almighty or by the inevitable workings of the laws of nature, they must in the end disappear from the American continent. Oliver Wendell Holmes observed in 1855 that the Indians were a "half-filled outline of humanity," a "sketch in red crayons of a rudimental manhood." It apparently had been the divine intention to place the Indians in America only until the white man, "the true lord of creation, should come to claim it." Thus, the impending disappearance of the Indians was not the fault of white men:

Theologians stand aghast at a whole race destined, according to their old formulae, to destruction, temporal and eternal. Philanthropists mourn over them, and from time to time catch a red man and turn him into their colleges as they would turn a partridge in among the barn-door fowls. But instinct has its way sooner or later; the partridge makes but a troublesome chicken, and the Indian but a sorry Master of Arts, if he does not run for the woods, where all the *ferae naturae* impulses are urging him. These instincts lead to his extermination; too often the sad solution of the problem of his relation to the white race. . . . Then the white man hates him, and hunts him down like the wild beasts of the forest, and so the red-crayon sketch is rubbed out, and the canvas is ready for a picture of manhood a little more like God's own image.[28]

In Francis Parkman's histories there is a pessimism similar to that of Holmes concerning the fate of the Indians. Parkman thought that the Indian had certain virtues but that they were not sufficient to outweigh his defects or to keep him from destruction. "Nature has stamped the Indian," wrote Parkman, "with a hard and stern physiognomy. Ambition, revenge, envy, jealousy, are his ruling passions; and his cold temperament is little exposed to those effeminate vices which are the bane of the milder races." On the other hand, his manly traits are "overcast by much that is dark, cold, and sinister, by sleepless distrust, and rankling jealousy." Some races are "moulded in wax, soft and melting, at once plastic and feeble. Some races, like some metals, combine the greatest flexibility with the greatest strength. But the Indian is hewn out of a rock. You can rarely change the form without destruction of the substance." Parkman views the approaching extinction of the Indian with regret because he can "discern in the unhappy wanderer the germs of heroic virtues mingled with his vices," but the future of the Indian is hopeless. "He will not learn the arts of civilization, and he and his forest must perish together."[29]

The nineteenth century was obsessed with the idea that it was race which explained the character of peoples. The notion that traits of temperament and intelligence are inborn in races and only superficially changed by environment or education was enough to blind the dominant whites. The Indians suffered more than any other ethnic minority from the cruel dicta of racism. The frontiersman, beset with the problem of conquering the wilderness, was in no mood to understand anything about the Indians except that they were at best a nuisance and at worst a terrible danger. The leading thinkers of the era were generally convinced that Indian traits were racially inherent and therefore could not be changed. The difference between the frontiersmen's view of the Indians and that of the intellectuals was more apparent than real. In general, the frontiersmen either looked forward with pleasure to the extinction of the Indians or at least were indifferent to it. The intellectuals were most often equally convinced with the frontiersmen that the Indians, because of their inherent nature, must ultimately disappear. They were frequently willing to sigh philosophically over the fate of the Indians, but this was an empty gesture.

What was needed to break through the misconceptions of the dominant whites was something more than humanitarianism—it was an understanding that the character of the Indians was the logical outcome of their social institutions, which had in turn been conditioned by their relationship with their physical environment, by the history of their relationships with other tribes of Indians, and later by their relationships with white civilization. What was needed was an attempt to see the Indian civilization, first of all, in terms of itself and not in terms of the values of the white race. In addition, the dominant whites needed to understand that the Indians could not suddenly transform their way of life and that both understanding of their culture and sympathy for their conditions were necessary on the part of the whites in order to enable the Indians to adjust to their new conditions. It was almost the end of the century before careful work had been begun by Franz Boas, who lived with a tribe, shared its values as much as it was possible for an outsider to do, and wrote about it in terms of its own values. Before Boas, three men in America were the most important of a small group of people who, in a careful and systematic way, had attempted to understand the inner workings of Indian tribal life. These men were Henry Rowe Schoolcraft, Lewis H. Morgan, and John Wesley Powell.

Henry Rowe Schoolcraft (1793-1864) was sent by the federal government in 1822 to serve as an Indian agent to the Chippewa Indians at Ste. Marie, a frontier settlement in the area between Lake Huron and Lake Michigan. One of his friends there was John Johnston, a successful Irish fur-trader who was an educated man and possessed a well-stocked library. Johnston was married to an Indian woman and his daughter, Jane D. Johnston, who was sent to England to be educated, became Schoolcraft's wife. In one of his books, Schoolcraft described his wife as "a highly educated lady, whose grandfather was a distinguished aboriginal chief-regnant, or king. . . ." Schoolcraft also tells us that his marriage to a woman with Indian blood

had the effect of breaking down toward himself . . . the eternal distrust and suspicion of the Indian mind, and to open the most secret arcana of his hopes and fears, as imposed by his religious dogmas, and as revealed by the deeply-hidden causes of his extraordinary acts and wonderful character.[30]

Schoolcraft began a study of the Chippewa language. He quickly became aware of a whole culture—a world in which ghosts appeared in sacred dreams, in which demons were omnipresent and had to be exorcised, in which men prospered or died from the spells cast upon them, in which medicine men had superhuman powers, such as the ability to plunge naked into roaring fires without being burned. He discovered the role of magic, of sex taboos—women were required to live in separate lodges when they were menstruating. He discovered such curious rituals as naked Indian women running around newly planted cornfields at night in order to assure the crop's freedom from blight or vermin. He discovered the complex world of the totem—a system of "coats-of-arms" in which family relationships and a feudal hierarchy of values were set up—a method of social organization which anthropologists would discover to have counterparts in primitive societies all over the world.[31]

Schoolcraft also discovered that Indian mythology was much more than a mere collection of marvelous tales—that it was the key to the explanation of Indian character. He remarks on the almost complete absence in white travelers' accounts of Indians of the role of legend in their culture, and he confesses his own slowness in realizing its central importance. "Surprise reached its acme," he tells us,

when I found him [the Indian] whiling away the tedium of his long winter evenings relating tales and legends for the amusement of the social lodge. These fictions were sometimes employed, I observed, to convey instruction or to impress examples of courage, daring or right action. But they were at times replete with wild forest notions of spiritual agencies, necromancy, and demonology. They revealed abundantly the cause of his hopes and fears, his notions of duty, and his belief in a future state.[32]

Schoolcraft was seriously handicapped in his desire to help the Indians by his conviction that civilization is inevitably the result of an agrarian economy and that a society based upon hunting must inevitably be barbarous. As long as the Indians insisted upon being hunters, Schoolcraft was convinced, they could never be "civilized." He says it is easy to understand why the Indians had never developed the "arts." "Of what use were these arts," he asks, "to a comparatively sparse population, who occupied vast regions, and lived, very well, by hunting the flesh and wearing the skins of animals? To such men a mere subsistence was happiness, and the killing of a few men in war glory." He continues:

It may be doubted whether the very fact of the immensity of an unoccupied country, spread out before a civilized or half civilized people, with all its allurements of wild game and personal independence, would not be sufficient, in the lapse of a few centuries, to throw them back into a complete state of barbarism.[33]

Thus, Schoolcraft is convinced that the Indians could be saved only if they could be induced completely to change their way of life—that is, if they could be induced to abandon hunting for farming. A society based upon hunting was "calculated to lead the mind from the intellectual, the mechanical, and the industrial, to the erratic, physical, and gross." As sympathetic as he was to the Indians, Schoolcraft disapproved almost wholly of their way of life and therefore came to welcome the system of reservations as the answer to the Indian problem. In his poem, *The Rise of the West, or a Prospect of the Mississippi Valley* (1841), Schoolcraft has this optimistic view of the Indian on his reservation:

> 'Tis done! the Indian is no more opprest,
> Free, on the bounding prairies of the west;
> No longer bound to pine in want and woe,
> Around his door the flowers of plenty grow;
> No longer doomed to feel the legal glave,
> And bitter taunt that marked him for a slave,
> His mind expatiates o'er a scene of rest
> With equal laws, and independence blest.[34]

In time, Schoolcraft came to realize that life on the reservation was much less idyllic than he had thought; but he never wavered in his conviction that as long as the Indian was a hunter there was no hope for him to be civilized. Thus, Schoolcraft interposed scarcely any objection to the destruction of those native customs which gave the Indian tribes cohesiveness and stability, nor did he see that change must come gradually if the Indian was to be able to adjust himself to it. Though he was wholly free from attempts to explain the character of the Indian on the basis of his race, Schoolcraft had no solution to the problem of the relationship of the whites with Indians based upon a respect for their culture. The ambivalence of his thought is perceptively pointed out by Roy Harvey Pearce. In the first edition of Schoolcraft's masterwork, *Historical and Statistical Information Respecting the History, Condition, and Prospect of the Indian Tribes of the United States* (1851-57), the cover of the first volume contains a gold-stamped picture of a ferocious Indian who has just scalped a white settler and is waving the scalp in one hand and holding his knife in the other as he stands over the prostrate form of his victim. For Schoolcraft, the Indian could only be a savage as long as he was a hunter.[35]

Lewis Henry Morgan (1818-1881) greatly expanded the researches of Schoolcraft. His works received a favorable reception. His *The League of the Iroquois* (1851) was described by John Wesley Powell as "the first scientific account of an Indian ever given to the world," and his later works were praised by Charles Darwin and Herbert Spencer. Morgan studied law, was admitted to the bar, and set up practice in Rochester, New York, in 1844, but clients were few. Meanwhile, Morgan interested himself in a social organization known as the Gordian Knot, which was a secret society, something like the Masonic orders except that it utilized Indian rituals. One of its members, Ely Parker, was himself an Indian, and he enlisted Morgan's serious interest in Indian ceremonies and customs.[36]

Parker was a man of great ability. He had been ridiculed for his defective English and had determined to obtain a white man's education. At first he had studied law, but he discovered that he could never be admitted to the bar because in New York law an Indian was ineligible to qualify as an attorney, and so he enrolled in Rensselaer Polytechnic Institute and became an engineer instead. Parker convinced Morgan that the society's conception of Indian ceremonies was almost wholly wrong. He took Morgan to visit the nearby Seneca reservation, and there Morgan became aware of the complexities of Indian tribal organization. The social club became a historical society, and the career of Morgan as an anthropologist was begun. Morgan is, in fact, sometimes described as the founder of American social anthropology.[37]

Morgan's interest in Indians led him at an early date to defend the Seneca tribe against white swindlers. The Ogden Land Company in New York hoped to persuade the chiefs of the Seneca reservation to give up a large part of their land by paying each of them a small sum of money. Some chiefs were influenced, after having been plied with whiskey, to sign a legal document favoring the sale. Other Indians had been elevated to chiefdom by a sham election instituted by the company. Morgan estimated that the company hoped to secure the land of the Indians for one-tenth of its market value. The secret society which Morgan had been instrumental in forming, now called the New Confederation of the Iroquois, raised money for the defense of the Seneca Indians. They collected signatures, exposed the fraudulent nature of the deal with the Indians, and convinced the United States Senate that the transaction should not be approved. As a reward, the Seneca tribe inducted Morgan into its membership and gave him the name Ta-ya-da-o-wu-kuh (One-Lying-Across). The name signified that Morgan bridged the gap separating the white man and the Indian.[38]

Morgan is principally known for his study of systems of kinship among Indian tribes. He discovered, for example, that an Iroquois warrior referred to the sons of other members of his own or related tribes as his "sons." Descent was reckoned and inheritance was determined through the female line. Property was owned and inherited, not individually, but through associate clans in a tribe and these, in turn, were divided into confederations. The system amounted to an approximation of the theory of representative government. Morgan believed that this arrangement had arisen from the practice of "primitive promiscuity" at some earlier point in the history of the tribes, a time when any male was eligible to cohabit with any female—a system which Morgan's critics sometimes facetiously described as "a thousand miles of wives." The institution of descent through the female line had developed, he believed, because it was impossible to determine who the father of a particular child was. Therefore, all the men in the tribe considered themselves each child's "father" and, eventually, all the members of the tribe considered themselves related by blood to one another. Modern anthropologists are no longer able to discern a clear line from the "primitive promiscuity" which Morgan assumed to the later practice of monogamy among the Iroquois, but his study is recognized as one of the pioneers in its field.[39]

After he married in 1851, Morgan was obliged to discontinue for several years his anthropological researches. "I laid aside the Indian subject," he said, "to devote myself to my profession." He was one of the men involved in building a railroad to the south shore of Lake Superior, and later he invested money in the newly established iron industry there. For a time, he went into politics and was elected as an assemblyman to the legislature of the state of New York. His success in business and politics, however, did not prevent his continuing his interest in the study of Indian life. In 1858 we find him sending out questionnaires to Indian agents all over the country to discover what systems of kinship and marriage ("consanguinity") were found in different tribes:

Morgan is remembered for two substantial works: his *Systems of Consanguinity of the Human Family* (1866) and his *Ancient Society or Researches in the Lines of Human Progress from Savagery through Barbarism to Civilization* (1877). More important than the specific conclusions at which he arrived was his demonstration that the Indians could be understood in a disciplined and scientific way, that their customs could not be explained with the clichés of racism. Morgan was also important because as a friend of the Indians he could not be dismissed as just another starry-eyed humanitarian. In 1876, after the Custer massacre, he strongly defended Sitting Bull and the Sioux. He pled with the federal government to make it possible for the

Indians to be self-supporting and to live in confidence that their treaties with the white man would not continue to be violated.[40]

Morgan's great value as an anthropologist was that he strove to see the Indians in terms of their own societies and not in terms of his own. The idea of evolution, though Morgan never explicitly avowed it—perhaps because of the objections of his religious friends and relatives—is clearly apparent in his work. He rejected Louis Agassiz's idea of "separate creations" of the races in different parts of the world with its corollary that Indians were a separate "species" from other races. He rejected the idea found among some Christian thinkers that the Indians represented a "postlapsarian degradation" from an originally noble type. He saw the Indians as subject to the same influences as the other races of mankind. "The history of the human race," he maintained, "is one in source, one in experience, one in progress." Schoolcraft was never wholly able to free himself from the notion of savagery as ineluctably connected with the Indians, but Morgan left such ideas behind.[41]

John Wesley Powell (1834-1902) was originally a geologist and explorer. He developed an interest in Indian languages, and through them an interest in general studies of the Indian. His *Introduction to the Study of Indian Languages* (1880) is recognized as a pioneer work of great value. He explicitly rejected race as an explanation of differences of culture. It was he who organized the Bureau of Ethnology of the Smithsonian Institution in 1879, and under his direction specialists in different areas began a scientific and comprehensive study of the culture of Indians.[42]

Schoolcraft, Morgan, and Powell were forerunners of a new attitude toward the Indians, but their point of view made little headway in their own time. It was well into the second quarter of the twentieth century before the champions of the Indian were able to persuade the federal government to free the Indians from restrictions inconsistent with their dignity—or to halt depredations upon the lands granted by solemn treaty to the Indians in perpetuity.[43]

We may imagine that, sad as the persecution of the Indians was in the United States, it was a necessary result of the ideas of the time. A comparison of the history of Canadian policy toward Indians with our own suggests that this conclusion is not justified. As early as 1670, the policy of the Hudson's Bay Company attempted to conserve Indian life and society. The reason may have been that it was useful to protect the Indians to make it possible for them to continue to trap animals in the fur trade, but a policy of friendly good will and fair dealing to the Indians was followed elsewhere as well. The Canadian government made treaties which it did not break. It respected the landholdings of the Indians, did not appropriate their communal funds or divert them into charges for "administration" as our own government did, and did not tolerate widespread corruption in the Indian Service. It provided a means for the orderly transition of the Indian into Canadian life, but it did not force the procedure by separating the Indians from their land. The American treatment of the Indian shows the nation at its farthest point from the ideals of political freedom and respect for individual rights which, in other areas, it was able to achieve."

XI

The Status of the Negro:
1865-1915

FOR A LONG TIME the opponents of racial injustice were obliged
to appeal almost exclusively to the altruism of the dominant
white race. They could, of course, point out the equivocal nature
of many of the racists' conclusions, but the racists had the immense advantage of the strong backing of scientists and social
scientists. A striking feature of the literature of racism in the
late nineteenth and early twentieth centuries is the patient way
in which the racists explain "scientific fact" to their opponents.
The attitude of the anti-racists is frequently hesitant, especially
when they are dealing with questions of inherent inequality
among the races. And often this "anti-racism" is—by modern
standards, at least—filled with ideas which are themselves racist.[1]

When a modern reader comes across the extreme racism of
southern political leaders of sixty years ago, he is likely to equate
their statements with those of the more extreme White Citizens
Councils of today. But the fact is that such men as Pitchfork Ben
Tillman of South Carolina, Tom Watson of Georgia, and James
K. Vardaman of Mississippi—all of whom frequently expressed
themselves in terms of coarse brutality—had far more backing
in the South than Citizens Councils do now. And their support-
ers were by no means limited to the South. In 1905, Tom Watson
closed an editorial attacking Booker T. Washington as follows:

What does Civilization owe to the negro?
Nothing!
Nothing!!
Nothing!!![2]

253

In more restrained language, eminent leaders in the sciences and social sciences were saying about the same thing.

The extreme racism of the early twentieth-century South was the chief evidence of the failure of the North to change the South's ideas concerning the Negro. The scales were, in fact, tilted in the opposite direction. So far as the question of race was concerned, the South appeared to be more successful than the North in getting the whole country to adopt its ideas. The task of elevating the Negro from slave to citizen was the most enormous one which had ever confronted the country, and by 1900 it was doubtful whether it would ever be accomplished. Even Lincoln, had he lived, might well have found the task of Reconstruction of the South too much for him.

For most of his life, Lincoln shared the traditional attitude of many of his contemporaries that the Negroes were inherently inferior. As much as he detested the institution of slavery, he doubted whether the Negro was fit for citizenship and, in any case, thought it would be impossible for him to attain equality in a society which he shared with the white man. In one of his debates with Stephen A. Douglas in 1858, Lincoln expressed an attitude concerning Negroes which was often quoted by southern apologists after the war:

I will say then that I am not, nor ever have been in favor of bringing about in any way the social and political equality of the white and black races, . . . that I am not nor ever have been in favor of making voters or jurors of negroes, nor of qualifying them to hold office, nor to intermarry with white people; and I will say in addition to this that there is a physical difference between the white and black races which I believe will for ever forbid the two races living together on terms of social and political equality. And inasmuch as they cannot so live, while they do remain together there must be the position of superior and inferior, and I as much as any other man am in favor of having the superior position assigned to the white race.[3]

Early in the war, Lincoln strongly resisted all appeals to identify the cause of the North with that of opposition to slavery. There were, of course, political reasons for his reluctance, since slavery still existed in some of the border states which were loyal to the Union, and to adopt antislavery as a cause would have jeopardized their support. It is unlikely, however, that Lincoln would have felt differently under other circumstances. For the first year or so of the war he clung tenaciously to the idea of linking emancipation of Negroes with the proposal to colonize them outside the nation. He cast about to find places where the Negro could be sent. He was opposed to Liberia because he believed the climate to be unhealthful and the cost of transporting Negroes such a distance too great. He seriously considered a province in Panama, then a part of the republic of Colombia, but when his interest became known several of the Central American governments vigorously protested any scheme to send Negroes there.[4]

Benjamin Quarles has pointed out that as the difficulties of colonization of Negroes multiplied, the point of view of Lincoln toward the war was changing. By the time of the Emancipation Proclamation in 1863 he had come to see that the purpose of the war was not merely to restore the Union as it was but to bring about a "new birth of freedom." Thus, in the last years of the war, says Quarles, Lincoln gradually set his policy in the direction of granting political rights to Negroes. In 1864, for example, he wrote a letter for the private consideration of the governor of the newly reconstructed state of Louisiana in which he broached the matter of allowing some Negroes to vote. He asked "whether some of the colored people may not be let in, as, for instance, the very intelligent, and especially those who have fought gallantly in our ranks. They would probably help in some trying time in the future to keep the jewel of Liberty in the family of freedom." On the other hand, Lincoln was not disposed to force the southern states to accept Negroes as voters. Thus, if Louisiana was unwilling to give Negroes the suffrage, he was not willing to punish her.[5]

As might have been foreseen, the South after the Civil War was strongly opposed to the enfranchisement of Negroes. As soon as they were able, several southern states passed laws, the

so-called "Black Codes," which were designed to limit drastically the rights of the newly liberated slaves. When the Black
Codes of South Carolina were published in 1866, H. Melville
Myers, the editor, explained in the preface why such laws were
necessary. The Negro race, he declared, at all times had "been
excluded, as a separate class, from all civilized governments and
the family of nations," since it was "doomed by a mysterious
and Divine ordination. . . ." The war had settled the matter of
the abolition of slavery, but this did not mean that Negroes
were to be considered as citizens. They were to be "equal before
the law in the possession and enjoyment of all their rights of
person—of liberty and of property," but they were not to be
voters and jurymen. "To institute . . . between the Anglo-Saxon,
the high-minded, virtuous, intelligent, patriotic Southerner and
. the *freedman* a social or political approximation more intimate
—to mingle the social or political existence of the two classes
more closely," said Myers, "would surely be one of the highest
exhibitions of treason to the race." Both whites and Negroes
were "distinctly marked by the impress of nature. They are
races separate and distinct, the one the highest and noblest type
of humanity, the other the lowest and most degraded."[6] Benjamin G. Humphreys, the new governor of Mississippi and still an
unpardoned ex-Confederate brigadier general, put the matter
succinctly. "The Negro is free, whether we like it or not. . . .
To be free, however, does not make him a citizen or entitle him
to social or political equality with the white man. But the constitution and justice do entitle him to protection and security in
his person and property."[7]

The Black Codes varied in their provisions, but generally
they forbade the Negroes the rights of holding office or of voting. Negroes were not eligible for military service; they could
not serve on juries nor could they testify in court except against
other Negroes. They were required to have passes in moving
from place to place and they were forbidden to assemble without proper permit by representatives of the law. If they refused
to work, they could be fined and hired out to work by labor

contractors. Young Negroes were bound out as "apprentices" until they attained the age of legal majority. The rights of Negroes were generally restricted to ownership and inheritance of property, suing and being sued in court, and marriage.[8]

The Black Codes led Congress to institute the drastic Reconstruction Act of 1867 in which the South was divided into five military districts and southern states were to be readmitted to the Union only after they had ratified the Fourteenth Amendment, which, among other things, decreed that

no state shall make or enforce any law which shall abridge the privileges or immunities of citizens of the United States; nor shall any state deprive any person of life, liberty, or property, without due process of law; nor deny to any person within its jurisdiction the equal protection of the laws.

The suffrage of those whites who had supported the Confederacy was drastically curtailed, and thus the South for a time was under the control of a Republican party made up of Negroes, whites loyal to the Union (the so-called scalawags), and northerners (the so-called carpetbaggers) who had come South as latter-day frontiersmen looking for business and political opportunities or as missionaries of northern altruism and philanthropy.

Thus began a program which was probably doomed from the beginning. When, in the generations following Reconstruction, any southerner was questioned concerning the rights of Negroes, he could point to the fearful excesses of Black Republicanism. He could explain the mixture of motives in the North—idealism concerning the ability of former slaves to assume the rights of government and vindictiveness toward the defeated white South—which led to the abandonment of the region to the evil opportunism of carpetbaggers and scalawags. What could be more right and natural, he could say, than that the white South should have put down "Negro government" as soon as it was able, by means legal or illegal?

More recent historians in the South have been much less inclined to see the Reconstruction period as an unimpeachable argument for white supremacy. The "excesses" of Reconstruction do not seem as bad as they once did, and such corruption as existed no longer seems to many historians the inevitable result of political participation by an inferior race. The "excesses," it has been pointed out, were hardly limited to the Radical Republicans. One observer has described Reconstruction as "a prolonged race riot." No accurate count of the Negroes killed during Reconstruction can be found, but one observer thinks that five thousand would be a conservative figure. General Sheridan estimated that thirty-five hundred whites and Negroes were killed in the ten years of disorders following the war.[9]

The sufferings of the South under Reconstruction were less extreme, it is now generally recognized, than the historians were for a long time ready to admit. Francis B. Simkins, a southern historian, has led the way to a more balanced view of the period. The radicalism of the Reconstructed legislatures, he maintains, was much less far-reaching than is generally supposed, because it hardly touched the basic matters of land ownership and social equality. A really radical program, Simkins points out, would have called for the confiscation of the land of the white Confederates to be distributed among the Negroes, but the efforts of the Freedmen's Bureau in this direction were "fitful and abortive." In addition, "no attempt was made to destroy white supremacy in the social . . . sphere or to sanction inter-racial marriages." Even those Negroes who were aggressive on the subject of their political rights in nearly all cases followed "the etiquette of the Southern caste system" in social relations.[10]

The mistakes of Reconstruction were frequently those of an inefficient idealism rather than of a thoroughgoing diabolism. The new legislators were inexperienced and badly led, even when they were not Negroes. There certainly were adventurers and swindlers among the Reconstructionists, but there were also many men of worthy character. Their chief weakness was that in their zeal for public improvements—particularly for building railroads and schools—they fell into the hands of dishonest promoters and skyrocketed the state debts. On the other hand, the

Reconstruction constitutions brought badly needed reforms to many of the states. Nearly all of them gave property rights to women, set up the first statewide systems of public education, placed the judiciary under popular control, created new tax systems with more nearly uniform methods of assessment, and established such welfare agencies as orphanages, asylums for the insane, and schools for the blind and deaf. In addition, they abolished imprisonment for debt and property qualifications for voting and holding office.[11]

There certainly was widespread corruption in the South during Reconstruction, but there were other places in the nation at this time where politicians had expensive spittoons in their offices. The notorious Tweed Ring of New York City easily matched any of the southern states in amount of rascality and corruption. And as C. Vann Woodward points out, the so-called "Redeemer governments" who restored white supremacy in the South in the 1870's were themselves guilty of a series of financial scandals. The treasurers of seven states either absconded or were accused of misappropriating funds, and in some states, particularly Mississippi, the corruption was greater than it had been with the carpetbaggers and scalawags.[12]

The evils of Reconstruction were real enough, and some of that evil stemmed from the fact that slavery was hardly the institution best calculated to make good citizens of the Negroes. Whether some kind of gradualist plan for Negroes could have been worked out it is difficult to say. The more serious error of the Radical Republicans was their unwillingness to restore voting powers to the white people of the South, an action which— more than the enfranchisement of the Negroes—embittered the region for generations. Deprived of control of local and state governments, the white southerners resorted to extralegal means to intimidate Negroes generally, but especially Negro officeholders and voters. The most famous of the organizations devoted to this campaign was, of course, the Ku Klux Klan. Organized in 1867, the Klan originated as a lark among young men in southern Tennessee who—so the story goes—chose this method of visiting their sweethearts attired in their version of the costume of knights of old and discovered accidentally that they were terrifying the Negroes.[13]

For a time the Klan was led by Nathan Bedford Forrest, one of the most respected of the former Confederate generals. At a Congressional investigation in 1871, Forrest maintained that he had been willing to accept Negro suffrage but objected to the fact that the vote was often denied to the southern whites. At the beginning, he said, the Klan had been careful to select its membership among the responsible white southerners—"worthy men," as he described them. The Klan "admitted no man who was not a gentleman." It took pains to exclude "rowdies and rough men . . . men who were in the habit of drinking, boisterous men, or men liable to commit error or wrong. . . ." But the Klan did not maintain its respectable leadership. Sometime in 1868 or 1869—the date is uncertain—Forrest resigned from the Klan and apparently did his best to disband and abolish it. By this time, however, the Klan was too useful to the southern whites to be thus easily destroyed. It became the organization of what Forrest called "wild young men and bad men." It spread over the South and by methods of terrorism—assassination, whipping, tarring and feathering—it sought to control the Negroes, the carpetbaggers, and the scalawags. In order to fulfil this role, the Klan was necessarily obliged to rely upon the lawless element of the community. In many parts of the South, the Klan was, in fact, thoroughly detested by responsible opinion. Prominent southerners of the time—men who were not scalawags—described the organization as composed of "reckless young men, without a great deal of standing in their community," as "a set of drunken and lawless vagabonds," and as "ignorant and without education to the last degree." In South Carolina, for example, the Klan flourished most in the hill country where the poor whites were especially powerful.[14]

The North finally wearied of its crusade to enforce the rights of Negroes in the South. Reconstruction was not officially over until 1877, when President Hayes withdrew the last troops from southern soil; but as early as 1872 the period of coercion had virtually come to an end. Troops were no longer sent to enforce federal election laws; all but a small number of former Confederates had had their civil rights restored; the Freedmen's Bureau was abolished. More and more, the southern white man was the arbiter as to how many rights the Negro should be permitted to enjoy. The North—preoccupied with its own rising industrialism and with the development of the West—was mostly willing to allow the white South to solve its race problems without federal intervention.[15]

The difference in attitude toward the Negro before and after the Civil War is striking. In the South the antebellum propagandists for slavery usually portrayed the Negro as occupying a condition for which God and nature had fashioned him—as loyal, devoted, willing to be led, childlike in his helplessness. The slaveholders were, in the words of Thomas R. Dew, a professor and later president of the College of William and Mary, "every where . . . characterized by noble and elevated sentiments, by humane and virtuous feelings." Those few masters who were cruel and mercenary were "those who have been unaccustomed to slavery. It is well known that northern gentlemen who marry southern heiresses are much severer masters than southern gentlemen."[16] In the North, as the abolitionist argument gained ground, the Negro was the pathetic victim of a cruel system; but this did not usually mean that he was the inherent equal of the white man. Harriet Beecher Stowe, for example, makes it quite clear in *Uncle Tom's Cabin* that, in spite of the Negro's humility and aptitude for religion, he is innately inferior. On the other hand, he was entitled to freedom and to benevolent consideration by the white man.[17]

The lofty strain is not generally found in the literature concerning the Negro which followed the Civil War—not in the South, and increasingly not in the North. The theme that the Negro must be benevolently guided by the whites is still found in the South, but it is frequently a muted note. What replaces it is, often enough, an undisguised hatred of the Negro which portrays him as little if any better than a beast. An important anti-Negro book written after the war was *Nojoque* by Hinton R. Helper, published in 1867. Helper was a North Carolinian, though not a member of the planter class. Before the war, he had warned the South that the plantation system and slave labor could not compete with the economic system of the North. When the war came, Helper remained loyal to the Union and was rewarded by being made consul at Buenos Aires. Though he was opposed to slavery, Helper violently hated Negroes and in *Nojoque* he expressed himself as appalled at northern attempts to make citizens of them. This book is one long Negrophobe oration. It has such section headings as "The Negro's Vile and Vomit-Provoking Stench." There is an extended treatment of the idea that the color white has always been in nature "a thing of life, health, and beauty," whereas the color black has always been "a symbol of ugliness, disease, and death." Sometimes Helper advocates removing all Negroes and Chinese to reservations in Texas and Arizona or colonizing them abroad, but sometimes his passion boils to the point where only extermination of "inferior" races will satisfy him. Natural forces, if left to themselves, he sometimes thinks, might dispose of the dark races. "We should so far yield to the evident designs and purposes of Providence," he declares, "as to be both willing and anxious to see the negroes, like the Indians and all other effete and dingy-hued races, gradually exterminated from the face of the whole earth." Yet "natural forces" were usually too slow for him. Concerning the struggle between the North and the South on the issue of slavery, he says: "It may not be questioned that an abundance of saltpetre, rightly applied to the woolly-heads, would have proved a most excellent means of unloosing the Gordian knot of American politics."[18]

A year after the appearance of *Nojoque*, a book written by a northerner, Dr. John Van Evrie's *White Supremacy and Negro Subordination* (1868), developed a similar theme. Van Evrie, a physician in New York City, was part owner of the firm which published *The Old Guard*, a Democratic monthly journal which was founded in 1863 in New York, defended the South and slavery during the war, and attacked the Reconstruction policies of the Republicans afterward. A frequent contributor to the magazine, Van Evrie was a little less violent than Helper on the subject of Negroes and more familiar with the arguments of scientists concerning race, but his estimate of Negro intelligence and ability was the same. He thought that education for the Negro, if it was possible at all, would do irrevocable damage to his brain. It would develop the forward portion of the cranium and give the Negro "a broad forehead and small cerebellum" similar to that of the white man. The relationship of the cranium to the body would thus be seriously altered, the Negro's center of gravity would be disturbed, and he would find it impossible to stand erect or to walk.[19]

Both Helper and Van Evrie reserved a special hatred for white advocates of Negro equality. Helper spoke of the "negro kissers" in Congress. The nation should never accept the Negro as a citizen: "God forbid that we should ever do this most foul and wicked thing." He denounced the "vile spirit of deception and chicanery" of the Radical Republicans and "the venal press and other peddlers of perverted knowledge."[20] Van Evrie warned the North that nothing could change the inferior Negro.

In short, even his sleeping and eating for a lifetime with Ben. Butler, or Wendell Phillips, or Thad Stevens, or in fact, the whole gang of Abolition mongrels and traitors who now darken and disgrace the Capitol of our country with their presence, would not change a single iota of his physiognomy from what it was six thousand years ago.[21]

When reconciliation with the North began to make headway in the South, the leaders of the New South movement were willing to concede that the Union was one and indivisible; but they were resolutely opposed to social equality for Negroes and almost as much so to their political equality, particularly in those areas where they might control elections. Sidney Lanier, for example, was a severe critic of the antebellum South and an advocate of co-operation with the North, but he had a low opinion of Negroes and did not envision them as citizens. In 1874, when Congress was debating the last of the Reconstruction measures, a bill to require that all races be admitted equally to hotels, waiting rooms, trains, ships, theaters, and other accommodations for the public, Lanier wrote a poem in which he had an old Georgia farmer express what apparently was his own opinion. The farmer declares that "this here oncivil rights is givin' me the blues," and continues:

When every nigger's son is schooled (I payin' of the tax,
For not a mother's son of 'em has more than's on ther backs),
And when they crowds and stinks me off from gettin' to the polls,
While Congress grinds ther grain, as 'twere, 'thout takin' of no tolls;
And when I stands aside and waits, and hopes that things will mend,
Here comes this Civil Rights and says, this fuss shan't have no end!
Hit seems as ef, jest when the water's roughest here of late,
Them Yanks had throwed us overboard from off the Ship of State.

If the Yankees persist in their attempts to make the Negro equal, the old farmer concludes the result will be a disaster:

I tell you, Jeems, I *kin* not help it—*maybe* it's a sin;
By God! ef they don't fling a rope, I'll push the nigger in![22]

Henry W. Grady, the leader of the New South movement and editor of the *Atlanta Constitution,* was a popular orator in all sections of the country in the 1880's. Calling for an end to sectional animosities, Grady still maintained that Negroes must be controlled by whites. "The supremacy of the white race of the South," he said in a speech in Dallas, Texas, in 1887,

must be maintained forever, and the domination of the negro race resisted at all points and at all hazards—because the white race is the superior race. This is the declaration of no new truth. It has abided forever in the marrow of our bones, and shall run forever with the blood that feeds Anglo-Saxon hearts.

In a speech before the Boston Merchants' Association in 1889, Grady called for the influx of northern capital and men into the South, a virgin field for economic development. "Give us your sons as hostages," he said. "When you plant your capital in millions, send your sons that they may help know how true are our hearts and may help to swell the Anglo-Saxon current until it can carry without danger this black infusion."[23]

The mass disenfranchisement of the Negro did not follow immediately after the withdrawal of federal troops. This event did not occur until the 1890's and, in some states, later still. For a generation, the Negro was tolerated as a voter in most parts of the South—uneasily, it is true—and both the conservative Redemptionists and the liberal Populists solicited his vote. The reasons for the ending of this period of tolerance are complex. The agricultural distress of the South may have made it more necessary to find a scapegoat. The increased racism of the North may have made the white South increasingly confident that disenfranchisement of the Negro—if it were handled in the right way—would not bring about federal intervention. Whatever the reasons, the southern Redemptionist conservatives—now known as Bourbons—and the Populists turned upon the Negroes in the period beginning in the 1890's and vied with one another to see how far they would go in ejecting him from any meaningful participation in politics.

The theme of how the Negro eventually came to lose what political rights he had in the South has been admirably traced by C. Vann Woodward in his *The Strange Career of Jim Crow* (1955). Woodward points to an essential part of the reason for the change when he says, "The South's adoption of extreme racism was due not so much to a conversion as it was to a relaxation of the opposition." Violent racism had been there all along, but it had been restrained by men who understood its danger. By the 1890's, however, the southern conservatives had lost much of their caution; the southern radicals of Populism had lost much of their idealism and zeal of reform. In addition, northern concern over the Negroes had declined.[24]

The task of the white southern political leaders was to enact laws which would disenfranchise the Negro without also disen-

franchising the poor white and still remain within the legal interpretation of the Fourteenth and Fifteenth Amendments. In
1890, the new state constitution of Mississippi provided that all
voters pay a poll tax of two dollars and that they also be required to display their ability to read any section of the state
constitution or to understand and interpret it when it was read
to them. The assumption was, apparently, that white registrars
would usually hold the Negroes strictly to the law but overlook
any deficiencies on the part of the whites.[25] The poor whites
of Mississippi were apprehensive—and with reason as it turned
out—that the literacy qualifications and other restrictions might
be used to disenfranchise them. To meet this difficulty, the Louisiana legislature in 1897 formulated the famous "grandfather
clause," an ingenious device. This law provided that the right to
vote should be exercised by persons who could read and write or
who held property. If a prospective voter could not meet the
foregoing qualifications, he could vote if he had voted on January 1, 1867, or if he was the son or grandson of someone who had
then voted. Since former slaves had been forbidden the vote in
1867, the law served to disenfranchise nearly all the Negroes. The
dramatic effect of these laws can be seen from the fact that the
number of registered voters fell in Louisiana from 127,000 in
1896 to 3,300 in 1900. It is little wonder that, as southern states
adopted grandfather clauses, a sense of helplessness pervaded the
Negroes. In a letter to a friend, John Spencer Bassett, the white
southern historian, described in 1899 the efforts to pass a grandfather clause in North Carolina as "an enamelled lie."[26]

For a long time the Supreme Court was unwilling to uphold
the Fifteenth Amendment's guarantee that the right to vote
should not be abridged because of race. James Weldon Johnson
commented on the efforts of the Negro to carry his case to the
Supreme Court in the generation before World War I:

More than once he took his case to the Supreme Court of the United
States, but the Court pointed out that he had failed to show that the
state had abridged or denied his right to vote or that persons who prevented him from voting had done so because of his *race, color or pre-*

vious condition of servitude. So, unable to prove that the committee
which had met him at the polls with shotguns was actuated by any
such base and unconstitutional motives, he found his case thrown out.
In the last analysis, he lost his vote because of the attitude of the
Supreme Court.[27]

It was eighteen years after the passage of the first grandfather
clause before the Supreme Court declared it unconstitutional.
The *Springfield* [Massachusetts] *Republican* commented in 1913
on the reluctance of the court. "Hitherto, no amount of legal
ingenuity has sufficed to extract from the United States supreme
court a direct, straightforward decision on the constitutionality
of the 'grandfather' clauses in the election laws of many states,
whereby the Negro voters have been disfranchised," said this
weekly journal. "The court has invariably disposed of cases designed to test the constitutionality of such laws on technical
grounds."[28] In 1915, when the court finally did declare the
grandfather clauses unconstitutional, the decision was almost
meaningless. The device had originally been contrived to persuade the southern poor whites to vote for poll taxes, literacy,
and ownership of property as requirements for voting. When
the grandfather clause was eliminated, the other devices for
limiting the vote remained and frequently operated against the
poor southern white as well as against the Negro. Later on, the
white primary replaced the grandfather clause in many southern
states as a device to restrict the Negro vote.[29]

The last attempt of the North in the nineteenth century to
secure the vote for Negroes in the South came in 1890. When
the southern states had been restored to the Union, they had
gained in their number of congressmen. Before the war, only
three-fifths of the Negro slaves had been counted for purposes
of determining how many congressmen a state should have, but
after the war the Negroes were fully counted. Thus, in 1880,
the South had 135 congressmen in the House of Representatives,
whereas in 1860 it had had only 108. The six New England
states, on the other hand, had declined from 41 to 40 congressmen. In 1890, the so-called Force Bill to insure the right of

Negroes to vote passed the House of Representatives, and it was championed in the Senate by Henry Cabot Lodge. Southern senators, with the aid of western senators who needed southern votes for free silver legislation, defeated the bill.[30]

Even ostensible friends of the Negro in the North sometimes counseled that he should cease his demands for the vote and concentrate on improvement of his race through education. In 1900, Bourke Cockran, an Irish-American congressman from Massachusetts, spoke at a race congress held in Montgomery, Alabama—the first important meeting of its kind held in the South since the end of the Civil War. Cockran startled his audience by calling for the repeal of the Fifteenth Amendment. The Reverend Mr. Edgar Gardiner Murphy, rector of St. John's Episcopal Church in Montgomery, presided at the conference and later wrote to Cockran:

> You will be surprised to know of the number of intelligent Negroes who have written in support of your contention. Most of the educated colored people in the South look upon the Fifteenth Amendment as I look upon it, as something that operates, whether unjustly or not, to range our white population against the Negro. They feel that if the Negro could be temporarily eliminated as a political force, the South could be freed from the nightmare of Negro domination and the whole South could work in sympathetic cooperation with him.[31]

Theodore Roosevelt, who was widely criticized in the South when as President he invited Booker T. Washington as a guest for dinner at the White House and also when he appointed a Negro postmaster in Charleston, South Carolina, privately expressed a low opinion of Negroes in his letters. In 1906, Roosevelt wrote to Owen Wister: "Now as to the negroes! I entirely agree with you that as a race and in the mass they are altogether inferior to the whites." Roosevelt went on to argue that it was inconsistent for southerners to argue that Negroes should not be allowed to vote and yet to count them in determining the number of congressmen they should have, but then he added: "Now remember, Dan, what I am going to say has nothing to do with the right of the negro to vote, or of his unfitness generally to exercise that right." Roosevelt never invited Washington to dinner a second time, and in later years he said he thought the invitation had been a "mistake." In a private letter he also condemned Negroes for cowardice in the Spanish-American War and ventured the opinion that this defect was inherent.[32]

A kind of fever chart in the history of American racism may be discovered by examining the annual statistics on lynching. For a long time, the word *lynch* had no connection with the death penalty or with Negroes. The name goes back to Colonel Charles Lynch of Bedford County, Virginia, who in the uncertain times of the American Revolution organized an informal court to deal with Tories and criminals on the Virginia frontier. The "court" limited itself to fines and whippings and did not hand down death penalties. When times became more peaceful, it was indemnified and exonerated by the Virginia legislature. "Lynch-Law" came to mean extralegal administration of punishment, particularly by whipping. In the 1850's, the term usually referred to the executions of horse-thieves and desperadoes by vigilance committees in the West. But during the Civil War and afterward during Reconstruction, the word *lynch* came to have something approaching its modern meaning—the killing of someone by a mob.[33]

It is a curious fact that in the early years of the 1880's— when statistics on lynching began to be kept—considerably more whites were lynched than Negroes. Between 1882 and 1888, 595 whites and 440 Negroes were lynched in the United States. But inexorably the figures changed. In 1889, 76 whites and 94 Negroes were lynched. By 1892, lynching reached its highest recorded point, with 69 whites and 162 Negroes suffering this fate. Thereafter the number declined, though for the next twelve years, from 1893 to 1904, an average of more than a hundred Negroes a year were lynched as compared with an average of 29 whites. In the thirty-three year period from 1883 to 1915, the annual toll of Negroes lynched never fell below 50 but once—in 1914, when the number was 49. In nine of these years the figures rose to more than a hundred. During the same period, the number of whites lynched was rapidly declining. In the years from 1906 through 1915, ten times as many Negroes (620) were lynched as whites (61).[34]

What was supposed to explain and justify the horrors of lynching as an instrument of "justice" was the raging urge of Negro men to rape white women. In 1942, a study of lynching disclosed that of the 3,811 Negroes lynched between 1889 and 1941, only 641, or less than 17 per cent, were even accused of rape, either attempted or committed. Negroes were lynched for such "crimes" as threatening to sue a white man, attempting to register to vote, enticing a white man's servant to leave his job, engaging in labor union activities, "being disrespectful to" or "disputing with" a white man, or sometimes for no discoverable reason at all. Mary Turner, in Georgia, was hanged and burned when she was almost at the point of childbirth because she threatened to disclose the names of the men who had killed her husband.[35]

To read the details of lynching is to be reminded of the torture of the Middle Ages. Indeed, the lynchers could sometimes have taught the torturers of that era some lessons. The victims were lucky indeed if they were merely hanged. In Paris, Texas, in 1893 a Negro had his eyes gouged out with a red-hot poker before he was burned to death. In Arkansas in 1921 a crowd of five hundred, including women, watched a Negro slowly burned to death. He was chained to a log and "fairly cooked to death" as small piles of damp leaves were burned under different parts of his body. When the victim would try to hasten his own death by swallowing hot ashes, his tormentors would kick the ashes out of his reach. The victim did not cry out or beg for mercy but answered questions a considerable time after the flesh had fallen away from his bones. A reporter from the *Memphis Press* described the scene in detail and noted how after the victim was dead there was a wild scramble of the mob to secure his bones as souvenirs. W. E. B. DuBois tells of seeing the fingers of a lynched Negro displayed in the windows of a butcher shop in

Atlanta. Sometimes victims had their teeth pulled out one by
one, their fingers and toes chopped off by axes while they were
still alive, and frequently they were castrated or otherwise muti-
lated. Anyone who is nostalgic for the superior virtue of the
past should read a history of lynching in this country.[36]

During this period a generation of flamboyant southern
political leaders arose whose major appeal was to the poor white
tenant farmers and whose stock in trade was hatred of the
Negro. One of these was James Kimble Vardaman of Mississippi,
who campaigned for governor in 1900 in an eight-wheeled
lumber wagon drawn by eight yokes of oxen. "We would be
justified," Vardaman declared, "in slaughtering every Ethiop
on the earth to preserve unsullied the honor of one Caucasian
home." The Negro was a "lazy, lying, lustful animal which no
conceivable amount of training can transform into a tolerable
citizen." One didn't inquire into the justice of killing predatory
animals. "We do not stop when we see a wolf," he reasoned, "to
find if it will kill sheep before disposing of it, but assume that it
will." He admitted the cruelty of this logic. But, he said, "I
am . . . writing . . . to present the cold truth however cruel it
may be."[37] Pitchfork Ben Tillman of South Carolina declared
in 1913 that from "forty to a hundred Southern maidens were
annually offered as a sacrifice to the African Minotaur, and no
Theseus had arisen to rid the land of this terror." He said he had
taken the oath as governor of South Carolina, "to support the
law and enforce it," but added that he "would lead a mob to
lynch any man, black or white, who ravished a woman, black
or white. This is my attitude calmly and deliberately taken, and
justified by my conscience in the sight of God." On another occasion, he declared that his opinion was "to hell with the Constitution" when it stood in the way of mob justice to rapists.[38]
Tom Watson of Georgia said that the Negro simply has "no
comprehension of virtue, honesty, truth, gratitude and principle." The South had "to lynch him occasionally, and flog him,
now and then, to keep him from blaspheming the Almighty,
by his conduct, on account of his smell and his color." Lynch

law was "a good sign"; it showed "that a sense of justice yet
lives among the people."[39] Negro-baiting became so profitable
politically that there is evidence that white politicians sometimes
subsidized Negro party activity in order to keep the opposition
strong enough to seem to be worth combating.[40]

A literary source of the most sordid kind of racism was to be
seen in the novels of Thomas Dixon, Jr. *The Clansman* (1905),
a story of Reconstruction days in South Carolina, reflects a violent hatred of Negroes. There is the following description of a
Negro rapist:

He had the short, heavy-set neck of the lower order of animals. His
skin was coal black, his lips so thick that they curled both ways up and
down with crooked blood-marks across them. His nose was flat and its
enormous nostrils seemed in perpetual dilation. The sinister bead eyes,
with brown splotches in their whites, were set wide apart and gleamed
ape-like under his scant brows. His enormous cheekbones and jaws
seemed to protrude beyond the ears and almost hide them.

The mulatto mistress of the northern senator in the novel, who
is apparently modeled upon Thaddeus Stevens, has "animal"
movements and the eyes of a "leopard." Another Negro in the
novel has a head which was "small and seemed mashed on the
sides until it bulged into a double lobe behind." His "spindle-
shanks supported an oblong, protruding stomach, resembling an
elderly monkey's which seemed so heavy it swayed his back to
carry it."[41]

As the tide of lynchings rose in the 1890's, Walter Hines
Page protested against them and correctly forecast where they
would lead. "The gravest significance of this whole matter," he
declared in 1893, "lies not in the first violation of the law, nor
in the crime of lynching, but in the danger that Southern public
sentiment itself under the stress of this new and horrible phase
of the race-problem will lose the true perspective of civilization."[42] In 1907, William Graham Sumner—hardly one to be
accused of an excessive sensibility—marveled that the country
had apparently come to accept as a matter of course lynchings

accompanied by torture. "It might have been believed a few years ago," he wrote, "that torture could not be employed under the jurisdiction of the United States, and that, if it was employed, there would be a unanimous outburst of indignant reprobation against those who had so disgraced us." He confessed that he did not understand why the country had been so little moved to protest against lynchings.[43]

Sometimes lynching was condoned or at least explained on the basis of the sexual nature of the Negro man. "The intelligent Negro may understand what social equality truly means," said Thomas Nelson Page in 1904, "but to the ignorant and brutal young Negro, it signifies but one thing: the opportunity to enjoy, equally with white men, the privilege of cohabiting with white women." The South understood the tendency of Negro men, and thus there was among the whites "universal and furious hostility to even the least suggestion of social equality."[44] A number of modern writers have attempted to explain and interpret the relationship between sexual attitudes and race prejudice, especially the violent kind exemplified in lynchings. John Dollard has mentioned the conviction of many southerners that Negro men have exceptionally large genitals and thus their raping of a white woman is a peculiarly horrible and brutal offense. Dollard speculates whether sexual jealousy on the part of white men may be a factor in lynchings. One still hears the idea expressed by white men in the Deep South that they wish they could be Negroes, at least on Saturday nights. Lillian Smith and Oscar Handlin have maintained that the puritanical code of religion in the South has in the minds of the whites invested Negroes with both the attraction and the horror of being completely free sexually. James Baldwin, the Negro author, is convinced that whites generally are obsessed with the Negro as a symbol of sexuality.[45]

The most open and avowed attacks on the rights of Negroes came from lynchings and from denial of the right to vote. More insidious in the denial of equality were the Jim Crow laws requiring separate facilities for Negroes. One of the last Reconstruction measures passed by Congress was the Civil Rights Act of 1875. It declared that all persons should be entitled to the full and equal enjoyment of public accommodations—in waiting rooms, trains, and ships, in theaters, hotels, and other businesses generally open to the public. In order to enforce the statute, Congress gave federal courts exclusive jurisdiction in cases which arose with regard to it.[46]

In 1883 the Supreme Court declared the Civil Rights Act of 1875 unconstitutional on the grounds that the Fourteenth Amendment applied only to the states and that segregation by private individuals or companies was legal under the Constitution.[47] In this case, the Supreme Court was following a pattern of decisions which had been set by lower courts and by its own previous decisions. In 1867, the Supreme Court of Pennsylvania ruled that a railway company could segregate a Negro if it chose to do so.[48] The Supreme Court of Ohio ruled in 1871 that school segregation was constitutional so long as equal facilities were provided, and three years later the Supreme Court of Indiana issued a similar decision.[49] In 1878, the Supreme Court held invalid, as a burden on interstate commerce, a Louisiana Reconstruction statute forbidding steamboats on the Mississippi River to segregate passengers according to race."[50] The best known of the "separate but equal" decisions is, of course, the *Plessy vs. Ferguson* case of 1896 in which the Supreme Court upheld the right of a railroad in Louisiana to segregate Negro passengers.[51]

Even under Reconstruction, the southern states did not generally attempt to have mixed schools for whites and Negroes. Louisiana and South Carolina were the only states with laws requiring mixed schools, and even in those states the law was not generally enforced. In Louisiana, P. B. S. Pinchback, a mulatto who was lieutenant governor of the state during Reconstruction, sent his children to school with the whites, but the white children made their lives miserable and finally caused them to withdraw. "They're good enough niggers," one of the white boys at school is said to have observed, "but still they're niggers; you can't teach 'em not to be black."[52] As public schools developed in the South, some states made a genuine effort to divide the money fairly between whites and Negroes. Northern philanthropy played an even more important part, particularly in aiding colleges. But from the 1880's until northern philanthropists came to the aid of Negro education early in the twentieth century, Negro education—like all education in the South—went through a lean and troubled period.[53]

In 1890, Henry W. Grady declared that separation of the races need not imply discrimination. To think that it did was a misconception of "fanatics and doctrinaires":

. . . the whites and blacks must walk in separate paths in the South. As near as may be, these paths should be made equal—but separate they must be now and always. This means separate schools, separate churches, *separate accommodations everywhere—but equal accommodations where the same money is charged, or where the State provides for the citizen.*

The South, Grady maintained, was keeping facilities for whites and Negroes approximately equal. He stated, for example, that in Georgia, though Negroes paid only one-fortieth of state taxes, 49 per cent of the school fund was devoted to Negro schools.[54] He did not mention other facilities for Negroes, but George Washington Cable said in 1885 that nearly all public accommodations for Negroes were dirty or unkempt. The Negro compartment on a train, he said, was "in every instance and without recourse, the most uncomfortable, uncleanest, and unsafest place: and the unsafety, uncleanness, and discomfort of most of these places are a shame to any community pretending to practice public justice."[55] In 1896, Supreme Court Justice John M. Harlan declared in his dissent to the *Plessy vs. Ferguson* decision that "there can be no doubt but that segregation has been enforced as a means of subordinating the Negro . . . [and] that the thin disguise of 'equal' accommodation . . . will not mislead anyone nor atone for the wrong this day done. . . ."[56]

Even before the decision of the court, Booker T. Washington had bowed to what he thought was the inevitable and asked the Negroes of the South not to press for integrated facilities. In 1895, he made a famous speech at the Cotton Exposition in Atlanta in which he attempted to conciliate the white South by, in effect, accepting the principle of segregation. "The wisest among my race understand," he said, "that the agitation of questions of social equality is the extremest folly. . . . In all things that are purely social we can be as separate as the fingers, yet one as the hand in all things essential to mutual progress." Washington had hoped that by agreeing to segregation he would lessen white fears concerning the right of Negroes to vote and to have equal educational facilities. Even so, he felt a great reluctance in making this concession. He tells us that on his journey to Atlanta to make the speech he felt "a good deal as . . . a man feels when he is on his way to the gallows."[57] From a long-range standpoint, the speech was a serious mistake. It was hailed with delight by many whites both in the South and in the North; on the other hand, it had no effect on the campaign of white southerners to deny the Negro the vote and the opportunity for an equal education.[58]

The phrase "separate and equal," comments Arthur Raper, "symbolizes the whole system, fair words to gain unfair ends." Only a year after the Plessy vs. Ferguson decision of 1896 we find James K. Vardaman in a campaign against Negro education in Mississippi. The state, he complained, was spending half a million dollars a year to prepare the Negro for "the higher duties of citizenship." Everybody knew that the Negro would not be allowed to be a citizen. His vote would either be "cast aside or Sambo will vote as directed by the white folks." Money spent on education of the Negro was a "positive unkindness to him." It rendered him "unfit for the work which the white man has prescribed, and which he will be forced to perform." Vardaman objected just as much to money sent by northern philanthropists for private Negro colleges in the South. "What the North is sending South is not money but dynamite," he exclaimed. "This education is ruining our Negroes. They're demanding equality." When he became governor in 1900, he drastically reduced the amount of state money spent for Negro schools. The only kind of education he thought suitable for the Negroes was vocational education and not much of that. The state colleges for Negroes in Mississippi were closed.[59]

The possibilities of segregation as a tool in the denial of rights to Negroes were almost unlimited. Public services which existed for whites were sometimes wholly nonexistent for Negroes. In many communities library facilities, for example, were and are supported by public funds but wholly limited to white patrons.[60] Usually, separate facilities were available for Negroes but they were vastly unequal. As late as 1936, the state of Mississippi was paying its white elementary public school teachers an average of three times as much as it paid its Negro teachers. The rest of the South was not this bad, but white teachers in the region were paid an average of over 60 per cent more than Negro teachers. White schools offered courses which Negro schools did not. White schools were frequently of sound construction, whereas Negro schools were frequently ramshackle affairs. John Dollard tells how a southern community as late as the 1930's built only the shell of a building for a Negro high school, and then the Negro members of the community were obliged to donate their time and money to build the interior of the building and to pay for the coal to heat it.[61]

In the South, segregation laws were also a means of denying Negroes the right to certain types of occupation. There were scores of ordinances like that of Atlanta which forbade barbers to shave or cut the hair of both whites and Negroes—they were obliged to choose one race or the other. This was a method of preventing Negro barbers from competing with whites for the white trade. In 1915, South Carolina passed a law forbidding factories and other places of business to employ Negroes to work alongside whites except as janitors or scrubwomen or in other menial positions. The law was aimed at preventing the state's industries, the growth of which was partly the result of the war

in Europe, from taking advantage of Negroes' willingness to
work at wages lower than those of whites—but wages which still
meant economic betterment and wider opportunities for the
Negroes.[62]

Where could the Negro turn at this time to have the injustices against him redressed? Not to the courts. Just as the
Supreme Court refused to pass on the constitutionality of the
"grandfather clause" which prevented Negroes from voting in
the South for many years, so it was also unwilling to examine
the question of whether segregated facilities for Negroes actually
were equal. In the 1890's a town in Georgia closed its Negro
high school but not its white high school. The Negroes of the
community in their suit did not challenge the segregation law,
but only asserted their right to a Negro high school if there was
a white one. The Supreme Court in 1899 denied the appeal of
the Negro plaintiffs and, in effect, left the matter of how much
education the Negroes were to receive wholly up to the states.[63]
In 1908, the Court had before it a case in which there was at
issue a Kentucky law aimed at Berea College's practice of educating Negroes along with whites. The Court refused to pass on
the constitutionality of the issue and, in effect, sanctioned laws
against integrated education even in private schools.[64]

The executive department of the federal government was
equally deaf to the pleas of Negroes. Grover Cleveland hailed
Booker T. Washington's speech of 1895 which had asked the
Negroes to accept segregation without protest.[65] William Mc-
Kinley remained silent as the southern states proceeded one after
another to disfranchise Negroes.[66] Theodore Roosevelt outgrew
the willingness he had displayed early in his first administration
to champion the cause of Negroes. By 1912, he apparently con-
curred when the Bull Moose convention which nominated him
refused to seat most of the Negro delegates, turned down a civil
rights plank for Negroes, and selected a "lily white" southerner
as his running mate.[67] William Howard Taft began his administration in 1909 by assuring the white South that he would ap-
point no federal officials in their region who would be offensive

to them, and of course the white South knew what he meant.[68]

It was the administration of Woodrow Wilson, however, which took the most drastic action against Negroes. In 1912, Josephus Daniels, who was then a North Carolina supporter of Wilson and was soon to become a member of his cabinet, was convinced that with the election of a southerner as President there was a chance that the South's attitudes and practices with regard to Negroes might be extended indefinitely in the North. It was in Wilson's administration and with his express approval that federal civil service workers were segregated by race in their employment, with separate eating and toilet facilities. When a Negro leader protested this segregation, Wilson all but ordered him out of his office because his language was "insulting." Post Office and Treasury officials in the South were given the freedom to discharge or downgrade Negro employees. In Atlanta, thirty-five Negroes were discharged from their jobs at the post office. "There are no Government positions for Negroes in the South," declared the Collector of Internal Revenue for Georgia in 1913. "A Negro's place is in the cornfield."[69]

The political leaders of the South were well aware that no one of them could survive in office if he were to champion the rights of Negroes. When Pitchfork Ben Tillman of South Carolina would rise in the Senate to engage in one of his coarse and violent diatribes, some other southern senators might silently leave the floor in protest, but no one of them dared directly to challenge him. Tillman gloried in his speeches that the white South had illegally deprived the Negroes of their rights:

We took the government away. We stuffed ballot boxes. We shot them. We are not ashamed of it. The Senator from Wisconsin would have done the same thing. I see it in his eye right now. He would have done it. With that system—force, tissue ballots, *etc.*—we got tired ourselves. So we called a constitutional convention, and we eliminated as I said, all of the colored people whom we could under the fourteenth and fifteenth amendments.

Tillman also claimed the support of large sections of opinion in the North for his statements on Negroes. He said that in his many speeches on the lecture circuit in the North he had met with enthusiastic crowds and wide acclaim for the opinions he expressed there. On the floor of the Senate, he taunted northerners for the race riots in their part of the country and for the hypocrisy of their avowal of the "brotherhood of man":

The brotherhood of man exists no longer because you shoot negroes in Illinois, when they come in competition with your labor, as we shoot them in South Carolina when they come in competition with us in the matter of elections. You do not love them any better than we do. You used to pretend that you did, but you no longer pretend it, except to get their votes.[70]

The virulent racism of southern politicians was reflected in a torrent of racist books and articles written in the style of Hinton R. Helper and John Van Evrie. A compendium of popular knowledge published in 1887 had a page of drawings entitled "The Levels of Intelligence," with a Negro resembling an ape representing the lowest level. Books pretending to have the last word of science concerning the importance of race and the nature of Negroes multiplied. Charles Carroll's *'The Negro a Beast'; or 'In the Image of God,'* (1900), William P. Calhoun's *The Caucasian and the Negro in the United States* (1902), William B. Smith's *The Color Line: A Brief in Behalf of the Unborn* (1905), and Robert W. Shufeldt's *The Negro, A Menace to American Civilization* (1907) were books passionately devoted to the theme of Negro inferiority; and, of course, magazine articles and pamphlets were legion. Popular novelists explained their characters on the basis of racist theory. Thomas Dixon, Jr. has already been mentioned. Another Virginian, Thomas Nelson Page, stated his opinions more calmly but had a similar low opinion of Negroes. He maintained that "the negroes *as a race* have never exhibited any capacity to advance; that as a race they are inferior," and the fact that there were a few Negro doctors and lawyers proved nothing but that they had white blood in their veins.[71]

Any age can display its fanatics, but what is more disappointing is the racism to be found among thoughtful and reflective men in the latter part of the nineteenth century and the early part of the twentieth. There was, for example, Nathaniel Southgate Shaler, who became dean of the Lawrence Scientific School at Harvard. In 1884 he wrote an essay, "The Negro Problem," published in the *Atlantic,* in which he viewed with sympathy the attempts in the South to disenfranchise the Negro. Shaler had been a pupil of Louis Agassiz; he subscribed to the old theory that a Negro child is just as bright as a white child up to the age of puberty, but beyond this point his "animal nature settled like a cloud over that promise." In addition, the Negro's innate and uncontrollable immorality made him "unfit for an independent place in a civilized state." What progress the Negro had made he owed to the discipline of slavery. As a free man, the Negro showed a strong tendency, which was probably ineradicable, to return to his naturally savage state. Convinced that the Negroes were a dying race, Shaler recommended that they be scattered over the United States to prevent their becoming an overwhelming burden for any one section. Because they were incapable of higher education, their schools should be limited to instruction in the lower trades, since "as a race they are capable of taking pride in handiwork."[72]

A racist work widely read and quoted in the South was Frederick L. Hoffman's *Race Traits and Tendencies of the American Negro,* published by the American Economic Association in 1896. Hoffman was a statistician for the Prudential Life Insurance Company in New York, who was convinced that the high incidence of tuberculosis, syphilis, gonorrhea, scrofula, and other diseases among Negroes would lead to their extinction as a race. He rejected the argument that better conditions would improve the health record of Negroes. For him, the "root of the evil" was the "immense amount of immorality, which is a race trait." "It is not in the *conditions of life*" that we should look for reasons for the poor health record of Negroes,

but in the *race traits and tendencies* that we find the causes of excessive mortality. So long as these tendencies are persisted in, so long as immorality and vice are a habit of life of the vast majority of the colored population, the effect will be to increase the mortality by hereditary transmission of weak constitutions, and to lower still further the rate of natural increase, until the births fall below the deaths, and gradual extinction results.

A Social Darwinist, Hoffman maintained that the only hope for the Negro was for him to be willing to subject himself to the same stern disciplines which had developed and conditioned the race of white men. "Instead of clamoring for aid and assistance from the white race," said Hoffman, "the negro himself should sternly refuse every offer of direct interference in his own evolution." Hoffman was proud of his own objectivity. He said that since he had been born in Germany and was not a native American he could write without "a personal bias which might have made an impartial treatment of the subject difficult."[73]

The idea that the Negroes were a dying race is frequently found in the literature of racism during this period. Albert Bushnell Hart, however, thought that Hoffman based his thesis "upon statistics of too narrow a range to permit safe deductions, or upon the confessedly imperfect data of the Federal censuses."[74] Some students of race have explained the belief in the coming extinction of the Negro, a belief which seems to have been especially strong in the North, as due to the special conditions of the time. The fact that most Negroes were extremely poor, together with the fact that heavy immigration was then coming from Europe and the immigrants had a high birth rate, led some observers to see a universal trend in what was a temporary condition. With the curtailment of immigration in the 1920's and the migration of Negroes from the South to the North with a consequent rise in their economic status, the disparity shown in the statistical comparison of disease and death among whites and Negroes did not seem so impressive. As late as 1919, we find E. A. Ross, the eminent sociologist, declaring that American Negroes were one-tenth of the population, whereas a century before they had been one-fifth. "The great bulk of negroes are in the South," he explained, "for in the North the climate does not suit them and they tend to die out."[75]

It is striking how often one finds among intelligent and sensitive people of the period—North as well as South—crude reflections of racism. One thinks of Henry Adams' contemptuous references to "niggers" and of John Fiske's account of a visit in 1877 to Baltimore, where he saw "elegant niggers" promenading on the streets. Rayford W. Logan has studied the files of eminent magazines of the last part of the nineteenth century and found in *Harper's, Scribner's, Century*, and to a lesser degree the *Atlantic* a fairly constant barrage of epithets applied to Negroes—such terms as nigger, niggah, darkey, coon, pickaninny, mammy, buck, uncle, aunt, high-yaller, yaller hussy, and light-complected yaller man. A standard device of humor was to give the Negro a fancy but revealing name—Colonel, Senator, Sheriff, Apollo Belvedere, George Washington, Abraham Lincum, Napoleon Boneyfidey Waterloo, Lady Adeliza Chimpanzee, Prince Orang Outan, Ananias, Piddlekins, Asmodeus, Bella Donna Mississipp Idaho, with the ultimate in the name Henri Ritter Demi Ritter Emmi Ritter Sweet-potato Cream Tarter Caroline Bostwick. Thomas Nelson Page wrote a humorous article for *Harper's* entitled "All the Geography a Nigger Needs to Know."[76]

Henry James, who explored moral issues in his novels and stories with perception and delicacy, was impervious to moral issues raised by the status of Negroes. On a visit to the South in 1907, he had the following reaction to the Negro porters he encountered in Washington:

I was waiting, in a cab, at the railway-station, for the delivery of my luggage after my arrival, while a group of tatterdemalion darkies lounged and sunned themselves within range. To take in with any attention two or three of these figures had surely been to feel one's self introduced at a bound to the formidable question, which rose suddenly like some beast that had sprung from the jungle. These were its far outposts; they represented the Southern black as we knew him not, and had not within the memory of man known him, at the North; yet all portentous and in possession of his rights as a man, was to be not a little discomposed. . . . One understood at a glance how he must loom, how he must count in . . . [the South.][77]

The studies of Reconstruction which began to appear in some numbers after the beginning of the twentieth century reflect among the historians mainly a criticism of the North for having allowed the Negroes in the South to vote and a sympathy for the South in having disenfranchised them. In a magazine article on Reconstruction in 1901, Woodrow Wilson said that the Negroes in the South had been "a host of dusky children untimely put out of school." Conditions had approached the stage of "ruin" until "at last the whites who were the real citizens got control again. . . ."[78] John W. Burgess, in a book on Reconstruction published in 1902, said the North was rapidly learning that there were "vast differences in political capacity" between the whites and the Negroes and that "it is the white man's mission, his duty and his right to hold the reins of political power in his own hands for the civilization of the world and the welfare of mankind." Congress had done a "monstrous thing" in giving the Negro the vote after the Civil War. "The claim that there is nothing in the color of the skin from the point of view of political ethics," he declared, "is a great sophism. A black skin means membership in a race of men which has never of itself succeeded to reason, has never, therefore, created any civilization of any kind."[79]

James Ford Rhodes, who wrote the first detailed study of the Reconstruction period, fully subscribed to the idea that the Negroes were innately inferior and incapable of citizenship. The promises of the Radical Republicans to the Negroes had "fostered the native laziness and improvidence of the race. . . ." Rhodes thought it a great pity that the North had been unwilling to listen to such men of science as Louis Agassiz who could have told them that the Negroes were unqualified for citizenship. "What the whole country has only learned through years of costly and bitter experience," declared Rhodes, "was known to this leader of scientific thought before we ventured on the policy of trying to make negroes intelligent by legislative acts: and this knowledge was to be had for the asking by the men who were shaping the policy of the nation."[80] William A. Dunning, in a study of Reconstruction published in 1907, declared that the Negroes "had no pride of race and no aspiration or ideals save to be like the whites." They were "impervious" to criticisms of maladministration in the southern legislatures which they dominated. The whole difficulty of Reconstruction, in fact, stemmed from the fact that the "antithesis and antipathy of race and color were crucial and ineradicable."[81] In 1917 Ellis Paxson Oberholtzer chided his fellow northerners for having failed to understand the racial problem in the South during Reconstruction. The southerners had attempted to tell the Yankees who came South, said Oberholtzer, that the Negro would work only under compulsion, that "God had made him lazy." The southerners pointed out that the Yankees knew little or nothing about the subject because they "had never seen a nigger except Fred Douglass," and Oberholtzer observes that the southerners' opinion "was founded in a good deal of truth." He himself says that the Negroes were "as credulous as children, which in intellect they in many ways represented. . . ."[82]

The decision in the South to segregate and disenfranchise the Negro encountered no really strong opposition in the North. "We must not try to enforce in the St. Charles Hotel in New Orleans," wrote Henry Martyn Field, a northern Presbyterian minister, "what cannot be enforced in the Fifth-avenue Hotel in New York."[83] As grandfather clauses and other restrictions radically diminished the vote of Negroes in the South, powerful men in the North looked on approvingly. An editorial in the *New York Times* in 1900 said that "Northern men . . . no longer denounce the suppression of the Negro vote in the South as it used to be denounced in the reconstruction days. The necessity of it under the supreme law of self-preservation is candidly recognized."[84] In 1907, when Kentucky forbade Berea College to educate Negro students in the same classes with whites, President Charles W. Eliot of Harvard called upon the North to be sympathetic to the southern view, saying,

Perhaps if there were as many Negroes here as there, we might think it better for them to be in separate schools. At present Harvard has about five thousand white students and about thirty of the colored race. The latter are hidden in the great mass and are not noticeable. If they were equal in numbers or in a majority, we might deem a separation necessary.[85]

There were, of course, men with different views in both the South and the North. But what is noticeable is that American thought of the period 1880-1920 generally lacks any perception of the Negro as a human being with potentialities for improvement. Most of the people who wrote about Negroes were firmly in the grip of the idea that intelligence and temperament are racially determined and unalterable. They concluded, therefore, that the failures of Reconstruction, the low educational status of the Negro, his high statistics of crime, disease, and poverty, were simply the inevitable results of his heredity. The defenders of the Negro were thus cast in the role of sickly humanitarians who refused to face facts. What was most needed at this time was a direct challenge to the intellectual bankruptcy of racist theory. Without such a challenge, one which would make sense to the hard-boiled disciplines of biology, anthropology, sociology, and psychology, the battle to improve the status of the Negro was a thankless and almost hopeless task.

XII

Anti-Immigration Agitation: 1865-1915

THE REASONS for hostility to immigrants in this country have not invariably been racial. The differences in customs and traditions of many of the immigrant peoples must, in the nature of things, have led to some suspicion of them. Xenophobia has changed according to conditions both here and abroad. After the French Revolution, there was prejudice in this country against French immigrants because they were thought to be atheists and revolutionaries. During the Know Nothing movement of the 1840's and 1850's, prejudice against the Irish was entangled with prejudice against Catholicism. The prejudice against German immigrants later in the century was associated in the public mind with dislike of socialism, with which the German immigrants were thought to be infected. But of all the reasons for prejudice against immigrants, it was race which eventually outdistanced the others and became, toward the end of the nineteenth century, by far the most powerful source of objection to them.[1]

The prejudice against immigrants has generally developed from two quite different sources. The workingmen's organizations were usually the first to become alarmed because immigrants, often coming from countries which had a low living standard, were willing to accept low wages when they came here. In addition, cultural and language differences made it difficult to organize the immigrants into unions. The fact that they were "cheap labor" made them, on the other hand, welcome to employers and, to a large extent, to middle- and upper-class groups

287

generally because they served as a brake on the labor demands of native American workmen. As more and more immigrants came, however, the alarm spread to upper-class spokesmen. The immigrant, so the opinion ran, had a long-range bad effect upon society. He placed his faith not in his own initiative, so the theory ran, but in the ward politician. When his cause was defeated at the polls, he frequently took to labor violence, anarchism, and radicalism. That this view of the immigrant differed sharply from that of the native workmen, particularly the union men, did not alter the fact that the immigrant more and more encountered prejudice from every level of American society.

Before the Civil War, the immigrant could be fairly certain of a welcome in the United States, wherever he came from, because his labor was needed. Perhaps Ralph Waldo Emerson went a little farther than many Americans would in his welcome to the immigrants, but many people were favorably disposed toward them. Let the immigrants come, Emerson said.

The energy of Irish, Germans, Swedes, Poles, and Cossacks, and all the European tribes—and of the Africans, and of the Polynesians,—will construct a new race, a new religion, a new state, a new literature, which will be as vigorous as the new Europe which came out of the smelting-pot of the Dark ages. . . .[2]

Oliver Wendell Holmes voiced a similar enthusiasm. "We are the Romans of the modern world,—the great assimilating people," he declared in 1858.[3]

Even before the Civil War, however, the welcome extended to the immigrant had begun to fade. "An Irish Catholic seldom attempts to rise to a higher condition than that in which he is placed," one northern commentator observed in the 1850's, "while the Negro often makes the attempt with success."[4] The tales of the primitivism of the Irish were legion. There was, for example, the story of the lady in Boston who had an Irish servant newly arrived from the old country who walked backward down the stairs because the only device she had ever known for getting down from an upper floor was a ladder. The Irish were "dirty Micks," "shanty Irish," "Paddies," and "yellow bellies." And postscripts to employers' notices began to appear: "No Irish need apply."[5]

The prejudice against the Irish and other immigrants expanded in the period after the Civil War. Sometimes the Irishmen's interest in politics and labor unions was given a very sinister turn by nativist spokesmen, and the racial characteristics later associated with Italians and other southern and eastern European immigrants were at first sometimes applied to the Irish. John Hay's novel, *The Bread-Winners* (1883), strongly represents the conviction that the Irish are inherently a deceitful and violent people. The villain of the story is Andy Offitt, an Irishman, whose

whole expression was oleaginous. It was surmounted by a low and shining forehead covered by reeking black hair, worn rather long, the ends being turned under by the brush. The mustache was long and drooping, dyed black and profusely oiled, the dye and the grease forming an inharmonious compound.

Offitt had "one of those gifted countenances which could change in a moment from a dog-like fawning to a snaky venomousness." Contrasted with Offitt is Matchin, the virtuous native American workman, a carpenter by trade. Offitt feels a "spontaneous hatred" for Matchin because of his "shapely build, his curly blond hair and beard, his frank blue eye"; in addition, Matchin's "steady-contented industry" excites in Offitt a "desire to pervert a workman whose daily life was a practical argument against the doctrines of socialism. . . ." Hay observes that native Americans rely on their own efforts and not on politics to advance their fortunes, while, on the other hand, "there was not an Irish laborer in the city but knew his way to his ward club as well as to mass." Offitt comes near to converting Matchin to the doctrines of socialism, but Matchin's native good sense—presumably aided by his superior racial character—saves him.[6]

In the West, and particularly in California, it was the Chinese who first bore the brunt of racism developing against immigrants. The Chinese came to California after the discovery of gold there in 1849. By 1852 there were twenty-five thousand in the state, and because their labor was considered helpful they excited no particularly unfavorable comment. As early as 1855, however, Bayard Taylor was sounding the alarm against the threat of Chinese immigration. It was his "deliberate opinion" that the Chinese were "morally, the most debased people on the face of the earth." Sexual practices which in other countries were "barely names, are in China so common that they excite no comment among the natives. Their touch is pollution, and harsh as the opinion may seem, justice to our own race demands that they should not settle on our soil."[7] As early as 1854, the Chinese in California were barred from testimony in the courts in cases involving whites. The reasoning of the Supreme Court of California in arriving at this decision was that since the Indians were not allowed to testify in the courts against whites and since the Chinese and the Indians were of the same race, the Indians having many centuries ago come from China, the law which applied to the Indians should also apply to the Chinese.[8]

Agitation against the Chinese as immigrants in California did not become strong until the 1870's. In 1868, the federal government had concluded the Burlingame Treaty with China which granted its citizens the right of immigration into this country on the same basis as that granted to other nations.[9] In 1870, however, came the first of the demonstrations of organized labor in California against the Chinese. The following year the demonstrations had become more serious and a number of Chinese were lynched. Dennis Kearney organized the Workingman's Party, one of the main planks in its platform being proposals for the exclusion of the Chinese. In 1876 both the city of San Francisco and the state of California memorialized Congress to repeal the Burlingame Treaty and exclude the Chinese.[10] It was not difficult to discover racist reasons in the anthropology of the times to explain Chinese "inferiority." Henry George, of single-tax fame, expressed an idea concerning the Chinese which was similar to that which had been advanced by Gratiolet with regard to the Negro. The Chinaman was capable of learning up to a certain point of adolescence, he asserted, but unlike the Caucasian he had a limited point of development beyond which it was impossible for him to go.[11] A device of the anti-Chinese propagandists was to write fictional accounts of the coming take-over of American civilization by a flood of Chinese immigrants.[12]

By 1879, the powerful aid of James G. Blaine had been enlisted in the Senate in the cause of Chinese exclusion. "Either the Anglo-Saxon race will possess the Pacific slope," he declared, "or the Mongolians will possess it." It was impossible for the Asiatic to come to the United States and "make a homogeneous element" with our population. "There is not a peasant cottage inhabited by a Chinaman. There is not a hearthstone, in the sense we understand it, of an American home, or an English home, or an Irish, or German, or French home." And thus he was unalterably opposed to the Chinese as immigrants.[13]

In 1882, the first of the exclusion acts against the Chinese was passed by Congress. At first the restriction laws proved unenforceable, and the Chinese continued to arrive in considerable numbers; but subsequent legislation in 1888 and 1892 closed the loopholes and from that time virtually all Chinese were excluded. In agitating for restrictive legislation, the labor unions played a major part. Terence V. Powderley, the head of the Knights of Labor, was one of the leaders in the battle. Samuel Gompers of the American Federation of Labor was also active. Gompers quoted Rudyard Kipling's opinion that the Chinese were a people "without nerves and without digestion" and his sinister prediction that they would "overwhelm the world." His years of experience with the Chinese as well as with other eastern races, said Gompers, was sufficient to convince him that "they have no standard of morals by which a Caucasian may judge them."[14]

The arguments against the Chinese as immigrants began to be extended to other immigrants as well. In the 1880's, immigration from southern and eastern Europe began to increase rapidly and to outdistance that from northern and western Europe and from Great Britain. When this happened, the uneasiness which California had felt concerning the Chinese spread to the East. Here, however, the peoples who mainly bore the brunt of prejudice were the Italians, the Jews, the Poles, the Serbians, the Hungarians, the Greeks, and other non-Teutonic peoples from Europe. The argument against the immigrants was not invariably racial. The immigrant was unused to an industrial society, so it was often said, and he was content with a low wage because he had never had anything else. He became the pawn of unscrupulous employers and politicians, it was maintained, and thus he inadvertently dragged down the standard of living and the moral tone of American workmen. Frequently the temptation was irresistible at this point to add the bald statement that the immigrant was often defective because of his race and thus he could not be assimilated into American civilization without having a bad effect upon it.

We find the racist argument in anti-immigration agitation not merely among the defenders of the status quo, but also among men who were to become famous for their concern for the welfare of the masses. As a young man in the 1880's, Woodrow Wilson was disturbed over the possible biological threat to the nation from the influx of inferior stocks of people. No longer, he declared, did the men of the "sturdy stocks" of northern Europe constitute the main body of "foreign blood" coming to the United States. Their place had been taken by immigrants from southern and eastern Europe, "men out of the ranks where there was neither skill nor energy nor any initiative of quick intelligence. . . ."[15] Frederick Jackson Turner was convinced that the coming of Italians, Poles, Russian Jews, and Slovaks was "a loss to the social organism of the United States." The influx of these peoples, he maintained, was "counter-acting the upward tendency of wages" and encouraging "the sweatshop system." The immigrants were "of doubtful value judged from the ethical point of view of the stocks that have hitherto made the nation." Turner was particularly disturbed over the fact that there were so many Jews among the immigrants. Their generations of life in crowded urban quarters, he said, had "produced a race capable of living under conditions that would exterminate men whom centuries of national selection had not adapted to endure squalor and the unsanitary and indecent conditions of a dangerously crowded population." The Jews, "a people of exceptionally stunted stature and deficient lung capacity," were nonetheless better able than native Americans to survive in the tenements and sweatshops of New York City.[16]

E. A. Ross, the sociologist, one of the most untiring of the advocates of a tight immigration policy, frequently based his arguments on race. "Observe immigrants not as they come travel-wan up the gang-plank, nor as they issue toil-begrimed from the pit's mouth or mill gate," he declared,

but in their gatherings, washed, combed, and in their Sunday best. You are struck by the fact that from ten to twenty per cent are hirsute, low-browed, big-faced persons of obviously low mentality. Not that they suggest evil. They simply look out of place in black clothes and stiff collars, since clearly they belong in skins, in wattled huts at the close of the Great Ice age. These oxlike men are descendants of those *who always stayed behind.*

Ross regarded President Cleveland's veto of the immigration restriction bill of 1893 as "one of the most disastrous actions ever taken by an American president," and in later years he was "shocked" at President Taft's "want of statesmanship" in vetoing similar legislation.[17] John R. Commons, the liberal economist at the University of Wisconsin, had views similar to those of Ross. "The peasantry of Europe to-day is in large part the product of serfdom and of that race-subjection which produced serfdom," he declared. "How different from the qualities of the typical American citizen whose forefathers have erected our edifice of representative democracy."[18]

Josiah Strong, the Social Gospel clergyman, contradicted himself on the problem of immigration. "Christianize the immigrant and he will be easily Americanized," he advised at one point. "Christianity is the solvent of all race antipathies." And yet Strong seems to have had trouble believing in his own rem-

edy. "There is now being injected into the veins of the nation a
large amount of inferior blood every day of every year," he declared in 1893. Five years later, he remarked that we should not
shut our eyes to the fact that "the foreign population, as a
whole, is depressing our average intelligence and morality in the
direction of the dead-line of ignorance and vice." The United
States was a mighty country, he said, but in attempting to absorb immigrants from southern and eastern Europe it was in
something of the predicament of a lion eating a diseased ox.
Someday, Strong warned, "we might have on our hands a very
sick lion."[19]

Jack London worried over the fate of an America overrun
by inferior immigrant races. The virtuous workmen in his novels
are always Anglo-Saxons. "Say, we old Americans ought stick
together, don't you think?" says Billy Roberts, the teamster
hero of The Valley of the Moon, to his sweetheart, Saxon Brown.
"They ain't many of us left. The country's fillin' up with all
kinds of foreigners." Later in the novel, a native American union
member attributes the failure of a strike to the ease with which
employers can hire immigrants at low wages. "There's nothin'
left for us in this country we've made an' our fathers an' mothers
before us," the native American worker declares. "We're all shot
to pieces. We can see our finish—we, the old stock, the children
of the white people that broke away from England an' licked
the tar outa her, that freed the slaves, an' fought the Indians,
an' made the West! Any gink with half an eye can see it
comin'."[20]

Many employers, on the other hand, thought immigration
was a good thing because it insured a continuing supply of cheap
labor. "All I want in my business is muscle," a large employer
of labor in California is reported as saying in the 1870's. "I
don't care whether it be obtained from a Chinaman or a white
man—from a mule or a horse!"[21] The more recent immigrant
was, in fact, often preferred to one who had been here long
enough to develop discontent. A tightfisted employer in Harold
Frederic's novel, The Damnation of Theron Ware (1896), ex-

emplifies this point of view in distinguishing between Irish and Italian workers. The Irish he thoroughly deplored because they were no longer satisfied with low wages. "I know 'em!" the employer declares.

I've had 'em in my quarries for years, an' they ain't got no idea of decency or fair dealin'. Every time the price of stone went up, every man of 'em would jine to screw more wages out of me. Why, they used to keep accounts o' the amount of business I done, an' figger up my profits, an' have the face to come an' talk about 'em, as if that had anything to do with wages.

The Italians are better employees. "I've got Eyetalians in the quarries now," says the employer. "They're sensible fellows: they know when they're well off; a dollar a day, an' they're satisfied, an' everything goes smooth."[22]

Some conservatives steadfastly continued to oppose the demand of labor for immigration restriction and to deny that the admission of immigrants in the past had depressed wages and living standards. In 1905 President Eliot of Harvard criticized Samuel Gompers for advocating restriction. "The Americans who have got into the good trades," said Eliot, "want to keep out all the newcomers from those trades." This prejudice against newcomers was based upon a false theory of economics. "Have wages fallen in the last 50 years or risen?" he asked. "Yet immigrants have been coming by the millions. Cannot we be satisfied to meet dangers of that sort when they actually arrive, without apprehending them beforehand?" Eliot chided the union members for a failure of confidence in their own abilities. "Our laboring class—if I may use such a term—hold a very unmannerly opinion about the newcomers. They have not confidence enough in their own superiority resulting from their own advantages." And he concluded by challenging the laboring men to respect themselves more.[23]

An event which profoundly altered the attitude of many conservatives toward immigrants was the Haymarket bombing in Chicago in 1886. Five of the six anarchists who were charged and condemned in the case were of foreign birth, a fact which was widely interpreted to mean that immigrants were dangerously radical. Marcus L. Hansen, in *The Immigrant in American History* (1940), denied that this inference was correct. These men, Hansen observed, were not typical immigrants. They were exiled revolutionists, not men who had come to this country of their own accord. In addition, said Hansen, the great majority of the immigrants in this country strongly repudiated the bombing. The immigrant press made it clear that it did not sympathize with violence or radicalism. Mass meetings of Germans and Scandinavians condemned the anarchists and affirmed their faith in American institutions. Immigrant church conventions pledged their loyalty and approved the methods by which the anarchists were convicted.[24]

Hansen believed that Samuel Gompers was able to keep the American Federation of Labor a cautious and conservative organization for nearly forty years, from 1886 until his death in 1924, because of the support of trade organizations in which immigrant membership was strong. Congressmen and senators who were foreign born, Hansen pointed out, were usually conservatives. An example was Norwegian-born Senator Knute Nelson of Minnesota, who for thirty years voted consistently with old-guard Republicans and commanded the almost unanimous support of Scandinavians in his state. The immigrant, Hansen concluded, was much more likely to be a conservative than a radical.[25]

Conservatives often had little direct knowledge of immigrants. It was easy for the suspicion to grow among them that these new and unfamiliar Italians, Poles, Hungarians, and Jews were dangerous to society by nature. That this change of attitude among conservatives began in the 1870's and greatly accelerated in the 1880's is borne out by Henry F. May's *Protestant Churches and Industrial America* (1949). In 1870 a labor crisis occurred in a New England town. Exasperated with union demands for higher wages, a factory management in North Adams, Massachusetts, imported Chinese laborers to replace the union men. Organized labor protested. The Protestant religious press, May points out, criticized the union men for objecting to the Chinese and reminded them of the racial issues which had been fought out in the Civil War. The *Congregationalist*, usually a mild and inoffensive journal, became passionate on behalf of the Chinese, whom it described as "youthful, pliable, faithful, quiet, neat to a degree" and praised for their willingness to accept wages "considerably less than those for which the Anglo-Saxons or the Celts, whom they have displaced, have refused to work." Several other religious magazines defended the company for bringing in the Chinese and charged that the labor "monopolists" were getting their just deserts.[26]

During the late 1870's, however, some alarm at the immigrant's supposed radicalism developed in the conservative religious press. When laboring men and inflationist farmers began to organize, these magazines began to suspect the sinister conspiracies of foreign agitators. The *Congregationalist* termed Ben Butler's Greenback-Labor candidacy for the Massachusetts governorship in 1884 an example of "French communism" opposed to "the good old Anglo-Saxon civilization." Despite considerable clerical hostility to immigrant groups, the Protestant press usually was opposed to immigration restriction, one reason being that labor favored it. In 1884, the *Congregationalist* was still steadfast in its opposition to immigration restriction except for Mormon converts and "socialist-anarchists," a stand which May says "represented prevailing church opinion." The Haymarket riot of 1886 did much to change the minds of the editors of the Protestant press. Josiah Strong depicted the immorality, labor unrest, and socialism of cities where there were large numbers of immigrants, and many of the Protestant religious journals began to examine their convictions. "By the end of the decade," May observes, "even conservative Protestants were beginning to agree with labor's demand for restriction, though different grounds were urged."[27]

The dismay of conservatives increased as industrialism proceeded and slums multiplied in the cities. They were generally unwilling to admit that these conditions were the result of complex economic forces. Rather, they sought the simple explanation that poverty and labor unrest were the inevitable results of the new racial character of the population. As early as 1865, E. L. Godkin had noted the tendency of American conservatives to place nearly all the blame for increased political corruption on the immigrants. If we ask a conservative what brought corruption into American life, said Godkin, he will "in nine cases out of ten, assure us that it is foreign immigration that has done it all; that, if no Irish or Germans had ever come to the country, no changes for the worse, either in government or society, would ever have taken place." Godkin, himself an immigrant from Ireland, chided the conservatives for their oversimplified view.[28]

By 1887, however, Godkin had decided that the conservatives might after all be right, although he was apt to attribute the trouble to the later immigrants, not to the Irish and Germans:

An American citizen [before the Civil War] who wrought with his hands in any calling was looked on, like other American citizens, as a man who had his fortunes in his own keeping, and whose judgement alone decided in what manner they could be improved. Nobody thought of him as being in a special degree the protégé of the State. In fact, the idea that he had a special and peculiar claim on State protection was generally treated as a piece of Gallic folly, over which Anglo-Saxons could well afford to smile. . . . We have changed all this very much. . . . There has appeared in great force, and for the first time on American soil, the dependent, State-managed laborer of Europe, who declines to take care of himself in the old American fashion. When he is out of work, or does not like his work, he looks about and asks his fellow-citizens sullenly, if not menacingly, what they are going to do about it. He has brought with him, too, what is called "the labor problem," probably the most un-American of all the problems which American society has to work over to-day.[29]

The more recent immigrants usually had to bear most of the conservatives' blame for the increased labor unrest. "The ranks of anarchy and riots," declared Chauncey Depew in 1892, "number no Americans. The leaders boldly proclaim that they come here not to enjoy the blessings of our liberty and to sustain our institutions but to destroy our government, cut our throats, and divide our property."[30]

In New England, the distrust of the immigrant reached the proportions of a movement in the 1880's and 1890's. This region was plagued by a series of troubles. Thousands of its young men emigrated to the West. Its agricultural communities found it difficult to compete with the more fertile land of the Midwest. Though its industry increased, the factory hands who manned it were drawn more and more from recent immigrants. These consisted now of southern and eastern Europeans and French Canadians rather than the Englishmen, Irishmen, and Germans of a generation before. In addition, these recent immigrants frequently had large families at a time when the size of the native American families was declining.

Some of the native New Englanders feared that they were suffering from biological decay. The idea that the Anglo-Saxon was unsuited for the American climate had been entertained before, particularly by Englishmen. Robert Knox, the Scottish physician and ethnologist, had argued in 1850 that the Anglo-Saxon was unsuited by nature for existence anywhere in the New World. "Already the United States man differs in appearance from the European," Knox declared. The women lost their teeth at an earlier age. The men had stringy muscles and a listless air. Infant mortality was higher, particularly in the South, and in New England the Anglo-Saxon birthrate was declining. All these factors were "warnings" to the Anglo-Saxon, Knox maintained, "that the climate was not made for him, nor he for the climate."[31]

In the 1850's the New Englanders had dismissed such ideas as nonsense, but in the 1880's they began to wonder themselves whether something might not be wrong and whether they would be overwhelmed by a flood of foreign immigrants. Dr. Nathan Allen, a physician of Lowell, Massachusetts, made a study in 1883 of the birthrate of native New Englanders as compared with that of more recent immigrants and sounded the alarm.

The following year Dr. John Ellis, another Massachusetts physician, devoted a book to the same subject. The prospect was, Ellis lamented, that the "glorious old state" would be "ruled by the foreign born and their descendants within a single generation. . . ." Ellis included in his book a letter from a physician who traced the trouble to the woman suffrage movement, the effect of which was to make woman dissatisfied with domestic life and "to tempt her into a fatuous struggle to compete with man in masculine pursuits, overtasking her powers of endurance and debilitating her nervous system." This writer also suggested that "true Christian parents" in New England should have "as many children as they can care for and properly rear," thus averting the disaster of turning the region over to "irreligious or to ignorant foreigners." In the latter years of the decade, the decline of New England native families was believed to be increased by a mysterious scourge of disease which swept the region, particularly the country districts where the proportion of old stock was highest. Some traced the epidemic of sickness to overeating of watermelons; others ascribed it to the pollution of the rivers. Whatever the cause, New Englanders of English extraction were depleted by a wave of this disease as well as by malaria and ague.[32]

Entirely aside from the problem of the immigrants, the old native Americans in New England felt the decline of their region as other regions demanded more of a voice in national affairs. The old New England families, Barbara Solomon has observed in an illuminating essay, had hopes of continuing to supply the leadership, not merely for their own region, but for the country at large. "They regarded the democratic faith of the Flowering as their inherited capital and tried to live by it," she points out. "From the start, however, they narrowed the range of democratic capacity to their own kind. Considering themselves as members of an upper class, 'the best blood in America,' they were proprietary in their obligation to the nation." When other sections of the country and the immigrants in their own section failed to appreciate this high-minded sense of stewardship and were reluctant to submit political and economic affairs to the direction of these men, they sometimes reacted with bitterness. Men whose families had long been high in the councils of the nation felt estranged from the life around them. Henry Adams found himself almost wholly an anachronism in the Washington of General Grant's administration. As a young man, Charles Francis Adams shared his brother Henry's sense of failure. In his diary, Barrett Wendell, another old-stock American, wrote that no one in his generation of native New Englanders had grown to manhood without being tempted to commit suicide.[33]

The idea of decay and of belonging to a dying race obsessed the old New Englanders. James Hosmer and John Fiske wrote nostalgically of the vanishing American of the New England country village. Brooks Adams was convinced that the decay had been worst where industrialism was most advanced. The effect of a manufacturing society, said Adams, was to destroy the old rugged virtues of courage and honor both in England and in America and to substitute for them a value system of the cash nexus. The Industrial Revolution had raised "a timid social stratum to the position of a ruling caste," one "which had never worn the sword, which had always been overridden by soldiers, and which regarded violence with the horror born of fear." The effects of this change could be detected by comparing the novels of Sir Walter Scott with those of Charles Dickens. Scott, who was born too early to feel the full effects of industrialism, proclaimed in his novels that courage and honor were the highest goals toward which man could aspire. In Dickens' novels we see "the destruction of this concept" and thus "all the chief attributes of the heroic mind" are lost. "Taken as a whole, the salient trait which runs through Dickens' writing is fear. Fear both of the unknown and of the known." A hysterical sentimentality pervaded Dickens' novels, Adams argued, a sentimentality representative of a degenerate age. The only remedy he could discover for the decline was a grim one. When the "energy of a race has been exhausted," he observed, it "must probably

remain inert until supplied fresh energetic material by the infusion of barbarian blood."[34]

Early in the 1890's a prominent New Englander studied the
decline of native stock in his region and placed the blame for it
on the influx of foreign immigrants. General Francis A. Walker
was a professor of political economy and history at Yale (1873-
81) and later president of the Massachusetts Institute of Technology (1891-97). He had been chief of the Bureau of Statistics
and Superintendent of the Census. In a statistical study, he advanced the startling thesis that the population of the United
States would have increased as rapidly from the years 1830 to
1880 if not a single immigrant had been admitted. He arrived at
this conclusion by assuming that the decline in the birthrate
had been caused solely by the fact that native Americans disliked
to bring up their children in an atmosphere polluted by sordid
Europeans. "They became increasingly unwilling," said Walker,
"to bring forth sons and daughters who should be obliged to
compete in the market for labor and the walks of life with those
whom they did not recognize as of their own grade and condition."[35]

From this thesis Walker advanced to the conclusion that all
of the industrial ills of the United States had only one real source
—the immigrant. With his appearance, said Walker, the free
states had been "for the first time . . . divided into classes." The
immigrants had "proved themselves the ready tools of demagogues in defying the law, in destroying property and in working violence." A learned clergyman had told Walker that when
a "socialistic mob" picketed the Massachusetts State House, he
heard no word spoken in any language which he knew—not in
English or German or French. Labor unions, Walker added, were
supported mainly by workers of foreign extraction who lacked
the "genius" of the native population. "If," he went on, "the
children and grandchildren of our population of thirty years
ago were alone concerned, it would still be true that the working
classes of this country had no occasion to ask favors in production and trade, or to ask to escape the utmost pressure of indus-

trial competition." Moreover, the immigrant's improvidence was made worse by his fecundity.[36]

In drawing up his indictment against European immigrants, Walker derived ideas both from the Social Darwinists and from the historians of the Teutonic origins school:

The entrance into our political, social, and industrial life, of such vast masses of peasantry, degraded below our utmost conceptions, is a matter which no intelligent patriot can look upon without the gravest apprehension and alarm. These people have no history behind them which is of a nature to give encouragement. They have none of the inherited instincts and tendencies which make it comparatively easy to deal with the immigration of the olden time. They are beaten men from beaten races; representing the worst failures in the struggle for existence. Centuries are against them, as centuries were on the side of those who formerly came to us. They have none of the ideas and aptitudes which fit them to take up readily and easily the problem of self-care and self-government, such as belong to those who are descended from the tribes that met under the oak-trees of old Germany to make laws and choose chieftains.[37]

Walker's point of view did not go unchallenged. Frederick Jackson Turner, for example, suggested that Walker had underestimated the number of Americans who immigrated from the end of the Revolution to 1820 and that he ignored the fact that "increase in wealth and luxury in any country tends to diminish the birth rate." In addition, Turner argued, the unwillingness of Americans to work in eastern industrial concerns had coincided with the "opening up, on a large scale, of the great West, whereby the native American energies found another outlet than in the common labor of factory and the railroad." Although Turner does not specifically attack Walker's thesis that the higher birthrate of the immigrants meant they would eventually displace the native Americans, he handled the identical argument when it was advanced by Francis Parkman, who feared that French Canadians would submerge and eventually overwhelm New England. Parkman's "extravagant apprehensions" were the result of a failure, said Turner, to note the equally high infant mortality rate of immigrants.[38]

Not many eminent men looked as closely at the logic of Walker's thesis as Turner did. John Fiske said that Walker's point of view was "very wise and thoughtful." In an article in the *Forum*, published in 1894, Sydney G. Fisher argued that Walker's thesis could also be used as the basis for the explanation of the decline of American literature from the great days of Emerson, Lowell, Holmes, and Longfellow. Literature of genius was "the expression of the deep, united feeling" of a people. The great period of the literature of New England had been from 1830 to 1860, before the full tide of alien immigration. "The only real literature we have ever had in the United States," Fisher declared, "arose during the period when the native feeling and homogeneousness of the country was strongest. . . ." Nowhere had this been more true than in New England. Now that the population of the region was 50 per cent foreign, there were only a few writers of any real merit within the region. "The high and deep tones are gone," Fisher lamented, "and it is not likely that we shall ever hear them again."[39]

It is in the light of theories like these that we can best understand the dislike—sometimes the downright loathing—for the immigrant which existed in minds otherwise cultivated, tolerant, and urbane. It shows up in many ways. For example, there is a persistent strain of anti-Semitism in Henry Adams. When he was editor of the *North American Review* and the magazine was in financial difficulties, his great fear was that it might perish on his hands or—even worse—"go to some Jew." In his personal letters, Adams refers on a number of occasions to his dislike of seeing rich Jews on transatlantic liners and in other public places. In the celebrated Dreyfus case, Adams was strongly anti-Dreyfus and expressed his satisfaction with "how emphatically the army, through the court-martial, set its foot on the Jews and smashed the Dreyfus intrigue into a pancake." Even when the innocence of Dreyfus was strongly established, Adams was reluctant to admit that French army officers had been guilty of perjury or of falsifying evidence. A "reasonable error" rather than a "conspiracy" on the part of the General Staff was, in Adams' opinion, the root of the difficulty. Henry James expressed strong anti-Semitic prejudices, and he seems to have felt little liking for other immigrants from eastern and southern Europe. When he returned to the United States for a visit in 1904, James recorded his dismay at the extent to which the "alien" had taken serene possession of the land.[40]

John Fiske lamented that New England was passing into the hands of "proprietors of an inferior type." Owen Wister recorded that a short story of his about a sleazy Jewish student at Harvard who is contrasted unfavorably with other students who are of native American stock brought him a letter of approval from William James. Henry Cabot Lodge recalled the gloomy turn of the tide of events when as a boy he and his fellow students at the Boston Latin School began to be overwhelmed by their more numerous Irish enemies in street fights. Barrett Wendell lamented the passing of the New Englander of native stock and lashed out at the immigrants. To an Englishman he wrote of his resentment against Mary Antin, a Jewish immigrant from Russia who had written books favorable to immigration. "She has developed an irritating habit of describing herself and her people as Americans," he complained, "in distinction from such folks as Edith and me, who have been here for three hundred years."[41] These examples of prejudice against immigrants, taken from the words of eminent men, could be matched and probably exceeded by popular nativist sentiment of the time. But we must justifiably have expected something better from men of learning and attainment.

Theodore Roosevelt's campaign against birth control was probably a reflection of the fears of certain old Americans that the native stock would be supplanted by the immigrants. In a letter to Cecil Spring-Rice, Roosevelt declared that of all the evil in America the worst was "the diminishing birth rate among the old native American stock." Roosevelt could scarcely find words to express his detestation of a person who deliberately chose not to have children. "Such a creature merits contempt as hearty as any visited upon the soldier who runs away in battle. . . ." Over the years Roosevelt continued to urge that Americans have big families, and the likelihood is that he was speaking especially to native Americans. "Willful sterility," he moralized, "inevitably produces and accentuates every hideous form of vice. . . . It is itself worse, more debasing, more destructive, than ordinary vice. . . . I rank celibate profligacy as not one whit better than polygamy."[42]

A serious campaign was initiated for the restriction of immigration. The Immigration Restriction League, formed in Boston in 1894, advocated federal laws to stem the tide. John Fiske was the first president, and the executive committee consisted of a number of conservative and wealthy New Englanders.[43] The next year Thomas Bailey Aldrich, in a widely discussed poem, "Unguarded Gates," published in the *Atlantic,* expressed the typical fears of the conservative restrictionist:

> Wide open and unguarded stand our gates,
> And through them presses a wild motley throng—
> Men from the Volga and the Tartar steppes,
> Featureless figures of the Hoana-Ho,
> Malayan, Scythian, Teuton, Kelt, and Slav,
> Flying the Old World's poverty and scorn;
> These bringing with them unknown gods and rites,
> Those, tiger passions, here to stretch their claws.
> In street and alley what strange tongues are loud,
> Accents of menace alien to our air,
> Voices that once the Tower of Babel knew!
>
> O Liberty, white Goddess! Is it well
> To leave the gates unguarded? On thy breast
> Fold Sorrow's children, soothe the hurts of fate,
> Lift the down-trodden, but with hand of steel
> Stay those who to thy sacred portals come
> To waste the gifts of freedom. Have a care
> Lest from thy brow the clustered stars be torn
> And trampled in the dust. For so of old
> The thronging Goth and Vandal trampled Rome,
> And where the temples of the Caesars stood
> The lean wolf unmolested made her lair.[44]

John W. Burgess, professor at Columbia University, expounded the same theme in the pages of the *Political Science Quarterly.*

What folly, on the part of the ignorant, what wickedness, on the part of the intelligent, are involved in the attempts . . . to pollute [the United States] with non-Aryan elements. . . . We must preserve our Aryan nationality in the state, and admit to its membership only such non-Aryan race-elements as shall have become Aryanized in spirit and in genius by contact with it, if we would build the superstructure of the ideal American commonwealth.[45]

Anti-immigration sentiment was strongest in New England and weakest in the South. We might have conjectured that the racial arguments used by the advocates of restriction would have gained a warm reception in the South, but there were not enough immigrants there for the issue to become a warm one. Some influential southerners hoped that the immigrant stream from Europe could be partially diverted in their direction. For this purpose, a number of southern states had set up elaborate commissions in the 1890's to advertise their attractions to prospective immigrants from Europe. This movement was strong enough to make Booker T. Washington fear the incursion of Europeans who might compete with Negro labor. In his speech at the Atlanta Exposition of 1900, Washington warned southerners of the consequences. White men should not "look to the incoming of those of foreign birth and strange tongue and habits for the prosperity of the South," he declared, but should rely upon Negroes, "people who have, without strikes and labour wars," for centuries performed the necessary labor to support the region's economy.[46]

The immigration commissions of the southern states received bad publicity when charges began to be heard that their real purpose was to foster systems of peonage for immigrants in the South. After several foreign countries had blacklisted southern states for their emigrants and the attorney general of the United States had censured the commissions' activities in 1907, they were generally abandoned by the state governments. When this happened, southerners seem to have decided that they did not want the immigrants anyway. Doubtless they were affected by the rising sentiment against the immigrant in the North. In 1906 the governor of Alabama is reported as thanking God that his state had only one-half of one per cent foreign born among its population. The same year James Horace Patten warned any fellow southerner who had enough patriotism to say to himself occasionally "my own, my native Southland," not to look to the "slum-loving, degraded peasantry" of Europe for new workers. In the large cities of the North, said Patten, such immigrants had substituted "boss despotism" for "popular government, as our Teutonic forefathers conceived it." "Are not our democratic institutions, our ideals, and our national character worth preserving," he asked, "even if it should be necessary to get along with a little less rapid exploitation of our resources?"[47]

Senator Tom Watson of Georgia predicted in 1906 that the day must come when the United States would have to reckon with its European immigrants. "Goths, Huns, Vandals, who lust for loot," these men "cannot be driven back by arguments." The time would come, warned Watson, when the order would go out for those defending the ramparts, "Put none but Americans on guard tonight." The same year the president of the Nashville Board of Trade advised the Southern Immigration Conference against admitting "that class of immigrants that breeds discontent and makes anarchists and midnight assassins. . . ."[48]

In spite of strong anti-immigration agitation, the only major restrictive legislation which was passed in the period before World War I was that for the exclusion of the Chinese. Toward the end of the nineteenth century, Japanese laborers began coming in considerable numbers to California. In 1906, the school board of San Francisco instituted a segregated system of education for Orientals. The Japanese government complained, and Theodore Roosevelt attempted to persuade the school authorities to change their policy. At first the school board refused to do so, but they later assented when Roosevelt worked out a "gentleman's agreement" restricting immigration from Japan. In 1907,

Japan agreed to refuse passports to laborers going to the United States for the first time, and thus Japanese immigration was reduced to one-tenth of its former figure.[49]

Otherwise, such restrictions as were placed upon immigration were relatively minor. Even in New England, where anti-immigration sentiment was strong, the movement was frequently on the defensive because there were enough people of the recent immigrant stocks to reply to the arguments of the restrictionists. Immigration into this country continued to be heavy—in 1907 rising to well over a million.[50] The end to large-scale immigration was to come after World War I had immensely increased racial antipathies in this country. In addition, the opponents of immigration would then be handed a new weapon—that of the intelligence tests devised by psychologists for the armed services. After World War I, when the anti-immigration chorus grew, many of the ideas of the earlier restrictions would be dusted off and used again, but until this happened the immigration movement continued relatively unchecked.

XIII

Imperialism and
The Anglo-Saxon

ALTHOUGH A BELIEF in the superiority of the Anglo-Saxon was not the ostensible cause for which the United States went to war with Spain in 1898, this theme often engaged the attention of proponents of the war. The war was no exception to Dr. Albert Shaw's thesis that "the power and persistence of ideas lie at the base of all historical movements."[1] The great theme of the war was, of course, that Spain was a malefactor nation who deserved the punishment of losing her colonies; but it was also argued that the peculiar virtues of the Anglo-Saxon made it desirable as well as necessary that he should expand his dominion abroad.

The war of 1898 was not the first American war in which an appeal had been made to the magnificent destiny of Anglo-Saxons. During the debates over expansion before and during the Mexican War, we can detect the emergence of race theories which later were to play so large a part in justifying war, expansion, and imperialism. As early as 1845, John O'Sullivan, the founder and editor of the *Democratic Review* and the supposed coiner of the phrase "manifest destiny," was convinced that the continent should belong to Americans because they were members of a superior race. Of Mexican territory he said:

The Anglo-Saxon foot is already on its borders. Already the advance guard of the irresistible army of Anglo-Saxon emigration has begun to pour down upon it. . . . A population will soon be in actual occupation of California, over which it will be idle for Mexico to dream of dominion.[2]

During the Civil War there seems to have been little emphasis upon Anglo-Saxon race themes. Sir Charles Lyell, an English sympathizer with the Confederate cause, explained the early southern victories as the result of "the prowess of the southern army, in which was not that large mixture of Celtic and German blood found on the Northern side."[3] Years after the war was over, one northern observer thought that it had been waged between two distinct races—the Goths of the North typified by the matter-of-fact and steady Grant and the Celts of the South typified by fire-eating southern gentlemen. The proponent of this novel view traced the cause of the war back to early immigration from separate parts of England.[4] As late as the 1920's, Clinton S. Burr explained the Civil War as representing a race war between the "yeomanry" of New England who were "Anglo-Saxon in the strictest sense of the word," on one side, and the "Normans" of the South, on the other.[5] The division of Yankees and Confederates into separate races, however, was never more than a curiosity as an idea.

In the 1840's the appeal to Anglo-Saxon supremacy had largely been a matter of emotion, of Fourth-of-July oratory, and was closely related to a belief in the unique merit of American political institutions. Moreover, Anglo-Saxon was not even firmly established as the name of the race to which most Americans belonged. Daniel Webster preferred to speak of the "Anglo-American race" which had "issued from the great Caucasian fountain."[6] By the time of the Spanish-American War, the idea of race superiority had deeply penetrated nearly every field—biology, sociology, history, literature, and political science. Then there was no doubt whatever concerning the name of the race. The supremacy of the Anglo-Saxon still figured in Fourth-of-July oratory, but it also had immense philosophic and scientific backing.

Social Darwinism provided ready and seemingly invincible arguments for the expansionist of 1898. Darwin himself had invested the westward movement of the American nation with all the force of a law of nature. "There is apparently much truth in the belief that the wonderful progress of the United States,

as well as the character of the people," Darwin had written in
The Descent of Man, "are the results of natural selection. . . ."
The nation was superior because "the more energetic, restless,
and courageous men from all parts of Europe" had emigrated
to the country during the previous ten or twelve generations.
Although various racial strains had contributed to the American
nation, it was the Anglo-Saxon strain which predominated.
"Looking to the distant future," Darwin added,

> I do not think that the Rev. Mr. Zincke takes an exaggerated view
> when he says: "All other series of events—as that which resulted in the
> culture of mind in Greece, and that which resulted in the empire of
> Rome—only appear to have purpose and value when viewed in connec-
> tion with, or rather as subsidiary to . . . the great stream of Anglo-
> Saxon emigration to the west."[7]

Disciples of Darwin often found it easy to fit the Spanish-
American War into their theories of struggle and natural selection. Some months after the war, at a dinner in New York
given in honor of the English sociologist Benjamin Kidd, that
gentleman is reported as having said: "In my judgment, the gun
fired by Admiral Dewey in the Bay of Manila was the most
important historical event since the battle of Waterloo." Following Kidd, Professor Franklin H. Giddings of Columbia University declared: "I find myself compelled to differ from the distinguished guest of the evening in his estimate of the battle of
Manila Bay. In my judgment it was the most important historical event since Charles Martel turned back the Moslems in
732 A.D." The shot at Manila Bay was of such vast importance
because "the great question of the twentieth century is whether
the Anglo-Saxon or the Slav is to impress his civilization on the
world."[8]

A vigorous expansionist, Giddings from the first moralized
on the great lessons of racial destiny to be derived from the war.
"We read to-day of the superiority of the Anglo-Saxon, and of
the decadence of the Latin race," he declared.

> A people that idly sips its cognac on the boulevards as it lightly takes

a trifling part in the *comedie humaine* can only go down in the struggle for existence with men who have learned that happiness, in distinction from idle pleasure, is the satisfaction that comes only with the tingling of the blood, when we surmount the physical and moral obstacles of life.

The American was superior because he was "at bottom a Saxon-Norman." In his veins coursed "the blood of the old untamable pirates."[9]

Two years after the war, Giddings was still lambasting Americans who had opposed it. "It seems never to have occurred to these gentlemen [the anti-imperialists]," Giddings declared, "that, if we *are* a nation of jingoes, bullies, and sensation lovers, it is a waste of breath to talk about what might have been if we had all been reasonable, long-suffering, diplomatic, and peace-loving." Instead of railing against "cosmic law," Giddings advised, the anti-imperialist "wise men" should "address themselves to the practical question: How can the American people best adapt themselves to their new responsibilities?"[10] If the "reservoir of energy" of the American people was not allowed to express itself in expansion, Giddings asked anti-imperialists to reflect, it might

discharge itself in anarchistic, socialistic, and other destructive modes that are likely to work incalculable mischief. . . . In those . . . millions who are descended from an earlier American stock, the primitive human passions have not been brought under absolute control, and the love of primitive occupations that partake of danger has not been eradicated. . . . It is not yet three hundred years since the colonists of our eastern coasts were performing their daily industrial tasks under the shadow of ever threatening danger from savage foes. . . . Are we to suppose that the offspring of such men, in so short an interval, have lost those instincts that lead men to prefer enterprises that call for physical courage and resourcefulness?[11]

Professor Harry H. Powers subscribed to the same heady doctrine. The Spanish-American War, he maintained, could be understood only as the first event in a decisive new era. The next generation would "see the entire world under the jurisdiction or within the 'sphere of influence' of half a dozen powers" which in turn would "continue the struggle for race supremacy with increasing definiteness and determination."[12] He had "no comment to make on the ethics of evolution," he declared, but would merely insist that war among the races was inevitable whether or not it was "congenial to our moral sense."[13] Before the American Academy of Political and Social Science, Powers spelled out just how much of an expansionist he was. From the "well-known biological principle that growth is a necessary consequence of life and . . . without it life cannot possibly persist," he drew a sensational inference. We must recognize, he said, that Americans "want the earth not consciously as a formulated program, but instinctively."[14] In the coming struggle, Powers foresaw the eventual victory of the Anglo-Saxon. In fact, his only real competitor was the Slav, who was "far below the Saxon" in every quality which could contribute to success "unless it be in his willingness to devote all his energies to national aggrandizement."[15]

War against Spain exactly fitted in with the theories of most of the men who had glorified the strength and virtue of the Anglo-Saxon. Even Brooks Adams, ordinarily pessimistic in his prophecies, was momentarily raised to a vast enthusiasm. "If an inference may be drawn from the past," exulted Adams, "Anglo-Saxons have little to fear in a trial of strength; for they have been the most successful of adventurers." Such movements as the Spanish-American War were "not determined by argument" but by "forces which override the volition of man."[16] "No man, no party, can fight with any chance of final success against a cosmic tendency; no cleverness, no popularity avails against the spirit of the age."[17]

Whitelaw Reid, editor of the New York Tribune, depended heavily on the determinist argument in favor of expansion and gave only a secondary position to moral arguments. He questioned whether a nation could set limits to its expansion. "When a tree stops growing," declared Reid, "our foresters tell us it is ripe for the axe. When a man stops in his physical and intellectual growth he begins to decay. When a nation stops growing it has passed the meridian of its course, and its shadows fall eastward.''[18] After Spain had ceded the Philippines to the United States, Reid insisted that the moral issue of imperialism had been settled. "The American people is in lawful possession of the Philippines, with the assent of all Christendom, with a title as indisputable as its title to California," he asserted, "and, though the debate will linger for a while, . . . the generation is yet unborn that will see them abandoned to the possession of any other Power." This conclusion was for him the only possible one.

The Nation that scatters principalities as a prodigal does his inheritance, is too sentimental and moonshiny for the nineteenth century, or the twentieth. . . . It may flourish in Arcadia or Altruria; but it does not among the sons of the pilgrims, or on the continent they subdued by stern struggle to the uses of civilization.[19]

Only a few extremists, however, carried the Social Darwinist argument to the point where war was justified for its own sake. Rear Admiral Stephen B. Luce had proclaimed in 1891 that war was one of the great agencies of human conflict and that "strife in one form or another in the organic world seems to be the law of existence. . . . Suspend the struggle, well called the battle of life, for a brief space, and death claims the victory."[20] Captain Alfred T. Mahan sometimes seemed close to the same assumption. In 1897, urging that the United States not be content with "passive self-defense," he reasoned thus: "All around us now is strife; 'the struggle of life,' 'the race of life,' are phrases so familiar that we do not feel their significance till we stop to think about them. Everywhere nation is arrayed against nation; our own no less than others." But Mahan drew back from an out-and-out glorification of war and took refuge in the argument that if one wants peace it is best to keep one's powder dry. "Let us worship peace, indeed," he conceded, "as the goal at which humanity must hope to arrive; but let us not fancy that peace is to be had as a boy wrenches an unripe fruit from a tree."[21]

It was easy to find men who called upon the eternal truths

of the Christian religion to justify expansion. Some came close to putting the seal of divine approval upon the doctrine of the survival of the fittest and the struggle for existence. The Reverend Oliver C. Miller of San Francisco, for example, declared that "bloodletting is still good for all nations. . . . For nation and individual the law of cleansing is the same. 'Without the shedding of blood there is no remission of sins.' "[22] Ex-Senator W. A. Peffer saw a more specific connection between the war and the divine will. "God must have intended that savage life and customs should yield to higher standards of living," he argued, "or he would have made the earth many times larger."[23] Lyman Abbott saw the hand of God in the increased power of the American people. "The real reason why the American navy beats the Spanish navy is because we have learned to use 'God's projectiles,' " he maintained, "and they have not learned in Spain. We have been taught how to lay hold of the muscles of the Almighty, and this knowledge is the fulcrum by which man and God work together to elevate the human race."[24]

It was the Reverend Josiah Strong, however, who saw most clearly the relationship between the war and God's plan for the favored races. For nearly twenty years he had been preaching the supremacy of the Anglo-Saxons and their eventual domination of the world. They were the "great colonizing race of the ages," he declared in 1893, and in fulfilment of their "mission" were carrying their civilization, "like a ring of Saturn—a girdle of light,—around the globe."[25] Anglo-Saxon expansion, he stated in 1900, was "God's great alphabet with which he spells for man his providential purposes." Anti-expansionists throughout American history, he argued, had clearly been in opposition to the will of God. "For a hundred years now, blind men have been quarreling with our national destiny or with divine Providence," said Strong.

They declared that Jefferson violated the Constitution in the purchase of Louisiana; they opposed the purchase of Florida; they were vehement in their opposition to the acquisition of Texas and California . . . ; they rejected Hawaii when offered as a gift, and would have had Dewey sail away from the Philippines, leaving an apple of discord to the European Powers, or dooming them to anarchy.[26]

On the other hand, he declared, men interested in discerning the will of God were more likely to favor the acquisition of foreign territory under the United States flag. "You will find that all American missionaries are in favor of expansion," Strong was told by a missionary friend in China.[27] It was true, Strong said, that many "excellent people" found it difficult to reconcile the war with an enlightened conscience, but to believe this was to believe that "force should never be used for moral ends." Such an argument was, of course, absurd. "Disciples of Count Tolstoi" and "philosophical anarchists," to be consistent, would be obliged to argue further that they did not believe "a loving parent" could wisely use force "to correct or restrain a wayward child. They would not have the police employ force to suppress a riot or to prevent robbery and bloodshed."[28] After the Philippines were ceded by Spain to the United States, Strong foresaw that the next area for Anglo-Saxon expansion would be closer home. "Our possessions cannot be any too extended in the Caribbean Sea," he declared, "provided only they come to us, as Captain Mahan says, by righteous means."[29]

Not all Americans were comfortable with the idea of the war as primarily an expansionist venture. Many who supported the war emphasized the wickedness of Spain and conceived of the United States as a liberator of enslaved peoples both in Cuba and in the Philippines. Reverend Washington Gladden, one of the foremost exponents of the Social Gospel in this country, declared that "to resist war [with Spain] was to stand in the way of the righteous retribution of God which ought to descend on a great malefactor." The relationship of the United States to the Cubans and the Filipinos after the war was a question which Gladden was willing to leave vague and unsettled. It is obvious, he argued, that "the constructive ideas of our civilization are Anglo-Saxon ideas. About that I should think there can be no dispute among intelligent men."[30] Apparently Gladden felt that the superior principles of the Anglo-Saxons would somehow apply themselves when the time came for colonial questions to be settled. Other Americans were convinced that the moral supremacy of the United States overrode other considerations. Much as the war was to be deplored, the National Education Association declared in a resolution,

the teachers of the United States recognize that it has been entered upon in the most unselfish spirit and from the loftiest motives. The cause of freedom and humanity, and the solidarity of both the American people and the Anglo-Saxon races is vastly increased by such an armed contest.[31]

Many of the proponents of expansion did not distinguish between determinist and moral arguments. Albert J. Beveridge, for example, argued that it was both useless and immoral to resist acquisition of foreign territory:

The American Republic is a part of the movement of a race,—the most masterful race of history,—and race movements are not to be stayed by the hand of man. They are mighty answers to Divine commands. Their leaders are not only statesmen of peoples—they are prophets of God. The inherent tendencies of a race are its highest law. They precede and survive all statutes, all constitutions. . . . The sovereign tendencies of our race are organization and government.

The spirit of our race was such that it "obeys that Voice not to be denied which bids us strive and rest not, makes of us our brother's keeper, and appoints us steward under God of the civilization of the world."[32] To Melville E. Ingalls, a friend and railroad president who disapproved of the war, Beveridge wrote: "Never forget that we are the only people on earth whose farmers buy the adjoining farm before they need it. We are of the blood which furnishes the world with its Daniel Boones, its Francis Drakes, its Cecil Rhodes—and its M. E. Ingalls."[33]

Theodore Roosevelt avoided the word "Anglo-Saxon," not only in his speeches but in his private correspondence. Perhaps the fact that he had Dutch ancestry caused him to dislike the term. Also, it was his habit on many occasions to cultivate a truculent anti-British attitude which made it inconvenient for him to recognize any racial bond between the two countries. When he was Assistant Secretary of the Navy, Roosevelt was introduced to Rudyard Kipling and "thanked God in a loud voice that he had not one drop of British blood in him," that his ancestry was pure Dutch. He added that he relied on American fear of the British to provide him with funds for a new navy.[34] Still, Roosevelt was nothing if not a politician. In addition to other objections to the term "Anglo-Saxon" he may have realized that it probably would antagonize those Americans who did not consider themselves members of the race.

What Roosevelt did, in effect, was to create a new ethnological division—the "American race" or "our race"—and then give it all the qualities which others attributed to Anglo-Saxons.[35] When Finley Peter Dunne's Mr. Dooley characterized Roosevelt's election in 1904 as an "Anglo-Saxon triumph," Roosevelt defended himself against the charge. He had never called the United States an Anglo-Saxon country, he insisted. Here in America was "a new and mixed race—a race drawing its blood from many different sources. . . ."[36] After this explanation was made, however, it was difficult to detect many differences between Roosevelt's new race and what others had been content to describe as Anglo-Saxons. To Roosevelt the early Texans were like "Norse sea-rovers." In wresting land from Mexicans and Indians, they showed both the faults and the virtues of a barbaric age. "They were restless, brave, and eager for adventure, excitement, and plunder; they were warlike, resolute and enterprising; they had all the marks of a young and hardy race, flush with the pride of strength and self-confidence." It is true, he admitted, that "they were utterly careless of the rights of others, looking upon the possessions of all weaker races as simply their natural prey."[37] But pioneers, Roosevelt argued elsewhere, should not be judged by ordinary moral standards. "Most fortunately," he observed, "the hard, energetic, practical men who do the rough pioneer work of civilization in barbarous lands are not prone to false sentimentality." Those who had complained about the lack of regard of the pioneers for the rights of Indians were usually people who didn't have enough initiative to go West in the first place.

Often these stay-at-homes are too selfish and indolent, too lacking in imagination, to understand the race-importance of the work which is done by pioneer brethren in wild and distant lands; and they judge them by standards which would only be applicable to quarrels in their own townships and parishes.[38]

Such views as these fitted in admirably with Roosevelt's enthusiasm for the war and for the administration of overseas territory. "The timid man," he proclaimed,

the lazy man, the man who distrusts his country, the over-civilized man, who has lost the great fighting, masterful virtues, the ignorant man, the man of dull mind whose soul is incapable of feeling the mighty life that thrills "stern men with empires in their brains"—all these, of course, shrink from seeing the nation undertake its new duties. . . .

A nation which "trained itself to a career of unwarlike and isolated ease" was bound, in the end, "to go down before other nations which have not lost the manly and adventurous qualities."[39] If the United States were to seek "slothful ease and ignoble peace," then "the bolder and stronger peoples" would pass us by and would "win for themselves the domination of the world."[40]

The theory of Anglo-Saxon superiority was invoked, not only to justify American expansion, but also to promote closer relations between the United States and England. The idea that the two countries should work together in matters of foreign policy because of their racial kinship was not, of course, new. In 1839, Thomas Carlyle had written to Emerson that the two Saxon countries, mother and daughter, should arrange an annual meeting of "All-Saxondom." At the moment, Carlyle argued, London was the best place for such a meeting, but the time might well come when Boston or New York would have its turn.[41] In 1850, Martin F. Tupper—a writer of popular verse in England—had expressed a friendly wish for closer and more familial relations between the two nations:

> Yes, Anglo-Saxon brother,
> I see your heart is right,
> And we will warm each other
> With all our loves alight . . .
>
> There's nothing foreign in your face
> Nor strange upon your tongue;
> You come not of another race
> From baser lineage sprung:
> No, brother! though away you ran,
> As truant boy will do,
> Still true it is, young Jonathan,
> My fathers fathered you![42]

An anonymous writer in Rhode Island answered this plea in another verse:

> Join then the Stripes, and Stars, and Cross,
> In one fraternal band,
> Till Anglo-Saxon faith and laws
> Illumine every land:
> And in broad day, the basking earth
> Shall thank the King of Heaven,
> That dear Columbia, blessed birth,
> To England's lap was given.[43]

In 1852, Tennyson published a poem, "Hands All Round," which stressed the mother-and-daughter relationship and oneness of blood:

> Gigantic daughter of the West
> We drink to thee across the flood,
> We know thee most, we love thee best,
> For art thou not of British blood?
> Should war's mad blast again be blown,
> Permit not thou the tyrant powers
> To fight thy mother here alone,
> But let thy broadsides roar with ours.
> Hands all round![44]

Before the Spanish-American War, the racial unity of the two peoples seems to have been noted more often in England than in this country. One of the few American disciples of Anglo-American unity was John Fiske, who, in 1880, stressed the advantages for the United States of close partnership with England. He called upon the English-speaking peoples to join as missionaries in the political regeneration of the world.[45] In 1890, James K. Hosmer, the American historian, appealed for an "English-Speaking Fraternity" powerful enough to withstand any coalition of European or Asiatic powers.[46] In 1897, Captain Mahan expressed his hope that the common race heritage of England and America would lead them to a common foreign policy.[47]

But in spite of occasional expressions of the need for amity and a joint policy with England, the mood of this country before the Spanish-American War was such as to make any alliance out of the question. The anti-British sentiment inherited from two wars with the mother country and the disposition of influential men in the British government to favor the cause of the South in the Civil War were enough to silence nearly all talk of close relations between the two nations. When he visited this country as a young man in 1889, Rudyard Kipling was surprised at the virulence of anti-British sentiment, although he tried to be good-humored about it. He recorded his impressions of the after-dinner oratory of a Fourth-of-July banquet in San Francisco:

I sat bewildered on a coruscating Niagara of—blatherumskite. It was magnificent—it was stupendous; and I was conscious of a wicked desire to hide my face in a napkin and grin. Then, according to rule, they produced their dead, and across the snowy tablecloths dragged the corpse of every man slain in the Civil War, and hurled defiance at "our natural enemy" (England, so please you!) "with her chain of fortresses across the world."[48]

An American friend of Kipling's attempted to explain to him after the banquet that the oratory really meant very little. "The skyrockets are thrown in for effect," he said, "and whenever we get on our hind legs we always express a desire to chaw up England. It's a sort of family affair." This explanation soothed Kipling and he, in turn, attempted to reassure his British readers. "When you come to think of it," he suggested,

there is no other country for the American public speaker to trample upon. . . . France has Germany; we have Russia; for Italy, Austria is provided; and the humblest Pathan possesses an ancestral enemy. Only America stands out of the racket; and therefore, to be in fashion, makes a sand-bag of the mother-country, and bangs her when occasion requires.[49]

Anti-British sentiment was strong enough in this country in 1895 to make the belligerent attitude of President Cleveland and Secretary of State Olney toward England immensely popular. In 1897, when Professor Albert V. Dicey, the English historian of law, advocated common citizenship for Americans and Englishmen, his proposal—by his own admission—"fell flat." He received a few expressions of sympathy and good will from prominent men in the United States, but he was told that such a project was hopeless from the start in the light of public opinion here.[50] Six months before the war, said Professor Franklin H. Giddings of Columbia, he had heard an American senator express the conviction that most of his constituents in the Mississippi Valley believed "that the British Empire ought to be blotted from the map of the world!"[51] Giddings doubted that animosity toward Britain in any part of the country really threatened war, but he did not believe the relations between the two countries had been a matter for serious concern.

One effect of the war was to reveal the need of the United States for the friendship of Great Britain. On paper, at least, Spain was a formidable military power for the United States to attack. She had nearly 200,000 troops in Cuba, whereas the United States Army consisted of 28,000 men scattered in small detachments from the Yukon to Florida. The navy had more battleships than Spain, but fewer armored cruisers and torpedo craft. The American army was badly equipped. There were enough Krag rifles for the Regulars, but the 200,000 volunteers called up by the President were issued Springfields and black powder. There was no khaki cloth in the country, and thousands of troops fought the summer campaign in Cuba clothed in the heavy uniform of winter garrison duty. In addition, France and Germany openly sympathized with Spain and there were real fears in this country of their intervention. After the United States won the war and just before his death in 1898, Bismarck is said to have remarked that God seemed to take care of drunkards, fools, and the United States.[52]

At this time, England was finding its "splendid isolation" precarious in the face of the growing challenge of both Germany and Russia; and the Boer War was already in the making. Accordingly, English policy was to court American friendship. Just before the war began, Earl Grey said to John Hay, the American ambassador to England: "Why do not the United States borrow our navy to make a quick job of Cuba? They could return us the favour another time." The offer was refused, but the fact that it had been made Hay found gratifying.[53] Joseph Chamberlain told Hay a few weeks before the beginning of the war that he was extremely desirous of a close alliance with the United States, or, if that were prevented by American traditions, "of an assurance of common action on important questions." Hay was in favor of as close an agreement with England as American public opinion would permit. "Shoulder to shoulder," he declared to President McKinley in reporting the offer, "we could command peace the world over."[54]

A few weeks later, on May 13, 1898, Chamberlain made an address in Birmingham, England, and bid specifically for an Anglo-American alliance. "Our first duty is to draw all parts of the empire into close unity," he declared, "and our next to maintain the bonds of permanent unity with our kinsmen across the Atlantic." This sentiment provoked loud cheers and Chamberlain went on to say,

There is a powerful and generous nation, speaking our language, bred of our race, and having interests identical with ours. I would go so far as to say that, terrible as war may be, even war itself would be cheaply purchased if in a great and noble cause the Stars and Stripes and the Union Jack should wave together over an Anglo-Saxon alliance.[55]

Almost without exception British newspapers endorsed Chamberlain's speech.[56] One authority on the Spanish-American War has described as "astonishing" its favorable reception in the American press.[57] Newspapers which had never been known to harbor any affection for the British suddenly proclaimed the power and beneficence of united Anglo-Saxon peoples. The *Chicago Tribune*, for example, expressed the general satisfaction:

There may never be such an alliance in formal written terms. And there may be. But what is unmistakable, not only inevitable, in the future but actual in the present, actual and potent, is this: that the two great branches of the Anglo-Saxon race are drawing nearer and nearer together for coöperation in peace, and, in logical sequence, in war as well. Every word that promotes that movement is to be welcomed and applauded. Well to the fore among such words are those spoken by Mr. Chamberlain, directly to an English audience, but indirectly and no less meaningly to all the world.[58]

The magazine campaign urging closer relations between the two countries was led by the *Century*. "This new interchange of sympathy realizes the statesman's noble vision of race patriotism," the magazine editorialized, "and signifies the extinction in America of the anti-British jingo."[59] In its reflections on Independence Day that year, the *Century* said the time had come for rejoicing that the two nations had become reconciled to one another. "The day," it continued,

will be distinguished by the omission of the occasional tirades against England. There is no progress of the world that is not marked by somebody's change of mind, and in the last three months even the most violent prejudices among our people against our English kinsmen have disappeared in the face of unmistakable evidence of her sympathy with America in the irrepressible conflict between the ideas of the sixteenth century and those of the nineteenth. . . . the two great divisions of the Anglo-Saxon race are "in closer sympathy than ever before."[60]

Prominent men in America individually campaigned for the new accord. Brooks Adams was convinced that "an Anglo-Saxon alliance, directed to attain certain common ends, might substantially make its own terms."[61] Barrett Wendell rejoiced that the family quarrel between the two nations was at an end and the peoples had both come to realize that the success of either meant the advancement of what was "noblest" in the other.[62] Albert J. Beveridge, speaking in the Irish stronghold of Boston, cautioned that the alliance should not exclude the issue of "justice to Ireland." If this difficulty could be removed, he believed, "an English-speaking people's league of God for the permanent peace of this warworn world" would be so momentous an event that the "stars in their courses" would fight for us and "countless centuries" would applaud.[63] Richard Olney, who had breathed defiance at Britain in 1895 as Cleveland's secretary of state during the Venezuela crisis, now adopted a quite different tone. Arguing that "family quarrels" were a matter of the past, Olney expressed his hope for Anglo-American diplomatic co-operation. "There is a patriotism of race as well as of country," he remarked.[64] John R. Dos Passos, a New York corporation lawyer, declared an alliance between England and America would be "as natural as marriage between man and woman. It consummates the purposes of the creation of the race."[65] Dos Passos seems to have felt that England was the bride in this marriage and that she should provide a dowry. As a measure of good faith in the proposed alliance Dos Passos suggested that England should deed Canada to the United States![66]

In July, 1898, a group of prominent men in London organized the Anglo-American League in order to keep alive the cordial relations which had been established.

Considering that the people of the British Empire and the United States are closely allied by blood, inherit the same literature and laws, hold the same principles of self-government, recognize the same ideas of freedom and humanity in the guidance of their National policy and are drawn together, by strong common interests in many parts of the world,

the League resolved at its first session, "this meeting is of opinion that every effort should be made in the interests of civilization and of peace to secure the most cordial and constant coöperation on the part of the two nations."[67]

Later in the same month an Anglo-American League was formed in New York with Whitelaw Reid as its chairman. The committee strove for a broad representation. It had three members of Cleveland's cabinet among its officers, and among its members were representatives of every administration from Lincoln's to McKinley's. An invitation to join the organization was sent to about fifteen hundred prominent Americans of every state in the Union in all fields of endeavor. The list included many well-known lawyers and judges, the editors of leading magazines and newspapers, college presidents, clergymen of all denominations, and business and industrial leaders. The league attempted, however, to include among its members representatives of groups which were not Anglo-Saxon. Carl Schurz, the German-American; Archbishop M. A. Corrigan, the chief Catholic prelate of New York; and the French-American, Frederic R. Coudert, were all issued invitations and all three of them accepted. Carl Schurz, besides his German ancestry, had the additional apparent handicap of being an opponent of the Spanish-American War, but was willing to concede that one good effect of the war was that it had brought England and the United States closer together. The Anglo-American League played its cards well. "Practically none" of the Americans who were asked for their endorsement declined to give it. Significantly, the American organization soft-pedaled the racial bond between the two countries. Its resolution read:

We, citizens of the United States of America, desire to express our most hearty appreciation of the recent demonstrations of sympathy and fellowship with this country on the part of citizens of the various countries comprised in the British Empire. We earnestly reciprocate these sentiments, recognizing as we do that the same language and the same principles of ordered liberty should form the basis of an intimate and enduring friendship between these kindred peoples. . . .[68]

A year later, the Transatlantic Society of America—an organization similar in aims but more local in character—was formed in Philadelphia.[69]

Two magazines were begun in 1899 with the specific purpose of cementing the Anglo-American friendship. In England, Lady Randolph Churchill began editing the *Anglo-Saxon Review,* an expensively printed monthly with articles designed to flatter the national consciousness of both countries. The magazine featured pictures of prominent men and women of both nations—George Washington's portrait was paired with that of Queen Victoria. The *Anglo-American Magazine* was jointly published in London and New York, its New York address being on Wall Street. Its cover contains a picture of Britannia with her lion and Columbia with her eagle standing staunchly together. Both magazines are filled with articles which emphasize the common racial bond of the two countries and praise the virtues of Anglo-Saxons.[70]

Expansion was a burning issue in this country only for the two years or so after Spain had ceded the Philippines in July, 1898. The movement for closer relations with England was checked even sooner. After the war had been won, there was no longer a need for foreign diplomatic support. Besides, England became involved in 1899 in the Boer War and suffered a series of defeats before achieving a rather humiliating victory. This turn of affairs put a noticeable damper on the sentiment in this country for Anglo-Saxon co-operation and encouraged the latent anti-British sentiment again to show its head. Significantly, the *Anglo-American Magazine* ceased publication in 1901 and the *Anglo-Saxon Review* in 1902. The issue of the government of the Philippines, however, had a longer life than either expansion or co-operation with England. The control of one country by another and the denial of rights of citizenship to the Filipinos were difficult ideas to reconcile with the Declaration of Independence and with American institutions. In order to make these opposing ideas of government compatible at all, the proponents of the acquisition of the Philippines were forced to rely heavily on race theories.

The argument of imperialists ran that some races are inherently incapable of self-government and that it would be a crime to saddle the Filipinos with the burdens of citizenship. "Fitness [for self-government] is not a God-given, natural right," declared Theodore Roosevelt, "but comes to a race only through the slow growth of centuries, and then only to those races which possess an immense reserve fund of strength, common sense, and morality."[71] "The testimony is absolutely overwhelming," argued Elihu Root, "that the people inhabiting the Philippine archipelago are incapable of self-government. . . ."[72] Albert J. Beveridge agreed with Root. The Filipinos, he said, "are not of a self-governing race. They are Orientals, Malays, instructed by Spaniards in the latter's worst estate."[73] The Filipinos were alleged by Senator Knute Nelson of Minnesota to be as yet "unfit for self-government, in the same sense that we have it," apparently the only sense to be considered a proper criterion. Unfitness for self-government, thought Senator Nelson, would make the granting of independence to them "the highest cruelty."[74]

Free institutions, it was argued, were desirable only for superior races. "The Declaration of Independence," stated Beveridge, "applies only to peoples capable of self-government. Otherwise, how dared we administer the affairs of the Indians? How dare we continue to govern them to-day?" If self-government was not possible for the Filipinos,

shall we leave them to themselves? Shall tribal wars scourge them, disease waste them, savagery brutalize them more and more? Shall their fields lie fallow, their forests rot, their mines remain sealed, and all the purposes and possibilities of nature be nullified? If not, who shall govern them rather than the kindest and most merciful of the world's great race of administrators, the people of the American Republic? Who lifted from us the judgment which makes men of our blood our brothers' keepers?[75]

Charles A. Gardiner, a member of the New York Bar, argued that Filipinos had no inherent political rights as Anglo-Saxons apparently did. "Natural rights of barbarians to a republican form of government—who can define them?" he demanded.

"None exists outside of Utopia or Plato's Republic. Whatever is granted, is an act of sovereign grace. Any government, or no government [for the Filipinos] rests with Congress. Any right, or no right, is in sovereign discretion."[76]

When anti-imperialists quoted Henry Clay's injunction, "I contend that it is to arraign the disposition of Providence Himself to suppose that He has created beings incapable of governing themselves,"[77] the imperialists with one accord cried "foul." Reverend Josiah Strong explained how scientific knowledge had outdated this theory.

Clay's conception was formed when the old carpenter theory of the universe obtained, before modern science had shown that races develop in the course of centuries as individuals do in years, and that an undeveloped race, which is incapable of self-government, is no more of a reflection on the Almighty than is an undeveloped child who is incapable of self-government. The opinions of men who in this enlightened day believe that the Filipinos are capable of self-government because everybody is, are not worth considering. This is a question of fact to be settled by weight of testimony. . . . I know of no witness, who has had personal observation of the Filipinos, who declares them to be capable of self-government. Admiral Dewey has said he believed them to be more capable of it than the Cubans. But this proves nothing; the Cubans have yet to demonstrate their capacity for government.[78]

Whitelaw Reid declared that great truths, such as Abraham Lincoln's dictum, "No man is good enough to govern another against his will," were not to be applied indiscriminately. There was a higher authority than Lincoln who had declared, said Reid, "If a man smite thee on thy right cheek, turn to him the other also." Yet he who acted literally on even this divine injunction, Reid argued, would be a "congenital idiot." In the Philippines "his corpse, while it lasted, would remain an object lesson of how not to deal with the present stage of Malay civilization and Christianity."[79]

Another factor which complicated the issues of imperialism was the supposed influence of the tropics on the health and character of white men. William Z. Ripley, for example, ex-

pressed in his influential *The Races of Europe* his conviction that
residence in the tropics was demoralizing for even the strongest
natures. "One of the most subtle physiological effects of a tropical climate is a surexcitation of the sexual organs," he declared,
"which in the presence of a native servile and morally undeveloped population often leads to excesses even at a tender age."[80]
Benjamin Kidd, an English sociologist, argued that "in the tropics
the white man lives and works only as a diver lives and works
under water."[81] Kidd did not conclude, however, that the white
man must leave tropical peoples in peace. He assailed the belief
that "the coloured races left to themselves possess the qualities
necessary to the development of the rich resources of the lands
they have inherited."[82] The tropics must be developed, he contended, and such development could "only take place under
the influence of the white man." The issue was larger "than any
mere question of commercial policy or national selfishness."[83]
The white man must supervise the exploitation of the tropics
from his own land, leaving physical labor for the colored and
not the white races.

Henry Adams had been convinced that the tropics were not
suited for white men, but he drew the Social Darwinist conclusion that he was obliged to go there anyway. "The European
in face of the tropics is a sweet study," he had written to Henry
Cabot Lodge in 1891.

He admits himself to be an abject failure there; he can make nothing
of it; he can't work; he can't digest; he can't sleep; he gets disease, and
he grumbles without ceasing; but he won't let anyone else go there.
He bars the Chinaman, hates the negro, and keeps sharp watch on the
Indian coolie. He won't let anyone alone. He can't keep his hands off
of stray land, even though he can do nothing with it. I find no fault
with him; on the contrary, he does only what he must do in the nature
of nature; but what the deuce can he make of it?[84]

The part of the argument which maintained that white men
could not live in the tropics without suffering a catastrophic decline seems to have been rejected by the imperialists. "It is said
we cannot colonize the tropics," said Whitelaw Reid, "because

our people cannot labor there." This might be so, he continued, if colonists from this country refused to obey elementary health precautions. The experience of other white colonists in the tropics, however, indicated that life there was not impossible. "Can we mine all over the world, from South Africa to the Klondike, but not in the Palawan? Can we grow tobacco in Cuba, but not in Cebu; or rice in Louisiana, but not in Luzon?"[85] Reid does not say so, but his strong implication is that one of the precautions the white man should take for his health in the tropics is to make sure that other races do the physical labor.

As long as the imperialists pledged the logic of necessity, as long as they argued that the Filipinos must inevitably come under the domination of the stronger race, they were deeply vulnerable to the arguments of their opponents. They could be charged with deserting the principles of the Founding Fathers and with being the enemies of American institutions. What was needed was some moral justification for imperialism, some rationale which drew upon ethical motives, some appeal to the traditions of American idealism. Most of the major American authors belonged to the side of the anti-imperialists. From across the seas, however, came the voice of a poet who said exactly what the imperialists needed to have said at this point of the argument.

In the February, 1899, issue of McClure's Magazine appeared Rudyard Kipling's "The White Man's Burden," a poem which one critic has said "circled the earth in a day and by repetition became hackneyed within a week."[86] American newspapers printed its heavily edifying message on their front pages as an exhortation to the United States to take up its onerous task of looking after the affairs of the dark peoples. It was not that Kipling was calling upon Anglo-Saxons to improve the moral or intellectual condition of the darker races. "Asia will never attend Sunday school, or learn to vote, save with swords for tickets," he declared elsewhere.[87] The import of his argument was not necessarily that the native races were to be uplifted. Rather, the idea behind "The White Man's Burden" was that the white races were taking upon themselves a task which might well be hopeless, but which their manly athleticism and moral rigor would not allow them to evade.

The advocates of expansion in this country found this creed most useful. If in some distant day the heathen in the Philippines could be taught to govern themselves without being a hindrance and menace to civilization, declared Whitelaw Reid, then so much the better. "Heaven speed the day!" But if this improvement did not take place, "we must . . . continue to be responsible for them ourselves—a duty we did not seek, but should be ashamed to shirk."[88] William Howard Taft spoke tenderly of our obligations to our "little brown brother," but left unanswered any question about the Filipino's growing up.[89] Some expansionists denied that they were also imperialists. "It is not imperialism when duty keeps us among these chaotic, warring, distracted tribes, civilized, semi-civilized and barbarous," argued Whitelaw Reid, "to help them, as far as their several capacities will permit, toward self-government on the basis of those civil rights."[90] The word *imperialism* had the bad connotations of "oppression," Beveridge pointed out, and therefore should not be used. He entitled one of his expansionist essays "For the Greater Republic, Not for Imperialism."[91]

Even the distinguished philosopher Josiah Royce was carried away, somewhat reluctantly it is true, by the argument that the white races should benevolently take charge of the affairs of natives of undeveloped countries. In 1908, he attempted to lay down some general rules of conduct for colonial administration, particularly for Americans in the Philippines. He cautioned against extremes of race theory. "While I deeply respect . . . the actual work of the sciences which deal with man, and while I fully recognize their modern progress," he declared, "I greatly doubt that these sciences as yet furnish us with the exact results which representative race-theorists sometimes insist upon."[92] "No doubt," he observed further, "if the science of man were exact, it would indeed include a race-psychology,"[93] but he doubted whether the present state of knowledge justified any very far-reaching conclusions regarding this psychology. After saying

this much, Royce moved on to the disappointing recommenda-
tion that Americans should emulate British colonial policy:

. . . The Englishman, in his official and governmental dealings with
backward peoples, has a great way of being superior without very often
publicly saying that he is superior. You well know that in dealing, as
an individual, with other individuals, trouble is seldom made by the
fact that you are actually the superior of another man in any respect.
The trouble comes when you tell the other man, too stridently, that
you are his superior. Be my superior, quietly, simply showing your superiority in your deeds, and very likely I shall love you for the very
fact of your superiority. For we all love our leaders. But tell me I am
your inferior, and then perhaps I may grow boyish, and may throw
stones. Well, it is so with races. Grant then that yours is the superior
race. Then you can afford to say little about the subject in your public
dealings with the backward race. Superiority is best shown by good
deeds and by few boasts.[94]

Some of the most effective satire of the anti-imperialists was
directed against the conception that imperialism was fundamentally a moral crusade with a benevolent concern for the interests of other races. "Does the white man, in his overflowing
philanthropy, want a burden?" inquired Goldwin Smith.

He has it at his own door. If he is a member of the British Parliament,
let him step out into Whitechapel or Houndsditch, or let him read
"The White Slaves of England," and see how in his own country the
alkali-worker, the nail-maker, the slipper-maker, the wool-comber, the
white-lead maker, the chain-maker live.

In the United States, Smith added, where "hatred of race has
mounted to such a pitch that the people of one race go out by
thousands to see a man of the other race burnt alive, and carry
away his charred bones or pieces of his singed garments as souvenirs; when they even photograph and phonograph his dying
agonies," there should be room enough for benevolence toward
other races to find some scope for its energies.[95] Smith resolutely
opposed the notion that what was happening in the Philippines
deserved the name of a moral crusade. "Boston does not go to

Manila," Smith observed. "To Manila go rough soldiers and commercial adventurers. . . . There have been complaints of the
multiplication of the haunts of dissipation and vice, while in
the coarser minds contact with a subject and despised race in
itself breeds insolence and, too often, inhumanity."[96]

Mark Twain satirized the civilizing mission of the Americans in his essay, "To the Person Sitting in Darkness."[97] The
Arena, one of the few anti-imperialist magazines of the period,
quoted a remark supposedly made in a moment of war-weariness
by a Negro soldier sent to help suppress Aguinaldo's rebels, "Dis
shyar white man's burden ain't all it's cracked up to be."[98] Finley
Peter Dunne, one of the most effective of the anti-imperialists,
had his Mr. Dooley suggest, "Take up th' white man's burden
and hand it to th' coons."[99] Even Theodore Roosevelt was willing
to admit that Dunne had scored in this sally. "As you know, I
am an Expansionist," he wrote in a letter to Dunne, "but your
delicious phrase about 'take up the white man's burden and put
it on the coons,' exactly hit off the weak spot in my own theory;
though, mind you, I am by no means willing to give up the
theory yet."[100]

Because so many famous American writers were anti-imperialist, it is easy to assume that there was more public opposition to expansion and the acquisition of the Philippines than
there actually was. Fred Harrington, in his "Literary Aspects of
American Anti-Imperialism, 1898-1902," has pointed out that
many men who were deeply opposed to imperialism nevertheless
were most guarded in their public utterances. Mark Twain, for
example, could easily have placed himself in the van of the anti-
imperialist writers, but he did not choose to do so. He wrote
much on the question of imperialism, Harrington observes, "but
it did not see the light of day, perhaps because of Mrs. Clem-
ens. . . ." It was only in 1901, after the imperialism crusade had
died down, that Twain came out into the open with his famous
essay.[101] William Dean Howells was a vice-president of the New
York Anti-Imperialist League, but he "produced no articles,
wrote no novels, let fall no quotable phrases that could have

helped the cause." Howells, too, may have been restrained by his wife, who had persuaded herself to believe in imperialism. Other anti-imperialists such as Thomas Bailey Aldrich, Hamlin Garland, Richard Watson Gilder, E. L. Godkin, and Herman E. von Holst expressed their views only privately.[102]

Harrington is rather at a loss to account for the public silence of these men. It may be, he conjectures, that they knew they would have difficulty in placing anti-imperialist pieces with any of the major magazines—*Harper's, Scribner's, Century, Lippincott's, McClure's,* and *Munsey's* were all firmly committed to expansion. Some smaller magazines such as the *Arena,* the *Dial, City and State,* the *Coming Nation,* and *Life,* however, were anti-imperialist; and the columns of the *Springfield Republican* and the *Boston Transcript* would also have been open to any protest these men might have cared to write. Harrington points out that some of these writers had dared popular disfavor before. Howells, for example, had spoken out against the injustice done to the anarchists after the Haymarket bombing in 1886.[103] The reasons for their silence probably were complex and personal. The trouble may have been that many of the anti-imperialists were paralyzed by the formidable logic of Social Darwinist race theories, against which they had only the weapons of moralists. In letters to sympathetic friends, they could employ moral arguments. In the public forum, however, the proponents of expansion relied on the supposedly immutable and objective findings of science which left moral arguments, by themselves, a little forlorn. In addition, many of these writers were older men and were losing their earlier buoyancy and their faith in man's ability to restrain the forces of rapacity and greed.

The direction of the anti-imperialist crusade was probably influenced by the accident of party alignment. As Richard Hofstadter points out, the foes of expansion were not inclined to attack the race theories upon which imperialists relied or to dispute the appeal to Social Darwinist ethics.[104] The Democratic party, the party of anti-imperialism, could ill afford to challenge the argument of Anglo-Saxon superiority, particularly in the

South. Party leaders inverted the race argument and used it to oppose expansion. They elected to campaign on the danger which inferior Cubans and Filipinos would represent to American institutions when they were given citizenship rights in the United States. The Philippines were tenanted by "a heterogeneous compound of inefficient Oriental humanity," declared one Democratic senator. The inhabitants differed from us in race, language, customs, and religion.[105] Why, asked Senator Benjamin Tillman, reading some stanzas from Kipling's poem, "The White Man's Burden," "should we mark their roads with our dead in a futile effort to call them from their 'loved Egyptian night,' " to force upon them "a civilization not suited to them and which only means in their view degradation and a loss of self-respect?"[106] "There is one thing that neither time nor education change," remarked the anti-imperialist Senator John W. Daniel of Virginia in 1899. "You may change the leopard's spots, but you will never change the different qualities of the races which God has created in order that they may fulfill separate and distinct missions in the cultivation and civilization of the world."[107]

To this racist argument of some of the anti-imperialists, the imperialists had a similar answer. "The frail of faith declare that these peoples [the Filipinos] are not fitted for citizenship," commented Albert J. Beveridge.

It is not proposed to make them citizens. Those who see disaster in every forward step of the Republic prophesy that Philippine labor will overrun our country and starve our workingmen. But the Javanese have not so overrun Holland; New Zealand's Malays, Australia's bushmen, Africa's Kaffirs, Zulus, and Hottentots, and India's millions of surplus labor have not so overrun England. Whips of scorpions could not lash the Filipinos to this land of fervid enterprise, sleepless industry, and rigid order.[108]

Whitelaw Reid agreed with Beveridge.

It is a bugbear that the Filipinos would be citizens of the United States, and would therefore have the same rights of free travel and free entry of their own manufactures with other citizens. The treaty did not make them citizens of the United States at all; and they never will be, unless you neglect your Congress.[109]

President McKinley, at one point, came near playing into the hands of anti-imperialist Democrats when he described American colonial policy toward the Philippines as "benevolent assimilation"—a phrase which a Republican senator was obliged to assure his perturbed colleagues did not exclude the President's intention to *differentiate* the Filipinos from the citizen body.[110]

Even had imperialism been the only issue confronting the country, the arguments of Democrats were hardly enough to convince the electorate that a change of administration was needed. To the anti-imperialism crusade of the Democrats, the Republicans responded with the rallying cry, "Don't haul down the flag!" Whatever chance the Democrats may have had when they chose imperialism as the chief issue of the election of 1900 was destroyed by other developments. An upswing in the foreign trade of the country and the discovery of extensive new gold deposits had enabled the Republicans to settle the money question. Industry was flourishing and wages were good. Higher prices for wheat, corn, and cotton allayed agricultural discontent. Very probably there was widespread agreement with the conditional idealism of the Republican party campaign plank which offered assurance that the Filipinos would have "the largest measure of self-government consistent with their welfare and our duties."[111] This plank was open to the interpretation that self-government was consistent neither with the welfare of the Filipinos nor with our duties, a conclusion with which great numbers of people would undoubtedly have agreed. Imperialism had conquered.

XIV

World War I and Racism

THE HATRED UNLEASHED by World War I inevitably found expression in the exacerbation of racial tensions in this country. Americans of German descent were not the only ones who felt the force of this hatred; all racial and ethnic minorities to some extent felt its power. In the early years of the century, great numbers of immigrants—particularly immigrants from southern and eastern Europe—passed through our ports. Under the best of circumstances, the assimilation of these people—many of whom spoke strange languages and observed strange customs—would have been difficult. In the South, the Negroes began to grow restive under the restrictions placed upon them. Many of them expressed their dissatisfaction by "voting with their feet" and migrating to the North. In 1900, 90 per cent or more of the Negroes lived in the southern states, but now they were moving to the North in increasing numbers. The war greatly accelerated this movement, as new industrial jobs opened up in the North. The fact that the immigrants and Negroes were available at cheaper wages inevitably caused them to be resented by working-class members of the older ethnic groups. The fact that they were potential voters was enough to alarm the middle and upper classes among the white citizens who did not yet suffer from direct economic competition.[1]

In 1915, the production of the film, *Birth of a Nation,* provided an immense impetus for the forces of racial bigotry. Quite as racist as Thomas Dixon's *The Clansman,* the anti-Negro novel upon which it was based, *Birth of a Nation* was a masterpiece of technical virtuosity and a landmark in the history of films. On the other hand, its version of history is frankly and crudely racist. The last half of the movie deals with the horrors of carpetbagger and Negro rule in South Carolina during the Reconstruction. Negroes are shown wildly reveling at elections, voting with both hands, and keeping the white man from the polls by force. As members of the state legislature, Negroes sit with their hats on and their bare feet on the desks as they drink liquor from flasks and pass an intermarriage law. The leading white Radical Reconstructionist in the North is shown with his Negro mistress. In the climax of the film, a renegade Negro pursues a young white girl through the woods. In order to avoid rape, she leaps to her death from a high rock. Her brother leads a mob to lynch the Negro and then organizes a unit of the Ku Klux Klan to regain control of society by white men. He breaks up a crowd of rioting Negroes just in time to save another white girl from forced marriage with the mulatto lieutenant-governor. The film was one of the great box-office successes of all time; millions of Americans flocked to see it and to absorb its "message."[2]

Another event which occurred at about the same time was the revival of the Ku Klux Klan. In 1915, Colonel William Joseph Simmons, a preacher in Atlanta, thought that the time had come for the Klan to ride again. His aim was to insure not merely that the white man should remain in control of state and local governments in the South but that the whole country should be aroused to the dangers which threatened from Negroes and from "hyphenated-Americans" of every kind. The purpose which was "pulsing in every fiber" of the Klan, said Simmons, was to "maintain Anglo-Saxon civilization on the American continent from submergence due to the encroachment and invasion of alien people of whatever clime or color." During the war itself the Klan grew slowly, and it became a major force only in the postwar years; but it was one more reflection of the increased racial tension of the time.[3]

The entry of the United States into the war in 1917 had both direct and indirect effects upon racist thinking. Directly, it stimulated wild flights of fancy among those Americans who would explain German militarism on the basis of the racial character of the German people. Of course, the old theories which had assumed the superiority of the Teutons had to be sharply revised. Now *Teuton* became a word of contempt, scarcely better than *Hun* or *Boche*. It was now taken for granted that the racial character of the Germans was quite different from that of the English and the Americans. The Germans were inherently murderous aggressors; the English and Americans had always been defenders of civilization. In 1920, George Creel, who had been director of the Committee on Public Information, a wartime federal agency, recalled the passions aroused.

Who does not remember the fears of "wholesale disloyalty" that shook us daily? There were to be "revolutions" in Milwaukee, St. Louis, Cincinnati; armed uprisings here, there, and everywhere; small armies hording thousands of rebellious enemy aliens into huge internment camps; incendiarism, sabotage, explosions, murder, domestic riot. No imagination was too meager to paint a picture of America's adopted children turning faces of hatred to the motherland.

All this led to demands for action. "People generally, and the press particularly," Creel recalled, "were keyed up to a high pitch, an excited distrust of our foreign population, and a percentage of editors and politicians were eager for a campaign of 'hate' at home."⁴

The anger against Americans of German descent was sharp but temporary. They were soon succeeded by a new scapegoat, immigrants from eastern Europe. The Austro-Hungarian Empire had included many of the ethnic groups which contributed heavily to the immigrant population in this country in the years before the war. The Bolshevist Revolution in Russia in 1917 helped to stamp firmly upon the minds of many Americans the supposed turbulent and anarchic character of the "Slavic race." It was only a step to include the Jews as also responsible for Russian Bolshevism, and one step more to find the immigrants from southern Europe equally unfit to partake of American citizenship.

Much of the sophisticated racism of the period during and following the war reflects the point of view and tone of two books both of which had been written years before, one in France and one in Germany: Count Arthur de Gobineau's *Essay on the Inequality of Races* (1853-55) and Houston Stewart Chamberlain's *Foundations of the Nineteenth Century* (1899). It is curious how many modern racists have taken their grandiose stance from one or the other of these men or from an amalgam of the two.[5]

Count Arthur de Gobineau (1816-1882) wrote his *Essay on the Inequality of Races* to defend the nobility of France against the modern ills of society—ills which stemmed, he thought, from racial mongrelization. The nobility was, in his view, descended from the ancient Teutons, but most of the people of France were descended from plebeian Gallo-Romans. With the French Revolution, the "race" competent to govern France had been defeated and supplanted by an inferior breed of men. Back of the *Essay* is a passionate desire derived from the racist theme of Teutonic superiority to justify the principles of monarchy and aristocracy.[6]

All history and all civilization, says Gobineau, are to be explained upon the basis of race. The only mystery is that men had so long remained ignorant of this appalling central fact of history. "Everyone must have had some inkling of this colossal truth," he declares, "for everyone must have seen how certain agglomerations of men have descended on some country, and utterly transformed its way of life; now they have shown themselves able to strike out in a new vein of activity where, before their coming, all had been sunk in torpor."[7]

Gobineau divides the races into three types—the white, the yellow, and the black. The whites are the great "masculine" race. In their pure state, the whites or "Aryans" had a "reflective energy" and an "energetic intelligence," "a perseverance that takes account of obstacles and ultimately finds a way to overcome them," and "an extraordinary instinct for order." They had "a remarkable, and even extreme, love of liberty." They were "openly hostile to the formalism under which the Chinese are glad to vegetate, as well as the strict despotism which is the only way of governing the negro."⁸

Among the members of the white race, the "principal motive is honor," but this is a word which "is unknown to both the yellow and the black man." The yellow race is passive, quiescent, lacking in energy, uninventive, and yet attached to institutions. It has a limited practical bent, knows and respects orders, and has at least some conception of the idea of freedom. Yellow men do not make good leaders but they do make good followers. "Every founder of a civilization would wish the backbone of his society, his middle class, to consist of such men." Thus, the yellow race is clearly superior to the black. To Gobineau, the Negro is inherently gluttonous, sensual, and stupid. His sensory organs are abnormally developed to compensate for his inferior intellect. Both the yellow and the black are "feminine" races.⁹

Though the whites are superior, Gobineau has misgivings about them as a "pure" race. All three races must be mixed, he maintains, if a truly great civilization is to be created. Race hybrids are, in fact, "the only members of our species who can be civilized at all." Thus, intermixture of races—the horror of most race theorists—is for Gobineau the key to progress as well as to degeneration. Civilization, he argues, is always in danger from two opposite threats—not enough race mixture or too much. At first, races "cannot overcome the natural repugnance, felt by men and animals alike, to a crossing of blood." Thus, the defects of each of the races perpetuate themselves. On the other hand, when the intermixture begins it is likely to go too far and the result is a mongrel people with the virtues of none of their parent stocks.¹⁰

It is the precise degree of intermixture of a people at any given time which explains the peculiarities of its civilization. "It would be unjust," says Gobineau, "to assert that every mixture is bad and harmful." If the three races had remained separate, the white race no doubt would have produced superior civilizations, but they would have had serious defects. "Artistic genius, which is equally foreign to each of the three great types," for

example, "arose only after the intermarriage of white and black."
Egypt and Assyria had too much black intermixture for the
highest artistic development, but Greece had just the right
amount at the time of its cultural ascendancy. Beauty as well
as artistic genius is the result of racial intermixture. Although
the whites are the most beautiful of the three original races, the
most beautiful people of all have come from "the marriage of
the white and black."[11]

If it were possible for a civilization to maintain the precise
degree of intermixture among the races which enabled it to rise
to eminence, it would never decay. "If the Romans of the later
Empire," for example, "had had a Senate and an army of the
same stock as that which existed at the time of the Fabii, their
dominion would never have come to an end. So long as they
kept the same purity of blood, the . . . Romans would have
lived and reigned." Yet the maintenance of the correct balance
of intermixture is almost impossible. Instead of ceasing when it
has created superior hybrids, intermixture continues until the
superior white ingredient is overwhelmed by the black and yellow races. Thus inferior hybrids are created which are "beautiful without strength, strong without intelligence, or if intelligent, both weak and ugly."[12]

Gobineau's sweeping theory of history is that civilizations
rise and flourish for a time while they have a fortunate balance
of racial intermixture, but this balance cannot continue forever. The reason a civilization declines is that "it has no longer
the same blood in its veins, continual adulterations having gradually affected the quality of that blood." A civilization will
"certainly die on the day when the primordial race-unit is so
broken up and swamped by the influx of foreign elements, that
its effective qualities have no longer a sufficient freedom of action." All this would suggest that Gobineau was a racial nationalist, but he was not. For him, it is not nations which create
civilizations; it is the small aristocratic minority within nations—for him, race is much more a matter of class than of nation. In addition, all modern nations represent, in his opinion, an

advanced stage of mongrelization. He has no hope that any of them can forestall impending calamity. With the rise of democracy, no aristocracy—no matter how superior—can hope to retain control.[13]

Consumed with passion for his great theme, Gobineau took little trouble to learn what scientific opinion was with regard to race. When Darwin's *The Origin of Species* was published, Gobineau contemptuously rejected it, partly because he was a pious Catholic who accepted the biblical account of creation and partly because he rejected on principle any theory which implied inevitable progress. *"Nous ne descendons pas du singe,"* he is reported to have said, *"mais nous y allons."* (We are not descended from the ape, but we are going in that direction.) His own theory assumed that degeneration was just as inevitable a biological process as progress—and much more common. Because of his indifference to biology, Gobineau was in turn neglected by the anthropologists. Among the serious students of race in the nineteenth century, he is frequently ignored altogether.[14]

Though his scientific importance was nil, his popular appeal was considerable, especially among those readers who were willing and eager to find the "key" to history in their most passionately held prejudices. The power of Gobineau was mainly in his style. He was an accomplished writer; he wrote several novels and all his work is animated by a fierce intensity and conviction.

Gobineau's racism emphasized the idea of social class, but an even more powerful racism—that based upon nationalism—was developing at the same time in Europe and eventually came to overshadow all other kinds. From an anthropological standpoint, no modern European nation represents an ethnic type distinct enough to be classified as a race. Yet what has been ridiculous as anthropology has nonetheless appealed to racists. The nationalists in countries which are composed of unusually diverse ethnic stocks have not been able to resist coining such anthropologically unintelligible terms as "the German race," "the French race," "the Italian race," "the English race," and even "the American race."

Nationalism and racism joined forces in several countries, but it was in Germany that Gobineau's theories were recast to make them conform to the new aggressive ethic. This task had taken some doing. For Gobineau, the Aryans had predominated in the ancient Germanic tribes, but the Teutons were only a minority of modern nations. There were more of them in modern France, he thought, than in modern Germany. "In France, about five-eighths of the total population play merely an unwilling and passive part in the development of modern European culture," he said, "and that only by fits and starts." On the rest of the European continent—in Germany, for example—the proportion of non-Teutonic peoples "is even higher." We find Gobineau arguing that the French are superior to the Germans, as one could see, he said, from the differences between Napoleon's armies in the 1812 invasion of Russia. Those contingents composed of German soldiers were more accustomed to cold weather, but they did not bear it so well as did the French soldiers. "The German officers, who perished by the hundreds, had just as high a sense of honour and duty as our soldiers had," says Gobineau, "but this did not prevent them from going under. We may conclude that the French have certain physical qualities that are superior to those of the Germans, which allow them to brave with impunity the snows of Russia as well as the burning sands of Egypt."[15]

In spite of Gobineau's reservations about Germans, the German nationalists often found his ideas too attractive to pass up. One of the most extravagant of these nationalists was the composer Richard Wagner. In 1880, Wagner read Gobineau's *Essay* and wrote that its theme "appeals to us with the most terrible force of conviction." Later, Wagner was a guest in Gobineau's home and became a devoted admirer. Yet however much he may have admired the man, Wagner had different racist ideas from those of Gobineau. For him, the ancient virtues of the Teutonic tribes were found not only among modern German aristocrats but also among virtually all Germans. Wagner admitted that the Germans had not always kept their ancient race pure, but he did not draw Gobineau's despairing conclusions. The battle was not yet lost. The blood of the noble Teuton had been allowed to deteriorate, but its essential nature was the same and it was to be found only in the German nation. The German people must be taught properly to revere their Teutonic blood.[16]

Wagner exalted race to the status of a religion. He maintained that the Germans are a race superior to all others, that the German language is superior to other languages and is the direct reflection of German racial qualities, that music peculiarly expresses the German soul. Christianity itself must give way to a religion based upon the great truths of ancient legends.

It is curious that Gobineau did not object to Wagner's version of Teutonism. One reason probably was that in his last years he was increasingly alienated from France. "The hatred of the French Revolution and the doctrine of the equality of man," says one of his biographers, "had thrown Gobineau into such antagonism against everything around him that he finally began to hate France down to her very historical roots."[17] And then, he was embittered by the circumstances of his retirement as a diplomat from the French foreign office. The government had pensioned him off before his time, and to add insult to injury had appointed as his successor the descendant of a Jacobin who had executed thousands of Royalists.

Whatever the reasons, Gobineau did without protest allow Wagner to recast his racial theory into German nationalist propaganda. And he himself became a patron saint of racism in Germany. The Gobineau Society, founded in Bayreuth, published new editions of his out-of-print works and devoted itself to the propagation of his theories.

Even Wagner was not the most grandiloquent prophet of German racism. That distinction belongs to his son-in-law, Houston Stewart Chamberlain (1855-1927), an Englishman who renounced his citizenship to become a citizen of Germany. How Chamberlain, whose father was an admiral in the British navy and three of whose uncles were officers of high rank in the army, came to detest everything English is not wholly clear. He tells us that in 1879, when he was a student in England, he had an experience with an election in which "rowdies with jailbird physiognomies" imported by the Conservative party to intimidate Liberal voters in Cheltenham knocked him down and beat him. "On that day," he says, ". . . I learned more about the English constitution and the English idea of liberty than I ever did later out of Hallam and Gneist. . . ."[18]

Chamberlain left England for Geneva, to study biology and physics, and then went to Dresden, where he came under the influence of German metaphysics and Wagnerian music. It was not until the 1890's that he developed the racial theories for which he is now chiefly known. Like Wagner, Chamberlain brings to racism a pseudo-religious exaltation and makes Christ a Teuton. His theory is that Aryan "blood" had penetrated to Galilee. For him language and race have mystic affinities, and therefore he finds deep significance in the fact that the Galileans spoke a dialect different from that of other Jews and comic to them. The reason that the Galileans found the Hebraic language difficult to pronounce was that they were Teutons. "Whoever makes the assertion that Christ was a Jew is either ignorant or insincere"; that is, he wishes "to curry favour with the Jews." But Chamberlain's chief argument for the belief that Jesus was a Teuton and not a Jew was that the ideas of Christianity are wholly consistent with those of the Teutonic peoples and inconsistent with those of the Jews.[19]

Chamberlain set himself to reconcile Christianity, the religion of humility and forgiveness, with aggressive German nationalism. Jesus, he said, had been misunderstood. "Whoever chooses conversion, whoever obeys the warning of Christ, 'Follow me!' must also when necessary leave father and mother, wife and child. . . . Here is no room for pity; whom we have lost we have lost, and with the hardness of the heroic spirit not a tear is shed over those who are gone: 'Let the dead bury their dead.' " He castigated what he regarded as the sickly humanitarianism which dares to call itself modern Christianity, with its ecumenical congresses emphasizing "tolerance." Christ, he tells us, "would never have sent an apostle to such a congress." Christ understood that "where the direction of the will is concerned . . . there is . . . no question of tolerance and never can be."[20]

After the fall of the decadent Roman Empire, Christianity, in Chamberlain's view, had found its true home among the Teutons. Nothing infuriated him more than the idea that the early Germanic peoples were barbarians and that their triumph over the Romans instituted the Dark Ages. One should read the accounts of the degeneracy of latter-day Rome if he thinks that the Romans were a civilized people. The true representative of ancient Rome in modern times, he maintains, is the Catholic church. He observes "with what peculiar exactitude the modern boundary of the universal Church of Rome corresponds with what I have pointed out as the general boundary of the Roman Imperium, and consequently of chaotic mongreldom." It is among the Germans that true Christianity flourishes. They alone have "the uncompromising character, the sense of absolute justice, the impelling will to triumph over all circumstances which accord with the characteristics and principles of Jesus."[21]

Chamberlain admires German philosophers, scientists, artists, and composers, but his greatest heroes are men of action. "Our European world is first and foremost the work not of philosophers and book-writers and painters," he says, "but of the great Teuton Princes, the work of warriors and statesmen." So far as racial theory is concerned, however, the question of who contributed the most to civilization is irrelevant because the Germans dominate every field of endeavor:

A Teuton writes a *Critique of Pure Reason,* but at the same time a Teuton invents the railway; the century of Bessemer and of Edison is at the same time the century of Beethoven and of Richard Wagner. Whoever does not feel the unity of the impulse here, whoever considers it a riddle that the astronomer Newton should interrupt his mathematical investigations to write a commentary to the Revelations of St. John, that Crompton invented the spinning machine merely to give himself more leisure for his beloved music, and that Bismarck, the statesman of blood and iron, caused Beethoven's sonatas to be played to him in the decisive moments of his life, understands nothing at all of the nature of the Teuton, and cannot in consequence rightly judge the part he plays in the history of the world in the past and at the present time.

Have other races accomplished nothing? Even Chamberlain does not go quite this far. He is willing to admit that the Chinese invented paper and printing, but he quickly adds that it was the Teutons who knew how to utilize such inventions and who first thought of making books.[22]

One of Chamberlain's habits is to appropriate the great men of other nations by discovering Teutonic characteristics in them. Anyone can walk through the collection of Roman busts in the Berlin Museum, he tells us, and discover how firmly established the Germans were in northern Italy where the Goths, Langobards, and Franks had mingled their blood. In later centuries, men who were thought to be Italians—men like Marco Polo, Copernicus, Galileo, and Bruno—were in reality Germans. Sometimes one can tell because they look like Germans, but even this is not always necessary. Dante, for example, was a "genuine Teuton" even though his face did not conform precisely with the ideal of German physiognomy. Chamberlain also can give a man Teutonic blood to indicate some of his tendencies and Latin blood to indicate others. Thus, Louis XIV was Teutonic when he defended the liberties of French Catholics against Rome, says Chamberlain, but non-Teutonic when he persecuted the Protestants.[23]

Chamberlain was aware that his grand generalizations could not be proved, but the lack of scientific evidence did not trouble him. Anthropologists had made the prodigious mistake, he said, of imagining that race is a matter of the shape of the skull, the color of the skin and eyes and hair, the shape of the limbs, and so forth. They did not realize that it is inward nature and not outer appearance which is the hallmark of race.

Since race cannot be determined by measurement of physical differences, Chamberlain argues that we should depend upon intuition. Such a procedure was not at all unscientific; Darwin himself had noted the importance of intuition. He had seen, says Chamberlain, that

the eye of the experienced breeder discovers things of which figures give not the slightest formation, and which the breeder himself can hardly express in words; he notices that this and that distinguished the one organism from the other, and makes his selection for breeding according; this is an intuition born of ceaseless observation.

How firmly Chamberlain is willing to rely upon intuition may be judged from his dismissal of the objections which had been raised to the theory that the Aryans are a racial type. "Though it were proved that there never was an Aryan race in the past," he declares, "yet we desire in the future that there may be one. That is the decisive standpoint for men of action."[24]

One of Chamberlain's persistent subthemes is anti-Semitism. He observes that Jews are "quite stunted" in their religious perceptions, a moral defect similar to physical defects which Darwin had observed among plants and animals. He says that German children, when a Jew suddenly comes into the room, will cry out because they realize instinctively that he is a sinister alien. Yet Chamberlain insists that he is not anti-Semitic because he does not advocate persecution. "Shall we then revile the Jews?" he asks in a characteristic passage. "That would be as ignoble as it would be unworthy and unreasonable."[25]

Chamberlain's most famous racist work was the two-volume *Foundations of the Nineteenth Century*, published in Germany in 1899. By 1910, it had gone through eight editions in Germany and had sold sixty thousand copies, a very large sale for a lengthy and expensive treatment of a serious subject. Wilhelm II described it as his "favorite book" and let it be known that he was reading it aloud to his sons. He had free copies distributed to officers of the German army, to the foreign diplomatic corps, and to schools and libraries throughout the country.

In 1912, Gobineau's *Essay on the Inequality of Human Races*, in an abbreviated version, was translated and published in this country. In 1911, Chamberlain's *Foundations of the Nine-*

teenth Century appeared here in translation. Theodore Roosevelt wrote a review of it and condemned Chamberlain as showing a "violent partiality" and having a "queer vein of the erratic in his temperament" which was exemplified by frequent lapses of "fairly bedlamite passion." And yet Roosevelt himself shows at least some susceptibility to the fears and hates which Chamberlain strove to arouse.

> Much that he [Chamberlain] says regarding the prevalent loose and sloppy talk about the general progress of humanity, the equality and identity of races, and the like, is not only perfectly true, but is emphatically worth considering by a generation accustomed, as its forefathers for the preceding generations were accustomed, to accept as true and useful thoroughly pernicious doctrines taught by well-meaning and feeble-minded sentimentalists.[26]

It is curious how many of the racists who flourished during and after World War I in this country closely reflected the ideas of Gobineau and Chamberlain. Most of the American racists had no particular regard for the Teutons—certainly not if one meant the old aristocracy of France or if one meant modern Germans. It may be that Gobineau's sense of doom and futility partially accounts for the influence of his *Essay*. For Gobineau, the decline of civilization was inevitable, but his readers did not usually draw this conclusion. Since Gobineau had no program to avert disaster, his readers could formulate one of their own. Though his ideas had to be changed a good deal, Gobineau was thus the spiritual father of the most diverse forms of racism. As early as 1856, a much abbreviated translation of the *Essay* had been published in this country as part of the southern campaign to defend slavery, but his idea that intermixture with Negroes was necessary for the whites to attain artistic genius was severely criticized. As we have seen, the *Essay* was used to buttress German racism and nationalism. For the American racists during and after World War I, Gobineau was one of the chief sources for anti-immigration arguments. Where Gobineau had deplored the "Gallo-Roman plebeians" of France, the

American racists substituted immigrants from eastern and southern Europe. They sometimes retained Gobineau's elegiac note that the great day of the superior "Nordic" race had passed, but they did not believe this wholly because, unlike Gobineau, they nearly all had a program through which civilization might be saved. American racists sometimes wrote in the confident and aggressive manner of Chamberlain, but what they chiefly gained from him was a method for countering the arguments of anthropologists which belittled the importance of racist theory. Like Chamberlain, the American racists argued that the truths of race could be learned from "intuition" and had no need of scientific verification.[27]

A book which was destined to serve as a model for many of the great number of racist books and articles which were to follow in the United States appeared in December, 1916. It was *The Passing of the Great Race*, by Madison Grant. Some years later, an enthusiastic follower of Grant recalled "the great impetus" given by this book to interest in race questions. "No one would have believed," said Charles Stewart Davison, "that twenty or thirty thousand copies of a book on racial descent and racial characteristics throughout the world would have been purchased and read in the United States." The book "marked the turning point" from previous indifference among Americans to the immense importance of racial differences. Davison's enthusiasm is understandable. Grant was certainly one of the most powerful racists this country has produced.[28]

Madison Grant (1865-1937) was a member of a family which on both sides had been prominent in New York City since Colonial times. His parents were wealthy and he was sent to Dresden, Germany, for part of his early education. He graduated from Yale and received the LL.B. degree from Columbia. Although he carried on a legal practice, the law was not his major interest. He devoted much of his time to various reform projects, some of which were of high value. Among his hobbies was the study of family history, and he was considered an expert genealogist. Although he was an officer of the American Eugenics

Society, an organization which frequently urged members of the upper classes to have more children, Grant himself remained a bachelor.[29]

Grant believed that the superior races in the United States were in danger of being overwhelmed by inferior immigrants. For twenty-five years Grant was a vice-president of the Immigration Restriction League. His purpose in writing *The Passing of the Great Race* was to alert Americans to the danger of the nation's losing its essentially "Nordic" racial character, a loss which he was certain could only be followed by the decline and ultimate extinction of its civilization. Grant, following William Z. Ripley, an American student of race, divided the population of Europe into three races: the Alpines, the Mediterraneans, and the Nordics. The Alpines were a brachycephalic people, short and sturdy, tending to be somewhat dark, and were especially numerous in central Europe. The Mediterraneans were a dolichocephalic dark group predominant in southern Europe. The Nordics, a dolichocephalic, blond, and tall race, were a minority everywhere except possibly in the Scandinavian countries; but there were many of them in northeast Germany, in England, and in the United States. Like Chamberlain, Grant refused to allow physical character to be the ultimate determinant of race. The physical characteristics of the Alpines and Mediterraneans, he says, are much more definite than those of the Nordics. While blondness is an indication of Nordicism, its absence is no sign that one is not a Nordic. "It often happens that an individual with all other Nordic characters in great purity has a skin of an olive or dark tint." Sometimes a Nordic may have "absolutely pure brunet traits" and along with them a "skin of almost ivory whiteness and of great clarity." A Nordic usually has blue eyes, but he may have brown or hazel ones. Stature is more important than skin color as a race determinant, but since "exceedingly adverse economic conditions may inhibit a race from attaining the full measure of its growth," a short person may be a Nordic. The fact that both Mediterraneans and Nordics are dolichocephalic does not mean that they are related but merely that there has been "a case of parallel specialization." On the other hand, a Nordic is not invariably dolichocephalic. With all this leeway,[30] Grant is at liberty to do what racists have generally done—to assign people to races just as he chooses.

So far as physical character is concerned, all this is merely bewildering, but when Grant extends the process to description of innate temperament and intelligence the full force of his racism becomes evident. In his *Races of Europe* (1899), Ripley had argued that each of the three European races has mental and temperamental traits peculiar to it, but he urged caution in the description of these inward characteristics. Grant, however, assigns all traits dogmatically. The Alpine race is "always and everywhere a race of peasants." They "tend toward democracy, although they are submissive to authority both political and religious" and thus are usually Roman Catholic. The Mediterranean is "inferior in bodily stamina to both the Nordic and the Alpine," but he is "probably the superior of both, certainly of the Alpines, in intellectual attainments." In the field of art the superiority of the Mediterranean race "is unquestioned although in literature and in scientific research and discovery the Nordics far excel it." This somewhat backhanded tribute to the Mediterranean race is not borne out in other parts of Grant's study. We discover elsewhere in the book that it has long since passed its peak of ability. Although it is given credit for the classical civilizations of Greek and Rome, it has "played a relatively small part in the development of the civilization of the Middle Ages or of modern times." Even its ancient glory was partly owing to the fact that it was "mixed and invigorated with Nordic elements, which probably predominated in the upper and ruling classes and imposed their guidance upon the masses."[31]

The Nordic race is a "race of soldiers, sailors, adventurers and explorers, but above all, of rulers, organizers and aristocrats in sharp contrast to the essentially peasant and democratic character of the Alpines." The Nordics are "domineering, individualistic, self-reliant and jealous of their personal freedom both in political and religious systems and as a result they are usually

Protestants." Chivalry and knighthood, feudalism, class distinctions, and racial pride—all these came from the inherent racial character of the Nordic. That Grant can find a Nordic almost anywhere goes without saying. "The Philistines and more probably the Amorites of Palestine may have been of Nordic race," he tells us. So may have been King David. "Certain references to the size of the sons of Anak and to the fairness of David, whose mother was an Amoritish woman, point vaguely in this direction." It is also significant that most artists have painted the two thieves as brunet in contrast to a blond Christ. "This is something more than a convention, as such quasi-authentic traditions as we have of our Lord strongly suggest his Nordic, possibly Greek, physical and moral attributes."[32]

Most of *The Passing of the Great Race* is devoted to explaining the rise and fall of civilizations on the basis of race. "In the Europe of today," he says, "the amount of Nordic blood in each nation is a very fair measure of its strength in war and standing in civilization." With trifling exceptions to the contrary, the same condition has prevailed throughout European history.

Both the Trojans and the Greeks were commanded by huge, blond princes, the heroes of Homer—in fact, even the Gods were fair haired —while the bulk of the armies on both sides were composed of little brunet Pelasgians, imperfectly armed and remorselessly butchered by the leaders on either side.

Similarly in Rome, the struggles "between Latin and Etruscan and the endless quarrels between patrician and plebeian arose from this existence . . . side by side, of two distinct and clashing races, probably Nordic and Mediterranean respectively." The decline of Spain was due to the dilution of the Nordic blood in the upper classes so that "the sceptre fell from this noble race into the hands of the little, dark Iberian, who had not the physical vigor or the intellectual strength to maintain the empire built up by the stronger race." Later, France suffered a similar fate. "When by universal suffrage the transfer of power was completed from a Nordic aristocracy to lower classes predominantly of Alpine and Mediterranean extraction, the decline of France in international power set in." In England, too, the Nordics were "in these days apparently receding before the little brunet Mediterranean type."[33]

Much of all this is, of course, a straight paraphrase of Gobineau and Chamberlain. It was an odd time—just before the United States was to declare war against Germany—for a strong statement of the doctrine of Nordicism to appear in this country. Grant is able to avoid the charge, however, that his theories were very much like those of the prophets of Teutonism in Germany. The truth was, Grant argued, that the Germans were not really Nordics. Great numbers of the Nordics of Germany had been slaughtered in the Thirty Years' War. Since the Nordics were pre-eminently fighters, the war "bore, of course, most heavily upon the big blond fighting man and, at the end of the war, the German states contained a greatly lessened proportion of Nordic blood." This decline explained the barbarism of the modern German army. "Today the ghastly rarity . . . of chivalry and generosity toward women, of knightly protection and courtesy toward the prisoners or wounded" among the Germans, Grant explains, "can be largely attributed to this annihilation of the gentle classes. The Germans of today, whether they live on the farms or in the cities, are for the most part descendants of the peasants who survived, not of the brilliant knights and sturdy foot soldiers who fell in that mighty conflict." And as Grant makes clear, the peasants were Alpines and the "gentle classes" were Nordics.[34]

One of Grant's contemporaries was able to dispose even more conveniently of the German claim to Nordic stock. Dr. William S. Sadler, a surgeon and professor of therapeutics at a noted school of medicine, suggested that not only had the Alpines displaced most of the Nordics in Germany in the Thirty Years' War, but many of the Nordics who were left later emigrated to the United States. Grant himself makes somewhat similar allowances for Americans of German descent, but he is more grudging about them—possibly because many Germans had come after the revolutions of 1848 and he detested all democratic movements. The Germans who had come to America, he said, were "for the most part of the Nordic race and while they did not in the least strengthen the nation either morally or intellectually, they did not impair its physique."[35]

If the Nordics were the superior race, one wonders why Grant feared they would not survive. One reason has already been suggested: the Nordics are brave warriors and are thus more likely to be killed in battle. After the war, Grant published a letter written to him by an American officer who had served in France and who commented on the effectiveness as soldiers of various ethnic groups in the A.E.F. "A fighting Italian is as rare as the dodo bird in spite of all the newspaper bull to the contrary," says the unnamed officer. "They are used entirely for road building and stevedore work about as far back of the lines as they can get." The fighting ability of American troops is

in direct proportion to the Americans in the various units. Get a draft outfit filled with the kind swept up from the east side and it is just about as unsafe as anything in the army; given an outfit like the Yankee division, or some of them with a full proportion of Americans, and there is nothing they are afraid of, nothing that will stop them short of death.

Grant himself remembers watching the regiments march away from New York on their way to Cuba in 1898 and says he could not help being impressed by the

size and blondness of the men in the ranks as contrasted with the complacent citizen, who from his safe stand on the gutter curb gave his applause to the fighting men and then stayed behind to perpetuate his own brunet type. In the present war, one has merely to study the type of officer and of the man in the ranks to realize that, in spite of the draft net, the Nordic race is contributing an enormous majority of the fighting men, out of all proportion to their relative numbers in the nation at large.[36]

A more serious long-range danger to the Nordics was the

peril of racial intermixture. The Nordic could triumph over other races only when his blood was pure. "It must be borne in mind," says Grant,

that the specializations which characterize the higher races are of relatively recent development, are highly unstable and when mixed with generalized or primitive characters tend to disappear. Whether we like to admit it or not, the result of the mixture of two races, in the long run, gives us a race reverting to the more ancient, generalized and lower type.

Thus, when blonds tend to mate with brunets, it is the brunet type which tends to predominate. One evidence that the darker races are older and more primitive is that "dark colored eyes are all but universal among wild mammals and entirely so among the primates, man's nearest relatives. It may be taken as an absolute certainty that all the original races of man had dark eyes." In addition, the Nordic cannot thrive in vast areas of the earth because "continuous sunlight affects adversely the delicate nervous organization." In tropical areas the Nordics "grow listless and cease to breed."[37]

The third reason the Nordic race was handicapped was its aversion to industrialism and urban environment.

Heavy, healthful work in the fields of northern Europe enables the Nordic type to thrive, but the cramped factory and crowded city quickly weed him out, while the little brunet Mediterranean can work a spindle, set type, sell ribbons or push a clerk's pen far better than the big, clumsy and somewhat heavy Nordic blond, who needs exercise, meat and air and cannot live under Ghetto conditions.

His race pride is itself a cause for his decline under these conditions, because native Americans of Nordic stock "will not bring children into the world to compete in the labor market with the Slovak, the Italian, the Syrian and the Jew." He is "too proud to mix socially with them and is gradually withdrawing from the scene, abandoning to these aliens the land which he conquered and developed." Thus the Nordic is "being literally driven off the streets of New York City by the swarms of Polish Jews. These immigrants adopt the language of the native American, they wear his clothes, they steal his name and they are beginning to take his women, but they seldom adopt his religion or understand his ideals."[38]

Grant has a number of remedies to suggest for the evils of race degeneration. The "laws against miscegenation must be greatly extended if the higher races are to be maintained," he warns. The task will prove difficult, because we have to contend with "a certain strange attraction for contrasted types" which is apparently instinctive. Nonetheless, we must forbid such marriages. The fit must be encouraged to have more children, the unfit to have fewer. People with deficiencies which can be passed on to their children must be sterilized. Before the discovery of the truths of eugenics, "much could be said from a Christian and humane viewpoint in favor of indiscriminate charity for the benefit of the individual." Without a plan for sterilization of the unfit, however, such charity was of "more injury to the race than black death or small pox." And for some not even sterilization would be enough. "The laws of nature require the obliteration of the unfit and human life is valuable only when it is of use to the community or race." It is a "mistaken regard for what we believed to be divine laws and a sentimental belief in the sanctity of human life," he says, which tends to prevent "the elimination of defective infants." Grant apparently has in mind other changes limiting the vote to certain races. He says that "as soon as the true bearing and import of the facts are appreciated by lawmakers, a complete change in our political structure will inevitably occur, and our present reliance on the influence of education will be superseded by a readjustment based on racial values."[39]

Although most of Grant's arguments are familiar, he was in some ways more astute than his predecessors in using anti-immigration arguments. For one thing, his use of the term *Nordic* rather than *Anglo-Saxon* gave him greater flexibility in appealing to American ethnic groups. An Anglo-Saxon was neces-

sarily one of English descent, but a Nordic could come from almost any of the countries of northern Europe. It is true that
Grant seems to be a bit cool toward the claims of the Germans
to being Nordic, but his bias, as we have seen, did not extend to
Americans of German descent. Grant's most obvious attempt at
mass support is his welcoming the Irish into the Nordic fold. It
is nonsense, he says, to speak of the Celtic race. He explains that
in spite of their Celtic language, "one fact stands out clearly"
concerning the Irish, that "all the original Celtic-speaking tribes
were Nordic." The Irish are, in fact, "fully as Nordic as the
English and the great mass of the Irish are of Danish, Norse and
Anglo-Norman blood in addition to earlier and pre-Nordic
elements."[40]

Grant's major conclusion is that the "Nordic" race in the
United States must protect the country from a fatal infusion of
inferior blood. "We Americans must realize," Grant declares,

that the altruistic ideals which have controlled our social development
during the last century and the maudlin sentimentalism that has made
America "an asylum for the oppressed," are sweeping the nation toward
a racial abyss. If the Melting Pot is allowed to boil without control and
we continue to follow our national motto and deliberately blind ourselves to all "distinctions of race, creed or color," the type of native
American of Colonial descent will become as extinct as the Athenian
of the age of Pericles, and the Viking of the days of Rollo.[41]

Though he is concerned with enlisting the support of the
Irish, Grant shows a rather surprising indifference to the opinions of southern native Americans. He observes that Massachusetts has produced more than fifty times as much genius per
hundred thousand whites as has Georgia, Alabama, or Mississippi.
The difference is partially to be explained by the difficulty the
Nordic has in adapting himself to a hot climate. Thus, one finds
in the South "an appreciably larger amount of brunet types
than in the North." By way of contrast to the brunet southerners, the native American New Englander is likely to have a
"clean-cut face," "high stature," and gray or blue eyes. Although

the poor whites of the southern mountains have physical traits which are "typically Nordic," they also have "aberrant . . . moral and mental characteristics." The reason is probably that the southern mountaineers are "to a large extent the offspring of indentured servants brought over by the rich planters in early Colonial times. . . . The persistence with which family feuds are maintained certainly points to such an origin." In addition, the Civil War had "shattered the aristocratic traditions which formerly secured the selection of the best men as rulers." Thus, he had noticed a "change in type of the men who are now sent by the Southern States to represent them in the Federal Government from their predecessors in ante-bellum times." The new senators and congressmen "lack the distinction and ability of the leaders of the Old South." One wonders what the southern senators and representatives in Congress whom Grant was soon to ask to help pass an immigration restriction law would have thought of this particular line of argument.[42]

Much of *The Passing of the Great Race* has little directly to do with the racial problems of the United States. The book has a lofty and mystical tone at times which reminds the reader of Gobineau's *Essay*. Grant is so convinced of his thesis that he does not need to stop and argue. In three hundred pages of text, he mentions only one man who might conceivably be said to qualify as an anthropologist—the early-nineteenth-century Alexander von Humboldt—and no contemporary biologists, sociologists, psychologists, or historians. In fact, relatively little of his book deals with modern times. Instead he writes a racial history of civilization extending back to the beginning of recorded time, with bewildering references to great numbers of tribes and reflections on their probable racial composition. The scholarship is overwhelmingly complex but sketchy on sources.[43]

Some of the reviewers of *The Passing of the Great Race* in American newspapers and periodicals were extremely enthusiastic. The review in the *Boston Transcript* spoke of its "profound learning" and declared that Grant's warnings "should be heeded before it is too late." Others praised the book but with reservations. The reviewer in the *Annals of the American Academy* said the position of the author "had much to recommend it," but that "so many extreme statements are made the reader often wonders what evidence there is." The review in the *Nation* observed that Grant's "concept of the truths of racial evolution" was on the whole "unanswerable" but that his enthusiasm had "led to occasional overestimates." The review in the *Dial* was one of the few which were openly hostile, commenting sarcastically that the alleged "science" of the book was "so pure that it is altogether imperceptible." In England, the reviews were much less favorable than in this country. The reviewer in the *Times Literary Supplement* wrote, "All that can be said of some of the statements brought forward by Mr. Grant as scientific evidence of his thesis is that they are incorrect." The London *Athenaeum* condemned the book's "race ecstasy" and said the fact "that a writer in democratic America should give currency to these doctrines is passing strange."[44]

The time was not quite ripe, however, for Grant's arguments to exert their maximum influence. In 1916, the United States was engrossed with the issue of the war in Europe. Since the main thesis of *The Passing of the Great Race* was immigration restriction and since immigration had declined to negligible numbers because shipping was then unavailable for this purpose, the immediate impact of Grant's book was nowhere near as great as it was to become after the war.

Grant's theorizing might perhaps have been recognized as the scientific mishmash it was if the racists had not been handed a formidable weapon at about the time that *The Passing of the Great Race* was published. The year 1916 also witnessed the perfecting of the Stanford-Binet scales of intelligence by Lewis Terman and his associates. Intelligence or the lack of it had been a counter in racist arguments for a long time. Now a powerful school of psychologists appeared which took up the old argument that intelligence is largely hereditary and is little affected by environment. They developed an impressive scheme of what seemed to be positive and objective proof. This system was, of course, extremely useful to the racists. All the nineteenth-century attempts to measure the physical character of races had ended in failure. Theories of innate character, though plentiful enough, had no substantial proof to back them. Now it scarcely mattered how the races differed physically; the point was that a method had been devised which seemed to prove that all the nonwhite races are intellectually inferior. This development helped to convince many men of imposing scientific reputation that Grant's thesis on the vast hereditary inequalities among races was correct, though perhaps not for the reasons he gave. Intelligence testing was to give racist theorizing a new lease on life—in fact, in the minds of many to make race the crucial determinant of human progress or retrogression.[45]

When mental tests were introduced into this country in the 1890's, one of the first experiments undertaken was an attempt to determine race differences. R. M. Bache, using tests which had been developed in Germany to measure quickness of sensory perception, compared twelve whites, eleven Indians, and eleven Negroes. The Indians had the quickest reactions, the Negroes were second, and the whites were third. But Bache calmly explained that the results proved the whites were the superior group. Their reactions were slower because they belonged to a more deliberate and reflective race than did the members of the other two groups.[46]

In 1897, B. R. Stetson compared five hundred white children with an equal number of Negro children in a test which evaluated memory. The Negro children made slightly higher scores, but this result was explained on the basis that they were older than the white children. This study was frequently quoted by later writers who saw in its result that Negroes may sometimes excel whites in "mechanical" intellectual processes requiring no extensive "cerebration." E. L. Thorndike, one of the pioneers of mental testing, explained that "the apparent mental attainments of children of inferior races may be due to lack of inhibition and so witness precisely to a deficiency in mental growth."[47]

In France, Alfred Binet, together with Théodore Simon, developed in 1905 a series of tests which were designed to measure degrees of intelligence. The original purpose of these tests was to recognize various degrees of feeblemindedness, but standards were set up for different age groups and the concept of mental age was introduced to indicate how a child might compare with other children of his age. The second Binet-Simon scale, which appeared in 1908, defined mental age more precisely by measuring it in terms of the ability of a child to answer a group of questions which 75 per cent of the children of his age could answer. Binet and Simon still regarded the chief value of mental tests as their ability to detect degrees of feeblemindedness in children. They admitted that environment and educational opportunity would inevitably affect the achievement scores and, therefore, they concluded that the tests would indicate the approximate intelligence only of those children who had closely similar environments.[48]

In spite of early warnings against interpreting tests as measuring hereditary intelligence without relation to environment, the temptation to do so was so strong that a great many psychologists succumbed to it. In 1912, William Stern introduced the idea of the intelligence quotient—the I.Q.—which was to be obtained by comparing one's mental age with his actual, or chronological, age. For example, if a ten-year-old child scored 100 on an examination, his mental age might correspond with his actual age. If he scored 80, his mental age was said to be eight years, and if he scored 120 his mental age was said to be twelve years. After the death of Binet, the center of intelligence testing shifted from France to the United States. In 1916, Lewis Terman and his associates published the Stanford-Binet scale of intelligence, a revision of the second Binet scale. The idea that the intelligence of a person could be expressed in terms of a number began to intrigue not only psychologists but the public at large.[49]

It requires an effort of the imagination to perceive the almost limitless horizon which seemed to stretch out before the psychologists. They hoped for tests that would make irrelevant the old question of which characteristics are the result of heredity and which of environment. In 1903, E. L. Thorndike observed that with "sufficient knowledge" we could "analyze any man's original mental nature into elements." In addition, we could determine what innate differences, if any, existed in the intelligence of different races. We could even discover whether there were innate differences in the mental processes "of the European stocks, of the Anglo-Saxon breed." If differences in innate intelligence could be measured, then a racial scale could eventually be worked out with considerable exactitude.[50]

One result of the intelligence tests was to show that the children of bank presidents and lawyers and college professors generally did much better than did the children of laboring men, a fact which was often interpreted to prove, not the fortunate effects of a good environment, but the supreme importance of a good heredity in the struggle for success. This conclusion had racial as well as class implications, since members of races were unevenly distributed among the social classes. In 1915, Lewis Terman observed that his tests showed that a low level of intelligence "is very, very common among Spanish-Indian and Mexican families of the Southwest, and also among negroes. Their dullness seems to be racial, or at least inherent in the family stocks from which they come." He admitted that the question had not been sufficiently studied, but he thought he knew what future studies would disclose. "The whole question of racial differences in mental traits will have to be taken up anew and by experimental methods," he said. "The writer predicts that when this is done there will be discovered enormously significant racial differences in general intelligence, differences which cannot be wiped out by any scheme of mental culture." Such tests would probably demonstrate that many children "are uneducable beyond the merest rudiments of training. No amount of school instruction will ever make them intelligent voters or capable citizens in the true sense of the word." Such children were the future "hewers of wood and drawers of water."[51]

An opportunity to employ intelligence tests on a mass scale

occurred in 1917 after the United States entered the war. The military services were interested in finding out which men would be the most effective in particular categories, especially as officers. A committee of psychologists—with Dr. Robert M. Yerkes as chairman—was asked to draw up a series of tests which would determine the intelligence and aptitudes of the great numbers of men then coming into the armed services. In all, more than 1,700,000 men were tested. So many extravagant claims and outright misinterpretations of these tests followed the publication of their results that it is necessary to examine them in some detail.[52]

There were two tests—the "army alpha" which was the test generally used, and the "army beta" which was a nonlanguage test taken by immigrants unfamiliar with English and by illiterates. The tests were designed to measure not mental age but general intelligence without respect to age. They were first tried out at selected camps to discover at what point about 5 per cent of the men would fall into the A category, the superior group from which officers would generally be chosen. It was hardly surprising, then, that when the tests were applied on a mass scale, 4.5 per cent of the men attained an A rating. Yet it was sometimes assumed that the tests had proved that only one man in twenty in the army was intelligent.[53]

Although the men were rated not by mental age but by the letters A—for superior—down through B, C, D, and E, an attempt was made to translate the scores of the army tests into mental age groups. The published report of the army psychologists lists mental ages according to the Stanford-Binet scale—without explaining how the scores had been transposed. Now, the mental tests given in the armed services could be interpreted to show the average intelligence of the men tested. Even this was not the full extent of the misinterpretation. The tests were used to "prove" what percentage of the American people were intelligent and what the average I.Q. was. There was still one more inconsistency in all this. The Stanford-Binet scale was based upon a few hundred tests and the army test on 1,700,000, but the

Stanford-Binet scale was used in order to measure the intelligence of the men in the army. Walter Lippmann pointed out the inconsistency of assuming that the average intelligence of men in the army was that of an immature child. "The average adult intelligence . . . cannot be less than the average adult intelligence." To assume that it could be was like saying that an "average mile was three quarters of a mile long." Lewis Terman, who was a member of the committee of psychologists, replied to Lippmann's criticism by saying that the army tests were established "independently of any other tests." Since Terman does not explain how this was done, it is no satisfactory explanation of the question of average mental age. The average adult mental age would have to be the average mental age and vice versa.[54]

The fact that the tests were constructed and administered, as the army report declared, "to minimize the handicap of men who because of foreign birth or lack of education are little skilled in the use of English," made it easy to exploit them for purposes of class and racial prejudice. Large claims were made for the effectiveness of the tests in measuring innate ability. The examinations "were originally intended, and are now definitely known, to measure native intellectual ability. They are to some extent influenced by educational acquirement, but in the main the soldier's inborn intelligence and not the accidents of environment determine his mental rating or grade in the Army."[55]

It is easy to see what a powerful tool was thus placed in the hands of the racists. The great lesson which many of the psychologists drew from the army tests was that intelligence is influenced relatively little by environment. The conclusion readily reached was that great numbers of people—in fact, the majority—were not capable of benefiting from improved education. The Negroes were the farthest removed from any possible hope. The tests, said Dr. Yerkes, "brought into clear relief . . . the intellectual inferiority of the negro. Quite apart from educational status, which is utterly unsatisfactory, the negro soldier is of relatively low grade intelligence." This discovery was "in the nature of a lesson, for it suggests that education alone will not place the negro race on a par with its Caucasian competitors."[56]

From all this, it can readily be seen how the army intelligence tests would provide a field day for racists who would argue that racial superiority and inferiority are simple facts which must be recognized. The end of the war would have brought difficult problems of adjustment even if this seemingly irrefutable scientific evidence for differences of intelligence among races had not been developed at this particular time. With the dislocations of the war and with the new status given to the importance of hereditary and racial differences, the early 1920's became the time when racist theories achieved an importance and respectability which they had not had in this country since before the Civil War.

XV

Racism in the 1920's

DURING THE WAR, the energies of the American people were mainly channeled into immediate practical objectives. When the victory had been won, however, the passions and resentments which usually had been restrained for the sake of national unity were freer to indulge themselves. The factory and industrial workers—many of whom were immigrants or the children of immigrants from southern and eastern Europe—were determined to improve their economic position, through strikes if necessary. The Negro, aware from his experience in Europe that ideas of racial caste were by no means universal, was determined to better his position in this country. And the Americans of the older ethnic groups were more and more intent upon holding the line against the rise in status of ethnic groups they believed to be inferior.

The unrest showed itself in the wave of strikes which began in 1919. Many Americans who participated in the postwar strikes were unquestionably of the older ethnic stocks. Among the 60,000 union members in Seattle and on the West Coast who struck in February, 1919, were many native-born American workers of north European stock. Other important strikes, however, were carried on largely by immigrants of more recent origin. In January, a strike of 35,000 New York garment workers began and spread through New England and the middle Atlantic states. In Lawrence, Massachusetts, the English-speaking employees mainly stayed at work while the "foreigners" went out. Many of the 376,000 workers who took part in the great steel strike of 1919 were representatives of the more recent immigrant stock. In addition to these disturbances, there was a relatively small—but at the time immensely significant—number of bombings by anarchists of the homes of judges, police superintendents, and other men in public life, and these bombings led to much comment on the innate character of the racial stocks which had come in recent years from Europe.[1]

Thus, a number of ominous signs appeared which reflected American race fears. There was a riot between whites and Negroes in Chicago in 1919 in which 23 whites and 15 Negroes were killed, 537 people injured, and 1,000 left homeless. Less than a year later, there was another major riot in Tulsa, Oklahoma. The Big Red Scare of the time led fourteen states in 1919 to follow the example set by the five which during the war had passed criminal syndicalism laws under which people were prosecuted for organization membership or for expression of opinion. That these fears of opinions were connected with fears of foreigners is suggested by the fact that during this year fifteen states also passed laws which required that English must be the sole language of instruction in all schools, public or private. In the summer of 1920, the Ku Klux Klan—which had been a relatively small organization since it was revived in 1915—began to pick up speed and to attract members on a large scale. By 1923 its membership was to be variously estimated at between three and six million persons, and it was to exert great influence not merely in the South but in a number of northern and western states. The Klan was an organization which stressed the supremacy of the white "Nordic" and the Protestant; it was opposed to the Negro, the Jew, and the Catholic. It was, moreover, only one of a number of superpatriotic organizations of the period pledged to the idea of 100-percentism. And the demands for immigration restriction rose in volume and vehemence.[2]

It was about this time that anti-Semitism became a really significant phenomenon in this country. In addition to the fulminations of the Klan, the *Dearborn Independent,* a magazine owned by Henry Ford and distributed to thousands of his dealers, began in May, 1920, to expose the "International Jew" who encouraged nations to go to war in order to batten on the profits of the munitions industry. "The Founding fathers were men of Anglo-Saxon-Celtic race," said the *Independent*. "Into the camp of this race comes a people that has no civilization to point to, no aspiring religion, no universal speech, no great achievement in any realm but the realm of 'get,' cast out of every land that gave them hospitality, and these people endeavor to tell the sons of the Saxons what is needed to make the world what it ought to be." As evidence of the conspiracy of the Jews, the magazine utilized the "Protocols of the Learned Elders of Zion," documents which purport to show widespread conspiracy to subvert governments but which are recognized by most authorities as forgeries.[3]

Less spectacularly, both Jews and Negroes suffered discrimination from sources which had traditionally been more tolerant of them. One sign of the change was the decision of a number of colleges and universities, particularly in the East, to institute quota systems for Jews. Columbia University, for example, suffered from the taunts of the alumni of schools where few of the students were Jews. A writer in 1921 mentions that those institutions which had sizable numbers of Jews were "made the butt of sly jokes by after-dinner speeches in rival universities, to the effect that such and such a college is safe from fire and flood, since He that keepeth Israel neither slumbers nor sleeps." A campus song put the matter more crudely:

> Oh, Harvard's run by millionaires,
> And Yale is run by booze,
> Cornell is run by farmers' sons,
> Columbia's run by Jews.[4]

Columbia acted to remove the basis of the charge by instituting a Jewish quota. New York University, Princeton, and Williams College also instituted a quota. President A. Lawrence Lowell of Harvard strongly supported a quota for Jews at Harvard and instituted a ban on Negroes' living in freshman dormitories—

where residence was compulsory—but he was overruled on both scores by a faculty committee and the Harvard Board of Overseers after widespread public protest.[5]

All these incidents suggest that racism was increasing in the United States in terms not merely of violence and open hatred but of subtle and insidious forms of discrimination. Our concern here is not to describe in detail the manifestations of American prejudice and nativism, but primarily to examine the debate over race within the academic disciplines. At first glance, these disciplines may seem somewhat remote from overt manifestations of violence. A man did not need to read an article or book on the biological, anthropological, psychological, or sociological aspects of race in order to participate in a race riot. Still, ideas have a way of trickling down. The academic disciplines would eventually provide a real defense against the ideas of the racists. At the time, however, they were in a state of confusion and unable effectively to combat the onrush of prejudice.[6]

There were plenty of zealots in the 1920's who frantically proclaimed a gospel of racism. We misinterpret the strength of the racism of the period, however, if we imagine that its most formidable proponents were emotional bigots like the Ku Kluxers. It is essential to understand that quite a large number of people eminent in the sciences and the social sciences were then genuinely convinced that races vary greatly in innate intelligence and temperament. It is futile to condemn these people as villains or hypocrites or fools. They were reflecting very powerful ideas of their time and drawing conclusions from them according to their lights. Often they expressed themselves in a calm and deliberate manner and deplored excesses of violence and discrimination. It is natural that in the histories of the period the views of the extremists have been accorded more attention, but it was mainly the academic writers on racial differences who made racism respectable.

The most powerful weapon of the racism of the period continued to be the intelligence test. Because mental tests were thought to be an objective measurement of innate ability and because they showed wide divergences in scores among races and nationality groups, they inevitably entered into the rising debate on the importance of race as a factor in national life. Then too, the tests seemed to make irrelevant all the arguments which had been developed over the past 150 years as to what race actually *is*. What did it matter now that anthropologists had been unable to find any scale by which races could be measured and distinguished from one another? The fact that the median scores for all races and ethnic groups in the country were lower than the scores of the native white Americans of English or north European stock was widely interpreted to mean one thing: all the non-Nordic races were inferior. One observer in 1922 said that everybody in America, even in the remotest villages, was learning the word *moron* and it "showed signs of running 'damn fool' out of the language. . . ." The menace of the "under-man" was widely discussed, and he often turned out to be a member of an "inferior" race.[7]

The psychologists followed the initial success of the army mental tests with a veritable avalanche of testing. In many of these studies, the racist implications were not far below the surface. E. L. Thorndike declared that "race directly and indirectly produces differences so great that government, business, industry, marriage, friendship, and almost every other feature of human instinctive and civilized life have to take account of a man's race." The original uncertainties about the effect of environment upon test scores all but disappeared. As late as 1940, Thorndike was willing to express the relative importance of heredity and environment in terms of percentages. Intelligence could be allocated "roughly" 80 per cent to the genes, 17 per cent to training, and 3 per cent to "accident."[8]

Dr. Carl C. Brigham, an assistant professor of psychology at Princeton, wrote one of the most bizarre of the studies of mental tests as applied to race. In *A Study of American Intelligence,* he accepted the division of Europeans into the three races of Nordic, Alpine, and Mediterranean and interpreted the army intelligence tests of 1917 and 1918 in such a way as to prove the superiority of the Nordic. The army had not attempted this sort of classification of the soldiers taking the test, but it had listed the national origin or descent of the soldiers. Brigham attempted to estimate the amount of Nordic, Alpine, and Mediterranean in each of the European nations. Sweden had 100 per cent Nordic blood, Norway had 90 per cent; Denmark, Holland, and Scotland followed with 85 per cent; England 80 per cent; Wales and Germany, 40 per cent; France and Ireland, 30 per cent; Poland and Spain, 10 per cent; Italy, Russia, and Portugal, 5 per cent. The nations with the highest Nordic blood contributed the largest number of soldiers with "A" and "B" ratings, so Brigham concluded the Nordics must be the most intelligent. "In a very definite way, the results which we obtain by interpreting the army data by means of the race hypothesis support Mr. Madison Grant's thesis of the superiority of the Nordic type."[9]

Looking back upon this test, one hardly knows which is its more curious aspect—Brigham's conviction that it was possible to express Nordic, Alpine, and Mediterranean "races" in terms of percentages for whole nations, or his conviction that intelligence was almost wholly unrelated to the quality of the education which different ethnic groups had received. How far he was willing to carry the argument that environmental differences were negligible in determining mental ability may be judged by the conclusion he drew from the fact that more recent immigrants from a given country did not do as well on these tests as those who had been here a considerable time. He discovered that immigrants who had been here twenty years did better on the tests than those who had been here fifteen; those who had been here ten years did better than those who had been here five. These facts did not lead him to conclude that perhaps environment might be a considerable factor; instead, he interpreted the figures as conclusive proof that the innate quality of the more recent immigrants was lower and was steadily declining. From the point of view of the racists among the advocates of immigration restriction, Brigham's study was a real triumph. Even Jewish immigrants did badly on the tests. "Our figures, then," Brigham concluded, "would rather tend to disprove the popular belief that the Jew is highly intelligent."[10]

A critic of Brigham's pointed out that not merely did northern Negroes do better than southern Negroes on the army tests, but the Negroes of some northern states did better than the whites of some southern states. The literate Negroes from Illinois had higher median scores than the literate whites from nine southern states; the literate Negroes from New York surpassed the literate whites from five southern states; the literate Negroes from Pennsylvania surpassed the literate whites from two southern states. None of this convinced Dr. Brigham that education and environment might radically change the intelligence scores. The superiority of the northern Negroes over southern Negroes was to be explained on the basis of their greater admixture of white blood and the fact that better opportunities in the North prompted the more intelligent Negroes of the South to migrate there. Dr. Robert M. Yerkes, who had been in charge of the army tests, agreed with Brigham's thesis that the higher scores of northern Negroes did not constitute an argument for the power of education and environment. He wrote a foreword to Brigham's book in which he endorsed the thesis that the tests proved that the Negroes were inferior in intelligence and that immigrants could be generally rated intellectually by the amount of Nordic blood in their veins.[11]

It was probably inevitable that the psychologists should devise scales for testing the "personalities" of race, now that the matter of racial intelligence medians had apparently been established. A study of the "will-temperament" of Negroes appeared in 1922. An elaborate racial personality study was made on Japanese schoolchildren and another on Chinese, Japanese, and Hawaiians; there was a study of the personalities of Indian children with the implication that the innate character of the race was thus disclosed. Psychologists attempted to measure such "racial" characters as "integrity," "kindliness," "courage," unselfishness," "reasonableness," "refinement," "cheerfulness and optimism," "motor inhibition," "non-compliance," and "finality of judgment." As one might have predicted, the tests generally showed that Negroes, Indians, Mexicans, and other nonwhite races were ordinarily inferior in their personality traits to the whites. The difficulty common to all the studies was that the researchers had discovered no means of determining the differences between traits caused by heredity and those caused by environment.[12]

Toward critics who doubted that scores in the tests were influenced only slightly by education and environment, a number of the psychologists were patronizing or even contemptuous. Lewis Terman placed such critics on a par with those "many excellent people who do not 'believe in' vaccination against typhoid and small pox, operations for appendicitis, etc." When Walter Lippmann questioned some of the conclusions which psychologists had drawn from the army tests, Lewis Terman brushed his objections aside. The fact was, said Terman, that "a majority of the psychologists of America, England and Germany are now enrolled in the ranks of the 'intelligence tests,' and all but a handful of the rest use their results." Further in the same article Terman argued that the racial implications of intelligence tests were undeniable: The "average Portuguese child carries through school and into life an IQ of about 80" as compared with 100 for the child of Nordic descent. Dr. William MacDougall, professor of psychology at Harvard, admitted that it could not be proved that intelligence was wholly or largely a matter of heredity, but he contended that all the evidence pointed in that direction. If Lippmann chose to argue that mental ability is not largely a matter of inheritance, he was "denying also the theory of organic evolution, and he should come out openly on the side of Mr. Bryan. For the theory of the heredity of mental qualities is a corollary of the theory of organic evolution." Terman also relegated Lippmann to the camp of William Jennings Bryan.[13]

MacDougall was perhaps the most indefatigable of the race theorizers among the psychologists of the time. He was a very different man from the intelligence testers, who stressed exact methods of experimental psychology. An Englishman who came to this country in 1920, he had a strongly teleological or purposive view of life and mind and a conviction that psychology ought to be useful to the historian, the sociologist, the anthropologist, the economist, and especially the intelligent political leader. He was a champion of the instincts theory of psychology and the great opponent of the behaviorists. MacDougall's *Introduction to Social Psychology* (1908) went through more impressions and editions than any other psychological work of its time, about twenty-five in all.[14]

When MacDougall directed his attention to the importance of race, his great theme was the superiority of the Nordics. In 1921, he published a series of his lectures at the Lowell Institute under the title *Is America Safe for Democracy?*, a warning to the nation on the perils of race intermixture. The book is a kind of compendium on racial psychology. We learn that the art of northern Europe is essentially "subjective" and "individualist" and that of southern Europe is "public," "formal," "ritualistic," and "conventional" because northern Europe is inhabited by Nordics whereas southern Europe is composed largely of Mediterraneans. The "herd instinct is relatively weak in the Nordic, strong in the Mediterranean peoples." Thus, Nordics are usually Protestants rather than Catholics because they are more fearlessly self-reliant than other races. They are also endowed preeminently with curiosity, a characteristic which makes them scientists and inventors par excellence. It is their Nordic blood which explains the fact that the Greeks were important innovators in science and philosophy, whereas the Mediterranean blood of the Romans explains their lack of talent in these fields. But curiosity has its price. We are told that the Swedes have a high rate of suicide because in that country the trait of curiosity is so strongly developed among the relatively pure Nordics that the people desire "to penetrate by their own act the impenetrable veil. . . ." Thus, a seeming defect is rationalized into a virtue.[15]

The racists could take comfort from many prominent biologists as well as from the psychologists. Some of the biologists regarded it as axiomatic that race mixture, at least among peoples widely different from one another, would lead to "disharmonies." These disharmonies were not necessarily produced by any defects of either race, but simply resulted from the fact that each of them was so unlike the other that to mix them led to physical, mental, and emotional deformities. Even biologists who recognized that the proof for this contention was lacking often thought that race mixture was bad because certain races were poor biological material, and therefore intermarriage with them would have "dysgenic" effects.

Dr. Charles B. Davenport, director of the Eugenics Record Office, a private organization at Cold Spring Harbor, New York, was probably the most positive advocate of the theory that race intermixture led to biological abnormalities. Although warning his readers that the subject had not been sufficiently investigated, Davenport proceeded to issue a series of disturbing conclusions. The Scotch, for example, were "long-lived" and had "internal organs . . . well adapted to care for the large frames." South Italians, on the other hand, had small, short bodies. The hybrids of these two "races" could be expected to yield "children with large frames and inadequate viscera—children of whom it is said every inch over 5' 10" is an inch of danger; children of insufficient circulation." In his conversations with dentists, he had discovered that "many cases of overcrowding or wide separation of teeth are due to a lack of harmony between the size of jaw and size of teeth—probably due to a union of a large-jawed, large-toothed race and a small-jawed, small-toothed race." Nothing was more striking, he added, than "the irregular dentations of many children of the tremendously hybridized American." Nor were physical defects alone to be dreaded. For example, "one often sees in mulattoes an ambition and push combined with intellectual inadequacy which makes the unhappy hybrid dissatisfied with his lot and a nuisance to others." Davenport feared for the future of the country since a "hybridized people are a badly put together people and a dissatisfied, restless, ineffective people. One wonders how much of the exceptionally high death-rate in middle life in this country is due to such bodily maladjustments;

and how much of our crime and insanity is due to mental and temperamental friction."[16]

The studies of J. A. Mjen were sometimes quoted as proof of the dysgenic effects of race mixture. Mjen studied the effects of intermarriage between Nordic Norwegians and Lapps in Norway and concluded that the resulting offspring were inferior to either of the parent stocks. It was not positive biological defects he discovered, however, but a lowered resistance to disease and a declining standard of morality, both of which could be explained as the effects of an unfavorable social environment, since intermarriage was frowned upon by both ethnic groups.[17]

Other studies did not bear out the thesis that race intermixture led to biological abnormalities. Eugen Fischer studied the effects of race crossing in German Southwest Africa between the Boers and Hottentots. The Boers had been dissatisfied with British rule in South Africa and had migrated far northward where they interbred with the Hottentots. The families studied by Fischer had an average of 7.7 children each, certainly an argument in favor of "hybrid vigor." In addition, the descendants of such unions tended to be greater in stature than either parent race. Dr. W. E. Castle, professor of zoölogy at Harvard, criticized the idea of racial disharmonies, citing the example of Pitcairn Island, where mutineers from Captain John Bligh's *Bounty* established a colony of Englishmen and native islanders in 1788. In 1901, there were 870 descendants of the Pitcairn Islanders, a group which was thoroughly mixed racially, and yet there seemed to be no evidence of disharmonic combinations among them.[18]

Dr. S. J. Holmes, professor of zoölogy at the University of California, was unconvinced by the findings of Fischer and Castle. He thought that scientists who could find no evidence for race disharmonies had confined their studies too exclusively to the first generation of offspring from race crossings:

Formerly inheritance was considered to be typically blending, and the subsequent generations of a racial cross were thought to be very much like the first. This is now known to be far from correct. Characters that appear to blend in the first generation of a cross segregate come out in various combinations in the second and subsequent generations, and we get in wide crosses a motley array of the most diverse forms. This is because the parent types differ in a considerable number of hereditary factors. The more different factors there are the larger the number of different combinations that can be made from them. And however harmonious the blend made in the first cross, the second generation is apt to produce many unfortunate combinations of traits.[19]

Dr. Edward M. East, professor of biology at Harvard, thought the studies of Fischer and Castle were open to another objection. Unlike races, East maintained, will produce a great variety of types. The "greater spread of the racial curve" would tend to produce some "men of iron," but it would also produce "weaklings" and "ne'er-do-wells," and the latter in far larger proportions. These ideas of Holmes and East were extremely interesting; all that was lacking was proof.[20]

Biologists who did not accept the theory of racial "disharmonies" nonetheless sometimes deplored race intermixture. They argued that since the psychologists had proved that races differ markedly in innate intelligence, it was logical to assume that crosses among them must represent offspring with at best an intermediate stage of intelligence between the two parent groups. Dr. Paul Popenoe, editor of the *Journal of Heredity*, criticized Fischer's use of the Boer-Hottentot mulattoes and Castle's use of the Pitcairn Islanders as evidence that racial crosses are not productive of evil results. These hybrid races might be "physically healthy," but mentally the case might be far different and would very likely prove that "miscegenation is an advantage to the inferior race and a disadvantage to the superior one."[21] Again, all that was lacking was proof.

Since the matter of racial "disharmonies" seemed to be debatable, many of the biologists who feared the harm of race mixture relied upon analogies with species among animals and plants. Any breeder could bear him out, said Dr. Michael F. Guyer, professor of zoölogy at the University of Wisconsin, that "race crossings" in the animal and plant worlds were generally bad:

The inferiority of the mongrel, in spite of possible hybrid vigor in the first generation, is universally recognized. No sensible farmer, for example, would seek to improve his Jerseys or his Herefords by crossing one with the other. It is true that in pure breeds of plant and animals we sometimes venture on a cross to introduce some new desirable character but we follow up such mixture by a rigid selection in which is eliminated all but the rare individuals having the desired characteristics, and we continue this elimination generation after generation to fix the characters again. It is obvious that no such selection as this would be possible among the progeny of human crosses.[22]

All this might seem very plausible—and it was an idea which was widely taken up by popular writers on race of the period—but, as we shall see, the biologists of a later time would come to believe that the analogy between man and lower organisms is almost wholly misleading.

The debates over the dangers of race intermixture were not, of course, merely academic. They took place against the background of a powerful movement drastically to reduce immigration from foreign countries. This movement might have been carried on without becoming involved in race theories, but with the mood of the times this was most unlikely. E. A. Ross, though in former years one of the most vociferous advocates among the sociologists of the idea of race superiority and inferiority, had by 1924 come to see clearly that the blatant racism used in the anti-immigration arguments could have only evil consequences for the nation. An opponent of large-scale immigration, he nonetheless attempted to combat the racist arguments and to argue immigration restriction wholly on its social and economic consequences. He declared:

The injury suffered by America has not come from an essential inferiority of the immigrants in respect to race fibre, but from their being unfamiliar with our language and institutions and ignorant of how to keep from being exploited economically and politically. It is particularly "the newer immigration," coming from southern and southeastern Europe, which has lacked the background of culture and experience needed for working our institutions.[23]

The census of 1920 had shown that there were nearly

14,000,000 people in the United States who had been born in some other country.[24] The proponents of immigration restriction might have developed an argument which did not imply the innate inferiority of any race. They might have contended that it was not possible to keep immigrants from being exploited as cheap labor if great numbers of them were allowed to come in. It might further have been argued that a readily available cheap labor force would, in turn, serve to depress the wages of workmen already here.

Not all the proponents of immigration were members of ethnic minorities, nor were they all moved chiefly by humanitarian considerations. Judge Elbert H. Gary, for example, had not had a reputation for racial tolerance. As head of the United States Steel Corporation he had defeated the strike of 1919 against a twelve-hour day and a seven-day week largely by pinning the Red label on the strikers and by exploiting race cleavages among the employees. But after an immigration restriction law was passed in 1920, Gary denounced it bitterly as "one of the worst things that this country has ever done for itself economically." This opposition, like the opposition of the National Association of Manufacturers to legislation restricting immigration, was probably due to a desire for cheap labor.[25]

This situation merely emphasizes strange alliances which had been developing for a long time on both sides of the immigration controversy. In favor of large-scale immigration were both high-minded defenders of the immigrants as real or potential good Americans and employers who wanted an uninterrupted supply of cheap labor. Opposed to large-scale immigration were conservative social thinkers who thought socialism and radicalism would flourish if immigration were not curtailed, and liberal thinkers who feared the effects of a continuing source of cheap labor upon the efforts of the unions to improve their status and power. We have already seen how this latter alliance developed in the late nineteenth and early twentieth centuries. Then, prominent advocates of reform—men like Josiah Strong, E. A. Ross, and John R. Commons—had found themselves on the same side of the argument with those conservative upper-class men who advocated immigration restriction. To cement this uneasy alliance, large amounts of racism were apparently necessary. The alliance continued into the 1920's, although the names of the leaders on both sides changed. Now upper-class conservatives like Madison Grant opposed immigration and a group of liberal thinkers—men who would have opposed Grant on every other conceivable issue—agreed with him that immigration must be stopped or at least radically curtailed. And here again it was a reliance upon racism which brought these two points of view, so different from one another, into a powerful alliance.

One "liberal" racist of the period was Dr. Henry Pratt Fairchild (1880-1956), professor of sociology at New York University. Fairchild was highly influential as an officer of various societies. He was at various times president of the American Eugenics Society, of the Population Association of America, and of the American Sociological Society. In addition, he served on many boards and committees, wrote, and lectured widely, convinced as he was that sociology ought to make its findings known to the public. He was a tireless worker in various "liberal" causes such as combating violations of academic freedom in colleges and universities and abuses of fair play in Congressional investigations. His position on economic questions was considerably left of center, since he believed in the principles of socialism.[26]

For several reasons, the attitude of Fairchild toward race is interesting. He was not usually dogmatic, positive, and inflexible. He took the trouble to read what his opponents, the race egalitarians, said, and he was aware—as many racists of his time were not—of the difficulties in the way of studying the phenomenon. He knew that race is not clearly definable, and he could appreciate all the claims of vanity which would cause distortions of any ethnic group's view of "outside" ethnic groups. As a humanitarian, he was quite aware that racism inevitably would be called in to justify any cruelty or oppression. And yet he thought the phenomenon of race character was real and must therefore be recognized.

It is true that behind his attempts at objectivity and fairness we can discover a history of prejudice, particularly in his early books. One detects in him a dislike for certain ethnic groups, particularly for the immigrants from southern and southeastern Europe. He apparently first became interested in race problems when in 1900, as a young man of twenty, he went to teach at the International College in Smyrna. His experience with the Greeks seems to have disillusioned him, because in his subsequent thesis at the University of Illinois on Greek immigration he had many harsh things to say of their character. "In general, dishonesty is one of the most serious faults of the race." "The Greek is much inclined to be indolent, egotistical, vain and superficial." While he displays some enterprise in business, his only ambition is to acquire sufficient means to "spend the last years of his life sitting in idleness in the clubs and coffee-houses, discussing politics and the thousand and one trivial things that a Greek can find to occupy his mind." Fairchild believed such characteristics were "inveterately Greek"—that is, that they were part of the racial character."

Fairchild's intellectual history might well be described as a series of attempts to understand social phenomena without the aid of race theories, an enterprise in which he never quite succeeded. Disliking the term "racism," he substituted the phrase "consciousness of kind," a conception introduced by Franklin H. Giddings to describe the attitude of sympathy toward members of the "in-group" as compared with hostility toward members of the "out-group." But since he thought that race was by far the strongest element of "consciousness of kind," the difference between his attitude and that of out-and-out racism is sometimes obscure. In the 1920's, Fairchild was one of the most active opponents of immigration, but—like E. A. Ross—he generally based his arguments on cultural and social factors. He emphasized the point that race is "a strictly biological term," that it has nothing to do with cultural traits. From this point he goes on to say that the cultural traits of southern and southeastern European immigrants make them difficult if not impossible to assimilate into the American national life. The only trouble with this line of thought is that it occasionally is not enough for Fairchild, and he keeps shifting back to what are essentially racist arguments.[28]

In another later book Fairchild says, for example, that it is an outstanding "practical question" whether race differences are merely matters of such bodily characteristics as color of skin and eye or whether they also refer to innate "intellectual, temperamental, and moral traits." His answer to the question shows an ambivalence which is practically an admission that such inner differences exist:

We may simply say that if these qualities are matters of inheritance at all, there is every reason to suppose that they are matters of racial inheritance, and important differences exist between races in these traits as well as in the external bodily traits. It may be observed in passing, that just as man's most significant evolution, that is to say, specialization, has been in his head, so the most striking racial criteria—skin color excepted—are located in the head. It would be most surprising and anomalous if all the significant variations between races were developed on the outside of the head, and none whatever in the brain, the most characteristic human organ.

If all this is true, it is certainly doubtful whether race is a "strictly biological term" which can be regarded as wholly unrelated to cultural traits.[29]

Fairchild sometimes argues that even though there may be no proof of innate differences of temperament among the races, the fact of race antipathy is not proof that the feeling is not instinctive, "for there are many instinctive reactions that develop only as the development of the individual calls for them, and this may be long after infancy." In one place, he says that race antipathy itself may indeed be an acquired characteristic and suggests "it can eventually be rooted out by education, exhortation, or some other social means." But after having admitted this much, he backtracks in another book by saying, "Of course the feeling [race antipathy] itself is not inherited; no feeling is. But it is wholly probable that the neural connections which cause a certain feeling to arise in response to a given stimulus are inherited." The results of inherent neural connections which respond to certain stimuli are identical with those which might be expected from inherited feelings of antipathy. "As a practical matter," says Fairchild, "it does not make much difference whether race feeling is innate or acquired."[30] It is difficult to see why Fairchild draws this conclusion. If race antipathy is innate, its effects at best can only be mitigated; if it is acquired, it is possible that man might in time reduce race tensions to negligible proportions.

When any pressure was put upon him, Fairchild was likely to decide that race antipathies definitely were innate, not acquired:

The principle has been propounded and urged by certain broad-minded and sympathetic persons that there should be no racial discrimination in any American legislation. Nothing could be more unsound, unscientific, or dangerous. Racial discrimination is inherent in biological fact and in human nature. It is unsafe and fallacious to deny in legislation forces which exist in fact.

Nor was he hesitant to argue that the United States should consider first of all the claims of the white race. In discussing the Negro race problem, he says there "can . . . be no doubt that if America is to remain a stable nation it must continue a white man's country for an indefinite period to come."[31] The tone of Fairchild's books is so different from the above remark that it is probably not so prejudiced as it sounds. As a northerner, Fairchild may not have known that "keeping the country white" was a common expression in the South which meant, in effect, denying political and other rights to Negroes. He probably meant that nonwhite races should not be allowed to become a majority in this country through immigration.

It must be admitted that the qualms which Fairchild occasionally had about race theory were not matched by many other racists of the 1920's. Among the real stalwarts was Dr. Henry Fairfield Osborn (1857-1935), the paleontologist. Like Madison Grant, with whom he was closely associated, Osborn came from

a prominent and well-to-do family—his maternal grandfather
was a very wealthy man. A biographical sketch of Osborn says
that his financially and socially secure background "accelerated
his career and helped to mold his benevolently autocratic character." In 1879 Osborn had gone to England to study comparative anatomy under Thomas H. Huxley. He met all the great
English biologists of the time, including Darwin, and developed
professional friendships which later proved to be useful to him as
a museum director. In 1908, he became president of the American Museum of Natural History, a post he held for twenty-five
years. He received almost every honor open to a scientist—membership in sixty-one societies and academies and twelve gold
medals. He was by no means only an administrator but also published widely in the field of paleontology.[32]

Osborn enthusiastically joined with Madison Grant in the
campaign to restrict immigration upon racial grounds, and he
wrote the preface to Grant's *The Passing of the Great Race*. Even
less than Grant did Osborn concern himself with the technical
difficulties of anthropology. He simply assumed as obvious that
racial inequalities of intelligence and temperament exist, that
they are enormous, and that civilization itself depends upon their
recognition. He wrote:

The true spirit of American democracy that *all men are born with
equal rights and duties*, has been confused with the political sophistry
that *all men are born with equal character and ability to govern themselves and others*, and with the educational sophistry that education and
environment will offset the handicap of heredity. In the United States
we are slowly waking to the consciousness that education and environment do not fundamentally alter racial values.

In "the increasing tide of Oriental and decadent European influence in current literature, . . . in the 'movies' and on the stage,"
he continued, "we witness with alarm . . . the decline of American standards of life, of conduct, of Sabbath observance, of the
marriage relation." It was the foreign element from which came
"grossly decadent and dissolute librettos" which were "saved
only from obscenity by the occasional hand of the censor" and

"ridiculed as Puritanism the original American standards." Under these circumstances, then, it was the Americans' "right and duty to maintain the predominance of our own race through the regulation of immigration. . . ." Such regulation was "not for a moment to be confused with racial prejudice or with religious and social bigotry."[33]

Like Grant, Osborn attributed nearly all of mankind's achievements to the Nordic race. The "Nordic tide which flowed into Italy" produced Raphael, Leonardo da Vinci, Galileo, Titian, Giotto, Donatello, Botticelli, Andrea del Sarto, Petrarch, and Tasso. "Dante's name, *Alighieri,* is also German, although the anthropologist Sergi recently denied his Nordic origin." How carefully Osborn chose his evidence for the existence of Nordic blood is apparent in his statement that "Columbus, from his portraits and from his busts, authentic or not, was clearly of Nordic ancestry." There followed a great file of Nordics through the history of other countries of Europe and some observations on the recently concluded Great War. The two great French military leaders of the war were Joffre and Foch, who were Nordics, but the apparently less able political leaders, Clemenceau and Poincaré, were of Alpine blood. The main point of Osborn's racist writings was that the Nordics in the United States were imperiled by the presence of millions of immigrants who came from a degenerate racial stock.[34]

Osborn was too vehement, however, to be typical of most of the biological and social scientists of his time who were disturbed over the problem of race degeneration. It is likely that if the racists could have done no better than this they would not have attracted the support of as many men as they did who were notable for their concern with objective truth. Most of the scientists concerned over race attempted to present their findings and conclusions more objectively. The biologist Dr. S. J. Holmes, for example, avoided the alarmist note. Though he thought that conclusions about race superiority and inferiority were inescapable, he was willing to admit that proof of such conclusions had not yet been presented. "We simply do not have the statistics to show," he said, "whether our inheritance has improved or deteriorated." On the other hand, degeneration had to be regarded as very probable:

But from our knowledge of the evolutionary factors at work in human society it is scarcely possible to avoid the conclusion that a certain amount of decadence is inevitable. We know that mental and moral defects are inherited; we know that the stocks with a record of intellectual achievement are multiplying with relative and increasing slowness; we know that the physically and mentally unfit reproduce more rapidly than under the conditions of more primitive civilization, and that their progeny are fostered and allowed to continue their defects. Amid all the influences tending to lessen the fertility of the more desirable classes of human beings there is scarcely any factor except natural selection which is working for the perpetuation of the best blood.[36]

All the men mentioned so far had relatively restricted audiences. Even Madison Grant's *The Passing of the Great Race,* although it had sold well for a book on a professedly scientific subject and had reached the attention of influential people, did not have a mass appeal. It was almost inevitable that someone would arise who would make the new "truths" of science concerning race available to great numbers of people. There were, in fact, a number of candidates for the honor: books and articles expounding the transcendent importance of race as a key to civilization poured from the presses in the 1920's. But the palm among the writers should go to Dr. Theodore Lothrop Stoddard. As much as any single person, he alarmed the nation over the perils of race.

Stoddard (1883-1950) was a member of an old New England family. His father, John Stoddard, was well known around the turn of the century for his popular series of illustrated travelogues, published as *Stoddard's Lectures.* John Lawson Stoddard, like many members of his family before, had intended to become a minister, but he lost his faith while he was a student and became a "scientific humanist." Later in life he was converted to Catholicism, but his son remained a somewhat militant agnostic.

Lothrop Stoddard graduated from the Harvard Law School in 1908, but he practiced law for less than a year. He returned to Harvard, where he received the M.A. degree in 1910 and the Ph.D. in 1914. His doctoral thesis was a study of the revolt of the Negroes against the French colonists in San Domingo in the late eighteenth and early nineteenth centuries, in which large numbers of white colonists were killed and a Negro state was set up. In one of his books, Lothrop Stoddard tells us that about 1910 he "became convinced that the key-note of the twentieth-century world-politics would be the relations between the primary races of mankind."[36]

Stoddard's central theme was that the white races—particularly the Nordics—were in danger of being inundated by the "inferior" races who had a much higher birthrate. The reason why the Nordics had been unaware of their position of utmost danger was that they had been lulled by the false doctrines of Jean-Jacques Rousseau. In spite of the fact that Rousseau was "neurotic, mentally unstable, morally weak, sexually perverted, and during the latter part of his life . . . undoubtedly insane," said Stoddard, he also "possessed great literary talents, his style, persuasiveness, and charm captivating and convincing multitudes." He was "a striking example of the 'tainted genius' " and had "accordingly exerted upon the world a profound—and in the main a baneful—influence, which is working indirectly but powerfully even to-day."

What Rousseau had done was to introduce the concept of the Noble Savage, an idea which led him naturally to the assumption of "the natural equality of all men." This, in turn, fostered the erroneous belief in the "absence of inborn differences between either individuals or races" and a faith in "the infinite power of laws, institutions, and other environmental factors to mould human beings, regardless of their origin or antecedents." Wedded to "sentimental abstractions," the social thinkers influenced by Rousseau had tended to "ignore those factors of race and culture which are the eternal, unchangeable bases of the entire problem." Ever since Rousseau, history had demonstrated the catastrophic effect of the idea of equality. "The tide set flowing by Rousseau and his ilk presently foamed into the French Revolution." In America, the results had been equally disastrous but delayed in their effects. Rousseau's equalitarian ideas "fitted in admirably with America's post-Revolutionary mood." The Americans had imagined that democracy was suitable for all races and thus had allowed the country to be peopled by hosts of inferior racial stocks. "Such were the unpleasant consequences of the equalitarian and cosmopolitan doctrines of Rousseau and his fellows as applied to America."[37]

The idea of the banefulness of Rousseau's influence was espoused by Irving Babbitt, a well-known professor of French at the time Stoddard was a student at Harvard and later a leader of the New Humanist movement. Babbitt traced many of the ills of contemporary America to the influence of Rousseau, but for him the problem was not one of race. He believed that Rousseau's conviction of the natural equality of man had led to the cult of the average man, and thus to the cult of mediocrity and anti-intellectualism. Babbitt's great idea was that the intellectuals of the country should renounce the belief in the equality of all men and substitute the classical idea of moderation, balance, and restraint, and thus create an intellectual—though not necessarily a social and political—elite. For Stoddard, however, the problem was much simpler. Where Babbitt had envisioned an aristocracy of intellect which the nation would eventually come to acknowledge and even to take pride in, Stoddard assumed that the aristocracy should be quite simply the members of the "Nordic race."

Stoddard cared little for the ideal of classical restraint. As a matter of fact, his ideas seem to be in some ways descendants of the conceptions of Rousseau, the man who for him was the archvillain of all history. There is an emphasis upon emotion, even primitive emotion, in Stoddard's writings. He thought it was only by an appeal to emotion that the tremendous tasks ahead could be accomplished. In one of his books, he quotes with apparent approval from W. J. Fielding's *The Caveman Within Us* to define the fundamentally irrational character of the human mind:

Do you know that this Cave-creature within you is *at bottom* absolutely unethical, anti-social, egotistical, primitive, and otherwise destitute of all the cherished virtues? In this, there is no cause for alarm. It merely proves that you are human; neither more nor less. And by getting an insight into the situation, you will be better able to adjust yourself to the problems of life. It will become a valuable guide in pursuing your destiny, as necessary in present-day life as is the chart of the navigator on the high seas.[38]

And what is this destiny that one must pursue? Stoddard is not speaking here of the cult of personal success. He is referring to the highest mission of the "scientific humanist," that of warning the Nordic race of the fate which will befall it and the civilization it carries within its blood unless it takes the necessary steps to avert disaster. The Renaissance humanists had failed, said Stoddard, because they had neither the desire nor the means to make their discoveries widely known. Concerned as they were with classics written almost entirely in Latin and Greek, they "had no practical way of enlisting the interest of the masses." And thus the earlier humanist movement had come to a sad end, while almost equally intolerant Catholics and Protestants battled one another and led Europe into a chaos of destruction. The new "scientific humanists" of the 1920's must not, he declared, make the same mistake. They must realize that their most important mission was to make clear the findings of science "to the masses of mankind" in order to keep civilization from being shattered.[39]

This campaign must not wait upon absolute scientific certainty. The need was much too urgent. Suppose, for example, says Stoddard, that "the weight of evidence indicates that intelligence is inherited." These findings would be of the utmost importance in our system of education. "We simply cannot afford to continue the inefficiency and injustice of present educational methods for twenty or thirty years until perfected tests may be thoroughly worked out." And, more important still, suppose that "biological research tends to show that the quality of the race is rapidly deteriorating." It follows that "we simply must take active steps to check the breeding of low-grade stocks and encourage the increase of high-grade strains; because if we do nothing but let biologists accumulate fresh data, it may turn out to be a case of locking the door after the horse has been stolen."[40]

In the campaign to enlist men's support for necessary eugenic measures, a high-minded devotion to truth was not enough. Here the importance of the emotional basis of human conduct becomes all important. We must recognize, says Stoddard, that

with most men the mainspring of action is impulse and prejudice rather than rational thought. Only a small minority are capable of thinking clearly and constructively when emotions are aroused. For this reason we can clearly foresee that, so far as the masses are concerned, heart will speak louder than head, and burning issues will be popularly treated on an emotional rather than a rational plane.

The scientist must not be reluctant to appeal strongly to emotion, "for intellect wholly untouched by emotion would be inhuman, presumably more diabolic than divine."[41]

Thus, the "scientific humanist" had a moral obligation to warn the "superior" white races that they might become extinct unless prompt measures were taken and—by implication—it did not matter if he adopted the techniques of the propagandist. The lower races had one tremendous advantage. Nature had given the less intelligent members of her species a higher birth-rate to compensate for their inability to compete. A rough kind of inverse ratio between intelligence and a high birthrate could be discerned. The conger eel, low on the evolutionary scale, could lay up to fifteen million eggs, far more than would ever reach maturity. As the species increased in intelligence, the birthrate dropped. The "Nordic race," being the highest race of all, thus naturally had the lowest birthrate.[42]

Stoddard was one of the most active propagandists for racism this country has produced. He wrote numerous articles for popular magazines—like *Collier's* and *Saturday Evening Post*—

and twenty-two books. His one great theme is that the Nordic has within his blood an almost exclusive power for civilization and progress. He has "clean, virile, genius-bearing blood, streaming down the ages through the unerring action of heredity, which, in anything like a favorable environment, will multiply itself, solve our problems, and sweep us on to higher and nobler destinies." But now the environment is unfavorable. In England, the Nordic has long been diminishing in importance because it was he who went out to fight the wars of conquest while the inferior Mediterraneans stayed placidly at home. "Today the small, dark types in England increase noticeably with every generation. The swart 'cockney' is a resurgence of the primitive Mediterranean stock, and is probably a faithful replica of his ancestors of Neolithic times." Even before the Great War had revealed that the Nordic race was in mortal danger, the revolt of inferior breeds abroad had indicated the nature of the terrible struggle ahead. In the Japanese defeat of Russia in 1904, "far-seeing white men recognized . . . an omen of evil import for their race-future." Whether the white man could hold his own in future conflicts with the colored races was an open question.[43]

The danger was close upon us because "in every quarter of the globe . . . the Bolshevik agitators whisper in the ears of discontented colored men their gospel of hatred and revenge. Every nationalist aspiration, every political grievance, every social discrimination, is fuel for Bolshevism's hellish incitement to racial as well as to class war." The Russian Revolution itself was merely another example of the struggle among the races. "The Russian people is made up chiefly of primitive racial strains, some of which (especially the Tartars and other Asiatic nomad elements) are distinctly 'wild' stocks which have always shown an instinctive hostility to civilization."[44]

Unlike most of the racists of his time Stoddard was as interested in foreign affairs as he was in American political affairs. He traveled widely and wrote topical accounts of political events abroad. One of his most widely read books was Volume VI of the popular *Harper's Pictorial History of the Great War*. In the

1920's, however, he had no clear message on American foreign policy. He did not have in mind an alliance of Nordic nations to rule the world. Like Madison Grant, he thought the Germans were mainly Alpines and not Nordics. He had no fondness for the English. He does speak vaguely of the necessity for an understanding within the "white world" over the dangers which would arise from the increased political aspirations of the colored peoples in Asia, in Africa, and in Latin America, but he had no concrete program to advocate.[45]

In specifically national affairs, Stoddard was much more definite. He was one of the most vociferous of the advocates of immigration restriction. "Can any one who knows the facts honestly deny," he asks, "that Englishmen, Scotchmen, and Scandinavians come to us with an inborn temperament and a social upbringing which predisposes them to true assimilation vastly more than is the case with, say, Russians, Sicilians, or Jugoslavs?" Some of the " 'pollyanna' optimists" were trying to delude us into believing that southern and eastern Europeans would make good American citizens. "That is just plain *bunk*. Every one who has honestly faced the facts knows that the immigrant masses which congest our industrial centres or have settled in blocks upon the land are, generally speaking, not 'good Americans.' They are still essentially 'aliens,' who are, for the most part, either indifferent or hostile to American ideals and institutions."[46]

Stoddard's books were widely and, on the whole, favorably reviewed. The reviewer in the *Nation and Athenaeum*, an English magazine, expressed what apparently was a minority view when he called *The Revolt against Civilization* a "farrago of scientific half-truths and journalistic nightmare," and deplored as "a symptom of the time that Mr. Stoddard is taken seriously." A number of anthropologists were aware of the fantastic nature of Stoddard's generalizations and the potential danger of his racism, but Stoddard had many admirers. The reviewer in the *New York Times* said of his *Social Classes in Post-War Europe* that it was "rich with collected facts and observations and il-

luminating with its philosophic discussion of their significance."
A reviewer in the *Bookman* thought *Re-Forging America* was "a
profoundly lucid and exhaustive study. . . ."[47]

In *The Great Gatsby* (1925), F. Scott Fitzgerald has a character named Tom Buchanan react to a book similar in theme to
many of Stoddard's. Buchanan is young, rich, brutal, complacent, and stupid. Like the reader to whom Stoddard said that the
"scientific humanist" should appeal, Buchanan reacts to social
questions with his emotions rather than with his intelligence.
After a dinner, the conversation turns to books.

"Civilization's going to pieces," broke out Tom violently. "I've
gotten to be a terrible pessimist about things. Have you read *The Rise
of the Colored Empires* by this man Goddard?"

"Why, no," I answered, rather surprised by his tone.

"Well, it's a fine book, and everybody ought to read it. The idea is
if we don't look out the white race will be—will be utterly submerged.
It's all scientific stuff; it's been proved."

"Tom's getting very profound," said Daisy, with an expression of
unthoughtful sadness. "He reads deep books with long words in them.
What was that word we——"

"Well, these books are all scientific," insisted Tom, glancing at her
impatiently. "This fellow has worked out the whole thing. It's up to
us, who are the dominant race, to watch out or these other races will
have control of things."

"We've got to beat them down," whispered Daisy, winking fero-
ciously toward the fervent sun.

"You ought to live in California—" began Miss Baker, but Tom
interrupted her by shifting heavily in his chair.

"This idea is that we're Nordics. I am, and you are, and you are,
and—" After an infinitesimal hesitation he included Daisy with a slight
nod, and she winked at me again. "—And we've produced all the things
that go to make civilization—oh, science and art, and all that. Do you
see?"

Later Nick Carraway, the narrator, observes that one of the
surprising things about the conversation is that Tom Buchanan
"could be depressed by a book."[48]

Madison Grant and Lothrop Stoddard exemplified in their

somewhat different ways the approach adopted by most of the prophets of race disaster in the 1920's. The background, the general outlook, and the specific opinions of the two men were similar. Both of them had family connections reaching back to the Colonial period; both were social and economic conservatives; both thought that race was the key to civilization and that the Nordics were vastly the superiors of other races. But they had different literary styles. Grant seems to have thought of himself as a kind of Moses and his pronouncements have a Mount Sinai character—he scans thousands of years of history, plots the rise and fall of civilizations according to the amount of their Nordic blood, and warns solemnly of the dangers to humanity which will arise unless the lower races are kept in check. Stoddard, on the other hand, was a man who considered himself in the forefront of particular battles, a member of the shock troops. He appeals less often to the grand sweep of history and more often to the opinions of contemporary biologists, sociologists, and psychologists who were concerned over the perils of race intermixture. He writes in a sharp, pungent, popular style, consciously using every technique of persuasion in order to convince as many people as possible that a concern over racial inequality was not bigotry but merely a matter of intelligence.

One of the men who followed the manner of Grant was Charles W. Gould, whose *America a Family Matter*, which appeared in 1922, is closely related to Grant's *The Passing of the Great Race*. Where Grant had drawn his examples from all ages back to the prehistoric, Gould concentrates on ancient Egypt, Greece, and Rome—tracing the fall of all three to the infusion of the blood of degenerate races. Like Grant, Gould draws many an ominous parallel with the immigrant situation in the United States. His style, however, is more emotional and violent than Grant's. Our degenerate time is "dragging on," he says,

but unless we can loose Orion's bands or stay the stars in their courses we cannot escape. Ten million malignant cancers gnaw the vitals of our body politic and to them we have wantonly added unnumbered other slaves—slaves of ignorance and vice—slaves who neither can nor will learn and understand free customs and free institutions. We can no more avoid the sweep of the eternal laws than could Rome.

And in his conclusion, he declaims:

Americans, the Philistines are upon us. Burst the fetters of our unseemly thraldom. Bar out all intruders. Repeal our naturalization laws. Deafen your ears to the clamor of demagogues. Make strong your hearts against the appeals of emotional humanitarianism. Repel the beguiling approaches of the grasping, who in short-sighted greed would at once rob the children and the children's children of those natural resources which we should guard as their patrimony, and worse—far worse—their right to sway and control law and government which is their heritage. . . . Arise—stand alert—trifle no more with Opportunity.[49]

Clinton Stoddard Burr's *America's Race Heritage* (1922) is in the same tradition of racism. It contains inspiring illustrations of Washington—"Of Unmixed English Ancestry"—and of other prominent early Americans, of the landing of the Pilgrims, of a typical pioneer cabin, of a buffalo hunt, to emphasize the proud traditions of a great race which must be protected against alien invasion. The immigrants from southern and eastern Europe are members of "races impregnated with radicalism, Bolshevism and anarchy. . . ." Bolshevism is fundamentally "an Asiatic conception which is repugnant to the Western mind." The "successive invasions by Turanian hordes" from Asia into Russia have "undoubtedly left at least a slight strain in the physical make-up of the Slav," and thus "the theory of community ownership is adopted more readily and unwittingly than among Western Europeans." Much of Russia's population is racially inferior. "The 'greasy' Ukrainians, the Cossacks and the peasantry of eastern Russia are undeniably Asiatic in origin." No wonder that "while our well-meaning citizens are regaling new immigrants with Americanization talks, some of their very folk are blowing up American citizens in Wall Street. . . ." Of course, it is race which explains these evil characteristics. "All this is merely the outward menace of a situation of deep biological significance," declares Burr. "The situation . . . in an insidious racial degree menaces the blood and character of our descendants to infinite generations; and thus imminently threatens, the stability, genius and promise of achievement of the American Commonwealth."[50]

The same thesis is expounded in Dr. Charles Conant Josey's *Race and National Solidarity* (1923). An assistant professor of psychology at Dartmouth, Dr. Josey writes in the lofty tone of conventional scholarship. Like Stoddard, Josey is equally concerned about the "menace" of the colored races abroad and that within America itself. He suggests a means of keeping the colored races in check which he would recommend to the colonial powers. It is as candid as it is ingenious. Western civilization, he says, "has rested for a long time on members of our group." Is this state of affairs really necessary? Must we "exploit our own laboring classes? Can we not shift many of the burdens they have carried to the backs of others and still maintain the richness and colorfulness of our culture?" The answer is that of course we can do this if only we are resolute enough.[51]

The key to the solution is to deny all subject races in colonial areas any representation in government and frankly to exploit their labor. The great revolution in industrial and manufacturing techniques makes it matter little "whether the laborer lives next door or in a foreign country." The natives must be rigidly controlled by the colonial powers; means must be employed to control the increase of their population. One way this might be done is subtly to combine with the humanitarians and to advocate the abolition of child labor in the colonies. This measure would make children become an economic liability instead of an asset to their parents. To make the measure more effective, it should be accompanied with the dissemination of birth control information.[52]

Josey admits that there might be difficulties in getting the American people "to regard as desirable a policy of deliberate exploitation," since "we hesitate to take advantage of our power to shift the burden of our culture from the backs of the exploited at home to other groups, or to safeguard our future by imposing restrictions on the weak." But these are minor objections in view of the great end to be achieved. "We must free our minds of many of our ethical and moral prejudices. In order to do so we must view our situation frankly in terms of the maximum good of our group and of the world." In the straight-faced manner of Jonathan Swift suggesting in "A Modest Proposal" the selling of Irish children as a meat delicacy for the table, Josey suggests a deliberate policy of exploitation. The difference is that whereas Swift did not mean his proposal to be taken seriously, Josey undoubtedly did:

We have found reasons for believing that the good of the world will best be served by the domination of the whites rather than the yellows. All these values are safeguarded by the programme suggested. It will intensify race consciousness. It will furnish us the means of a rich culture without internal exploitation. It will set free larger numbers of our citizens to indulge in creative enterprises. It will insure to the world the continued domination of the whites. It will insure to the world the contributions the white race seem so pre-eminently able to make. Surely, then, it is our duty to take measures to safeguard our future.[53]

The chief political objective which the racists of the 1920's had in mind, however, was immigration restriction. One of the most tireless workers on this subject was Dr. H. H. Laughlin, who was associated with another racist, Dr. Charles B. Davenport, at the Eugenics Record Office at Cold Spring Harbor, New York. Laughlin worked closely with the House Committee on Immigration and was its leading expert on eugenics. In one of his reports for Congress, Laughlin developed the thesis that immigrants had a disproportionate percentage in American insane asylums, jails, and poorhouses, a fact which was evidence that they had "inborn socially inadequate qualities." And let no one imagine that these inferior people would not intermarry extensively with superior Americans of native stock. "The committee of the Eugenics Research Association has had the matter in hand," said Laughlin, "and has failed to find a case in history in which two races have lived side by side for a number of generations and have maintained racial purity. Indeed, you can almost lay it down as an essential principle that race mixture takes place whenever there is racial contact."[54]

One of the most effective of the racist propagandists was Kenneth L. Roberts. He had been a captain of the Intelligence Section of the Siberian Expeditionary Force of the U.S. Army in 1918 and 1919. Before his military service, Roberts had been a writer and editor for magazines, and he later became well known as a writer of fiction. After the war, the *Saturday Evening Post* sent him to Europe to examine plans there for large-scale emigration to America. His central thesis was that most of the people who planned to come here were unfit material for citizenship. His articles were collected in 1922 in the volume *Why Europe Leaves Home*. "Any promiscuous crossing of breeds invariably produces mongrels," declared Roberts, "whether the crossing occurs in dogs or in humans, and whether it takes place in the Valley of the Nile or on the Arctic plain or in the shadow of Rome's seven hills or along the stern and rock-bound shores of New England." He found it difficult to believe that anyone could be "fatuous enough to believe that . . . pouring all the races of Europe in a human melting-pot" would enable us to "keep on producing the same breed of men that founded America, laid down its scheme of government, wrenched its farms and its cities from the wilderness, and produced its scientists, statesmen, artists, pioneers, authors and explorers." America had been "founded and developed by the Nordic race, but if a few more million members of the Alpine, Mediterranean and Semitic races are poured among us, the result must inevitably be a hybrid race of people as worthless and futile as the good-for-nothing mongrels of Central America and Southeastern Europe."[55]

One of the racists, Dr. Alfred E. Wiggam, made an effort to reconcile racism with ideas of religion. Wiggam was less concerned with *Realpolitik* than Stoddard and Josey and more concerned with presenting the new biological gospel in terms that would be acceptable to conventional moral ideas. Accordingly, he writes in the style of a folksy philosopher who wants to benefit mankind by making available for popular use the discoveries of genetics. He sets out to convince the nation of the importance of its having a higher birthrate among the "well born" and a lower birthrate among the unfit. The indiscriminate propagation of the mentally and morally unfit and of the inferior races ought to be discouraged.

Wiggam attempts to square this idea with the truths of religion. In former times, he says, God spoke to man through a burning bush, through tablets etched on stone, and through prophecies and dreams. But now

He has given men the microscope, the spectroscope, the telescope, the chemist's test tube and the statistician's curve in order to enable men to make their own revelations. These instruments of divine revelation have not only added an enormous range of new commandments—an entirely new Decalogue—to man's moral codes, but they have supplied him with techniques of putting them into effect. . . . The first warning which biology gives to statesmanship is that the advanced races of mankind are going backward; that the civilized races of the world are, biologically, plunging downward; . . . that your vast efforts to improve man's lot instead of improving man are hastening the hour of his destruction; . . ."[56]

This message, far from being antithetical to the Christian gospel of love and concern for one's fellow man, Wiggam finds wholly in line with the truths taught by Jesus. Jesus did not subscribe to the facile doctrine that all men are created equal. "He pointed out that some men have one talent, some two and others five. He also recognized its tremendous practical consequences when He made the five talent man ruler over many cities and dismissed the man of one talent brains and one talent morals from five talent social responsibility." Far from opposing the modern campaign for race betterment, Jesus would have favored it. "Had Jesus been among us," Wiggam declares,

he would have been president of the First Eugenics Congress. He would have been the first to grasp what our writers and poets and artists ought to-day to grasp, the great idealistic and spiritual significance of Darwin's generalizations, Weismann's microscope, Gregor Mendel's peas, Bateson and Castle's guinea pigs, Davenport and Laughlin's hu-

man pedigrees, Morgan's *Drosophilae*, Galton, Pearson, Woods and
Pearl's biometrical calculations. . . . With these in his hands He would
have cried: "A new commandment I give unto you—the biological
Golden Rule, the completed Golden Rule of science. *Do unto both the
born and the unborn as you would have both the born and the unborn
do unto you.*"

And Wiggam's books were popular successes—both *The New
Decalogue of Science* (1922) and *The Fruit of the Family Tree*
(1924) were best sellers.[57]

In the translation of these new "truths" of race to the area
of legislation, naturally some caution had to be employed. There
were large groups of immigrants from southern and eastern European countries in a number of states, and they could have done
considerable harm to any political leader who spoke openly in
the manner of Madison Grant, Lothrop Stoddard, or even Alfred
E. Wiggam. Thus we find that the political leaders who favored
immigration restriction spoke with more circumspection. Warren G. Harding, in one of his campaign speeches for the Presi-
dency in 1920, cautiously enunciated the doctrine of racial "differences" in advocating an immigration restriction law. "There
is abundant evidence of the dangers which lurk in racial differences," he declared. "I do not say racial inequalities, I say racial
differences." No one could "tranquilly contemplate the future
of this Republic without anxiety for abundant provision for
admission to our shores of only the immigrant who can be assimilated and thoroughly imbued with the American spirit." He
favored such modification of the country's immigration laws as
would guarantee "not only assimilability of alien-born, but the
adoption by all who come of American standards, economic and
otherwise, and a full consecration to American practices and
ideas." After he was elected, Harding attempted to bridge the
unbridgeable by urging in a speech in Alabama that Negroes be
allowed to vote while at the same time warning the nation vaguely of the perils of race. "Whoever will take the time to read
and ponder Mr. Lothrop Stoddard's book on 'The Rising Tide
of Color,' " said Harding, ". . . must realize that our race prob-

lem here in the United States is only a phase of a race issue the whole world confronts. Surely we shall gain nothing by blinking the facts. That is not the American way of approaching such issues."[58] But Harding does not spell out what Americans should do with such "facts."

Calvin Coolidge expressed the racist implications of immigration restriction more bluntly. In a popular article written in 1922, when he was Vice-President, he argued that biological laws show us that Nordics deteriorate when mixed with other races. But neither Harding nor Coolidge was as forthright as James J. Davis, Secretary of Labor under both administrations, who said that the older immigrants to America were the beaver type that built up America, whereas the newer immigrants were rat-men trying to tear it down; and obviously rat-men could never become beavers.[59]

The leader of the campaign in Congress for immigration restriction was Representative Albert Johnson, a Republican from the state of Washington. Until he became involved in politics, Johnson had been an editor of a small daily newspaper in the town of Gray's Harbor, a center of the lumber industry. Before antiradicalism gave Johnson his big start in politics, he was known chiefly as a booster, a glad-hander, and a foe of conservation laws. In 1912, the I.W.W. began a strike against the lumber companies and Johnson led an armed citizens' movement against the strikers, ran the union leaders out of town, and secured the recall of the town's mayor who had been sympathetic to the strike. All this happened while Johnson was running for Congress, and he turned his campaign into a crusade against the I.W.W., which he saw as a foreign conspiracy to subvert American institutions. He was elected to Congress and continued to serve his district for the next twenty years. Johnson was too violent to suit some of the more aristocratic and educated workers in the campaign against immigration. One observer says that he had "an ordinary intellect" and that "a certain opportunism made him vacillate at times, and some of his more earnest associates thought he drank too much." On the other hand, he "exuded a certain crude vigor, people liked him, and above all he embraced the two bitterest aversions of his timber-rich constituency in southwestern Washington—a hatred of the Wobblies and a hatred of the Japanese."[60]

Johnson began to exert important influence in March, 1919, after the new Republican Congress assumed control. At this time he became chairman of the House Committee on Immigration. Greatly impressed by *The Passing of the Great Race*, Johnson consulted with Grant both in New York and in Washington on the form which bills against immigration should take. What Grant—a fastidious member of society—thought of Johnson's crudeness has not been recorded, but other scientific men obviously thought of him as a hero. As a rather surprising climax to a career not conspicuously scientific, Johnson was elected president of the Eugenics Research Association at Cold Spring Harbor, New York, in 1923.[61]

The campaign for restriction of immigration gained steadily in power. Although the race argument was probably in most peoples' minds, politics demanded that restriction should not seem to be directly aimed at any particular race or nationality. Accordingly, the Immigration Act of 1921 was set up under a "national origins quota," which limited the number of immigrants from any given country in Europe to 3 per cent of the immigrants from that country who were living here in the year 1910. This law was criticized as too liberal and in 1924 a more stringent immigration act was passed, one which reduced the annual quota of each nationality group from 3 to 2 per cent and by using the census of 1890 instead of that of 1910 favored the older immigrant stocks—the English, Irish, German, and Scandinavian immigrants—over the newer immigrant stocks, those from Italy, Austria, Russia, Poland, and other southern and eastern European countries. In addition, the law excluded Japanese immigrants altogether, extending the ban which had previously existed against other Orientals. Even so, the bill was not as stringent as many advocates of restriction would have liked, since both Canada and Latin American countries were exempted from the quota. Because of difficulties of determining national origins quotas, the figure of 150,000 annual immigrants set by the bill did not go into effect until 1929. Until the late twenties, a yearly average of 287,000 immigrants were permitted to enter.[62]

Even with its "defects," the immigration restrictionists hailed the Act of 1924 as a great victory. In signing the bill, President Coolidge tersely commented, "America must be kept American," apparently implying that the basis of unity of the country was racial. In a statement to the press, Senator David A. Reed—who had introduced the Senate version of the act—explained that "the races of men who have been coming to us in recent years are wholly dissimilar to the native-born Americans," that "they are untrained in self-government—a faculty that it has taken the Northwestern Europeans many centuries to acquire," and that it was best for America "that our incoming immigrants should hereafter be of the same races as those of us who are already here, so that each year's immigration should so far as possible be a miniature America, resembling in national origins the persons who are already settled in our country." Secretary of Labor Davis described American immigration policy as having passed through three phases: (1) the ideal of "asylum"; (2) the economic attitude; (3) the biological ideal. The *Chicago Tribune* said that the act was "a Declaration of Independence, not less significant and epoch-making for America and the world than the Declaration of 1776."[63]

The act was also significant in ways which were not immediately obvious. The heavy reliance upon racism, the perpetual appeals to the truths of biology, anthropology, sociology, and psychology, could hardly fail to arouse in reflective people—especially those who were working in the disciplines concerned—the question of whether such conclusions were in fact justifiable. The racists, particularly the advocates of Nordic superiority, might seem at the time to have had things much their own way, but a revolt against their ideas was beginning to gain momentum. Although race problems would continue to bedevil the nation for a long time to come, it would be progressively more difficult to call upon the names of eminent men in the sciences and social sciences who were convinced of innate racial inequalities and of the necessity for keeping the inferior races in a subordinate position in society. The idea that races have innate characteristics of mentality and temperament would suffer a crushing series of defeats at the hands of the biological and social scientists of the next generation.

XVI

The Scientific Revolt Against Racism

ALL ATTEMPTS to construct any theory of history or civilization upon racial theory, all attempts to describe accurately the differences of character, temperament, and intelligence among the races, have been failures. Race theory has frequently lent itself to the crudest kind of manipulation by the people who wished to justify a scheme of exploitation or discrimination. It was in the 1920's that the racists first met a serious check among the sciences and among the academic disciplines generally. One can hardly help wondering—now that the claims of the racists are widely recognized as having little or no scientific backing—why the opposition to racism was so long in developing. Were not the effusions of the nineteenth-century racists, for example, extreme enough to call for a more sober scrutiny among serious thinkers?

One reason was that the scientists themselves frequently spoke of race in personal and emotional tones rather than in terms of fact. There could hardly be a subject more likely to involve prejudice than that of race. Unlike religious, political, or social ideas, human differences which we have elected to call racial differences are a part of our physical endowment which we are born with and cannot change. All of us belong to one race or another or to a combination of races, and thus all of us are involved to some extent in an emotional attachment to the idea that our own race is at least potentially equal to others. Much of the debate over the merits and defects of races has taken place in a peevish and ill-tempered atmosphere, one in which the opponents frequently "get personal" and tell members of other

409

races home truths about themselves. The usual response to a racist attack has been for the victim to reply in kind against the race of his opponent—not to question the dogma of racism. In England, when complacent racists derided the Irishman for being a furious and mercurial Celt, the Irishman responded by calling the Englishman a boorish and sluggish Anglo-Saxon. Some of the most distinguished men have been unable to save themselves from this particular dead end of logic. The Negro leader, W. E. B. DuBois, in bitterness and frustration over prejudice against members of his race, responded at one point by appealing to a counter-racism based upon the supposed superiority of Negroes to whites. In the Nordic controversy over immigration in the 1920's, one Italian journalist was so outraged by the poor opinion of the "Mediterranean race" held by the eminent biologist, Dr. S. J. Holmes, that he was moved to write an indignant letter. He said he was sorry that the Italians—who included such men as Dante, Columbus, and Leonardo da Vinci—had made the mistake of introducing civilization to the crude and barbarous peoples of northern Europe.[1] This kind of response to racism, though it may have salved the feelings of the people who engaged in it, did nothing more than attempt to supplant one kind of racism with another.

Even distinguished men of science who were famous for their skepticism of ideas which could not be backed up by proof had for a long time a curious leaning toward and tolerance for the illogic of racism. They could see the absurdities to which it sometimes led, but they were reluctant to part with it as a tool for speculation about human differences. The state of the sciences of biology and anthropology was such in the nineteenth and early twentieth centuries that few men of reputation in the field were willing to hazard the opinion that race theory is useless in explaining the character of peoples. They protested against some of the conclusions of the racists with regard to particular peoples, but they did not reject racism itself. In the nineteenth century, Thomas Henry Huxley revolted against appeals to race in England as justification for denying home rule for Ireland. He declared that "the arguments about the difference between Anglo-Saxons and Celts are a mere sham and delusion." We are unable to determine which qualities we have brought into the world with us and which are dependent upon the circumstances of our environment, says Huxley, and more nonsense has been written on the matter of the racial basis of national character than on any other subject. But then Huxley proceeds to take back with his right hand what he has given with his left: "Do not let what I have said mislead you into the notion that I disbelieve in the importance of race. I am a firm believer in blood, as every naturalist must be. . . . I believe in the immense influence of the fixed hereditary transmission which constitutes a race."[2] With opinions like these, Huxley had little influence in checking racist theorizing.

The uncertainty of students of the subject over the meaning of race and the extent of its importance helps to explain why so little was done in the nineteenth century to study the development of racial theory itself. In 1910, Lord Cromer wondered that so little had been done in any country on the subject. "I am not aware," he wrote, "that any competent scholar has ever examined into the question of the stage in history at which difference of color . . . acquired the importance it now possesses as a social and political factor."[3] The probable reason why so few such studies were attempted was that there was such a chaos of conflicting opinions among the scholarly disciplines involved that a researcher would have experienced great difficulty in developing any secure intellectual position from which to view the phenomenon of race.

Of course, there were some men in the nineteenth century who realized that reflections on the character of races lent themselves readily to the self-aggrandizement of one's own people and the denigration of others. Doubtless, many of the eminent men in history and literature who ignored the race theorizing then so much in the air did so because they recognized its tendentious character. John Stuart Mill explicitly rejected racism. "Of all vulgar modes of escaping from the consideration of the

effect of social and moral influences on the human mind," he declared in 1848, "the most vulgar is that of attributing the diversities of conduct and character to inherent natural differences."[4] But neither Mill nor any other man of real eminence in
the nineteenth century made any sustained attempt to show how
and why racism lent itself to the most flagrant kinds of special
pleading.

Virtually all of the systematic critics of racism in the nineteenth century were Europeans, and it is a pity that most of
them are unknown. They were usually ignored by their contemporaries, holding as they did opinions which were opposed
by men of great reputation as scientists, social scientists, or historians. When the tide of intellectual opinion turned against
racism, the early opponents tended to be forgotten for a different reason—their ideas were now merely a part of the generally
accepted opinion. One such man was Theodor Waitz, a German,
who carefully studied the theories of race which had been propounded by 1859—his study came too early to include Darwin—
and decided that there was no way of determining definitely
what the innate characters of races are. He argued that it is probable that all races are capable of civilization and he criticized in
detail the theories of race which had assumed natural superiority
and inferiority.[5]

In England, William Dalton Babington studied race theories
based upon national character. In 1895, two years after his death,
his essays on race questions were published. In stodgy prose but
nonetheless in a sensible way, Babington examined the question
of whether an accurate description of the intelligence and temperament of races could be developed and decided that such a
project was not feasible and that nearly all that had been written
on the subject was valueless. Two years later, John Mackinnon
Robertson published in England *The Saxon and the Celt*, one of
the wittiest and most devastating books of the century on the
subject of race. Robertson had the verve and pugnacity of a self-
made man. He left his lower-class home at the age of thirteen
and from that time on made his own way, developing into a man

of considerable learning with a great talent for satire. He wrote an extensive critique of the vanity and self-praise implicit in the writings of the historians of the Teutonic origins and Saxon schools of thought. Unfortunately for his development as a historian of race theories, Robertson became involved in many other controversies. He was a free thinker and—in something of the manner of Colonel Robert Ingersoll in this country—delighted in pointing out the mistakes of Moses. He was an anti-Baconian in the Shakespeare-Bacon controversy and devoted a great deal of time to it. He became a Member of Parliament and there was known for championing various causes—for example, opposition to the Boer War. Undoubtedly, these activities tended to restrict his activities as a writer on historical questions.[6]

In the United States, William Z. Ripley, a lecturer on anthropology at Columbia, published in 1899 *The Races of Europe,* an impressively lengthy and thorough volume with many pictures to illustrate the physical types found on the Continent. Ripley believed that mental and emotional qualities are inherited racially, but he was much more cautious than most anthropologists of the period in describing these qualities. He criticized the geographers for imagining that there was such a thing as the "Aryan race." He rejected the idea that craniology is an exact science. He subjected to mild ridicule theories of Anglo-Saxon or Teutonic superiority. It was high time to call a halt, he declared, when "vulgar" theories of race were "made sponsor for nearly ever conceivable form of social, political, or economic virtues or ills, as the case may be."[7] Ripley undoubtedly helped to introduce Americans to some of the many complexities of racial theory.

In 1905, Jean Finot published his *Le Préjugé des Races* in France. His approach emphasized the scientists and not the historians. He studied with particular care the attempts to develop systems of race classification on the basis of bodily characteristics. His book contains extensive quotations from such explosive racists as Gobineau, Ammon, La Pouge, and Houston Stewart Chamberlain, for the purpose of showing the dangers of extremism. "Inexorable doctrines on the inequality of human beings, adorned with scientific veneer," Finot declares,

are multiplied to infinity. Based on craniological differences, the largeness or smallness of the limbs, the colour of the skin or the hair, etc., they endeavor to appeal to a sort of pseudo-science, with its problematic laws, unexamined facts and unjustifiable generalizations, as a guarantee of their audacious theories. . . . Despotic, cruel, and full of confidence in their laws, the creators and partisans of all these doctrines do their best to impose them as dogmas of salvation and infallible guides for humanity.

In England, Rev. John Oakesmith, an Episcopal clergyman, published *Race and Nationality* in 1919. Oakesmith tells us that his study was greatly influenced by Finot, and he applies Finot's methods of criticism to English and American racists. His book is well written and has the additional merit of being the first attempt of a writer to deal in detail with the literature of modern racism from the standpoint of religion.[8]

No single one of these books had much influence upon the exuberant racism of the period—nor, indeed, did all of them together. It is quite important to recognize why they did not. The critics of racism could show defects in the logic of racist theorizing, but they were unable to give an alternative explanation that would suffice to show why it is that races differ so much all over the world in their ideas and attitudes, a question which has puzzled thinkers at least as far back as Julian the Apostate. If racism did not explain why one race was bold and adventurous and another was submissive and sedentary, what did explain it? Henry Adams said what many an intelligent and well-read person must have thought when, early in the twentieth century, it had become apparent that all the attempts to classify the races on the basis of bodily character were a failure. "History offered a feeble and delusive smile at the sound of the word *race*," said Adams in *The Education of Henry Adams;* "evolutionists and ethnologists disputed its very existence; no one knew what to make of it; yet, without the clue, history was a fairy tale."[9]

Most of the racists of the period hardly bothered to recognize the existence of their opponents, and when they did they dismissed them as sentimental humanitarians. William MacDougall probably typified the racists of the period when he specifically criticized the works of Robertson, Finot, and Oakesmith:

> These authors, who deny all importance to racial composition and differences of innate endowment, may conveniently be classed over against their opponents, the race-dogmatists, as the "race-slumpers." It is characteristic of them that they in the main avoid the straight issues and content themselves with exposing the errors of the race-dogmatists. They make much of the undeniable truth that none of the civilized peoples of the world are of pure race, but rather are all alike the products of repeated blendings of races and peoples. They point out that, if any racial peculiarities of mental constitution exist, they are so obscure that no one has been able to define them and measure them, as the physical anthropologists have succeeded in defining and measuring certain physical qualities as indicators of race. They point to the fact that in many instances men born of primitive and even savage parents have shown themselves capable of acquiring all the elements of culture of the most highly civilized communities, and of playing an honorable part in the complex life of such a community. . . . Especially they avoid the direct issue by demonstrating at length the obvious truth that race and nationality are not coincident. This is merely a red herring drawn across the track to put us off the scent. The "race-slumpers" have shown, it must be admitted, that the facile generalizations of many historians upon race and national character have been of the most flimsy nature, often erroneous and sometimes absurd. We must recognize with them that these flimsy assumptions have worked harm; and we must agree with them in condemning in the most outspoken way the evil work of the more extreme race-dogmatists.
>
> But when Mr. Oakesmith concludes that the practical value of "race" is purely subjective; that "race" is merely an emotion, like that of the soldier who is proud of his regiment's history; when the "race-slumpers" assert or imply, as they do, that all men are born with the same mental endowments, that all human stocks are of equal value, and that the anthropologic composition of a people is of no influence upon the course of its history, then we must part company from them.[10]

The theory that race explains the character of an individual or a society or a civilization was absolutely essential to Mac-

Dougall and the other racists of his time. Yet, the theory he opposed was in fact the one which was steadily to gain strength. More and more, the attempt would be made to explain human societies not upon the basis of their biological inheritance but upon social processes, a method of study which amounted to an emphasis upon environment. Edward B. Reuter has explained the change thus: "Social traits were seen to form and change in the experience of living together; the problem of social research was seen to lie, not in the biological characters or cultural traits which get whatever meaning they have in social relations and their changes, but in social and human attitudes, values, and experiences."[11]

The great shift of emphasis from biology to social process as an explanation for cultural differences was a gradual one, and the increasing emphasis on the latter did not necessarily imply a rejection of the former. As we have seen, the Teutonic origins of government theory of history declined not so much because historians rejected the importance of race as because they found more fruitful the study of environmental factors. In sociology, too, a similar shift went on. We have seen that Herbert Spencer, for example, attached great importance to race theories in explaining the character of societies, but he was also among the first to realize the value of collecting information to discover what differences exist between classes, social groups, and societies generally, a search which inevitably led him to a close study of environmental factors and which caused later racist thinkers to regard him as harmful, or at least a dubious support for their side.[12] One can detect a gradual shift from an emphasis on heredity and biology in explaining human societies to an emphasis upon purely cultural factors.

The rise of cultural anthropology had the utmost importance for race theory because the close and detailed knowledge of the community life of primitive peoples showed how directly ideas and customs are interrelated, and how fallacious is the idea that any society can be meaningfully interpreted in terms of its racial inheritance. A few students of race in the nineteenth century were able to see the great importance of the cultural approach. "According to the usual opinion," wrote Theodor Waitz in 1859,

the stage of culture of a people or of an individual is largely or exclusively the product of its or his faculty. We maintain that the reverse is at least just as true. The faculty of man does not designate anything but how much and what he is able to achieve in the immediate future, and it depends upon the stages of culture through which he has passed and the one he has reached.[13]

Soon after Waitz had written this perceptive comment, Sir Edward Burnett Tylor (1832-1917) began a series of studies in England which would transform the approach of serious students toward the primitive peoples. Like Spencer and Robertson, Tylor did not have a university education. His parents were well-to-do Quakers, and the regulations then in force prevented him from aspiring to a university education. Instead he worked in his father's brass factory until he was twenty-three, when ill health forced him to travel. He went to Mexico, where he became interested in prehistoric civilization. A modern admirer of Tylor, Paul Radin, believes that Tylor's lack of a university education was a positive advantage, since he was more critical than he otherwise might have been of the tendency of historians to generalize too broadly on the subject of the characteristics of peoples. He developed his own methods of study, one of which emphasized the careful examination of particular cultures. "The condition of culture among the various societies of mankind . . . ," Tylor declared, "is a subject apt for the study of laws of human thought and action." Thus, Tylor intensively examined the state of knowledge, the religion, the art, and the customs of certain primitive societies. Radin believes that Tylor practically created from its foundation the new science of modern anthropology, and that his book, *Primitive Culture*, published in 1871, has stood the test of time in its field better than any other work of the period.[14]

Most of the early work of developing methods of studying

primitive cultures was done in Europe, but in this country some of the most significant events in the history of cultural anthropology were to take place and these were to have, in turn, a tremendous effect upon race theories. The leader in this field was Dr. Franz Boas (1858-1942), who was born and educated in Germany but who decided to become an American citizen in his twenty-ninth year and did nearly all of his significant work here. The racists of the 1920's rightly recognized Boas as their chief antagonist. Although his opinion was then a minority one, he never wavered before the onslaughts of biological interpretations of history and civilization. More importantly, he was able to meet his opponents with arguments which could not be brushed aside as humanitarian twaddle. It is possible that Boas did more to combat race prejudice than any other person in history.[15]

Boas grew up in a family whose members were encouraged to develop their ideas independently of authoritative pronouncements. He was born in Minden, Westphalia. His parents had rejected their Jewish faith, having "broken through the shackles of dogma," although his father "retained an emotional affection for the ceremonial of his parental home without allowing it to influence his intellectual freedom." One of the important memories of Franz Boas' student days was his reaction to the statement of one of his friends that everyone had the obligation to accept the traditions which have been handed down to us. "The shock that this outright abandonment of freedom of thought gave me," said Boas, "is one of the unforgettable moments of my life."[16]

"The background of my early thinking," Boas tells us, "was a German home in which the ideals of the revolution of 1848 were a living force." His mother was an unusual woman, founder of the first Froebel Kindergarten, and a friend of a number of the prominent "forty-eighters." Boas attended the universities at Heidelberg, Bonn, and Kiel, and one of his extracurricular activities was to engage in dueling, from which he received several deep facial wounds—the scars of which in later years he would attribute, if questioned, to polar bear clawings he had received in an expedition to Baffinland. There is a story, which cannot be authenticated, that Boas revealed to a friend that the scars were caused by a duel which followed an anti-Semitic insult from another student in a public café. The story is that Boas threw the student out the door and was challenged. The next morning his adversary offered to apologize, but Boas insisted upon the duel. "Apocryphal or not," says A. L. Kroeber, "the tale absolutely fits the character of the man as we later knew him in America."[17]

Boas received the doctorate in 1881, when he was twenty-three, in the field of physics. His thesis was called *Contributions to the Understanding of the Color of Water*, and in the course of his investigations he used photometric methods to compare intensities of light, a procedure which led him to consider "the quantitative values of sensations." He tells us that he "learned to recognize that there are domains of our experience in which the concept of quantity, of measures that can be added or subtracted like those with which I am accustomed to operate, are not applicable." Boas' discovery is important because it conditioned his attitudes toward his anthropological work throughout his life: on the one hand, he had an enormous respect and capacity for patient and detailed work; on the other, he realized that there are limits to our ability to record sense data accurately, an important discovery for the future anthropologist.[18]

The variations of perception among human beings led him to the "writings of philosophers," and he says, "my previous interests became overshadowed by a desire to understand the relation between the objective and the subjective world." There was a gradual shift from physics toward physical and then cultural geography. In 1883 Boas went to Baffinland, a journey which launched him on his career as an anthropologist. The Germans, as their contribution to an international program of polar exploration, had estabished a meteorological station in Baffinland. This expedition turned out to be most significant for the future development of Boas' ideas. He elected not to stay with the other members of the party. In fact, he rarely saw them. Instead, he chose to live among the Eskimos themselves. He became "an Eskimo among Eskimos," he tells us, and the experience "had a profound influence upon the development of my views . . . because it led me away from my former interests and toward the desire to understand what determines the behavior of human beings."[19]

When he got back to Germany, Boas set out to write a systematic account of the distribution of Eskimo tribes. He was a docent in geography at the University of Berlin, and while he was there he became acquainted with Rudolph Virchow, who was an opponent of the extravagant race theories of the time and who became, by Boas' own account, the great single influence in his scientific development. On a trip to the United States in 1887, Boas called upon the editor of the magazine *Science* and was asked to become one of the assistant editors. At the time, he was on leave from the University of Berlin, but he decided soon afterward to resign his position there and to become an American citizen. His reasons for changing his citizenship, his disciple and colleague A. L. Kroeber says, were a matter partly of his career and partly of his convictions. He thought that in Germany he would be too closely restricted to the routine activities of a university teacher without opportunities for field research. As an "enthusiastic republican and ardent individualist," he was attracted to the "ideal of American democracy." In addition, he did not feel that he could in conscience submit to the formal demand in Germany that he declare his religious affiliation. In America, he taught at Clark University for four years, worked as chief assistant of the Department of Anthropology at the Chicago Exposition of 1893, an enterprise which had considerable importance since the collections for the Fair were extended and expanded to become the Field Museum. In 1895, Boas went as curator of ethnology and somatology to the American Museum of Natural History in New York; in 1896, he began teaching at Columbia, and by 1899 he was made professor of anthropology there; in 1901, he became curator of the Museum.[20]

One can only be amazed at the amount of work that Boas was able to do. He was an authority in anthropometry and in Indian languages, and he is the only anthropologist to attempt a mastery of two such different fields. We have already encountered his work as an anthropometrist, in directing the measurement of 17,000 immigrants and the children of immigrants, a study which showed that children do not necessarily reproduce the cranial and other features of their parents if they grow up in a different environment, findings which made all attempts to classify races on the basis of craniology so impossible as to be preposterous. In linguistics, he was a specialist in American Indian languages. It was he who initiated the program which resulted in the publication in 1911 of the *Handbook of American Indian Languages,* in three volumes, which contains grammars of nineteen different tongues. Three of the treatments are wholly Boas'; in a fourth he was an avowed and in three others an unavowed collaborator; all the rest but three are by men whom he trained. It is little wonder that a specialist in native languages describes Boas as "Papa Franz," as "the ancestor in learning, of all those in this country who work in descriptive linguistics." For Boas, an adequate command of the language of the tribe an anthropologist wished to study was an essential because "much information can be gained by listening to conversations of the natives and by taking part in their daily life, which, to the observer who has no command of the language, will remain entirely inaccessible."[21]

All of this is, of course, impressive, but it only indirectly explains why Boas eventually wielded so tremendous an influence in combating racism. To understand this point, it is necessary to consider Boas' approach to the problem of studying primitive peoples. Ruth Benedict wrote a tribute to Boas' contributions as an ethnologist which explains briefly the radical difference between his methods of studying other cultures and those of earlier students. When he went to live with the Eskimos, she says, he thought that their culture could be explained as a natural reaction to their environment, but he learned that such an explanation was not only extremely inadequate, but unacceptable.

He learned that the facts of experience could not be explained merely by reference to laws of physical or material substances; they depended even more largely upon man-made conventions, products of the human mind. These cultural inventions could fly in the face of objective reality, they could be rational or irrational. They had their own *rationale*, however, and he believed this could be discovered only by tracing them in detail in specific cultures, following them into the grammatical categories of the language, tracing their diffusion from tribe to tribe and from continent to continent, and identifying the same convention as it was expressed for instance in religion and in social organization.[22]

In this approach, Boas carried Tylor's ideas to what now seems their logical conclusion. "Tylor was busy in his library putting together travellers' accounts of strange people and bringing order out of chaos whatever the problem he touched," Ruth Benedict explains, "whether it was a minimal definition of religion or the connection between matriolocality and odd bits of behavior." Boas once said to her, she recalls, that Tylor "thought that scraps of data from here, there, and everywhere were enough for ethnology." In time, Boas learned that a much more thorough investigation of the language, beliefs, and customs of a primitive tribe was necessary if it was to be truly understood. This meant an "insistence on inclusive and systematic field investigation by the anthropologist himself," and this point—which to us now seems obvious—was "the greatest forward step in methodology anthropology has taken in the whole course of its history." Of course there had been previous good observers of primitive life, but "no one had envisaged intensive investigation of the mental life of man as it expressed itself in all aspects of culture, conceived as a study on a par with investigations of the natural world." A major result of this thoroughgoing method was a series of studies which culminated in Boas' *The Mind of Primitive Man* (1911), a study which has set the basic tone of all subsequent serious work in anthropology.[23]

Boas' approach was, it need hardly be said, poles apart from the conventional one which tended to judge all other cultures and particularly those of primitive peoples by standards foreign to them. Instead of attempting to discover from their ideas and institutions why other peoples thought and felt and acted as they did, the usual procedure was to judge them according to the extent to which their ideas and practices coincided with those of our own culture. Boas' attitude was equally far from the attempt to correlate race and culture, from the assumption that every race or culture represented a stage of progression either lower or higher in the same scale.

One reason why Boas' influence on race theories is not immediately obvious is that, having dropped the idea that race is the determinant of culture, he used a language very different from that of his opponents. They wanted to know whether or to what extent the bodily inheritance or race of an individual person or a group determined mental or temperamental characteristics. Boas' assumption is that no serious student of the problem has been able to establish such a correlation and that it certainly has been possible partially to explain mental and temperamental characteristics on the basis of culture. It is this latter task which Boas and his disciples set out to accomplish, a task which in effect bypassed questions which to the racists were crucial.

Thus, when Boas speaks of race theories it is generally with the reluctance of a man who feels torn away from his essential task of examining the effects of a given culture upon a given people. A. L. Kroeber thinks that Boas' ideal as a researcher came from Rudolph Virchow, an ideal which Boas occasionally expressed as a motto: "icy enthusiasm." Boas utilizes almost none of the arts of persuasion except an unflinching reliance upon logical argument. Kroeber explains Boas' "alleged lack of eloquence or aesthetic form" as the refusal of a proud man to make even partial compromises which would have seemed to be a weakness. Although Boas refused even to consider form as such, says Kroeber, "his writing possesses an inner and very genuine form to a high degree; but it is a form similar to that expressed by decision, economy, and elegance in a mathematical demonstration—qualities which can win applause only before the most expert of selected audiences." And yet—on race questions, at least—Boas was no cloistered expert. He spoke out again and again in the 1920's against racists like Madison Grant, Henry Fairfield Osborn, and Lothrop Stoddard. In the 1930's and until his death in 1942, he was one of the most active of the American opponents of Nazi race theories.[24]

What happened to race theories so prominent in American life and thought in the 1920's? In one sense, of course, nothing happened, since millions undoubtedly still believe that character and intelligence and human worth are largely matters of race. But in the academic disciplines there has been a sharp swing away from race interpretations of either individuals or cultures. Although we still have race problems aplenty in this country, we no longer have many psychologists, sociologists, historians, or creative writers with any considerable reputation who rely upon race theories to "explain" human nature.

As we have seen, mental tests were once thought to be one of the most conclusive of the proofs of innate differences among races. What do psychologists now think of their racist implications? Although a number of psychologists seem to have imagined in the 1920's that a method of determining the intellectual potential of any person or even of any race had finally been attained, the conclusion was hardly drawn before it had to be modified. For one thing, psychologists became aware of the extent to which intelligence tests reflected the ideals and standards of a particular culture. Bertrand Russell has pointed out how difficult it is to maintain an objective attitude even to the matter of the intelligence of animals. His reading of American students of animal intelligence, he tells us, led him to believe that the animals reach decisions by a frantic method of trial and error. The animals which German psychologists studied, he adds, seem to scratch their heads and come to reasoned conclusions. If objectivity is difficult to attain in studying animals, it is much more so in studying human beings.[25]

The more psychologists studied the results of mental tests,

the more certain they became that no kind of racial scale of intelligence could be worked out. This conclusion did not mean, as some of the racists maintained, that the psychologists argued that everyone who does not have some abnormality is born with an approximately equal potential for intelligence; but it does mean that differences in intelligence cannot be established along racial lines. By 1927, opinion among the psychologists had changed to such an extent that Boas could say, "All our best psychologists recognize clearly that there is no proof that the intelligence tests give an actual insight into the biologically determined functioning of the mind."[26]

In 1931, Thomas Russell Garth reviewed the vast literature which had developed on the subject of mental differences among races and came to the conclusion that "there are no sure evidences of real racial differences in mental traits." Garth admitted that his work had begun with "a silent conviction that he would find clear-cut racial differences in mental processes," but after diligent work he concluded "it is useless to speak of the worthlessness of so-called 'inferior peoples' when their worth has never been established by a fair test." Otto Klineberg extended Garth's researches and has put the matter, if anything, more firmly still. One of the most interesting of the experiments conducted on the supposed racial character of intelligence concerned Indian children in Oklahoma whose parents and grandparents had become wealthy because oil was discovered on their land. The tests were particularly interesting since the advantages of wealth were largely a matter of geographical accident and not of biological selection. The Indian children who came from these homes were equal or superior to children in the general population, clearly an indication that some factor other than innate ability was at work.[27]

In these circumstances, some of the psychologists who had argued for a racial scale of intelligence began to give ground and even to reverse themselves. C. C. Brigham, who had written a well-known analysis of the army tests in 1922 and had come to the conclusion that Nordic immigrants were superior men-

tally to Alpines and Mediterraneans, later completely changed
his mind. "Comparative studies of various national and racial
groups may not be made with existing tests . . . ," he admitted.
"In particular one of the most pretentious of these comparative
racial studies—the writer's own—was without foundation." Occasionally, a psychologist still appears who resurrects all the
arguments of inferiority of some races, particularly of Negroes,
based upon intelligence tests. The psychologists generally reject
these arguments, not because they contend that racial intellectual
equality has been proved but because they are so far unimpressed
by the success of attempts to distinguish between the effects of
heredity and those of environment.[28]

As among the psychologists, so among the biologists and
geneticists the alarm over the effect of intermixture between "inferior" and "superior" races had largely subsided by the end of
the 1920's. Dr. Charles M. Davenport was still attempting in
1929 to show by studying race crossing in Jamaica between
whites and Negroes that the results were biologically disharmonic—that the progeny of such unions were biologically unsound. But Davenport's study was received with almost complete skepticism by biologists and anthropologists. All the ideas
of Grant and Stoddard and Osborn about the allegedly unstable
and recessive nature of the superior traits of the Nordic failed
to find any permanent respectability among the biological sciences, simply for want of proof. Franz Boas replied to Lothrop
Stoddard's fears that the "superior" traits of Nordics would be
lost through intermixture:

Where is the proof of the development of specialized hereditary capacities? Where is the proof that such capacities, if they exist, are recessive? How can it be shown that such specialized characteristics in
selected mating will be bred out? Not a single one of these statements
can be accepted.[29]

The frequent appeal to the analogy of dogs and horses in
commenting upon the race mixture among people came to seem
much less persuasive than it once had. For one thing, as the science of genetics developed, the idea that heredity is a mysterious

and wholly independent force declined. As Dr. H. S. Jennings expressed this idea, both heredity and environment play essential and necessarily unified parts in producing an individual organism. The habit of thinking of heredity "as an entity," as "a force, something that itself does things" is "an error that has induced clouds of misconception." Rather than make this kind of mistake, says Jennings, it would be better to have no such notion as "heredity." Of course, it must not be concluded that the biologists have proved all races to be equal, but there is no longer a significant trend among them toward the alarmist view that race mixture represents a biological peril. Among modern students of this subject, Dr. Theodore Dobzhansky of Princeton and Dr. L. C. Dunn of Columbia have been particularly active in attempting to allay what now had become largely popular fears over the dangers of race intermixture. "The extent to which genetic differences between peoples have contributed to the emergence of differences between their cultures . . . is," Dr. Dubzhansky admitted in 1956, a problem which

has not been solved, and it cannot be solved by dogmatic pronouncements. Such pronouncements have been numerous, while careful and unprejudiced studies have been conspicuously few. This is a matter for the future. For the time being, there is no convincing evidence that even the common denominators of all cultures are directly conditioned biologically.[30]

Deprived of their support from psychology and biology, some of the racists of the 1920's began to show signs of giving ground. Of course, not all of them did so. Madison Grant and Lothrop Stoddard seem never to have lost their confidence in race as the prime determinant of civilization. Madison Grant wrote a book in 1931 tracing the Colonial stock back to its Nordic foundations. In *Clashing Tides of Colour* (1935) and *Into the Darkness* (1940), Stoddard continued his racial analyses— although now considerably modified. Stoddard interviewed Hitler in 1940 and wrote an account which amounted to a partial vindication of the Nazis, arguing that many of their ideas were excellent but that they had gone much too far in their fanaticism.[31]

Neither were all the social scientists convinced that the concept of race was without validity in explaining mental and cultural differences. Dr. Ernest Hooton, professor of anthropology at Harvard, protested against those who have

gone to the extreme of denying any significance to the hereditary physical complex of which race consists, maintaining that it is nothing more than a combination of bodily trivialities produced by the vagaries of purposeless heredity or "faked" by leavening environmental agencies which tend to cast all men within an area in the same mold. In taking this view, I think that these students are guilty of emptying the baby out with the bath water.

Also, Hooton was convinced that it was not invalid to draw conclusions from intelligence tests concerning the intelligence of races. The tests proved at least, he believed, that "racial differences do exist, but they may not be as great as differences between nationalities." Elsewhere, Hooton protests against the fallacies of racist theorizing. In substance, his opinion is that race differences may be important but that we have no means of determining what they are.[32]

Among the most interesting shifts of opinion is that of Henry Pratt Fairchild. In 1944, he made one of his last attempts to formulate his views on the importance of race. Obviously, he says, he objects to the "inhumanity, arrogance, and brutality of the activities carried on under the name of what has come to be called 'racism,'" but he also objects to "an opposing school of thought, for which there is perhaps no better name than 'anti-racism.'" In their zeal for human brotherhood, says Fairchild, the anti-racists "frequently fall into almost as unscientific procedure as the champions of race superiority themselves. Science gives no more support to their assumption that race is nothing than it does to the claim that race is everything." These difficulties show up dramatically, Fairchild declares, in current attitudes among psychologists toward intelligence tests. He admits that the tests "have probably not completely succeeded in eliminating the effects of experience and environment," but he thinks they have "partially succeeded in doing so." All this means, concludes Fairchild, that

> we do not yet know scientifically what the relative intellectual ability of the various races of men is. Some different tests, equally valid, might give the Negro a higher score than the white. Until we do know, probably the best thing is to *act* as if all races had equivalent mental ability, but we must keep open minds, and be prepared sometime to have it proved that, in some particulars at least, there are marked divergences.[33]

Most contemporary social scientists have exhibited more skepticism than Fairchild did concerning the value of mental tests in detecting race differences. In reading his objections to race equalitarianism, however, one may overlook or undervalue his significant admission that we ought to "act as if all races had equivalent mental ability. . . ." This is the direction, indeed, which the attitude toward race has taken. Most contemporary students of the subject have assumed that the more we act as if races are innately equal the more we become aware of their potential for development. The more we act as if certain races are inferior to ourselves, the more difficult we make it for them to develop their capabilities. As time has passed, we seem to be no nearer than we were to developing a means of separating the effects of heredity from those of environment, and the emergence of increasing numbers of men and women of great ability from all races makes us aware of how much we have undervalued the human potential for development.

What chiefly happened in the 1920's to stem the tide of racism was that one man, Franz Boas, who was an authority in several fields which had been the strongest sources of racism, quietly asked for proof that race determines mentality and temperament. The racists among the historians and social scientists had always prided themselves on their willingness to accept the "facts" and had dismissed their opponents as shallow humanitarians who glossed over unpleasant truths. Now there arose a man who asked them to produce their proof. Their answer was a flood of indignant rhetoric, but the turning point had been reached and from now on it would be the racists who were increasingly on the defensive. As frequently happens in the history of thought, after a change of opinion occurs one can only wonder why it was so long delayed. It is true that Boas did not accomplish the task of laying the ghost of racism all by himself. There were others at about the same time who were becoming strongly aware of the illogic of racism. But it was clearly Boas who led the attack.

The shift of the scientists and social scientists with regard to race did not occur because of any dramatic or sudden discovery. Racism had developed into such a contradictory mass of the unprovable and the emotional that the serious students eventually recognized that as a source of explanation for mental and temperamental traits of a people it was worthlesss. Once this point was accepted, the top-heavy intellectual structures of racism began to topple, one after another.

XVII

The Battle Against Prejudice

AN ADEQUATE HISTORY of the rebels against racial prejudice would be a lengthy book, but—at least up until the last forty years or so—it would consist mainly of a discouraging repetition of humanitarian protests against injustice, protests which were generally either derided or ignored. It may be, however, that we owe more than we realize to early opponents of racism. Prejudice against ethnic minorities in this country has been immensely strong. Sometimes it has approached the point at which it seemed doubtful whether some ethnic groups were to be considered human at all, but there has always remained a nagging doubt that they *might* be. Prejudice never reached the point in this country, as it did in Nazi Germany, at which there was a widespread and concerted effort to destroy a whole people. That it did not is largely owing to the people who kept the conscience of the nation alive with regard to the injustice done to minority groups.

Of white men who spoke out against racism in the nineteenth century, none was more remarkable than George Washington Cable. In his novel, *The Grandissimes* (1879), Cable achieved a real stroke of imagination when he chose the period at the beginning of the nineteenth century when the Creoles of Louisiana were adjusting with great difficulty to the alien Americans who had recently acquired sovereignty. The Creoles of 1803 were in a position similar to that of the white South during Reconstruction—in the face of conquest by "foreigners" they were forced to reconsider ideas which they had previously taken for granted. Arlin Turner in his biography of Cable has rightly observed that the novel is "still a powerful attack on the traditional Southern attitude toward the Negroes" and has commented upon Cable's ironic treatment of the southern conviction that the slaves were "the happiest beings on earth."[1] The story of Bras-Coupé, the Negro who would not accept slavery, is an impressive indictment of the Black Code.

Cable was intelligent enough to realize that if the Negro was segregated in every area of public life, he must inevitably be deprived of his rights as a citizen. *The Silent South* (1885) is an indictment of those southerners who stood by while the extremists decided how far they would go in relegating the Negro to a subordinate position. Cable asks for nothing less for the Negro than full rights of citizenship. Of the practice of excluding Negroes from jury service, he asks whether a white man would be convinced that he would get a fair trial from a jury entirely composed of Negroes:

Assuming that their average of intelligence and morals should be not below that of jurymen as now drawn, would a white man, for all that, choose to be tried in one of those courts? Would he suspect nothing? Could one persuade him that his chances of even justice were all they should be, or all they would be were the court not evading the law in order to sustain an outrageous distinction against him because of the accident of his birth? Yet only read white man for black man, and black man for white man, and that—I speak as an eye-witness—has been the practice for years, and is still so today; an actual emasculation, in the case of six million people both as plaintiff and defendant, of the right of trial by jury.[2]

Cable argued for an integrated educational system in the South, especially in view of the fact that the poverty of the region would render it impossible to maintain two segregated systems of real quality. He chided the South for "the huge bugbear of Social Equality" and "absurd visions of all Shantytown pouring its hordes of unwashed imps into the company and companionship of our own sunnyheaded darlings. What utter nonsense! As if our public schools had no gauge of cleanliness, decorum, or moral character!"³ Cable's chief point is that the South "cannot afford to tolerate at large . . . a class of people less than citizens" and that the Negro should be allowed to "be free to become in all things, as far as his own personal gifts will lift and sustain him, the same sort of American citizen he would be if, with the same intellectual and moral calibre, he were white."⁴

Cable's views were too far in advance of his time to have much chance of adoption. In opposing them, Henry W. Grady took a somewhat indulgent view—speaking of the "singular tenderness and beauty" of Cable's fiction but calling his ideas on race "sentimental rather than practical." In a rather low blow, Grady questioned Cable's right to call himself a southerner because his parents were northerners and because of his obvious affection for New England. Cable had once written that he had gone to New England and felt that he "had never been home till then." Grady caught him up on this admission and said that a man so "out of harmony with his neighbors as to say, even after he had fought side by side with them on the battle-field, that he never felt at home until he had left them, cannot speak understandingly of their views on so vital a subject as that under discussion." Grady says he is certain that though the Negro schools will be separate, the southern whites will "insist on perfect equality in grade and efficiency." Other critics of Cable in the South were considerably less tolerant, and he eventually left the region altogether and spent his last years in New England.⁵

Where Cable discussed calmly and objectively the irrationality of racism, Mark Twain made its irrationalism the subject of satire. He emphasizes the absurdities of racism, an approach which, though less direct and exhaustive than that of Cable, is often more effective because it seems to have no design upon the mind of the reader. Twain did not arrive at his stand against racism until some years after he had reached his majority. As a young man, his ideas of Negroes, for example, were not different from what one might expect of one who had grown up in a slaveholding society. "I reckon I had better black my face," he wrote back home on a visit to Syracuse, New York, in 1854, "for in these Eastern States niggers are considerably better than white people," and he mentioned the "infernal abolitionists" he found everywhere there.[6] In later years, however, Twain had changed his mind. In 1869, we find him commenting on a lynching in the South in which the victim had later been found to have been innocent:

Ah, well! Too bad, to be sure! A little blunder in the administration of justice by Southern mob-law; but nothing to speak of. Of course, every high-toned gentleman whose chivalric impulses were so unfortunately misled in this affair . . . is as sorry about it as a high-toned gentleman can be expected to be sorry about the unlucky fate of "a nigger." But mistakes will happen, even in the conduct of the best regulated and most high-toned mobs, and surely there is no good reason why Southern gentlemen should worry themselves with useless regrets, so long as only an innocent "nigger" is hanged, or roasted or knouted to death, now and then.[7]

Twain is at his best in satirizing racism in *The Adventures of Huckleberry Finn* (1884). One of his better touches is the often quoted comment of Tom Sawyer's Aunt Sally when Huck—whom she believes to be Tom—invents an accident on a river steamer to explain the delay of his arrival in Louisiana:

"We blowed out a cylinder-head."
"Good gracious! anybody hurt?"
"No'm. Killed a nigger."
"Well, it's lucky; because sometimes people do get hurt. Two years ago last Christmas your uncle Silas was coming up from Newrleans on the old *Lally Rook,* and she blowed out a cylinder-head and crippled a man. And I think he died afterwards. He was a Baptist."[8]

In a later novel, *Pudd'nhead Wilson* (1894), Twain dealt more directly with race questions. This is the story of Roxana, a Negro nurse of a white child. Roxana's own child is so fair as to be indistinguishable from whites. To insure that her child shall be reared as a white, Roxana substitutes him in the crib for the white baby and takes the white baby as her own child. The child who is part Negro grows up mouthing all the shibboleths of white supremacy and the child who is white grows up to be humble and self-effacing in the tradition of a Negro servant. Thus Twain is able to show that qualities which are thought of as racial are the result of cultural conditioning.[9]

To the problems of the "heathen" abroad, Twain turned a ready sympathy and the attention of a shrewd and humorous intelligence. He was particularly good at exposing pretentious moral fervor on the part of the dominant white people who were certain they knew what the people "sitting in darkness" needed. On shipboard, he once heard a group of people at church services singing the hymn "From Greenland's Icy Mountains." One of the lines reads, "They call us to deliver their land from error's chains." Twain comments: "The call was never made."[10] To a Jew who once complimented him for the absence in his works of anti-Semitic utterances, Twain replied in characteristic fashion that there were no reflections upon the character of Jews in his books "because the disposition was lacking." And he added:

I am quite sure that (bar one) I have no race prejudices, and I think I have no color prejudices nor caste prejudices nor creed prejudices. Indeed, I know it. I can stand any society. All that I care to know is that a man is a human being—that is enough for me; he can't be any worse.[11]

In one of his novels, William Dean Howells dealt sympathetically, although by modern standards in somewhat gingerly fashion, with the theme of miscegenation. *An Imperative Duty* (1892) is the story of Rhoda Aldgate, who has been reared in the North by an aunt who has kept her from the knowledge that her mother back in New Orleans was an octoroon. Olney, the hero, is a physician who falls in love with Rhoda before he learns of her Negro ancestry, but he does not allow the knowledge to prevent their marriage. The couple go to Rome where Rhoda passes for white and "is thought to look so very Italian that you would really take her for an Italian."[12]

At this point, however, Howells apparently felt obliged to

make concessions to the idea that race determines character and temperament. In the last pages of the book, he suggests that the marriage is not wholly a happy one because in Rhoda there is a "war between her temperament and her character." All of us, Howells observes, consist of hereditary mixtures "where all strains are now so crossed and intertangled that there is no definite and unbroken direction any more . . . ," but apparently Rhoda's condition is worse. It is true that the "confusion" in her disposition was "only a little greater than in most others." Her husband's chief regret is that his wife is given to melancholy and morbidity. It was too bad, Olney reflects, that "her mother's race had not endowed her with more of the heaven-born cheerfulness with which it meets contumely and injustice." Apparently, she had inherited her "hypochondria of the soul" from the "Puritanism of her father's race"; it had "sickened in her" and led her to have an overly sensitive conscience. To anyone who has read much of Howells, Rhoda's conscience will seem to be no more abnormally developed than that of his other heroines, but he apparently thought that in this instance he was confronted with a racial trait. Just as Rhoda is a Howellsian heroine, so Olney is a Howellsian hero. Therefore, the problem is less severe for him than we might imagine because—like all of Howells' heroes—he has a great sense of duty and is "not a seeker after happiness." The story is well meant, but it would hardly soothe anyone's fears over the evils of racial intermixture. It is significant that no mention is made of Olney's and Rhoda's having children.[13]

In 1899 Stephen Crane wrote "The Monster," a powerful indictment of bigotry. Henry Johnson, a young Negro coachman, rushes into a burning house and saves the son of Dr. Treadway. In the process, Johnson is horribly burned and survives as a grotesque and misshapen figure with his mind seriously affected. The doctor insists on having Johnson remain on his premises in gratitude for his act of sacrifice, but because Johnson's hideousness frightens people the doctor is severely criticized by the people of the northern town, first for not quietly allowing Johnson to die and, second, for not sending him away somewhere so he will not be seen. Eventually, the doctor himself becomes a pariah in the town. This is one of Crane's best stories; it is strange that it is not better known.[14]

One of the men who quietly challenged prejudice against Negroes was the artist, Winslow Homer. In 1875, he went South to Petersburg, Virginia, where he sought out the Negroes for portraits. One of his pictures, entitled "The Cotton Pickers," is a detailed rendering of two Negro women working in the fields. The white people of Petersburg asked him to hold an exhibition, but they were puzzled and hurt that so many of his pictures were of Negroes. A southern matron looked at "The Cotton Pickers" and, with dismay, turned to Homer and said: "Mr. Homer, why don't you paint our lovely girls instead of those dreadful creatures?" Exaggerating his Yankee accent, Homer is said to have replied: "Because they are the purtiest." His pictures of Negroes are careful representations. Unlike many of the artists of the nineteenth century, he did not paint them as if they were white men with black faces. He carefully portrayed their distinctive bodily and cranial characteristics. He painted them seriously and sympathetically, not as a subject for low humor.[15]

A staunch friend and advocate of Negroes was Thomas Wentworth Higginson. During the Civil War, he commanded a Negro regiment of the Union army and wrote a most informative and revealing account of his experiences. He tells how at first he thought of the Negro soldiers under his command as an indistinguishable mass, but he says that "as one grows more acquainted with the men, their individualities emerge; and I find, first their faces, then their characters, to be as distinct as those of whites." Higginson was convinced that Negroes are not inherently stupid and that they should be made citizens. Back in Newport, Rhode Island, toward the end of the war, he became a member of the local school board and was the leading figure in the decision no longer to segregate Negroes in the schools.[16]

He was also the friend of immigrants, no matter what country they came from. To the charge that many immigrants could not be assimilated into American life, Higginson replied that there could be no "omelet without breaking of eggs" and thus "no fusing of all nations except by bringing the nations here to be fused. If the patricians of those races will not come—and why should they, since they have more exclusive privileges at home? —we must accept the plebeians, in the knowledge that they may provide us with patricians in their grandchildren a century hence." It was unfair, he maintained, to point only to the high proportion of crime among the immigrants. The prisons had a larger proportion of immigrants rather than of native Americans because the immigrants represented "a poorer and less befriended class." The "eminent scoundrels, who are rich and shrewd enough to keep out of prison" were most often native Americans using the immigrants as their "tools." A "successful swindler" did more real harm to society than "twenty men convicted of drunkenness or petty larceny." And as for crimes of violence, "it is not among the vehement Italians that lynchings occur, but in those portions of the Union least touched by foreign immigration. Let us make law, then, to regulate those landing on our shores; but let us not forget that the ancestors of our lawmakers also landed here."[17]

The immigrants themselves began to discover that they were not without resources. The development of consciousness of political power, first among the Irish and later among other immigrants, eventually extended in some degree to all minorities. Rudyard Kipling wrote a poem about the Irish immigrant in America which illustrated this point:

There came to these shores a poor exile from Erin;
    The dew on his wet robe hung heavy and chill;
Yet the steamer which brought him was scarce out of hearin'
    Ere't was Alderman Mike inthrojucin' a bill.[18]

Before scientific criticism of racist theory had gained much headway, immigrant groups were making it politically dangerous for their elected representatives to champion the old shibboleths against foreigners. There were a good many people in the United States who were not Anglo-Saxons, and they had votes. They were unlikely to be moved by appeals to the magnificent destiny of Anglo-Saxons.

What were some of the ways in which this power of immigrant groups, eventually to become an important tool in combating racism, was first exercised? During the Spanish-American War, Finley Peter Dunne satirized the inaccuracy of the description of Americans as the great representatives of the Anglo-Saxon race. His character, Mr. Dooley, indicates the real ingredients of the American nation:

I'm wan iv th' hottest Anglo-Saxons that iver come out iv Anglo-Saxony. . . . I tell ye, whin th' Clan an' the Sons iv Sweden an' th' Banana Club an' th' Circle Francaize an' th' Pollacky Benivolent Society an' th' Benny Brith an' th' Coffee Clutch that Schwartzmeister r-runs an' th' Turnd'yemind an' th' Holland society an' th' Afro-Americans an' th' other Anglo-Saxons begin f'r to raise their Anglo-Saxon battle cry, it'll be all day with th' eight or nine people in th' wurruld that has th' misfortune iv not bein' brought up Anglo-Saxons.[19]

The opposition to co-operation with England among Irish and German groups in this country may not always have been sensible and closely reasoned, but it did serve as a damper to some of the more extravagant claims of racial unity in which its proponents indulged themselves. John Hay, the secretary of state in 1900, confided in a private letter that anti-British sentiment was making his work extremely difficult. He spoke of the "diseased state of the public mind," of the "mad-dog hatred of England prevalent among newspapers and politicians," about the pleas of congressmen to him that nothing the State Department did should lend itself to the charge of "subservience to Great Britain." Hay felt that in the alliance he had "wrung great concessions" from England without any compensation on our part. "That we should be compelled to refuse the assistance of the greatest power in the world, *in carrying out our own policy*," he exclaimed, "because all Irishmen are Democrats and some Germans are fools—is enough to drive a man mad."[20]

In 1902, an official of the Transatlantic Society of America

—an organization devoted to promoting political and economic co-operation between America and England—was forced to confess that in New England the society was shunned by men with political ambitions. "While Irish societies can obtain any number of brilliant American speakers to address them without fear or favor on any occasion," he lamented,

this society has never been able to secure either for love or adequate compensation, the services as orator of any prominent American public man who has political ambition or a political future. These public men will not go on record or do anything which may bring them any consequences from the all powerful Irish vote in America.[21]

German-American immigrants caused almost as much trouble in the Middle West, where they held mass meetings in protest against an "Anglo-Saxon alliance."[21]

Sometimes the Anglo-Saxon propagandists made an attempt to placate the Irish and German minority groups by making them honorary Anglo-Saxons. One exponent of the idea of racial manifest destiny was willing to substitute a new compound word in place of Anglo-Saxon—one which would include English-Americans, Irish-Americans, and German-Americans. George Brinton Chandler spoke of the magnificent future of the "Teuto-Celts" in America and in the world.[22] A Canadian enthusiast included the Irish but for some reason left out the Germans when he declared that "the Anglo-Saxon-Celtic people headed by John Bull and Brother Jonathan are God's chosen peoples."[23] Other propagandists for Anglo-American unity of policy appealed to the self-interest of the Irish and of other minority groups. The *Arena*, one of the magazines strong on the Anglo-Saxon theme, hopefully reminded Irishmen that if the United States had an alliance with England, she might then be able "to exert a moral influence" on behalf of their compatriots in Ireland.[24] The *Anglo-American Magazine*, a periodical whose two chief themes were the superiority of the Anglo-Saxon race and the necessity for close co-operation with England, did all it could, nevertheless, to avoid giving offense to minority groups in this country, particularly to the Irish. One article observed that many American newspapers owned or edited by Irishmen were "outright advocates of improved relations with Great Britain and generous promulgators of Anglo-Saxon union," and it advised Englishmen "to realize more intelligently the tone and scope and merits of Irish-American sentiment and character."[25]

More astute observers at the turn of the century realized that an alliance or understanding between the United States and England based upon their racial affinity would be vehemently attacked by American minority groups. While the Spanish-American War was still in progress and the feeling between the two nations was at its peak of cordiality, James Bryce in England took occasion to explain in an article in the *Atlantic* why the racial bond was not a secure basis of accord. It was in "community of ideas and feeling," in "similarity of instinctive judgments," he argued, "that an Anglo-American accord must be established." "The sense of identity has deeper and better foundations," he tactfully explained, "than the pride of Anglo-Saxon ancestry and the spirit of defiance to other races."[26]

The opponents of the doctrine of Anglo-Saxon superiority may not have been powerful enough to prevent a rising sentiment for immigration restriction, but they did force the proponents of restriction to change their tactics. The idea that the immigrant from southern and eastern Europe was an inherently inferior human being—anarchist, slum-loving, beyond the reach of argument in his degradation—was received with skepticism by thoughtful people and with hostility by the groups themselves as they increased in size and in political awareness. As was natural, many of the defenses of the immigrants came from representatives of their own groups or from their children or grandchildren—people like Finley Peter Dunne, John P. Altgeld, Jacob Riis, Mary Antin, and Theodore Dreiser.[27]

Not all defenders of the immigrant groups were of this high caliber. Some of the historians whose ancestors had not been English went to ludicrous lengths in their anxiety to prove the Americanism of their own particular group. George Washington, Thomas Jefferson, and Abraham Lincoln were sometimes discovered really to have been Germans, Irishmen, or Dutchmen. When this metamorphosis could not be managed, they were at least shown to have some German, Irish, or Dutch blood. The famous battles of American history were reappraised with the glory of victory ascribed to this or that ethnic group. Because their insecurity was sometimes great, the historians of recent immigrant stock—as Edward N. Saveth has pointed out—exceeded in their "jingoism" the historians of the older American stocks.[28]

The process of defense of ethnic minorities begun by the Americans of Irish and German stock spread to the others. In the election of 1912, one of the presidential candidates discovered that some of his reflections on the character of the Italian and Hungarian immigrants in his writings of the 1880's and 1890's were being recalled to his disadvantage. Woodrow Wilson needed the support of the Italian and Hungarian groups in the cities of the North. An editor of an Italian paper wanted to know what Wilson had to say about his previous statements concerning the racial inferiority of Italian immigrants. Wilson replied tactfully that he had merely been "deploring the coming to this country of certain lawless elements which I had supposed all thoughtful Italians themselves deplored. . . . Certainly, the Italians I have known . . . have constituted one of the most interesting and admirable elements in our American life." To Hungarians who might be offended, Wilson soothingly declared that he counted himself "very unfortunate if I have been so awkward in my way of expressing what I had to say as to bring injustice to a people whom I admire and respect."[29]

Less than a year later, Wilson's ambassador to England, Walter Hines Page, was having similar trouble with minority groups in this country. In a speech in Southampton, England, in August, 1913, Page declared that the United States was and always had been "English led and English-ruled." His remark stirred up a storm in America, particularly among the Irish. In a private letter to Wilson, Page protested—with some justice—

that his praise of the English element in American life need not imply disrespect to other ethnic components. What he failed to take into account, however, was that there was a strong tradition in American thought which imputed all the virtue of the nation to its English stock and cast aspersions on other elements. The mayor of Boston thundered that Page's speech was an insult to Ireland and the Irish. Senators from New York, Massachusetts, and Oregon protested in the halls of Congress. To Wilson, Page said that he supposed he would have "to abolish the word 'English' " from his vocabulary.[30] In such ways as these political leaders learned to be more circumspect in their care for the feelings of minorities.

Doubtless, the minorities have been—and sometimes still are—supersensitive. Efforts have been made to bowdlerize or remove from libraries those books thought to be unfavorable to this or that ethnic group. Shakespeare's *Merchant of Venice* and Dickens' *Oliver Twist* have come under fire for their presentation of the Jew as an evil stereotype. Italian groups have protested when the villains of stories and movies have been Italians. More recently, Negro groups have objected to stories which they believe reflect adversely on the race. "Little Black Sambo," with its supposed connotations of condescension toward Negroes, has disappeared from many children's libraries and anthologies. Somewhat surprisingly, Twain's *The Adventures of Huckleberry Finn* is sometimes charged with race prejudice in its presentation of Nigger Jim. Stephen Foster's "Old Folks at Home," in some modern versions, appeals to "O, brothers" instead of "O, darkies."[31] An outstanding writer of fiction from the South has told me that she has learned she must be very careful in choosing stories to read before northern university audiences not to select one in which a character uses the word "nigger." Such sensitivity is understandable, but it is an attempt to make an unfavorable stereotype disappear simply by banishing it. Perhaps ethnic minorities will become more tolerant if racism declines to a point where they will realize that such aspersions reflect nothing more than the ignorance or evil of the characters who employ them or that they are important solely from the standpoint of past history.

The status of ethnic minorities in this country—though still very far from perfect—is a great deal better than it was, say, in 1900 or, for that matter, in 1920 or 1940. As we have seen, part of the reason for change has been that scientists and scholars as well as humanitarians have had time to look carefully at the old racist shibboleths and to recognize them for what they are. Many people are now aware that the idea that some races are inherently inferior and the idea that race determines temperament have virtually no foundation in science. In addition, there have been other forces which have led to the decline of the power of racism in this country.

Some of these forces have been impersonal. The great expansion of the economy and the consequent rise of a large middle class have made many people more secure in their status and thus less subject to hatred of other groups who also have what the sociologists sometimes call "upward mobile" aspirations. Among many of the ethnic groups there has been widespread intermarriage, and this tendency has led to greater acceptance all around of ethnic groups hitherto thought of as wholly separate. The greater role of minorities in American life has been accompanied by a flowering of talent among many groups which in the nineteenth century were regarded as inherently inferior. The old notion that Italians, for example, may succeed in art and music but not in science or law seems horrible to many people, but chiefly it seems quaint. One sometimes still encounters the notion that Negroes may succeed as entertainers or sportsmen but not as anything else, or one hears that Negroes succeed in any endeavor only when they have white intermixture. Both statements are now widely recognized for what they are—expressions of prejudice. As Irishmen, Germans, Jews, Italians, Chinese, Greeks, Armenians, Poles, Hungarians, Latin Americans, Negroes, Indians, and other ethnic minorities have found success in the areas of politics, science, and the arts, they have to some extent elevated the status of their ethnic groups along with them. In addition, they have served as implicit refutations of the whole doctrine of racism.

What has happened abroad has also had an important effect upon racist ideology in this country. In the 1930's and 1940's, the country was treated to the spectacle of just how far a nationalism based upon race might go in Germany and, to a lesser extent, in Italy. The racist mouthings of Hitler, Goering, Goebbels, and their racist philosopher Alfred Rosenberg were a compound of horror and absurdity. Americans realized with a shock, especially after World War II, that the Nazis had meant exactly what they said—that they were perfectly willing to carry out their beliefs by a program of genocide—by killing literally millions of Jews and other peoples they regarded as inferior. The recognition that race prejudice is not merely regrettable but also highly dangerous was no longer limited to the minorities who suffered from discrimination or to the students of racism.

In addition, the international role of America itself has caused many an American to be more concerned about the way we treat our own minorities. With the coming of World War II and of the struggle afterward to buttress the countries abroad against the spread of communism, Americans have inevitably been obliged to re-evaluate some of their own attitudes. The establishment of the United Nations in this country may have made some Americans more responsive to foreign opinion. The influx of a great many students from abroad—particularly from the new nations of Africa and the Far East—has also contributed to an awareness of our own weaknesses.

We owe something to impersonal forces in the decline of racism, but the trouble with impersonal forces is that they can as easily work one way as another. We owe far more to the people and the organizations motivated by a concern for the equality of all. Their number has increased enormously in the last generation and it continues to grow. It includes those who have made an intensive study of the problems of race and of caste problems of particular ethnic groups. It includes people and organizations dedicated to the welfare of particular minorities or to civil liberties generally. It includes many people who have no particular connection with any organization or cause but who are concerned over the evils of discrimination and injustice.

Organizations have served an indispensable function in combating prejudice. They have planned programs, co-ordinated the activities of individual people, and massed support on specific issues. The National Association for the Advancement of Colored People (NAACP) is the oldest of the modern organizations specifically dedicated to the cause of the rights and welfare of Negroes. A race riot in Springfield, Illinois, the home of Abraham Lincoln, had killed scores of Negroes and driven many more from the city in 1908. In response to this injustice and others like it, the NAACP was founded in 1909. At first, it was largely a white organization, W. E. B. DuBois being the only nonwhite officer, and for many years it had a white president. Only a few years after its founding, however, there were a large number of Negroes on its executive board. In its more recent history, both Negroes and whites have played an extensive role in its activities. The National Urban League, founded in 1910, is an organization principally devoted to the problems of Negroes. It has been supported mainly by philanthropic foundations and has served the function of research and planning and of advising other Negro groups. Other organizations, such as B'nai B'rith, the National Conference of Christians and Jews, the American Civil Liberties Union, and many others, have actively concerned themselves with matters of racism and of prejudice.

More slowly than they should have but with increasing strength and conviction, religious organizations have become active in questions of racial injustice in this country. Protestants, Catholics, and Jews have each had their peculiar problems to overcome in joining this particular crusade. The major Protestant denominations have been handicapped by the fact that their membership is frequently middle and upper class, and thus relatively few of the people likely to be the victims of racism have been members of their congregations. Virtually all Protestant denominations have separate Negro churches, and thus the areas of association for religious purposes have been very small. The congregation of a Protestant church is likely to be a closely knit group in which religious worship is augmented by social activity. Moreover, the minister is frequently—whatever creeds or constitutions may say—under the control of opinion within the local congregation.

Up until quite recent times the attitude of the Protestant churches toward racial prejudice was timid and conservative. There were, of course, individual voices that spoke up against bigotry. In the 1920's and 1930's, the Federal Council of Churches, while forthright and courageous in dealing with industrial problems, was inclined to falter on the subject of race. "Its pronouncements on race," observes a historian of the attitudes of Protestant churches on social questions in this period, "very often go no further than the 'separate but equal' formula. . . ."[32] Such work as the churches did in this area was largely confined to betterment of slum conditions for Negroes and other groups, solicitation of funds for denominational Negro colleges, and extensive missionary and educational activities abroad. The churches were moving toward a more positive position, but there were occasional indications of a tremendous lag. In 1932, for example, a Southern Baptist leader, the representative of four million Baptists, refused at a meeting in a northern city to sit at a banquet table where there was a Negro.[33]

Especially in the years following World War II, the Protestant churches have taken a much more active role in combating racism. One sees this not merely in the resolutions against racial inequalities and against discrimination but also in the life of the church itself. Churches which were previously content to pass resolutions have now gone out to solicit Negroes to become members. Not seldom the Protestant ministers have been in advance of community opinion, and a good many elders, deacons, and vestrymen must often have wondered what had got into their ministers to make them so militant on the subject of rights of ethnic minorities, particularly of Negroes. It was a Baptist minister who was physically attacked by white segregationists when in 1956 he led a Negro child by the hand into a white school in Tennessee which had been integrated by a court decision.[34] In the summer of 1963, as demonstrations against segregated facilities mounted, high officials in the northern Presbyterian and Episcopal churches allowed themselves to be arrested in Baltimore for participating in a demonstration at a private amusement park.[35] There is still much to do to convince the ordinary Protestant church member that racial prejudice should be a matter of concern to him, but the future on this score looks more hopeful than it ever has in the past.

Like the Protestants, the Catholics have been handicapped by problems special to them. In the nineteenth century, The Catholic church was largely an immigrant church in this country and the Irish, the Italians, the Poles, and other immigrants were often in direct competition with Negroes for jobs. An American historian pointed out that in the 1840's and 1850's the Irish were faithful to the Democratic party and were unconcerned over the evils of slavery. "How the Irish rushed en masse to the polls of our State only seven years ago," wrote Horace Greeley in the *New York Tribune* in 1854,

to vote down the right of colored men to the elective franchise! No other class of our citizens was so zealous, so unanimous in its hostility to Equal Suffrage without regard to color. "Would you have your daughter marry a naygur?" was their standing flout at the champions of democracy irrespective of race and color.

In Boston the Irish, with the warm approval of their press, broke up abolition meetings.[36] The immigrant groups who were Catholic were more likely to protest the discrimination leveled against them than to concern themselves with injustices suffered by other minority groups, particularly by Negroes. More importantly, they were not then in a position of sufficient power to influence American opinion.

Even before the Civil War there were Catholic opponents of

slavery and voices raised against racial injustice, but they became stronger after the war. In the late nineteenth century,
Archbishop John Ireland, of St. Paul, Minnesota, was an advocate of nondiscrimination against Negroes. In 1891, he declared
that the only answer to the problem of race was "to grant our
colored citizens practical and effective equality with white citizens." First of all, the Negro should have political equality. If
his education did not fit him for political participation, "let us
for his sake and our own, hurry to enlighten him." Archbishop
Ireland wished to "open to the Negro all industrial and professional avenues—the test for his advance being his ability, but
never his color. I would in all public gatherings, and in all public
resorts, in halls and hotels, treat the black man as I treat the
white."[37]

In recent years, the Catholic church has taken a strong
position in favor of racial equality. The acceptance of Negro
students in Catholic colleges and universities has been cordial
and widespread. In the Deep South, even when they were a relatively small minority and when there was strong community opposition, the Catholics have shown courage and foresight in their
widespread willingness to integrate their schools. Though there
are many critics among the Catholics who maintain that the
church has been too cautious on racial matters, their record in
comparison with that of Protestants is very good indeed. Even
severe Protestant critics of Catholics have recognized that their
record in the field of race relations has been an enviable one.[38]

The Jews have experienced persecution similar to that visited
on racial minorities. The fact that to the anthropologists the
Jews are not a race has made little difference to racial bigots.
Both individual Jews and Jewish organizations have shown themselves generally willing to combat prejudice against other minorities and not merely against themselves. B'nai B'rith has worked in co-operation with the Southern Regional Council and other
groups concerned with the lessening of discrimination against
Negroes. The Jews have produced a large number of the leading combatants against racism. It is no accident that Franz Boas,

probably the man who did more than any other to lay the ghost of racism in scientific disciplines, was a Jew. One of the most dedicated and effective of the workers in the cause of equality for Negroes is Harry Golden, the editor of the *Carolina Israelite*.

The change of American racial attitudes sometimes seems glacially slow, but if we examine the changes which have occurred over a period of years we may be astonished at how widespread and pervasive the change has become. A little more than fifty years ago, Negroes were not allowed on the New York stage in plays in which white actors appeared. Their parts were taken by white actors in blackface, but beginning in 1910 they began to be admitted. When this change eventually reached the South, curious concessions were sometimes made to old prejudices. In the printed programs, the white actors' names were presented with a courtesy title of Mr., Mrs., or Miss, but the Negro actors had their names printed without such titles. Southern newspapers began to put titles before the names of Negroes—sometimes beginning in the section reserved for social news for Negroes and sometimes in the obituary column. They began to print the picture of the valedictorian of the Negro high school as well as pictures of Negroes charged with crime. These—and hundreds of other changes, sometimes trivial in themselves—have constituted the foreshadowings of more important changes to come.[39]

The two most important setbacks in recent history to growing racial amity in this country occurred during World War II. One was the illegal and discriminatory treatment accorded to Japanese Americans during the war. Fearful of an invasion by the Japanese and of widespread espionage and subversion among the Japanese Americans, the federal government undertook after the disaster at Pearl Harbor to arrest American citizens of Japanese ancestry and to send them to special camps set up for them. This was a measure of panic, and the uprooting of these people is a harmful blot on the national record. The Nisei, as they were called, were obliged to dispose of their property, often at prices far below the true value. The other spectacular failure of racial relations in this country during the war took place in Detroit, where there was a serious race riot against Negroes in 1943. The influx of thousands of Negroes as the new war industries opened up led to tension. The riot started over the issue of a Negro's presence at a bathing beach. At about the same time, another serious riot occurred in Beaumont, Texas.[40]

Significant changes came in the status of American Indians with the New Deal in 1933. Up until then the federal government had either itself exploited the Indians or else permitted others to exploit them. It was a sorry record of autocracy and mismanagement. Indian tribal funds were appropriated by the federal government to pay the costs of the Indian Bureau—an easy way of reneging on old treaties. From 1900 to 1930, more than a hundred million dollars had been taken by the government from the Indian tribal funds for this purpose.[41] The oil boom in Oklahoma led to a system of white "guardians" appointed by the courts to take care of the financial interests of the Indians who owned land on which oil was discovered and who did not understand legal and economic complexities. John Collier has estimated that 90 per cent of the 265 million dollars in oil leases paid out between 1915 and 1931 to the Osage Indians went, in fact, to the white "guardians." Until 1933, the Indian was forbidden to incorporate or to organize politically, and thus he was helpless against depredation. The Indian Bureau could expel from Indian lands any anthropologist, journalist, or "agitator" without giving any reason, a power which it made it difficult for anyone known to be critical of the Bureau to obtain information upon which to base any study. After 1917, the Bureau began a new program of liquidation of the Indian title to reservation lands, a program which was expanded under the notorious Albert B. Fall, secretary of the interior under the administration of President Harding and a chief figure in the Teapot Dome scandals. In the 1920's, the Bureau launched a campaign against the "obscenity" of the rituals of the Pueblo Indians, forbade Indian children to attend them, and accused white allies of the Indians of being "agents of Moscow."[42]

Some amelioration came to the Indians under the administration of President Hoover, but the more important changes came when John Collier was appointed Indian Commissioner in 1933. With the backing of Secretary of the Interior Harold L. Ickes and of President Roosevelt, Collier instituted a whole new program for the Indians—based upon government protection for their land, giving them the right freely to organize their societies, aiding them in developing their holdings with grants of money and of credit. The program to break up the Indian tribal organization, the drive to liquidate tribal lands, the prejudice against allowing them the freedom to practice their own pagan religion were all discarded. In 1961, for the first time, a trained anthropologist, Philleo Nash, was appointed Indian Commissioner. The Indian problem is still not solved. We have yet to devise a method by which the Indian's right to his land may be protected but which will also give him access to the advantages of education and of modern life generally. On the other hand, for the last thirty years the rights of the Indians have been immeasurably more respected than they were at any other previous period.[43]

Race relations for the Negroes also began to improve. The lynching rate continued high all through the 1920's. In the ten years from 1918 through 1927, there were 455 persons lynched in America and of these 416 were Negroes. Eleven were Negro women. Burning Negroes to death was still common—forty-two of the above victims were burned alive and others were either beaten to death or cut to pieces. The bodies of sixteen others were burned after death. In the 1920's there were pathetic advertisements in the newspapers—such as that of the NAACP in 1922— with such comments as the following: "Do you know that the United States is the *Only Land on Earth* where human beings are BURNED AT THE STAKE? In Four Years, 1918-1921, Twenty-Eight People were publicly BURNED BY AMERICAN MOBS."[44] Since the 1930's, lynchings have declined greatly in numbers, though the figures may not tell the whole story. Some observers have thought that the decline may be somewhat less significant than it seems. Lynchings have generally been defined as the action of a mob in depriving a person of his life without due process of law. As lynchings grew in public disfavor, a method sometimes employed was to have a small group of white men seize a Negro and kill him in a secluded place with few or no spectators. Such a method would not technically be a lynching and thus might not show up in the statistics.[45] There is no doubt, however, that though lynching may not have declined as much as the statistics would indicate, it has declined very markedly in the last thirty-five years.[46]

The struggle of Negroes to gain the right to vote in the South has been a long and tortuous one. The "grandfather clause" was eliminated by the Supreme Court in 1915, but a method even more successful in preventing Negroes from voting was instituted in the 1920's. Primary elections, in which candidates of a single party are selected, originated in this country toward the end of the nineteenth century and became widespread in the first two decades of the twentieth. The inspiration for the white primary came from a decision of the Supreme Court in 1921. Justice McReynolds declared that a primary was not part of an election and thus the federal Corrupt Practices Act which had the purpose of limiting the campaign expenses of senatorial candidates was not applicable to this kind of election.[47] The Texas legislature took the hint and, in 1923, barred Negroes from the polls in any Democratic primary in the state. Since election in a Democratic primary was virtually tantamount to election to office in Texas and in the other southern states, the white primary prevented the Negroes from any meaningful participation at the polls.[48]

By 1932, all of the southern states which had comprised the Confederacy had one or another version of the white primary, though exclusion of Negro voters was not uniformly enforced.[49] In 1927, Texas' white primary law had been invalidated by the Supreme Court as a violation of the Fourteenth Amendment, but the decision turned out to be meaningless. It was the mandatory provision of the state which made the practice of excluding

Negroes from the primaries unconstitutional. Texas promptly
repealed the mandatory law but left the door open for political
parties to restrict their membership as they chose, and the Central Committee of the Democratic party in Texas promptly decided to eliminate Negroes. In 1935, the Supreme Court upheld
this practice, ruling that the restrictions which a political party
required of its members were a matter in which "the state need
have no concern."[50] Thus, the Negroes were exactly where they
were before—in effect, denied a meaningful vote because of their
race. Six years later, in 1941, the Court reversed itself and held
that white primaries were unconstitutional in elections which
involved federal offices.[51] In 1944, the Court went farther and
declared that it was unconstitutional to exclude Negroes or other
minorities from voting in primaries for state and local offices as
well.[52] All subsequent efforts of southern states to regulate the
primaries explicitly on the matter of race have failed.[53]

Intimidation and artful dodges on the part of state and local
officials still keep Negroes from voting in many parts of the
South. In 1961 the Civil Rights Commission estimated that in
approximately a hundred counties in eight southern states Negro citizens were prevented—by outright discrimination or by
fear of physical violence or economic reprisal—from exercising
the right to vote. Some southern states require the passing of
literacy tests; others require that a candidate for the vote be able
to explain to the satisfaction of local electors any section of the
federal or state constitutions. With the past history of discrimination against Negroes in voting, anyone would be justified in
skepticism as to whether white voters were examined with as
much rigor as Negro voters. There is, in fact, much evidence
that the law in many places is nothing more than a device to exclude Negroes from voting.[54] Legislative gerrymandering of Congressional and state districts has frequently kept the votes of
Negroes from being adequately counted. The cities, where the
largest number of Negro voters live, are frequently grossly un-
derrepresented in Congress and in state legislatures. One effect
of the system is to prevent full and meaningful participation of

Negroes in elections. The system of unfair legislative apportionment is itself under attack in the courts at present and the chances seem good that the system may be on its way out.[55] All these obstructions to Negro voting should not obscure the fact that the number of Negro voters in the South is steadily rising.[56]

Up until 1938, the Supreme Court had been just as unwilling to examine into the question of whether segregated educational facilities for Negroes were equal to white facilities. In 1938, Lloyd Gaines, a Negro, was successful in his suit before the Court in his contention that the fact that Missouri did not admit Negroes to its law school and had no law school for Negroes violated his right to equal treatment under the law. The system of evading the constitutional issue by paying tuition grants to schools out of the state which would accept Negroes was thus invalidated.[57] In 1940, a suit was instituted, under the general direction of the NAACP, on the matter of the inequalities between the salaries of white and Negro teachers in the public schools. All of the southern states and several of the border states maintained a dual system and the salaries of white teachers were much higher than those of Negro teachers. The court ruled that these inequalities were unconstitutional. At first, a number of states in the South simply ignored the decision—Maryland was the only state which complied immediately—but gradually other states accepted the law.[58]

From 1938 to 1954, the Court refused to rule on the constitutionality of segregation itself; but clearly, in 1950, it had set a direction in the tenor of its decisions in which it was virtually impossible, at least in higher education, for states to meet the constitutional requirements with segregated facilities. In that year, it ruled that even though Texas had gone to considerable expense to set up a separate law school for Negroes, it was unequal in fact and not merely because its physical facilities were deficient. The fact that Negroes would be excluded from the association among the state's lawyers and officials which the older and well-established white law school could provide made the Negro institution of its very nature unequal to the white school.[59]

Also in 1950, the Court ruled that the practice at the University of Oklahoma in segregating a Negro student—he was required to sit in a chair outside the door of the classroom and also segregated in the library and in the dining hall—was a denial of equal protection which handicapped him in the effective pursuit of his graduate studies. These restrictions, said Chief Justice Vinson, "impair and inhibit his ability to study, to engage in discussion and exchange views with other students, and, in general, to learn his profession." To the argument that the white students would, in any case, refuse to associate with the Negro, the Court replied that even if they did the matter would be irrelevant so far as his right to attend the school was concerned: "There is a vast difference—a constitutional difference—between restrictions imposed by the state which prohibit the intellectual commingling of students, and the refusal of students to commingle where the state presents no such bar."[60]

These decisions led in 1954 to the most famous of all the civil rights decision with regard to education. On May 17 of that year—known as the new emancipation day or "Black Monday" depending on the way one looked at it—the Court ruled that "separate educational facilities are inherently unequal" and that the plaintiffs in the case had been "deprived of the equal protection of the laws guaranteed by the Fourteenth Amendment."[61] Thus, the old *Plessy vs. Ferguson* decision of 1896—with its unrealistic conception of "separate but equal" facilities—was finally laid to rest. On the basis of the 1954 school segregation case, the Court soon afterward banned as unconstitutional all segregation in transportation facilities, on public golf courses, beaches, parks, and playgrounds.[62] Thus, a new era for the Negro citizen began.

There has been, of course, vigorous opposition to the Court's decisions on segregation. Virtually every legal strategy has been tried—massive resistance, tuition payments, the governor's interposition of his own authority, the closing of parks, the governor's standing in the door of the University of Alabama to protest the admission of Negroes, the closing of schools in a particular area, as in Prince Edward County, Virginia. All of these devices, except that of closing local parks and schools, have been overthrown by subsequent court decisions and there is not much chance that the abandonment of facilities for public education and recreation will ultimately succeed.

A sobering note must accompany these victories. Though the southern states have been unable to devise any method which would permit segregation, they have been able by various tactics to retain much *de facto* segregation, particularly in the schools. The number of Negroes in previously all-white schools in the Deep South is very small—probably no more than 0.5 per cent of the Negro school age population in this area.[63] Alabama, the last of the states to yield to integration on the college level, has admitted Negro students to its state university. In colleges and universities, the record has been better than it has been in public schools, but it is far from complete compliance. It is clear that the widespread implementation of the Court's decision is an event still in the future.[64]

In other ways, Negroes have gained in the courts rights which previously were denied them. In the 1930's, the Supreme Court began to bring pressure to bear upon the lower courts in cases in which police brutality was used to obtain confessions and cases in which Negroes were excluded from jury service. In 1935, in the famous Scottsboro case in Alabama in which several Negroes were convicted of rape under allegedly flimsy evidence, the Supreme Court overruled the conviction because Negroes had been systematically excluded from the jury.[65] Obviously, the lower courts wished to have their convictions sustained by the Supreme Court, so Negroes began to be called for jury duty in the South in cases in which the defendant was a Negro and there was a likelihood that he might appeal a conviction from an all-white jury. In 1948, the Court ruled that racially restrictive covenants could not be enforced in equity by state courts against Negro purchasers and, in 1953, that breach of a restrictive covenant by a white covenanter was not legally liable for damages.[66]

It is still legal in about half of the states of the Union—in-

cluding all the southern ones and many of the far western ones—
to forbid members of different races, usually the white and the
Negro, to intermarry.[67] Immigration is still on a quota basis and
the restrictions reflect the racial prejudices of those who formulated the law, since the northern and western European nations
are given much higher quotas than are other nations.[68] American
Indians still suffer many serious handicaps and much remains
to be done to make available to them the advantages of education and a high standard of living which other segments of the
population enjoy.[69] The system of migrant labor in agriculture
makes it impossible for a large number of people, most of whom
are Latin Americans, to protect themselves against economic
exploitation and lack of educational opportunities.[70] Automation
and other readjustments in industry have made unemployment
among unskilled workers rise even when the economy is boom-
ing, and this problem inevitably has implications for those racial
minorities in which the number of unskilled workers is large.[71]
The problems which directly or indirectly involve the racial
issues are still very much with us, and it will require heroic
efforts on our part to solve them.

In the months before this book went to press, questions of
civil rights agitated the whole country. Demonstrations of Negroes and their sympathizers occurred both in the Deep South—
where they are most likely to provoke violent retaliation and
therefore where until recently they have been the most infre-
quent—and in many areas of the North, where it has sometimes
been assumed that minority problems are not serious. In August,
1963, a mass demonstration for civil rights in Washington
brought the nation's attention to the deep dissatisfaction which
Negroes feel about discriminatory laws and practices. On the
other hand, there has been an upsurge of violence by the advocates of white supremacy. In June, 1963, Medgar Evers, an
official of the NAACP in Mississippi, was shot and killed in
Jackson. Also in June, Governor George C. Wallace of Alabama
stood in the door of the University of Alabama in an unsuccessful attempt to prevent the registration of two Negro stu-

dents. Mississippi has been in turmoil since the violence which accompanied the enrolment of the first Negro student at the University of Mississippi in 1962. In September, 1963, came demonstrations in Birmingham which were violently put down. On November 22, the nation was deprived of perhaps the most effective spokesman for civil rights in history with the assassina- • tion of President John F. Kennedy. He died while the civil rights bill which he sponsored was pending in Congress.

The battle against racism is still far from won. As Martin Luther King has put the case for Negroes, "We have come a long, long way, but we still have a long, long way to go."[72] There have been important victories. More and more people real- ize that the old arguments about the superiority or inferiority of this or that race no longer have impressive backing behind them. A cause for hope is that the leaders of the battle against racial in- justice are as dedicated as they have ever been and are, in addi- tion, much more numerous. They include not only skilful spokesmen for specific racial minorities—though these are essen- tial. They also include more and more powerful allies among all Americans, whatever their race. The fusion of all the forces op- posed to racism has meant that the number of people concerned about its injustices has grown large enough so that the nation is increasingly willing to do something about them. Racism, the most serious threat to the idea of equality before the law and to the individual development of one's own capabilities, is now on the defensive as it has never been before. With the proper resolu- tion, it can be changed from a major to a minor problem of our national life.

Notes

CHAPTER I

1. *The Hymns of the Rigveda*, trans. Ralph T. H. Griffiths (Benares, India, 1896), I, 488-90; Adolf Kaegi, *The Rigveda: The Oldest Literature of the Indians* (Boston, 1886), pp. 43-45.

2. See Thomas H. Huxley, "The Methods and Results of Ethnology," *Fortnightly Review*, I (1865), 267.

3. Hutton Webster, *Ancient Civilization* (New York, 1931), p. 16; Gerald Massey, *A Book of the Beginnings* (London, 1881), I, 454.

4. Ezra 10:1-15; Ruth Benedict, *Race: Science and Politics* (New York, 1940), p. 163; Jer. 13:23; A. A. Roback, *A Dictionary of International Slurs (Ethnophaulisms) with a Supplementary Essay on Aspects of Ethnic Prejudice* (Cambridge, Mass., 1944), p. 283.

5. Gen. 9:24; *The Jewish Encyclopedia* (New York, 1925), VI, 186.

6. Ovid, *Metamorphoses*, trans. Rolfe Humphries (Bloomington, Indiana, 1955), pp. 26-40; *Hippocrates, with an English Translation by W. H. S. Jones* (New York, 1923), pp. 111, 115.

7. "Politica," in *The Works of Aristotle Translated into English under the Editorship of W. D. Ross* (Oxford, 1921), X, 1327b 21.

8. Vitruvius Pollio, *The Ten Books on Architecture*, trans. Morris Hicky Morgan (Cambridge, Mass., 1914), p. 173; Dorothy Moulding Brown, *Indian Fireside Tales* (Madison, Wisconsin, 1947), p. 48.

9. A. L. Kroeber, "Caste," *Encyclopedia of the Social Sciences* (New York, 1931), III, 254-57; *Hippocrates . . .*, p. 115; for other sources on the lack of racial prejudice in ancient Greece and Rome, see T. J. Haarhoof, *The Stranger at the Gate: Aspects of Exclusiveness and Cooperation in Ancient Greece and Rome, with Some References to Modern Times* (Oxford, 1948), *passim*; Frank M. Snowden, Jr., "The Negro in Ancient Greece," *American Anthropologist*, L (January-March, 1948), 31-44; Robert Schlaifer, "Greek Theories of Slavery from Homer to Aristotle," *Harvard Studies in Classical Philology*, XLVII (1936), 166-204; William Linn Westermann, *The Slave Systems of Greek and Roman Antiquity*, "Memoirs of the American Philosophical Society," XL (1955), 44.

10. *The Works of the Emperor Julian with an English Translation by Wilmer Cave Wright* (London, 1923), III 176AB, 209DE, III 178A.

11. *Ibid.*, III 143DE, III 116AB, II 292C.

12. Acts 17:26; *The City of God by Saint Augustine*, trans. Marcus Dods (New York, 1950), pp. 530-31; Charles Norris Cochrane, *Christianity and Classical Culture: A Study of Thought and Action from Augustus to Augustine* (Oxford, 1940), pp. 276-77.

13. See Frederick Hertz, *Nationality in History and Politics: A Study of the Psychology and Sociology of National Sentiment and Character* (New York, 1944), p. 57.

14. Hugo Valentin, *Antisemitism Historically and Critically Examined*, trans. A. G. Chater (New York, 1936), p. [27]; Matt. 27:25; Howard Clark Kee and Franklin W. Young, *Understanding the New Testament* (Edgewood Cliffs, N.J., 1957), pp. 172-73. The fourth chapter of Acts is also sometimes cited as proof that the Christians charged the Jews as the principal offenders in the death of Christ. See *The Catholic Encyclopaedia* (New York, 1907-1912), VIII, 402; Cecil Roth, *A Short History of the Jewish People: 1600 B.C.-A.D. 1935* (London, 1936), pp. 143-45, 183.

15. Valentin, *op. cit.*, p. [27].

16. See Joshua Trachtenberg, *The Devil and the Jews: The Medieval Conception of the Jew and Its Relation to Modern Anti-semitism* (New Haven, 1943), p. 42; "The Prioress's Tale," *The Complete Works of Geoffrey Chaucer*, ed. F. N. Robinson (Boston, 1933), p. 195.

17. Quoted in A. Lukyn Williams, *Adversus Judaeos, A Bird's-Eye View of Christian Apologia until the Renaissance* (Cambridge, 1935), p. 387; Emil Weller, *Die ersten deutschen Zeitungen* (Stuttgart, 1872), p. 52; Trachtenberg, *op. cit.*, pp. 50-52.

18. Gonzalo Fernandez de Oviedo, *Historia general y natural de las Indias, Islas y Tierra Firme del Mar Oceano*, ed. José Amador de los Rios (4 vols.; Madrid, 1851-1855), *Primera Parte*, Lib. 2, cap. 6; Lib. 4, cap. 2; quoted in Lewis Hanke, *The Spanish Struggle for Justice in the Conquest of America* (Philadelphia, 1949), p. 11.

19. Ecclus. 34:18; Hanke, *op. cit.*, p. 21.

20. Hanke, *Bartolomé de las Casas: Bookman, Scholar & Propagandist* (Philadelphia, 1952), p. 33.

21. Hanke, *The Spanish Struggle for Justice in the Conquest of America*, pp. 49, 113; Francis Augustus MacNutt, *Bartholomew de Las Casas: His Life, Apostolate, and Writings* (Cleveland, 1909), pp. 208, 212, 232-34, 237-38, 244-45.

22. Hanke, *The Spanish Struggle for Justice in the Conquest of America*, pp. 129-31; MacNutt, *op. cit.*, p. 304.

23. Quoted in A. Wolf, *A History of Science, Technology, and Philosophy in the 16th & 17th Centuries* (New York, 1935), pp. 583 ff.

24. Paracelsus, *Explicatio totius astronomiae* (Geneva, 1658), II, 655, 658; quoted in Don Cameron Allen, *The Legend of Noah; Renaissance Rationalism in Art, Science, and Letters* (Urbana, Illinois, 1949), p. 133; J. Lewis McIntyre, *Giordano Bruno* (London, 1903), pp. 267-68; Lucilio Vanini, *Oeuvres philosophiques de Vanini*, trans. M. X. Rousselet (Paris, 1842), p. 214; *Revue Anthropologique*, XXV (1915), 21.

25. Isaac de la Peyrère, *Men Before Adam. Or a Discourse upon the twelfth & thirteenth, and fourteenth verses of the fifth chapter of the epistle of the Apostle Paul to the Romans. By which are prov'd that the first men were created before Adam* (London, 1656); an account of the life of La Peyrère is found in Jean Pierre Niceron, *Memoires pour servir à l'histoire des hommes illustres dans la Republique des Lettres* (Paris, 1730), XII, 56-84; D. R. McKee, "Isaac de la Peyrère, a Precursor of the Eighteenth Century Critical Deists," *PMLA*, LIX (1944), 464-66.

26. Lynn Thorndike, *A History of Magic and Experimental Science* (New York, 1941), pp. 145-78, also chap. xiv; McKee, *op. cit.*, pp. 458-59.

27. Thorndike, *op. cit.*, V, 33-34.

CHAPTER II

1. *The Original Writings and Correspondence of the Two Richard Hakluyts* (London, 1935), 2nd Ser. lxxvi, II, 245; see Louis B. Wright, *Religion and Empire: The Alliance Between Piety and Commerce in English Expansion 1558-1625* (Chapel Hill, 1943), p. 47.

2. *The Discoverie of the Large and Bewtiful Empire of Guiana by Sir Walter Raleigh*, ed. V. T. Harlow (London, 1928), pp. 143-44; see Lewis Hanke, *Bartolomé de las Casas: Bookman, Scholar & Propagandist* (Philadelphia, 1952), pp. 53-54.

3. Hanke, *op. cit.*, pp. 54-58; *A True and Sincere Declaration of the Purpose and Ends of the Plantation Begun in Virginia* (London, 1610), quoted in Keith Glenn, "Captain John Smith and the Indians," *Virginia Magazine of History and Biography*, LII (October, 1944), 229.

4. Quoted in Ezra Hoyt Byington, "John Eliot, the Puritan Missionary to the Indians," *Papers of the American Society of Church History*, VIII (1897), 115; see Carolyn Thomas Foreman, *Indians Abroad* (Norman, 1943), pp. 23-24.

5. James Alton James, *English Institutions and the American Indian* ("Johns Hopkins University Studies in Historical and Political Science," Twelfth Series [1894]), pp. 510-11.

6. Ezra Hoyt Byington, *The Puritan as a Colonist and Reformer* (Boston, 1899), pp. 207-8, 117.

7. *Ibid.*, p. 126; see also pp. 138-39.

8. Quoted in S. Bannister, *British Colonisation and Coloured Tribes* (London, 1838), pp. 50 ff.

9. Curtis P. Nettels, *The Roots of American Civilization: A History of American Colonial Life* (New York, 1938), p. 220; Daniel Wait Howe, *The Puritan Republic of the Massachusetts Bay in New England* (Indianapolis, 1899), pp. 78-79.

10. "A Narrative of the Captivity and Restauration of Mrs. Mary Rowlandson," in *Narratives of the Indian Wars, 1675-1699*, ed. Charles H. Lincoln (New York, 1913), pp. 119-21.

11. Increase Mather, "*Decennium Luctuosum,* 1699," in *Narratives of the Indian Wars, 1675-1699*, p. 208; Cotton Mather, "A Brief History of the War with the Indians in New-England," in *The History of King Philip's War, by the Rev. Cotton Mather, D.D.*, ed. Samuel G. Drake (Boston, 1862), pp. 208-9.

12. John Cotton, *The Way of Congregational Churches Cleared* (London, 1648), Pt. I, p. 78; quoted in Herbert W. Schneider, *The Puritan Mind* (New York, 1930), p. 39.

13. Quoted in Byington, *The Puritan as a Colonist and Reformer*, p. 144.

14. Increase Mather, "The History of King Philip's War . . . ," pp. 37-40.

15. *Ibid.*, pp. 41-42.

16. William Douglass, *Summary, Historical and Political, of the First Planting, Progressive Improvements, and Present State of the British Settlements in North America* (Boston, 1758), II, 131; Louis B. Wright, *The Cultural Life of the American Colonies: 1607-1763* (New York, 1957), pp. 160-61.

17. Quoted in Hoxie Neale Fairchild, *The Noble Savage: A Study in Romantic Naturalism* (New York, 1928), p. 11.

18. Benjamin Bissell, "The American Indian in English Literature of the Eighteenth Century," *Yale Studies in English*, LXVIII (1925), 4.

19. Fairchild, *op. cit.*, pp. 12-14.

20. See Theodore Parker, *The American Scholar*, ed. George Willis Cooke (Boston, 1907), pp. 224-25; James, *op. cit.*, p. 14.

21. *A Study of History* (New York, 1948), I, 211.

22. *Necessity of Reformation, Epistle Dedicatory*, quoted in Thomas Jefferson Wertenbaker, *The Puritan Oligarchy: The Founding of American Civilization* (New York, 1947), pp. 74-75.

23. Frederick Hertz, *Nationality in History and Politics* (New York, 1944), p. 59; see also Everett V. Stonequist, "Race Mixture and the Mulatto," in Edgar T. Thompson, ed., *Race Relations and the Race Problem* (Durham, 1939), pp. 247-48.

24. *Nationalism in the Soviet Union* (London, 1933), p. 123.

25. Hertz, *op. cit.*, p. 59; quoted in A. Mitchell Hunter, *The Teaching of Calvin* (2d ed. rev.; London, 1950), pp. 158, 159, 159n.

26. John Lawson, *History of Carolina* (London, 1709); quoted in Brewton Berry, *Race Relations: The Interaction of Ethnic and Racial Groups* (Boston, 1951), p. 248.

27. *The Writings of Colonel William Byrd*, ed. John Spencer Bassett (New York, 1901), pp. 99-101.

28. Nettels, *op. cit.*, p. 232.

29. Oscar Handlin, *Race and Nationality in American Life* (New York, 1957), pp. 6-11.

30. See *Ibid.*, p. 13.

31. There is a discussion of these points in Guion G. Johnson, "A History of Racial Ideologies in the United States with Reference to the Negro" (MSS in the New York Public Library, 1943); Guy B. Johnson, "Patterns of Race Conflict," in Edgar T. Thompson, ed., *Race Relations and the Race Problem*, pp. 125-26.

32. William Waller Hening, *The Statutes at Large of Virginia* (Richmond, 1810-1823), I, 146; J. C. Hurd, *The Law of Freedom and Bondage in the United States* (Boston, 1858), I, 229; Johnson, *op. cit.*, p. 9.

33. Sermon, February 19, 1731. *Works*, ed. Alexander Campbell Fraser (Oxford, 1901), IV, 405.

CHAPTER III

1. *"Nouvelle Division de la Terre, par les differentes Especes ou Races d'hommes qui l'habitent, envoyée par un fameux Voyageur à M. l'Abbé de la **** à peu près en ces termes," Journal des Sçavans*, April 24, 1684, pp. 133-40.

2. *Ibid.*, pp. 134-36.

3. *The Scientific Revolution 1500-1800: The Formation of the Modern Scientific Attitude* (Boston, 1954), pp. 167, 275.

4. *Ibid.*, pp. 301-2.

5. Eric Voegelin, "The Growth of the Race Idea," *Journal of Politics*, II (July, 1940), pp. 301-2.

6. Gottfried W. von Leibnitz, *Otium Hanoveranum sive Miscellanes ex ore* . . . (Leipzig, 1718), p. 37; quoted in M. F. Ashley Montagu, *Man's Most Dangerous Myth: The Fallacy of Race* (New York, 1942), p. 19.

7. John C. Greene, "Some Early Speculations on the Origin of Human Races," *American Anthropologist*, LVI (February, 1954), 33.

8. Linnaeus' brief discussion of the races of man is found in his *Systema naturae per regna tria naturae* (Lyons, 1735). A translation from the section on race from the 1789 edition of this work is found in Earl W. Count, ed., *This Is Race: An Anthology Selected from the International Literature on the Races of Man* (New York, 1950), pp. 355-57; see also Linnaeus, *The "Critica Botanica" of Linnaeus (1737)*, trans. Arthur Holt (London, 1938), pp. 196-97.

9. George Louis Leclerc Buffon, *Natural History, General and Particular* . . . , trans. William Smellie (3rd ed.; London, 1791), VIII, 34-35.

10. *Ibid.*, III, 201, 204; see Greene, *op. cit.*, p. 33.

11. Buffon, *op. cit.*, III, 151-53.

12. "An Inaugural Dissertation by John Hunter, M.D., F.R.S.," 1775, included in *The Anthropological Treatises of Johann Friedrich Blumenbach* . . . , trans. and ed. Thomas Bendysshe (London, 1865), p. 372; see entry on John Hunter, *Dictionary of National Biography* (London, 1908-1909), X, 290.

13. *"De Generis Humani Varietate Nativa."* (3rd ed.; Göttingen, 1795), in *The Anthropological Treatises of Johann Friedrich Blumenbach* . . . , pp. viii, 264-65.

14. *Ibid.*, pp. 115-16, 204; see Hippocrates, "Airs, Waters, Places," *Hippocrates with an English Translation by W. H. S. Jones* (New York, 1923), p. 111.

15. Blumenbach, *op. cit.*, pp. 210-11, 221.

16. Quoted by K. F. H. Marx, "Life of Blumenbach," in *The Anthropological Treatises of Johann Friedrich Blumenbach*, pp. 30, 57, 306, 309-10.

17. *Dictionary of American Biography* (New York, 1928), XVII, 344-45.

18. *An Essay on the Causes of the Variety of Complexion and Figure in the Human Species* (rev. ed.; Philadelphia, 1788), pp. 13, 23, 38, 240n.

19. *Ibid.*, pp. 91-93, 93n; Whitfield J. Bell, *Early American Science: Needs and Opportunities for Study* (Williamsburg, Va., 1955), p. 26n.

20. *An Essay on the Causes of the Variety of Complexion and Figure in the Human Species* (2nd ed. rev.; New York, 1810), pp. 83, 92, 95; see William Stanton, *The Leopard's Spots: Scientific Attitudes toward Race in America 1815-59* (Chicago, 1960), pp. 5-6. I am especially indebted in this and the following chapters to this valuable study.

21. "Observations intended to favour a supposition that the black Color (as it is called) of the Negroes is derived from the LEPROSY. Read at a Special Meeting July 14, 1797," American Philosophical Society, *Transactions*, IV (1799), 289-97; quoted in Stanton, *op. cit.*, pp. 6-7.

22. James Boswell, *Boswell's Life of Johnson* . . . (Oxford, 1934-50), III, 201-2.

23. *Notes on Virginia*, in *The Writings of Thomas Jefferson* (Washington, 1903), II, 192-93; Oliver Goldsmith also thought that whites were superior because of their ability to blush; see his *An History of the Earth* (2nd ed.; London, 1778), II, 232.

24. Jefferson, *op. cit.*, II, 194-96.

25. *Ibid.*

26. *Ibid.*, II, 199-201.

27. *The Works of Voltaire: A Contemporary Version with Notes by Tobias Smollett*, rev. and modernized by William F. Fleming (New York, 1901), XXXIX, 223-25.

28. *Ibid.*, 240-41.

29. *Sketches of the History of Man Considerably Enlarged by the Last Additions and Corrections of the Author* (Edinburgh, 1788), I, 12-13.

30. *Ibid.*, I, 25-29.

31. *Ibid.*, I, 40-42.

32. *Ibid.*, I, 75-77.

33. *Ibid.*, I, 78.

34. Charles White, *An Account of the Regular Gradation in Man* . . . (London, 1799), p. iv, [1].

35. *Ibid.*, pp. 42-43, 54-55, 59, 94-95.

36. *Ibid.*, pp. 58-59, 61, 63, 73.

37. *Ibid.*, pp. 65-66, 71, 74, 82.

38. *Ibid.*, p. 34.
39. *Ibid.*, p. 129.
40. *Ibid.*, p. 136.
41. *Ibid.*, pp. xiv, 133, 137-38.
42. *An Essay on the Causes* . . . (rev. ed., 1788), pp. 202-3.
43. *An Essay on the Causes* . . . (2d ed. rev.; New York, 1810), pp. 269-70, 275-77, 277n.
44. *Ibid.*, pp. 275-77.
45. Letter to M. Henri Gregoire, *The Writings of Thomas Jefferson*, XII, 254-55.

CHAPTER IV

1. James Cowles Prichard, *Researches into the Physical History of Man* (4th ed.; London, 1851); John Addington Symonds, "On the Life, Writings and Character of the late James Cowles Prichard, M.D., F.R.S.," in *Miscellanies* . . . (London, 1871), p. 124.
2. Quoted in Symonds, *op. cit.*, pp. 121-22.
3. *The Eastern Origin of the Celtic Nations* . . . (London, 1831); *An Analysis of the Egyptian Mythology* . . . (London, 1819); see article on Prichard in Earl W. Count, ed., *This Is Race: An Anthology Selected from the International Literature on the Races of Man* (New York, 1950), p. 707.
4. See article on Prichard in *Encyclopaedia Britannica*, 11th ed. (1910), XXII, 315.
5. *Lectures on Physiology, Zoology, and the Natural History of Man, Delivered at the Royal College of Surgeons* (London, 1819), pp. 125-26, 365, 475-76.
6. *Ibid.*, pp. 353, 554.
7. See Erik Nordenskiöld, *The History of Biology: A Survey*, trans. Leonard Bucknall Eyre (New York, 1929), p. 343.
8. An account of Morton's battles with his opponents on the subject of the unity or diversity of origin of human races is found in William Stanton, *The Leopard's Spots: Scientific Attitudes toward Race in America 1815-59* (Chicago, 1960), *passim*. For Silliman's opinion, see p. 26.
9. Letter of November 27, 1849, quoted by Henry S. Patterson, "Memoir of the Life and Scientific Labors of Samuel George Morton," in Josiah Clark Nott and George R. Gliddon, *Types of Mankind* . . . (Philadelphia, 1854), p. xlvii n.
10. "Additional Observations on Hybridity in Animals and on Some Collateral Subjects, Being a Reply to the Objections of the Rev. John Bachman, D.D.," *Charleston Medical Journal and Review*, V (November, 1850), 758; *Crania Americana; or, A Comparative View of the Skulls of Various Aboriginal Nations of North and South America, to Which is Prefixed an Essay on the Varieties of the Human Species* (Philadelphia, 1839), pp. 5-6.
11. Louis Agassiz, "Sketch of the Natural Provinces of the Animal World and Their Relation to the Different Types of Man," in Nott and Gliddon, *op. cit.*, pp. lviii-lxxvi.
12. Quoted in J. C. Hall, "An Analytical Synopsis of the Natural History of Man," introduction to Charles Pickering, *The Races of Man; and Their Geographical Distribution* (London, 1851), p. xxxiv; see Stanton, *op. cit.*, p. 103.
13. *The Quadrupeds of North America* (New York, 1851-54); see Stanton, *op. cit.*, pp. 123-25.
14. "Reply to the Letter of Samuel George Morton . . . ," *Charleston Medical Journal and Review*, V (1850), 274.

15. *The Doctrine of the Unity of the Human Race Examined on the Principles of Science* (Charleston, S.C., 1850), p. 116.

16. "An Examination of Prof. Agassiz's Sketch of the Natural Provinces of the Animal World, and Their Relation to the Different Types of Man, with a Tableau Accompanying the Sketch," *Charleston Medical Journal*, X (1855), 482-534; see Stanton, *op. cit.*, pp. 171-72.

17. *The Doctrine of the Unity of the Human Race Examined on the Principles of Science*, pp. 291-92.

18. *Ibid.*, p. 212; "A Reply to the Letter of Samuel George Morton, M.D., on the Question of Hybridity in Animals Considered in Reference to the Unity of the Human Species," *Charleston Medical Journal and Review*, V (July, 1850), 507; Morton, "Additional Observations on Hybridity in Animals and on Some Collateral Subjects, Being a Reply to the Objections of the Rev. John Bachman, D.D.," *Charleston Medical Journal and Review*, V (November, 1850), 759; see Stanton, *op. cit.*, pp. 143-44.

19. Stanton, *op. cit.*, pp. 68, 80-81.

20. Quoted in *ibid.*, p. 143.

21. *Ibid.*, pp. 162-63.

22. Nott and Gliddon, *op. cit.*, pp. 405, 457-59, 461.

23. See Benjamin Robert Haydon, *Life, Letters, and Table Talk*, ed. Richard H. Stoddard (New York, 1876), pp. 292-93.

24. *Richmond Enquirer*, July 6, 1854, quoted in Stanton, *op. cit.*, p. 194; George Fitzhugh, *Sociology for the South, or the Failure of Free Society* (Richmond, Va., 1854), p. 95.

25. Theodor Waitz, *Introduction to Anthropology*, ed. J. Frederick Collinwood (London, 1863), *passim*; [Asa Gray], "Darwin on the Origin of Species," *Atlantic Monthly*, VI (1860), 109-16, 229-39, 406-25; Nott, quoted in Stanley, *op. cit.*, p. 183; see also p. 189.

26. Charles Darwin, *The Descent of Man* (New York, 1874), p. 203.

27. [Robert Chambers], *Vestiges of the Natural History of Creation* (London, 1844), pp. 226-27.

28. Darwin, *The Descent of Man*, chaps. viii, xix, and xx.

29. *Ibid.*, p. 167.

30. The search has been described in Jean Finot, *Race Prejudice*, trans. Florence Wade-Evans (London, 1906); Ruth Benedict, *Race: Science and Politics* (rev. ed.; New York, 1943); Jacques Barzun, *Race: A Study in Modern Superstition* (New York, 1937).

31. Pallas, *Act. Academy St. Petersburg, 1780*, part ii, p. 69; the evidence against a correlation between climate and race is summed up in Dominique Alexandre Godron, *De l'Espèce et des Races dans les Etres Organisés et Specialement de l'Unité de l'Espèce Humaine* (Paris, 1859), II, 246 ff.; Benedict, pp. 37-38.

32. Barzun, *op. cit.*, pp. 52-53; Thomas Kenneth Penniman, *A Hundred Years of Anthropology. With Contributions by Beatrice Blackwood and J. S. Weiner* (2d ed. rev., London, 1952), p. 56; *The Anthropological Treatises of Johann Friedrich Blumenbach*, trans. and ed. by Thomas Bendysshe (London, 1865), p. 236.

33. Quoted in Charles Hamilton Smith, *The Natural History of the Human Species: Its Typical Forms, Primeval Distribution, Fileations and Migrations* (Boston, 1851), pp. 16-18; *Congressional Globe*, 40th Congress, 2nd Session, pp. 266-67.

34. See article on "Physiognomy," *Encyclopaedia Britannica*, 1957 ed., XVII, 886-87; *The Life and Letters of Charles Darwin* (New York, 1899), I, 101.

35. See John D. Davies, *Phrenology, Fad and Science: A 19th-Century American*

Crusade (New Haven, 1955), *passim;* for the paragraphs on phrenology which follow, I am especially indebted to this excellent study.

36. Merle Curti, *The Growth of American Thought* (New York, 1943), p. 341.

37. *American Journal of Science,* XXIII (1833), 356.

38. Davies, *op. cit.,* p. 16; Mark Twain, *The Adventures of Huckleberry Finn* (New York, 1948), p. 179.

39. Davies, *op. cit.,* pp. 145-46.

40. Morton, "On the Size of the Brain in Various Races and Families of Man," in Nott and Gliddon, *op. cit.,* pp. 301-2; Morton, *Crania Americana,* p. 262; Morton, "On the Origin of the Human Species," in Nott and Gliddon, *op. cit.,* p. 310; see table in Nott and Gliddon, *op. cit.,* pp. 260-61.

41. "On the Size of the Brain in Various Races and Families of Man," in Nott and Gliddon, *op. cit.,* pp. 309-10.

42. Quoted in Nott and Gliddon, *op. cit.,* p. 453.

43. Bachman, *The Doctrine of the Unity of the Human Race* . . . , p. 229; Nott and Gliddon, *op. cit.,* pp. 453, 464.

44. See Charles S. Johnson and Horace M. Bond, "The Investigation of Racial Differences Prior to 1910," *Journal of Negro Education,* III (July, 1934), 329-30; John H. Van Evrie, *White Supremacy and Negro Subordination* (New York, 1868), pp. 93-94.

45. See Penniman, *op. cit.,* p. 42; Barzun, *op. cit.,* pp. 57-58.

46. Barzun, *op. cit.,* p. 161; Ernest A. Hooton, *Up from the Ape* (New York, 1931), p. 400.

47. A. H. Keane, article on "Ethnology," *Chambers' Encyclopedia* (Philadelphia, 1889), IV, 440-41; Ranke, quoted in Marcus Hirschfeld, *Racism,* trans. and ed. by Eden and Cedar Paul (London, 1938), pp. 132-33; Broca, *Memoires d'Anthropologie* (Paris, 1871-80), IV, 356; quoted in Barzun, *op. cit.,* p. 169.

48. F. Tiedemann, "On the Brain of the Negro," *Royal Philosophical Transactions* (1838), pp. 520-24; Nott and Gliddon, *op. cit.,* pp. 453-54.

49. Darwin, *The Descent of Man,* p. 247; Charles S. Johnson and Horace M. Bond, *op. cit.,* p. 331; Robert Bennett Bean, "Some Racial Peculiarities of the Negro Brain," *American Journal of Anatomy,* V (1906), 353-432; Franklin P. Mall, "On Several Anatomical Characters of the Human Brain," *American Journal of Anatomy,* IX (1909), 1-32.

50. Raymond Pearl, "Biological Factors in Negro Mortality," *Human Biology,* I (1929), 229-49; Montagu, *op. cit.,* p. 63; Benedict, *op. cit.,* pp. 102-3; see Dr. Carl F. Schmidt's article on the brain in *Encyclopaedia Britannica,* 1957 ed., IV, 14.

51. Fiske, *The Destiny of Man Viewed in the Light of his Origin* (Boston, 1884), p. 49; *Iconographic Encyclopaedia* (Philadelphia, 1886), I, 20; Bean, *The Races of Man: Differentiation and Dispersal of Man* (New York, 1935), pp. 94-95.

52. Blumenbach, *op. cit.,* p. 305; Peter A. Browne, *The Classification of Mankind, by the Hair and Wool of their Heads, with an Answer to Dr. Prichard's Assertion, that "The Covering of the Head of the Negro is Hair, . . . and Not Wool"* . . . (Philadelphia, 1850), pp. 1, 8, 20; quoted in Stanton, *op. cit.,* pp. 151-52; William Van Amringe, *An Investigation of the Theories of the Natural History of Man* (New York, 1848), p. 397.

53. Prichard, *op. cit.,* I, 88-97; A. H. Keane, *Chambers' Encyclopedia* (Philadelphia, 1889), I, 45.

54. Murray, *Transactions of the Royal Society of Edinburgh* (1861), p. 567; Darwin, *The Descent of Man,* I, 211.

55. *Systems of Consanguinity and Affinity of the Human Family* (Washington, 1871), p. 508.

56. Finot, *op. cit.*, p. 54.

57. Topinard quoted in William Z. Ripley, *The Races of Europe* (New York, 1899), pp. 111-12; Powell quoted in A. H. Keane, *Chambers' Encyclopedia*, IV, 439.

CHAPTER V

1. Henri, Comte de Boulainvilliers, *Essais sur la Noblesse de France contenans une dissertation son origene et abissement* (Amsterdam, 1732), *passim*; see Jacques Barzun, *The French Race: Theories of Its Origins and Their Social and Political Implications Prior to the Revolution* (New York, 1932), pp. 137 ff.; see also Ruth Benedict, *Race: Science and Politics* (New York, 1940), pp. 174-76.

2. See H. Mattingly, introduction to *Tacitus on Britain and Germany: A New Translation of the "Agricola" and the "Germania"* . . . (London, 1948), p. 9; quoted in T. P. Peardon, *The Transition in English Historical Writing, 1760-1830* (New York, 1933), p. 104; see also p. 20.

3. David Hume, *The History of England* (London, 1754-62), I, 229; Peardon, *op. cit.*, p. 30.

4. *An Enquiry into the Foundation of the English Constitution; or, An Historical Essay upon the Anglo-Saxon Government both in Germany and England* (London, 1745), pp. 11-13.

5. See Peardon, *op. cit.*, p. 115n; Sharon Turner, *The History of the Anglo-Saxons, from Their First Appearance above the Elbe, to the Death of Egbert* (London, 1799), pp. 71-72; see Peardon, *op. cit.*, pp. 218-23.

6. See Barzun, *op. cit.*, p. 204; quoted in Charles Morgan, *The Liberty of Thought and the Separation of Powers, A Modern Problem Considered in the Context of Montesquieu* (London, 1948), p. 14; see F. T. H. Fletcher, *Montesquieu and English Politics 1750-1800* (London, 1939), *passim*.

7. Hume, *op. cit.*, I, 201-2.

8. See Paul Merrill Spurlin, *Montesquieu in America: 1760-1801* (Baton Rouge, 1940), p. 29n.

9. *The Rise and Progress of the English Commonwealth* (London, 1832), I, 4.

10. *The Saxons in England: A History of the English Commonwealth till the Period of the Norman Conquest* (London, 1849), I, vi; see G. P. Gooch, *History and Historians in the Nineteenth Century* (New York, 1952), p. 269.

11. *History of the United States from the Discovery of the American Continent* (Boston, 1860), VII, 93; VIII, 271; *The History of the Constitution of the United States* (New York, 1882), II, 284; Michael Kraus, *A History of American History* (New York, 1937), p. 225.

12. *The Rise of the Dutch Republic, A History* (New York, 1855), I, v-vi; see John Mildmay, ed., *John Lothrop Motley and His Family* (New York, 1910), p. 42.

13. Motley, *The Rise of the Dutch Republic*, I, 4, 6, 9, 17.

14. *Ibid.*, I, 7, 17.

15. *Ibid.*, II, 143.

16. *History of the Conquest of Mexico and History of the Conquest of Peru* (Modern Library, New York, n.d.), p. 829; *William Hickling Prescott: Representative Selections with Introduction, Bibliography, and Notes*, eds. William Charvat and Michael Kraus (New York, 1943), pp. 70-71.

17. *Unpublished Letters to Gayangos in the Library of the Hispanic Society of America*, ed. Clara Louisa Penney (New York, 1927), p. 82; *William Hickling Prescott: Representative Selections* . . . , p. cxii.

18. *William Hickling Prescott: Representative Selections* . . . , pp. 79-80.
19. *The Correspondence of William Hickling Prescott: 1833-1847*, ed. Roger Wolcott (Boston, 1925), pp. 177, 414; *Unpublished Letters to Gayangos* . . . , p. 64; *The Conquest of Mexico*, Book VI, chap. viii; *William Hickling Prescott: Representative Selections* . . . , pp. 74, 79.
20. *The Correspondence of William Hickling Prescott*, pp. 3, 501.
21. See Frank Freidel, *Francis Lieber: Nineteenth-Century Liberal* (Baton Rouge, 1947), p. 235.
22. *On Civil Liberty and Government* (Philadelphia, 1859), pp. 21, 295; see Bernard Edward Brown, *American Conservatives: The Political Thought of Francis Lieber and John W. Burgess* (New York, 1951), pp. 47-48.
23. *The Stranger in America* . . . (Philadelphia, 1835), pp. 188-210; Frank Freidel, "Francis Lieber, Charles Sumner, and Slavery," *Journal of Southern History*, IX (1943), 75-93; Freidel, *Francis Lieber: Nineteenth-Century Liberal*, p. 235; Brown, *op. cit.*, pp. 47-48.
24. *Francis Parkman: Representative Selections*, ed. William L. Schramm (New York, 1938), pp. 380-82.
25. *The Races of Men: A Fragment* (Philadelphia, 1850), p. [7].
26. *Ibid.* pp. 24, 177.
27. *Ibid.*, pp. 26-27, 216-20.
28. *Ibid.*, pp. 41, 89-90, 216, 253.
29. George Templeton Strong, *Diary*, eds. Allan Nevins and Milton H. Thomas (New York, 1952), II, 348; Carl Wittke, *The Irish in America* (Baton Rouge, 1956), p. 43; Ray Allen Billington, *The Protestant Crusade: 1800-1860* (New York, 1938), *passim*.
30. *English Traits* (Boston, 1903), pp. 46-48.
31. William Stubbs, *Lectures on Early English History*, ed. Arthur Hassall (New York, 1906), pp. 3-4; Thomas Babington Macaulay, *The History of England from the Accession of James II* (Philadelphia, [1887]), p. 22; Knox, *Races of Man* . . . , pp. 45, 128; Edward A. Freeman, *Old-English History* (London, 1881), pp. 28-29; Freeman, *Comparative Politics* . . . (London, 1873), p. 298; Freeman, *The Origin of the English Nation* (New York, 1879); Freeman, *Lectures to American Audiences* . . . (Philadelphia, 1882), p. 85.
32. "Race and Language," *Historical Essays* (3rd Ser., 2nd ed.; New York, 1892), p. 191.
33. *Seventeen Lectures on the Study of Medieval and Modern History and Kindred Subjects* . . . (London, 1887), p. 96; quoted in Gooch, *op. cit.*, p. 321; *Letters of William Stubbs, Bishop of Oxford, 1825-1901*, ed. William Holden Hutton (London, 1904), pp. 185-86.
34. For examples of Freeman's race prejudices, see W. R. W. Stephens, *The Life and Letters of Edward A. Freeman* (New York, 1895), II, 8, 234, 236-37, 254, 428; Green, review of Freeman's *Norman Conquest*, see *Saturday Review*, XXVIII (Sept. 5, 1869), 322; Green, *Short History of the English People* (London, 1875), pp. 27, 30; see John M. Robertson, *The Saxon and The Celt* (London, 1897), pp. 223-24; see Frederic E. Faverty, *Matthew Arnold: The Ethnologist* (Evanston, Ill., 1951), p. 20.
35. Letter to *Nation*, XI (Sept. 22, 1870), 192.
36. *A Short History of the Roman People* (Boston, 1890), pp. 317-18; *The Life of Agricola and Germany by P. Cornelius Tacitus*, ed. William Francis Allen (Boston, 1882).
37. "The Place of the Northwest in General History," *Papers of the American Historical Association*, III (1889), 340-42.

38. *Ibid.*

39. *The Young Henry Adams* (Cambridge, Mass., 1948), p. 256.

40. *Letters of Henry Adams, 1858-1891,* ed. Worthington Chauncey Ford (New York, 1930), I, 237; "The Anglo-Saxon Courts of Law," in *Essays in Anglo-Saxon Law* (Boston, 1876), *passim.*

41. "The Anglo-Saxon Courts of Law," p. 1; quoted in Samuels, *op. cit.,* p. 257.

42. *Letters of Henry Adams,* 1858-891, I, 236; *North American Review,* CXIV (January, 1872), 193; *North American Review,* CXVIII (January, 1874), 176-77; quoted in Samuels, pp. 247-48; see Edward N. Saveth, *American Historians and European Immigrants: 1875-1925* (New York, 1948), pp. 13-121. This excellent study has been most useful to me.

43. "The Anglo-Saxon Courts of Law," pp. 1, 26.

44. *Letters of Henry Adams, 1892-1918,* ed. Worthington Chauncey Ford (Boston, 1938), II, 333.

45. *Ibid.,* II, 80.

46. See the brief article in *Herbert Baxter Adams, Tributes of Friends, with a Bibliography of the Department of History, Politics and Economics, 1876-1901* (Baltimore, 1902), p. 46.

47. In the foregoing tributes, the emphasis is usually on the kindly personal qualities of Herbert Baxter Adams and his willingness to encourage his students.

48. Herbert Baxter Adams, "The Germanic Origin of New England Towns" ("Johns Hopkins University Studies in Historical and Political Science," Vol. I [1883]), Section 2, pp. 5-38; "Saxon Tithingmen in America," *Ibid.,* Section 4, pp. 1-23.

49. "Saxon Tithingmen in America," pp. 10-11.

50. H. B. Adams himself spent a great deal of time tracing his own ancestors.

51. *Greater Greece and Greater Britain and George Washington: The Expander of England. Two Lectures with an Appendix* (London, 1886), pp. 88, 100; *Lectures to American Audiences . . . ,* p. 17.

52. *Lectures to American Audiences . . . ,* p. 200; *Some Impressions of the United States* (London, 1883), pp. 137-38.

53. *Greater Greece and Greater Britain . . . ,* p. 90; *The Life and Letters of Edward A. Freeman,* II, 234-42.

54. Albert Bushnell Hart, "Methods of Teaching American History," in *Methods of Teaching History,* ed. G. Stanley Hall (2d ed.; Boston, 1902), p. 3; Saveth, *op. cit.,* p. 430.

55. "Germany, Great Britain, and the United States," *Political Science Quarterly,* XIX (March, 1904), 2; *Germany and the United States: An Address Delivered before the Germanistic Society of America, January 24, 1908* (New York, 1909), p. 8.

56. *Political Science and Comparative Constitutional Law* (Boston, 1890), I, 33, 37-38; *Sanctity of the Law* (New York, 1928), p. 231; "The Ideal of the American Commonwealth," *Political Science Quarterly,* X (September, 1895), 407, 419-20; "Letters of Sanford B. Dole and John W. Burgess," *Pacific Historical Review,* V (1938), 74.

57. *Political Science and Comparative Constitutional Law,* I, 45-46.

58. *Reminiscences of an American Scholar: The Beginnings of Columbia University* (New York, 1934), pp. 242, 397; Herbert Baxter Adams, *The Study of History in American Colleges and Universities* (Bureau of Education, Circular of Information No. 2 [Washington, D.C.: Government Printing Office, 1887]), p. 75; Burgess, *The Causes of the European Conflict* (Chicago: The Germanistic Society of Chicago, 1914), p. 2.

59. Burgess, "Germany, Great Britain, and the United States," p. 12; *Germany and the United States* . . . , p. 5; Albert Weinberg, *Manifest Destiny* (Baltimore, 1935), pp. 369, 429; Henry F. Pringle, *Theodore Roosevelt: A Biography* (New York, 1931), pp. 577 ff.

60. Quoted in Brown, *American Conservatives* . . . , p. 131; "John W. Burgess," *New England Historical and Genealogical Register*, LXXV (July, 1931), 331.

61. "The Anglo-Saxon Land Law," in Henry Adams, ed., *Essays in Anglo-Saxon Law*, p. 54.

62. *Studies in History* (Boston and New York, 1884), pp. 113, 131, 185; see Saveth, *op. cit.*, pp. 53-54.

63. "Certain Accepted Heroes and Other Essays," in *Essays in Literature and Politics* (New York, 1897), p. 200; *Congressional Record*, 54th Congress, 1st Session, p. 2818.

64. Lodge, *Early Memories* (New York, 1913), p. 18; *A Short History of the English Colonies in America* (rev. ed.; New York, 1902), pp. 228, 245, 262.

65. John Fiske, *American Political Ideas Viewed from the Standpoint of Universal History* (New York, 1885), p. 50; James K. Hosmer, *A Short History of Anglo-Saxon Freedom: The Polity of the English Speaking Race* (New York, 1890), *passim*.

66. See chaps. xii and xiii of this book.

67. Edward Channing, "The Genesis of the Massachusetts Town, and the Development of Town-Meeting Government," *Proceedings of the Massachusetts Historical Society*, 2nd Ser., VII (1891-92), 250.

68. Edward Channing and Albert Bushnell Hart, *Guide to the Study of American History* (Boston, 1896), pp. 1-4.

69. Quoted in Worthington Chauncey Ford, article on Charles Francis Adams, *Dictionary of American Biography* (New York, 1928), I, 51; Saveth, *op. cit.*, pp. 29-30.

70. Herbert Levi Osgood, "Scientific Anarchism," *Political Science Quarterly*, IV (March, 1889), 30-31; *The American Colonies in the Seventeenth Century* (New York, 1904), pp. xxv-xxvi.

71. Frederick Jackson Turner, "The Significance of the Frontier in American History," *Annual Report of the American Historical Association for the Year 1893* (Washington, 1894), p. 199.

72. Charles A. Beard, "The Teutonic Origins of Representative Government," *American Political Science Review*, XXVI (February, 1932), 28-44; William Archibald Dunning, *A History of Political Theories Ancient and Mediaeval* (New York, 1902), p. xvi.

73. *The American as He Is* (New York, 1908), p. xvi.

CHAPTER VI

1. See article on "Aryans," *Encyclopaedia Britannica*, 11th ed. (1910), IV, 240-41; Arthur John Arberry, *Asiatic Jones: The Life and Influences of Sir William Jones* . . . (New York, [1946]), *passim*.

2. Isaac Taylor, *The Origin of the Aryans* . . . (New York, 1890), pp. 6-7, 131-32.

3. Quoted in Jacques Barzun, *Race: A Study in Modern Superstition* (New York, 1937), p. 135.

4. *Lectures on the Science of Language*, 1st Ser. (London, 1861), pp. 211-12; *Auld Lang Syne* (New York, 1899), p. 192.

5. *The Races of the Old World, a Manual of Ethnology* (London, 1863), *passim*.

6. See Frank H. Hankins, *The Racial Basis of Civilization: A Critique of the Nordic Doctrine* (New York, 1926), pp. 15-20.

7. Müller, *Biographies of Words and the Home of the Aryas* (London, 1888), pp. 120-21; Ripley, *The Races of Europe: A Sociological Study* (New York, 1899), p. 103n.

8. *An Essay Towards Facilitating Instruction in the Anglo-Saxon and Modern Dialects of the English Language for the Use of the University of Virginia* (New York, 1851), p. 4; *The Commonplace Book,* annotated by Gilbert Chinard ("The Johns Hopkins Studies in Romance Literatures and Languages" [Baltimore, 1926]), II, 212; Letter of June 5, 1824, Jefferson, *Writings,* eds. Andrew A. Lipscomb and Albert Bergh (Washington, 1903-6), XVI, 42-44. I am indebted for Jefferson's ideas on race to D. F. Tingley's excellent study, "The Rise of Racialistic Thinking in the Nineteenth Century" (Master's thesis, University of Illinois, 1952), pp. 80-83.

9. *Writings,* ed. Lipscomb and Bergh, XVI, 43-44; *Writings,* ed. Paul Leicester Ford (New York, 1892-99), VII, 415-16.

10. *An Essay Towards Facilitating Instruction . . . ,* pp. 20-24; see John B. Henneman, "Two Pioneers in the Historical Study of English—Thomas Jefferson and Louis F. Klipstein: A Contribution to the Study of English in America," *PMLA,* VIII (1893), xliii-xlix; Morgan Callaway, Jr., "The Historic Study of the Mother-Tongue in the United States: A Survey of the Past ("University of Texas Studies in English," No. 5 [Austin, 1925]), pp. 7-8; Philip A. Bruce, *History of the University of Virginia, 1819-1919: The Lengthened Shadow of One Man* (2 vols.; New York, 1920), II, 161.

11. Callaway, *op. cit.,* pp. 17-18; Francis A. March, "Recollections of Language Teaching," *PMLA,* VIII (1893), xix-xx; March, "The Study of Anglo-Saxon," *Report of the [U.S.] Commissioner for the Year 1876* (Washington, [1877]), p. 479.

12. Howard Mumford Jones has traced the history of the way race theory was utilized in the teaching of the Anglo-Saxon language; see his *Ideas in America* (Cambridge, Mass., 1944), pp. 132-236, and his *The Theory of American Literature* (Ithaca, New York, 1948), pp. 78-117; Furness, "English in the High School," *Modern Language Notes,* I (November, 1886), 109.

13. Garnett, "The Position of Old English in a General Education," *Academy,* V (March, 1890), 120-22; White, "Claims for English as a Study," *Education,* XII (January, 1892), 278.

14. Callaway, "The Present-Day Attitude Toward the Historic Study of the Mother-Tongue" ("University of Texas Studies in English," No. 5 [Austin, 1925]), p. 52.

15. March, "Recollections of Language Teaching," p. xxi; Chadwick, *The Study of Anglo-Saxon* (Cambridge, England, 1941), pp. 55-56.

16. Child, quoted in March, "The Study of Anglo-Saxon," p. 479n; Cook, *The Higher Study of English* (New York, 1906), pp. 39-41.

17. *Ibid.,* pp. 114-15.

18. "On the Teaching of English," *Atlantic Monthly,* LXXXI (April, 1898), 107.

19. Lanier, "The Proper Basis of English Culture," *Atlantic Monthly,* LXXXII (August, 1898), 166; George R. Carpenter, Franklin T. Baker, and Fred N. Scott, *The Teaching of English in the Elementary and the Secondary School* (2d ed.; New York, 1904), pp. 215-26.

20. "Anglo-Saxon in the High School," *Academy,* V (April, 1890), 165-66.

21. (New York, 1898), pp. 2-3, 4, 6.

22. Pattee, quoted in Howard Mumford Jones, *The Theory of American Literature,* p. 100; Wendell, letter to H. M. Kallen, October 11, 1919, *Barrett Wendell and*

His Letters, ed. M. A. DeWolfe Howe (Boston, 1924), p. 319; Wendell, *A Literary History of America* (New York, 1900), p. 141.

23. *A Literary History of America,* pp. 28, 293; *Stelligeri and Other Essays Concerning America* (New York, 1893), p. 126.

24. *A Literary History of America,* p. 28.

25. *Ibid.,* pp. 4, 64.

26. Letter to F. J. Stimson, December 18, 1904, *Barrett Wendell and His Letters,* p. 162; *A Literary History of America,* p. 502.

27. (New York, 1886), I, viii, 16.

28. *Ibid.,* I, 1, 36-37, 62.

29. *Ibid.,* I, 46, 22.

30. B. J. Whiting, *et al.,* eds., *The College Survey of English Literature* (New York, 1945), I, 5-6.

31. George B. Woods, *et al.,* eds., *The Literature of England: An Anthology and a History* (4th ed.; Chicago, 1958), I, 20, II, 2.

32. "Teaching American Literature in American Colleges," *American Mercury,* XIII (March, 1928), 328-29.

33. Macy (New York, 1913), p. 3; Jones, *The Theory of American Literature,* p. 79.

34. *Prejudices, Fourth Series* (New York, 1924), p. 27.

35. *Prejudices, Second Series* (New York, 1922), pp. 143-50.

36. *Ibid.,* p. 71; *A Book of Prefaces* (New York, 1927), p. 213; *Prejudices, Fourth Series,* pp. 17-40.

37. (New York, 1927, 1930).

CHAPTER VII

1. "The Growth of the Race Idea," *Journal of Politics,* II (1940), 314.

2. See *Revolution and Counter Revolution,* ed. Eleanor Marx Eveling (Chicago, 1907), pp. 91, 137-38; M. M. Bober, *Karl Marx's Interpretation of History* (Cambridge, 1927), pp. 68-69.

3. *First Principles* (4th ed.; New York, 1902), p. 537; see Don Martindale, *The Nature and Types of Sociological Theory* (Boston, 1960), pp. 66-67; *Encyclopedia Americana,* 1960 ed., XXV, 387.

4. *Ibid.*

5. See C. E. M. Joad, "Herbert Spencer," *Encyclopedia of the Social Sciences* (New York, 1930), XIV, 295.

6. Letter to J. A. Skilton, January 10, 1895. *Life and Letters of Herbert Spencer,* ed. David Duncan (New York, 1908), II, 77.

7. This is a persistent theme of Spencer's, but it is developed most comprehensively in his *The Man Versus the State* (New York, 1884); see also *Life and Letters of Herbert Spencer,* II, 6-7.

8. *First Principles,* p. 511; *Social Statics, Abridged and Revised; Together with The Man Versus the State* (New York, 1893), pp. 260-61; *Encyclopedia Americana,* 1960 ed., XXV, 387.

9. See his letter to Auberon Herbert, June 16, 1890, *Life and Letters of Herbert Spencer,* I, 402.

10. *Principles of Sociology* (New York, 1880-96), I, Part 2, 685.

11. "The Comparative Psychology of Man, Read Before the Anthropological Institute, June 22, 1875," in *Essays: Scientific, Political, and Speculative* (3rd ed., 3 vols.; London, 1878), I, 426-27.

12. *Ibid.*, p. 427.

13. *Ibid.*, pp. 425-26.

14. Letter to E. Cazelles, May 3, 1871, *Life and Letters of Herbert Spencer,* I, 204.

15. See Edward Livingston Youmans, ed., *Herbert Spencer on the Americans and the Americans on Herbert Spencer* (New York, 1883), pp. 19-20.

16. Letter to Kentaro Kaneko, August 26, 1892, *Life and Letters of Herbert Spencer,* II, 16-17.

17. See J. Arthur Thomson, *Herbert Spencer* (New York, 1906), pp. 169, 178, 205; *Life and Letters of Herbert Spencer,* II, 47; J. Rumney, *Herbert Spencer's Sociology* (London, 1934), pp. 6-7.

18. *Principles of Sociology,* II, Part 3, 584-85; for other examples of Spencer's anti-imperialism, see *Life and Letters of Herbert Spencer,* I, 380-81; II, 121, 135-36, 190.

19. See Ferdinand Canning Scott Schiller, "Herbert Spencer," *Encyclopaedia Britannica,* 11th ed. (1910), XXV, 637; Osborn, preface to Madison Grant, *The Passing of the Great Race* (New York, 1918), p. vii.

20. Charles H. Cooley, "Reflections upon the Sociology of . . . Herbert Spencer," *Sociological Theory and Social Research* (New York, 1930), pp. 263-89.

21. See Richard Hofstadter, *Social Darwinism in American Thought: 1860-1915* (Philadelphia, 1945), pp. 34-35.

22. *The Challenge of Facts and Other Essays* (New York, 1914), p. 55; see also pp. 27-28; *The Forgotten Man and Other Essays,* ed. Albert Galloway Keller (New Haven, 1919), p. 475; *Earth-Hunger and Other Essays,* ed. Albert Galloway Keller (New Haven, 1913), p. 215.

23. Quoted in Harris E. Starr, *William Graham Sumner* (New York, 1925), pp. 62-63, 433; Sumner, *The Challenge of Facts and Other Essays,* pp. 302-3.

24. *Life and Confessions of a Psychologist* (New York, 1923), pp. 436, 438.

25. *Adolescence* (New York, 1904), II, chap. xviii, esp. pp. 647, 651, 698-700, 714, 716-18, 748.

26. *Ibid.*, pp. 698-700; "How Far Are the Principles of Education along Indigenous Lines Applicable to American Indians?" *Pedagogical Seminary,* XV (September, 1908), 365-69.

27. Edwin C. Boring, "The Influence of Evolutionary Theory upon American Psychological Thought," in *Evolutionary Thought in America,* ed. Stow Persons (New Haven, 1950), p. 270.

28. *Hereditary Genius: An Inquiry into Its Laws and Consequences* (rev. ed.; New York, 1891), pp. 24, 38, 39, 41.

29. *Ibid.*, pp. 338-39, 346.

30. *Ibid.*, pp. 4, 357-59.

31. *The Jukes: A Study in Crime, Pauperism, Disease, and Heredity* (4th ed.; New York, 1910).

32. James M. Baldwin, *Mental Development in the Child and in the Race* (New York, 1895), chap. i; Boring, *op. cit.*, pp. 278-79.

33. *Hereditary Genius* . . . , pp. 352, 357.

34. L. Sears, "The Study of Anglo-Saxon," *57th Annual Meeting of the American Institute of Instruction* (Boston, 1887), pp. 76, 79.

35. *Commonwealth or Empire: A Bystander's View of the Question* (New York, 1902), p. 14.

36. *The Social Unrest: Studies in Labor and Socialist Movements* (New York, 1903), p. 234.

37. *Early Memories* (New York, 1913), p. 3.

38. *The Heredity of Richard Roe* (Boston, 1911), p. 116.

39. *Democracy and Empire, with Studies of their Psychological, Economic, and Moral Foundations* (New York, 1900), p. 84.

40. "Pity" (with F. H. Sanders), *American Journal of Psychology*, XI (July, 1900), 534-91; *Educational Problems* (New York, 1911), II, 73, 77-79, 148, 185-86; *Pedagogical Seminary*, XXX (September, 1923), 259.

41. *The Course of American Democratic Thought in Intellectual History Since 1815* (New York, 1940), p. 204.

42. *Glimpses of the Cosmos* (New York, 1913-18), II, 352; VI, 312; *Outlines of Sociology* (New York, 1898), pp. 92-94.

43. The review is published in *Man*, IV (March 1, 1884), 100-101.

44. *Glimpses of the Cosmos*, V, 315; *Pure Sociology* (2d ed.; New York, 1911), p. 568.

45. *Hereditary Genius* . . . , p. 330.

46. *Applied Sociology* (Boston, 1906), pp. 110, 236.

47. "Social Darwinism," *American Journal of Sociology*, XII (1907), 710.

48. *Applied Sociology*, pp. 110, 236.

49. *Glimpses of the Cosmos*, IV, 252.

50. *Applied Sociology*, pp. 107-8; Auguste Comte, *System of Positive Polity*, trans. F. Harrison (London, 1875), II, 378.

51. Ludwig Gumplowicz, *The Outlines of Sociology*, trans. Frederick W. Moore (Philadelphia, 1899), pp. 145-48; the conflict theory of society of Gumplowicz and Ratzenhofer is summarized in Ward, *Pure Sociology*, pp. 205-26.

52. *Pure Sociology*, p. 205.

53. Quoted in Samuel Chugerman, *Lester F. Ward, The American Aristotle: A Summary and Interpretation of His Sociology* (Durham, N.C., 1939), pp. 145-46.

54. *Pure Sociology*, pp. 213, 215-16, 237-40.

55. *Ibid.*, pp. 76-77, 359-60.

56. See Bernhard J. Stern, ed., "The Letters of Ludwig Gumplowicz to Lester F. Ward," *Sociologus*, I (1933), 3-4.

57. Charles Hunt Page, *Class and American Sociology: From Ward to Ross* (New York, 1940), p. 34; Hofstadter, *op. cit.*, p. 62.

58. Cited in Edward S. Corwin, "The Impact of the Idea of Evolution on the American Political and Constitutional Tradition," in *Evolutionary Thought in America*, ed. Stowe Persons, p. 188; Charles H. Cooley, "Genius, Fame and the Comparison of Races," *Annals, American Academy of Political and Social Science*, IX (1897), 317-58; Ward quoted in Page, *op. cit.*, p. 60.

59. *Human Nature and the Social Order* (New York, 1902), pp. 209-10, 268, 288.

60. "Ward-Ross Correspondence," *American Sociological Review*, III (June, 1939), 387, 391.

61. Quoted in W. J. Ghent, *Our Benevolent Feudalism* (New York, 1902), p. 156; E. A. Ross, *Principles of Sociology* (rev. ed.; New York, [1930]), pp. 108-9; *Foundations of Sociology* (5th ed.; New York, 1917), pp. 341-43; *Sin and Society* (New York, 1907), p. 53; *Seventy Years of It* (New York, 1936), pp. 55, 95, 299.

62. *What Is America?* (New York, 1919), pp. 19-20; *Seventy Years of It*, pp. 95, 299.

63. "The Causes of Race Superiority," *Annals, American Academy of Political and Social Science*, XVIII (July, 1901), 67, 83, 85, 88-89.

64. *Social Control: A Survey of the Foundations of Order* (New York, 1932), pp. 423-24; *Changing America: Studies in Contemporary Society* (New York, 1919), pp. 13-14.

65. "The Causes of Race Superiority," p. 88.

66. *Seventy Years of It*, pp. 126, 145; *The Old World in the New: The Significance of Past and Present Immigration to the American People* (New York, 1913), p. 293.

67. *Seventy Years of It*, p. 144; *Social Control*, pp. 33-34. Ross's opinions about the effect of climate upon character suggest comparison with the ideas of Blumenbach in the eighteenth century. In 1795, Blumenbach argued that the tropical sun had the effect of stimulating the action of the liver. "Hence . . . the temperament of most inhabitants of tropical countries is choleric and prone to anger." *The Anthropological Treatises of Johann Friedrich Blumenbach*, trans. Thomas Bendysshe (London, 1865), p. 211.

68. *The American Mind: An Interpretation of American Thought and Character Since the 1880's* (New Haven, 1950), p. 246.

69. *Races and Immigrants in America* (New York, 1907), pp. 7, 11, 46, 136, 173.

70. For examples, see the discussions of Lester F. Ward, Charles H. Cooley, E. A. Ross, and John R. Commons in Merle Curti, *The Growth of American Thought* (New York, 1948); Charles A. Beard, *The American Spirit* (New York, 1948); and Henry Steele Commager, *The American Mind*.

CHAPTER VIII

1. *The Education of Henry Adams* (New York, 1918), p. 225.

2. *Applied Christianity: Moral Aspects of Social Questions* (Boston, 1891), p. 297.

3. *Means and Ends of Education* (4th ed.; Chicago, 1903), pp. 47-48.

4. *The Letters of William James*, ed. Henry James (Boston, 1920), II, 44.

5. Quoted in Panchanan Mitra, *A History of American Anthropology* (Calcutta, 1933), p. 59.

6. *The Autobiography of Benjamin Franklin: A Restoration of a "Fair Copy"* by Max Farrand (Berkeley, Calif., 1949), p. 149.

7. Quoted in *The Pulpit of the American Revolution*, ed. J. W. Thornton (2d ed.; Boston, 1876), p. 403.

8. Quoted in Gilbert Chinard, *Thomas Jefferson: The Apostle of Americanism* (Boston, 1929), p. 428.

9. "Good Advice in Bad Verse," quoted in *American History Told by Contemporaries*, ed. A. B. Hart (New York, 1901), III, 203.

10. *The Works of Thomas Jefferson*, ed. H. A. Washington (New York, 1884), VIII, 45.

11. Quoted in Merle Curti, *The Growth of American Thought* (New York, 1943), pp. 663-64.

12. *Congressional Globe*, 27th Congress, 3rd Session, App., p. 74; quoted in Albert K. Weinberg, *Manifest Destiny, A Study of Nationalist Expansionism in American History* (Boston, 1935), p. 73.

13. See Weinberg, *op. cit.*, pp. 161, 178.

14. Washington Gladden, *Recollections* (New York, 1909), pp. 118-19, 165, 167; Dr. A. B. Beaven, formerly president of the Federal Council of Churches of Christ in America, quoted in G. Bromley Oxnam, *Personalities in Social Reform* (New York, 1950), p. 74.

15. *Christian Nurture* (rev. ed.; New York, 1876), pp. 212-14.

16. *The Collected Works of Theodore Parker,* ed. Frances Power Cobbe (London, 1864), VII, 31.

17. *Ibid.,* VI, 244; V, 328.

18. *Theodore Parker, The American Scholar,* ed. George Willis Cooke (Boston, 1907), pp. 199, 249.

19. *Ibid.,* pp. 249, 247, 224-25.

20. *Ibid.,* pp. 178, 217.

21. *Ibid.,* pp. 244, 228.

22. Robert Knox, *The Races of Men: A Fragment* (Philadelphia, 1850), p. 11.

23. Robert Baird, *The Progress and Prospects of Christianity in the United States of America* (London, [1851]), p. 5.

24. See Curti, *op. cit.,* pp. 670-71.

25. Quoted in Charles A. Beard, *The American Spirit: A Study in the Idea of Civilization in the United States* (New York, 1948), p. 554.

26. *The Times and Young Men* (New York, 1901), pp. 201-3.

27. *Ibid.,* pp. 216-17.

28. *Our Country: Its Possible Future and Its Present Crisis* (New York, 1885), p. 110.

29. *The Times and Young Men,* p. 75; *Our Country . . . ,* p. 176.

30. *The New Era; or The Coming Kingdom* (New York, 1893), pp. 54-55; *Our Country . . . ,* p. 178; John Fiske, *American Political Ideas Viewed from the Standpoint of Universal History* (New York, 1885), pp. 129-52.

31. *Our Country . . . ,* p. 168.

32. *Ibid.,* pp. 174-75; see also *The New Era,* chap. iv, and *Expansion Under New World-Conditions* (New York, 1900), p. 27.

33. *Our Country . . . ,* pp. 178, 218.

34. *The Challenge of the City* (New York, 1907), pp. 205, 104; *The New Era,* p. 77.

35. John Haynes Holmes, "Josiah Strong," *Dictionary of American Biography* (New York, 1936), XVIII, 150; Ely, quoted in Strong, *Our Country,* p. 234.

36. Genesis 49:24; A. B. Grimaldi, "Professor John Wilson: The Father of the Rediscovery of Israel," *Our Race Quarterly,* II, 2nd Ser. (December, 1910), 78; Charles A. L. Totten, "The Romance within the Romance; or the Philosophy of History: Tea Tephi, David's Daughter, Jeremiah's Ward," *Our Race Quarterly,* III, 1st Ser. (March 20, 1891), 58.

37. Mrs. E. C. Daubeney, *Jeshurun: An Elementary Paper on Our British Israelitish Origin* (London, [187?]), pp. 13-14.

38. On his American tour in 1882, Edward A. Freeman, the historian, mentioned the Anglo-Israelites briefly. "I will not believe," he declared, "that the Anglo-Israelites are other than an insular curiosity. If I am shown one on American soil, I shall ask to see his brother who believes that the earth is flat and that the sun is only three miles from it. . . . I cannot bring myself to believe that there is a single Anglo-Israelite in the New World." *Lectures to American Audiences . . .* (Philadelphia, 1882), pp. 100-101; Edward Hine, letter dated December 1, 1884; quoted in Alexander Beauford Grimaldi, *Memoir of Edward Hine* (London, 1909), pp. 21, 23. History does not record that Robert Ingersoll spent his last years as a convert to British Israelism.

39. See the files of *Our Race Quarterly.* Its title changed to *Our Race, Its Origin and Its Destiny.*

40. *The Christian Conquest of Asia; Studies and Personal Observations of Oriental Religions* (New York, 1899), pp. 237-39.

41. *Anglo-Saxon Supremacy* (Boston, 1915), pp. 176-77, 239. For other examples of Brandt's attitude concerning Anglo-Saxon responsibilities, see pp. 19, 127-28.

42. For example, Walter Rauschenbusch declares, "I want to pay the tribute of honor to three men who were pioneers of Christian social thought in America twenty-five years ago: Washington Gladden, Josiah Strong, and Richard T. Ely. These men had matured their thought when the rest of us were young men, and they had a spirit in them which kindled and compelled us." *Christianizing the Social Order* (New York, 1912), p. 9.

43. *Recollections*, pp. 368-69, 373-74.

44. *The Christian Society* (New York, 1894), p. 22.

45. *Christianity and the Social Crisis* (New York, 1907), p. 222; *Christianizing the Social Order*, p. 154.

46. *Christianity and the Social Crisis*, p. 74; *Christianizing the Social Order*, p. 278; "The Problem of the Black Man," *American Missionary*, LVIII (March, 1914), 732-33; see Rayford W. Logan, *The Negro in American Life and Thought: The Nadir, 1877-1901* (New York, 1954), pp. 271-72; see also Purvis M. Carter, "The Astigmatism of the Social Gospel" (Master's thesis, Howard University), *passim*.

47. "Our Indian Problem," *North American Review*, CLXVII (December, 1898), 719-28; *Christian Union*, editorial in the issue of June 12, 1890; both these items are quoted in Logan, *op. cit.*, pp. 272-73.

CHAPTER IX

1. Alice Payne Hackett, *Sixty Years of Best Sellers, 1895-1955* (New York, 1956), pp. 16, 17, 27, 102-3, 106.

2. *History of English Literature*, trans. N. Van Laun (Chicago, n.d.), I, 8-12.

3. *Ibid.*, I, 90-91, 104-5; see Sholom Jacob Kahn, *Science and Aesthetic Judgment: A Study in Taine's Critical Method* (London, 1953), pp. 89-94.

4. Wilson, "Decline of the Revolutionary Tradition: Taine," in his *To the Finland Station: A Study in the Writing and Acting of History* (New York, 1940), p. 48; Taine, *op. cit.*, I, 130-59; see Kahn, *op. cit.*, p. 89.

5. Taine, *op. cit.*, I, 144-45, 151; Kahn, *op. cit.*, p. 89.

6. Taine, *op. cit.*, I, 80, 84, 427.

7. Wilson, *op. cit.*, pp. 47-48.

8. *Ibid.*, p. 44.

9. See Franklin Walker, *Frank Norris: A Biography* (New York, 1932), p. 94.

10. *Studies and Appreciations* (New York, 1900), pp. 197, 199.

11. See Lars Ahnebrinke, *The Influence of Emile Zola on Frank Norris* (Uppsala, Sweden, 1947), *passim;* both Norris' and London's frank glorification of raw courage and brutality in their heroes may owe something to the descriptions of the Saxons and Normans in the early chapters of Taine's *History of English Literature.*

12. "The Responsibilities of the Novelist," in *The Complete Edition of Frank Norris* (New York, 1928), VII, 21-22.

13. Quoted in Walker, *op. cit.*, pp. 67-68.

14. Joan London, *Jack London and His Times: An Unconventional Biography* (New York, 1939), p. 170.

15. Owen Wister, *Roosevelt: The Story of a Friendship 1880-1919* (New York, 1930), pp. 29, 40.

16. Quoted in Walker, *op. cit.*, pp. 230-31.

17. *Adventure* (New York, 1921), p. 106.

18. The most famous of Wister's tales dealing with lynch law is *The Virginian* (New York, 1902).

19. *The Complete Edition of Frank Norris*, X, 35-42.

20. Walker, *op. cit.*, p. 57.

21. (New York, 1913), p. 26.

22. *Ibid.*, pp. 27-34.

23. Joan London, *op. cit.*, p. 209.

24. Kidd, *Social Evolution* (New York, 1894), p. 268; see Richard Hofstadter, *Social Darwinism in American Thought 1860-1915* (Philadelphia, 1945), pp. 80-84.

25. Quoted in Joan London, *op. cit.*, pp. 212-13.

26. *Ibid.*, p. 284.

27. (New York, 1906), p. 171.

28. *Roosevelt: The Story of a Friendship*, pp. 134-35.

29. *Ibid.*, pp. 136-38.

30. *The Valley of the Moon* (New York, 1913), pp. 15, 102-3.

31. Article in San Francisco *Wave*, February 20, 1897, reprinted in *The Complete Edition of Frank Norris*, X, 87; "Grettir at Drangey," *The Complete Edition of Frank Norris*, IV, 146.

32. "La Tinaja Bonita," in *Red Men and White, The Writings of Owen Wister* (New York, 1928), [Vol. 1], p. 215; "The Right Honorable the Strawberries," *When West Was West, The Writings of Owen Wister*, [Vol. 6], pp. 160-61; *The Virginian*, pp. 4, 16, 116.

33. *Moran of the Lady Letty, A Story of Adventure Off the California Coast* (New York, 1898), pp. 71-72, 216; *A Man's Woman*, p. 49; *Blix: Moran of the Lady Letty, The Complete Edition of Frank Norris*, III, 3-4.

34. Ernest Marchand, *Frank Norris: A Study* (Palo Alto, California, 1942), p. 108n; quoted in Walker, *op. cit.*, p. 142; *Moran of the Lady Letty*, p. 184.

35. *Moon-Face and Other Stories* (New York, 1906), p. 60; *Adventure*, p. 90; *The Valley of the Moon*, p. 129.

36. *The Virginian*, pp. 350, 452.

37. *Lady Baltimore*, pp. 260-61.

38. London, *Adventure*, p. 47; Wister, *The Virginian*, p. 366; London, *The Sea-Wolf*, pp. 24-25, 47.

39. *The Mutiny of the Elsinore* (New York, 1924), pp. 148-49.

40. *The Complete Edition of Frank Norris*, X, 198, 201.

41. *Ibid.*, p. 199.

42. *Ibid.*, pp. 199, 207.

43. *The Virginian*, p. 372; "The Evolution of the Cow-Puncher," *The Writings of Owen Wister*, [Vol. 1], p. xxi.

44. *Ibid.*, pp. xxii-xxiv.

45. *The Sea-Wolf*, p. 149; *The Scarlet Plague* (New York, 1915), p. 147.

46. *The Mutiny of the Elsinore*, p. 226.

47. "The Evolution of the Cow-Puncher," p. xxxii.

48. *Ibid.*, pp. xxii-xxiv.

49. *Burning Daylight* (New York, 1910), p. 151.

50. *Collected Writings Hitherto Unpublished in Book Form, The Complete Edition of Frank Norris*, X, 99.

51. *A Man's Woman*, pp. 105-6.

52. *The Sea-Wolf*, pp. 34, 50, 75, 98, 243.

53. *The Octopus: A Story of California* (New York, 1901), pp. 502-5.

54. "The Unexpected," in *Love of Life and Other Stories* (New York, n.d.), p. 127.

55. *Ibid.*, pp. 138-44.

56. *The Valley of the Moon*, p. 41.

57. *The Mutiny of the Elsinore*, pp. 75-77; *Adventure*, p. 199.

58. "The Responsibilities of the Novelist," p. 101.

59. *The Sea-Wolf*, pp. 95-96.

60. *The Effects of Tropical Light on White Men* (New York, 1905), *passim*; London, *The Mutiny of the Elsinore*, pp. 148-49.

61. *The Mutiny of the Elsinore*, p. 149.

62. "The Evolution of the Cow-Puncher," pp. xxvi-xxvii.

CHAPTER X

1. Ray Allen Billington, *Westward Expansion: A History of the American Frontier* (New York, 1949), p. 46; William T. Hagan, *American Indians* (Chicago, 1961), pp. 14-15.

2. "The Northwest Ordinance, July 13, 1787," in Henry Steele Commager, ed., *Documents of American History* (New York, 1949), p. 131.

3. Quoted in B. Schrieke, *Alien Americans* (New York, 1936), p. 31.

4. *Narratives of the Perils and Sufferings of Dr. Knight and John Slover* (Cincinnati, 1867), pp. 62-71; quoted in Albert K. Weinberg, *Manifest Destiny: A Study of Nationalist Expansionism in American History* (Baltimore, 1935), p. 77.

5. *The Writings of Thomas Paine*, ed. Moncure Conway (New York, 1894-96), III, 431.

6. Quoted in Jedidiah Morse, *A Report to the Secretary of War of the United States on Indian Affairs* (New Haven, 1822), p. 282.

7. Billington, *op. cit.*, p. 297; Harold E. Fey and D'Arcy McNickle, *Indians and Other Americans: Two Ways of Life Meet* (New York, 1959), pp. 62-63.

8. See Frank E. Stevens, *The Black Hawk War, Including a Review of Black Hawk's Life* (Chicago, 1903), *passim*.

9. Grant Foreman, *Sequoyah* (Norman, 1938), pp. 11-15.

10. "Worcester *v.* Georgia, 6 Peters, 515 (1832)," in Commager, *op. cit.*, pp. 258-59; Grace Steele Woodward, *The Cherokees* (Norman, 1962), p. 171.

11. Quoted in John Collier, *The Indians of the Americas* (New York, 1947), pp. 208-9.

12. Billington, *op. cit.*, pp. 314-16; Houston, *New York Herald*, January 30, 1848; quoted in Weinberg, *op. cit.*, p. 498.

13. Collier, *op. cit.*, p. 213.

14. *Ibid.*, p. 224; *Commissioner's Annual Report* (1872); quoted in Fey and McNickle, *op. cit.*, p. 48.

15. Collier, *op. cit.*, p. 223; Duncan, *Congressional Globe*, 28th Cong., 2nd sess., App., p. 178; quoted in Weinberg, *op. cit.*, p. 163.

16. (New York, 1881), p. 338.

17. *Congressional Record*, 46th Cong., 2nd sess., p. 4262; quoted in Weinberg, *op. cit.*, p. 91.

18. Hagan, *op. cit.*, p. 133; Billington, *op. cit.*, p. 667; Collier, *op. cit.*, p. 238.

19. "Dow, Jr.," *Illinois State Register*, July 17, 1846; quoted in Weinberg, *op. cit.*, p. 168; Morton, *Crania Americana . . .* (Philadelphia, 1839), p. 6; Morton, "Some Observations on the Ethnology and Archaeology of the American Aborigines," *American Journal of Science and Arts* (1846), p. 9; Josiah Clark Nott and George

R. Gliddon, *Types of Mankind* . . . (Philadelphia, 1856), pp. 69, 461-64; Patterson, "Memoirs of the Life and Scientific Labors of S. G. Morton," in *Types of Mankind* . . . , p. xxxviii.

20. *The Winning of the West* (New York, 1889-96), I, 334-35; quoted in Hermann Hagedorn, *Roosevelt in the Bad Lands* (Boston, 1921), p. 355.

21. Alexis De Tocqueville, *Democracy in America,* trans. Henry Reeve, ed. Henry Steele Commager (New York, 1947), p. 28.

22. Jedidiah Morse, *op. cit.,* pp. 67-73.

23. *Ibid.,* pp. 80-81.

24. *The Complete Works of J. Fenimore Cooper* (Leatherstocking ed.; New York [1893?]), XXVIII, 443; XXVI, 308-9.

25. *The Complete Works* . . . , III, 77-88; IV, 471.

26. *Ibid.,* XXVII, 257, 112-13.

27. Agassiz, "The Diversity of Origin of Human Races," *Christian Examiner* (1850), p. 144; for the ideas on races in the Currier and Ives lithographs I am indebted to an unpublished paper by Morton J. Cronin.

28. See Cephas and Evangeline Warner Brainerd, eds., *The New England Society Orations* (New York, 1901), I, 298.

29. *The Conspiracy of Pontiac and the Indian War after the Conquest of Canada,* in *The Works of Francis Parkman* (Frontenac ed.; New York, 1915), XIV, 45-48.

30. *Information Respecting the History* . . . *of the Indian Tribes* . . . (Philadelphia, 1851-57), I, viii.

31. See H. R. Hayes, *From Ape to Angel: An Informal History of Social Anthropology* (New York, 1958), pp. 3-14.

32. *Ibid.,* p. 8.

33. *Algic Researches* (New York, 1839), I, 18-20; quoted in Roy Harvey Pearce, *The Savages of America: A Study of the Indian and the Idea of Civilization* (Baltimore, 1953), p. 122.

34. *The Rise of the West, or a Prospect of the Mississippi Valley, a Poem* (New York, 1841), p. 17.

35. Pearce, *op. cit.,* p. 128.

36. Hayes, *op. cit.,* pp. 16-18.

37. *Ibid.,* p. 17.

38. *Ibid.,* p. 18.

39. *Ancient Society: Or Researches in the Lines of Human Progress from Savagery through Barbarism to Civilization* (Chicago, 1877), pp. 66 ff.

40. See Hayes, *op. cit.,* p. 23.

41. Quoted in Hayes, *op. cit.,* p. 46; see Pearce, *op. cit.,* p. 128.

42. See Wallace Stegner, *Beyond the Hundredth Meridian: John Wesley Powell and the Second Opening of the West* (Boston, 1954), *passim.*

43. Collier, *op. cit.,* pp. 261 ff.

44. *Ibid.,* pp. 296-97.

CHAPTER XI

1. See esp. chaps. vii and xvii.

2. *Tom Watson's Magazine,* I (June, 1905), 298; quoted in C. Vann Woodward, *Tom Watson: Agrarian Rebel* (New York, 1938), p. 380.

3. Speech at Charleston, Illinois, September 18, 1858. *The Collected Works of Abraham Lincoln,* ed. Roy P. Basler (New Brunswick, 1953), III, 145-46.

4. Benjamin Quarles, *Lincoln and the Negro* (New York, 1962), pp. 108-12.

5. Letter to Michael Hahn, March 13, 1864, *The Collected Works of Abraham Lincoln*, VII, 243.

6. See the preface of H. Melville Myers, comp., *Stay Law and . . . Freedmen's Code* (Charleston, 1866).

7. Cited in Hodding Carter, *The Angry Scar, The Story of Reconstruction* (New York, 1959), p. 52.

8. A readily available source on the Black Codes of South Carolina is Louis M. Hacker, ed., *The Shaping of the American Tradition* (New York, 1947), p. 629; Merle R. Eppse, *The Negro, Too, in American History* (Chicago, 1938), p. 238.

9. Guy B. Johnson, "Patterns of Race Conflict," in Edgar T. Thompson, ed., *Race Relations and the Race Problem* (Durham, 1939), p. 138.

10. "New Viewpoints of Southern Reconstruction," *Journal of Southern History*, V (February, 1939), 52-56.

11. Simkins, *op. cit.*, p. 51; Hacker, *op. cit.*, p. 593.

12. *The Strange Career of Jim Crow* (New York, 1955), p. 57.

13. John Hope Franklin, *From Slavery to Freedom* (2d ed.; New York, 1956), *passim*.

14. Nash K. Burger and John Bettersworth, *South of Appomattox* (New York, 1959), pp. 125, 128, 134, 139; Francis B. Simkins and Robert H. Woody, *South Carolina During Reconstruction* (Chapel Hill, 1932), pp. 459-62.

15. Hacker, *op. cit.*, p. 596.

16. *An Essay on Slavery* (Richmond, 1849), pp. 91, 96-97; this is a reprint of the rare *Review of the Debate* [on the abolition of slavery] *in the Virginia Legislature of 1831 and 1832* (Richmond, 1832).

17. *Uncle Tom's Cabin; or, Life Among the Lowly* (Philadelphia, 1895), pp. 208, 351; J. C. Furnas, *Goodbye to Uncle Tom* (New York, 1956), pp. 314-15, 328, 375.

18. *Nojoque; A Question for a Continent* (New York, 1867), pp. 15, 81, 106, 208.

19. *White Supremacy and Negro Subordination; or, Negroes a Subordinate Race and (So-Called) Slavery Its Normal Condition. With an Appendix, Showing the Past and Present Condition of the Countries South of Us* (New York, 1868), p. 94.

20. *Nojoque . . .*, p. 472; *The Negroes in Negroland: The Negroes in America; and Negroes Generally. Also, the Several Races of White Men Considered as the Involuntary and Predestined* (London, 1868), pp. viii-xiii.

21. *White Supremacy and Negro Subordination*, n.p., section between the Preface and Table of Contents.

22. "Civil Rights," 1874. *Centennial Edition of Sidney Lanier* (Baltimore, 1945), I, 40-41.

23. *Joel Chandler Harris' Life of Henry W. Grady, Including His Writings and Speeches* (New York, 1890), pp. 100, 197.

24. (New York, 1955), pp. 51 ff.

25. See Gunnar Myrdal, et al., eds., *An American Dilemma: The Negro Problem and Modern Democracy* (New York, 1944), p. 484.

26. *Louisiana Constitution*, Art. VIII, Par. 1; John Spencer Bassett, *Expansion and Reform, 1899-1926* (New York, 1926), pp. 24-26; Letter of Bassett to Herbert Baxter Adams, Feb. 18, 1899, in W. Stull Holt, ed., "Historical Scholarship in the United States, 1876-1901, as Revealed in the Correspondence of Herbert B. Adams," "Johns Hopkins University Studies in Historical and Political Science," LVI, No. 4 (1938), 265.

27. *Negro Americans, What Now?* (New York, 1934), pp. 56-67.

28. *Springfield Republican*, November 20, 1913; cited in Sinclair Kennedy, *The Pan-Angles, A Consideration of the Federation of the Seven English-Speaking Nations* (New York, 1914), p. 66.

29. Bassett, *Expansion and Reform, 1889-1926*, pp. 24-26.

30. *Ibid.*, pp. 22-23.

31. Quoted in James McGurrin, *Bourke Cockran* (New York, 1948), pp. 213-18; cited in John La Farge, *No Postponement* (New York, 1950), pp. 82-83.

32. Letter from Roosevelt to Wister, April 27, 1906. Quoted in Owen Wister, *Roosevelt: The Story of a Friendship 1880-1919* (New York, 1930), p. 253; letter of Roosevelt to Curtis Guild, Jr., October 28, 1901, quoted in Henry F. Pringle, *Theodore Roosevelt: A Biography* (New York, 1931), p. 249. For an account of Roosevelt's attitude toward Negroes, see Seth M. Scheiner, "President Theodore Roosevelt and the Negro, 1901-1908," *Journal of Negro History*, XLVII (July, 1962), 169-82. Owen Wister criticized Roosevelt for his appointment of Negroes to southern post offices and for inviting Booker T. Washington to dinner. Of Washington's invitation to dinner, Wister has one of the southern women in one of his novels say that the event had given local Negroes an exaggerated notion of their own importance. "The very next day some of the laziest and dirtiest where we live had a new strut, like the monkey when you put a red flannel cap on him—only the monkey doesn't push ladies off the sidewalk." *Lady Baltimore* (New York, 1906), p. 91.

33. J. E. Cutler, *Lynch-Law* (New York, 1905), chap. ii, particularly pp. 29-30.

34. *The Negro Year Book*, 1937-1938 (Tuskegee, Alabama, 1938), p. 156.

35. Jessie Daniel Ames, *The Changing Character of Lynching* . . . (Atlanta, 1942), *passim*.

36. Rayford W. Logan, *The Negro in American Life and Thought: The Nadir 1877-1901* (New York, 1954), p. 221; *Memphis Press*, January 27, 1921, quoted in James Weldon Johnson, *Along This Way: The Autobiography of James Weldon Johnson* (New York, 1933), p. 317; W. E. B. Du Bois, "My Evolving Program for Negro Freedom," in Rayford W. Logan, ed., *What the Negro Wants* (Chapel Hill, 1944), p. 53.

37. *Greenwood* [Miss.] *Commonwealth*, July 15, 25, 27, August 26, 1897, March 29, December 6, 1901; quoted in Albert D. Kirwan, *Revolt of the Rednecks in Mississippi Politics: 1876-1925* (Lexington, Kentucky, 1951), pp. 146-47.

38. *59 Cong., 2 Sess.*, 1441; Tillman to *New York Sun*, November 4, 1913, cf. *Congressional Record, 57 Cong.*, 1 Sess., 5102. Quoted in Francis B. Simkins, *Pitchfork Ben Tillman: South Carolinian* (Baton Rouge, 1944), pp. 396-97.

39. *Weekly Jeffersonian*, Thomson, Georgia, May 15, 1913, January 4, 1917, and February 12, 1914; Thomas E. Watson, *Sketches: Biographical, Historical, Literary* (Thomson, Ga., 1912); quoted in Woodward, *op. cit.*, p. 340.

40. Robert W. Winston, *It's a Far Cry* (New York, 1937), chap. xiii.

41. *The Clansman* (New York, 1905), pp. 57-58, 93, 145, 208, 216, 249, 292-93.

42. "The Last Hold of the Southern Bully," *Forum*, XVI (November, 1893), 308.

43. Quoted in Walter White, *Rope and Faggot: A Biography of Judge Lynch* (New York, 1929), p. 7.

44. *The Negro: The Southerner's Problem* (New York, 1904), pp. 112-13.

45. Lillian Smith, *Killers of the Dream* (New York, 1949), pp. 116-20, 127-28; Oscar Handlin, *Race and Nationality in American Life* (New York, 1957), pp. 124-32; John C. Dollard, *Caste and Class in a Southern Town* (New Haven, 1937), pp. 160-61; James Baldwin, *In Another Country* (New York, 1960), *passim*.

46. *Stat.* L, Chap. 114.

47. *109 U.S. 3 (1883)*.

48. See "The Philadelphia and West Chester Railroad Company *v.* Miles," *American Law Review*, II, 358.

49. *21 Ohio 198 (1871); 48 Indiana 327 (1874)*.

50. *95 U.S. 485 (1878)*.

51. *163 U.S. 537 (1896)*.

52. Myrdal, *op. cit.*, p. 579; Edwin R. Embree, *Brown America: The Story of a New Race* (New York, 1931), p. 89.

53. Myrdal, *op. cit.*, pp. 887-90.

54. *The New South* (New York, 1890), pp. 244-46.

55. *The Silent South together with The Freedman's Case in Equity and The Convict Lease System* (New York, 1885), p. 26.

56. *163 U.S. 537 (1896)*.

57. *Up from Slavery* (New York, 1924), pp. 213, 223.

58. See Basil Mathews, *Booker T. Washington* (Cambridge, Mass., 1948), p. 91.

59. *Greenwood* [Miss.] *Commonwealth*, July 1, 1897, cited in Kirwan, *op. cit.*, pp. 145-46; quoted by Ray Stannard Baker, *Following the Color Line; an Account of Negro Citizenship in the American Democracy* (New York, 1908), p. 247; Ralph McGill, "The South Has Many Faces," *Atlantic Monthly*, CCXI (April, 1963), 86.

60. See *Wilson Library Bulletin*, XXXVI (April, 1962), 668-69.

61. Doxey A. Wilkerson, *Special Problems of Negro Education* (Washington, 1939), pp. 23-25.

62. *Cr. C, 22, 167 (1915), XXIX, 79 (1916), XXIX, 706*; cited in Charles S. Johnson, *Patterns of Negro Segregation* (New York, 1943), pp. 171-72.

63. *175 U.S. 528 (1899)*.

64. *211 U.S. 45 (1908)*.

65. Mathews, *op. cit.*, p. 91.

66. Logan, *op. cit.*, p. 89.

67. Scheiner, *op. cit.*, pp. 169-82; W. E. B. DuBois, *Dusk of Dawn: An Essay toward an Autobiography of a Race Concept* (New York, 1940), p. 234.

68. Henry F. Pringle, *The Life and Times of William Howard Taft* (New York, 1939), I, 390; Simkins, *op. cit.*, p. 418; W. E. B. DuBois, *Dusk of Dawn*, pp. 232-33.

69. C. Vann Woodward, *The Strange Career of Jim Crow*, p. 77; DuBois, *op. cit.*, pp. 236-37; *Atlanta Georgian and News*, October 7, 1913, cited in Arthur S. Link, *Woodrow Wilson and the Progressive Era 1910-1917* (New York, 1954), p. 65.

70. *Congressional Record, 56* Cong., 1 Sess., 2245; cited in Simkins, *op. cit.*, p. 395; George Frisbie Hoar, *The Lust of Empire* (New York, 1900), p. 9.

71. R. S. Peale, ed., *The Home Library of Useful Knowledge* (Chicago, 1887), p. 534; Page, *Old South; Essays Social and Political* (New York, 1892), pp. 313-15, 316, 320, 338, 342; Wister, *Lady Baltimore, passim*; Gertrude Atherton, *Senator North* (New York, 1900), *passim*.

72. "The Negro Problem," *Atlantic Monthly*, LIV (November, 1884), pp. 697, 700-706; see also his "The African Element in America," *Arena*, II (November, 1890), 66, and his "The Nature of the Negro," *Arena*, III (December, 1890), 25.

73. (New York, 1896), pp. v, 95, 327-28.

74. *The Southern South* (New York, 1910), pp. 10-11.

75. *What Is America?* (New York, 1919), p. 7; see also S. J. Holmes, "The Trend of the Racial Balance of Births and Deaths," in Edgar T. Thompson, ed., *Race Relations and the Race Problem* (Durham, 1939), p. 62.

76. Henry Adams, letter to John Hay, November 2, 1901, *Letters of Henry*

Adams, 1892-1918, ed. Worthington C. Ford (Boston, 1938), II, 358; John Fiske, letter of February 25, 1877, *Letters of John Fiske*, ed. Ethel F. Fiske (New York, 1940), p. 360; Logan, *op. cit.*, pp. 240, 266; Page, *Harper's*, LXXIV (May, 1887), 993.

77. *The American Scene* (New York, 1907), pp. 360-61.

78. "The Reconstruction of the Southern States," *Atlantic Monthly*, LXXXVII (January, 1901), 2-11.

79. *Reconstruction and the Constitution 1866-1876* (New York, 1902), pp. viii-ix, 133.

80. *History of the United States from the Compromise of 1850 to the Final Restoration of Home Rule at the South in 1877* (New York, 1906), V, 558; VI, 39.

81. *Reconstruction Political and Economic 1865-1877* (New York, 1907), pp. 211-13.

82. *History of the United States Since the Civil War* (5 vols.; New York, 1917-37), I, 73.

83. *Bright Skies and Dark Shadows* (New York, 1890), pp. 131-32, 151.

84. *New York Times*, May 10, 1900, cited in Woodward, *op. cit.*, p. 55.

85. Quoted in Gilbert Thomas Stephenson, *Race Distinctions in American Law* (New York, 1910), p. 164.

CHAPTER XII

1. Howard Mumford Jones, *America and French Culture: 1750-1848* (Chapel Hill, 1927), pp. 543-45; Oscar Handlin, *Boston's Immigrants 1790-1865: A Study in Acculturation* (Cambridge, Mass., 1941), pp. 210-11.

2. Quoted by Stuart P. Sherman in *Essays and Poems of Emerson with an Introduction by Stuart P. Sherman* (New York, 1921), p. xxxiv.

3. *The Autocrat of the Breakfast Table* (Boston, 1858), p. 21.

4. Quoted in Charles S. Johnson, "Race Relations and Social Change," in Edgar T. Thompson, ed., *Race Relations and the Race Problem* (Durham, N. C., 1939), p. 281.

5. Ray Allen Billington, *The Protestant Crusade: 1800-1860. A Study of the Origins* (New York, 1938), *passim*.

6. *The Bread-Winners, A Social Study* (New York, 1883), pp. 74-75, 86-87.

7. Mary Roberts Coolidge, *Chinese Immigration* (New York, 1900), p. 501; for the pages which follow on anti-Chinese agitation, I am deeply indebted to Donald Fred Tingley, *The Rise of Racialistic Thinking in the United States in the Nineteenth Century*, University of Illinois dissertation (Urbana, 1952), pp. 226-57; Taylor, quoted in Samuel Gompers and Herman Gutstadt, *Meat vs. Rice; American Manhood against Asiatic Coolieism, Which Shall Survive* (San Francisco, 1908), p. 30.

8. *People v. Hall (4 Cal. 399), October term (1854)*; cited in Tingley, *op. cit.*, p. 233.

9. William M. Malloy, comp., *Treaties, Conventions, International Acts, Protocols and Agreements Between the United States of America and Other Powers, 1776-1909*, in *Senate Document No. 357*, 61 Cong., 2 Sess. (1909-1910), p. 235; cited in Tingley, *op. cit.*, p. 233.

10. See Tingley, *op. cit.*, pp. 237, 247.

11. *Report of the Joint Special Committee to Investigate Chinese Immigration, Senate Report No. 689*, 44 Cong., 2 Sess. (1876-1877), p. 289; cited in Tingley, *op. cit.*, p. 240.

12. Pierton W. Dooner, *Last Days of the Republic* (San Francisco, 1880); Robert Wolton, *A Short and Truthful History of the Taking of California and*

Oregon by the Chinese in the Year A. D. 1899 (San Francisco, 1882), esp. pp. 10-11, 13, 58-59, 79, cited in Tingley, *op. cit.*, p. 252.

13. Quoted in Gompers and Gutstadt, *op. cit.*, p. 22.

14. "Chinese Exclusion Act," (1882), in Henry Steele Commager, ed., *Documents of American History* (New York, 1949), pp. 110-11; Gompers and Gutstadt, *op. cit.*, pp. 17, 29.

15. *History of the American People* (New York, 1902), V, 212-14.

16. Chicago *Record-Herald*, September 25, 1901, quoted in Edward N. Saveth, *American Historians and European Immigrants, 1875-1925* (New York, 1948), pp. 128-29; this study has been extremely helpful to me.

17. *The Old World in the New: The Significance of Past and Present Immigration to the American People* (New York, 1913), pp. 285-86; *Roads to Social Peace: The Weil Lectures, 1924, on American Citizenship* (Chapel Hill, 1924), p. 49.

18. *Races and Immigrants in America* (New York, 1907), pp. 10-11.

19. *Our Country: Its Possible Future and Its Present Crisis* (New York, 1885), pp. 45-46, 210; *The New Era; or The Coming Kingdom* (New York [1893]), p. 77; *The Twentieth Century City* (New York, 1898), p. 98.

20. *The Valley of the Moon* (New York, 1913), pp. 24, 154.

21. Secretary of the Connecticut Board of Agriculture, *Tenth Annual Report (1876-1877)*, p. 48, quoted in Marcus L. Hansen, *The Immigrant in American History*, ed. Arthur M. Schlesinger (Cambridge, Mass., 1940), p. 169.

22. *The Damnation of Theron Ware, or Illumination* (New York, 1896), p. 46.

23. Article in the *Boston Herald*, December 16, 1905. In clippings of the Immigration Restriction League in the Harvard library.

24. Hansen, *op. cit.*, pp. 89-92.

25. *Ibid.*, pp. 90-92.

26. "China at North Adams," editorial in the *Congregationalist*, June 30, 1870, p. 204; see also July 14, 1870, pp. 3-4, 220. See also *Watchman and Reflector*, July 7, 1870, p. 6; July 14, 1870, p. 6; *Christian Union*, June 25, 1870, p. 406. The above sources are cited in Henry F. May, *Protestant Churches and Industrial America* (New York, 1949), p. 57.

27. *Congregationalist*, October 30, 1878, p. 348, cited in May, *op. cit.*, p. 96; see also p. 123.

28. "Aristocratic Opinions of Democracy," *North American Review*, C (January, 1865), 201.

29. "Some Political and Social Aspects of the Tariff," *New Princeton Review*, III (March, 1887), 172-73.

30. *Orations, Addresses and Speeches of Chauncey Depew*, ed. John D. Champlin (New York, 1910), III, 264-73.

31. *The Races of Men: A Fragment* (Philadelphia, 1850), pp. 56-57.

32. Allen, "Changes in New England Population," *Popular Science Monthly*, XXIII (August, 1883), 433-44; Dr. John Ellis, *Deterioration of the Puritan Stock and Its Causes* (New York, 1884), pp. 3, 22; H. Winn to John Ellis, September 8, 1883, quoted in Ellis, *op. cit.*, p. 3; Hansen, *op. cit.*, p. 171. The idea that Anglo-Saxons and Europeans generally are not suited for the climate of the United States is also discussed in the following sources: Louis Schade, *The Immigration into the United States from a Statistical and National-Economical Point of View* (Washington, 1865); James Hunt, "On the Acclimatisation of Europeans in the United States of America," *Anthropological Review*, VIII (April, 1870), 109-37; Friedrich Kapp, "Immigration," *Journal of Social Science: Containing the Transactions of the American Association*, II (1870), 1-30; Edward Jarvis, "Immigration," *Atlantic Monthly*, XXIX (April, 1872), 454-68.

488   *Notes to Pages 301-8*

33. Barbara Soloman, "The Intellectual Background of the Immigration Restriction Movement in New England," *New England Quarterly,* XXV (March, 1952), 33; see also Soloman, *Ancestors and Immigrants: A Changing New England Tradition* (Cambridge, Mass., 1956), *passim; The Education of Henry Adams: An Autobiography* (New York, 1918), pp. 255-313; *A Cycle of Adams Letters,* ed. Worthington C. Ford (Boston, 1920), I, 102-3, 10-11, 239; unpublished diary, quoted in *Barrett Wendell and His Letters,* ed. Mark De Wolfe Howe (Boston, 1924), p. 47.

34. Hosmer, *A Short History of Anglo-Saxon Freedom* (New York, 1890), pp. 277-78, 303, 352; Fiske, *American Political Ideas Viewed from the Standpoint of Universal History. Three Lectures Delivered at the Royal Institution of Great Britain in May, 1880* (New York, 1885), pp. 25-26; Brooks Adams, *America's Economic Supremacy* (New York, 1900), pp. 111-13; Brooks Adams, *The Law of Civilization and Decay: An Essay on History* (New York, 1897), p. xi.

35. *Restriction of Immigration. A Publication of the Immigration Restriction League,* No. 33 (New York, 1899), pp. 441-42.

36. "Immigration and Degradation," *Forum,* XI (August, 1891), 641; *Restriction of Immigration,* p. 448; *Discussions in Economics and Statistics,* ed. Davis Dewey (New York, 1899), II, 326.

37. "Restriction of Immigration," *Atlantic Monthly,* LXXVII (June, 1896), 828.

38. Chicago *Record-Herald,* September 25, 1901, quoted in Saveth, *op. cit.,* p. 128; "An Unfamiliar Essay by Frederick J. Turner, 'The Rise and Fall of New France,'" ed. Fulmer Mood, *Minnesota History,* XVIII (December, 1937), 398.

39. Letter of February 1, 1898, *Letters of John Fiske,* ed. Ethel Fiske (New York, 1940), p. 669; Fisher, "Has Immigration Dried Up Our Literature?" *Forum,* XLVI (January, 1894), 562-67.

40. Henry Adams, letter of May 26, 1875, *Letters of Henry Adams, 1858-1891,* ed. Worthington C. Ford (New York, 1930), I, 267; letter of January 13, 1898, *ibid.,* p. 114; September 25, 1899, *ibid.,* II, 241; also see Saveth, *op. cit.,* p. 82.

41. Fiske, *American Political Ideas Viewed from the Standpoint of Universal History,* pp. 17-18; Wister, *Philosophy Four, a Story of Harvard University* (New York, 1903); see Wister's introduction to *Safe in the Arms of Croesus, The Writings of Owen Wister* (New York, 1928), VIII, x-xi; Lodge, *Early Memories* (New York, 1913), p. 86; Wendell, letter of March 31, 1917, *Barrett Wendell and His Letters,* p. 282.

42. Letter of August 11, 1899, *The Letters and Friendships of Sir Cecil Spring-Rice,* ed. Stephen Gwynn (New York, 1929), I, 293; Roosevelt, *Presidential Addresses* (New York, 1910), III, 288; "Race Decadence," *Outlook,* XCVII (April 8, 1911), 766.

43. Clippings, Immigration Restriction League, Harvard library; Oscar Handlin, *The Uprooted* (New York, 1951), pp. 287-88; Saveth, *op. cit.,* pp. 38-39.

44. *Atlantic Monthly,* LXX (July, 1892), p. 57.

45. "The Ideal of the American Commonwealth," *Political Science Quarterly,* X (September, 1895), 407.

46. Handlin, *The Uprooted,* pp. 288-89; Booker T. Washington, *Up from Slavery* (New York, 1901), pp. 220-21.

47. *Nation,* LXXXV (December 19, 1907), 557; "Report of Hon. Charles W. Russell, Assistant Attorney-General, Relative to Peonage Matters, Oct. 10, 1907," *Annual Report of the Attorney General of the United States for the Year 1907* (Washington, 1907), pp. 207-15.

48. Quoted in the *Wilmington* [N.C.] *Morning Star,* September 30, 1906. In clippings of Immigration Restriction League.

49. Gilbert Thomas Stephenson, *Race Distinctions in American Law* (New York, 1910), pp. 159 ff.; see Henry F. Pringle, *Theodore Roosevelt: A Biography* (New York, 1931), p. 407.

50. *Statistical Abstract of the United States* (Washington, 1920), p. 817.

CHAPTER XIII

1. "The Monroe Doctrine and the Evolution of Democracy," *Proceedings of the Academy of Political Science,* VII (1917), 471.

2. "Annexation," *United States Magazine and Democratic Review,* New Ser., XVII (July and August, 1845), 9.

3. Letter to Thomas S. Spedding, March 12, 1865, *Life, Letters, and Journals of Sir Charles Lyell, Bart.,* ed. Mrs. [Katherine Murray (Horner)] Lyell (London, 1881), II, 397.

4. H. G. Cutler, "The American Not a New Englishman, but a New Man," *New England Magazine,* New Ser., IX (September, 1893), 24-31.

5. *America's Race Heritage* (New York, 1922), p. 39.

6. *The Works of Daniel Webster* (16th ed.; Boston, 1872-77), II, 214.

7. *The Descent of Man, and Selection in Relation to Sex* (London, 1871), I, 179. The passage quoted and endorsed by Darwin is from Rev. Foster B. Zincke, *Last Winter in the United States* (London, 1868), p. 29.

8. Reported in Josiah Strong, *Expansion Under New World-Conditions* (New York, 1900), pp. 185-86.

9. *Democracy and Empire, with Studies of their Psychological, Economic, and Moral Foundations* (New York, 1900), pp. 243, 305.

10. *Ibid.,* pp. 270-71.

11. *Ibid.,* p. 274.

12. "The War as a Suggestion of Manifest Destiny," *Annals of the American Academy of Political and Social Science,* XII (September, 1898), 183-84.

13. *Ibid.,* pp. 182-83.

14. *Ibid.,* p. 180.

15. *Ibid.,* pp. 186-87.

16. "The Spanish War and the Equilibrium of the World," *Forum,* XXV (August, 1898), 651.

17. Tyler Dennett, *John Hay* (New York, 1933), p. 278.

18. *Problems of Expansion as Considered in Papers and Addresses* (New York, 1900), p. 152.

19. *Our New Duties: Their Later Aspects* (New York, 1899), pp. 5-6.

20. "The Benefits of War," *North American Review,* CLIII (1891), 677.

21. *The Interest of America in Sea Power, Present and Future* (Boston, 1897), pp. 18, 267.

22. *San Francisco Examiner,* April 25, 1898. Quoted in Morrison I. Swift, *Imperialism and Liberty* (Los Angeles, 1899), p. 72.

23. "A Republic in the Philippines," *North American Review,* CLXVIII (1899), 319.

24. *City and State,* June 9, 1898. Quoted in Swift, *op. cit.,* p. 71.

25. *The New Era; or The Coming Kingdom* (New York, [1893]), p. 69.

26. *Expansion Under New World-Conditions,* p. 212.

27. *Ibid.,* p. 249.

28. *Ibid.*, p. 276.

29. Strong mentions that Mahan had read several chapters of his *Expansion Under New World-Conditions* before publication and had given him "the benefit of his valuable criticism." See Preface, p. 10.

30. *England and America. Addresses delivered in England during the Summer of 1898* (London, [1898]), p. 70.

31. *Educational Review,* XVI (September, 1898), 204.

32. *For the Greater Republic, Not for Imperialism. An Address Delivered at the Union League of Philadelphia February 15, 1899* ([Philadelphia? 1899?]), pp. 4-6.

33. Beveridge to Ingalls, September 21, 1898. Quoted in Claude G. Bowers, *Beveridge and the Progressive Era* (Cambridge, Mass., 1932), p. 77.

34. Rudyard Kipling, *Something of Myself for My Friends Known and Unknown* (New York, 1937), pp. 121-22.

35. Roosevelt did this explicitly and in such a way as to make his purpose quite clear. "Our object is not to imitate one of the older racial types," he declared in a speech to the Knights of Columbus in New York, "but to maintain a new American type and then to secure loyalty to this type." *The Works of Theodore Roosevelt,* ed. Hermann Hagedorn, National Ed. (New York, 1926-1927), XVIII, 402.

36. *Theodore Roosevelt and His Times Shown in His Own Letters,* ed. Joseph B. Bishop (New York, 1920), I, 347.

37. *Nat. Ed.,* VII, 115.

38. *Ibid.,* IX, 57.

39. *The Strenuous Life: Essays and Addresses* (New York, 1900), pp. 6-7.

40. *Ibid.,* p. 20.

41. *The Correspondence of Thomas Carlyle and Ralph Waldo Emerson, 1834-1872,* ed. Charles E. Norton (3rd ed.; Boston, 1883), I, 247.

42. "A Word to the Yankees," *Anglo-Saxon,* I, Part 3 (1849), 26.

43. *Anglo-Saxon,* p. 29.

44. First published in the London *Examiner,* February 7, 1852. Reprinted in *The Suppressed Poems of Alfred Lord Tennyson, 1830-1868,* ed. J. C. Thomson (London, 1910), p. 103.

45. *American Political Ideas Viewed from the Standpoint of Universal History. Three Lectures Delivered at the Royal Institution of Great Britain in May 1880* (New York, 1885), p. 135.

46. *A Short History of Anglo-Saxon Freedom. The Polity of the English-Speaking Race. Outlines in its Inception, Development, Diffusion, and Present Condition* (New York, 1890), pp. 343, 351 ff.

47. Mahan, *op. cit.,* p. 34.

48. *American Notes* (New York, [1910?]), p. 65.

49. *Ibid.,* pp. 66-67.

50. "England and America," *Atlantic Monthly,* LXXXII (October, 1898), p. 441.

51. *Democracy and Empire,* p. 277.

52. Samuel Eliot Morison and Henry Steele Commager, *The Growth of the American Republic* (3rd ed. rev.; New York, 1942), II, 332.

53. Hay to McKinley, April 4, 1898. Quoted in Charles S. Olcott, *The Life of William McKinley* (Boston, 1916), II, 130.

54. *Ibid.*

55. See London *Times,* May 14, 1898, for a complete text of the speech.

56. See Bertha A. Reuter, *Anglo-American Relations during the Spanish-American War* (New York, 1924), p. 153.

57. *Ibid.,* p. 155.

58. Quoted in Reuter, *op. cit.,* pp. 155-56.

59. "A Service of England to America," an editorial, *Century Magazine,* LVI (June, 1898), 314.

60. "Reflections Appropriate to 'the Fourth,'" an editorial, *Century Magazine,* LVI (July, 1898), 474. For articles having similar themes see B. O. Flower, "Proposed Federation of Anglo-Saxon Nations," *Arena,* XX (August, 1898), 222-38; Julian Ralph, "Anglo-Saxon Affinities," *Harper's Magazine,* XCVIII (February, 1899), 385-91; Carl Schurz, "The Anglo-American Friendship," *Atlantic Monthly,* LXXXII (October, 1898), 433-40; Lyman Abbott, "The Basis of an Anglo-American Understanding," *North American Review,* CLXVI (May, 1898), 513-21; Sir Richard Temple, "An Anglo-American *versus* a European Combination," *North American Review,* CLXVII (September, 1898), 306-17.

61. "The Spanish War and the Equilibrium of the World," p. 650.

62. Letters to Sir Robert White-Thomson, April 4, 1898, and December 17, 1899, *Barrett Wendell and His Letters,* ed. M. A. DeWolfe Howe (Boston, 1924), pp. 120, 137.

63. *The Meaning of the Times and Other Speeches* (Indianapolis, 1908), pp. 43-44.

64. "International Isolation of the United States," *Atlantic Monthly,* LXXXI (May, 1898), 588.

65. *The Anglo-Saxon Century and the Unification of the English-Speaking People* (New York, 1903), p. 101.

66. *Ibid.*

67. *An American Response to Expressions of English Sympathy,* printed for the Anglo-American Committee (New York, 1899), Introduction; quoted in Reuter, p. 159.

68. *Ibid.,* pp. 160-61.

69. Theodore C. Knauff, "The Transatlantic Society of America," *Anglo-American Magazine,* VII (April, 1902), 255-62.

70. For examples in the *Anglo-Saxon Review* see Arnold White, "England and America: 'Strangers Yet,'" VII (December, 1900), 8-22; for Anglo-Saxon bias see especially editorial comments in the column, "Impressions and Opinions," appearing in each issue of the magazine. In the *Anglo-American Magazine* see Eaton B. Northrup, "The Courage of Destiny," I (January, 1899), 78-90; Arthur Ernest Davies, "The New Nationalism," VI (July, 1901), 17-31; Jack London, "The Salt of the Earth," VIII (August, 1902), 1-16; William MacLeod Raine, "The Anglo-Saxon Heritage," VIII (December, 1902), 29-30.

71. *Nat. Ed.,* X, 248.

72. *Speech at Canton, Ohio, October 24, 1900* ([Washington? 1900?]), p. 16.

73. *Congressional Record,* 56th Congress, 1st Session, p. 708.

74. *Congressional Record,* 55th Congress, 3rd Session, p. 297.

75. *For the Greater Republic, Not for Imperialism,* p. 14.

76. *Our Right to Acquire and Hold Foreign Territory. An Address Delivered Before the New York State Bar Association at its Annual Meeting at Albany, January 18th, 1899* (New York, 1899), p. 42.

77. *The Life and Speeches of the Hon. Henry Clay,* ed. Daniel Mallory (Hartford, Conn., 1853), I, 386.

78. *Expansion Under New World-Conditions,* pp. 289-90.

79. *Our New Duties: Their Later Aspects* (New York, 1899), p. 24.

80. *The Races of Europe* (New York, 1899), p. 562.

81. *The Control of the Tropics* (New York, 1898), p. 54.

82. *Ibid.,* p. 85.

83. *Ibid.*, p. 53.

84. *Letters of Henry Adams, 1858-1891,* ed. Worthington Chauncey Ford (Boston and New York, 1938), II, 511.

85. *Problems of Expansion as Considered in Papers and Addresses,* p. 148.

86. Charles Burke Elliott, *The Philippines to the End of the Military Régime* (Indianapolis, 1916), p. 370.

87. Quoted in Erin Graham, "Kipling the Colonial," *Anglo-American Magazine,* VIII (September, 1902), 15.

88. *Problems of Expansion as Considered in Papers and Addresses,* p. 62.

89. A phase invented by William Howard Taft. See Mrs. Dauncey Campbell, *The Philippines: An Account of Their People, Progress, and Condition* (Boston, 1910), p. 110.

90. *Our New Duties: Their Later Aspects,* p. 20.

91. *For the Greater Republic, Not for Imperialism,* pp. 16-17.

92. *Race Questions, Provincialism, and Other American Problems* (New York, 1908), p. 10.

93. *Ibid.*, p. 35.

94. *Ibid.*, pp. 25-26.

95. *Commonwealth or Empire: A Bystander's View of the Question* (New York, 1902), p. 43.

96. *Ibid.*, pp. 57-58.

97. *North American Review,* CLXXII (February, 1901), 161-76.

98. Peter MacQueen, "When Will the War Cease?" *Arena,* XX (December, 1899), 702.

99. *Mr. Dooley in the Hearts of His Countrymen* (Boston, 1899, reprinted 1914), p. 225.

100. Letter, Theodore Roosevelt to F. P. Dunne, June 16, 1900. F. P. Dunne MSS., quoted in Elmer Ellis, *Mr. Dooley's America: A Life of Finley Peter Dunne* (New York, 1941), pp. 146-47.

101. "Literary Aspects of American Anti-Imperialism, 1898-1902," *New England Quarterly,* X (1937), 661.

102. *Ibid.*, p. 666.

103. *Ibid.*, p. 667.

104. *Social Darwinism in American Thought, 1860-1915* (Philadelphia, 1945), p. 166.

105. *Congressional Record,* 55th Congress, 3rd Session, p. 922.

106. *Ibid.*, p. 1532.

107. *Ibid.*, p. 1424.

108. *For the Greater Republic, Not for Imperialism,* pp. 10-11.

109. *Problems of Expansion as Considered in Papers and Addresses,* p. 43.

110. *Congressional Record,* 55th Congress, 3rd Session, p. 923.

111. Kirk H. Porter, *National Party Platforms* (New York, 1924), p. 234.

CHAPTER XIV

1. Ira D. Reid, *The Negro Immigrant: His Background, Characteristics and Social Adjustment, 1899-1937* (New York, 1939), *passim.*

2. See Deems Taylor, *A Pictorial History of the Movies* (New York, 1943), p. 46.

3. See J. M. Mecklin, *The Ku Klux Klan: A Study of the American Mind* (New York, 1924), *passim.*

4. *How We Advertised America: The First Telling of the Amazing Story of*

the Committee on Public Information that Carried the Gospel of Americanism to Every Corner of the Globe (New York, 1920), pp. 167-69.

5. Gobineau, *The Inequality of Human Races*, trans. Adrian Collins (London, 1915); this is an abridged version of *Essai sur l'Inégalité des Races Humaines* (4 vols.; Paris, 1853-55); Chamberlain, *Foundations of the Nineteenth Century*, trans. John Lees (London, 1913).

6. See Oscar Levy, "The Life Work and Influence of Count Arthur de Gobineau, an Introductory Essay," in Gobineau, *The Renaissance*, trans. Paul V. Cohn (London, 1927), pp. v-vi.

7. *The Inequality of Human Races*, p. xiv.

8. *Ibid.*, p. 146; see Frank H. Hankins, *The Racial Basis of Civilization: A Critique of the Nordic Doctrine* (New York, 1926), pp. 38 ff.; for additional studies of Gobineau, see Jacques Barzun, *Race: A Study in Modern Superstition* (New York, 1937), pp. 72 ff.; Ruth Benedict, *Race: Science and Politics* (New York, 1940), pp. 85 ff.

9. *The Inequality of Human Races*, pp. xv, 27-28, 74-75, 93, 205.

10. See Hankins, *op. cit.*, pp. 35-37, 43-44.

11. *The Inequality of Human Races*, p. 208.

12. *Ibid.*, p. 33.

13. *Ibid.*, pp. 101-2.

14. See Hankins, *op. cit.*, pp. 33, 59; Barzun, *op. cit.*, pp. 84-85.

15. *The Inequality of Human Races*, pp. 152-53, 196; Hankins, *op. cit.*, p. 53.

16. See Leon Stein, *The Racial Thinking of Richard Wagner* (New York, 1950), pp. 36-37.

17. Levy, *op. cit.*, pp. xi-xii, xxxiv, xxxv; see Barzun, *op. cit.*

18. *England and Germany* (n.p., 1914), pp. 17-18.

19. See Lord Redesdale, "Introduction," Chamberlain, *op. cit.*, I, 201-17.

20. Chamberlain, *op. cit.*, I, 193-94, 214, 233.

21. *Ibid.*, I, 320.

22. *Ibid.*, I, 551-52; II, 336 ff.

23. *Ibid.*, I, 538n., 539; II, 224.

24. *Ibid.*, I, 536, 266n.

25. *Ibid.*, I, 324.

26. "Review of *The Foundations of the Nineteenth Century*," *Outlook*, XCVIII (July 29, 1911), 728-31.

27. Gobineau, *The Moral and Intellectual Diversity of Races, with Particular Reference to Their Respective Influence in the Civil and Political History of Mankind* (Philadelphia, 1856). This also is an abridged translation.

28. Davison in Madison Grant, *The Alien in Our Midst* (New York, 1930), pp. 68-69.

29. See obituary in *New York Times*, May 31, 1937, p. 15.

30. Ripley, *The Races of Europe: A Sociological Study* (New York, 1899), *passim*; Grant, *The Passing of the Great Race* (2d ed.; New York, 1918), pp. xii, 20-21.

31. Ripley, *op. cit.*, pp. 1-2, 515-16; Grant, *op. cit.*, pp. 153, 165.

32. *Ibid.*, p. 230.

33. *Ibid.*, pp. 154, 159, 193, 197, 208.

34. *Ibid.*, pp. 184, 186.

35. Sadler, *Long Heads and Round Heads, or What's the Matter with Germany* (Chicago, 1918), pp. 48 ff.; Grant, *The Passing of the Great Race*, p. 87.

36. "The Fighting Ability of Different Races," *Journal of Heredity*, X (1919), 30; *The Passing of the Great Race*, p. 74.

37. *The Passing of the Great Race,* pp. 17, 18, 24, 38-39.

38. *Ibid.,* pp. 91, 209.

39. *Ibid.,* pp. 49-50, 60.

40. *Ibid.,* pp. 3, 64, 175.

41. *Ibid.,* p. 263.

42. *Ibid.,* pp. 39-40, 43, 83-84, 99.

43. *Ibid., passim.*

44. *Boston Transcript,* December 9, 1916, p. 7; *Annals of the American Academy,* LXX (March, 1917), 330; *Nation,* CIV (April 19, 1917), 466; [London] *Times Literary Supplement,* May 3, 1917, p. 209; *Dial,* May 17, 1917, p. 24; [London] *Athenaeum,* (July, 1917), p. 13.

45. One of the best accounts of intelligence testing and its application to race theory is Otto Klineberg, *Race Differences* (New York, 1935), *passim;* a useful bibliography of this subject is Thomas Russell Garth, *Racial Psychology: A Study of Racial Mental Differences* (New York, 1931), pp. 222-32.

46. "Reaction Time with Reference to Race," *Psychological Review,* II (1895), 474-86.

47. See C. S. Johnson and H. M. Bond, "The Investigation of Racial Differences Prior to 1910," *Journal of Negro Education* (1934), p. 39; Thorndike, *Educational Psychology* (New York, 1903), p. 139.

48. Edwin G. Boring, "The Influence of Evolutionary Theory upon American Psychological Thought," in Stowe Persons, ed., *Evolutionary Thought in America* (New Haven, 1950), pp. 289-90.

49. *Ibid.*

50. Thorndike, *op. cit.,* p. 139.

51. *The Measurement of Intelligence: An Explanation of and a Complete Guide for the Use of the Stanford Revision and Extension of the Binet-Simon Intelligence Scale* (Boston, 1916), pp. 90-91.

52. Yerkes, "Psychological Examining in the United States Army," National Academy of Sciences, *Memoir,* XV (1921), 790 ff.

53. Lippmann, "The Mental Age of Americans," *New Republic,* XXXII (October 25, 1922), 212.

54. Lippmann, "The Mental Age of Americans," p. 213; Terman, letter to *New Republic,* XXXIII (January 17, 1923), 201.

55. Yerkes, *op. cit.,* p. 794.

56. *Ibid.,* p. 870.

CHAPTER XV

1. See John Higham, *Strangers in the Land: Patterns of American Nativism 1860-1925* (New Brunswick, N.J., 1955), pp. 222 ff.; this is an excellent study and has been most useful to me.

2. *Ibid.,* pp. 227, 260.

3. Quotations from the *Dearborn Independent* are in *The International Jew,* IV (1920), 50-51; see Keith Sward, *The Legend of Henry Ford* (New York, 1948), pp. 140-60.

4. See Francis Edward Clark, "Our Dearest Antipathies," *Atlantic Monthly,* CXXVII (February, 1921), 241; quoted in Heywood Broun and George Britt, *Christians Only: A Study in Prejudice* (New York, 1931), p. 73.

5. Broun and Britt, *op. cit.;* Horace M. Kallen, *Culture and Democracy in the United States: Studies in the Group Psychology of the American Peoples* (New York,

1924), p. 189n; *New York Times*, June 17, 1922, 1:6; April 10, 1923, 1:6; *Nation*, CXIV (1922), 708; Harry Starr, "The Affair at Harvard," *Menorah Journal*, VIII (1922), 263-76; Harris Berlock, "Curtain on the Harvard Question," *Zeta Beta Tau Quarterly*, VII (May, 1923), 3-5; see Milton L. Barron, ed., *American Minorities: A Textbook of Readings in Intergroup Relations* (New York, 1957), pp. 133-44.

6. An introduction to the complexities of modern theory is found in Leslie Clarence Dunn and Theodore Dobzhansky, *Heredity, Race, and Society* (New York, 1956), *passim*; see also Joseph Edward Clark, *The American Critique of the Democratic Idea, 1919-1929*, dissertation (Stanford University, 1958), *passim*.

7. Alvin Johnson, "The Highbrow 'Revanche,'" *New Republic*, XXXI (August 2, 1922), 277.

8. *Individuality* (Boston, 1911), p. 34; "Colored Pupils in High Schools," *School and Society*, XVIII (November 10, 1923), 569-70; *Educational Psychology* (New York, 1921), III, 207 ff.; *Human Nature and the Social Order* (New York, 1940), p. 320; see Merle Curti, *The Social Ideas of American Educators* (New York, 1935), p. 491.

9. (Princeton, 1923), p. 182.

10. *Ibid.*, pp. 155, 190.

11. William C. Bagley, "The Army Tests and the Pro-Nordic Propaganda," *Educational Review*, LXVII (April, 1924), 184; Yerkes, "Psychological Examining in the United States Army," National Academy of Sciences, *Memoir*, XV (1921), 778; Brigham, *op. cit.*, p. 192; see Yerkes' introduction to Brigham, *op. cit.*, pp. vii-viii; see also Yerkes, "Testing the Human Mind," *Atlantic Monthly*, CXXXI (1923), 358-70; Arthur Sweeney, "Mental Tests for Immigrants," *North American Review*, CCXV (1922), 600-612.

12. S. J. MacFadden and J. F. Dashiel, "Racial Differences as Measured by the Downey Will-Temperament Individual Tests," *Journal of Applied Psychology*, VII (1922), 30-53; Marvin Darsie, "The Mental Capacity of American-born Japanese Children," *Comparative Psychology Monographs*, III (1925), No. 15.

13. Terman, *The Measurement of Intelligence: An Explanation and a Complete Guide for the Use of the Stanford Revision and Extension of the Binet-Simon Intelligence Scale* (Boston, 1916), p. 23; "The Great Conspiracy or the Impulse Imperious of Intelligence Testers, Psychoanalyzed and Exposed by Mr. Lippmann," *New Republic*, XXIII (December 27, 1922), 116-17, 120; MacDougall, letter to *New Republic*, XXXIV (May 23, 1923), 346.

14. J. C. Flugel, *A Hundred Years of Psychology: 1833-1933 with Additional Part on Developments 1933-1947* (2d ed., London, 1951), pp. 271-72; A. A. Roback, *History of American Psychology* (New York, 1952), p. 256.

15. (New York, 1921), pp. 79, 82-83, 100-102.

16. American Philosophical Society, *Proceedings*, LVI (1917), 364-68.

17. "Harmonic and Disharmonic Race Crossings," in *Eugenics in Race and State* (Baltimore, 1923); see also "Biological Consequences of Race-Crossing," *Journal of Heredity*, XVII (1926), 175-85.

18. Fischer, *Die Rehobother Bastards und das Bastardierungsproblem bein Menschen* (Jena, 1913), p. 280; Castle, *Genetics and Eugenics: A Text-Book for Students of Biology and a Reference Book for Animal and Plant Breeders* (Cambridge, Mass., 1921), pp. 267-69; see Castle, "Biological and Social Consequences of Race-Crossing," *American Journal of Physical Anthropology*, IX (April-June, 1926), 145-56.

19. *Studies in Evolution and Eugenics* (New York, 1923), pp. 223-24.

20. *Heredity and Human Affairs* (New York, 1927), p. 162.

21. *Applied Eugenics* (New York, 1924), pp. 300-301.

22. *Being Well-Born: An Introduction to Heredity and Eugenics* (2d ed.; Indianapolis, 1927) pp. 410-11.

23. *Roads to Social Peace* (New York, 1924), pp. 48-49.

24. *Statistical Abstract of the United States* (1921), p. 484.

25. Oscar Theodore Barck, Jr. and Nelson Manfred Blake, *Since 1900: A History of the United States in Our Times* (rev. ed.; New York, 1925), p. 276; Gary quoted in *Literary Digest*, LXXVII (May 5, 1923), 9; see Higham, *op. cit.*, p. 315.

26. See obituaries in *New York Times*, October 3, 1956, p. 33 and *American Sociological Review*, XXI (December, 1956), 783.

27. *Greek Immigration to the United States* (New Haven, 1911), pp. 24, 29, 68-69.

28. *Immigration: A World Movement and Its American Significance* (rev. ed.; New York, 1925), pp. 398-401; *The Melting-Pot Mistake* (New York, 1926), p. 21.

29. *The Foundations of Social Life* (New York, 1927), pp. 113-14.

30. *Ibid.*, pp. 188-89; *The Melting-Pot Mistake*, p. 74.

31. *The Melting-Pot Mistake*, pp. 239-40.

32. *Dictionary of American Biography*, Supplement I, ed. Harris E. Starr (New York, 1944), p. 584.

33. "The Address of Welcome to the Second International Congress of Eugenics, New York, September 22-28, 1921, by Osborn, President of the Congress," in Madison Grant, ed., *The Alien in Our Midst* (New York, 1930), pp. 203-9.

34. Letter to *New York Times*, April 8, 1924, p. 18.

35. *Studies in Evolution and Eugenics* (New York, 1923), pp. 75-76.

36. *Scientific Humanism* (New York, 1926), *passim; The Rising Tide of Color against White World-Supremacy* (New York, 1920), p. [v].

37. *The Revolt against Civilization: The Menace of the Under Man* (New York, 1923), pp. 128-29; *Re-forging America: The Story of Our Nationhood* (New York, 1927), p. 37, 131.

38. Quoted in Stoddard, *Scientific Humanism*, pp. 25-26.

39. *Scientific Humanism*, pp. 173-74.

40. *The Revolt against Civilization* . . . , p. 132.

41. *Scientific Humanism*, pp. 93-94, 96.

42. *The Rising Tide of Color* . . . , p. 161; *The Revolt against Civilization* . . . , p. 17.

43. *The Rising Tide of Color* . . . , pp. 89, 166-67, 171, 305.

44. *The Rising Tide of Color* . . . , p. 220; *The Revolt against Civilization* . . . , p. 220.

45. *The Rising Tide of Color* . . . , pp. 201-2; 307-8.

46. *Re-forging America* . . . , pp. 103, 233.

47. *Nation and Athenaeum*, XXXI (August 26, 1922), 714; for anthropologists' reactions, see Franz Boas' review of *The Rising Tide of Color*, *Nation*, CXI (December 8, 1920), 656; Alexander Goldenweiser's review of *Racial Realities in Europe*, *New York Tribune*, November 2, 1924, p. 4; *Bookman*, LXV (July, 1927), xii.

48. (New York, 1953 ed.), pp. 13-14, 21.

49. *America a Family Matter* (New York, 1922), pp. 125, 164-65.

50. *America's Race Heritage* (New York, 1922), pp. 3, 6, 27, 206, 234.

51. (New York, 1923), p. 207.

52. *Ibid.*, pp. 208-11.

53. *Ibid.*, p. 211.

54. Higham, *op. cit.*, pp. 313-14; *Hearings, Biological Aspects of Immigration*, Sixty-Sixth Congress, 2nd Sess., April 16-17, 1920, p. 15.

55. *Why Europe Leaves Home* (Indianapolis, 1922), pp. 22, 230-31.
56. *The New Decalogue of Science* (Indianapolis, 1923), pp. 17-18.
57. *Ibid.,* pp. 44-45.
58. See speech reported in *New York Times,* Sept. 15, 1920; see also speech in Birmingham, Alabama, reported in *New York Times,* October 27, 1921, p. 11.
59. Coolidge, "Whose Country Is This?" *Good House-Keeping,* LXXII (February, 1921), 14; Davis, *The Iron Puddler: My Life in the Rolling Mills and What Came of It* (New York, 1922), pp. 28, 61; quoted in Higham, *op. cit.,* pp. 318-19.
60. See Higham, *op. cit.,* pp. 177-78, 307.
61. *Eugenical News: Current Record of Race Hygiene,* VIII (1923), 53; cited in Higham, *op. cit.,* pp. 313-14.
62. See "Immigration Act of 1924, May 26, 1924," in Henry Steele Commager, ed., *Documents of American History* (New York, 1949), pp. 372-74; Samuel Eliot Morison and Henry Steele Commager, *The Growth of the American Republic* (New York, 1942), II, 187-88; Higham, *op. cit.,* p. 324.
63. Coolidge and Reed quoted in *Literary Digest,* LXXXI (May 10, 1924), 12; Higham, *op. cit.,* pp. 323-26.

CHAPTER XVI

1. Letter to *New York Times,* April 17, 1924, p. 30; see Elliott M. Rudwick, *W. E. B. Du Bois: A Study in Minority Group Leadership* (Philadelphia, 1960), pp. 194-96.
2. "The Forefathers and Forerunners of the English People," *Anthropological Review,* VIII (April, 1870), 203.
3. *Ancient and Modern Imperialism* (London, 1910), p. 4.
4. *Principles of Political Economy with Some of Their Applications to Social Philosophy,* ed. Sir W. J. Ashley (New York, 1929), p. 324.
5. *Introduction to Anthropology,* trans. J. Frederick Collingwood (London, 1863), *passim.*
6. Babington, *Fallacies of Race Theories as Applied to National Characteristics: Essays by William Dalton Babington, M.A.* (London, 1895), *passim;* Robertson, *The Saxon and the Celt* (London, 1897), *passim;* see also his *Criticisms* (2 vol.; London, 1903), *passim,* and "The Illusion of Race," *Contemporary Review,* CXXXIV (July, 1928), 28-33.
7. *The Races of Europe: A Sociological Study* (New York, 1899); for criticisms of racism, see pp. 1, 213-15, 219-20, 522-23, 529.
8. Finot, *Race Prejudice,* trans. Florence Wade-Evans (London, 1906), p. [3]; Oakesmith, *Race and Nationality: An Inquiry into the Origin and Growth of Patriotism* (New York, [1919]), *passim.*
9. (Modern Library, New York, 1931), pp. 411-12.
10. *Is America Safe for Democracy?* (New York, 1921), pp. 29-31.
11. "Racial Theory," in Edgar T. Thompson and Everett C. Hughes, eds., *Race: Individual and Collective Behavior* (Glencoe, Illinois, 1958), pp. 525-36.
12. J. Rumney, *Herbert Spencer's Sociology: A Study in the History of Social Theory* . . . (London, 1934), p. 58; for an objection to Spencer's environmentalist theories see Henry Fairfield Osborn's introduction to Madison Grant, *The Passing of the Great Race* (rev. ed.; New York, 1918).
13. Quoted in Franz Boas, "The Question of Racial Purity," *American Mercury* (October, 1924), III, 163.
14. Tylor, *The Origins of Culture* (New York, 1958), p. 1; Radin, "Introduction," pp. ix, xiii; this is a reprint of Part I of *Primitive Culture: Research into the*

Development of Mythology, Philosophy, Religion, Language, Art and Custom (London, 1871).

15. The July-September issue of *American Anthropologist*, XLV, n.s. (1943) contains a series of tributes to Boas by his associates and former pupils.

16. "An Anthropologist's Credo," *Nation*, CXLVII (August 27, 1938), 201.

17. "Franz Boas the Man," *American Anthropologist*, XLV, n.s. (July-September, 1943), 8.

18. "An Anthropologist's Credo," pp. 201-2.

19. *Ibid.*

20. Kroeber, *op. cit.*, pp. 10-11.

21. Murray B. Emeneau, "Franz Boas as a Linguist," *American Anthropologist*, XLV, n.s. (July-September, 1943), 35-36, 38; Boas quoted, pp. 35-36.

22. "Franz Boas as an Ethnologist," *American Anthropologist*, XLV, n.s. (July-September, 1943), p. 27.

23. *Ibid.*, pp. 27-28; Boas, *The Mind of Primitive Man* (New York, 1911).

24. Kroeber, *op. cit.*, pp. 16, 22; for some of Boas' articles and books deploring racism, see "Lo, the Poor Nordic," *New York Times*, April 13, 1924, IX, 19; *Aryans and Non-Aryans* (New York, 1934); "Race," *Encyclopedia of the Social Sciences*, XII (New York, 1937); *Race and Democratic Society* (New York, 1945); *Race and Nationality* (New York, 1915); "Race Problems in America," *Science*, n.s., XXIX (May 28, 1909), 839-49; "This Nordic Nonsense," *Forum*, LXXIV (October, 1925), 502-11.

25. "Can Scientific Man Survive?" *Saturday Review*, XL (December 21, 1957), 24.

26. Boas, "Fallacies of Racial Inferiority," *Current History*, XXV (February, 1927), 681.

27. Garth, *Race Psychology: A Study of Racial Mental Differences* (New York, 1931), p. 211; Klineberg, *Race and Psychology* (UNESCO Pamphlet, Paris, 1951), pp. 1-40.

28. Brigham, "Intelligence Tests of Immigrant Groups," *Psychological Review*, XXXVII (1930), 165.

29. Review of *The Rising Tide of Color*, *Nation*, CXI (December 8, 1920), 656.

30. Jennings, *Prometheus; or Biology and the Advancement of Man*, p. 34; Dobzhansky, *The Biological Basis for Human Freedom* (New York, 1956), p. 119.

31. Grant, *The Conquest of a Continent, or The Expansion of Races in America* (New York, 1933); Stoddard, *Clashing Tides of Colour* (New York, 1935); *Into the Darkness* (New York, 1940).

32. *Up from the Ape* (New York, 1931), pp. 501-2, 595.

33. "The Truth about Race," *Harper's*, CLXXXIX (October, 1944), 418-25.

CHAPTER XVII

1. Cable, *The Grandissimes* (New York, 1880); Turner, *George W. Cable: A Biography* (Durham, N.C., 1956), p. 93.

2. *The Silent South together with The Freedman's Case in Equity and The Convict Lease System* (New York, 1885), p. 19.

3. *Ibid.*, p. 34.

4. *Ibid.*, p. 16.

5. *Joel Chandler Harris' Life of Henry W. Grady, Including His Writings and Speeches* (New York, 1890), pp. 286-87.

6. *Mark Twain's Letters, Arranged with Comment,* ed. Albert Bigelow Paine (New York, [1917]), I, 104.

7. *Buffalo Express,* September 23, 1869; quoted in Philip Foner, *Mark Twain: Social Critic* (New York, 1958), p. 218.

8. *The Writings of Mark Twain* (New York, 1899-1922), III, 306-7.

9. *Ibid.,* V.

10. *Mark Twain's Notebook Prepared for Publication with Comments by Albert Bigelow Paine* (New York, 1935), p. 277.

11. Quoted in Howard Mumford Jones, *Ideas in America* (Cambridge, Mass., 1944), pp. 228-29.

12. *An Imperative Duty: A Novel* (New York, 1892), pp. 149-50.

13. *Ibid.,* pp. 148-49.

14. *The Monster and Other Stories* (New York, 1899).

15. See Jean Gould, *Winslow Homer: A Portrait* (New York, 1962), p. 158.

16. *Army Life in a Black Regiment* (Lansing, Mich., 1960), p. 24; Mary Thacher Higginson, *Thomas Wentworth Higginson: The Story of His Life* (Boston, 1914), pp. 253-54.

17. *Book and Heart: Essays on Literature and Life* (New York, 1897), pp. 155-56, 159.

18. Quoted in William Z. Ripley, "Race Factors in Labor Unions," *Atlantic Monthly,* XCIII (March, 1904), 305.

19. *Mr. Dooley in Peace and in War* (Boston, 1898), p. 56.

20. William Roscoe Thayer, ed., *The Life and Letters of John Hay* (New York, [1915]), II, 234-35.

21. Theodore C. Knauff, "The Transatlantic Society of America," *Anglo-American Magazine,* VII (April, 1902), 261; Charles Waldstein, *The Expansion of Western Ideals and the World's Peace* (New York, 1899), p. 20.

22. "The War's Legacy to the American Teacher," *Anglo-American Magazine,* II (July, 1899), 32.

23. William G. Mackendrick, *The Destiny of Britain and America* (6th ed., rev.; Boston, 1926), p. 4.

24. B. O. Flower, "The Proposed Federation of the Anglo-Saxon Nations," *Arena,* XX (August, 1898), 231.

25. Edwin Ridley, "The Irish-American," *Anglo-Saxon Magazine,* I (April, 1899), 369; for other articles with the theme of wooing the Irish, see Robert Stein, "The Royal Anti-Catholic Declaration and Anglo-Saxon Union," VII (March, 1902), 201-11; Robert Stein, "Placate the Irish," VIII (August, 1902), 27-48.

26. "The Essential Unity of Britain and America," *Atlantic Monthly,* LXXXII (July, 1898), 27.

27. See Finley Peter Dunne, "In the Interpreter's House," *American Magazine,* LXXIV (July, 1912), 383; John P. Altgeld, *Live Questions: Including Our Penal Machine and Its Victims* (Chicago, 1890), p. 11; Mary Antin, *They Who Knock at Our Gates* (New York, 1914), p. 82; Theodore Dreiser, *A Hoosier Holiday* (New York, 1916), pp. 68-69.

28. See Edward N. Saveth, *American Historians and European Immigrants, 1875-1925* (New York, 1948), pp. 202-3; see also pp. 204, 216-17; Marcus L. Hansen, *The Immigrant in American History* (Cambridge, Mass., 1940), pp. 147-48.

29. Ray Stannard Baker, *Woodrow Wilson: Life and Letters* (New York, 1931), III, 286-87; compare these comments of Wilson with those in this study on p. 292.

30. Burton J. Hendrick, ed., *The Life and Letters of Walter H. Page* (New York, 1925), III, 89-91.

31. See, for example, John Haynes Holmes, "Sensitivity as Censor," *Saturday Review of Literature*, XXXII (February 26, 1949), 9 ff.

32. Paul A. Carter, *The Decline and Revival of the Social Gospel* (Ithaca, 1956), pp. 195-96.

33. *Ibid.*, p. 196.

34. "Clinton Minister Lives His Faith," *Christian Century*, LXXIII (December 17, 1956), 1470.

35. *Presbyterian Life*, XVI (August 1, 1963), 24-28.

36. New York *Tribune*, August 26, 1854, quoted in Allan Nevins, *Ordeal of the Union: A House Dividing* (New York, 1947), II, 330.

37. Quoted in John La Farge, *No Postponement; U.S. Moral Leadership and the Problem of Racial Minorities* (New York, 1950), pp. 145-46.

38. Harold E. Fey, "Catholicism and the Negro," *Christian Century*, LXI (December 20, 1944), 1476-79.

39. See Bernard Sobel, ed., *The Theatre Handbook and Digest of Plays* (New York, 1940), p. 569.

40. Carey McWilliams, *Prejudice; Japanese Americans: Symbol of Racial Intolerance* (Boston, 1944), *passim*.

41. See John Collier, *Indians of the Americas* (New York, 1947), pp. 246-47.

42. *Ibid.*, pp. 242-43, 246-58.

43. *Ibid.*, pp. 261 ff.

44. Walter White, *Rope and Faggot: A Biography of Judge Lynch* (New York, 1929), p. 21; the advertisement is reproduced in James Weldon Johnson, *Along This Way: The Autobiography of James Weldon Johnson* (New York, 1933), facing p. 372.

45. Florence Murray, ed., *The Negro Handbook* (New York, 1949), pp. 91-92.

46. See statistics on lynching in *World Almanac and Book of Facts* (New York, 1963), p. 311.

47. 266 *U.S.* 232 *(1921)*.

48. George W. Spicer, *The Supreme Court and Fundamental Freedoms* (New York, 1959), pp. 90-95.

49. Gunnar Myrdal, *et al.*, eds., *An American Dilemma: The Negro Problem and Modern Democracy* (New York, 1944), pp. 480-81.

50. 273 *U.S.* 536 *(1927)*; 295 *U.S.* 45 *(1935)*; Spicer, *op. cit.*, pp. 90-91.

51. 313 *U.S.* 299, 318 *(1941)*; Spicer, *op. cit.*, p. 91.

52. 321 *U.S.* 649 *(1944)*.

53. O. D. Weeks, "The White Primary: 1944-1948," *American Political Science Review*, XLII, No. 3 (June, 1948), 500-510; also Donald S. Strong, "The Rise of Negro Voting in Texas," *ibid.*, pp. 510-12; Spicer, *op. cit.*, pp. 92-95.

54. *Excerpts from the 1961 Commission on Civil Rights Reports Including All the Findings and Recommendations Made by the Commission in Its Five-Volume Report* (Washington, [1961]), pp. 5, 15-17.

55. *Ibid.*, p. 17.

56. *Voting: 1961 Commission on Civil Rights Report* (Washington, [1961]), pp. 21-22.

57. 305 *U.S.* 337 *(1938)*.

58. Decision of the United States Circuit Court of Appeals of June 18, 1940, in the case of Melvin Alston vs. the School Board of Norfolk, Va.; Myrdal, *op. cit.*, p. 320.

59. 339 *U.S.* 629 *(1950)*.

60. 339 *U.S.* 637 *(1950)*.

61. 347 *U.S.* 483 *(1954)*.

62. *352 U.S. 903; 350 U.S. 877; 350 U.S. 879.*

63. *Education: 1961 Commission on Civil Rights Reports* (Washington, [1961]), p. 4.

64. *Statistical Summary of School Segregation-Desegregation in the Southern and Border States,* Southern Education Reporting Service, Nashville, Tenn., November, 1962, p. 2.

65. Myrdal, *op. cit.,* p. 549.

66. *346 U.S. 249 (1953).*

67. See *U.S. News and World Report,* LV (September 2, 1963), 9.

68. "President Recommends Revision of Immigration Laws," *Department of State Bulletin,* XLIX (August 19, 1963), 298-300.

69. John Collier, "Slow Recovery Since Wounded Knee," *Saturday Review,* XLVI (June 15, 1963), 31-32.

70. "Vagabond Kings," *Reporter,* XXVII (May 9, 1963), 12-14.

71. "Jobs for Negroes: How Much Progress in Sight," *Newsweek,* LXII (July 15, 1963), 68-70.

72. L. D. Reddick, *Crusader without Violence: Martin Luther King* (New York, 1959), *passim.*

Bibliographic Essay

Maghan Keita

CHAPTER I

For a fuller discussion of the evolution of racial theory, useful sources include Herodotus, *The Histories* (London: Penguin, 1954); A. B. al Jahiz, *The Life and Works of Al Jahiz* (Berkeley: University of California Press, 1969); George Washington Williams, *History of the Negro Race in America, 1619–1880* (1883, reprinted New York: Arno Press, 1968); W.E.B. Du-Bois, *The World and Africa* (New York: International Publishers, 1946; C.G. Woodson, *African Background Outlined* (New York: Negro Universities Press, 1960, c. 1936). Post 1963 sources include Edith Sanders, "The Hamitic Hypothesis," *Journal of African History* 10, 4 (1969); Frank Snowden, *Blacks in Antiquity* (Cambridge, Mass.: Harvard University Press, 1970) and *Before Color Prejudice* (Cambridge, Mass.: Harvard University Press, 1983). Some attention might also be given to revisions in the translations of primary sources and the rationale for those revisions, e.g., *Rig Veda, Talmud.*

W.E.B. DuBois's concept in the 1897 essay "The Conservation of Races" (in Howard Brotz, *Negro Social and Political Thought, 1850–1920,* New York: Basic Books, 1963), that race is culture and is not solely biologically driven is also attested to in Nehemia Levtzion and J.F.P. Hopkins, eds., *Corpus of Early Arabic Sources for West African History* (Cambridge: Cambridge University Press, 1981) in which the authors of several of the primary texts speak of "black Jews." By the same token, it would seem that the Emperor Julian's prescriptions were only racialist/ racist if they are judged by modern standards.

CHAPTER II

The theoretical notions of race that evolve in the English-speaking colonies of the western hemisphere bear the stamp of the Enlightenment as revealed in the early works of such people as Cotton Mather, *Another Tongue Brought In, To Confess the Great Saviour of the World* (Boston: B. Green, 1707) and

503

Cadwallader Coldin, *The History of the Five Nations Depending on the Province of New York* (New York: William Bradford, 1727). Elisabeth Tooker's "League of the Iroquois: Its History, Politics, and Ritual" and Bruce Burton's "The Iroquois Had Democracy Before We Did" provide analytical insight into the discussions of early Anglo-American and the conceptualization of democratic structures. Tooker's voluminous work on the Iroquois and confederated Native American nations sheds much light on ambivalent English attitudes as does Ronald Takaki's *"The Tempest* in the Wilderness: The Racialization of Savagery," *The Journal of American History* 79, 3 (December 1992). Jack Forbes' *Africans and Native Americans,* also provides another dimension to the discourse and lends weight to the need to expand the parameters of discussion to include more than simply "black" and "white."

In this regard, reflections on the interesting issue of intermarriage between Moors and Jews are alluded to in the literature of the medieval and Renaissance periods in works such as *Tristan, Morte d'Arthur, Chanson de Roland, Poema de Mio Cid,* and of course, *Othello.* Many of the major romantic epics of the medieval age include intermarriage as the central theme. See Maghan Keita, "The Return of the Black Knight: The African in Arthurian Lore" (unpublished manuscript).

Secondary tests that also speak to intermarriage include Charles Edward Chapman's *A history of Spain, founded on the Historia de Espana y de la civilizacion espanola of Rafael Altamira* (New York: Macmillan, 1918). Added to this should be the works of Edwyn Hole, *Andalus: Spain under the Muslims* (London: R. Hale, 1958). Works following Gossett's publication are Thomas F. Glick, *Islamic and Christian Spain in the Early Middle Ages* (Princeton: Princeton University Press, 1979); Stanley Lane-Poole, *The Moors in Spain* (London: Darf Publishers Limited, 1984); S.M. Imamuddin, *Muslim Spain 711–1492 A.D.: A Sociological Study* (Leiden: E.J. Brill, 1981); Salma Khadra Jayyusi, ed., *The Legacy of Muslim Spain* (Leiden: E.J. Brill, 1992); and Richard A. Fletcher, *Moorish Spain* (New York: H. Holt, 1992). The primary sources in Arabic also attest to the frequency, if not the facility, of unions between Muslim and Jew. See Levtzion and John Hunwick, *Sharia in Songhay: the Replies of Al-Maghili to the Questions of Askia Al-Haji Muhammad* (London: Oxford University Press, 1985); Elias Saad, *Social History of Timbuktu* (Cambridge: Cambridge University Press, 1983); Jamil M. Abun-Nasr, *A History of the Maghrib in the Islamic Period* (Cambridge: Cambridge University Press, 1987); and Maghan Keita, "Scholarship as a Global Commodity: African Intellectual Communities in the Medieval and Renaissance Periods," *Proceedings of the PMR Conference* 14 (1989). While these sources fundamentally concern Africa, they also chronicle and synthesize works that encompass a significant sector of the Islamic world.

Jan Carew's "The End of Moorish Enlightenment and the Beginning of the Columbian Era," *Race & Class* 33, 3 (1992) ties the African and European segments together quite nicely. His text and notes speak not only to issues Islamic/Jewish unions, but also to those that involve Christians as well as Jews and Moslems. Also see Jan Read, *The Moors in Spain and Portugal* (Totowa, N.J.: Rowman and Littlefield, 1975).

The "20 Negars" who arrive at Jamestown in 1619 were not slaves, but indentured servants. See John Hope Franklin and Alfred A. Moss, Jr., *From Slavery to Freedom* (New York: McGraw-Hill. 1988); Eric Williams, *Capitalism and Slavery* (New York: Russell & Russell, 1961); and John Blassingame, *The Slave Community* (New York: Oxford University Press, 1979). Blassingame's *Black New Orleans* (Chicago: University of Chicago Press, 1973) begins to show the complexities that marked black life in the early years of the American experiment. T.H. Breen and Stephen Innes also provide a compelling account of these complexities in *"Myne Owne Ground": Race and Freedom on Virginia's Eastern Shore, 1640–1676* (New York: Oxford University Press, 1980).

CHAPTER III

The notion that social relations could be scientifically observed and predicted was inherent in the Count de Buffon's statement that there are "Negro tribes so primitive that they cannot count beyond the number three." Claudia Zaslavsky's *Africa Counts: Number and Pattern in African Culture* (Boston: Prindle, Weber & Schmidt, 1979) concerns African abstract and philosophical thought and explains different numeric and metric systems within the African context; as does V.Y. Mudimbe, *The Invention of Africa* (Bloomington: Indiana University Press, 1988) and *The Idea of Africa* (Bloomington: University of Indiana Press, 1994); and Jahnheinz Jahn, *Muntu* (New York: Grove Press, 1961). These works open a panorama on the vast and complex questions that center on intellectual culture in African societies.

Benjamin Banneker's 1791 letter to Thomas Jefferson concerning the latter's observations on Negro inferiority in the "Letters of Benjamin Banneker" is a powerful, if oblique refutation of Jefferson's beliefs. In Herbert Aptheker, ed., *A Documentary History of the Negro People in the United States* (New York: Citadel Press, 1990). Banneker was surrounded by the rhetoricians and savants of America's early black community who were numerous and outspoken. Among them were Richard Allen and Absalom Jones (1787) of the early African American church and protest movements and black abolitionist David Walker's "Walker's Appeal" (1829).

More black voices were raised in the late eighteenth and early nineteenth centuries. Maria W. Stewart, Henry Highland Garnett, E.W.

Blyden, Martin R. Delany, Frederick Douglass, and Alexander Crummell were among the most prominent and prolific.

The anthropology of the nineteenth century had its roots in the work of the eighteenth-century Egyptologist Constantin de Volney, *Travels Through Egypt and Syria* (New York: John Tiebout, 1798); Vivant Denon, *Travels in Upper and Lower Egypt . . . During the Campaigns of General Bonaparte* (1803; reprinted, New York: Arno 1973); and Abbé Henri Gregoire, *An Inquiry Concerning the Intellectual and Moral Faculties and Literature of Negroes* (Brooklyn: Thomas Kirk, 1810). Martin Bernal's *Black Athena: The Afroasiatic Roots of Classical Civilization* (New Brunswick, N.J.: Rutgers University Press, 1987) is also quite useful here.

CHAPTER IV

The most negative elements of nineteenth century anthropological theory are marked by the works of the Count de Gobineau; they have a definitive link to George Morton, George R. Gliddon, and Josiah Nott and the establishment of the American School of Ethnology. See Michael Biddliss, "Gobineau and the Origins of European Racism," *Race* 7 (January 1966), and *Father of Racist Ideology: The Social and Political Thought of Count Gobineau* (New York: Weybright and Talley, 1970).

Frederick Douglass responds to Glidden, Morton, and Nott et al. in 1854 in the "Claims of the Negro Ethnologically Considered," reprinted in Eric Foner, ed., *The Life and Writings of Frederick Douglass*. Douglass's work is followed by many more scholars of color through the close of the nineteenth century. They include Edward Wilmot Blyden, *The People of Africa* (New York: Anson Press, 1871) and George Washington Williams, *History of the Negro Race in America* (1883, reprinted New York: Arno Press, 1968). Also see Dickson D. Bruce, Jr., "Ancient Africa and the Early Black American Historians, 1883–1915," *American Quarterly* 36 (Winter 1984), and David McBride, "Africa's Elevation and Changing Racial Thought at Lincoln University, 1854–1886," *Journal of Negro History* 62 (1977).

For an examination of the ways in which the Bible has been used to justify racist thought, see George Frederickson, *The Black Image in the White Mind* (Hanover, Conn.: Wesleyan University Press, 1971); see also Stuart Gilman, "Degeneracy and Race in the Nineteenth Century: The Impact Of Clinical Medicine," *The Journal of Ethnic Studies* 10 (Winter 1983) on scientific inquiry and prognostication on social behavior in the nineteenth century.

In the forefront of the black construction of race were the intellectuals of the African Methodist Episcopal Church (A.M.E.). In 1888, C.A.A. Taylor, writing in the *A.M.E. Democrat,* took up the definition and development of "the Negro Race." In 1892, William Walroud Moe offered the provocative "The Boasted Inherent Superiority of the Anglo-Saxon Race on Trial, with the Universally Authoritative Acknowledgement of the Unique Ethiopian Race." Moe's work appeared in the A.M.E. *Church Review.* Between 1892 and 1895, Bishop Benjamin Tucker Tanner wrote several pieces that examined the invention of race from a decidedly black standpoint. To illustrate the case, Tanner moved his readers from biblical chronology through an examination of Darwinian theories. Tanner's work included several essays and correspondence in the A.M.E. *Church Review* and a monograph, *The Color of Solomon—What?* (Philadelphia: A.M.E. Book Concerns, 1895). In 1895, George Wilson Brent wrote on "The Ancient Glory of the Hamitic Race" in the *Church Review.*

CHAPTERS V, VI, AND VII

The anthropological arguments of the eighteenth and nineteenth centuries were also played out in the idiosyncrasies of "whiteness," the emergence of the field of linguisitcs, and a new literary genre. Both W.E.B. DuBois's *Black Reconstruction* (1935, New York: Atheneum, 1992) and Rayford W. Logan's *Betrayal of the Negro* (New York: Collier, 1965) are excellent sources in chronicling black achievement and resiliency on one hand, and white resistance to black participation in the democratic process at every level, on the other. DuBois's work, in particular, is a direct challenge to the Dunning-Burgess ideology.

Alice Littlefield et al. illuminate the evolution, permutations, and demise of race as a concept in "Redefining Race: The Potential Demise of a Concept in Physical Anthropology," *Current Anthropology* 23 (December 1982). Theodore W. Allen, *The Invention of the White Race* (London: Verso, 1994); David Roediger, *The Wages of Whiteness* (London: Verso, 1991); and Ruth Frankenberg, *The Social Construction of Whiteness* (Minneapolis: University of Minnesota Press, 1993) are useful in defining race as a social rather than biological construction. Again, Martin Bernal's *Black Athena* should prove quite useful to discussions on philology, the study of language, and comparative studies of language.

As mentioned previously, the work of Jack Forbes on the differences between blacks and whites, whites and Native Americans, and Native Americans and blacks, poses some very interesting issues. In addition to *Africans and Native Americans,* see his "The Manipulation of Race, Caste and Identity: Classifying AfroAmericans, Native Americans and Red-Black People," *Journal of Ethnic Studies* 17 (Winter 1990).

Notions of the homogeneity of "New England letters" are explored in the works of Gloria Horseley-Meacham, "Bull of the Nile: Symbol, History, and Racial Myth in 'Benito Cereno'," *The New England Quarterly* 64 (June 1991); Toni Morrison, *Playing in the Dark* (Cambridge: Harvard University Press, 1992); Eric Sundquist, *To Wake the Nations: Race in the Making of American Literature* (Cambridge: Belknap Press of Harvard University Press, 1993); and Shelley Fisher Fishkin, *Was Huck Black? Mark Twain and African American Voices* (New York: Oxford University Press, 1993).

The strength of "racist explanations of civilization" is underlined in a review of the major texts on "civilization" beginning with the works of Arnold Toynbee, *A Study of History* (London: Oxford University Press, 1946). The recent *The Bell Curve* by Richard Herrnstein and Charles Murray (New York: Free Press, 1994) rests on the precedent of a number of works which equate, specifically, the "decline of American civilization" with racial interpretations of intelligence and aptitude testing.

CHAPTERS VIII, IX, AND X

Some of the issues central to an examination of "the Social Gospel and Race," "Literary Naturalism and Race," and "the Indian in the Nineteenth Century" are supported by reference to the following sources:

Horace Bushnell's proclamation concerning "better and finer material" parallels Cecil Rhodes' 1887 statement on the Anglo-Saxon: "the best, the most human, most honourable race the world possesses. . . ."

The racial implications of the social gospel had both secular and sacred application that are illustrated in the works of Carl Peters, Thomas Carlyle, Thomas Macauley, Frederick Lugard, and numerous others. See Philip D. Curtin, ed., *Imperialism* (New York: Harper & Row, 1971).

Gloria Horsley-Meacham's "Bull of the Nile," and Laura Brown's "Reading Race and Gender: Jonathan Swift" *Eighteenth Century Studies* 23 (Summer 1990) are particularly helpful in exploring "Literary Naturalism and Race." Again, the work of Jack Forbes on race and Native Americans should be quite helpful in expanding on issues of "Indians" and the complexities that might be explored in literary, historical, sociological, political, and economic arenas.

CHAPTER XI

Within the context of "the Status of The American Negro: 1865–1915," there are numerous interpretations of the period of Reconstruction. Again, see W.E.B. DuBois's *Black Reconstruction*, Rayford Logan's *The Betrayal of the Negro*, and Eric Foner's *Reconstruction: America's Unfinished Revolution*,

1863–1877 (New York: Harper & Row, 1988). Here, Roediger and Allen are useful as are the works of C. Vann Woodward: *Origins of the New South, 1877–1913* (Baton Rouge: Louisiana State University Press, 1951) and *The Strange Career of Jim Crow* (New York: Oxford University Press, 1974).

Attitudes toward black troops and their conduct in the Spanish-American War are explored in a number of works written before 1963. These include Miles V. Lynk, *The Black Troopers or the Daring Heroism of the Negro Soldiers in the Spanish-American War* (Jackson, Tenn.: M.V. Lynk Publishing House, 1899); Edward A. Johnson, *History of Negro Soldiers in the Spanish-American War and Other Items of Interest* (New York: Johnson Reprint Corp, 1899); William Troy, *Loyalty of the Colored Man to the United States Government [in] the Late Conflict with Cuba, the Spanish Government and the Philippines* (Philadelphia: Christian Banner Print, 1900); Booker T. Washington, *A New Negro for a New Century* (Chicago: American Publishing House, 1900); Louis Harlan, *The Booker T. Washington Papers* (Urbana: University of Illinois Press, 1972); and Stephen Bonsal, *The Negro Soldier in War and Peace* (New York: North American Review, 1907). In sources that appear after 1963, the most prominent is John Hope Franklin's *From Slavery to Freedom;* Alan Margolis, "The Role of the Negro American Soldier in the Spanish-American War," (M.A. Thesis: Queens College, Department of History, 1975); Marvin Fletcher, "The Black Volunteers in the Spanish-American War," *Military Affairs* 33 (April 1974); Reuben L. Wright, *The Role of the Buffalo Soldiers During the Spanish-American War* (Fort Leavenworth, Kansas; U.S. Army Command and General Staff College, 1992).

CHAPTERS XII, XIII, XIV, XV, AND XVI

The final chapters of Gossett's work move the reader through the influx of new immigrants and questions of race and imperialism into World War I and its racism and the racism of the subsequent years. The work closes with an exploration of the ways in which science has been enlisted in the denunciation of racism and an exposition on the "battle against prejudice."

In many ways, these topics fit together nicely and more recent material underlines the themes of the final two chapters. White men in the tropics is a concern of Philip Curtin, *Death by Migration: Europe's Encounter with the Tropical World in the Nineteenth Century* (Cambridge: Cambridge University Press, 1989); Alfred Crosby, *The Columbian Exchange: Biological and Cultural Consequences of 1492* (Westport, Conn.: Greenwood, 1972); and William McNeill, *Plagues and Peoples* (Garden City, N.Y.: Anchor Press, 1976).

The "Brown brothers" reply to imperialism (from the American side) in the records of the African Methodist Episcopal Church and the writings of its bishops, such as Reverdy Ransom, *The Pilgrimage of Harriet Ransom's Son* (Nashville: The Sunday School Union, undated); and Henry McNeal Turner, *Respect Black: The Writings and Speeches of Henry McNeal Turner* (New York: Arno Press, 1971). Another critical piece of reading is Lawrence Little's doctoral dissertation, "A Quest for Self-Determination" (Ohio State University, 1993). These works also coincide with black notions on the construction of race, including DuBois's "Conversation of Races"; Douglass' Ethnologically Considered"; and Blyden's *The Races of Africa*.

There are a number of works on women and imperialism. Among them are Janet Schaw, *Journal of A Lady of Quality*, Evangeline Walker Andrews, ed. (New Haven, Conn.: Yale University Press, 1934); Lady Flora Lugard, *A Tropical Dependency* (London: J. Nisbet & Co. Limited, 1905); Jenny Sharpe, *Allegories of Empire* (Minnesota: University of Minnesota Press, 1993); and Napur Chaudhuri and Margaret Strobel, eds., *Western Women and Imperialism* (Bloomington: Indiana University Press, 1992). While this literature's primary concern is the agency of European and Euro-American women in the colonial process, it is also witness to an emerging discourse on the agency of colonized women in the context of imperialism.

The fascination for the "Nordic warriors" of the Spanish-American War and beyond are tempered by references to works such as *Harlem on the Rhine,* and Arthur Barbeau and Florette Henri, *The Unknown Soldiers* (Philadelphia: Temple University Press, 1974). These pieces are supported by a critical and historical reading of Erich Maria Remarque's *All Quiet on the Western Front* (Boston: Little, Brown, 1929) and Myron Echenberg's *Colonial Conscripts: The Tirailleurs Senegalais in French West Africa, 1857–1960* (Portsmith: Heinemann, 1991).

The "prophets of race disaster" are offset by the works of the Harlem Renaissance and associated literary movements of the 1920s. These include Alain Locke's *New Negro* (c. 1925, New York: Atheneum, 1992); Nathan Huggins's *Harlem Renaissance* (New York: Oxford University Press, 1971) and *Voices from the Harlem Renaissance* (New York: Oxford University Press, 1976); David Levering Lewis's *When Harlem Was in Vogue* (New York: Knopf, 1981); and Ann Douglas's *Terrible Honesty: Mongrel Manhattan in the 1920s* (New York: Farrar, Strauss and Giroux, 1995).

Index

Abbott, Lyman, 176, 193, 196, 316
Abolitionists and race, 66
Abyssinians, 170
Acquired characteristics, inheritance of, 6, 38, 152, 163-64, 200
Adam and Eve, 15, 44, 47, 50
Adams, Brooks, 301, 314, 325
Adams, Charles Francis, 119, 301
Adams, Henry, 103, 177, 283, 301, 304, 331, 414
Adams, Herbert Baxter, 106-8, 111, 121
Adams, John Quincy, 230
Africa, 36
Agassiz, Louis, 59-60, 242, 281
Alabama, 233, 237, 361
Aldrich, Thomas Bailey, 306, 336
Allen, Nathan, 292
Allen, William F., 101-2, 117
Alpine race, 354-55, 357, 374, 396, 402, 426
Altgeld, John P., 441
American Civil Liberties Union, 446
American Eugenics Society, 384
American Historical Association, 107
American literature, 134, 138, 140-42, 198, 202, 304
American Philosophical Society, 41
American race, 319, 345
American Revolution, 40, 117, 135, 179
American Sociological Society, 162, 384
Americans, 122, 135, 137, 151, 179, 200, 313, 358-59, 361
Angels, 33
Anglo-American League, 326-27
Anglo-American Magazine, 440
Anglo-Israelites, 190-92
Anglo-Saxon, 25, 87, 90-93, 95-96, 99-100, 116, 118, 135-36, 138-39, 140, 142, 163, 168, 170, 181, 185, 188-89, 191-92, 196, 221-22, 224-27, 291, 297, 299, 360, 410-11, 439

Anglo-Saxon language and literature, 103, 126-33
Anglo-Saxon Magazine, 328
Anglo-Saxon obligations to "inferior" races, 313, 329-33
Anglo-Saxon Review, 328
Anglo-Saxon solidarity, United States and England, 128, 320-25, 327-28, 440
Anglo-Saxon supremacy, 310-12, 314, 316-18, 320, 326, 334, 337, 413, 440
Animal analogies and race, 4, 11-13, 32-33, 42, 45, 49, 145, 175, 382, 405
Anthropology, 35, 37, 56
Anti-British sentiment, 322-23, 439-40
Anti-imperialism, 313, 317-18, 330-31, 334-38
Antin, Mary, 305, 441
Aristotle, 6
Army alpha and beta tests, 367-68, 374, 377
Artistic ability and race, 43, 51-52, 223, 343, 355
Aryans, 3-4, 118, 123-26, 151, 164, 187, 194, 214, 342, 346, 348, 351, 413
Asiatics, 6-7, 35
Assyria, 344
Astrology and race, 14-15
Atheism, 44, 51
Audubon, John James, 61
Augustine, 9
Austro-Hungarian Empire, 341
Aztecs, 182-83

Babbitt, Irving, 392
Babel, 47
Babington, William Dalton, 412
Babylon, 46
Bache, R. M., 364
Bachman, John, 60-63, 75
Baird, Robert, 184
Baldwin, James, 273

511

Baldwin, James Mark, 157
Bancroft, George, 88
Barbour, F. A., 133
Barrows, John H., 192
Bassett, John Spencer, 266
Battle of Wounded Knee, 236
Bean, Robert Bennett, 78, 80
Beard, Charles A., 121
Beauty and race, 38, 42, 45-46, 344
Bedouins, 170
Belford, James B., 236
Belgians, 38
Benedict, Ruth, 5, 421
Benton, Thomas Hart, 179
Beowulf, 130, 133, 139, 141, 168
Berea College, 278, 285
Berkeley, George, Bishop, 31
Bernier, François, 32-34
Beveridge, Albert J., 318, 326, 329, 333, 337
Bible and race, 4-5, 10-12, 15, 21-22, 25, 41, 44, 46-47, 50, 62-64, 67
Binet, Alfred, 364-65
Biology, 33-35
Birth of a Nation, 339-40
Birthrate and race, 170-71, 188, 195, 200, 300, 305-6, 391, 394, 400, 403
Bismarck, Otto von, 324
Bissell, Benjamin, 24
Black Codes, 256-57
Black Hawk War, 231
Blaine, James G., 291
Blood and race, 11
Blumenbach, Johann Friedrich, 37-39, 70, 80
B'nai B'rith, 446, 449
Boas, Franz, 245, 418-26, 429-30, 449
Boche, 341
Bodin, Jean, 14
Boer War, 324, 328
Boers, 380-81
Bolshevist Revolution, 341, 395, 399
Bond-servants, 29
Bopp, Franz, 123
Boulainvilliers, Henri Comte de, 84
Brace, Charles Loring, 125
Brachycephalic, 76, 354
Brackenridge, Hugh, 229-30
Brains and race, 77-80
Brandeis, Louis, 207-8
Brandt, John, 192-93
Brigham, Carl C., 374-75, 426
British-Israel Association, 191
Broca, Paul, 69, 76, 81
Brooks, John Graham, 158
Browne, Peter A., 80-81
Bruno, 15
Bryan, William Jennings, 377

Buffon, George Louis Leclerc, 35-36, 39, 44-46
Bureau of Ethnology, Smithsonian Institution, 251
Bureau of Indian Affairs, 233-34, 451
Burgess, John W., 110-12, 114, 120, 284, 307
Burlingame Treaty, 290
Burr, Clinton Stoddard, 311, 399-400
Bushnell, Horace, 180, 185, 196
Butler, Nicholas Murray, 122
Byrd, William, 27
Byrhtnoth, 132-33

Cable, George Washington, 275, 431-34
Caedmon, 101, 130
Cain, 15, 50
Caledonians, 46
California, 234
Callaway, Morgan, Jr., 130
Calvin, John, 26
Calvinism, 34, 194
Camper, Peter, 69-70
Canaan. *See* Ham
Canada, 94, 118, 326
Canadian policy toward Indians, 252
Caribs, 34
Carlyle, Thomas, 170, 320
Carpetbaggers, 257, 340
Cartwright, Major John, 127
Castle, W. E., 380
Catholic church, 349
Catholics, 9, 11-16, 22-27, 96-97, 157, 185, 195, 287-88, 350, 355, 371, 378, 393, 446, 448-49
Caucasians, 37-38, 65, 68, 118, 179, 181, 237, 271, 291, 311, 369
Celts, 8, 89, 95-97, 99-100, 112, 139-40, 152, 184, 297, 311, 361, 410-11
Chadwick, Munro, 131
Chamberlain, Houston Stewart, 145, 347-53, 413
Chamberlain, Joseph, 324-25
Chambers, Robert, 67-68
Chandler, George Brinton, 440
Channing, Edward, 118-19
Characterization in fiction and race, 198, 203
Chaucer, 11, 200
Chemistry, 33, 39
Cherokees, 232-33
Child, Francis J., 131
China, 4
Chinese, 34, 75, 262, 289, 290-91, 294, 297, 308, 342, 350, 376
Chippewas, 245
Choctaws, 233
Chosen people, Americans, 179

Christianity and race, 9-10, 30-31, 152, 170, 176, 178, 180-81, 186-87, 189, 193, 293, 316-18, 330, 347-49, 403, 414
Cicero, 137
Cid, El, 139
Civilization and race, 66, 152-53, 183-85, 188, 194, 225, 244, 315, 317-19, 337, 340-44, 349, 355-56, 388, 393, 395, 398-99, 409-10, 412
Clay, Henry, 330
Cleveland, Grover, 278, 293, 323
Climate and race, 5-7, 14, 16, 31, 36-39, 41, 45-48, 69, 137, 171-72, 225, 282, 299, 361-62
Cockran, Bourke, 268
Collier, John, 452
Colonial period and race, 17-31, 142
Color and race, 4, 7, 28, 37-38, 41, 46, 65, 69, 342, 354, 361, 386, 414
Combe, George, 73
Commager, Henry Steele, 172
Commons, John R., 172-74, 293, 383
Comte, Auguste, 164
Conrad, Joseph, 141
Consanguinity, 82, 249-50
Cook, Albert S., 131-32
Cooley, Charles H., 153, 167-68
Coolidge, Calvin, 405, 407
Cooper, James Fenimore, 198, 239, 240-41
Corrigan, M. A., 327
Cotton, John, 21-22
Crane, Stephen, 436-37
Crania, 12, 37, 48, 58, 73-74
Craniology, 37-38, 69, 73-76, 78-79, 206-7, 413-14, 421
Creeks, 233
Creel, George, 341
Creoles, 431
Cromer, Evelyn Baring, 411
Crusades, 10
Cuba, 324
Cubans, 317, 330, 337
Cultural anthropology, 417-18, 421-23
Curate of Los Palacios, 11
Currier and Ives prints, 242
Custer massacre, 250
Cuvier, Georges Léopold Chrétien Fréderic Dagobert, Baron, 82

Danes, 45, 133, 139, 361
Daniel, John W., 337
Daniels, Josephus, 279
Darwin, Charles, 33, 66-68, 71, 78, 81, 145-46, 148, 151, 159-60, 176, 205, 248, 311-12, 345, 350-51, 412
Davenport, Charles B., 379, 401, 426

Da Vinci, Leonardo, 16
Davis, Hugh, 30
Davis, James J., 405
Davison, Charles Stewart, 353
Decadence of white non-Anglo-Saxon races, 312, 314, 341
Declaration of Independence, 41
Democracy, 132, 134-37, 173-75, 194-95, 205, 345, 378, 388
Deniker, Joseph, 78
Depew, Chauncey, 298
De Soto, Hernando, 184
Determinism, 145-46, 162, 167, 174, 199, 314
Dew, Thomas R., 261
Dicey, Albert V., 323
Dickens, Charles, 301
Dickinson College, 41
Dixon, Thomas, Jr., 272, 280, 339
Dobzhansky, Theodore, 427
Dolichocephalic, 76, 354
Dollard, John, 273, 277
Dos Passos, John R., 326
Douglass, Frederick, 66, 285
Douglass, William, 22
Drake, Sir Francis, 24-25, 318
Dreiser, Theodore, 141, 441
Dreyfus case, 304
Droysen, Johann Gustav, 111
Dubois, Pierre, 9
DuBois, W. E. B., 270, 410, 446
Dugdale, Richard, 157
Duncan, Alexander, 235
Dunn, L. C., 427
Dunne, Finley Peter, 319, 335, 439, 441
Dunning, William A., 121, 284
Dutch, 229, 318-19
Dwight, Timothy, 179

East, Edward M., 381
Education and race, 18-19, 73, 237, 372, 388, 432
Edwards, Jonathan, 180
Egypt, 4, 77, 344, 346, 398
Eliot, Charles W., 285, 295
Eliot, John, 19, 21-23, 27, 228
Elite, cult of, 156, 344, 392, 401
Elizabeth I, 17
Ellis, John, 300
Ely, Richard T., 172, 190
Emerson, Ralph Waldo, 72, 97, 142, 288
English, 17, 135
English Common Law, 207
English literature, 138-41, 200
English race, 345
Enlightenment, philosophy of, 34
Environment, 7, 34, 40, 366, 388, 412, 427

Epictetus, 43
Equality of races, theory of, 41, 154,
    163-64, 427, 432
Eskimos, 62, 79, 420-21
Ethnic sensibilities, 443-44
Eugenics, 155, 157-60, 162-63, 167, 178,
    360, 393-94, 403
Eugenics Research Association, 401, 406
European race, 32, 35
Evers, Medgar, 458
Evolution, 66, 68, 144-45, 148, 151, 173,
    176-77, 185, 190, 197, 303
Ezra, 4

Facial features and race, 32, 69-70
Fairchild, Henry Pratt, 384-87, 428-29
Fall, Albert B., 451
Fielding, W. J., 392
Fifteenth Amendment, 70, 266, 268
Filipinos, 315, 317, 328-30, 332-33, 337-
    38
Finns, 75-76, 187
Finot, Jean, 413-15
Fischer, Eugen, 380
Fisher, Sydney G., 304
Fiske, John, 79, 110, 117, 188, 283, 301,
    304-6, 322
Fitzgerald, F. Scott, 397
Fitzhugh, George, 66
Ford, Henry, 371
Forrest, Nathan Bedford, 260
Fourteenth Amendment, 266, 274, 453
Fowler, W. C., 128
France, 150, 157, 324, 346-47, 352, 356-
    57
France, Anatole, 79
Franklin, Benjamin, 179
Frederic, Harold, 294
Freedmen's Bureau, 258, 261
Freeman, Edward A., 98, 100, 104, 108-
    10, 116, 121, 131
French, 9, 24, 27-28, 94-95, 98, 118,
    135, 138, 200-201, 230, 312-13, 342,
    346
French-Canadians, 170, 303
French race, 345
Furness, Horace H., 129

Gabriel, Ralph W., 160
Galileo, 33
Gall, Franz Joseph, 71
Galton, Francis, 155-59, 162, 168
Gardiner, Charles A., 329
Garland, Hamlin, 336
Garnett, James M., 129
Garrison, William Lloyd, 180
Garth, Thomas Russell, 425
Gary, Elbert H., 383

Gates, Lewis E., 201
Genealogy, 158-59
Geography and race, 14, 32, 40, 60, 62
George, Henry, 290
Georgia, 232-33, 361
German race, 345
Germans, 8, 38, 102, 112-13, 137-38,
    152, 287, 298, 311, 341, 346-47, 352,
    357-58, 361, 396, 429
Germany, 342, 346, 357
Gibbon, Edward, 85
Giddings, Franklin H., 159, 312-13, 323,
    385
Gilder, Richard Watson, 336
Gladden, Washington, 176-77, 180, 193-
    94, 317
Gliddon, George Robin, 64-65
Gneist, Heinrich Von, 348
Gobineau, Arthur Count de, 145, 324-
    47, 351-53, 362, 413
God, 33-35
Godkin, E. L., 298, 336
Golden, Harry, 450
Gompers, Samuel, 291, 295-96
Gould, Charles W., 398
Grady, Henry W., 196, 264, 274, 433
Grandfather clause, 266-67, 285, 453
Grant, Madison, 153, 353-64, 384, 387,
    389-90, 396-98, 404, 424, 426-27
Gratiolet, 75, 290
Gray, Asa, 67
Great chain of being, 47
Greeks, 5-8, 39, 94, 112, 344, 355-56,
    378, 385, 398
Greeley, Horace, 72, 448
Green, John Richard, 100
Greenback-Labor Party, 297
Greenland, 36
Grey, Edward, 324
Gumplowicz, Ludwig, 165-67
Guyer, Michael F., 318

Haeckel, Ernst, 81
Hair and race, 80-81
Hakluyt, Richard, 17
Hall, A. R., 33
Hall, G. Stanley, 154-55, 157, 159
Ham, sons of, 5
Handlin, Oscar, 29, 273
Hansen, Marcus L., 296
Harding, Warren G., 404-5
Harlan, John M., 275
Harrington, Fred, 335-36
Hart, Albert Bushnell, 110, 119, 282
Hawthorne, Nathaniel, 142
Hay, John, 324, 439
Haymarket bombing, 295, 297, 336
Helper, Hinton, 262, 280

Heredity, 144, 159, 177, 214, 366, 426-27
Hero, Anglo-Saxon, 208-22, 224-26
Heroine, Anglo-Saxon, 208-13, 217, 220
Herron, George T., 176, 193-94
Hertz, Frederick, 26
Higginson, Thomas Wentworth, 437-38
Hindus, 77
Hine, Edward, 191
Hippocrates, 6-7
Hispaniola, 12
Histories and race, 84-122, 174, 183, 243, 284-85, 342, 345, 373, 409, 413-14
Hoffman, Frederick L., 281
Hofstadter, Richard, 336
Holmes, Oliver Wendell, 207-8, 243, 288
Holmes, S. J., 380, 389, 410
Holst, Herman E. von, 336
Home, Henry. *See* Kames, Lord
Homer, Winslow, 437
Hooton, Ernest A., 76, 428
Hosmer, James K., 110, 117, 301, 322
Hottentots, 34, 380-81
Houston, Sam, 233
Howe, Samuel Gridley, 72
Howells, William Dean, 335-36, 435-36
Hugo, Victor, 137
Humanists, 393-94
Humboldt, Alexander von, 362
Hume, David, 85-86
Humphreys, Benjamin G., 256
Hun, 341
Hunter, John, 36, 39
Huxley, Thomas Henry, 69, 81, 388, 410

Illinois, 231
Imagination and race, 42-43, 223-24
Immigrants: anarchists, 295-96; assimilation, 135-38, 155, 288, 291-92, 339, 404, 437-38; defense of, 441-43; inferiority of, 294, 354, 360, 382, 388-89, 396, 398-99, 402; labor unrest, 296-99, 302-3, 307, 370-71, 383; political corruption, 298
Immigration, restriction of, 120, 169, 173-74, 306-9, 352-54, 362-63, 382-83, 385, 387, 401, 404-7, 458
Immigration Restriction League, 306, 354
India, 3, 7
Indian and Negro compared, 238, 241
Indian culture, 246-50
Indians: conversion to Christianity, 12-13, 17-19, 21-24, 26-28; decline in number, 234-35; defense of, 12-13, 23, 28, 34-35, 39, 41, 43; explanation of race differences, 7; hatred of, 12-13, 20-21, 24; inferiority of, 73; loss of

land, 230-37, 239, 251, 319, 451-52; reservations, 228, 231, 247; separate origin of, 44, 46; South American, 92; Southwest, 366; tribal funds appropriated, 451
Individualism and race, 188
Industrialism and race, 188, 292, 359
Ingersoll, Robert, 187, 191
Innate inferiority, 173, 177, 184, 229, 364, 444
Intelligence and race, 7, 37, 43-45, 47-49, 59, 65, 75, 94, 150, 244, 280, 355, 363-68, 373-76, 381, 388, 408-9, 424-29
Intelligence, scales of: Binet-Simon, 365; Stanford-Binet, 363, 365, 367
Intermarriage, racial, 25-28, 31, 151, 182, 245, 344, 352, 401-2, 435-36, 458
Interracial sexual relationships, 25, 30
Ireland, John, Archbishop, 449
Irish, 97, 109-10, 122, 138, 152, 170, 287-89, 294, 298, 361, 438-41
Iroquois, 40, 250
Israelites, 25
Italian race, 345
Italians, 189, 200, 204, 294, 358-59, 410

Jackson, Andrew, 223
Jackson, Helen Hunt, 235, 237
Jamaica, 49, 426
James I, 18
James, Henry, 283, 305
James, William, 178, 305
Jamestown, Virginia, 29
Japanese, 79, 308-9, 376
Japanese Americans, 450
Jefferson, Thomas, 42-43, 51-53, 87, 126-27, 154, 179
Jennings, H. S., 427
Jeremiah, 5
Jesus, 10, 25, 348, 403
Jews, 4-5, 10-12, 14-15, 21, 46, 97, 100, 170, 190, 207-8, 292-93, 304-5, 341, 348, 351, 359-60, 371-72, 375, 402, 435, 445-46, 449-50
Johnson, Albert, 405-6
Johnson, Guy B., 30
Johnson, James Weldon, 266-67
Johnson, Samuel, 42
Jones, Howard Mumford, 140-41
Jones, Sir William, 123
Jordan, David Starr, 159, 168
Josey, Charles Conant, 400-402
Jukes family, 157
Julian the Apostate, 8-9, 414

Kaffirs, 34, 79

Kames, Lord, 45-47, 50-51
Keane, A. H., 81
Kearney, Dennis, 187, 290
Kemble, Fanny, 73
Kemble, John Mitchell, 87-88
Kennedy, John F., 458
Kidd, Benjamin, 205, 312, 331
King, Martin Luther, 459
King Philip (the Indian), 21
King Philip's War, 20-21
Kipling, Rudyard, 155, 202-3, 319, 322, 332, 438
Kirkland, Mrs. Caroline Stansbury, 137
Klineberg, Otto, 425
Kneeland, Samuel S., 70
Know Nothing movement, 97, 287
Knox, Robert, 95-97, 184, 299
Kohn, Hans, 26
Kroeber, A. L., 423-24
Ku Klux Klan, 259-60, 340, 371, 373

La Farge, John, 105
La Follette, Robert, 172
Laffiteau, Father, 44
Laissez faire society, 147-48, 152-53, 161, 168, 174
Lamarck, Jean Baptiste, 152, 163-64, 199
Language and race, 55, 125, 129-30, 133, 138, 141-42
Lanier, Sidney, 130, 132, 263-64
Laplanders, 32, 34, 36, 45-47
Lardner, Ring, 141
Las Casas, Bartolomé de, 12-14, 17, 23, 92
Latin temperament, 139, 171
Laughlin, H. H., 401
Lavater, Johann Kaspar, 71
Lawrence, Sir William, 56
Lawson, John, 27
League of Nations, 177
Leibnitz, Gottfried Wilhelm von, 34
Lice and race, 81
Liddell, Mark H., 132
Lieber, Francis, 90, 93
Lincoln, Abraham, 254-55, 330
Linnaeus, Carolus, 35, 82
Lippmann, Walter, 368, 377
"Little brown brother," 155, 333
Literary ability and race, 43, 52, 223
Literary history and race, 134-35, 137-39, 140-41, 143
Livy, 200
Locke, John, 50
Lodge, Henry Cabot, 103, 110, 115-16, 159, 196, 268, 305, 331
Logan, Rayford W., 283
Lombroso, Cesare, 204
London, Jack, 198-99, 202-6, 209, 211-14, 216-27, 294

Lowell, A. Lawrence, 372-73
Lucan, 46
Luce, Stephen B., 315
Luther, Martin, 26
Lyell, Charles, 311
Lynching, 125, 166, 269-73, 434, 438, 452-53

MacDougall, William, 377-78, 415
McKinley, William, 278, 338
Maclean, John, 39
Macy, John, 141
Maeterlinck, Maurice, 141
Mahan, Alfred T., 315, 317, 322
Maine, Sir Henry, 101
Malabar, 46
Malays, 329
Mall, Franklin P., 78
Manifest destiny, 310, 314-18, 328, 333, 335, 440
Mann, Horace, 72
March, Francis A., 130
March on Washington, 458
Marshall, John, 232-33
Marx, Karl, 144-45, 187, 205
Maryland, 30, 39
Massachusetts, 19, 361
Massachusetts Bay, 18, 25
Mather, Cotton, 229
Mather, Increase, 20-21, 31
Mating of men and apes, 49
May, Henry F., 296-97
Measurement of race differences, 69, 73, 76, 82-83, 125, 155, 363-64, 376
Mediterranean race, 354-55, 357, 374, 378, 402, 410, 426
Memory and race, 42
Mencken, H. L., 141-43
Mendel, Gregor, 159
Metternich, Prince von, 71
Mexican War, 233
Mexicans, 44, 218, 222, 233, 319, 366
Mexico, 182, 184, 310, 417
Middle Ages, 9-10
Mill, John Stuart, 411-12
Miller, Oliver C., 316
Milton, John, 50, 137
Mississippi, 233, 277
Mr. Dooley. *See* Dunne, Finley Peter
Mjen, J. A., 380
Mommsen, Theodor, 111
Mongolians, 39, 291
Monkeys and apes and race, 4, 15, 48-50, 206, 345
Monstrous races, 9, 11
Montagu, M. F. Ashley, 79
Montesquieu, Charles Louis, Baron, 86
Morgan, Henry Lewis, 82, 245, 248-51
Morse, Jedidiah, 238

Morton, George Samuel, 58-59, 63, 70, 73-74, 237
Moslems, 9-10
Motley, John Lothrop, 89, 90
Mulattoes, 30-31, 49-50, 61, 272, 340
Müller, Friedrich Max, 124-25
Munger, Theodore, 176, 193
Murray, Andrew, 81
Musical ability and race, 42, 49

National Association for the Advancement of Colored People (NAACP), 446, 452, 455
National Conference of Christians and Jews, 446
National Education Association, 318
National Urban League, 446
Nationalism and race, 122, 345-46, 353
Natural selection, 145-46, 312
Nazis, 126, 424, 427-28, 445
Neanderthal man, 79
Negroes: in Africa, 255; defense of, 40-41, 51-52; education, 274-78, 286, 376, 437, 544-57; epithets, 283; hatred of, 262; inferiority, 15, 31, 36, 42-45, 65, 70, 80, 254, 256, 261-64, 269, 280-81, 286, 376; legal redress, 278, 457; origin of, 5-7, 15-16, 36-41, 45-51, 58-61; segregation, 256, 277, 279, 285-86, 437, 455-57; slavery of, 3, 28-30, 41-42, 63-64; suffrage, 255-56, 259, 265-67, 276, 284-85, 404, 453-55; understood by southerners, 261, 285
Nelson, Knute, 296, 329
Neoclassicism and race, 139-40
New England, 18-20, 31, 142, 170, 182-83, 299, 305, 309, 361
New England towns and race, 118-19
New Jersey, 39
New York Anti-Imperialist League, 335
Newgate, 52
Newton, Isaac, 50, 53
Nietzsche, Friedrich Wilhelm, 134, 205
Noah, 44
Noble savage, 24-25, 391
Nordic race, 353-62, 374-89, 391-96, 402, 405, 407, 410, 426-27
Normans, 106, 111, 116, 127, 131, 133, 135, 139-40, 200
Norris, Frank, 198, 201-4, 209-10, 212, 214-15, 219-21, 224
Norsemen, 139, 361
Nott, Josiah Clark, 64-65, 74-75, 77, 237

Oakesmith, John, 414-15
Oberholtzer, Ellis Paxson, 285

Odor and race, 11, 42
Old, Jacob, 20
Olney, Richard, 323, 326
Organic selection theory, 157-58
Organic view of society, 144-46, 161
Orientals, 32, 329, 337
Osborn, Henry Fairfield, 153, 387-89, 424, 426
Osgood, Herbert Levi, 120
O'Sullivan, John, 310

Page, Thomas Nelson, 273, 280
Page, Walter Hines, 272, 442-43
Pain, sensitivity to, 49
Paine, Thomas, 230
Palgrave, Sir Francis, 87
Pallas, Peter Simon, 69
Pancoast, Henry S., 134
Paraguay, 34
Parker, Ely, 248-49
Parker, Theodore, 180-83, 185, 196
Parkman, Francis, 90, 94, 243-44, 303
Parrington, Vernon L., 143
Patmore, Coventry, 130
Pattee, Fred Lewis, 134
Patten, James Horace, 308
Patterson, Henry S., 237
Paul III, Pope, 13
Paul IV, Pope, 15
Pearce, Roy Harvey, 248
Pearl, Raymond, 78
Peffer, W. A., 316
Pennsylvania, 39, 41
Persia, 124
Peru, 13, 17
Peter the Venerable, 11
Peyrère, Isaac de la, 15
Phaedrus, 43
Philadelphia, 40
Philippines, 315, 317, 328-30, 333-35, 337-38
Phrenology, 71-73
Physical environment determines moral character, 137
Physics, 33
Physiognomy, 15, 70-71
Pictet, Adolphe, 124
Pilate, 10
Pinchback, P. B. S., 274
Pinkerton, John, 86
Pitcairn Island, 380-81
Plato, 8, 137
Plessy vs. Ferguson, 274-75, 456
Pocahontas, 18
Poe, Edgar Allan, 142
Political ability and race, 6, 14
Polygenetic origin of races, 8, 15, 44-51, 54, 58-60, 63-67

Polynesians, 79
Popenoe, Paul, 381
Populists, 265
Portuguese, 222, 377
Powderley, Terence V., 291
Powell, John Wesley, 85, 245, 248, 251
Powers, Harry H., 313
"Praying Indians," 19-21
Predestination, 34
Pregnancy, blackness of white women in, 38
Prescott, William Hickling, 90-93, 182-83
Prichard, James Cowles, 54, 81
Priestley, Joseph, 127
Princeton, 39
Prioress, Chaucer's, 11
Protestants, 15, 18-19, 22, 24-27, 97, 184-86, 188, 297, 350, 356, 378, 393, 446-48
Puritans, 25, 108, 110, 131, 179, 182-83, 196, 229, 389

Quakers, 152, 228
Quarles, Benjamin, 255
Quincy, Josiah, 72

Race, 94, 97, 415; antipathy, 62, 386-87; conflict theory of society, 165, 167, 205, 314-15; as religion, 347-48; riots, 280, 371, 451
Race-crossing, advantageous, 144, 147, 151, 288, 301-2, 312, 343-44, 352, 355, 376, 380; degenerative effects, 150-51, 205, 343, 359-60, 379, 381-82, 389-90, 393, 402-3, 405, 426-27; productive of sterility, 49, 61
"Race-slumpers," 415
Races: earliest, 55; doomed to disappear, 230, 235, 242-44, 281-82, 301; hierarchy of, 56-57, 67, 69, 135, 142, 144, 150, 154, 156, 160, 164, 166, 169, 170, 177, 179, 187, 194, 196-97, 219, 256, 334, 337, 343, 349, 350, 352, 364, 374, 458; homogeneity, 134; number of, 32, 35, 37, 82, 342, 345, 354, 374; orthognathous, 70; prothognathous, 70
Racial justice, 197
Radin, Paul, 417
Raleigh, Sir Walter, 17, 24
Rape, 166, 272
Raper, Arthur, 276
Ratzenhofer, Gustav, 165
Rauschenbusch, Walter, 176, 180, 193-95
Recapitulation theory, 149, 154-55
Reconstruction, 257-60, 274, 285-86, 340

Reed, David A., 407
Reid, Whitelaw, 314, 327, 330-31, 333, 337
Religion and race, 46, 51
Representative government and race, 104-5, 113, 138, 173, 329-30, 360, 399-400, 402, 407
Retzius, Anders, 75-76
Reuter, Edward B., 416
Rhodes, Cecil, 318
Rhodes, James Ford, 284
Richardson, Charles F., 137-38
Rig-Veda, 3
Riis, Jacob, 441
Ripley, William Z., 126, 330, 354, 413
Roberts, Kenneth L., 402
Robertson, John MacKinnon, 412-13, 415, 417
Roland, 139
Rolfe, John, 18
Romans, 7, 14, 43, 52, 113, 121, 342, 349, 355, 378
Rome, 7-8, 349, 356, 398
Roosevelt, Theodore, 114, 168, 237-38, 268-69, 278, 305-6, 308, 318-19, 329, 335, 352
Root, Elihu, 329
Rosenberg, Alfred, 445
Ross, E. A., 168-72, 282, 293, 382-83, 385
Rousseau, Jean Jacques, 148, 391-92
Rowlandson, Mrs. Mary, 20
Royce, Josiah, 333
Rush, Benjamin, 39, 41
Russell, Bertrand, 424
Russia, 346
Russians, 187, 395, 399

Sadler, William S., 357
Saint-Hilaire, Geoffroy, 57, 58
St. Paul, 9
Samoyedes, 34
Sandys, Sir Edwyn, 8
Sanskrit, 123
Savagery, natural, 229, 237
Saveth, Edward N., 442
Scalawags, 257
Scandinavians, 46
Schoolcraft, Henry Rowe, 63, 245-48, 251
Scott, Sir Walter, 301
Scott, Winfield, 233
Schurz, Carl, 327
Sears, L., 158
Semitic race, 164
Senecas, 249
Separate, but equal, 274-76, 433, 456
Sequoyah, 65

Sexual attraction between races, 166
Sexual differences among races, 48, 55, 171
Sexual selection, 68
Shakespeare, 50
Shaler, Nathaniel Southgate, 281
Shaw, Albert, 310
Silliman, Benjamin, 58, 72
Simkins, Francis B., 258
Simmons, William Joseph, 340
Simon, Théodore, 364-65
Sioux, 236, 250
Sitting Bull, 250
Slav, 112, 341
Slavery and race, 7, 28-31, 36, 40-43, 50, 52, 181
Slovak, 359
Smith, Goldwin, 158, 334
Smith, Lillian, 273
Smith, Samuel Stanhope, 39-41, 51
Socialism and race, 206, 287, 383
Sodomy, 12
Solomon, Barbara, 300
Southern Immigration Conference, 308
Southern Regional Council, 449
Spain, 310, 324, 328, 356
Spalding, Bishop, 178
Spaniards, 12-13, 17, 23-24, 92, 181-82, 184, 222, 230, 329
Spanish-American War, 312-14, 322, 325, 358, 439
Spanish Inquisition, 11-12
Species, 35
Spencer, Herbert, 145-53, 167, 173, 205, 248, 416-17
"Sports," 55, 59
Spring-Rice, Cecil, 305
Spurzheim, Johann Gaspar, 71-73
Squire, Samuel, 86
Stanton, William, 66
Stern, William, 365
Stetson, B. R., 364
Stoddard, Theodore Lothrop, 390-98, 400, 402, 404, 424, 426-27
Stowe, Harriet Beecher, 261
Strong, Josiah, 176, 178, 185-90, 192-93, 196-97, 293-94, 297, 316, 330, 383
Stubbs, William, 98, 100, 104, 121, 131
Sumner, William Graham, 153-54, 161, 167, 173, 272
Swedes, 75-76, 378
Syrian, 359

Tabula rasa, 34
Tacitus, 84, 86, 101-2, 107, 118, 121-22, 130, 137
Taft, William Howard, 155, 278, 333
Taine, Hippolyte, 153, 199-202
Talmud, 5

Tartars, 187, 395
Taylor, Bayard, 290
Taylor, Henry Osborn, 105
Temperament and race, 7, 42-43, 46, 59, 171, 173, 244, 342, 355, 376, 385, 388, 396, 408-9, 415, 444
Tennyson, Alfred Lord, 321
Terence, 43
Terman, Lewis, 363, 365-66, 368, 377
Teutonic origins, 84-122, 130, 138, 207, 303, 413, 416
Teutonic temperament, 139-40, 171, 173
Teutons, 138, 170, 181, 222, 341, 346-47, 349-50
Thorndike, E. L., 364, 374
Tiedeman, F., 77
Tillman, Ben, 253, 271, 279, 337
Tocqueville, Alexis de, 238
Tories, 127
Totten, Charles A. L., 191
Touch, sense of, 49
Toussaint L'Ouverture, 156
Toynbee, Arnold, 25
Transatlantic Society of America, 327, 439
Treitschke, Heinrich Von, 106, 111, 120
Tribal societies, 234, 249
Tropics and race, 28, 173, 225, 331-32
Tupper, Martin, 321
Turner, Arlin, 432
Turner, Frederick Jackson, 119-20, 143, 188, 292, 303-4
Turner, Sharon, 86
Twain, Mark, 72, 142, 335, 434-35
Tyler, Moses Coit, 110
Tylor, Edward Burnett, 417, 422

Ugliness in races, 39, 42, 45-46
United Nations, 445
Unity of human race, 34-38, 51, 57-58, 60-61, 63, 66-67, 70
Urban II, Pope, 10
Utes, 236

Van Baer's law, 145
Van Evrie, John, 262, 280
Vanini, Lucilio, 15
Vardaman, James K., 253, 271, 276
Virchow, Rudolph, 423
Virginia, 18-20, 29-30, 39-40
Vitruvius, 6-7
Voegelin, Eric, 144-45
Voltaire, 44

Wagner, Richard, 346
Waitz, Theodore, 66, 412, 417
Walker, Francis A., 302-4
Walker, Francis C., 234
Wallace, George C., 458

Ward, Lester F., 160-68
Washington, Booker T., 253, 268-69, 276, 278, 307
Watson, Tom, 253, 271, 308
Webster, Daniel, 74-75, 116, 311
Wendell, Barrett, 134-36, 301, 305, 326
Wheatley, Phyllis, 43
Whigs, 127
White, Andrew D., 110
White, Charles, 47-51, 56
White, True W., 130
White Citizens Councils, 253
"White Man's Burden, The," 323, 337
White primary, 453-54
White race, 7, 342-43; supremacy of, 264-65, 343, 387
White races, differences among, 124, 157
Whitman, Walt, 72, 142
Wiggam, Alfred E., 402-4

William and Mary College, 19, 27
Williams, Roger, 19, 228
Wilson, Edmund, 200-201
Wilson, John, 190
Wilson, Woodrow, 279, 284, 292, 442
Winslow, Governor, 19
Wister, Owen, 198-99, 202, 206-9, 211-13, 215-16, 218-19, 224, 226-27
Woodward, C. Vann, 259, 265
Workingman's Party, 290
Worms, Bishop of, 10
Wovoka, 236

"Yellow Peril," 206
Yerkes, Robert M., 367-68, 376

Zeus, 8
Zola, Emile, 201